Defenders of the truth

*The battle for science
in the sociobiology debate
and beyond*

ULLICA SEGERSTRÅLE

OXFORD
UNIVERSITY PRESS

OXFORD
UNIVERSITY PRESS

Great Clarendon Street, Oxford OX2 6DP

Oxford University Press is a department of the University of Oxford. It
furthers the University's objective of excellence in research, scholarship, and
education by publishing worldwide in

Oxford New York

Athens Auckland Bangkok Bogotá Buenos Aires Calcutta Cape Town
Chennai Dar es Salaam Delhi Florence Hong Kong Istanbul Karachi
Kuala Lumpur Madrid Melbourne Mexico City Mumbai Nairobi Paris
São Paulo Singapore Taipei Tokyo Toronto Warsaw

with associated companies in Berlin Ibadan

Oxford is a registered trade mark of Oxford University Press in the UK and
in certain other countries

Published in the United States by Oxford University Press Inc., New York

© Ullica Segerstråle 2000

The moral rights of the author have been asserted

Database right Oxford University Press (maker)

First published 2000

A catalogue record for this book is available from the British Library

Library of Congress Cataloguing in Publication Data
Data applied for

ISBN 0 19 850505 1
Typeset in Minion by Footnote Graphics Warminster, Wilts
Printed in Great Britain on acid-free paper
by T.J. International Ltd, Padstow

Contents

Preface

This book is directed at all those who are interested in an in-depth analysis of the tangled web called the sociobiology debate and the continuation of some of its core concerns in the so-called Science Wars. It spans developments in the sociobiology controversy and its various ramifications over a quarter of a century. I happened to be a witness to the beginning and evolution of this conflict, and as a sociologist found it to be a fascinating case study of the ways of science.

Over these twenty-five years, the academic climate has become somewhat more receptive to biological arguments. The vehement protests against sociobiology have transformed themselves into more general scientific and philosophical criticisms. At the same time, the Human Genome Project has become the target of many of the political and moral concerns raised earlier by sociobiology. And after a quarter of a century, sociobiology itself has come full circle with E. O. Wilson's *Consilience*, expanding the philosophical intent of *Sociobiology* that earlier was obscured by more immediate political concerns.

But there are many 'sociobiologies', of which Wilsonian sociobiology is just one. *Defenders of the Truth* strives to put the emergence of sociobiology and the reactions to it in a larger scientific context, occasionally entering also the territory of philosophy of biology.

The title of the book refers to the strong commitments felt by the scientists involved in this debate. How does a sociologist establish truth? The way I have proceeded is through interviews and discussions, and by reading the work of the protagonists and mainstream evolutionary biologists, including occasional unpublished letters and documents. I can also speak as an attendant of several of the early discussions about sociobiology at Harvard and elsewhere, and as an observer at some meetings of the Sociobiology Study Group. All this is put in perspective, and the protagonists of the sociobiology debate followed up to the present day. However, the controversy did not only involve biologists. Accordingly, I have obtained the views of a broad range of academics in different fields.

As a matter of historical record, I want to mention the people I have interviewed formally or informally over the years (many of these at the height of the controversy in the early 1980s), or who in conversation provided a crucial piece of the puzzle for my understanding of what the sociobiology controversy was all about:

Richard Alexander, Eric Ardener, Jonathan Beckwith, Brian Bertram, Nick Blurton-Jones, Noam Chomsky, Stephen Chorover, Tim Clutton-Brock, Leda Cosmides, Jonathan Cullen, E. Curio, Martin Daly, Nick Davies, Bernard Davis, Richard Dawkins, Irven

DeVore, John Edsall, John Eisenberg, Madhav Gadgil, Nathan Glazer, Stephen J. Gould, Penelope Greene, William Hamilton, Stuart Hampshire, Paul Harvey, Richard Herrnstein, Timotsu Hidaka, Robert Hinde, Jerry Hirsch, Jonathan Hodge, Bert Hölldobler, Ruth Hubbard, Pierre Jaisson, Jerome Kagan, John Krebs, Thomas Kuhn, Robert Lange, David Layzer, Edmund Leach, Bernie LeBoef, Richard Levins, Jeffrey Levinton, Richard Lewontin, Charles Lumsden, Salvador Luria, Brendan Maher, Aubrey Manning, David Maybury-Lewis, John Maynard Smith, Ernst Mayr, David McClelland, Peter Medawar, Mary Midgley, Peter O'Donald, George Orians, Karl Popper, Don Price, John Rawls, Vernon Reynolds, Mark Ridley, Walter Rosenblieth, Paul Shorman, B. F. Skinner, Larry Slobodkin, David Sloan Wilson, John Staddon, Stanley Tambiah, John Thoday, Lionel Tiger, Robert Trivers, John Turner, Leigh van Valen, George Wald, Sheldon White, Margo Wilson, Vero Wynne-Edwards, Nur Yaiman, and John Ziman.

There are several persons whose interest and moral support have been important to me during my work: Christopher Badcock, Bernard Barber, Jerome Barkow, Pat Bateson, Randall Collins, Richard Dawkins, Irven DeVore, Loren Graham, Bill Hamilton, Jonathan Hodge, Sarah Blaffer Hrdy, David Hull, John Maynard Smith, Everett Mendelsohn, Robert Morton, Frank Sulloway, Ernst Mayr, David Riesman, Michael Ruse, George Williams, Edward O. Wilson, John Ziman, and Harriet Zuckerman. There are many others who over the years in one way or other have helped me in my work and provided important feedback. To them I express my deepest gratitude. Needless to say, the responsibility for any errors in the book is all mine.

Parts of my research have been presented on different occasions over the years. I would particularly like to thank Vincent Falger and Peter Meyer from the European Sociobiological Society, and Gary Johnson from the Association for Politics and the Life Sciences, for their encouragement and for providing a friendly critical audience. I also want to thank the directors of the summer courses in ethics and sociology of science at the Inter-University Centre for Post-Graduate Studies in Dubrovnik, Aant Elzinga and Thomas Brante, who for many years created a stimulating atmosphere for intellectual debate. I would also like to mention the valuable discussions and useful advice from my colleagues at the Zentrum für Interdisziplinäre Forschung at the University of Bielefeld, Germany, where I participated in the group project "Biological Foundations of Human Culture" under the directorship of Peter Weingart, particularly Pete Richerson, Sandy Mitchell, and Leda Cosmides.

I wish to acknowledge the kind permission of Kluwer Academic Publishers to use parts of my article 'Colleagues in Conflict', *Biology and Philosophy* 1 (1), 1986, 53–87, in Chapters 3 and 8 in this book, and JAI Press for permission to reprint excerpts from my book chapter 'Truth and Consequences in the Sociobiology Controversy and Beyond', in V. Falger, P. Meyer, and J. van den Dennen, *Sociobiology and Politics*, Research in Biopolitics, Vol. 26, 1998, pp. 249–73, in Chapters 18 and 19. Parts of Chapter 14 appeared earlier under the title, 'Reductionism, Bad Science', and Politics: A Critique of Anti-Reductionist Reasoning', in *Politics and the Life Sciences* 11 (2), 1992, 199–214.

I appreciate the encouragement of my editor at Oxford University Press (UK), Michael Rodgers, and I thank Marie-Anne Martin for undertaking the arduous task of indexing *Defenders of the Truth*.

Finally, I want to acknowledge the financial support of the Finnish Academy, whose Senior Researcher grant helped me get the book started, and the collegial support of my colleagues from the Philosophy Colloquium and the Center for the Study of Ethics in the Professions at my home university, Illinois Institute of Technology in Chicago.

CHAPTER 1

The sociobiology debate as a battle for truth

Scientific and moral truth—together or apart?

> Emotional cerebration appears to have the paradoxical capacity to find equal support for opposite sides of any question. It is particularly curious that in scientific discourse, as in politics, the emotions seem capable of standing on any platform. Different groups of reputable scientists, for example, often find themselves in altercation because of diametrically opposed views of what is true. Although seldom commented on, it is equally bewildering that the world order of science is able to live comfortably for years, and sometimes centuries, with beliefs that a new generation discovers to be false (Paul MacLean, 1970).[1]

This book is about different visions of science and different conceptions of the responsibility of a scientist. The characters in my story are all defenders of the truth—it is just that they have different conceptions of where the truth lies. The truth of these scientists is multifaceted: epistemological, methodological, moral, political, metaphysical, even esthetic. Still, these aspects are not randomly combined—rather, they cluster into identifiable, organized world views, complete with different stocks of taken-for-granted knowledge.

My aim in this book is to take the reader along toward a deeper understanding of the sociobiology controversy, and through it, the world of science in general. I am interested in what Peter Medawar once called 'a view through the keyhole'. Controversies, where scientists attack one another's scientific world views and justify their own, may well be some of the best keyholes we have. But I am not doing this alone. My assistants in this detective task are many of the participants themselves, and their immediate and more distant academic colleagues, whom I had the opportunity to interview at the height of the controversy and sometimes later, too. Of course, I reserve the right to try to make sense of what my informants have told me. (In the same way, I am looking forward to feedback from them and others.)

It is now a quarter of a century since the sociobiology controversy started around Harvard zoologist E. O. Wilson and his book *Sociobiology: The New Synthesis*. It is high time to take stock of the situation. What was really going on? The received view is that it was a politically motivated nature–nurture controversy between hereditarians and 'environmentalists' (who should these days actually be called 'culturalists' or 'nurturists' so as not to be confused with the later ecologically oriented environmentalist movement). That is the way it appeared, and the way it was presented. But the reality was much more complex.

Watchers of this unfolding drama have noted the relentlessness with which the critics kept attacking their targets, who were accused not only of 'incorrect' political and moral stances, but also of 'bad science'. What were the actual motivations of Wilson and some other leading sociobiologists? And what were the motivations driving the critics of sociobiology, particularly the Sociobiology Study Group of Science for the People? I will devote part of this book to examining the scientific and moral/political commitments of the participants, starting with the sociobiology debate as it evolved around Wilson in the Harvard setting. We will then meet the British 'sociobiologists' (how they disliked that name!), and follow the international traffic and interchange of ideas as the protagonists partly shift and the 'camps' become increasingly transatlantic.

Clearly, however, the debate was not merely 'about' individual scientists and their different commitments. This was a debate about the nature of science, the relationship of science to society, and the nature of acceptable knowledge at a particular time—it was just expressed as a conflict between individuals. The controversy about sociobiology can in many respects be seen as the scientific community's discussion with itself. Some of the concerns about science underlying the sociobiology debate would later come to the surface in the so-called Science Wars of the 1990s (see Chapter 17, and Segerstråle, 2000).

Since the beginning of the sociobiology controversy the general climate has changed toward greater acceptance of genetical arguments, and with the expectation of the Human Genome Project soon mapping our DNA. The protagonists in the original controversy have gone on to partly new issues, but from the point of view of their original, overall agendas, much remains the same. For some scientists, the sociobiology controversy was an opportune vehicle to promote larger moral-cum-scientific agendas existing *before* the beginning of this particular conflict. Part of this book is dedicated to identifying these, and showing how for the participants in the debate, their moral/political values were coupled to their scientific positions.

The critics of sociobiology employed a particular style of textual exegesis which I call 'moral reading', aimed at revealing the true meaning of sociobiology. For them, the political truth of sociobiology was obvious. For the sociobiologists, it was not. For scientific practitioners in this field, the new theories and approaches of sociobiology represented an exciting and legitimate new way of understanding evolution. For a long time, however, the climate was such that the critics' interpretation of the true meaning of sociobiology came to overrule their targets' protests. The critics profited from the prevailing post-war taboo on biological explanation of behavior. (In a parallel way, in the 1960s a shy graduate student in England called Bill Hamilton had encountered enormous difficulties in getting anybody to even listen to his idea of studying the genetics of altruism. 'Genetics' was a tainted word after the war, and to combine it explicitly with a human term like 'altruism' was considered absolute anathema.)

Politically, the dichotomies in the sociobiology controversy were not necessarily clearly between the left and the right, although it was often presented this way. The actual dividing line went, rather, between a particular type of New Left activist on the one hand and traditional liberals and democrats on the other. These positions, in turn, were connected to different conceptions of 'good science'. The result was various types of oppositions between the two larger camps in the sociobiology controversy: here we had positive 'planters' vs critical 'weeders', naturalists vs experimentalists, and modelers vs molecular-level reductionists. What was initially confusing was that these conflicts erupted within the very *same* field of evolutionary biology and that the quarreling parties all called themselves evolutionary biologists. Even more confusing was the fact that hardline molecular-level reductionists accused the modelers of 'reductionism'. Mix in Marxist claims of a rather special nature, and you have a web so tangled that political accusations may appear as a sheer heuristic device to get a handle on things!

The most important dividing line in the sociobiology debate, however, did not go between these larger camps, but between two completely different attitudes to *the relationship between scientific and moral truth*. And this division tended to coincide with the Atlantic Ocean. On the one hand, we had Wilson and his American critics who believed in the ultimate coupling of science and moral values—what I call a 'hyper'-Enlightenment quest. On the other, we had the British 'sociobiologists', notably Dawkins and Maynard Smith, who in their 'regular' Enlightenment quest were striving hard to keep science *separate* from moral concerns.

Usually, different conceptions of science do not come into direct confrontation, and so different fields can sustain their own standards, suited to their particular field of inquiry. But this arrangement was totally disrupted in the sociobiology controversy. It became obvious that what seemed plausible and reasonable to scientists in some fields was not so to scientists in other fields. And this may not have been based only on scientific convictions. In fields heavily relying on argumentation, such as evolutionary biology, values easily enter scientific discussion through *plausibility arguments*.

The sociobiology controversy also had a strong metaphysical component—in fact, this may have been a reason for its appeal. Many scientists seemingly could not resist the chance to discuss the nature of human nature. Others were inescapably attracted to the issue of free will and determinism. Sociobiology with its gene talk seemed to fit very nicely under a generalized label of 'genetic determinism'. And this was something that sociobiologists had difficulties extricating themselves from, not the least because of the undereducation of the general public in matters biological (and the way in which the critics of sociobiology reinforced false dichotomies).

The strong moral component of the subject matter attracted especially those scientists who in their scientific work strived to combine the pursuit of scientific and moral truth. Other scientists, who believed in a strict separation between their scientific and moral/political lives, typically stayed away from the controversy. (This included leading left-wing scientists.) What, then, drove the members of the Sociobiology Study Group to spend so much time on criticizing sociobiology? There is no doubt that the critics of sociobiology believed in what they were doing. But this did not mean that they had abandoned scientific competition and the academic quest for recognition—quite the contrary. The critics simply took the quest for credit to its logical next level—the moral realm—and continued their academic prospecting there.

In fact, for *both* parties, the sociobiology debate presented a good opportunity to gather moral brownie points from concerned academic colleagues and the general public. While the critics chanced on unmasking racists and sexists (the worse the villain, the bigger the symbolic reward), the defenders of sociobiology could reap recognition from those who believed in the virtue of positive, traditionalist science. I am not necessarily attributing conscious motives here; I see the behavior of the participants as an expression and extension of more universal scientific optimization strategies.

The sociobiology debate as academic engineering

What happens to scientific ideas that go against established orthodoxy at a particular time? Max Planck took a dark view, in his famous formulation, '[a] new scientific truth does not triumph by convincing its opponents and making them see the light, but rather because its opponents eventually die, and a new generation grows up that is familiar with it' (Planck, 1949). Thomas Kuhn put his own spin on the Planck problem by suggesting that what we have are 'paradigms', scientific orthodoxies, supplanting each other over time. Is it then more or less a matter of luck if a scientist can break through with an unorthodox contribution at an inopportune time? No. Sometimes it just requires clever engineering.

Wilson has taken center stage in the sociobiology controversy because of the upheaval around his book and perhaps a certain Harvard mystique. Meanwhile 'everybody' knows that the mathematical theory underlying sociobiology was formulated by Bill Hamilton in a two-part paper in 1964. (What they don't know is the background story to Hamilton's famous paper, discussed in Chapter 4.) This has led some biologists to argue that Wilson 'did not say anything new'—implying that the credit for the sociobiological revolution should go mostly to those who *did* say 'something new'. But this misses the point, well expressed by John Krebs (1985), that Wilson's important contribution consisted in the fact that he created a field by showing its scattered practitioners that it *existed*. And Wilson not only gave the field a name, he also advocated its feasibility and importance in a social climate suspicious of evolution and the genetics of behavior.

But did he need a scandal to do it? Those who have bought into the 'sandwich model' of *Sociobiology*—political conspiracy version—believe so. According to it, Wilson had put 25 chapters of filling between his all-important first and last chapters. On this view, Wilson's aim was really political: he wanted to legitimize the social status quo. There is another version of the sandwich model, however, the animal behaviorist one. And here we have just the opposite vision of 25 chapters of wonderful information and pictures of animals surrounded by two thin, rather uninteresting slices about humans. The critics focused on the bread, the animal behaviorists on the filling. *Chacun à son gout*!

Then there are those who suspect a publicity stunt: that Wilson's last chapter on humans was included to generate scandal and create a general interest in his big coffee-table tome. The praise Wilson got from his biological colleagues indicates that

Sociobiology would probably have sold well enough even without the controversy—just like Wilson's *The Insect Societies,* another coffee-table book, published with the same press. On this view, then, Wilson did not really need a scandal—although nobody doubts that the controversy helped sell his book and spread the idea of sociobiology.

But there were others who *did* need a scandal—and those were Wilson's two Harvard colleagues, Gould and Lewontin. They had become increasingly disenchanted with neo-Darwinism and wanted to explore alternative approaches. The problem was that, although they 'knew' that an adaptationist, gene-oriented approach was both scientific-ally and morally/politically wrong, at this point they did not have a good scientific alternative to offer. What to do? They wanted to be heard, and as scientists, they wanted to make a mark scientifically. Solution: create a stirrup around sociobiology, present it as both morally dubious and scientifically wrong—and in this way create a climate where people will want to hear what you have to say. On this view, as much as it represented truly held beliefs for many, the moral and political outrage around sociobiology was at the same time a Trojan horse devised to smuggle doubts about adaptationism into the scientific discussion and have them taken seriously. Later, as more supporting arguments had been amassed, the Trojan horse would be slowly dismantled.[2]

But the horse kicked back, as it were. An unintended consequence of all this criticism was that it provoked a response and thereby helped strengthen the sociobiological approach. The *morally* motivated criticism in the sociobiology controversy in fact helped speed up the process of articulation and clarification of many of the *scientific* issues underlying sociobiology and evolutionary biology, such as the status of adaptation, the unit of selection, and the relationship between culture and biological evolution.

Over 25 years, the sociobiology controversy has finally graduated to a genuine scientific controversy; the moral/political aspect has now been largely abandoned. Or has it? What we currently see is a heated battle about the nature of evolutionary theory, in which each statement at least in principle, and often in practice, has seeming moral/political implications as well. Still at stake are questions about the status of adaptation and the true unit of selection, and about the relationship between develop-ment and evolution. The battle, however, has broadened into questions regarding the Modern Synthesis itself and the kind of truth it is capable of generating. The ontological quest of the critics of sociobiology has expanded into an all-out critique of those scientists who are restricting themselves to gene-selectionist modeling, including the assertion that gene-selectionism is not currently the dominant neo-Darwinist para-digm. In turn, their escalating efforts to divide the world into (sensible) 'Us' and (unreasonable) 'Them' reflects a deeper divide between those who would wish for evolutionary biology to answer Why? questions and those who think a science ought to restrict itself to How? questions. In this sense, the sociobiology controversy can be seen as part of a larger battle for the soul of science in one of the few fields where it might still be fought.

In one respect we have seemingly come full circle. Gene selectionists, who may just have thought that they had finally convinced their colleagues of the usefulness of their own approach, now have to contend with a new challenge from 'neo-group selection', typically applauded by critics of sociobiology. The sociobiology debate continues . . . in yet another dialectical movement in the search for truth, and with unmistakable moral and metaphysical overtones.

Wilson, too, has come full circle. His latest book *Consilience*—the synthesis of syntheses—argues for an unified effort of all realms of human knowledge to solve the problems of mankind and the Earth. Wilson's great humanist ambition in *Sociobiology*—to save mankind through increased knowledge of human nature—is now re-emerging. This idea was almost totally suppressed by the (now rather speciesist-seeming!) political debate around his book. Perhaps after a quarter of a century, Wilson will be given another chance, and the serious discussion he intended can begin.

The sociobiology debate as opera

In a recent conversation with an artist I wondered aloud what the right art form would be for a presentation of the sociobiology controversy. In the early days of the debate, when the atmosphere at Harvard was thick with anti-sociobiological feeling, I had entertained myself by thinking of it as a murder mystery. 'Opera!' was her immediate answer.[3]

Opera. She was right. Here we had individuals passionately believing in their causes, telling us in beautiful arias about their longings. The object of desire this time was not a woman, but Truth. There were changing scenarios, but predictable overall themes and tendencies of the main characters, resulting in quite enjoyable duets—and occasionally trios and even quartets. There were rousing choruses appearing at suitable moments. The story itself had all the ingredients of good drama: there were triumphs and dis-appointments, intrigues and coups, and even a whiff of gang warfare *à la* the Capulets and Montagues. But above all, it involved deeply felt emotions. For those involved, the sociobiology controversy touched the very core of what it meant to be a scientist. For the audience, it was slightly embarrassing, although intuitively understandable and often quite enjoyable.

This book, then, deals with the libretto, as it were. I invite the reader to imagine the actual staging, complete with musical scores. Here I only give a few preliminary hints and highlights. The opera has three acts: I, 'What happened in the sociobiology debate?'; II, 'Making sense of the sociobiology debate'; and III, 'The cultural meaning of the battle for science'.

The opera opens with the early upheaval around Wilson's *Sociobiology*. For Chapter 2 we need lots of smoke on the scene, shouting and the clanking of swords. A pitcher of ice-water is indispensable for the reconstruction of the 1978 AAAS meeting in Washington, DC. Chapter 3 brings in a would-be tragic twist: the necessity with which the early protagonists in this story, E. O. Wilson and Richard Lewontin, were on a collision course before the beginning of the controversy. A duet might do it, with both protagonists blindfolded. The next two chapters take us away from the political storm to the creators of sociobiological theory. This brings us over the Atlantic, to Bill Hamilton, George Price, and John Maynard Smith, and back again to a different part of

Harvard—this time the Anthropology Department. The scene opens with Bob Trivers and Irven DeVore playing poker. Before that, we have had a brief encounter with a lumbering robot and his friend, the Chicago gangster. The most dramatic moment, however, is a sad scene with Hamilton as a lonely graduate student struggling with the mathematics of altruism, which nobody seems to be interested in. He is sitting on a bench at Waterloo Station, surrounded by dubious-looking types. Papers are crumpled and tossed, hair is pulled. He sings a long lament divided in two parts, Part I and Part II.

By Chapters 6 and 7 the political dust has cleared enough for a would-be serious scientific discussion to take place. A lot of finger-pointing now goes on as everybody accuses everybody else of error. The high point is Stephen J. Gould's delivery of his and Lewontin's 'Spandrels of San Marco' paper to the Royal Society. Here an architecturally inspired aria will do fine, preferably with a chorus repeating the rousing Latin chant: 'Nullius in Verba, Nullius in Verba'. In the distance we can now see two figures walking on the top of the chapel of King's College, Cambridge. They are Pat Bateson and Gould empirically investigating Gould's spandrels claim. Bateson almost falls off the roof when he pulls at a ceiling rose and finds it only loosely attached. In Chapter 8, Wilson emerges again, looking conspiratorial, this time carrying complicated-looking but fragile metal constructions in both hands. He has now, with Charles Lumsden's help, created genes–mind–culture models to demonstrate that his sociobiological project is in principle workable and worthwhile. But what do others think of the result? Lewontin sneers, Medawar hums, Edmund Leach giggles, and Maynard Smith counts. All flee when Nap Chagnon and his Yanomamö Indians arrive. They have come to protect the models.

Chapter 9 shows that the political connotations of sociobiology will simply not go away. The cast now includes more prominently Steven Rose, 'Britain's Lewontin', dressed all in leather, sustaining a two-front battle against both Wilson and Dawkins. The point where the high opera comes closest to collapsing into a Gilbert and Sullivan operetta, however, is the Nabi episode—a subintrigue in *Nature* involving a pseudonym which may or may not be Lewontin's. Act I ends with Rose threatening Dawkins with a law suit.

Act II switches mode completely. We are no longer dealing with an unfolding story, we stop temporarily to let in a sociologist. She claims, incredibly, that this highly emotional spectacle, full of gossip, intrigue, and innuendo, can in fact be analyzed and made sense of as scientific behavior. She even insists that what we have witnessed is actually rather typical, and that we might learn something about the way science works from looking more closely at these actors and trying to understand how they think and reason.

This sociologist starts out where she believes the real action is: in a workshop of the critical industry. In Chapter 10, hectic activity is going on. The goal is to show that sociobiology is both morally and scientifically corrupt, which is taken-for-granted truth, but needs to be revealed to others. Noam Chomsky briefly visits, but decides not to buy the product. In Chapter 11 we find ourselves in a beautiful garden, with primroses and the Pale Brindled Beauty Moth. Avid gardeners abound. Some are planting pretty flowers but others are following immediately in their footsteps, weeding out what the former have planted. The two types of gardeners are sent by two different firms, both named Defenders of the Truth, but their truths are different, and so are their strategies.

In Chapter 12 we meet a group of scientists who have taken unusual roles in the debate. They have retained a critical stance while refusing to buy into the rhetoric of the anti-sociobiologists: Peter Medawar, John Maynard Smith, Pat Bateson, and Salvador Luria. We hear them out. Chapter 13 opens with communicative naturalists clashing with critical experimentalists. But it gets worse: soon the whole academy divides into two camps, who live in two separate worlds of truth and 'known facts'. This time we see lots of people running around with blindfolds.

In Chapter 14 more smoke has to be brought on stage. We are here dealing with fairly hairy epistemological and ontological issues relating to sociobiology and IQ research as science: what exactly is it that the opponents of these fields object to? The high point here is the Reductionist Lament against Reductionism. Chapter 15 brings out the protagonists of the two camps onto different balconies to receive tribute from their respective crowds cheering below. The protagonists are pointing at each other and shouting things across the scene. At particularly apposite jeers the crowds toss gold coins up on their favorite's balcony. The protagonists go on, in seeming ceaseless interchange, both sides accumulating piles of moral capital from the continuing conflict. Act II ends with Stephen J. Gould getting the Optimization Award for most effective simultaneous pursuit of scientific and moral aims, with E. O. Wilson as a close second.

In Act III, we are transported to the present. The sociologist has partly gone back to reporting, but she refuses to stop analyzing. Chapter 16 takes stock of the progress of sociobiology and the fate of the protagonists in the controversy. We note a scene with Wilson journeying to different topics, getting his suitcase relabeled from 'bad sociobiologist' to 'good environmentalist', all the time carrying the gene–culture co-evolution models around in a secret compartment. This is registered by the choir, who hesitantly tries to make 'co-evolution' rhyme with 'revolution' as Wilson is crowned the moral victor in the sociobiology controversy. Meanwhile, we see Gould and Dawkins involved in a dramatic-seeming duel duet with impeccably co-ordinated singing, while both keep systematically shooting beside the target.

In Chapter 17 we hear the clanking of swords again. There is a lot of movement on the scene as the chapter establishes the continuity of the sociobiology controversy with the Science Wars. The chapter ends with everybody on the same side, raising the banner of Truth against the barbarians—constructivists and relativists—now at the gate, although there is some traffic in and out a backdoor.

Chapter 18 is dominated by a scene with a bridge which has been destroyed in the middle. People on one side are trying to use all kinds of ingenuity to bridge the gap, but are easily rebuffed by the people on the other side, who seem to consider this a hostile takeover. Many seem to believe that the gap is best left as it is, but we see lots of people swimming over in both directions. Wilson, a veteran strategist at bridging the Two Cultures, appears on the scene with a hat with inbuilt ear plugs and blinders. He has decided not to be distracted any longer by people saying he cannot do it. Finally, we see him landing from the ceiling in a hot-air balloon labeled *Consilience*. He sings a persuasive solo about his plan, which is to invite members of both sides to see the big picture. Sound of bassoons in the background.

Chapters 19 and 20, the finale, address the connection between fact and values, science and belief, and even the status of evolutionary biology as a science. Different points of view are delivered in dramatic alto voices. The scene is almost unbearably smoky by now. Enlightenment and hyper-Enlightenment advocates run around with candles. Demons abound. Even the Pope pops up. Suddenly, through a hidden opening in the scene floor, Truth and Clarity emerge. The scene is flooded by light. The smoke clears. Everybody claims victory and gets out. Truth and Clarity smile. They have seen it so many times before.

Well, admittedly the scene with Truth and Clarity is still beyond this book. Maybe it can be added in a future edition.

PART ONE

What happened in the sociobiology debate?

CHAPTER 2

The storm over *Sociobiology*

The creation of the sociobiology controversy

What can make a six-pound, 12″ × 12″ hardcover academic book a hot seller? Give it an intriguing name, provide it with full-page drawings and an appealing cover. But there is still the price factor. How does one convince academics and the general public that this is a book that they absolutely need to have? The answer is, of course, controversy.

For controversy to happen, there should not only exist clear potential opponents to the book's central message but also a general climate sympathetic to such criticism. The critics should be qualified ones, that is, of the same authority as the author, and they should represent the book's message as being so offensive as to upset any decent person. Finally, they should continue their attack long enough for the book and its author to get solidly onto the index of evil scholarship. For Harvard University Press, the events around the publication of *Sociobiology* could not have been more propitious had it engineered the whole publicity campaign itself. But let us start from the beginning.

In the early summer of 1975, the distinguished Harvard entomologist Edward O. Wilson published a very large tome, *Sociobiology: The New Synthesis*. In his book, Wilson defined sociobiology as a new discipline devoted to 'the systematic study of the biological basis of all social behavior'. Among animal species Wilson explicitly included our own species *Homo sapiens*, and the final chapter of his work looked exclusively at humans. In this chapter Wilson suggested that human sex role divisions, aggressiveness, moral concerns, religious beliefs, and much more, could be connected to our evolutionary heritage, as it is represented today in our underlying genetic dispositions.

In November 1975, a group called the Sociobiology Study Group, composed of professors, students, researchers and others from the Boston area launched an attack on Wilson's *Sociobiology*, which by then had received widespread publicity and positive reviews. The first public statement by this group was a letter in the *New York Review of Books* (Allen *et al.*, 1975), in response to the evolutionist C. H. Waddington's sympathetic account of Wilson's book in an earlier issue (Waddington, 1975). The dramatic nature of this letter lay not only in its strong language, but also in the fact that among the co-signers could be found the names of some of Wilson's colleagues, working in the same department at Harvard, particularly Richard C. Lewontin and Stephen J. Gould.

The political tone of the letter was evident: Wilson's attempt to include the human species as a legitimate object of analysis in terms of the concepts of the newly developed discipline of sociobiology was linked to former 'biological determinist' theories which had lent themselves to abuse for political reasons. As the critics formulated it:

> These theories provided an important basis for the enactment of sterilization laws and restrictive immigration laws by the United States between 1910 and 1930 and also for the eugenics policies which led to the establishment of gas chambers in Nazi Germany. The latest attempt to reinvigorate these tired theories comes with the alleged creation of a new discipline, sociobiology (Allen *et al.*, 1975).

Wilson was presented as an ideologue supporting the status quo as an inevitable consequence of human nature, because of his interest in establishing the central traits of a genetically controlled human nature. He was criticized for not making evident to the 'innocent reader' what was fact and what was speculation, and for playing down the absence of direct evidence of a genetic foundation for human behavioral traits. According to the critics, despite Wilson's claims that he presented a wealth of new information, his supposedly new science had no scientific support and in reality concealed political assumptions. The critics charged that in order to 'graft speculation about human behavior onto a biological core', Wilson used 'a number of strategies and sleights of hand'. Finally, the letter writers stated their own position on human nature:

> We are not denying that there are genetic components to human behavior. But we suspect that human biological universals are to be discovered more in the generalities of eating, excreting and sleeping than in such specific and highly variable behaviors as warfare, sexual exploitation of women and the use of money as a medium of exchange (Allen *et al.*, 1975).

Wilson's response was that the letter's co-signers had utterly distorted the content of his message, and that their accusations were all false (Wilson, 1975c). He provided examples of how he had been quoted out of context so that his true meaning had been distorted, and he invited the readers to check for themselves. As one might guess, his critics were not persuaded, and wrote a longer position paper with detailed criticism (Sociobiology Study Group of Science for the People, 1976a), which in turn was rebutted by Wilson (Wilson, 1976a). From here the sociobiology controversy soon escalated, polarizing the academic community in much the same way as the IQ controversy some five years earlier. Before long the dispute had become a media event, with coverage on the front page of *Time* magazine.

Instead of checking for themselves, however, it seems that many academics rather took the critics' interpretation at face value. The price of $25 for the big book may have been unattractive, and the prospect of reading it even more daunting for someone who had no interest in evolutionary biology as such. In the prevailing academic climate many simply assumed that the critics had done a fair job of singling out the offensive parts of the book and subjecting it to justified political criticism. And since many of the signers were university professors (four of them from Harvard), the critique had the necessary back-up of authority to be taken seriously. Finally, for anyone who took a culturally formed human nature for granted, the critics' eloquent, accusatory style succeeded in making sociobiology sound highly suspect. I can say all this with great understanding, since I myself, trained as a sociologist (and a chemist/biochemist), but unfamiliar with reasoning in evolutionary biology, started off believing that the critics were right—indeed, that they had said all there was to say about sociobiology, and that the case was closed.

There were other reasons why the critics' interpretation, rather than Wilson's protests about his innocence, quickly came to prevail. Most academics are not in the habit of checking sources, unless they have a *specific* reason for it (such as refereeing an article or writing a book review), and as long as the conclusion fits with their taken-for-granted assumptions. So, also in the case of *Sociobiology*, people rather let the critics read the book 'for' them. Why read the original when the critics' conclusion was eminently plausible?

Controversies involving sensitive political issues exhibit something of the social psychology of witch hunts. Once they have started, it does not help much that the targets themselves protest and try to demonstrate their innocence. The original inter-pretation tends to stick, and those who criticize it as incorrect or unfair—or worse, try to defend the target—run the risk of being identified themselves as supporters of the same unpopular cause that got the target in trouble in the first place. (Defend someone as not being racist, and you automatically come under suspicion for racism yourself.) This was exactly what happened in the sociobiology controversy.

Missing: serious scientific criticism

Few of Wilson's colleagues in the United States came to his defense. Arguably, they would not have had to defend sociobiology itself, but merely his right to do what he did as an evolutionary biologist. But Wilson had been charged with the worst of possible crimes: he had been connected with racism and genocide. Not only do scientists not like controversy in general, but here was the additional danger that anybody who spoke up would be tarred with the same brush.

What is more, many of Wilson's American colleagues may have genuinely thought that the climate was not yet ripe for the promulgation of biological theories of human behavior. They only needed to look at the demonstrations and polemics around University of California, Berkeley professor Arthur Jensen in the early 1970s, following his suggestion in the *Harvard Educational Review* (Jensen, 1969) that one should not dismiss a priori the hypothesis that the 15-point difference in IQ between white and black populations might have a genetic component.[1] His infamous article was entitled: 'How much can we boost IQ and scholastic achievement?' and started with the pro-vocative statement: 'Compensatory education has been tried and it apparently has failed' (Jensen, 1969).[2]

And closer to home, there had been the uproar over Harvard psychologist Richard Herrnstein's 1971 article in *The Atlantic Monthly*. Herrnstein had conjectured that in a future society with increased emphasis on equality of opportunity, there would exist a social stratification based on 'IQ-classes' instead. In fact, his argument was not new; it had been made before by the British sociologist Michael Young in his tongue-in-cheek report *The Rise of the Meritocracy, 1870–2033* (Young, 1958). But in the contemporary

American context, the article took on an air of scandal—which may have been the idea, too, considering the timing. During 1971–2, Herrnstein's article gave rise to a series of letters and addresses, not only in its original journal but also in *The Harvard Crimson*, a weekly newspaper. His lectures were interrupted, and posters around Harvard yard pictured him as 'wanted' for racism. Herrnstein himself went so far as to suggest that his negative national reputation was the reason why in 1972 Harvard University was chosen as the site for the national convention of the SDS, Students for Democratic Society (Herrnstein, 1973).[3]

But even without making a connection to Jensen or Herrnstein, many may have thought it ill-advised of Wilson to include a discussion of humans in his book. After all, at this time, a cultural or environmentalist explanation of human behavior was taken for granted, or at least was the official position, in academia. In such a climate, any claim about a genetically founded human nature would understandably be associated with earlier only-too-well-known uses of biology for various unsavoury political purposes: Social Darwinism, eugenics, sterilization laws, and, just as the critics claimed, Nazi genocide. And, to the extent people bothered to look at Wilson's infamous last chapter, it did indeed seem speculative—there was then, and is now, little hard evidence about humans. What is more, the first chapter of *Sociobiology*, entitled 'The Morality of the Gene', was already a slap in the face of academic orthodoxy. Wilson appeared to blatantly commit the 'naturalistic fallacy'—deriving *ought* from *is*, a notorious scholarly fault, by arguing that better knowledge about our biological heritage was a moral and social imperative.

Considering, then, the plausible political interpretation of this sort of writing at the time, the critics' charges of dangerous consequences made sense. But did the hypothesized political *effect* of the first and last chapters also imply a political *intent* on the part of the author? This was what the Sociobiology Study Group seemed to suggest, at least, and this appears also to have been unproblematically accepted by others. Few in academia or outside knew Wilson well, and he himself avoided public debate (even though he lent himself to occasional interviews). So, while people had little direct information to go on, it was indeed puzzling why anyone would want to argue so ardently for a biologically founded human nature when so little was known and claims of this kind had such clearly perceived political connotations. The critics' insinuation that Wilson had a political agenda seemed eminently plausible. For some it may not even have mattered what Wilson's true intent was—what was important was the *perceived* pernicious political effect of his message. That, alone, was enough to merit serious action.

And, once the controversy had started, most of those who knew Wilson, his colleagues at Harvard and in biology at large, did not try to correct the impression that had been formed. In his autobiography, Wilson himself complains about the avoidance patterns of his colleagues (Wilson, 1994, p. 338). I can remember at least two of Wilson's American biology colleagues who were reluctant or refused to be interviewed by me about their views on sociobiology. The sociobiology debate soon fell into a standard interpretive framework: it came to be seen as a typical political nature–nurture controversy with progressive environmentalists pitted against conservative hereditarians; the good guys against the bad guys. This impression was continuously reinforced by the critics.

But the critics had not only criticized sociobiology on political grounds. They had also said that it was bad *science*. In fact, this was an equally important part of their over-all message, and part of their motivation in attacking Wilson in the first place. In later chapters, we will examine the various types of scientific issues involved. At this point, we may just note that if what the opponents to sociobiology really wanted was effective scientific critique, they chose a very bad strategy. At least, this was the opinion of Ernst Mayr, observing the controversy from his own office in the Museum of Comparative Zoology at Harvard. He was quite irritated with the critics—not because of their attack on sociobiology, but because of the way they botched the job. 'Why could these crooked Marxists not be honest!' he said in interview in 1981. He worried that, because of the political attack, people might believe that the critics did not have any good *scientific* arguments. Yet it would have been 'so easy' to criticize sociobiology on scientific grounds, according to Mayr. (Later, he did indeed offer such a criticism himself; Mayr, 1983.)

Perhaps even more damaging to the potential scientific debate about sociobiology was the absence of any serious critical reviews in scholarly journals. There was a clear reason for this. According to Mayr, just because of the political criticism, several people who had been severely critical of sociobiology and had taken their time preparing reviews for scientific journals, now simply tore them up. They did not want their genuinely scientific disagreements to be seen as in any way supportive of the Sociobiology Study Group's political attack on sociobiology. Mayr knew of at least three such cases (Mayr, interview).

Thus, the political allegations of the critics sent shock waves through the academic community and from the very beginning undermined serious scientific discussion about the real merits and shortcomings of sociobiology. Interestingly, there was later even some admission that the critics' initial strategy had misfired. 'Other people may have listened more if we had presented our arguments differently,' Lewontin said in the spring of 1976, while Gould conceded: 'Our rhetoric was at fault' (Lewin, 1976). In any case, the lack of scientific critique was only temporary: soon Gould and Lewontin changed their strategy and went full steam ahead with various scientific attacks on sociobiology. Arguably, though, Gould and Lewontin's new focus on the field's scientific shortcomings was not a real substitute for the continuing lack of genuinely scientific critique. In their writings, these two Harvard critics never quite abandoned their original moral/political condemnation of sociobiology.

The Sociobiology Study Group as a whole did in fact early on make an attempt to present their own serious objections to sociobiology in more detail to the general public. It was just that this attempt failed. Ever since 28 May 1975 when *Sociobiology* had been mentioned on the front page of *The New York Times*—a noticeboard for world events and important scientific breakthroughs—the group had been set to do something. They wanted to restore balance after what they deemed an overblown publicity campaign by

Harvard University Press in cahoots with the media (cf. Beckwith, 1981–2; Alper *et al.*, 1978).

Lewontin told me in one of my interviews what happened next. As a representative of the Sociobiology Study Group, he called Boyce Rensberger, the science editor at *The New York Times* responsible for the front-page article on *Sociobiology*, and suggested that Rensberger now also write something on the mounting criticism of sociobiology. But Rensberger responded that this would be premature. According to Lewontin, his exact words were: 'There is no controversy yet.' But Lewontin did not easily let *The New York Times* editor off the hook. In November, when the letter to *The New York Review of Books* was in press, Lewontin called him again. And this time he could say: '*Now* there is controversy!' (Lewontin remembered this with some triumph in his voice.)

And Rensberger finally did agree to write about the critical opposition to socio-biology. He asked if there was any material written by the Sociobiology Study Group that he might use. It was now that Lewontin, in response to Rensberger's request, sat down and over a weekend composed a long critical position paper for the Sociobiology Study Group, which was then rapidly dispatched to Rensberger. Lewontin admitted that this longer critique of sociobiology was really his single-handed work, although he had let a couple of other group members briefly look at it.

The result was a big disappointment. Lewontin felt terribly cheated. Rather than highlighting the essence of the critics' objections to sociobiology, Rensberger had pro-duced a 'sensationalistic' piece.[4] What was more, the science editor had misrepresented the fact that it was he himself who had asked for the material. Worst of all, he had made Lewontin into the chief opponent of Wilson! (This was a label that Lewontin really disliked and tried to erase whenever he had a chance.) In other words, the critics' early attempt to use *The New York Times* as a vehicle for their critical attack on sociobiology had badly misfired.

This meant that although a detailed scientific criticism of *Sociobiology* was already available in November, neither the academic world nor the general public were aware of the Sociobiology Study Group's serious critique. (The long critique was later published as an article in *BioScience* with a rebuttal by Wilson, but not until March 1976.) This is not to say that there was not a hectic samizdat activity operating from Lewontin's Harvard office, where the long critique was distributed to callers from a box on the floor. Considering the traffic around Lewontin (and his box), his correspondence, and the many invitations he received to speak up against the evils of sociobiology during this early stage of the controversy, there is no doubt that it was he who was seen as Wilson's chief opponent, whether he liked it or not. For many, Lewontin became the upholder of good and moral science against bad and dangerous pseudoscience.

The Sociobiology Study Group in action

Let us now take a look at the early stages of the controversy and the composition of the Sociobiology Study Group itself. According to several members, the Sociobiology Study

Group was spontaneously formed upon the announcement of Wilson's book as an 'event' on the front page of *The New York Times* on 28 May 1975 (for example, Ruth Hubbard, interview). What offended the group in that article was among other things the statement:

> Sociobiology carries with it the revolutionary implication that much of man's behavior toward his fellows . . . may be as much a product of evolution as is the structure of the hand or the size of the brain (Rensberger, 1975a).

And the positive public presentation of Wilson's book did not stop there. In less than a month, *The New York Times Book Review* carried an upbeat review of *Sociobiology*, suggesting that 'we are on the verge of breakthroughs in the effort to understand our place in the scheme of things' (27 June 1975), which was also duly noted by the group of critics.

It was the accumulation of these kinds of laudatory statements that made the Sociobiology Study Group feel the need to take away what they saw as a 'screen of approval' around sociobiology (Hubbard, interview; Allen *et al.*, 1975). Thus it was probably for maximal shock effect that in their letter the critics created a direct contrast between the above quote on purported scientific 'breakthroughs' and the strongest possible counterstatement they themselves could mobilize: their political allegation involving Nazi Germany.

For the purposes of the Sociobiology Study Group, Conrad Waddington's review of *Sociobiology* in the 7 August issue of *The New York Review of Books* was extremely timely. The group had not so far been able to reach a larger public with their criticism, at least not through the most obvious medium, *The New York Times*. Now it was possible for them to formulate their criticism of Wilson as a letter to *The New York Review of Books*, protesting against Waddington's largely positive review of Wilson's book. Writing this letter was a strategic move in launching the attack on sociobiology, since the correspondence section of this journal routinely works as a forum for sociopolitical polemics. Of course, in the same forum, Waddington would have been expected to reply to the critics' broadside against sociobiology. And considering his broad sympathies with the aims of evolutionary biology (even though he was partly critical of Wilson), he might have declared the critics badly mistaken in their claim that Wilson's aim was political. This, in turn, may or may not have influenced the course of events in the sociobiology controversy. However, a reply from Waddington was not forthcoming. In the meantime, this eminent evolutionist had died.

Who were the members of the Sociobiology Study Group? The initial co-signers of the letter were sixteen Boston-area academics, ranging from professors to students. (Indeed, Elizabeth Allen, the first signatory to the much-quoted reference of Allen *et al.*, was but a pre-medical student at Brandeis at the time.) The professors involved were Jon Beckwith, professor at Harvard Medical School; Stephen Chorover, professor of psychology, MIT; David Culver, professor of biology at Northwestern (visiting at Harvard Medical School); Stephen J. Gould, professor in the Museum of Comparative Zoology, Harvard; Ruth Hubbard, professor of biology, Harvard; Anthony Leeds, professor of anthropology, Boston University; and Richard Lewontin, professor of biology, Harvard. Among the rest were, in addition to Allen, a teacher (Barbara Beckwith); a research assistant (Margaret Duncan, Harvard Medical School); a resident fellow (Hiroshi Inouye, Harvard Medical School); a graduate student (Chuck Madansky, Harvard Medical School); a research associate (Miriam Rosenthal, Harvard School of Public Health); a doctor (Reed Pyeritz, Peter Bent Brigham Hospital, Boston); and a psychiatrist (Herb Schreier, Massachusetts General Hospital). Some obvious 'missing' names among Boston-area radicals were Noam Chomsky, Salvador Luria, George Wald, and Richard Levins. These all had their own reasons for not being on the list. Levins was very ill at that moment and the others chose not to participate for reasons that we will return to in Chapters 10 and 12.

Later, the Sociobiology Study Group associated itself with Science for the People, or rather, with its Boston chapter. Science for the People (SftP) was a national forum for left-wing academic activism (Walsh, 1976). With regard to sociobiology, the most active other chapter existed at Ann Arbor, where Richard Alexander, another sociobiologist, met some early opposition. That chapter also published a book, *Biology as a Social Weapon* (Ann Arbor Collective for Science for the People, 1977). SftP arranged campaigns and meetings and published a bimonthly journal. In addition to sociobiology, issues taken up by SftP included such things as environmental hazards, Third World problems, and various academic controversies as they arose (or were created), such as the IQ controversy, the recombinant DNA debate, and the controversy over the XYY ('criminal') gene. For a surprisingly long time, however, the favorite target of SftP seems to have been sociobiology and Wilson.

The early association between the Sociobiology Study Group and SftP also meant that the original group was now joined by other academic activists, such as Joseph Alper, a chemist at the University of Massachusetts, and Robert Lange, a physicist at Brandeis. One of the first things this enlarged group (now called the Sociobiology Study Group for Science for the People) did was to produce the above-mentioned position paper. The Sociobiology Study Group and its individual members published articles and book reviews, wrote letters and pamphlets, gave lectures and arranged public meetings at Harvard and elsewhere. The group also met regularly on a monthly basis in the homes of its members. I was generously granted permission to be an observer in the group and attended two or three of its meetings. These meetings discussed strategies in the criticism of sociobiology, reported successes, and noted what needed to be done next, and who would do it. One of the more memorable group meetings was held in May 1976 at the house of Stephen Chorover, with Noam Chomsky as a guest. There had been some concern and puzzlement that Chomsky, a perceived political ally and devastating left-wing critic, had so far not written any critique of sociobiology. Chomsky had now been invited because the group hoped that he would lend his considerable critical talents to the common cause. It did not work out that way, however. Chomsky could not be co-opted. We will return to this in Chapter 10.

To give a sense of the content and tone of the public meetings arranged by the Sociobiology Study Group at the height of its influence, I will give the example from a representative gathering in the geology lecture room at Harvard in November 1979. On the program were various lectures relating to the general topic of 'biological determinism', which accommodated also Evelyn Fox Keller, invited from nearby Northeastern University to speak on women and mathematics; she criticized a new psychometric study purporting to show sex differences in math ability. Most of the other lectures dealt with sociobiology, such as a paper on sociobiology and sex roles by SftP member Freda Salzman, and a long and surprisingly academic-sounding presentation—despite its horrifying content on Nazi practices—by Stephen Chorover. (Many of the talks in fact related to the presenters' own articles or books, in preparation or in print.) One talk documented the recent use of sociobiological arguments by European right-wing groups (this gave rise to a report in *Nature* entitled 'Sociobiology Critics Claim Fears Come True', Dickson, 1979). Overall, just as in the monthly group meetings, the atmosphere was one of righteous moral indignation at dangerous 'biological determinist' theories and their creators.

There was one surprising incident, though, at this public meeting. Irven DeVore from the Harvard anthropology department, the only representative of 'the enemy' present, spoke up. He testified to the relative innocence of sociobiologists in regard to the contexts in which their ideas had been put by others. Here he referred particularly to a film, *Doing What Comes Naturally*, commercially produced by Hoebel–Letterman Productions in 1976, where various statements by himself, Robert Trivers, and Wilson had been used to prove points about human behavior and differences between the sexes in a way of which these sociobiologists themselves totally disapproved. (This film was one of the favorite traveling exhibits presented by the critics as examples of the evils of sociobiology; the soundtrack had been transcribed by Chorover in February 1978 just in time for the meeting of the American Association for the Advancement of Science; more about this later.) Although I believe that many respected DeVore's courage, his comment did not seriously affect the audience's sense of political outrage, which had been successfully reinforced by the evening's rousing talks.

It was not only the Sociobiology Study Group that arranged meetings. There were also occasions organized by academic departments on quite short notice—for instance, the sociology department led a well-attended panel symposium in one of Harvard's largest lecture halls, and later sponsored a talk by invited anthropologist Marshall Sahlins, who presented what was to become his book *The Use and Abuse of Biology* (1976). No wonder the sociologists and anthropologists were upset—Wilson seemed to want to make these fields, too, part of evolutionary biology. There were also talks arranged outside the university, for instance in a place called the Cambridge Forum in Harvard Square, where among others Gould spoke on the panda's thumb as a critique of sociobiological adaptationism, and where also debates on the continuing IQ controversy were arranged, such as one between Harvard Medical School colleagues Bernard Davis and Jon Beckwith in 1976, to which we will return in Chapter 11.

But there were still more hostile critics of Wilson than the members of the Sociobiology Study Group. The most vocal· were the members of CAR (International Committee Against Racism). On a number of occasions, this organization picketed in

Harvard Square and handed out flyers calling for demonstrations against Wilsonian sociobiology. These flyers, sporting CAR's logo of a clenched fist, said such things as 'Sociobiology, by encouraging biological and genetic explanations for racism, war and genocide, exonerates and protects the groups and individuals who have carried out and benefited from these monstrous crimes' and 'But in 1975, E.O. Wilson laid claim to the title of chief of this group [Harvard's 'master race' ideologues], when in *Sociobiology* he postulated genes for all social life, including war, business success, male supremacy and racism.'[5]

From the beginning, the Sociobiology Study Group was also monitoring the reception of the controversy in academia. The group members were quick to react with letters of protest in places like *Science* whenever they perceived a misrepresentation of their own position. For instance, they felt that the science journalist Nicholas Wade had been unfair and biased in his early overview of the controversy (Wade, 1976), and had been too easily persuaded by Wilson's claims that the critics had completely distorted his message. The Sociobiology Study Group was therefore concerned to point out that they had not misrepresented Wilson. For this purpose, they composed a multi-authored letter with Beckwith as the first signer. (This was a deliberate action in order to play down the role of Lewontin; this measure was democratically discussed at a group meeting I attended.) The letter invited the readers of *Science* to check for themselves. According to the co-signers, 'There is politics aplenty in *Sociobiology*, and we who are its critics did not put it there' (Alper *et al.*, 1976).

One of the high points for the Sociobiology Study Group was undoubtedly the meeting for the American Association for the Advancement of Science (AAAS) in Washington, DC in February 1978. There biologist George Barlow and anthropologist James Silverberg organized a two-day symposium on sociobiology (later published as a book by Westview Press: *Sociobiology: Beyond Nature/Nurture?*, Barlow and Silverberg, 1980). The organizers believed this to be 'the first symposium in which competent advocates and critics of sociobiology have come together and spoken responsibly', but admitted that 'some of our participants were at first reluctant to appear, fearing harrassment' (Barlow and Silverberg, 1980, p. xxv). Science for the People had seized this opportunity to propagate their own viewpoints on sociobiology and arrange their own parallel sessions and discussions. They had been allowed to set up tables in the corridor outside the lecture rooms and were even granted the use of the rooms during the breaks between the ordinary sessions.

According to two leading members of SftP, the Sociobiology Study Group sold a total of 1000 of their papers (there was even a Critique of Sociobiology packet available for $2.00), talked to people, and showed their parade exhibit—the film *Doing What Comes Naturally*, which was was well attended (Beckwith and Lange, 1978). As Jonathan Beckwith and Robert Lange proudly described it in their report from this conference: 'SftP did well on the floor, raising points, challenging speakers, etc. and many people attended our countersessions. All in all, people felt like we put in a good showing and influenced a lot of people' (Beckwith and Lange, 1978). Indeed, if the organizers considered it an achievement to have both sociobiology advocates and some of their academic critics on the same panel, Science for the People saw the very fact that the symposium had been arranged as a relative victory for their own cause:

> The very fact of the AAAS sponsoring this symposium on the 'controversy' is an indication of the success we have had in making the claims of the sociobiologists controversial. What caught many of us in Science for the People by surprise at the AAAS meetings was the extent of the spreading negative reaction to sociobiology. At this meeting, and at another recent meeting in which we participated at Wellesley College, sociobiologists seemed very much on the defensive. Many have rushed to dissociate themselves from Wilson. At the AAAS meeting, the discrediting of human sociobiology was reflected in the content of the symposium itself, in numerous private and public discussions which Science for the People held with those attending the meetings and in the receptivity to our ideas and literature (Beckwith and Lange, 1978).

The two-day symposium featured about twenty speakers in all. As a member of the audience, I can say that for those who anticipated a public showdown, it was somewhat disappointing to sit through rather technical talks dealing with animal sociobiology. (Lectures of more popular interest by advocates were probably those by Steven Emlen, David Barash, Richard Dawkins, and Wilson, and among the scientific and political critics, those by Stephen J. Gould, developmental psychologist Stephanie Shields, and the anthropologist Eleanor Leacock; cf. Beckwith and Lange, 1978.) But there was anticipation in the air, particularly in the session where both Wilson and Gould were to speak. The ballroom was filled to capacity. Would Gould demolish sociobiology? Would Wilson stand up to Gould? By now, the audience wanted some action. The result exceeded anybody's expectations.

What happens is a total surprise. The session has already featured Gould, among others, and Wilson is one of the later speakers. Just as Wilson is about to begin, about ten people rush up on the speaker podium shouting various epithets and chanting: 'Racist Wilson you can't hide, we charge you with genocide!' While some take over the microphone and denounce sociobiology, a couple of them rush up behind Wilson (who is sitting in his place) and pour a jug of ice-water over his head, shouting 'Wilson, you are all wet!' Then they quickly disappear again. Great commotion ensues but things calm down when the session organizer steps up to the microphone and apologizes to Wilson for the incident. The audience gives Wilson a standing ovation. Now Gould steps up to the microphone saying that this kind of activism is not the right way to fight sociobiology—here he has a Lenin quote handy, on 'radicalism, an infantile disorder of socialism'. For his valiant handling of the situation, Gould, too, gets a standing ovation. (The audience does not quite know how to react to any of this but applauding seems somehow right.) Wilson—still wet—gives his talk, in spite of the shock of the physical attack. He explains his own non-political background motivation for *Sociobiology* and produces various types of studies in support of the idea of a genetic basis for human behavior. After all the action, his calmly delivered talk is something of an anticlimax.

Who were these disrupters of the peace? It turned out they belonged to CAR. In their report, Beckwith and Lange evaluated the incident as follows: 'While our general feeling was that the anti-Wilson-Sociobiology sentiments were not seriously diminished by the

CAR action, it did provide Wilson with at least a momentary respite from the criticisms and restored some respect to his position. Furthermore, the press coverage of the opposition to sociobiology focused excessively on this incident' (Beckwith and Lange, 1978). According to them, 'One of us rose at the end of Wilson's talk to dissociate ourselves from the CAR action.'

But how much of a surprise was this incident really for the Sociobiology Study Group/SftP? While Beckwith and Lange in their account give the impression that the demonstrators were rushing into the ballroom from outside, Wilson states that they rose from their seats *in the audience* and returned to them afterwards. He also noted that they were carrying placards with anti-sociobiology slogans (Wilson, 1994, p. 348). Clearly, there were ties between CAR and the Sociobiology Study Group/SftP (for instance, Sociobiology Study Group member Rosenthal's article had been used as a CAR flyer); probably even an overlap in membership. It seemed to me, sitting towards the back, that among the ice-water squad at AAAS I recognized at least one female face from the monthly meetings of the Sociobiology Study Group that I had attended.

Could the sociobiology debate have been avoided?

When I asked Lewontin in one of my interviews whether the whole controversy might not have been avoided had there been better communication, he answered: 'This is the kind of question that does not even arise for someone like me.' I understood this to mean that the events were all part of the great unfolding of historical materialism or something along those lines, and he made me feel terribly un-Marxist for venturing such a naive question. However, the question is obviously legitimate, since a controversy involves conscious actions on both sides and chances are that a lack of communication is not accidental. With hindsight, I believe that 'bad communication' is indeed one way of characterizing the sociobiology debate. On the other hand, I do not think that the controversy could have been avoided.

Like good novels or mysteries, the sociobiology controversy involves hypothetical 'what-if' scenarios. Let us look at some of these. Might the controversy have been avoided, had the contending parties only sorted out their differences early on? One of the obvious candidates for a what-if scenario is Wilson's chance meeting with Gould in the late spring of 1975. According to Wilson, Gould then warned him that there might be political upheaval because of *Sociobiology*, upon which Wilson invited Gould to come to his office to explain more closely what this meant. But Gould did not follow this up. Wilson was angry and disappointed that he had not been informed about the mounting opposition—according to Wilson's own what-if scenario, he imagined that he could have helped dispel incorrect interpretations of the book's message in this way (Wilson, interview in 1981). Of course, soon after 28 May Gould had joined the Sociobiology Study Group, and we can assume that his allegiance to that group prevented further interaction with 'the enemy'.

Wilson seems to have been totally unaware of the impending letter attack by the Sociobiology Study Group. As he himself said in his response to the letter in *The New*

York Review of Books, 'in spite of the fact that I have been on friendly terms with some of the signers of the letter for years, and two share the same building with me at Harvard University, I did not know of the letter's existence until three days before it appeared in print' (Wilson, 1975c). He went on to say that had the critics only contacted him in time, he could have calmed their fears of political abuse of sociobiological statements. He could also have showed them an article that he had written and which had been ready for a couple of months before the letter emerged (this was his article on altruism published in *The New York Times Magazine* on 13 October; Wilson, 1975b). According to Wilson, that article contained explicit warnings about taking sociobiological views as a justification for existing social practices. There was, for instance, the following statement, which Wilson now repeated in his response:

> The moment has come to stress that there is a dangerous trap in sociobiology, one which can be avoided only by constant vigilance. The trap is the naturalistic fallacy of ethics, which uncritically concludes that what is, should be. The 'what is' in human nature is to a large extent the heritage of a Pleistocene hunter-gatherer existence. When any genetic bias is demonstrated, it cannot be used to justify a continuing practice in present and future societies. Since most of us live in a radically new environment of our own making, the pursuit of such a practice would be bad biology; and like all bad biology, it would invite disaster (Wilson, 1975b).

Thus, although shocked over the political interpretation of a work which he himself intended to be provocative primarily for social scientists, Wilson presented himself as willing to rectify any misunderstandings early on. But just as in a good novel, it was too late.

People have had a hard time believing that Wilson could have been so politically out of touch. As he said himself, 'the political objections forcefully made by the Sociobiology Study Group of Science for the People in particular took me by surprise' (Wilson, 1978c). He repeated this in his autobiography, where he commented on Maynard Smith, who in interview with me in 1981 had voiced just such incredulity. Maynard Smith had told me:

> And it was also absolutely obvious to me—I *cannot* believe Wilson didn't know—that this was going to provoke great hostility from American Marxists, and Marxists everywhere . . .

To this Wilson responded:

> But it was true. I was unprepared . . . In 1975 I was a political naif: I knew almost nothing about Marxism as either a political belief or a mode of analysis, I had paid little attention to the dynamism of the activist left, and I had never heard of Science for the People. I was not even an intellectual in the European or New York-Cambridge sense (Wilson, 1994, p. 339).

This was also the genuine feeling I got at the time of interviewing Wilson in late 1981 (and also earlier, in 1977, when I interviewed him for a term paper). What is more, after his first outburst of disbelief, Maynard Smith changed his mind in that very same interview. He concluded that Wilson may, after all, have been politically innocent, for the following reason:

> I think this is the difference between a European and an American. No European with his degree of culture and general education [would have been unaware of the political implications] (Maynard Smith, interview).

Wilson may also have been unaware of the fact that he had chosen a most unfortunate name for his new discipline. He himself seems to have wanted to make connections to various existing precedents in biology, as he explained in the last chapter in *The Insect Societies* (Wilson, 1971a) and at the 1978 AAAS symposium (Wilson, 1980b, p. 295). For Wilson, sociobiology was the systematic study of the biological basis of all social behavior. For his critics, however, the term 'sociobiology' had an immediate and different connotation: it was associated with German *Sozialbiologie* and the Nazi legacy. It was not a coincidence that Chorover in his 1979 book *From Genesis to Genocide* felt free to employ the same term 'sociobiology' both for Wilsonian sociobiology and the Nazi biology with which he compared it.

But considering Wilson's eagerness to straighten out misconceptions, we can further presume that had someone only told Wilson at the manuscript stage about the ease with which his message would be misinterpreted—for instance his colleague Stephen J. Gould, with whom he sustained a half-collegial relationship throughout the sociobiology controversy—he would surely have included the caveat from his 1975 article (Wilson, 1975b) in *Sociobiology* itself. It would not have detracted anything from what Wilson *himself* regarded as the book's major message. But as it happened, those who looked through Wilson's manuscript were mainly fellow biologists who concentrated on the scientific aspects of the book. And in that regard, *Sociobiology* was already challenging enough. Wilson's synthesis was a formidable piece of work.

Still, might not even some biologist reader of the manuscript have raised the red flag at Wilson's last chapter on humans? It does not seem so. It is apparent from the many positive reviews of *Sociobiology* that biologist readers were not initially as disturbed by this chapter as Wilson's political critics. Talking to biologists, I quickly learnt that they were rather unsurprised to see a final chapter on humans. For them, humans are also an animal species—only more difficult to study, since culture gets in the way. Some even saw a final chapter on humans as a kind of 'reward' after long work on animals! At least the biologists that I interviewed at the International Ethology Congress in Oxford in 1981 were not at all shocked by Wilson's last chapter, or, for that matter, other pur-ported sociobiological sins. 'Everybody does it!' was an often-heard comment when I brought up the critics' charges of speculation, advocacy, and many other things which had been presented as deeply scientifically and politically suspect in Wilson.

One could argue, of course, that a political warning ought really not to have been needed. Wilson had only to remember what had recently happened to other academics who had suggested the link possibility of hereditary influences on human behavior. Should not the political uproar around intelligence testing, beginning with Arthur Jensen in 1969 and continuing with Richard Herrnstein in 1971 and 1972 have sent a warning signal to Wilson? The answer is that it did. A careful reading of *Sociobiology* shows that Wilson was extremely cautious when it came to matters of intelligence; in fact, he played down the social significance of IQ-type intelligence (p. 554). And not only did he not make overtly racist statements, but he also approvingly cited the modern position that 'race' is not a meaningful biological concept. In order to make Wilson into a racist, one would have to interpret his text. (As we shall see in Chapters 3, 10, and 15, much effort did indeed go into such an exercise.)

Thus, ironically, Wilson may have thought that he had covered himself rather well from political assaults just because of his deliberate caution with regard to such 'obvious' political matters as race and the genetic basis for intelligence. Also, for someone positive-minded like Wilson, the very idea of scrutinizing his own (or others') texts for potential negative political connotations may not have come naturally. It was this lack of a critical political mindset, presumably shared by countless of his fellow naturalists, for which Wilson was severely punished. He did not foresee that by the very fact of invoking the idea of a genetically controlled human nature, however positive his long-term ambition with *Sociobiology* may have seemed to himself, he was treading on dangerous political ground.

Wilson's precautions in regard to race and IQ passed largely unnoticed. Those who relied only on the critics' quotations and interpretations of Wilson's text—and those were the majority—certainly never became aware of them. (Obviously, it was not in the critics' interest to quote Wilson's direct statements about intelligence and race, since these were annoyingly politically correct.) Instead, much effort went into making Wilson say what he 'ought to', so that his statements would better fit the picture the critics wished to paint. (This was usually achieved by quoting Wilson out of context, or by patching different parts of the text together; we will see examples of this in Chapter 10.)

The best example is perhaps Chorover's *From Genesis to Genocide*. In 1984 I was able to shock my class of well-intended liberal students at Smith College by giving them the assignment to compare Chorover's representation of passages of *Sociobiology* with Wilson's original text. The students, who were deeply suspicious of Wilson and spontaneous champions of his critics, embarked on this homework with gusto. Many students were quite dismayed at their own findings and angry with Chorover. This surely says something, too, about these educated laymen's relative innocence regarding what can and cannot be done in academia.

There were also other recent precedents. In the 1960s and early 1970s, the proliferation of popular books on ethology, starting with Konrad Lorenz' *On Aggression* and Robert Ardrey's *The Territorial Imperative* in 1966, had met with stern resistance from academic opinion leaders, even though (or perhaps just because) they had been enormously popular with the general public. Other books in this genre included Desmond Morris' *The Naked Ape* (1967), Lionel Tiger's *Men in Groups* (1969) and Tiger's and Robin Fox's *The Imperial Animal* (1971). These books typically postulated a human nature rooted in an earlier hunter-gatherer existence, and thereafter set out to explain a number of aspects of current social behavior as reflections of the 'human biogram' (an expression coined by Tiger and Fox). Typical of the criticism, again, was that descriptions of purported innate behavioral tendencies were immediately seen as justifications for existing social inequalities. (For reminiscences of these attacks, see Tiger and Fox, 1973; Tiger, 1996.) It did not seem to help much that they wrote clarifying articles on their true position in places such as *The New York Magazine*.

The best example of the opposition to this popular ethological genre is probably *Man and Aggression*, a book of critical reviews of Lorenz and Ardrey edited by the anthropologist Ashley Montagu as early as 1968. Montagu was something of a veteran when it came to holding up the banner for culture against hereditarian views on behavior. He had been involved in the post-Second World War campaign against racism resulting in the UNESCO statement in 1952 (see the last section of this chapter). As a seeming antidote to Lorenz' book and the harm it had caused, in 1976 Montagu himself wrote a book called *The Nature of Human Aggression*, and in 1978 he edited *Learning Non-Aggression* (this book collected available anthropological evidence against the idea of innate aggressiveness in humans). Therefore, when *Sociobiology* came along and the controversy around it started, it seemed only to continue this same discussion about innate traits of human behavior, including aggression, which made it the natural next candidate for Montagu. In 1980, he edited *Sociobiology Examined*, a volume of critical reviews and essays on sociobiology, just as he had done in 1968 with regard to the Lorenz and Ardrey books.

Again, Wilson was well aware of the academic reaction against Lorenz and the more popular ethological writers. This is exactly why in *Sociobiology* he took pains to *distance* himself from ethology. He drew a contrast between modern, scientifically based sociobiology and the 'advocacy' of the 1960s' authors. He also emphasized the difference between sociobiological reasoning relying on the modern conception of gene–environment interaction and the Lorenzian concept which was based on the old-fashioned view of 'instinct'. In fact, Wilson may even have overdone the contrast between ethology and sociobiology. This was the view among some ethologists and behavioral ecologists at the International Congress of Ethology in Oxford in 1981, and it was certainly the feeling of Irenäus Eibl-Eibesfeldt, the 'heir' of Konrad Lorenz, who in his précis of his own book *Human Ethology* (1979) in the *Behavioral and Brain Sciences* included critical remarks on sociobiology (Eibl-Eibesfeldt, 1979).[6]

But Wilson was unsuccessful also in his attempts to distance himself from the ethologists. The critics' interpretive framework was broader than Wilson's. They were concerned about any attempt to apply evolutionary explanations to human culture; whether these were ethological or sociobiological did not matter to them, and they disputed that Wilson's approach was any more scientific than that of the ethologists, despite Wilson's criticism of them (Allen *et al.*, 1975). In 1976 Lewontin made a direct connection between earlier ethological attempts and newer sociobiological claims. According to him, both of these wished to 'Darwinize' human culture, an attempt which had become increasingly popular and respectable over the last decade:

> By Darwinizing culture biologists both assert their intellectual hegemony and provide a cheap diet of easy explanation for the starving multitudes in the social sciences. . . .

Beginning in 1966 with the appearance of Ardrey's *The Territorial Imperative* (1966) and Lorenz's *On Aggression* (1966) elaborated in a more specifically genetic mode by such papers as Trivers' on reciprocal altruism (1971) and parent-offspring conflict (1974) which were themselves extensions to a human context of Hamilton's theory of social behavior (1964). Darwinizing social behavior was announced as a full-fledged science in 1975 by the publication of Wilson's *Sociobiology: The New Synthesis* (1975) (Lewontin, 1976a; [I have substituted numbers for references with name and year]).

This appeared in a paper which Lewontin delivered to the annual meeting of the Philosophy of Science Association in 1976 (which meant that the paper was ready in 1975 in order to get included in the Proceedings for that meeting). The paper is unusual as an early critique of sociobiology in that it manages to keep the criticism at a level of scientific principle *without* political allegations. (Wilson did not see this paper until a longer version of it appeared as 'Sociobiology as an Adaptationist Program' in 1979, which he regarded as 'good criticism', a view shared by Ernst Mayr; interviews in 1981.) But if Lewontin so disliked the overall approach of *Sociobiology*, could he not have said so straightforwardly, in good time, and in person? After all, Wilson and he were colleagues working in the same building. And if he had said something, would not Wilson have taken it seriously and tried to do something about it? This raises the question: when did Wilson become aware of Lewontin's serious objections to his work?

Here we get into an interesting situation of conflicting accounts. Wilson and Lewontin appeared to have different recollections of the time of Lewontin's first confrontation with Wilson about Wilson's book. In one of my interviews with Lewontin he volunteered to tell me about this. This was Lewontin's version: Wilson had been eager to ask for his opinion of *Sociobiology*, and therefore, when Lewontin was around for some other purpose, Wilson had asked him what he thought about the book. In Wilson's presence, Lewontin now went through *Sociobiology*, pointing to all the errors in it: '*This*, and *this*, and what do you say about that.' (When Lewontin recounted this, he got rather agitated, and made it sound almost as if Wilson had violated some holy law.) According to Lewontin, his criticism had made Wilson quite unhappy, since Wilson had probably hoped for his support. When I asked about the timing of this incident—was it before or after the letter appeared—Lewontin recalled that this meeting had taken place before the letter. His voice was so casual that I got the impression that Lewontin had indeed alerted Wilson to the 'errors' of his book in good time.

This is not at all how Wilson remembered the incident. According to Wilson, Lewontin never said anything about the book to him until it had come to Wilson's attention that the letter would be published, just a few days before the event. And, according to Wilson, it was at that point that Wilson, when he saw Lewontin around, practically dragged him to his office and asked: What the hell is going on? And, in Wilson's recollection, it was only then, under pressure, that Lewontin pointed out Wilson's scientific 'errors'.

These accounts are not necessarily contradictory. In both cases, we are dealing with a point in time when the book had already been published. What we get is, rather, different impressions as to how prepared Wilson was for the total onslaught by his Harvard colleagues. Lewontin is painting a picture of himself as an important scientific authority, whose opinion Wilson had sought at some reasonable time, while Wilson keenly remembers his sense of betrayal at being kept in the dark until the last minute. In either case, however, it is clear that Lewontin did not spontaneously confront Wilson, but preferred an indirect to a direct approach.

The prevalence of the 'environmentalist' paradigm

To understand the strong political reaction to sociobiology we have to go farther back than the mid-1970s. The real question is, perhaps, why was it that at the time academia was dominated by an environmentalist/culturalist paradigm, and why was environmentalism perceived as linked to progressive politics? Although the critics of sociobiology acted as if this was the natural state of affairs, in reality we are dealing with a historical contingency, not a logical necessity. The prevailing environmentalism had to do with the post-Second World War situation and particularly with the famous UNESCO agreement in 1952, which effectively put a ban on biological research in human behavior. It was exactly this taboo that Wilson, and before him, Arthur Jensen and supporters of research in the heritability of behavior, were breaking.

The situation in the 1970s was in marked contrast to the beginning of this century, when hereditarian explanations prevailed in American academia, and where hereditarian explanations were used for both conservative and progressive social policy recommendations (for example, the famous opposition between William Graham Sumner and Lester Ward). What were, then, the historical reasons for the later shift to 'official' environmentalism? Although the explicit declaration of environmentalism as the politically and intellectually correct approach happened with the UNESCO statement in 1952, scholars have located the actual shift as far back as the late 1920s and 1930s (for an overview of relevant scholarship, see Degler, 1991).

Among the many factors seen as responsible for the shift in the general political atmosphere in the United States during this time have been mentioned such things as the growing social influence of the immigrants and the northern urban blacks after the Great Migration, and the Great Depression of the early 1930s. The latter made it particularly hard to support the idea of an innate relationship between economic status and biological fitness, a popular Social Darwinist argument at the time. Also, during the 1930s, the support for the eugenics movement, which had earlier in the century been strong in the United States, was dwindling rapidly amidst reports of escalating Nazi sterilization practices. In 1938, the American Anthropological Association took an unusual action and passed unanimous resolution denouncing 'racism' (Degler, 1991, p. 203). (At this time, the term 'race' was used to denote also what we now call an ethnic or cultural group.) An indicator of the new intellectual climate was that during the 1930s and 1940s earlier popular terms like 'heredity' and 'instinct' largely disappeared from the social science literature, and there was a dramatic decrease in articles on race and sex differences (Degler, 1991, pp. 203, 205).

But there were scientific reasons as well for the shift toward environmentalism in the explanation of social behavior. Before the Second World War, the biological paradigm, which had been predominant at the beginning of the century, was already in decline. It was becoming apparent that genetics was more complicated than earlier assumed, which meant, for instance, the assumptions about deterioration of the genetic potential in a population due to 'race-crossing' could not be scientifically supported any longer (Barkan, 1992; Degler, 1991). The relatively swift transition from hereditarianism to environmentalism in the 1930s may in fact have been largely due to the efforts of the anthropologist Franz Boas and his students Ruth Benedict, Margaret Mead, and others, who all actively promoted the idea of culture over biology (Barkan, 1992; Degler, 1991).

The turning point came with the UNESCO statement on race in 1952, after which it was no longer possible to legitimately refer to race as an explanatory factor for human behavior. The historian of biology, William Provine, noted the strong political drive for an environmentalist attitude in academia during this time (Provine, 1973). He pointed out that, based on available evidence, the strictly academic attitude in fact ought to have been an *agnostic* one, since at that time there were little or no new data about the nature of racial differences. However, in the climate after the Second World War, it made more political sense to emphasize the point that no differences existed. According to Provine, the UNESCO statement was also carefully crafted to make just that point (Provine, 1973; Degler, 1991, p. 204).

With this, the climate in society and academia had shifted in favor of environmental explanations, so much so that it was taken for granted by a new generation of scholars. This is how the historian Elazar Barkan describes the situation:

> [T]he substance of the debate had dramatically changed. Any hereditarian explanation of social or cultural characteristics or ability was prone to be classified as racist. Naturalism and biological reductionism were generally viewed with suspicion, an attitude which has remained to the present, as the heated debates of sociobiology since the mid seventies illustrate . . .
>
> UNESCO's statement provides only one illustration of the shift between the end of World War I and 1950 which saw biological explanations replaced by cultural analysis. Rigid views of hierarchies among human groups largely yielded to relativism and indeterminism. The minority of academics who dissented from the new convention protested against a surrender to 'cultural determinism'. But the revolution spread to a constituency far wider than universities or intellectuals (Barkan, 1992, pp. 342–3).

This same view was expressed by Lewontin in a Public Television Nova program on 2 February 1975. He contrasted the current situation in academia with the anti-racist attitude adopted by the post-war generation:

> [T]hose of us who've grown up since the thirties and forties began to believe that that was the typical attitude of academics; that they were liberal, they were anti-elite, they didn't believe in racism and so on, because we didn't know so much about the history of the thirties (Lewontin, 1975b).

But recently, Lewontin charged, the American academics had gone back to their old attitudes toward race, criminality, poverty, and so on, using 'untrue statements, facts which are not facts, logic which is not logic, to prove that there are important genetic differences between races' (Lewontin, 1975b).

During the two decades after the UNESCO statement, environmentalism inspired both politics and science. In the 1960s the student and Civil Rights movements and a series of social policy measures under the banner of the Democratic party's Great Society initiative, such as the famous Head Start program, fueled the hope that social progress could be achieved through changing the social environment. (Soon it became apparent that this was more difficult than anticipated.)

Meanwhile, the rules were slowly changing. The landmark Civil Rights Act in 1964 forbade discrimination in hiring practices and thus effectively legislated equal opportunity. But this initial notion of a 'colorblind' society (Martin Luther King's famous dream), was quickly developed further into various federally enforced initiatives to actively promote the hiring of blacks and (certain) ethnic minorities, with the explicit aim of overcoming past discrimination. To enforce the government's new program of Affirmative Action, an Equal Employment Opportunity Commission was established to oversee compliance with the new federal regulations for anyone receiving federal funds. This Commission started enforcing compliance in 1972. By then, two things had happened. Affirmative Action had been extended to encompass also small businesses, state and local employees, and universities. Moreover, a number of important precedents had been established in federal court rulings. On the basis of one of these, a new idea of 'quota' had become acceptable as one possible avenue for employers to comply with Affirmative Action (for a brief overview of relevant legislation and court rulings, see Murray, 1984, pp. 93–4). The quota system, in turn, occasionally led to charges of 'reverse discrimination' against white males. The most famous of these was the Bakke case in 1978, where the Supreme Court—with one vote's majority—upheld University of California's right to use 'diversity of the student body' as a justification for racial preferences in admission.

In the new political climate created by Affirmative Action, although 'everybody' supported the idea of promoting the hiring of minorities, there was an implicit (and sometimes explicit) battle between those who held on to the original, individualist American Dream, and those who believed in the rights of (certain) minority groups to receive restitution for past discrimination. Thus, in a paradoxical way, in contrast to the UNESCO statement and the post-war climate, in the early 1970s the focus had shifted once again toward an emphasis on *group* membership—this time because of a federal initiative with concrete economic implications.

A concern for the smooth sailing of Affirmative Action and a wish to sustain its original rationale to bring restitution for past discrimination could perhaps explain the persistent attempts of the critics to scrutinize sociobiological theory for inherent emphasis on inequality, racism, and sexism. (Wilson himself, meanwhile, was interested in emphasizing a universal, biologically based human nature.) A very real but hidden issue in the sociobiology debate, and something which connected it with the IQ debate, may thus have been Affirmative Action. Some of the polemics in the larger debate become more understandable if we assume that the critics saw themselves as contributing to the new cause by showing how racist and sexist attitudes permeated respectable-seeming science.

Thus, paradoxically, by the early 1970s, the emphasis on race or ethnic group had again become a socially significant issue, this time because of federally enforced hiring practices. Meanwhile, in 1972—unlike twenty years earlier—some new data had finally been obtained that could be used to emphasize the biological unity of humans and underlying similarity between different races. Research on the distribution of human blood factors showed that in human populations there was a within-group variation of about 85 per cent compared with a between-group variation of only about 15 per cent; that is, most of human biological differences were between individuals of the same population (geographic group or race), not between populations (Lewontin, 1972b, 1974a). This led most biologists to the conclusion that race was indeed not a biologically meaningful concept. Thus, the potential political significance of these research results was that they could now be used to undermine any attempts to scientifically justify racial discrimination, by simply questioning the whole concept of 'race' and racial differences. (This point was later emphasized particularly by Wilson's Harvard colleague and co-warrior, Bernard Davis.)[7]

But we have to remember the total situation. These new findings in biology were not easily registered in a social and academic climate with taboos on biological explanations as such. Other non-biologists may not even have been aware of recent developments in biology and genetics. At the beginning of the sociobiology controversy, who knows how many academic or non-academic non-biologists were still thinking in terms of an antiquated opposition between 'nature' and 'nurture', instead of modern gene–environment interaction, or believed that races represented some kind of immutable 'types' instead of populations with wide genetic variation among their individual members.

A good illustration of the fact that the academic intelligentsia was holding on to the 'total' environmentalist position established by the UNESCO statement was the Resolution against Racism published in 1973 as an advertisement in *The New York Times*. This resolution was signed by over 1000 academics from different institutions all over the United States. It declared that all humans have been endowed with the same intelligence and condemned recent research by Jensen and others as both unscientific and socially pernicious. It stated that 'racist' researchers deserve no protection under the name of academic freedom, and urged liberal academics to resist 'racist' research and teaching. Interestingly, this resolution did not argue on the basis of the new revolutionary data on blood groups; instead, it quoted Lewontin's earlier 1970 critique of Jensen as an example of the fight against racism in academia.

This kind of black-out situation for biological information, combined with the usual time it takes for scientific advances to become 'general knowledge', might explain why at the beginning of the sociobiology controversy the Sociobiology Study Group was able to stir up such emotion with its attacks on Wilson and others. Its formulations fed right into entrenched general beliefs and biological ignorance at a time when any attempt at biological explanation was anathema. Thus, what was attacked was not really sociobiology, but 'sociobiology', as stereotyped by the critics and feeding into political fears and antiquated popular conceptions about biology among academics and the public alike.

Finally, it is hard to escape the conclusion that there was a *need* for the sociobiology controversy among left-wing academics at the time—if simply to sustain the momentum gathered in the earlier IQ controversy. After the vigorous campaigns against Jensen and Herrnstein, the academic left required somebody new to epitomize the political evils of 'biological determinism'. Wilson (or, rather, 'Wilson') became the new focus for the activist cause and *Sociobiology* the new totem for scattered radicals to rally around. Wilson's massive book was already good for pedagogical purposes: it was quite something to be able to point to an over 500-page, purportedly serious scientific treatise (although cast in presentable coffee-table format) as one more exemplar of biology in the service of ideology. The attack on *Sociobiology* would set a warning example for other academics: see what happens to those who venture out on dangerous political ground!

But there was more to the sociobiology controversy than politics. Although the Sociobiology Study Group made valiant efforts to construe Wilson as a political offender (see especially Chapter 10), we can hypothesize that Wilson would soon enough have been dropped in favor of a new and more suitable political target, had there not been among the critics also colleagues with serious *scientific* disagreements with Wilson. As I shall argue in this book, it was in large part the fundamental differences between Wilson and his leading opponents in regard to the meaning of science that made the criticism of sociobiology so acrimonious. In the next chapter, we will examine the conflict between Wilson and his most vehement adversary, Richard Lewontin—one of the better reasons why the sociobiology controversy could not really have been avoided.

CHAPTER 3

Colleagues on collision course: Wilson's and Lewontin's contrary moral-cum-scientific agendas

A clash among titans?

The public's fancy was captured early on by the fact that the author of *Sociobiology* and his chief opponent were both Harvard biologists with laboratories one above the other in the same building. Indeed, one of the questions I was often asked was, 'Do they talk to each other?' (Incidentally, they didn't.) Considering the eminence of these two scientists, no wonder that science journalists employed such dramatic descriptions as 'a clash among titans' (Wade, 1976). The question is, of course, whether it is correct to reduce the sociobiology controversy to a conflict between these protagonists. Although I believe it is quite proper to speak of Wilson and Lewontin as the chief opponents in this controversy, it is important to point out that the sociobiology debate represented a much larger conflict in science. As an academic controversy, this opposition has often been considered as primarily a 'nature' vs 'nurture' perspective on human behavior. I will try to show that the sociobiology debate represented a contrast between two fundamentally different views of 'good science'.

Singling out these two opponents in this chapter, then, does not amount to reducing the sociobiology debate to a personality conflict. Even though we are dealing here with quite contrasting personalities, the thing to keep in mind is that Wilson and Lewontin are scientists with strong cognitive commitments (one scientific colleague aptly described them as 'twenty-four-hour scientists'). This means that we should try to understand the various types of scientific, moral, and political convictions that motivated Wilson and Lewontin as scientists, and also how these convictions ultimately led the colleagues onto a collision course. Moreover, even though it will become obvious that Wilson and Lewontin had their own idiosyncratic scientific profiles, many of their scientific and moral/political convictions were *shared* by the larger 'camps' in the sociobiology controversy; in fact, one might say that Wilson and Lewontin epitomize two different total scientific world views. We will return to this in Chapters 13 and 14.

In this chapter, we will look more closely at the nature of the disagreement between

Wilson and Lewontin and how it reflected a clash between their personal long-term moral-cum-scientific agendas, rather than between personalities as such. I will show how, for both Lewontin and Wilson, their larger agendas involve a *coupling* of scientific and moral interests. We will see how Wilson and Lewontin were on a countercourse *before* the beginning of the sociobiology controversy, and how the different nature of their moral-cum-scientific agendas made a head-on collision in 1975 inevitable.

My attempt to identify the exact nature of the opposition between these two protagonists also means that I dismiss the popular conception of the sociobiology controversy as simply a 'nature–nurture' conflict, where progressive environmentalists were fighting conservative hereditarians. The situation was much more complicated, not the least because Wilson, although he emphasized the role of genes, was a typical modern gene–environment *interactionist* and regarded himself as a political liberal. (Indeed, much mischief has been done by sustaining the rhetorical idea that socio-biologists are 'genetic determinists'.) It cannot be denied, however, that on top of the scientific beliefs that he shared with many modern evolutionary biologists, Wilson had a highly unusual (at least among his contemporaries) moral agenda of his own. It was this agenda that was misunderstood and misconstrued by the Sociobiology Study Group.

Wilson's positive program

Sociobiology: The New Synthesis was a large, ambitious book. There is little doubt that through it, Wilson saw himself as creating (or solidifying) a new 'paradigm'. Theoretical ideas and empirical studies from the last few decades were drawn together in one huge construction, by which animal social behavior was viewed as genetically controlled and evolving through natural selection. In writing *Sociobiology*, Wilson specifically used modern population biology, for he saw this as the theoretical under-pinning of any claims about the evolution of social behavior. As a modern biologist, Wilson was especially interested in employing the mathematical formulas of population genetics, through which evolution by natural selection could be expressed as a change in the gene frequencies of traits.

At once, we start to see the seeds for controversy between Wilson and Lewontin, for just the year before (in 1974) Lewontin, a population geneticist, had published a major book of his own, criticizing most of the current claims made in his particular field. In this work, *The Genetic Basis of Evolutionary Change*, Lewontin spelled out the problems faced by his field in view of certain new scientific findings, and suggested that funda-mental theoretical revisions would have to be made within that field for it to produce valid predictive statements. Lewontin's point, especially, was that simple older formulas used for calculation in population genetics were incorrect, because they did not consider recently detected complex interactions between individual genes. Erroneously, genes were still being treated as akin to separate beans within a bag (the individual organism).

We have seen that Sociobiology Study Group criticized Wilson on both political and scientific grounds. Therefore, it is important to note that in *Sociobiology* Wilson did not ignore the kinds of criticisms raised by Lewontin. On the contrary, he approvingly discussed exactly Lewontin's points (Wilson, 1975a, p. 70). Nevertheless, Wilson explicitly decided to go ahead and use existing formulas provisionally, waiting for better ones to be developed. As I will show below, this was because, for Wilson, population biology was a means to a larger goal; for Lewontin it was an end in itself. Wilson saw nothing wrong with making do with what existed; Lewontin believed one should categorically discard the available formulas, except for the limited cases where they were *known* to be applicable.

But the usefulness of population genetic formulas as provisional tools would have been a rather strange issue to form a basis for a serious controversy. After all, Wilson and Lewontin were not in disagreement about the theoretical correctness of Lewontin's criticism. It is only when matters are put in the context of the larger agendas of these two scientists that it becomes clear that this decision of Wilson's, while boosting his own scientific and moral goals, came to effectively undermine those of Lewontin.

What was the larger scientific agenda influencing Wilson in his 1975 book? Here it is necessary to introduce Wilson's academic background. After completing his undergraduate work and an MSc in biology at the University of Alabama, Wilson came to Harvard as a graduate student in the early 1950s, became a Junior Fellow in Harvard's prestigious Society of Fellows, and joined the Harvard Faculty in 1958, rising to professor of zoology in 1964 and the Frank Baird, Jr. professorship of science in 1976. While at Harvard, Wilson came to 'inherit' the grand scientific ambitions of L. J. Henderson and W. M. Wheeler: the former the influential founder of the Harvard Society of Fellows, and the latter the eminent Harvard entomologist and popularizer of the 'super-organism' concept. The great scientific dream of these two men was to integrate the social and natural sciences on the basis of equilibrium theory (Russett, 1966). Wilson, a student of Wheeler's student, C. M. Carpenter, carried on with this mission, and this is why the comparison of social behavior in different species became central to him. Indeed, Wilson had already spoken of the importance of such an integrated theory in the last chapter of his book *The Insect Societies*, published in 1971. He hoped that the post-Second-World-War developments in cybernetics and especially optimization theory would provide the tools needed for this enterprise (cf. Haraway, 1981–2).

Along with the scientific agenda, Wilson also inherited a particular philosophical style: the coupling of scientific and moral notions. Wheeler (who was a socialist, believing in the ideas of Kropotkin) had seen the co-operation in insects as a good model for human society. For this reason, in developing sociobiology, Wilson made the problem of 'altruism' absolutely central. He presented various models for the solution of this problem, including suggestions which were not at all in vogue among mainstream sociobiologists at that time. Thus he came to integrate knowledge into an idiosyncratic synthesis, in many respects different from the work of the other students of animal behavior. For instance, Wilson inherited his mentors' fondness for holistic explanations, substituting the old metaphysical holism with a 'new holism' based on communication theory (cf. Wilson, 1975a, p. 7), and gave much more prominence to 'group selection' explanations than did some of his English colleagues (like Richard Dawkins, author of *The Selfish Gene*).

Therefore, we might say that Wilson took over a basic philosophy—unfortunately one that initially made him unaware of the fact that, in mixing science and social concerns, he was skating across dangerously thin philosophical ice. In particular, he cheerfully ignored the barrier separating facts from values. Brazenly, he started *Sociobiology: The New Synthesis* with the following statement:

> Camus said that the only serious philosophical question is suicide. That is wrong even in the strict sense intended. The biologist, who is concerned with questions of physiology and evolutionary history, realizes that self-knowledge is constrained and shaped by the emotional control centers in the hypothalamus and limbic system of the brain. These centers flood our consciousness with all the emotions—hate, love, guilt, fear, and others— that are consulted by ethical philosophers who wish to intuit the standards of good and evil. What, we are then compelled to ask, made the hypothalamus and limbic system? They evolved by natural selection. That simple biological statement must be pursued to explain ethics and ethical philosophers, if not epistemology and epistemologists, at all depths.

And in the last chapter he suggested that 'a genetically accurate and hence completely fair code of ethics' must wait for further contributions of evolutionary sociobiology (Wilson, 1975a, p. 575).

As one can imagine, this kind of move created immediate suspicion among his critics, and incredulity among many of his colleagues (which is, for instance, reflected in Maynard Smith's generally sympathetic review of *Sociobiology* in 1975). Lewontin, in interview, suggested that Wilson ought to read Hume: 'it would be good for him'. He guessed that some friend or critic must have pointed out this problem to Wilson. Indeed, Wilson retracted his position even before the start of the controversy in an article in *The New York Times Magazine*, where he warned about the 'dangerous trap' of believing that something that was good for us in our hunter-gatherer existence is automatically still good for modern man (Wilson, 1975b). As we saw in the last chapter, it was already too late. What is more interesting is that Wilson later seems to have snapped back again to his original position. This is, for instance, reflected in his 1985 papers which he wrote with Michael Ruse (Ruse and Wilson, 1985a, 1986). I will return to these matters in my discussion of the cultural significance of the sociobiology debate in Part III of this book.

While it is possible to argue that Wilson was to some extent a product of his own intellectual heritage, there is no doubt of a stronger force driving Wilson: his personal moral agenda. Wilson's zeal in making sociobiology a truly predictive science, encompassing all of social behavior, was intimately tied to an old desire of his: to prove the (Christian) theologians wrong. He wanted to make sure that there could not exist a separate realm of meaning and ethics which would allow the theologians to impose arbitrary moral codes that would lead to unnecessary human suffering. He believed that there must exist a natural ethics for humans and was on the lookout for it. For Wilson, any new scientific knowledge which could allow human beings increased control over their lives would take power away from the theologians who wanted to run other people's lives.

To explain such an ambition, we have to go back to the deeply religious environment of Wilson's childhood and adolescence. Raised as a Southern Baptist, he went through a conversion experience at a revival meeting at the age of 15 and was 'born again' by being baptized. (Wilson, interview, 1981; cf. Wilson, 1985, 1994.) He had a sense of religious awe, but, in retrospect, this was 'more of a blind emotional acceptance . . . a rite of transition . . . a special form of allegiance to the tribe in front of the shaman' (Wilson, interview). And very soon he was reconverted and became a free thinker. The reason for this was partly 'the fraudulent activity of the Church', partly his own discovery of evolution:

> When I was 17, I saw that a lot of things that had inspired me earlier were really theatrical staging. And then I had been exposed to evolution, and because I had discovered that what I most loved on the planet, which was life on the planet, made sense only in terms of evolution and the idea of natural selection, and that this was a far more interesting, richer and more powerful explanation than the teachings of the New Testament. That was not difficult to arrive at (Wilson, interview).[1]

From this time on, Wilson devoted himself fully to his favorite subject: the study of ants. But he learned an important lesson from the evangelical preachers: 'the love of language . . . to be able to talk, to move people with language' (ibid.). As we shall see, this ambition is indeed reflected in Wilson's prose, which on occasion assumes an 'evangelistic' tone, and may entice author and reader alike to move between what is and what might be.

The lesson that Wilson had derived from this experience was that religion could not claim to possess privileged knowledge of correct ethical values for humankind: it had better be kept on a leash by materialist science. Thus, in the notorious passage from *On Human Nature*, the 1978 work that Wilson devoted to humans, where he says that 'the genes hold culture on a leash'—it is really *religion*, not culture *per se* that Wilson is talking about. This is clear also from the full context:

> But to the extent that principles are chosen by knowledge and reason remote from biology, they can at least in principle be non-Darwinian. This leads us ineluctably back to the second great spiritual dilemma. The philosophical question of interest that it generates is the following: Can the cultural evolution of higher ethical values gain a direction and momentum of its own and completely replace genetic revolution? I think not. The genes hold culture on a leash. The leash is very long, but inevitably values will be constrained in accordance with their effects on the human gene pool. The brain is a product of evolution. Human behavior—like the deepest capacities for emotional response which drive and guide it—is the circuitous technique by which human genetic material has been and will be kept intact. Morality has no other demonstrable ultimate function (Wilson, 1978a, p. 167).

Thus, contrary to his critics' belief, it was not a conservative political desire to support the existing social order that was driving Wilson. It was rather his wish to make scientific materialism triumph over irrational religious dogma that made him state his case so strongly and even exaggerate the power of evolutionary biology. In this way he ended up presenting this field as a 'harder' scientific one than it is at present.

Wilson's moral aim was a quantitative explanation of all aspects of human social behavior. He was also interested in being able to formulate a trajectory of mankind's future (as a substitute for divine prophecy, as he explained at a symposium for theologians and scientists; Wilson, 1980a). The best foundation for both of these objectives was population genetics, which he regarded as the 'hardest' branch of evolutionary biology. (More specifically, Wilson planned on using existing formulas developed by Fisher.) Therefore, unlike many other sociobiologists (for example, Dawkins in *The Selfish Gene*), Wilson could not really 'afford' to leave the cultural realm as a separate one, sitting on top of the genetic one, even if he entertained this as a theoretical possibility; materialism had to be guaranteed. This is why Wilson extended orthodox population biology to encompass human social behavior as well. But here Wilson encountered a severe problem: how to account for rapid cultural change in human populations on the basis of changes in gene frequencies which, according to prevailing theory, require much longer time spans. His solution was to postulate a 'multiplier effect' which would speed up the process. According to Wilson, there was some evidence for such an effect from animal studies (Wilson, 1975a, pp. 11–13).

For Wilson, then, the 'coupling' of his moral and scientific concerns was a long-term project. His scientific work carried moral implications, but in order to make these persuasive it had to be shown to come as close as possible to the 'hard' science ideal.

Lewontinian's critical agenda

Just as the key to understanding Wilson is his strong devotion to a positive agenda involving evolutionary theory as a total explanatory scheme, so the key to understanding Lewontin is the latter's equally strong devotion to a critical agenda, with regard to both science and society.

Although Lewontin's interest in Marxism was well known at the time of the sociobiology controversy (Marxism for him was both a philosophical and sociopolitical program), it seems that Lewontin's Marxist stance was in fact linked to a more general critical concern of his: the *correct* depiction of reality in theory and models. This can be clearly seen particularly from his 1974 book. While for Wilson the criterion for a good theory was testability, for Lewontin a theory in addition to being testable has to be a *true* account of an underlying process in the real world. Thus, for instance, Lewontin was against statistical calculations and constructs, for the reason that these did not have a real basis in nature or, alternatively, presumed a stochastic universe without proper causal laws (see, for example, Lewontin, 1974b, 1977a; Levins and Lewontin, 1980). Furthermore, while Wilson considered parsimony a fundamental scientific principle, and believed that deliberate oversimplification was crucial for theory formation (see, for example, Wilson, 1971b), for Lewontin a theory rather ought to be made more *complex* in order to accurately capture reality (Levins and Lewontin, 1980). Thus, Lewontin was concerned with 'correct' epistemology, methodology, and ontology because, for him, incorrect approaches prevent us from finding out the underlying truth about the world.

It is not difficult to see why Wilson's explicit choice of approach in *Sociobiology* on many counts was absolute anathema to Lewontin's meta-scientific convictions in general. And because Wilson chose to include human society in his sociobiological scheme, he came to include assumptions about human nature and society which clashed with Lewontin's sociopolitical convictions as well. Indeed, Lewontin's devotion to Marxism in practice often worked as a 'coupled' moral-cum-scientific agenda, and it was this coupled agenda that in effect came to clash with the Wilsonian one.

Unlike the case of Wilson, when it comes to Lewontin there are few comprehensive moral statements—one has to tease out Lewontin's critical program from his general writings and his attacks on others. However, there are clues to be found. It appears that Lewontin was convinced (as are many other scientists) that 'good science' is un-problematic, but 'bad science' is in need of explanation. But additionally it seems that he was convinced that it was the political bias of scientists that was the cause of 'bad science', at least in fields that have serious sociopolitical implications. Therefore, he saw his specific task as twofold: 1) to demonstrate the 'scientific error' of scientists with 'incorrect' political beliefs, and 2) to unmask these beliefs in their scientific text and show how the latter 'errors' led to the former one. Lewontin's general strategy as a critic (later on to be seen in his attack on Wilson) was especially clearly spelled out in his criticism of Jensen in 1970:

> I shall try, in this article, to display Professor Jensen's argument, to show how the structure of his argument is designed to make his point and to reveal what appear to be deeply embedded assumptions derived from a particular world view, leading him to erroneous conclusions (Lewontin, 1970a).

Later, in a review of research on cognitive abilities (Lewontin, 1975a), Lewontin attacked the 'carelessness, shabbiness and intellectual dishonesty' in this field. It 'could not' be a genuine scientific desire that was motivating the students of IQ, because, according to Lewontin, the only truly scientifically interesting questions about cognitive traits could be asked at the molecular level. Therefore it 'must' be their underlying sociopolitical bias that was driving them to bad research.

But he did not remain content with simply demonstrating how ideological bias leads to scientific error, which could be regarded as one type of abstract Marxist analysis. For Lewontin, there was a moral issue involved as well (cf. 'dishonesty'). Obviously, then, Lewontin refused to take the position that the sociopolitical bias of a scientist may have an unconscious effect on the results. This would, for instance, be the standpoint of his colleague Stephen J. Gould.[2] Lewontin was quite explicit about how he disagreed with Gould in a book review of the latter's *The Mismeasure of Man*:

> Like Kamin, I am, myself rather more harsh in my view. Scientists, like others, sometimes tell deliberate lies because they believe that small lies can serve big truths (Lewontin, 1981b).

The strong moralistic tone in Lewontin's criticism suggests that his conversion to Marxism was not able to override a basic, idiosyncratically Lewontinian style of thought, or alternatively, that his attitude in fact represents a viable Marxist position in an American context. I will examine this more closely in Chapters 11 and 14.

Thus, Lewontin took the position that scientists producing 'bad science' in socio-politically relevant fields should be held morally responsible for holding incorrect scientific beliefs. An illustration of this is the following excerpt from a Public Television Nova program transcript in February 1975. Here we can see a surprisingly ahistorical (for a Marxist) standard, modern science, being used to prove that the nineteenth-century Swiss–American biologist, Louis Agassiz, was a deliberate liar:

> In the late 19th century, such eminent zoologists for example as Louis Agassiz, the founder of the Agassiz Museum at Harvard, said, with no basis in fact, he knew there was no basis in fact, and therefore you can only say he must have been telling a lie, that the skulls of negroes hardened up and closed earlier . . . And that was the reason why one shouldn't try to teach black people things. Now, Louis Agassiz knew that was not true, or at least he could, had no evidence that it was true, and we know now that it is not true, that the sutures of blacks and whites close at about the same time . . . We also know that brain size has nothing to do with intelligence: that your brain doesn't swell as you learn. But Louis Agassiz put out this pap, and as one of the great zoologists of the 19th century, of course, people believed him (Lewontin, 1975b).

Indeed, this bold analysis gave rise to a letter exchange between Lewontin and a former colleague, a mathematics professor, who took strong exception to this kind of reasoning. According to this colleague, one would need to know whether Agassiz, in fact, knew the skull suture argument to be false. Did Lewontin possess such evidence? From Lewontin's answer, it appears that Lewontin did not see a compelling need for evidence of this type when he passed a moral verdict:

> He was a liar because lying can involve two things. One is saying something which you know not to be true; the other, especially for a scientist, is to claim something as a matter of fact when you know that there has never been one particle of empirical evidence offered in its favor. I do not know which of these two categories of liars Mr. Agassiz falls into, but he certainly falls in one of them, since there never was and never can be a demonstration that the skull sutures of blacks close before the skull sutures of whites since the reverse is true, although there is no significant difference.

Thus, Lewontin basically reiterated what he had already said, and used current knowledge to attribute moral guilt to earlier scientists (cf. Lewontin 1977b, p. 10). He did not consider whether a scientist such as Agassiz may have sincerely (but mistakenly) believed that he had reasonable grounds for claiming what he did. Such an uncharitable attitude might be usefully called 'moral presentism'. As we shall see, Lewontin was not the only one among the Sociobiology Study Group who reasoned in this way.

In what ways exactly did Wilson's *Sociobiology* incur Lewontin's ire? *Prima facie*, both intellectually and socially, there are reasons to believe that Wilson would have expected a different kind of response. The sociobiology controversy has obscured the point that Wilson and Lewontin in fact shared many beliefs about evolutionary mechanisms, as well as many concerns about evolutionary biology as a field. This was because they had in part a common history. It was, ironically, Wilson himself who brought Lewontin to Harvard in the early 1970s, hoping that they could continue their common interest in creating necessary new theory in evolutionary biology, theory of a 'holistic' kind. The reason was that both Wilson and Lewontin had been part of a small group of radical young evolutionary biologists who, at the beginning of the 1960s, attempted to break with the prevalent tradition and develop something new:

> In the early '60s we gathered at [Robert] MacArthur's place in Vermont. We were about a half dozen people, all the same age. We formed a little group, a self-conscious little group in the early '60s . . . We talked deliberately about how one would create a new population biology based on modeling and how one would go into these areas that were unformed and make order for the first time . . . (Wilson, interview).

(Other members of this small group included Richard Levins, Robert MacArthur, and L. B. Slobodkin.)

The situation in evolutionary biology at this time was, according to Wilson, one of stagnation (1975a, p. 64). What unified the evolutionary biologists in the 'new phase' was, among others, a 'holistic' interest in evolutionary ecology, that is, in the actual evolutionary history of a species in its (changing) environment. At the end of the 1960s, Lewontin (1968), Levins (1968), and MacArthur and Wilson (1967) had contributed to the development of the new theory (Wilson, 1971b). Lewontin's theoretical approach at this point was game theory, while his concern with the molecular underpinnings of genetics had led him to seminal discoveries of the variation which exists in virtually every population of organisms (Lewontin and Hubby, 1966). Wilson and MacArthur, meanwhile, had been working on island biogeography.

This subject was 'terribly messy', it was 'a major unformed field, full of various fragments of information, just like the social sciences today; it had no structure like population genetics . . . ' (Wilson, interview). Exactly for this reason, Wilson felt the challenge to go into this field and provide it with structure, and his collaboration with MacArthur was most fruitful—Wilson 'knew what the real world was like' and MacArthur was a sophisticated modeler. And equally important: both of them were 'visionaries', according to Wilson (Wilson, interview). (Sadly, MacArthur died of cancer in 1972.) Once the field of biogeography was structured, it was only natural for Wilson to be on the lookout for other 'messy fields'. Social behavior was a clear candidate. But for rigorous structuring, he would need the help of top-notch population geneticists. Therefore, it is no wonder that Wilson was interested in bringing Lewontin to Harvard from Chicago ('he was the best'; Wilson, interview), hoping for a concentration of efforts in the development of new theory in evolutionary biology. And, with the help of Ernst Mayr, the doyen among evolutionists, Wilson was successful. He even took pains to convince Harvard that Lewontin, who he knew had become a Marxist under Levins' tutelage, would not cause trouble at Harvard (Wilson, interview).

Wilson soon realized he had made a mistake. He recalled how he had telephoned the biology department at Chicago to ask about this specific point and how he had been reassured by their response that Lewontin would be able to keep politics and science separate at Harvard. Wilson later reckoned that Chicago must have been only too eager to get rid of Lewontin. 'I was had!', was how he laughingly recalled it in interview. Later on, Wilson and Lewontin together brought in Richard Levins, another member of the original group of 'revolutionaries' in evolutionary biology, who had become Lewontin's Marxist tutor. Conceivably, what Wilson wanted to do by bringing in Lewontin and Levins was to strengthen the field of evolutionary biology at his university, a new field that he wished to give form and structure to as quickly as possible. The takeover attempt of Harvard's biology department by 'Caligula'—Wilson's name for Jim Watson, who wanted to eliminate traditional biology in favor of molecular biology at Harvard—was still fresh in Wilson's memory (cf. Wilson, 1994; see also Chapter 14).

Why, then, did Lewontin feel obliged, almost literally, to bite the hand that fed him? This can only be attributed to the development of his own critical agenda at that time. While he was not in principle against an attempt to create an integrated sociobiology (see Lewontin, 1976a), it was his own changed attitudes to large-scale model-building in conjunction with his concern with 'correct' epistemology, methodology, and ontology that made him opposed to Wilson's synthesis. Rather soon after his game-theoretical efforts, Lewontin's interests in the molecular basis of genetics took over, and his position henceforth was that 'God is in the details', that is, good science is based on carefully established facts, not on ambitious models (see Chapter 6). In addition, *Sociobiology* happened to emerge at a time when the fight against racism triggered by the Jensen and Herrnstein controversies was still going on, albeit at a lower level of intensity, and in which Lewontin had high stakes as a scientific and moral/political critic.

At Chicago, Lewontin had taken upon himself to expose 'racist' research, and in 1973, already at Harvard, he was one of the 1000 signatories of the 'Resolution Against Racism' advertisement in *The New York Times* (28 September 1973), urging for a stop to 'racist' research. What was more, the text of the resolution cited Lewontin's 1970 critique of Jensen as an example of the fight against racism in academia. His attitude in the 1975 article criticizing research in cognitive abilities (Lewontin, 1975a) was essentially the same. In the meantime, Lewontin himself had contributed research which could be used to dismiss suggestions such as the one by Arthur Jensen that there may be a genetic basis for cognitive differences between different racial groups.

One of Lewontin's major discoveries in the 1960s had been of the genetic variation within and between animal populations and the fact that variation within a population is much greater than between populations. For humans, Lewontin (1972b) found that the same was true at least for blood-group data. In turn, this came to be accepted by liberals and left-wing academics as definitive counter-evidence to any biological basis for differences between races. Race was declared not to be a biologically useful concept. Later, Luigi Cavalli-Sforza and his colleagues continued such a line of research in their documentation of the genetic similarities and differences in different language groups.[3]

Consistent with his moral/political agenda, Lewontin in the Nova program on Public Television in February 1975 took earlier and contemporary scientists to task for 'lying' about genetic differences while posing as experts. And, in this program, Lewontin warned the public against a new racism raging in academia, and told them to watch out for 'experts' attempting to legitimize the status quo. This explains why Wilson's book, *Sociobiology*, appearing when it did, depending as it did on population genetics, and full of claims about humankind, was Lewontin's natural target for critical examination of political messages and racist implications.

But just how did *Sociobiology* now feed into Lewontin's anti-racist agenda? Wilson prided himself on being a fairly liberal thinker—the sort of person who naturally falls to the left of center politically. There was no overt racism in *Sociobiology*. And, indeed, it is difficult to see how Wilson, in stressing population genetics which is expressly based on *individual* variation, could be construed as a racist emphasizing *group* differences, especially since Wilson explicitly quoted Lewontin's famous 1972 paper dealing with blood-group data. Wilson even added:

> There is no *a priori* reason for supposing that this sample of genes possesses a distribution much different from those of other, less accessible systems affecting behavior (Wilson, 1975a, p. 550).

Lewontin drew a connection by association. When interviewed in *The Harvard Crimson* on 3 December 1975, he said: 'Sociobiology is not a racist doctrine, but any kind of genetic determinism can and does feed other kinds, including the belief that some races are superior to others.' This was enough reason why sociobiology had to be stopped. Starting in *The New York Review of Books*, with a stream of articles and addresses, with and without co-thinkers, Lewontin anathematized the Wilsonian program.

Where did Lewontin's specific logic of critique come from? For this, we have to look at some influential factors in Lewontin's scientific background long before he became a Marxist. Like Wilson, Lewontin inherited a moral-cum-scientific agenda from his mentor, in this case the eminent Russian–American geneticist, Theodosius Dobzhansky. And like Wilson, Lewontin also 'transformed' the original agenda. For Dobzhansky, 'population thinking' was both a scientific and a moral/political issue. Scientifically, it had to do with the accurate depiction of evolutionary processes on the basis of Mendelian genetics. Morally/politically, an emphasis on the importance of variation within a population—that is, individual genetic differences instead of group averages or 'types'—would combat easy stereotyping and racism. Additionally, Dobzhansky had a social vision based on science: increased knowledge of individual genetic differences would help both individuals and society maximize their potential, because in this way individual capabilities would be matched to social needs (see, for example, Dobzhansky, 1968, 1973a,b). Thus, Dobzhansky used a biological argument to support the traditional American ideology of individual liberalism. A typical example is the following:

> A class or caste society leads unavoidably to misplacement of talents. The biological justification of equality of opportunity is that a society should minimize the loss of valuable human resources, as well as the personal misery resulting from misplaced abilities, and thus enhance its total adaptiveness to variable environments (Dobzhansky, 1968).

Lewontin, however, took over only part of his thinking: the opposition to typological thinking and group averages in science, and the opposition to racism in society. What he did not accept, because of his new ideological commitments, was the necessary counterpart to this view: the stress on individual *genetic* differences. Any significant influence of the genes, within or between groups, would be bad, and therefore had to be discounted as a significant causal factor. No doubt one reason for this was precisely the ease with which the 'innocent layman' and academics alike might still be caught in typological thinking, or, like Jensen, feel free to extrapolate from individual differences to group differences—a scientific error with social implications. Ironically, therefore, apart from Wilson, the prime targets of Lewontin's attacks as a critic have been exactly those scientists who have explicitly voiced Dobzhansky-style beliefs about the social value of identifying individual genetically based talent (such as the late Harvard microbiologist Bernard Davis, one of Wilson's staunch supporters).

For Lewontin, typological thinking had to do with more than race differences: it was applicable to *any* assertion about inherent differences between human groups, be these based on race, sex, class, or ethnicity. The fight against typological thinking had been expanded into a fight against 'biological determinism' in general (cf. Lewontin, 1977b). According to Lewontin, the pronouncements by American academics about inherent differences between groups had always served to uphold the social status quo. In the United States, the groups typically discriminated against had been blacks and southern and eastern European immigrants, so it was not surprising that 'the academic science produced by white northern European culture has consistently shown the racial superiority of white northern Europeans' (Lewontin, 1977b). Lewontin continued his demonstration by holding the early American IQ testers responsible for the ethnic quotas established in the notorious Immigration Act of 1924, using Kamin (1974) as his reference.

Thus, for Lewontin, the fight against typological thinking in general meant not only an attack on research explicitly intended to establish an innate basis for group differences, but also an attack on any research on differences in innate ability between *individuals*. The reason was the ease with which such differences might be correlated with some social category, like race, sex, ethnic group, or class, and thereby be used as grounds for discriminatory social practices in the service of the social power-holders.

Now we can start understanding how it was at all possible for Wilson's claims to come under scrutiny for racist implications. While Wilson's sociobiological program, for it to be amenable to the formulas of population genetics, was dependent exactly on a postulated genetic variation in human behavioral traits—that is, genetic differences between individuals—it was precisely this feature of the program that Lewontin, in order to combat racism and 'biological determinism' would have to oppose. And while Wilson's moral-cum-scientific agenda motivated him to accept the existing research in human behavioral genetics at face value, Lewontin's critical agenda made him dismiss most of the research in this field as not meeting minimum scientific standards (cf. Lewontin, 1975a). It is ironical to reflect on the fact that Wilson, when deciding to import Lewontin to Harvard, must have believed himself quite safe from potential criticism for racist research, not only because he knew that Lewontin knew that he was not a racist, but also because in *Sociobiology* he explicitly endorsed Lewontin's own recent findings about human variation.

One further feature of Lewontin's specific logic has to be emphasized. It seems that for him 'good science' was modern science and 'bad science' was old-fashioned science. But, in addition, good science was defined as the type of science Lewontin was doing in his laboratory. I quote once more from the Nova program. Stating that recently the old attitudes of American academics, especially racist geneticists and psychologists, had come to the fore again, Lewontin concluded:

> So we have the same old story, untrue statements, facts which are not facts, logic which is not logic, to prove that there are important genetic differences between races. Yet everything that modern genetics, the kind of genetics that goes on in our lab, for example, tells us is that Darwin was right in the first place. That most of the genetic variation that occurs in the human species and indeed in most species, is between individuals within any group, and rather little of it is between groups.

We can now see why it was 'necessary' for Lewontin (and the other critics) to describe Wilson as an old-fashioned and bad scientist in *The New York Review of Books* letter and the ensuing longer criticism in 1976, and as presenting facts that were not facts. As in the Agassiz case, Lewontin discounted the possibility that Wilson may have himself believed in the plausibility of the behavioral genetic evidence on *scientific* grounds. The aim here was the same as in Lewontin's criticism of Jensen some five years earlier: to show how ideological assumptions lead to 'bad science'. A corollary of Lewontin's position is also worth noting: it appears that he believed that modern science—his own science—would be immune from the influence of ideology, or at least, that he himself, because of his ideological awareness, would be beyond moral criticism for disseminating 'facts that are not facts'. As I will argue in Chapter 8, such a precarious position may well have backfired and contributed to the clash between Lewontin and Wilson in conjunction with *Genes, Mind and Culture*.

So, while Lewontin had genuine meta-scientific disagreements with Wilson, he was here forced by his own logic and critical strategy, as well as by his commitment to the public in the Nova program, to look for scientific and moral 'errors' in his colleague. This is why Wilson was said to have 'old-fashioned' views of genes and not to be aware of the current problems of adaptation. This was a serious misrepresentation of Wilson, since he in fact discussed these matters at length in his book. Wilson also made it quite explicit that it was for heuristic reasons that he chose particular theories as building blocks for his program.

These charges really struck home. It was especially hurtful for Wilson to be thus described as a bad scientist. He wished the critics had acknowledged his general scholarship and then said that he had gone too far speculating about humans (Wilson, interview). It was probably at least in part because of the slight on his professional abilities that Wilson was spurred on in his theorizing about human sociobiology.

This is, then, the story of two colleagues acknowledged as leading evolutionists, former partners in the aim to take over and reform their discipline, but later fundamentally divided over epistemological strategies, moral concerns, and their evaluation of worthwhile science. In addition to the scientific and moral interests involved, one has to allow for personality differences and for differences in scientific taste, which border on esthetic conceptions, a matter which we will turn to now.

A matter of taste

What about personality differences? Wilson has always emphasized that he is terribly shy. From interviews and also from his recent autobiography, *Naturalist* (Wilson, 1994), it becomes obvious that Wilson is more interested in other species than humans. Indeed, this was true even at the peak of the sociobiology controversy. Just after Wilson, together with Lumsden, had published *Genes, Mind and Culture*, he said he could not wait to get back to his ant studies. Interestingly, while Wilson's most conspiratorial critics perceived him as obsessed with human sociobiology, he declared in interview that the place where he was really happiest was at the edge of the rainforest—alone. (He added being with his family as something of an afterthought.) This romantic side of Wilson never came to the attention of the critics, and it is not clear that they would have understood the kind of motive driving Wilson anyway (see Chapter 13 for an analysis of the differences between naturalists and experimentalists). The only person who might have been able to explain Wilson to the Sociobiology Study Group was Stephen J. Gould, since he and Wilson, after all, shared a naturalist interest. However, for other reasons, Gould chose not to mediate in the sociobiology controversy.

It is perhaps because he perceived himself as shy that Wilson made much of Lewontin as an 'alpha male', at least in personal conversations. This is the way that Wilson described his colleague's behavior in his 1994 autobiography:

> Unafflicted by shyness, at committee meetings he almost always seated himself near the head or center of the conference table, speaking up more frequently than others present, questioning and annotating every subject raised. He was the boy prodigy you surely encountered at least once in school, the first to raise his hand, the first reaching the blackboard to crack the algebra problem . . .
>
> He would pivot from one role to another, first the thoughtful and cautious dean, now the lecturer expanding a philosophical idea, then the hearty joking companion, and abruptly, on occasion, the angry radical. To accentuate a point, he would raise his hands above his head with fingers opened, and as his voice evened out and the argument unfolded, slide them back to the table top palms down, at first placed side by side and then eased apart, the mood having turned reflective, then quickly up again to chest level and windmilled one around the other, the subject grown more complex and the listener thereby commanded to pay close attention. He spoke in whole sentences and paragraphs . . . While he spoke he turned about to make eye contact with each listener within range, flashing the grin, signaling a confidence in his choice of words, revealing an attention to technique as well as substance (Wilson, 1994, pp. 342–3).

This is marvelous ethology, worthy of a naturalist. Wilson was obviously sensitive to Lewontin's nonverbal cues. Incidentally, his statement that Lewontin spoke 'in whole sentences and paragraphs' was a great acknowledgement—Wilson typically attributed such capabilities to people he admired. (In our interviews he described Robert McArthur and Richard Levins as people who spoke 'in whole paragraphs'—presumably even higher praise. Wilson much admired Levins for his originality and for being a great 'visionary'—and even for the purity of his Marxist vision; Wilson, interview in 1981.)

It is interesting that in his autobiography Wilson so thoroughly scrutinized not only the objective achievements of Lewontin, which he generously described, but also the latter's self-confidence and style. It seems, indeed, that Wilson had the keen sense of being in constant competition with his colleague. Wilson once in interview referred to their relationship as 'sibling rivalry'. Considering Lewontin's boyish appearance, it is perhaps surprising to learn that he and Wilson were born in the same year, 1929. Now we can better understand the depth of opposition between these two colleagues: they were part of the same scientific generation, they spoke to the same issues in evolutionary biology, they had even a common ambition at one point—but they later ended up on diametrically opposite sides.

But there is more. For a reader of Wilson's autobiography, it becomes obvious that naturally shy Wilson in fact was deadly ambitious—he was driven by the quest to be the best. What is more, it seems that Wilson in fact often deliberately threw himself into adrenaline-producing situations: for instance, in his youth he competed as a long-distance runner. After giving up the running prospect early in his life, later visions of great intellectual feats gave him the needed stimulation. Note, for instance, his description of how he felt about the very idea of formulating a comprehensive sociobiological theory: 'Once again I was roused by the amphetamine of ambition' (Wilson, 1994, p. 323). It was unusual—and honest—of Wilson to reflect on the role of ambition in his life. (His critics, meanwhile, acted as if they themselves were exempt from such base considerations as ambition and competition, which, of course, they were not; see Chapter 15.) Indeed, Wilson appears to have actively *sought out* particular persons to serve the role as immediate competitors—before Lewontin, it was Jim Watson that was Wilson's stimulating challenge (Wilson, 1994).[3]

In contrast to Wilson, Lewontin had nothing to say about any sense of competition with his colleague. Neither did he compare personal styles, except for noting that Wilson preferred written polemics ('Ed is better in writing, he is not so good on his feet', Lewontin, interview. Wilson, in his autobiography, noted Lewontin's considerable public presence and wit.) Indeed, in my three long interviews with Lewontin, he persistently criticized Wilson for only one thing: failing to do 'serious' science. Indeed, from the very beginning of the controversy, in an interview in *Harvard Gazette*, Lewontin insisted that Wilson's sociobiological theory 'does not belong in the corpus of natural science, because he provides so many ways and gimmicks to make his theory work, it is by nature self-confirming and violates scientific method' (Lewontin, 1976b). Thus, whatever his nonverbal cues of dominance, Lewontin's relationship to Wilson probably had less to do with primate-type competition than with the basic fact that he disapproved of Wilson on *intellectual* grounds.

Also, and importantly, unlike his Science for the People colleagues, Lewontin in private did not condemn Wilson on *political* grounds. Indeed, listening to him speaking in strongly disapproving tone of his colleague, one got the impression that Wilson had violated some holy principle of 'good science', of which Lewontin was the self-appointed enforcer. Or rather, incredible as it may sound, particularly since they were the same age, I got the impression that Lewontin genuinely felt that Wilson had 'disobeyed' him and his rules. (Indeed, in 1974, Lewontin had devoted a whole book to laying down the rules for acceptable science.) It seems, then, that although Lewontin could keenly perceive the political dangers of sociobiology—and often did so—his fundamental objection to sociobiology was scientific.

What about differences of scientific taste? Lewontin paid more attention to 'keeping it clean', while Wilson was especially attracted to 'unformed' areas in evolutionary biology, where he could bring about order. Indeed, he had already started this in the field of biogeography. Here it is interesting to note that Wilson considered himself the *scientifically* radical and Lewontin the *scientifically* conservative:

> Lewontin had always struck me as being the conservative in that little group. He was in a field that was already highly developed, he adored Theodosius Dobzhansky, his teacher, he took pride in the advanced and sophisticated nature of the field he was in, population genetics, which is the best developed . . . while the rest of us were talking about fields which had not been formulated yet . . . Lewontin always struck me as not being a visionary. He never said 'we are going to create new ways of thinking'. He was always, even in the '60s, sitting in the safe domain, questioning and so on. He is very IQ bright, he is not creative-bright . . . I think that is what he meant when he once said that Levins is brighter than him . . . he cannot conceive of new ways of thinking the way Levins and MacArthur did . . . Although, I don't want to do him an injustice—he has done some extremely ingenious things—but I always had the feeling that, even before his radical days, he was always hugging the coast . . . (Wilson, interview).

Thus, the situation could be described as an opposition between a purist, critical, logical approach with slightly negative overtones (Lewontin), and a practically oriented, opportunistic, speculative, and generally 'positive' model-building approach, where judgment is postponed until later (Wilson). From the protagonists' own perspectives, the first approach is 'serious science' (Lewontin) or 'too safe' (Wilson), while the latter one is either 'creative and risky' (Wilson) or 'not serious' (Lewontin). It is obvious that the scientists' perceptions of themselves and of one another were related to their different conceptions of 'good science' and the way they saw themselves as contributing to scientific progress.

The differences in the two colleagues' scientific taste were also reflected in the moral/political part of their respective agendas. Lewontin's emphasis on the need for 'correct' facts made it an additional moral/political obligation for him to criticize 'bad science'. (In turn, the importance of correct facts was tied to Lewontin's view that true knowledge did not lend itself to political abuse; see also Chapters 11 and 14.) The situation was less problematic for Wilson: the idea was simply to do more science, and it was science rather than 'unaided intuition' that ought to guide our social progress and ethical choices. For Wilson, science could be objective if scientists tried hard enough;

and the democratic process would lead to sensible choices of application of results (see, for example, Wilson, 1978b). In other words, there was also a fundamentally different conception of the social role of the scientist tied in with Wilson's and Lewontin's meta-scientific concerns. In Chapter 11, we will return to a more general discussion of the contrast between 'planters' and 'weeders', for which Wilson and Lewontin can serve as prototypes.

The story does not end here. We will follow through the controversy about socio-biology, especially human sociobiology, centering on the work *Genes, Mind and Culture*, which Wilson published in 1981 together with Charles Lumsden, a young Canadian physicist. That episode is a good example of the various factors entering into the Wilson/Lewontin clash. In fact, we will see how the earlier conflict between their moral-cum-scientific agendas came to a head with this new book. First, however, we will leave the Harvard setting and look at the broader scientific context of the sociobiology controversy. How did the polemics in this debate relate to prevailing views on important scientific issues within evolutionary biology at the time, such things as the role of adaptation and the unit of selection? Here, we will specifically consider the British connection. It will become apparent that the sociobiology debate around Harvard was a rather idiosyncratic American phenomenon, which had little basis in the United Kingdom, but 'had to be imported'—an expression I often encountered in interviews with British scientists.

CHAPTER 4

The British connection

From group selection to kin selection: collective conversion or scientific stampede?

Sociobiology was exactly what it said it was: a synthesis of the theoretical developments and empirical studies in animal social behavior over the previous thirty years. Many of Wilson's fellow biologists were duly grateful to him for ploughing through and processing an enormous amount of existing literature 'for' them. They also appreciated many of his insights. In fact, Wilson describes how his 'new colleagues' in vertebrate studies encouraged his idea of writing a synthesis, although he was not a specialist in their field (1975a, p. v; 1994, p. 330). The testimony to his success, again, is the poll conducted in 1989 among the officers and fellows of the international Animal Behavior Society. Wilson tells us that they 'rated *Sociobiology* the most important book on animal behavior of all time, edging out even Darwin's 1872 classic, *The Expression of the Emotions in Man and Animals*' (Wilson, 1994, pp. 330–1).

For many, Wilson's most important contribution was that he had introduced to a larger audience the ideas of some important architects of sociobiology. Who were these theorists? If, indeed, the central problem of sociobiology was altruism (as Wilson maintained), there were many individuals who had tried to model altruism in genetic terms. And several of these were British. That was already true for two out of three of the founders of mathematical population genetic neo-Darwinism developed in the 1930s, R. A. Fisher and J. B. S. Haldane, who, like the American Sewall Wright, had also included brief discussions of the conditions for altruism among their other theoretical efforts.[1]

A later wave of explanations for altruism also had a strong British flavor. There was the Scottish field ecologist Vero Wynne-Edwards' (1962) group selectionist model, playing an important role in stimulating discussion about the level of selection. There was Bill Hamilton's (1964) idea of inclusive fitness, which urged us to look at 'kin selection' instead of 'individual selection'. And there was (the American) Bob Trivers' (1971) concept of 'reciprocal altruism' applicable to unrelated individuals. Another model that Wilson mentioned, although more in passing (p. 129), was Maynard Smith's and Price's (1973) model of animal conflict (here there was a combined British–American input). However, he did not emphasize their important idea of an evolutionarily stable strategy (ESS). (It was rather Dawkins who, one year later, in *The Selfish Gene* was to make ESS a cornerstone of his book.) Finally, Wilson (p. 341) also introduced Trivers' (1974) idea of 'parent–offspring conflict', thus including game theory among the family of socio-biological models. But Wilson did not explicitly use the term 'game theory' to explain these kinds of conflicts, and we see no trace of such things as animal 'strategies'. (Again, it was Dawkins who explicitly embraced and explained the logic behind these new approaches.)

What has been observed by many is that between the mid-1960s and the mid-1970s or so, something like a paradigm shift happened in the world of evolutionary biology. Although I believe that Thomas Kuhn's term has been overused and misapplied, I think it may be unusually applicable to the shift from a group-selectionist to a kin-selectionist mode of reasoning. This shift can be seen at many levels: most clearly in the long-term change in focus in evolutionary explanation. According to Geoffrey Parker, for instance, around 1965 you had to be a group selectionist if you wanted to get published at all; ten years later, you had difficulty getting published if you were *not* a kin selectionist (interview, 1981; Parker, 1981). At the level of academic departments, it took the form of a loaded atmosphere and careful maneuvering. I have heard individual testimonies to this, and descriptions of how, particularly in certain British departments, voices were hushed and doors were closed when the old guard approached—the old guard being the representatives of the group-selectionist orthodoxy.

If at the personal level a criterion for paradigm shift is a 'Gestalt switch' or 'religious conversion' for an individual scientist, then for many this was exactly what it felt like. For some, kin selection theory had a deep metaphysical meaning. (Indeed, one American biologist at a conference-dinner gathering in the late 1980s adopted a quasi-religious tone in his discussion of the significance of Hamilton's 1964 paper. He had already given us xeroxes of Hamilton's brief 1963 summary, 'the most important paper published in the twentieth century'). For others, kin selection represented a dangerous ideological step in the wrong direction and was sternly resisted for this reason. A testimony to the fact that group selection and kin selection were 'total' interpretative frameworks was the rift this caused between Harvard anthropologist Irven DeVore and his mentor and friend, anthropologist Sherwood Washburn. DeVore had become an avid kin selectionist, while Washburn resisted the idea with his whole being (DeVore, interview 1982). (I will return to Washburn's conflict with Hamilton in Chapter 7.)

But there was also the straight intellectual 'conversion'. Maynard Smith, after struggling through the math of Hamilton's paper, suddenly got the point and exclaimed to himself: 'Of course; why didn't I think of that!' (personal communication). And here we have Wilson's testimony as to his own conversion experience. Wilson had taken Hamilton's article in the *Journal of Theoretical Biology* with him on a long train ride from Boston to Miami in the spring of 1965 (he worked especially well on trains):

> My first response was negative. Impossible, I thought; this can't be right. Too simple. He must not know much about social insects. But the idea kept gnawing at me that afternoon . . . As we departed southward across the New Jersey marshes, I went through the article again, more carefully this time, looking for the fatal flaw I believed must be there. At intervals I closed my eyes and tried to conceive of alternative, more convincing explanations of the prevalence of hymenopteran social life and the all-female work force. Surely I knew enough

to come up with something. I had done this kind of critique before and succeeded. But nothing presented itself now. By dinnertime, as the train rumbled on in Virginia, I was growing frustrated and angry. Hamilton, whoever he was, could not have cut the Gordian knot. Anyway, there was no Gordian knot in the first place, was there? I had thought there was just a lot of accidental evolution and wonderful natural history. And because I modestly thought of myself as the world authority on social insects, I also thought it unlikely that anyone else could explain their origin, certainly not in one clean stroke. The next morning, as we rolled on past Waycross and Jacksonville, I thrashed about some more. By the time we reached Miami, in the early afternoon, I gave up. I was a convert, and put myself in Hamilton's hands. I had undergone what historians of science call a paradigm shift (Wilson, 1994, pp. 319–20).

It was good that he persisted. The theory of kin selection which he first 'resisted with all his ability' Wilson would later describe as the most important element for his sociobiological theory (Wilson, 1994, p. 315). (Still, the conversion seems to have been somewhat incomplete, since Hamilton finds himself counted in together with group selectionists of various kinds in Chapter 5 of Wilson's *Sociobiology*.)

But what was everybody converting *from*? To get a sense of the intellectual climate in the early 1960s, let us listen to Hamilton's own description. According to him, '[m]any Cambridge biologists seemed hardly to believe in evolution or at least seemed to be skeptical of the efficacy of natural selection'. He takes as an example Professor Sir Vincent Wigglesworth's formulation in his *The Life of Insects,* 1964:

> Insects do not live for themselves alone. Their lives are devoted to the survival of the species whose representatives they are . . . Indeed, we have now reached the aim and purpose . . . of the life of insects (Wigglesworth quoted in Hamilton, 1996, p. 22).

Hamilton comments that Wigglesworth never interested himself in anything beyond proximate explanations—how the insect body is engineered—which means he could have little professional reason to discuss ultimate explanations ('aim and purpose'). Still, the citation illustrates 'the Cambridge atmosphere of the time, an atmosphere that Wigglesworth breathed and influenced', which in biology translated to automatic support for adaptation at the species level (p. 22).

It was this vague good-for-the-species formulation that Wynne-Edwards tried to put on more solid ground with his 1962 book *Animal Dispersion in Relation to Social Behaviour.* Many have pointed out the service that the Scottish ecologist rendered the biological community through his effort to give some kind of explanation and at least show a mechanism by which group selection *might* come about. (Wynne-Edwards suggested that animals deliberately, 'altruistically', regulate their numbers for the good of the group. They get their information about population density by displaying together in large crows.) A brief summarizing article in *Nature* (Wynne-Edwards, 1963) was rapidly criticized by Maynard Smith, however, who presented kin selection as an alternative to group selection (Maynard Smith, 1964). George Williams in 1966 declared higher levels of selection unnecessary and told people to focus on the individual. He followed up with an edited book, *Group Selection*, in 1971, and Maynard

Smith wrote an important critical article in *Quarterly Review of Biology* in 1975. Wynne-Edwards recanted. But as Dawkins (1989, p. 297) has noticed, it was not long before Wynne-Edwards re-recanted! One reason was the strength he had found in David Sloan Wilson's work on group selection. Indeed, when I visited Wynne-Edwards in 1981, he was extremely happy with the turn of events. D. S. Wilson had just published a book that seemingly supported a group-selectionist view (D. S. Wilson, 1980).

Not many followed in the footsteps of Wynne-Edwards' particular model of group selection, but an indicator that the kin-selection approach had not yet won over the hearts and minds of the biological community is Hamilton's address to an international conference on Biosocial Anthropology in 1973 (published as Hamilton, 1975). There he spoke of 'the *consensus of biologists* . . . in believing that the generally significant selection is at the level of competing groups and species' (italics added). As a contrast to this he said: 'I shall argue that lower levels of selection are inherently more powerful than higher levels and that careful thought and factual checks are always needed before lower levels are neglected. In this I follow a recent critical trend in evolutionary thought' (here he referred to Williams' 1966 book and to a 1970 article by Lewontin on the units of selection).

According to Hamilton, Darwin himself was mostly concerned with individual fitness and left the question open when it came to group selection. He treated for instance the 'family group' in the social insects as the unit of selection, but realized that altruistic traits would be counterselected within a group, while in competition between groups, the more altruistic group would be fitter. Nevertheless, remarkably, after a while 'almost the whole field of biology stampeded in the direction where Darwin had gone circumspectly or not at all'—that is, in the direction of group selection. The rediscovery of Mendelism or its incorporation in evolutionary theory seemed to have had no effect, Hamilton noted. The result was the following:

> From about 1920 to 1960 a curious situation developed where models of 'Neodarwinism' were all concerned with selection at levels no higher than that of competing individuals, whereas the biological literature as a whole increasingly proclaimed faith in Neodarwinism, and at the same time stated almost all its interpretations of adaptation in terms of 'benefit to the species'. The leading theorists did occasionally point out the weakness of this position but on the whole concerned themselves with it surprisingly little (Hamilton, 1996, p. 331).

How could such a situation have come about? Hamilton's own suggestion is that it was 'Marxism, trade unionism, fears of "social darwinism", and vicissitudes of thought during two world wars'. Natural selection can easily be seen as having reactionary implications, he said, 'unless "fittest" means the fittest species (man) and "struggle" means struggle against nature (anything but man)'. Under these circumstances, Hamilton believed, benefit-of-the-species arguments were simply euphemisms for natural selection. Researchers were talking good-for-the-species group selection in order to be able to do research at all! (There was an added benefit, too, speculated Hamilton: these kinds of arguments provided an escape from inner conflict for readers and writers alike; p. 331.)

But of course it was not too long before 'almost the whole field of biology stampeded' in the *opposite* direction. In fact, many may have rushed into kin selection without even bothering to understand it seriously or reading Hamilton's paper first hand (see, for example, Darlington, 1971; Seger and Harvey, 1980; May and Robertson, 1980; Grafen, 1982).

Bill Hamilton: the lonely figure

Most people know Bill Hamilton's 1964 two-part paper, 'The Genetical Evolution of Social Behaviour' as furnishing the scientific world with the concept of 'inclusive fitness' and starting it thinking in terms of kin selection instead of group selection, and this in quantitative terms. As Wilson put it:

> Hamilton had traveled that high road of science once described by the great biochemist Albert Szent-Györgyi, 'to see what everyone had seen and think what no one has thought'. But I am reasonably sure that had Hamilton expressed kin selection in merely abstract terms, the response to his formulation would have been tepid ... Yet Hamilton did succeed dramatically (although few learned about the theory until I highlighted it in the 1970s). He did so because he went on to tell us something new about the real world in *real, measurable terms*. He provided the tools for real, empirical advances in sociobiology (Wilson, 1994, p. 317, italics added).

Some may also associate Hamilton with gene selectionism, or 'the gene's eye' view. Hamilton had, indeed, introduced the gene's eye perspective in his final remarks of his 1964 paper and also in his short 1963 paper, a view which was later 'brilliantly developed by Richard Dawkins' (Hamilton, 1996, p. 27). Still, in his autobiographical notes, Hamilton was concerned to point out that his intent was not to establish a gene-selectionist approach. He wanted to find a solution to the problem of altruism that would be based on the idea of the whole organism, *individual fitness*. Hamilton saw himself as extending the ideas of R. A. Fisher (p. 21).

Ever since his undergraduate days, Hamilton had been obsessed with the genetics of altruism. He was a student at Cambridge in Fisher's department of genetics (Fisher himself had retired in 1957, around the time Hamilton began his studies). When he started, he did not even know that others had tried—and largely abandoned the idea. As he says himself: 'Clearly the fact that I had proceeded initially unaware of most of the tentative approaches of various Neodarwinian forerunners means that I was more hopeful of the idea's explanatory power than had been the forerunners—the three great pioneers of modern evolutionary theory, J. B. S. Haldane, R. A. Fisher, and Sewall Wright, who ... gave to altruism at most a few lines' (p. 2). Haldane had primarily made some verbal statements, written up in the popular journal *New Biology* (1955). But according to Hamilton, the principle of the genetics of altruism had in fact been foreshadowed much earlier by Fisher (1930) (p. 49). Hamilton also recognized Williams and Williams' early (1957) attempt to elucidate the natural selection of altruistic behavior among sibs (p. 50).[2]

The one mathematical treatment of altruism that Hamilton had found seemed like a nonstarter. Its author was Haldane, who had once seriously tried a group-selectionist approach, quite apart from his kin-selectionist 'pub joke' about laying down his life for two brothers or eight cousins (later published in *New Biology*). Hamilton tells us that as an undergraduate he had looked into Haldane's group-selection formulas 'as an arithmetic exercise', but soon 'proved it a failure'. He could show that the conditions under which this group-selectionist mode for altruism would work were even more severe than Haldane had believed (p. 22).

Hamilton's dismissive attitude to Haldane's group-selection model can be explained on the ground that he was 'allergic' to group selection. 'Fisher was my hero', he says in his autobiographical notes. Fisher represented the individualist approach that he craved (p. 21). Consequently, Hamilton saw himself as essentially extending Fisher's argument in his own work. But his lecturers disapproved of Fisher; they were all group selectionists. (Somebody even told Hamilton that Fisher was not worth looking into, that 'he was good with statistics but knew nothing about biology'.) This meant that Hamilton had to discover Fisher's writings on evolution all by himself (p. 21).

If people only knew the circumstances under which Hamilton produced his famous paper for the *Journal of Theoretical Biology*! His was an extremely lonely existence—so lonely that he sometimes found himself working on park benches, and late at night in Waterloo Station—just to be among people. In the park, the wind often grabbed 'his miserable arithmetics' and scattered it over the lawns. He was having difficulties with the mathematics in what was to become the famous paper 'The Genetical Evolution of Social Behaviour, I and II'—which, a decade later, was destined to become *Current Contents*' most cited paper ever. But this was by no means obvious in the early 1960s to the struggling, shy graduate student, who felt himself intellectually so desperately alone, doubting his own abilites, and wondering from time to time if he was not, after all, some kind of 'crank'. How come nobody had seen what he had seen, he asked himself? All this is told in moving detail in Hamilton's introductory essays to Volume I of his collected works, *Narrow Roads of Geneland*.

Hamilton's own narrow road in geneland had been full of obstacles from the very start. The genetics of altruism was clearly an idea whose time had not come. Absolutely nobody seemed to want to hear about genetics and altruism—at least not in the same sentence. Hamilton failed to interest any genetics department, including the famous Galton Laboratory at University College London (p. 4). Finally he obtained a scholarship at the London School of Economics, which allowed him to pursue his study of altruism on the condition that he also enrolled in human demography in their department of sociology (p. 4). Later, when he outgrew his advisers, it was arranged that he would be part-supervised at the Galton Laboratory, now as a PhD student.

Hamilton reflects that the London School of Economics was probably rather embarrassed by his interest in genetics. In the post-war period, genetics as a field was suspect, and this was, after all, LSE—a stronghold of leftist thought. Hamilton felt the coolness of the chair of sociology toward him. (It certainly did not help that he gave the London School of Economics Department of Sociology as the address for his first published paper, 'The Evolution of Altruistic Behavior', appearing in 1963 while the longer paper was still in press) (p. 5).

What was even more clear to Hamilton, however, was that his Galton Laboratory supervisor, Professor Lionel Penrose, FRS, was suspicious of him: how else could one explain Penrose's and his secretary's persistently 'gloomy' avoidance behavior? (p. 17). Perhaps Penrose thought of him as a rabid eugenicist? The two of them had never discussed this, but Hamilton believed that he may have mentioned his admiration for Galton's pioneering work, which may have been a *faux pas*. Mentioning Galton seemed, of course, a rather obvious thing to do in the Galton Laboratory, but times were extremely sensitive. In fact Penrose himself, the head of the institution, had taken a strongly anti-eugenical stance. After the war, he had taken care to change the image of the institution, making its research mainstream genetics and renaming its journal the *Annals of Eugenics* the *Annals of Genetics* instead (p. 14).

To make matters worse, Penrose was exactly one of the persons that Hamilton had earlier approached to ask for sponsorship for studying the problem of altruism. Penrose had not only refused point blank, but even said that he doubted that there was such a problem to be studied in the first place. He had, however, offered Hamilton work on some more standard problems in genetics, but Hamilton had declined that offer (p. 14). Now Hamilton had suddenly appeared, despite all, through a back door as it were. Hamilton did not feel welcome:

> Although supervised at the Galton laboratory for 2 years I never had a desk there nor was ever invited to give any presentation to explain my work or my occasional presence to others. I think virtually no one I passed in the corridors or sat with in the library knew my name or what I was doing. Probably this was largely my own fault. I was a student who, if not offered or invited, wouldn't request, and I think I didn't ask for desk space either there or at LSE. In fact, I had no idea at the time what was normal for graduate students. . . . I just wanted access to libraries plus some pittance of support; these together would give me freedom to follow my puzzles (Hamilton, 1996, p. 11).

It is not hard to understand why Hamilton spent very little time in the Galton Laboratory. He did not even have a desk there. Hamilton worried whether he would ever get a PhD. Whatever happened, he would have to show something for his three years of scholarship support. It was now 1962. His paper's fate was unclear. He had submitted it to the *Journal of Theoretical Biology*, but was still waiting for an answer. Hamilton decided to write a brief version with the main points of the paper ('Hamilton's rule', $k > 1/r$, inclusive fitness, and the gene's eye view) and submit it somewhere for more rapid publication. He decided on *Nature*.

The response came back almost by return. The topic was too specific for *Nature*, Hamilton was told, and he was encouraged to try 'a psychological or socialogical [*sic*] journal' instead (p. 3). Hamilton took that to mean that 'there existed a prejudice against my topic' in *Nature* and resubmitted the paper to the *American Naturalist*, where it was accepted in 1962 and published in 1963 (Hamilton, 1963). At least he had something in print. The long paper was still under review. By now, Hamilton was exhausted and decided that a total change of scene would do him good. He wrote to Warwick Kerr in Brazil, and in 1963 he got himself invited as a visiting scholar there (p. 29). Over the next decade or so he would make three trips to Brazil, sometimes with his family, conducting field studies and teaching biology in Portuguese.

What happened to the manuscript he had submitted to the *Journal of Theoretical Biology*? 'I forget whether in 1963 I was in preparation to go to Brazil or had already left when the editor's reply arrived saying that my paper was generally acceptable to the journal but needed major revision and in particular must be split into two', Hamilton tells us (p. 29). That request for revision was very frustrating to him after the struggle he had already had with the paper. And as Hamilton explained, with his adjustment to the new conditions, learning Portuguese and teaching duties, his revision and division work went slowly. He sent back the revised manuscript in early 1964. It was accepted, and finally published in July 1964, in two parts as requested (p. 29).

Back from Brazil, Hamilton landed a job at Imperial College, on the basis of his publications alone—he did not yet have his PhD. He found the students rather un-interested in his ideas, but meanwhile his fame as a theorist was growing. Still, there were signs that he was not appreciated. Finding himself passed over for promotion, he decided to pack up and leave. This time, he did not go to Brazil but to America, where he would stay for six years (1977–84), spending a short time at Harvard in 1978 but otherwise mostly at the University of Michigan, Ann Arbor, where Richard Alexander had arranged a position for him.

At least until the mid-1970s, Hamilton seems to have been more appreciated in America than in his own country. And one important American who liked his theory was E. O. Wilson. Wilson tells a story of how he tried to make the British academic world pay more attention to Hamilton in 1965, when Hamilton was still a graduate student. Wilson had 'discovered' Hamilton in that year, and had a chance to meet Hamilton in person just before a meeting of the Royal Entomological Society in London, where Wilson was invited to give a paper. Sympathizing with 'young Hamilton', who told him about his difficulties in getting a PhD, Wilson decided to devote a significant portion of his talk to Hamilton's contribution. He took a certain pleasure in knowing that in the audience would be the top figures in British entomology. Wilson ended up spending a third of his hour-long presentation on Hamilton. He had also prepared responses to the objections he expected to hear—and got. 'It was a pleasure to answer them', recounts Wilson. 'When once or twice I felt uncertain I threw the question to young Hamilton, who was seated in the audience. Together we carried the day' (Wilson, 1994, pp. 320–1).

There is no doubt Wilson did his enthusiastic and persuasive best. Did it have an effect on the audience? Probably some, since Wilson was, after all, a world expert. On the other hand, the top figures included Vincent Wigglesworth, the very person Hamilton had cited as a staunch upholder of the 'official' group-selectionist idea. The boost by Wilson may have had indirect effects, such as making Hamilton's road to his PhD smoother (he already had a job). Also, 'young Hamilton' could certainly do with some encouragement from an older colleague.

Perhaps it was memories like this (and later friendships formed at the Man and Beast conference in Washington in 1969, see Chapter 5) that made America later appear a clear choice for Hamilton. Still, going to the United States during this time of course also meant arriving during the heated beginning of the sociobiology controversy. In one sense, Hamilton had only jumped from the ashes into the fire. At the University of Michigan there was almost immediately a student demonstration against him (personal communication). Ann Arbor had a vigorous group of anti-sociobiologists, involved with the local chapter of Science for the People, in which anthropologists were particularly active. (This group, Ann Arbor Collective of Science for the People, had in 1977 published *Biology as a Social Weapon*). On the other hand, around Alexander had gathered a vigorous group of graduate students who were interested in discussing ideas and eager to learn from Hamilton. The move to America may have been wise: on the crest of an ever-growing fame, Hamilton returned in triumph to Oxford in 1984, for a Royal Society Research Fellowship in Zoology.

As we see, the story has a positive ending. But could not someone have helped this struggling graduate student earlier on? Were there not people who would have understood his scientific quest? How is it possible that no one spotted his genius? Here we come to one of the strange twists of the Hamilton story—the non-meeting between Hamilton and Maynard Smith.

Maynard Smith and the missed opportunity

The story of the non-contact between Hamilton and Maynard Smith is a sad one, from the perspective of both Hamilton and Maynard Smith. Here was a graduate student with a quest that nobody seemed to share at the time: an interest in a genetic basis for altruism. People who were in a position to support him backed away because of the dangerous word 'genetics'. At the same time he was outside the then current orthodoxy of genetics itself and rebuffed by the leaders in the field. Could he have tried to tailor his own academic program? At Cambridge, he had asked to be allowed to combine genetics studies with a course in anthropology. Edmund Leach gave his absolute veto, and the genetics department, too, refused co-operation. Nobody explained why. Perhaps this was a true expression of the gap between the Two Cultures at the time, vividly described by C. P. Snow just around then (1959) and supposedly reflecting the situation particularly at Cambridge. The ones who ended up supporting Hamilton (Norman Carrier and John Hajnal at LSE) did so because of an unusual quality of their minds which transcended academic entrenchments, fashions, and fears: they simply *liked* intellectual puzzles and wanted them solved! (All this can be gleaned from Hamilton's autobiographical notes.)

But there were, of course, at least two people in the world who would—or at least should—have been quite interested in Hamilton, had they known about his existence. They were J. B. S. Haldane and John Maynard Smith. Haldane himself had retired from University College in 1957 and emigrated to India. But what about Maynard Smith? He was, after all, Haldane's student and close colleague.

Here the story gets really bizarre. Hamilton, although he was officially the student of

Cedric Smith in the department of genetics at University College, spent very little time there; as we saw, he did not have a desk and did not receive feedback from anybody about his work. If anything, he spent most of his time *outside* University College, feeling terribly alienated. So where was Maynard Smith during this time? It turns out he was, in fact, working in the very same building, but in the zoology department! (Maynard Smith was at University College from 1951 to 1965, when he left for Sussex University.)

Hamilton and Maynard Smith did in fact meet, once. Hamilton remembers this vividly. For him, it was an important meeting: Maynard Smith was an established professor who might have taken an interest in his ideas and perhaps become an adviser. Maynard Smith cannot remember the meeting at all, but is willing to reconstruct what might have happened; of course, he later also heard the story from Hamilton himself. It was not really a formal meeting, rather, the geneticist Cedric Smith introduced his student to his zoology colleague Maynard Smith, saying something along the lines: 'Here is Bill Hamilton, he is working on the genetics of altruism.' To this, Maynard Smith had responded politely but without particular enthusiasm. 'Genetics of altruism' did not ring any bell. And the shy graduate student went away, rejected once again.

Maynard Smith has felt bad about this for years. One of the reasons seems to be that he prides himself on being able to bring out undiscovered people who have something important to say. He told me, for instance, how he got Cambridge University Press to publish Kimura's theory of neutral selection—Kimura himself had been rather doubtful that his controversial work would ever be published. And it was also Maynard Smith who uncovered the whereabouts of the elusive George Price, whom we will meet in the next section, the result of which was the 1973 Maynard Smith and Price paper.

So, in principle, Maynard Smith could have encouraged Hamilton. But he didn't. According to himself, he was not interested in genetics of altruism at that time— nobody was in a serious way—and Hamilton was a very unassuming and shy person. As we see, Maynard Smith doesn't even remember meeting him. People do not carry labels with 'genius' on their foreheads. This was, then, a sadly missed opportunity for interaction, and they did not meet again. According to Maynard Smith's wife Sheila, a geneticist working 'down the corridor' from Hamilton's supervisor's office in the same lab, she never saw Hamilton around (Sheila Maynard Smith, personal communication). (This reinforces my belief in what I call scientific 'corridor life'—the way one may get to know people and learn things by sheer proximity and regularly bumping into people. Hamilton, with his non-institutional existence, did not become part of this corridor life.)

The story continues, however, and the plot thickens. In 1962 Vero Wynne-Edwards had published his *Animal Dispersion in Relation to Social Behaviour*, the first explicit formulation of a possible mechanism for the workings of group selection. In November 1963, he followed up with an article published in *Nature* (Wynne-Edwards, 1963). Some responses to this followed in March 1964, accompanied by a rejoinder by Wynne-Edwards. One such response was Maynard Smith's communication 'Group Selection and Kin Selection' (Maynard Smith, 1964), a paper often referred to. In the popular literature I have seen the situation presented as Hamilton introducing the concept 'inclusive fitness' and Maynard Smith the term 'kin selection', both in the same year.

Wait a minute! How come that it was, after all, possible to contribute articles on biological topics to *Nature*, one year after the editor had declared that it was not? Hamilton himself reflected on the fact that he may have provided an unfortunate correspondence address for his article: The London School of Economics, Department of Sociology. We can perhaps take this as a sign of Hamilton's early rather innocent conception of academic life and the lack of an adviser to give him 'insider' advice; after all, Hamilton was mostly operating on his own. (In fact, it is a testimony to the quality of his papers that they were published under these conditions.)

There are even better reasons. Wynne-Edwards was an established professor, giving the then prevailing view of 'the good of the species' empirical support in his well-received 1962 book. The editor of *Nature* may have felt justified—indeed, obliged—to spread the word to his readers. Once that was published, it was only natural to have some polite controversy. Because Maynard Smith's communication, after all, was not an article: it was formulated as a letter, directly addressing and challenging the notion of group selection. In that letter, Maynard Smith wrote as follows: 'I will contrast group selection with something I will call kin selection. Kin selection has been treated by Haldane and Hamilton.' (Here he gave a reference to Haldane 1955 and Hamilton 1963.)[3]

I asked Maynard Smith about this received impression that 'kin selection' was his term, parallel to Hamilton's 'inclusive fitness'. But Maynard Smith waved away such an interpretation. He took no credit for the term 'kin selection' he said. In fact, he saw his response to Wynne-Edwards as an opportunity to introduce *Hamilton's* new idea. Moreover, 'kin selection' was not even his invention. It had come about in a group discussion after a recent seminar devoted to discussing Wynne-Edwards' ideas. Many of the people present felt that something was wrong with that idea of group selection. Maynard Smith had presented Hamilton's idea of inclusive fitness from his 1963 paper as an alternative, and people got interested. What shall we call this type of selection, they wondered, to distinguish it from group selection? Maynard Smith remembers that someone then—it was certainly not he, he believed it was Arthur Cain, but Cain could not recall it—came up with the name 'kin selection' (Maynard Smith, interview in 1998).

In other words, Maynard Smith saw himself as someone who at an early point was drawing attention to Hamilton's contribution in order to show that Wynne-Edwards was wrong. Meanwhile, he knew that Hamilton's big *Journal of Theoretical Biology* paper was forthcoming and would clarify any details further. How did he know that? The answer is: he was the reviewer. Yes, it was Maynard Smith himself who had caused so much trouble for Hamilton by asking him to correct some things, to add some examples, and particularly, to split the paper in two—a request that Hamilton considered particularly gratuitous.

A close friend of Hamilton, who shall remain anonymous, had told me that Hamilton believed that his long paper had been unnecessarily delayed by that request, while in the meantime Maynard Smith had been able to send off his own quick 1964 kin-selection contribution to *Nature*. (As we saw, Maynard Smith's brief communication had appeared in March and Hamilton's article in the *Journal of Theoretical Biology* did not appear until July that year.) What might be said to this? We can certainly sympathize with Hamilton's frustration. Still, *auditur et altera pars*.

I asked Maynard Smith directly about this matter. His answer threw a totally different light on the case. Maynard Smith told me that he had in fact tried to *help* Hamilton by asking for the paper to be split! The paper was a long and difficult one. In fact, it had first gone to other reviewers, none of whom could make any sense of it. Finally it had landed with Maynard Smith as a last resort, in the hope that he would understand it. The paper began with a lot of mathematical formulas which used an unusual notation system. Maynard Smith could not figure out what the author wished to convey. A particular problem was that Hamilton had used a typewriter which did not clearly distinguish between two types of circles used in the notation, open and closed ones, but this distinction seemed crucial to the presentation. Just as Maynard Smith was about to abandon the paper, he too, his eyes fell on a sentence which contained the term 'inclusive fitness'. In a flash he grasped the paper's basic idea and exclaimed to himself: 'Of course; why didn't I think of that!' The paper was obviously an intellectual break-through.[4]

But something had to be done with the manuscript. As it stood, nobody would have the time and patience to struggle through Hamilton's paper long enough to ever get to the important point about inclusive fitness, the paper's core. What to do? Maynard Smith reasoned as follows: if the paper were to be cut in two, and Part II *started* with the introduction of the term 'inclusive fitness', referring back to its mathematical deriva-tion in Part I, then perhaps at least some people would get Hamilton's important message even with cursory reading.

What about the kin-selection communication to *Nature*? We have already heard Maynard Smith's story. The stimulus came from Wynne-Edwards, whose idea was con-sidered so important that it was given space in *Nature*. It is hard to see how there can be anything wrong with a scientist quickly writing a *letter* rebutting an idea he perceives to be erroneous (group selection) by suggesting a scientific alternative (kin selection), particularly since Maynard Smith did mention Hamilton's 1963 paper. (And had Hamilton not lost time by his move to Brazil, his 1964 paper, too, might have been in print by March, and could have been referred to, accordingly, by Maynard Smith.)[5]

In the next section we will meet a person with whom both Hamilton and Maynard Smith collaborated and whose contribution was crucial to the development of socio-biology. That is sociobiology's hidden genius, George Price.

George Price: the fundamentalist scientist

Had George Price lived to see the controversy about sociobiology, he would have understood it very well. He had a very keen sense of the social and political implications of sociobiological reasoning. In fact, it was exactly because he had read Hamilton's 1964 paper and was worried about it that he had advanced into sociobiological theorizing in the first place, trying to find an acceptable alternative. But he had also worked on subjects that interested Maynard Smith. Thus, when Price moved to the United Kingdom in the late 1960s, he soon became a collaborator with both Hamilton and Maynard Smith. For Hamilton, Price's formulas opened up the way for a new, more elegant and general derivation of the idea of inclusive fitness. For Maynard Smith, Price contributed some of the important ideas for the evolutionarily stable strategy. And Price's third achievement was the role he assumed as mediator between Hamilton and Maynard Smith, resulting in a better understanding between them.

Price was a self-taught genius, who saw his gift of doing population genetics as a miracle.[6] He was the epitome of the type of scientist for whom it was imperative to connect his scientific and moral concerns. This tendency got stronger later, when it was infused with a religious conviction. Price appears to have been an absolutely uncompromising person, taking both his science and religious conviction extremely seriously. For him, neither scientific theories nor the text of the Bible were metaphorical; they were literal truth and had consequences in the real world. With regard to science, this meant that evolutionary theories had social implications, and when it came to Christianity, Christian charity had to be acted on. This drove Price on the one hand to develop brilliant new theories, on the other to help the poor and homeless in London. These, then, were the circumstances under which he worked with Hamilton and Maynard Smith. The following account is based on what I have heard from Hamilton and Maynard Smith, and on Hamilton's moving description of Price in his autobiographical notes.

How did the American George Price end up in London? He had been corresponding with Hamilton about his 1964 paper, and later a divorce and a large insurance sum for an accident he had suffered enabled him to relocate to London to pursue his intellectual interests. As Hamilton describes it, 'he arrived in London as an ardent and outspoken atheist and a general sceptic' (Hamilton, 1996, p. 320).

Price had studied Hamilton's kin-selection papers closely and been deeply disturbed —according to Hamilton, 'as deeply shocked as the Victorian lady and her friends had been by evolution itself' (p. 175):

> By suggesting to him that life evolved purely by natural selection would not be nearly as benign as he had previously supposed, the papers seem to have had a profound effect on him. Could this limited nepotistic altruism be the best, the most 'humane', that evolution could achieve? If so, the prospect for humanity seemed stark. He set to work to try to understand genetics and to verify what I had done. Once he had convinced himself that something at least close to what I claimed was true, he became very depressed. Was it the limit, or was there something else? (Hamilton, 1996, p. 320.)

Price's response had been to try to develop a different formula, which he had sent to Hamilton. That formula was not a correction of kin selection, but was rather 'a strange, new formalism that was applicable to every kind of natural selection. Central to Price's approach was a covariance formula the like of which I had never seen', Hamilton tells us (p. 172). The formula was correct, and clearly totally original.[7] And Price had other ideas, too; for instance an application of Hamilton's kin-selection model to spiteful behavior. Moreover, his covariance formula was applicable to group selection, Price had informed Hamilton.

Group selection was not exactly Hamilton's cup of tea. 'Up to this contact with Price, and indeed for some time after, I had regarded group selection as so ill defined, so woolly in the uses made by its proponents, and so generally powerless against selection at the individual and genic level, that the idea might as well be omitted from the toolkit of the evolutionist', observed Hamilton (1996, p. 173). Nevertheless, it would fall to Hamilton to follow up on Price's various hunches. A few months before Price died, Hamilton called him and told him that, thanks to his formula, he now had a far better understanding of group selection and had 'a far better tool for all forms of selection acting at one level or at many than I had ever had before' (p. 173). This greatly pleased Price. Hamilton was later to use this approach of nested analysis of levels of selection to rederive his idea of inclusive fitness (Hamilton, 1996, pp. 324, 326).[8]

Together, Hamilton and Price had also been able to pull off a major academic coup: a successful collusion against the (new) editor of *Nature*! Price had sent in his covariance formula to *Nature*; it had been rejected, but the reviewers seemed confused, which Hamilton took as a sign that the paper might be resubmitted. Hamilton in the meantime had worked out Price's suggestion about spiteful behavior and now had a paper ready himself. Why not try to publish that in *Nature*? And why not go one step further, and give the new editor a chance to publish Price's and Hamilton's papers together?

> I suggested a plan to George; he agreed, and very shortly we swung into action. His revised paper went to *Nature*, mine followed quickly; his came back not even reviewed; weeks later back came mine; mine was accepted! I now wrote to *Nature* regretting that I must withdraw it because the powerful new method I had used and cited had been recently refused by *Nature* and I could not proceed until that method was published somewhere. There followed a telephone call from the editor saying he was ringing me because he did not know how to contact Dr Price....
>
> The happy ending is that *Nature* took both papers.... Yet, if in 1970 George and I had combined instead of splitting, if we had sent a single paper deriving the covariance formula, re-establishing kin selection with it, and finally exemplifying spite, all in one glorious synthesis, I am fairly sure that the joint effort would have been rejected (Hamilton, 1996, p. 176).

Hamilton noted that Price and he were certainly 'neither *Nature*'s first nor last colluding evolutionists'. Desperate measures were obviously needed with a journal that continued accepting exceedingly few evolutionary papers, 'and those it does still mostly flow via favoured cliques and topics' (p. 176).

But it was not only with Hamilton that Price was involved during his London stay. Maynard Smith had earlier been a peer reviewer of a manuscript of Price's on animal fighting and found it extremely interesting.[9] Price's work actually inspired Maynard Smith's own work on game theory, which he pursued during a stay at the University of Chicago. When the time came to write up the material, back in London, Maynard

Smith wanted to give Price credit and also get in contact with him for further development of ideas (Maynard Smith, 1976b/1989, p. 205).

But where was he? Nobody knew. Price at the time had no affiliation and was in fact living in a flat without a telephone in Soho. Result: Maynard Smith went and banged on his door (interview, 1998). It turned out that Price had not pursued the paper further (despite Maynard Smith's review recommendations to do so). Maynard Smith tried to persuade Price to write up his ideas in a more accessible form. Price seemed reluctant; he told his visitor he was too busy with other things. Finally he agreed to do a joint paper—the famous paper on the strategy of animal conflict which established the idea of an ESS (Maynard Smith and Price, 1973).

This placed Maynard Smith in something of a quandary. He had got important ideas from Price, but he could not quote them in his own writing, since they were not published anywhere (and there was not even a publication forthcoming). He wanted to go ahead and publish, but he would have to find a way to somehow refer to Price. We remember Hamilton's 'collusion' with Price to get *Nature* to publish both his and Price's papers, when he was relying on Price for his own paper, and Price's paper had already been rejected. But Hamilton had at least a paper to work with. Maynard Smith had nothing.

Maynard Smith solved the problem in an unusual way. He published his game-theoretical work, 'Game Theory and the Evolution of Fighting' as the first essay in a small volume of collected reprinted essays (Maynard Smith, 1972). Price's name does not appear in the notes and references. However, in the Acknowledgements introducing the book Maynard Smith says:

> The essay on 'Game theory and the evolution of fighting' was especially written for this book. I would probably not have had the idea for this essay if I had not seen an unpublished manuscript on the evolution of fighting by Dr George Price, now working in the Galton Laboratory at University College London. Unfortunately, Dr Price is better at having ideas than at publishing them. The best I can do therefore is to acknowledge that if there is anything to the idea, the credit should go to Dr Price and not to me (Maynard Smith, 1972, p. viii).[10]

Price had explained that he was too busy to publish because of other things. What were those 'other things'? Hamilton and Maynard Smith soon learnt that Price had started taking care of the people on the street, helping them with money and trying to find them jobs. In fact, the reason he had moved to Soho from a rather posh earlier apartment was exactly in order to be closer to his flock. (Not surprisingly, he was being rapidly drained of the resources he had initially brought from America.) At the same time, however, he was involved in a scrupulous exegesis of the Bible, particularly the New Testament. This he considered his *real* work.

> George believed that the discovery he had made in evolutionary theory was truly a miracle. God had given him this insight where he had no reason to expect it. . . . Because it was a formula missed by the world's best population geneticists throughout the past 60 years, it was clear to him that he had somehow been chosen to pass on a truth about evolution to a

world that was, somehow, just now deemed ready to receive it. How was he supposed to do it? How much was he expected to tell and how? He . . . decided it was right to treat the matter in just the way he saw divine Truth being handled in the Testaments—that is, . . . perceived only slowly by disciples . . . Through such first interpreters, through such glass, so darkly, along with religious truth, evolutionary truth was supposed to filter outwards. In this process I believe I was chosen to be his first initiate (Hamilton, 1996, p. 323).

Hamilton commented in passing that Price did not choose to be obscure in his scientific writing. But Maynard Smith was to experience at least some unusual scientific consequences of Price's newfound religiosity. As mentioned, the paper that they worked on, 'The Strategy of Animal Conflict', eventually published as Maynard Smith and Price (1973), was the protomodel for the famous Evolutionarily Stable Strategy. The model animals involved were called 'Hawk' and 'Dove'. At least, this was the case when they started their collaboration. But in the middle of this Price went through his religious conversion and now declared that 'Dove' could no longer be used because of its religious connotation. This is why their paper discusses Hawk and *Mouse* instead! (In later papers, Maynard Smith as the single author returned to Hawk and Dove.)

I have here presented a rather abstract story of Price and his moral-cum-scientific quest. In reality, he was living in increasingly chaotic conditions. The homeless that he tried to help let him down in different ways. He was evicted by his landlord and got permission to live in his office in the Galton Laboratory (Cedric Smith, Hamilton's supervisor, had given him this office space). But Price was followed to his new sleeping quarters by his clientele; shouting and disruption followed, and Price was asked to move out. Meanwhile, Price was becoming increasingly depressed with what he saw as his lack of success with helping people in the truly Christian fashion. (Some of his protegés had blatantly abused his kindness.) He was also playing a dangerous game with God. Dependent on thyroxin tablets against hypoglycemia, he sometimes stopped taking them, waiting to see if God would somehow supply him with the chemical through a miracle. That would be a sign that he should continue with his social work. On two occasions, Price did get his medicine in an unexpected way. The third time God did not intervene. Price committed suicide shortly after Christmas 1974. His note said that he was feeling depressed and did not want to become a burden to his friends (Hamilton, 1996).

The funeral was attended only by Hamilton and Maynard Smith and a handful of the people Price had tried to help during his life in London. 'Price took his Christianity too seriously', declared the preacher. 'Like Saint Paul?', mumbled Hamilton quite audibly. Maynard Smith, who told me this, was impressed by what he considered a very apposite remark.

Whatever else this story shows, it is an example of how a moral connection between scientists, in this case Hamilton and Price, was able to establish trust between them and thus supersede other differences, such as Hamilton's 'allergy' to group selection. Personal trust in this case led Hamilton to take Price seriously and let himself be convinced by him. Eventually, this resulted in Hamilton not only deriving group-selection models from Price's formula but also arriving at a more comprehensive approach to his own notion of inclusive fitness.

Equally interesting is that Price contributed to a reconciliation not only between Hamilton and Maynard Smith, but also in a sense helped reconcile the approaches of their evolutionist predecessors, Fisher and Haldane. Remember that Price's group-selectionist approach in fact depended on Haldane's original group-selectionist models —exactly those models that Hamilton had earlier dismissed as an undergraduate. But now, thanks to Price, Hamilton was *de facto* building on *Haldane* to develop a more general model for inclusive fitness, which Hamilton had originally seen as a deliberate extension of *Fisher*. It may be through intermediaries like Price that a type of convergence sometimes can happen between two seemingly competing approaches in science.

'Hamilton and I are not teaching our students to hate each other', said Maynard Smith cryptically towards the end of my recent interview. Hate each other? That statement seemed somehow disconnected from our general discussion. What did he mean? Did he mean that Haldane and Fisher, who did hate each other (this was rather well known), had taught their students, too, to do so? 'Oh yes,' said Maynard Smith. Later, I reflected once again on that fated original meeting between Hamilton and Maynard Smith. Could it have been that when young Hamilton was introduced to Maynard Smith there was, after all, more to it than merely the unfortunate fact that Maynard Smith did not see the genetics of altruism as a promising problem, while Hamilton was too shy to make him see that it was? Might Maynard Smith's hackles have been raised at a perceived connection between Hamilton and Fisher (Hamilton's undergraduate degree from 'Fisher's department' at Cambridge, or the very fact that Hamilton used Fisher's formulas)? In other words, did a possible 'Fisher' cue activate a behavioral rule instilled by Haldane in him: 'Do not collaborate with students of my enemy'? (Never mind that Hamilton was not really a student of Fisher—behavioral rules work on cues!)

This is sheer speculation, all triggered by Maynard Smith's own remark. Perhaps all is well that ends well. And Maynard Smith's recommendations probably did help to highlight the significant point of Hamilton's paper, when as a reviewer he was finally confronted with Hamilton's work. One indicator is a much-thumbed copy of *Group Selection* (Williams, 1971), borrowed from a huge American research university. There Hamilton's paper is republished (with corrections) in its two parts. Part II has been dutifully marked and underlined by students. Part I remains in pristine condition.

A tempest in a teacup? Dawkins and the British debate

The critics of Wilson's *Sociobiology* had barely got started before they were hit by a new book to put on the Index: Richard Dawkins' *The Selfish Gene* (1976a). Unlike Wilson's tome, this book was modest-sized, and probably intended mainly for Britain, whose general public has traditionally been much more interested in evolutionary ideas than the American one. Undoubtedly the title was catchy. It elegantly captured the essence of the book's scientific message, at the same time as it was dangerously titillating. It contained that forbidden word 'the gene' in connection with a trait that seemed to be uniquely human. In the British post-war climate, Hamilton had encountered great opposition to his idea of the genetics of altruism. On the face of it, Dawkins had put himself in exactly the same position as Hamilton fifteen years earlier—only worse.

But times had changed—in Britain at least. Also, unlike Hamilton, but much like Wilson, Dawkins directed himself to the educated layman. Think about the British reading public as people who in general enjoy both puzzle-solving and reading about nature and evolution, and who are willing to be taken on even farfetched logical excursions as long as an author makes good his promise to reveal the mystery in a lucid way.

The Selfish Gene was duly appreciated in its home country (Dawkins, 1979a, 1989a, viii). It took the sociobiology controversy as it had evolved in the United States to make *The Selfish Gene* into a dangerous political manifesto. The critics' predefinition of what Dawkins' book was really 'about' was so forceful that it was initially impossible for Dawkins to 'counterdefine' their message of his book. For the critics, again, it was not hard to find suitable passages to quote. The absolute favorite has been the one about 'lumbering robots' and 'survival machines', which has made regular reappearances in the anti-sociobiological literature as an example of the extreme genetic determinism of sociobiology. This is what Dawkins himself said about these passages:

> I had forgotten the great computer myth, as well as the great gene myth, or I would have been more careful when I wrote of genes swarming 'inside gigantic lumbering robots . . .' and ourselves as 'survival machines—robot vehicles blindly programmed to preserve the selfish molecules known as genes' (Dawkins, 1982, p. 16).

What was *The Selfish Gene*, then, 'really' about? That book aimed at elucidating the logic of a 'gene's eye' perspective, an important aid in understanding the new socio-biological ideas of inclusive fitness, kin selection, behavioral strategies, and so on. Dawkins himself said that he wished to explicate the new developments in evolutionary theory and show the logic of the gene's eye perspective, a view implicit in the writings of the pioneers of neo-Darwinism in the 1930s and made explicit by George Williams and Bill Hamilton in the 1960s:

> For me their insight had a visionary quality. But I found their expressions of it too laconic, not full-throated enough. I was convinced that an amplified and developed version could make everything about life fall into place, in the heart as well as in the brain. I would write a book extolling the gene's-eye view of evolution. It should concentrate its examples on social behavior, to help correct the unconscious group-selectionism that then pervaded popular Darwinism (Dawkins, 1989, ix).

And so he did. *The Selfish Gene* was written 'in something resembling a fever of excitement' (Dawkins, 1989a, p. x). True to the British tradition of lucid exposition (and his own experience as a teacher), Dawkins brings in vivid examples and hypothetical scenarios, he entertains, he anthropomorphizes, he stretches the reader's imagination —all in the service of explaining evolutionary theory. Dawkins wants to present the *logic* of the gene's eye perspective—how we may look at evolution in a new way, considering the interest of a gene in producing replicas of itself rather than working for the survival of the individual organism. And, because it is a logical explanation, it does not matter what a gene is—it can, for instance, be a piece of the genome, and it can be working together with a lot of other genes (I will return to this in Chapter 7).

But Dawkins' ambitions were completely misunderstood by the political critics of sociobiology. An example of what Dawkins himself identified as the critics' 'wanton eagerness to misunderstand' is a statement dealing with 'philanderer genes'. This was how Steven Rose interpreted a particular passage in *The Selfish Gene* (interestingly, he managed to slip it into his review of a quite different book, Wilson's *On Human Nature*):

> although he does not go as far as Richard Dawkins (*The Selfish Gene*...) in proposing sex-linked genes for 'philandering', for Wilson human males have a genetic tendency towards polygyny, females toward constancy (don't blame your mates for sleeping around, ladies, it's not their fault they are genetically programmed). Genetic determinism constantly creeps in at the back door (Rose, 1978, quoted in Dawkins, 1982, p. 10).

Rose's review implied, according to Dawkins, that he and Wilson 'believe in the existence of genes that force human males to be irremediable philanderers who cannot therefore be blamed for marital infidelity. The reader is left with the impression that those authors are . . . died-in-the-wool hereditarians with male chauvinist leanings' (Dawkins, 1982, p. 10).

In what ways was Dawkins misunderstood? His original passage was not about humans, and it was not about genes. It was a *model* of a *strategy* (Dawkins actually had a bird in mind, he informs us). The philanderer strategy was one of two hypothetical alternatives, and the point of the exercise was to discuss the conditions under which philandering or faithfulness would be favored by natural selection. The model did not assume that philandering in males was more typical than faithfulness. Dawkins attributed Rose's 'multiple compounded misunderstanding' to a deep belief in 'the gene myth'. For Rose, genetic determinism was 'determinism in the full philosophical sense of irreversible inevitability' (Dawkins, 1982, p. 10).

So, Dawkins' logical description of a general mechanism was seen as a justification for a particular type of action. Rose's interpretation had a lot in common with the stance of the Sociobiology Study Group on matters of this sort. Considering his close connection with Lewontin and their collaboration on a number of issues, it is only fair to call Rose 'Britain's Lewontin'. We will meet Rose throughout this book as one of the most avid critics of sociobiology.

One reason why the treatment received by Dawkins appears particularly unfair is that, unlike Wilson's *Sociobiology*, *The Selfish Gene* from the outset explicitly *excluded* human behavior and warned the reader not to be mistaken about the author's intentions with the book:

> This brings me to the first point I want to make about what this book is not. I am not advocating a morality based on evolution. I am saying how things have evolved. I am not saying how we humans morally ought to behave. I stress this, because I know I am in danger of being misunderstood by those people, all too numerous, who cannot distinguish a statement of belief in what is the case from an advocacy of what ought to be the case (Dawkins, 1976a, p. 3).

This had absolutely no effect on the critics of sociobiology. Under the common umbrella of such terms as 'biological determinism' or 'reductionism', Dawkins and Wilson were presented as delivering the same message. What is more, because the critics kept collapsing Wilson and Dawkins, the impression may have been created that Dawkins *scientifically* was 'the same' as Wilson. Aside from the fact that both men were interested in presenting the latest theories and empirical research in evolutionary biology to a larger public, and both were using that dangerous-sounding term 'gene', Dawkins and Wilson in fact represented quite different 'sociobiologies'.[11]

Dawkins aimed at systematically explicating the logic of Darwinian theory from the gene's eye perspective, building on Williams and Hamilton. Wilson, again, although he recognized Williams' contribution, considered the gene-selectionist approach too narrow. (In fact, he told Dawkins that he thought Dawkins' ideas were reductionist; Dawkins, 1981a, p. 578.) So while Dawkins in *The Selfish Gene* fully embraced kin selection, Wilson's particular brand of sociobiology regarded kin selection as just one of the many possible mechanisms for altruistic behavior, on a par with group selection. This is one of the reasons why Dawkins declared *Sociobiology* to be, 'in many respects prerevolutionary in attitude: not the new synthesis, but the last and greatest synthesis of the old, benevolent regime' (Dawkins, 1981a, 1982, p. 56) But Dawkins also gave Wilson credit. In interview in 1981 he pointed out that Wilson and he were drawing on much the same material, but that Wilson had included a lot of interesting theories and an ecological dimension which was totally lacking in his own book.

Finally, we have the different 'last chapters' of the two books. While Wilson used his last chapter to extrapolate his sociobiological modeling to human society, Dawkins put a deliberate stop to this by declaring culture a separate realm. He even postulated a different non-genetic mechanism for the transmission of human culture, including a new unit for transmission, 'meme'. (Dawkins says that the reason why he developed the idea of 'meme' was a logical one: he had found one more possible replicator in addition to genes.) Dawkins' general efforts to keep humans separate were recognized by an early reviewer of *The Selfish Gene*, the moral philosopher Bernard Williams:

> Dawkins is refreshingly free of two connected errors which rampage through
> popularizations on these subjects: that there is a straight extrapolation from the behaviour
> of systems under natural selection to anything at all about human society; and that nothing
> basic about human life is determined by culture. He explicitly and repeatedly denies both
> these falsehoods, and is very cautious in tracing any analogies between human social habits
> and genetically determined behaviour patterns in other species (Williams, 1976).

Obviously, Rose and other critics read a very different book.

Among biologists in the United Kingdom there was a general impression that the sociobiology controversy did not emerge spontaneously in their country, but 'had to be imported'. At least, this is what I was told at the International Congress of Ethology in Oxford in 1981. Here Rose was seen as a main agent, although his criticism was regarded as a rather isolated phenomenon (someone joked that Rose was now trying to spread the sociobiology controversy to Australia, too). Domestic or imported, some visible discontent with sociobiology could, however, be found elsewhere. For instance, there was a critical article on sociobiology and a letter contributed by the Science as Ideology Group of the British Society for Social Responsibility in Science (1976a, b). I was also told of some student demonstrations against sociobiology, typically by students with little interest in animal behavior (this I heard from a former protester).

Among fellow biologists, ethologist Patrick Bateson had early on pointed out the danger of the shorthand 'genes for' such and such a trait. He criticized sociobiologists for misleading use of language and giving people the impression that there was a simple one-to-one correspondence between genes and behavior (Bateson, 1981). And, indeed, this seemed to be just what people believed. Dawkins describes how he and John Maynard Smith participated in a public debate with two radical critics of 'sociobiology' (Dawkins' quotation marks) in front of a student audience. Maynard Smith tried to educate the suspicious audience about the logic of genes 'for' traits. He wanted to illustrate the idea of a gene *making a difference* (for instance 'a gene that makes a difference between blue and brown eyes'). His aim was to show that a single gene in this way could in fact control even a very complex learned behavior pattern (in itself dependent on many genes):

> Maynard Smith reached for a hypothetical example and came up with a 'gene for skill in tying shoelaces'. Pandemonium broke loose at this rampant genetic determinism! The air was thick with the unmistakeable sound of worst suspicions being gleefully confirmed. Delightedly sceptical cries drowned the quiet and patient explanation . . . (Dawkins, 1982, p. 23).[12]

Bateson, himself a developmental biologist, also felt that Dawkins was paying too little attention to other than evolutionary aspects of behavior (Bateson, 1978). Indeed, this is a criticism of sociobiology that remains even today (Bateson, personal communication). The question is whether it was a matter of conviction or emphasis: for instance, did Dawkins' focus on the gene's eye's view mean that he truly *believed* this was the most important type of explanation and that, say, development was of secondary interest? Dawkins in 1982 indicated that it was a matter of emphasis (p. 99).

The answer demonstrates another interesting difference between Dawkins and Wilson. Wilson did, in fact, consider an evolutionary explanation to be the 'deepest' one. But Dawkins was, after all, trained as an ethologist and a student of Niko Tinbergen, known for his insistence on the famous four questions: the equal importance and complementarity of questions about immediate causes, development, evolution, and function of a particular behavior (Tinbergen, 1963). In fact, with his multi-dimensional approach Tinbergen is often held up as a kind of antidote to sociobiology's seeming extreme emphasis on genes. (Ernst Mayr, similarly, distinguishes between 'proximate' and 'ultimate' causes; Mayr, 1963). How, then, did a Tinbergen student choose to embark on the seemingly narrow course of exclusively evolutionary explanation, deliberately leaving out the richness of multilevel description? I recently asked Dawkins exactly this. He was unperturbed. According to him, ultimate explanation, after all, deals with *one* of Tinbergen's four questions! Dawkins saw himself as a 'functional ethologist', that is, someone who is interested in the adaptive explanation of how a particular behavior may have evolved.

If the 'imported' criticism was political, the 'domestic' criticism of *The Selfish Gene* was largely of a *moral* nature. I encountered several criticisms of the very idea of calling the book *The Selfish Gene*. The fiercest critique of Dawkins came from the philosopher Mary Midgley (1979), to whom I shall return below. Molecular biologist Gunther Stent had already written a review condemning Dawkins' notions both of 'altruism' and 'gene' (Stent, 1977). People appeared to have rather emotional reactions to the new technical use of the term 'altruism'. Others who reacted to the use of the term 'selfish' were the philosopher Stuart Hampshire and the anthropologist Vernon Reynolds (interviews in 1981).

I was perhaps most surprised to see Karl Popper's reaction. I had written to him, asking to talk to him about the testability of sociobiological theory. Was it or was it not testable? This had been one of the strongest criticisms against people like Wilson, and Popper was obviously the man to see—especially since he had just declared that Darwinism was, after all, testable (Popper, 1978, 1980). He had changed his mind after originally declaring it to be a metaphysical research program.

It turned out to be harder than I imagined to get Popper to discuss sociobiology. It began in a rather surrealist way. I received a phone call in England: 'This is Karl Popper', said the voice, 'I am not a determinist!' Well, I had not accused him of being one! When we later got together, drinking polite Viennese coffee outside his house in Buckinghamshire, it turned out to be well-nigh impossible to get him to talk about sociobiology at all. As soon as I brought it up, he just dismissed it as 'ideology'—he had seen it all before. I tried to point out that there was new theory, that there were differences between Wilson and Dawkins, and so on. When I mentioned *The Selfish Gene*, Popper immediately took issue with the title. Why emphasize selfishness—why not call the book 'The Co-operative Gene'! After all, genes also have to co-operate! After that, he simply changed the topic to what *he* wanted to discuss: determinism in physics.

And Popper was not alone. The philosopher Stuart Hampshire, whom I interviewed around the same time, commented on the choice of 'selfish' in the title. The anthropologist Vernon Reynolds (who didn't like sociobiology in any form) also thought that 'selfish' was a poor choice. There may, indeed, have been more widespread opposition to this title, because in his next book, *The Extended Phenotype*, Dawkins went out of his way to emphasize that genes of course co-operate, and that they are, in fact, selected exactly *for* their ability to co-operate with one another. Also, he noted that he had no control of the fact that in the German and Japanese editions of *The Selfish Gene* the cover depicted humans like puppets pulled by strings; however, he had registered his protest.

Bernard Williams' positive review had shown that moral philosophers did not *necessarily* feel that they had to take issue with the title of Dawkins' book. In fact, one philosopher, John Mackie, not only refrained from criticism but actually made use of Dawkins' 'Chicago gangster theory of life' in his *Philosophy* article called 'The Law of the Jungle', having to do with reciprocal altruism (Mackie, 1978). But seeing Dawkins approvingly quoted in this way in a leading philosophy journal triggered a strong response in the philosopher Mary Midgley. What followed was a violent attack on *The Selfish Gene*. According to Midgley:

> [Dawkins'] central point is that the emotional nature of man is exclusively self-interested, and he argues this by claiming that all emotional nature is so. Since the emotional nature of animals clearly is not exclusively self-interested, nor based on any long-term calculation at all, he resorts to arguing from speculations about the emotional nature of genes . . .
> (Midgley, 1979, p. 439).

She went on to say: 'Genes cannot be selfish or unselfish, any more than atoms can be jealous, elephants abstract or biscuits teleological' (p. 439).

Dawkins, not surprisingly, was taken aback with what he called the 'inexplicable hostility' of Midgley (Dawkins, 1981a). He wrote a sharp response, noting that she 'raises the art of misunderstanding to dizzy heights', and further, that her understanding of sociobiology was inadequate. In his answer, Dawkins—ever the patient tutor!—took the opportunity to educate not only Midgley but readers in general about typically misunderstood points in sociobiological reasoning and *The Selfish Gene* in particular.

Dawkins informs Midgley that his book is about the evolution of life, not the emotional nature of humans. In fact, he is quite uninterested in humans, 'a particular, rather aberrant species' (Dawkins 1981a, p. 562). Moreover, in sociobiology 'selfishness' and 'altruism' are defined in purely behavioral terms, having to do with the effect of an act. 'Did Midgley, perhaps, just overlook my definition? One cannot, after all, be expected to read every single word of a book whose author one wishes to insult', Dawkins wonders, but concludes that 'no such excuse can be made', because he had explained it all on the very first pages of his book (p. 564). And, Dawkins points out, even if Midgley misunderstood him as saying that *genes* had a selfish emotional nature, it would not follow that he thought that *humans* were selfish, too. And even if he thought humans were selfish, it would not follow that he approved of it. 'Of course, to the extent I am interested in human ethics . . . I disapprove of egoism', Dawkins adds (p. 564).

From Dawkins' response we also learn the actual background to his Chicago gangster theory of life. He had used it as an example in his book to illustrate 'the fundamental principle, that *individual* behaviour, altruistic or selfish, is best interpreted as a manifestation of selfishness at the *gene* level' (p. 566, my italics). In effect, *The Selfish Gene* was an argument for rejecting the traditional group-selectionist explanation for altruism ('the selfish group'), presenting instead 'the selfish individual', or—better and simpler—'*The Selfish Gene*' as the correct alternative. 'If anybody had suggested to me that it was possible to misread that passage as saying that people are essentially Chicago gangsters I would have laughed', says Dawkins. But Midgley did achieve 'this superhuman feat of misunderstanding' when she wrote: 'telling people that they are *essentially* Chicago gangsters is not just false and confused, but monstrously irresponsible' (Midgley, 1979, p. 455), Dawkins noted (1981a, p. 566).

In fact, the example was intended as an illustration of game-theoretic thinking. Three strategies were postulated, called 'Cheat', 'Sucker', and 'Grudger'. The game-theoretical analysis led to two stable solutions, it was a 'bistable' system in which either Cheats or

Grudgers—whichever reached more than a critical frequency in the population—would do better than the other. According to Dawkins, Midgley had reacted emotionally to Mackie's talk about Cheats, Suckers, and Grudgers, not noticing that Mackie may have made an important contribution to biology! He may have suggested a mechanism through which group selection would, after all, have a chance to work—that is, by 'differentially extinguishing groups of cheats at the expense of groups of Grudgers (reciprocal altruists)' (p. 569).[13] (Midgley had reported: 'Dawkins concluded that Cheats and Grudgers would exterminate Suckers, and Grudgers might well do best of all', p. 440.)

Midgley had also commented on Dawkins' science. Early on in her article she had said: 'There is nothing empirical about Dawkins. Critics have repeatedly pointed out that his notions of genetics are unworkable' (p. 439). According to Dawkins, however, there were no references to such geneticists (Dawkins, 1981, p. 571). But more importantly, he was only following prevailing conventions in his field, such as the deliberate simplification of 'one gene, one strategy', the shorthand of 'genes for' a trait, and so on. Admittedly, these could lead to typical misunderstandings (pp. 570–3). The puzzle was, however, why Midgley kept invoking other evolutionary biologists such as Wilson and Maynard Smith against what Dawkins was saying. Why was this philosopher intemperately attacking one particular biologist for doing exactly what most of his professional colleagues were doing (p. 571)?

It can be seen as a sign of the times and the 'collective consciousness' among the critics of sociobiology that Midgley's article was later republished (without Dawkins' response) in Ashley Montagu's 1980 *Sociobiology Examined*, a collection of critical essays on sociobiology.

What was it that made Midgley so angry with Dawkins? I asked her this question at the time, visiting her and her husband in their home in Newcastle upon Tyne. I wanted to find the reason for Midgley's nasty tone and seemingly active misreading of him. Did she imagine Dawkins as some kind of fascist type, a Michelin man urging people to be selfish? 'Well, something like that,' she laughingly admitted, 'and are you now telling me that he is is quite reasonable?' I tried to describe Dawkins and his views as best I could; I saw my role as trying to tell both these two perfectly charming people that they had built up quite untenable images of each another (I had just spoken to Dawkins before I visited Midgley).

But the story turned out to be more complicated. Midgley told me she did not really wish to go after *Dawkins* as much as she wanted to quench any attempt by *moral philosophers* to use selfish genery as a backup for their purposes. She had seen this kind of thing happen before, and it had to be nipped in the bud:

> If such a toy is handed to moral philosophers, and they aren't promptly slapped, they will use it for a very long time. They like a little bit of empirical backing, and off they go (Midgley, interview in 1981).

She told me she had become terribly depressed and upset after reading Mackie's article, and it was this mood that made her write in that particularly hostile way: 'I can see that it may have looked a bit arbitrary as far as Dawkins is concerned. . . . I might, had I calmed down, written a more balanced article, and would then have said: I am jolly glad, of course, that some Darwinism is spread about, and I can see the advantage of people being taught kin selection, and things of that sort. I am still not sure it would have been sensible to do it. If you want to put up a very clear signpost for moral philosophers . . . you have to do it this way ' (Midgley, interview).

So, Midgley was *not* against Darwinian explanation as such, which is what probably many believed who read her review. In fact, she regarded herself as having done a 'balanced review' of Wilsonian sociobiology in her *Beast and Man* (1978). Unfortunately, she said, she had not yet read Dawkins when she wrote that book, and later did not have the time to do a separate review of Dawkins. When she was suddenly confronted with the philosopher Mackie's usage of Dawkins, she felt forced to strike hard. Still, she reflected, although her tone might have been different, she was still 'disturbed about Dawkins'. 'This is bloody awful' was what she had thought when she read *The Selfish Gene*. According to Midgley, people like Dawkins and Desmond Morris made Darwinism sound so crude, and made it so much harder for people like her who tried to explain that Darwinism was not so crude. The reason she disliked selfish gene explanations was that they were too genetic and atomistic; she herself preferred psychological and ethological explanations instead. She thought motivations were important.

Midgley, then, had a clear aim in her review: to criticize Dawkins to such an extent that no philosopher would ever want to use him as scientific backing for philosophical theorizing! She felt she had to do something strong, because Dawkins had, overall, received very good reviews for his book. To me, again, it seemed as if she, just like the critics of Wilson, had been reading Dawkins in a particular moral/political spirit (what I call 'moral reading', see Chapter 10). Her article does, indeed, give the impression of someone who is intent on drawing the *worst* possible inferences from Dawkins' statements. In conversation, however, Midgley actually seemed somewhat critical of the American critics of *Sociobiology*; she thought they went too far. The similarity between Midgley's and the Sociobiology Study Group's approach was that both were holding sociobiological authors responsible for the interpretation of their books by others.

To get a sense of the general standards in the relevant biological community at the time, I asked two of Dawkins' colleagues, John Krebs and Nick Davies, about their views on Dawkins' decision to call the book *The Selfish Gene*. Davies thought it was a clever move: the book would surely get attention in this way, and its scientific message would spread. In Krebs' opinion the title was somewhat exaggerated, and he could see the reason for the reaction of the critics. He said he had even spoken to Dawkins about that.

And what of those objections by 'geneticists'? In conversation, Midgley had in fact told me about geneticists at the University of Newcastle where she was teaching. I had also heard from Vernon Reynolds that Peter O'Donald, the Cambridge geneticist, was very critical of the selfish gene idea; this was confirmed by John Krebs. In O'Donald's contribution to an early volume discussing sociobiology from different angles, the technical reason for his criticism becomes apparent: the muddle created by having two types of 'fitness'—population genetic and inclusive fitness (O'Donald, 1982). Dawkins' response can be found in *The Extended Phenotype* published the same year: an excruciatingly detailed (and highly useful) treatment of five different meanings of 'fitness' (Dawkins, 1982, Chapter 10).

Finally, what was it that made Dawkins write in a style that provoked such strong reactions? Besides his quest for clarity, he had another motive. Dawkins later explained that the reason he sounded so 'evangelist' in *The Selfish Gene* was that he needed forcefully to rebut *group selection*, still going strong, by bringing in gene selectionism as an alternative (Dawkins, 1979a). Dawkins, then, did have a conscious goal, but it was not the gospel of selfishness that his moral critics assumed. On the other hand, anyone reading Trivers' Foreword to the book may indeed be excused for believing that Dawkins was really referring to human behavior:

> Whole industries have grown up in the social sciences dedicated to the construction of a pre-Darwinian and pre-Mendelian view of the social and psychological world. . . . Whatever the reasons for this strange development, there is evidence that it is coming to an end. . . . One by one Dawkins takes up the major themes of the new work in social theory: the concepts of altruistic and selfish behavior, the genetical definition of self-interest, the evolution of aggressive behavior [Trivers here continues the list] . . . In short, Darwinian social theory gives us a glimpse of an underlying symmetry and logic in social relationships which, when more fully comprehended by ourselves, should revitalize our political understanding and provide the intellectual support for a science and medicine of psychology. In the process it should also give us a deeper understanding of the many roots of our suffering (Trivers, 1976, pp. vi–vii).

Trivers' use of the term 'social theory' to refer to new sociobiological thought clearly gave the impression that he was explicitly talking about humans. And of course he was, while Dawkins was not, and could say so.

CHAPTER 5

The 'deep background' of sociobiology

Harvard discovers Hamilton: Bob Trivers and Irven DeVore

There is no doubt that Bob Trivers was a major factor in the spread of the gospel of sociobiology, both as a contributor to the theory and as a promoter of Hamilton's theory on the Harvard scene in the early 1970s. It was there he developed his theories of reciprocal altruism (Trivers, 1971) and parent–offspring conflict (Trivers, 1974), and functioned as an enthusiastic teacher of undergraduates. Yet his situation was precarious. He was still working on his PhD, which he obtained in the early 1970s in the biology department, after which he became an assistant professor working with Irven DeVore in the anthropology department. In 1977 he was denied tenure. Assistant professors at Harvard do not usually get tenure, but everybody agreed that Trivers was exceptionally bright. The problem was that he suffered at the time from painful spells of schizophrenia, which impaired his normal functioning. Although his colleagues knew about this and sympathized with it, Harvard may have decided to err on the side of caution.[1] Trivers became a professor at the University of California, Santa Cruz, from where he later moved to Rutgers University—a move arranged by his biosocial anthropological colleagues Lionel Tiger and Robin Fox.

The force behind Trivers, the man that kept him going during the dark times, was Irven DeVore. In a moving interview in 1982, DeVore described himself as a 'facilitator', a role that he consciously assumed. (I will be following DeVore, unless other references are given.) The point was to keep Trivers going. Interestingly, DeVore, acting on a human impulse, would soon be rewarded by Trivers taking an intense interest in the new theory of kin selection. According to DeVore, Trivers had once told him that because of him (Trivers), Hamilton had become more popular in America than in his own home country.

This may well have been the case. Trivers' name appeared everywhere—particularly after the storm had broken out over *Sociobiology*. (Trivers vigorously defended Wilson and his book on several public occasions, *Omni*, 1985, p. 78). Even before the emergence of that book, Trivers was energetically promoting kin-selectionist thinking. He was also the author of the Preface to *The Selfish Gene*. In that preface, Trivers foresaw a revolution in science which would soon affect the social sciences (here he seems to have been too optimistic). He dreamed about a unified social theory grounded in natural selection (*Omni*, 1985, p. 78). In addition to his scholarly articles, he figured in the popular press, notably in *Time* magazine's article on sociobiology in 1977. Trivers also appeared in the notorious film *Doing What Comes Naturally*, which was shown by Science for the People on various occasions and whose transcript was widely distributed.

One way in which *The Selfish Gene* was being propagated was by being assigned as required reading in Trivers' and DeVore's undergraduate course. Michael Rodgers, the Oxford University Press editor of Dawkins' book, remembers how he shipped 400 copies from the United Kingdom to Harvard—there was not yet an American edition.

The fact that DeVore and Trivers joined forces in the first place involves a rather weak causal chain. Trivers came to Harvard in 1961 on a scholarship to study mathematics and prepare for a career as a civil rights lawyer (*Time*, 1 August 1977, p. 56).[2] In his junior year, however, he had a schizophrenic episode and was hospitalized. When he was restored to health, it was important that he should have a job. DeVore was approached because of his connection with an organization called the Educational Development Center in Newton, Mass., a producer of educational material for schools, for whom Jerome Bruner, Barbara Smuts, and Jon Seger also worked.

Trivers was given the task of writing a book on animal behavior for fifth graders. He had never cared much for biology, but he had found DeVore's book *The Primates* lying around and started looking at it with great interest. He was a fast learner. 'Bob wrote a gem of a book', said DeVore. Later, Trivers became strongly influenced by William Drury, who had been taught by Ernst Mayr—in fact Trivers 'went out and apprenticed himself' to Drury, according to DeVore. Trivers was fascinated with altruism. The breakthrough came in 1966 when Trivers read both Wynne-Edwards and David Lack at the same time, wildly shifting between a group-selectionist and an individual selectionist paradigm. In the end, group-selectionism lost. 'I was inflamed by the truth', said Trivers (Bingham, 1980).

6 months after his 'conversion', Trivers was introduced to Hamilton's 1964 paper by Ernst Mayr (Bingham, 1980). Soon it was Trivers who was teaching DeVore the intricacies of kin-selection theory. DeVore did not at first know what Trivers was talking about—Hamilton was so hard to understand. It didn't fit with the usual way of thinking. But suddenly he realized what Trivers was saying, said DeVore. 'He absolutely led me by the nose. I pulled the graduate students together—this may really be hot! I was the car, he was the engine.'

At one point Trivers came to a halt in his studies of Hamilton's 1964 paper; something was wrong. He contacted Ed Wilson about this, asking if Wilson could help him with a problem he was having with Hamilton's mathematics in regard to Hymenoptera. Wilson could not. Trivers cracked it on his own. As Trivers later rather proudly told me, Hamilton had told him that he was one of two people in the world who had found that error in Hamilton's paper. The other was Hamilton (Trivers, personal communication).[3]

DeVore soon felt that others should also learn about the new ideas. This led to what DeVore called the 'Simian Seminars', weekly meetings of researchers and graduate students. Nobody was doing this at the time, said DeVore. They all had the sense of being pioneers. (Hamilton himself had not yet reached the fame that he would later attain. And *Sociobiology* and *The Selfish Gene*, which popularized his ideas, were still some years away.)

But Trivers and DeVore had their share of student protests, too, before the 'official' sociobiology controversy. They had started a new major course for undergraduates in Harvard's General Education program in the early 1970s, 'The Biological Basis of Social Behavior'. Their first lecture was picketed. There were about 200–300 students and 40–50 picketing. 'So years later when Ed was being attacked, I had already been teaching this course.' The name of the course was deliberately chosen to provoke discussion among the students. 'We were no fools. We knew that there would be protest', said DeVore. But they had developed a strategy for handling this. At the picketed first session, Trivers and DeVore struck a deal with the students. They told them that they would be allowed to come with any objections to the course during the fourth lecture, but until then they would have to attend and listen quietly. What was the strategy? 'We started deliberately with all kinds of criticisms. By the fourth week, there was no protest—because the protesters were already taking the course for credit!', DeVore grinned.

When the storm over *Sociobiology* erupted, nobody paid attention to the fact that DeVore did not share Wilson's views in several important respects. Of course, Wilson and DeVore were friendly colleagues, and among other things, had been teaching an undergraduate course together. Still, this did not mean that DeVore shared Wilson's grandiose synthetic ambitions. He was basically embarrassed by the emphasis on genes in conjunction with human behavior, and thought it was very unfortunate that because of this sociobiology had now become connected to IQ and other controversial issues. Also, he felt that Wilson did not have a comprehensive enough grasp of anthropology:

> When *Sociobiology* was nearing completion, Ed sent me the last chapter. It was not that I disagreed with him. I wanted him to have written a different book. I felt it was nothing like the whole story. Ed was naïve in many ways in those days. It was not that he had no respect for the social sciences; he had so many other things on his plate. I kept thinking that Trivers and I should have done this!

Wilson's idiosyncratic handling of anthropological information often put DeVore in a quandary. I had a glimpse of this during my interview with him in his office. DeVore took a phone call, and briefly answered some question. 'That was Wilson!', DeVore told me. 'He asked me: "*Isn't it true that* cousin incest is a taboo in almost all societies?" He always does that!' It was typical of Wilson to call him up to check some fact just in this way. The problem was, you never knew what he was going to do with the information you provided, DeVore complained. And then he always *thanked* you in his acknowledgements!

Visitors from England were particularly welcome in DeVore's department. Maynard Smith remembers visiting Harvard in the 1970s. He walked into DeVore's office and found DeVore, Trivers, and others engaged in what looked like a promising game of poker. That may have created a special bond between Maynard Smith and this group. Maynard Smith was no mean poker player himself, having put himself through college in this way, as he revealed in interview in 1998. But the poker game may have signaled something more general. Maynard Smith, after all, was a game theorist, and so was Trivers, both thinking in terms of the strategy of conflict. But while the British type of sociobiology, and particularly *The Selfish Gene*, was permeated with various kinds of 'strategies', this kind of vocabulary was totally absent from Wilsonian sociobiology (just as card playing presumably was from Wilson's lab—and life).

The different default settings of their way of thinking, however, did not prevent Wilson and Trivers from being on very good terms with each other. It is clear that Wilson, too, provided important support for this brilliant, unpredictable man. Wilson had served on Trivers' doctoral committee in zoology, and no doubt encouraged him—encouraging others was second nature to Wilson. Wilson describes how Trivers used to appear in his lab without warning:

> He would stride through my office door and sit down, oblivious or uncaring of the old Harvard custom of making appointments. Thereupon I figuratively fastened my seatbelt and prepared for swift and rocky travel to some unknown destination. Then would come a flood of ideas, new information, and challenges, delivered in irony and merriment. Trivers and I were always on the verge of laughter, and we broke down continually as we switched from concept to gossip to joke and back to concept. Our science was advanced by hilarity. My own pleasure in these exchanges was tinged with a sense of psychological risk, as though testing a mind-altering and possibly dangerous drug (Wilson, 1994, p. 325).

What did they talk about? One would assume that much of it would have been relevant to the content of *Sociobiology*, then in progress. We now get into what DeVore himself called the 'deep history' of *Sociobiology*. According to DeVore, when writing the book Wilson had not really appreciated the importance of Hamilton's kin-selection theory; he was thinking more in terms of group selection. As the book was coming close to finishing

> Wilson gave Trivers chapters to read. . . . It was a muddle! It was almost the eleventh hour. Trivers worked very hard with *Sociobiology*. He pored over those chapters, . . . he tried to make Ed rewrite the inclusive fitness discussion, particularly since Ed comes up with a very misleading treatment of kin selection and group selection. For Trivers kin selection and individual fitness were extensions of Darwinism. Group selection was opposed to that. . . . Ed finishes the book. *Sociobiology* has a very prominent treatment of inclusive fitness theory! (DeVore, interview 1982.)

'What would have happened to the book if Trivers had not been there to help?', I asked. 'It would have been a crooked model!', said DeVore.

When I finally ran into Trivers at a meeting in 1993 I asked him about this. Was it true that he had, in a sense, 'saved' Wilson by helping make the book more kin selectionist at the last minute? Trivers told me that he did not see things that way. He recalled merely that he had asked Wilson if he understood Hamilton's maths concerning haplodiploidy in Hymenoptera, after which he told me the story about the error he had found in Hamilton's paper. I did not probe deeper. If we take a look at the acknowledgements in *Sociobiology*, however, we can see that Wilson recognizes Trivers as follows: 'I am especially grateful to Robert L. Trivers for reading most of the book and discussing it with me from the time of its conception' (Wilson, 1975a, p. v). Trivers is the only person who gets this kind of recognition in *Sociobiology*.

It turned out that when DeVore said that without Trivers' help it would have been a 'crooked model', he had something quite specific in mind—namely John Crook himself! And here DeVore gave a quick glimpse of his own development. By the late 1960s, he was pretty much fed up with primate studies. 'The generalities we were making were only holding for a year,' DeVore commented, 'plus the field had attracted a lot of pedestrian types, butterfly collectors.' John Crook and colleagues were much more influential. He and Wilson both agreed that Crook was the man with the right approach:

> Ed and I taught a seminar about 1969–70. After *The Insect Societies*, he was working on a synthesis of biology, sort of grand principles. Ed and I were both saying: *what is the best model we have? Crook's model of mammals and primates!*

'Sociobiology is a word that gives me terrible trouble', said DeVore. When he and Washburn had been working with baboon troops in 1958–9, they had simply assumed that the group was the unit of selection: 'There was no other theory around.' Later, Crook had developed his ecological approach to animal behavior (duly admired in the field; see, for example, Maynard Smith, 1982c). According to DeVore, Crook himself had been very baffled when he saw the new name 'sociobiology' given to the study of animal behavior. 'They take the scheme I developed [and give it a new name]... I don't call that sociobiology, I call that the end of behavioral ecology!', had been Crook's reaction. DeVore added: 'I really think that you have to divide the world into pre- and post-Bill Hamilton.'[4]

There were many reasons why DeVore did not like the term 'sociobiology'. For instance, because of *Sociobiology* DeVore, the fierce champion of kin selection and the 'British paradigm', often found himself identified as a supporter of the *Wilsonian* type of sociobiology! This is what he had constantly to contend with at conferences. 'We call you the natural selection mafia!', people told him. 'We were all supposed to be followers of E. O. *Wilson!*' DeVore said exasperatedly.

So DeVore ran into trouble because of his apparent association with Wilson's socio-biology, although he was, in fact, a convert to kin selection himself. At the same time, his belief in kin selection created tension with other colleagues. Most dramatically, it had created an irreparable rift between him and his mentor and friend, the primato-logist Sherwood Washburn. Washburn was a staunch believer in group selection for humans, and regarded DeVore's conversion to kin selection as absolute apostasy. (We will return to Washburn in Chapter 7.) DeVore's new kin selectionist interests also caused trouble for him with other leaders in the field of primate behavior, such as Cambridge ethologist Robert Hinde. DeVore told me that Hinde had strongly criticized him at two different conferences. More precisely, Hinde had attacked him in public and then apologized profusely in private, which DeVore found rather odd. (The first was a Great Apes conference in Austria; the other was a meeting in Cambridge where DeVore had been a stand-in for Jane Goodall.) DeVore explained that he had been interested in seeing how the leaders at Cambridge, Hinde and Peter Marler—a generation older than him—would take the whole kin selection revolution. 'They took it badly,' he said.

In an interesting aside, DeVore said he believed that some sociobiologists might be trying to work out their personal problems in their science. For instance, he knew that Trivers came from a large family and always felt he was 'underinvested in' by his parents. 'I would also say he had a religious background,' DeVore added. He speculated that what we do in science may be connected with our early childhood; in fact he had discussed this with Wilson. 'Ed's lifelong fascination was with islands. His father was a pilot. My interest in evolution goes back to the same time. Some of us are trying to work out our personal problems through science. He is one of those who can give this working out universal proportions.'

And what about DeVore himself? His parents 'had instilled in him an almost pathological altruism'. His father was a Methodist minister, and he himself had started out to be a preacher, but given it up in his junior year. 'What I was really interested in was the evolution of human behavior over time.' He went to the University of Chicago, but there Robert Redfield, whom he had hoped to learn from, became ill and died. DeVore was persuaded to become the teaching assistant of another professor, Sherwood Washburn. DeVore had no interest in primates, Washburn's specialty, but Washburn wanted him to go to Africa and help him in research. 'If you come with me, I'll get you a grant to study pygmies', he promised. When Washburn later left for California, he persuaded DeVore to teach there. At the time there was an explosion of interest in animal behavior. 'He was highly opinionated and a son of a bitch', said DeVore affectionately.

In retrospect, the meeting between Trivers and DeVore can perhaps be construed as a happy chance. What mattered was what DeVore did with Trivers' untamed brilliance. Trivers' career was, in a sense, similar to DeVore's own—neither of them had been a biologist from the start, but ended up with this subject by a circuitous route. Both perhaps had some kind of unresolved problem with altruism. Maybe it was this similarity that initially made DeVore take a particular interest in young Trivers, and appoint himself his 'facilitator'. Which, in turn, led to DeVore's discovering kin selection at a point when he felt the need for a satisfactory explanatory theory. Which, in turn, helped DeVore inspire disciples such as John Tooby and Leda Cosmides. And, eventually, DeVore's efforts to 'keep Trivers going' were also to benefit *Sociobiology*—which Trivers may have helped straighten out more than he gave himself credit for.

Mutual aid

The emergence of sociobiology as a field turns out to be rather more complex than the 'standard model', which has E. O. Wilson in *Sociobiology* singlehandedly synthesizing the theories and empirical studies of the last thirty years, creating 'sociobiology'. Of course Wilson wrote his tome, with an almost superhuman effort (and, as he gracefully acknowledged in the early pages of his book, with a lot of help from his friends). There is no doubt that Wilson was an extremely successful articulator of important ideas in evolutionary biology in 1975. Still, a closer look shows that in the early 1970s the whole field of animal behavior was 'stampeding'—to use Hamilton's expression—in the direction of the new ideas of kin selection and reciprocal altruism. In this picture, sociobiology as a field emerges less as a one-man synthesis than as the outcome of a *collective process*, feeding on mutual influences between colleagues, and affected by certain 'catalytic' events.

Who else was trying to achieve a similar kind of synthesis of the new developments in the field of social behavior as Wilson did in *Sociobiology*? Many have noted a surge of books and articles published in the mid-1970s. It has been further suggested that some of these books were simply overshadowed by *Sociobiology*. The anthropologist Sherwood Washburn (1978b) mentioned three such books: John Alcock's *Animal Behavior: An Evolutionary Approach*, Jerram Brown's *The Evolution of Behavior*, and Eibl-Eibesfeldt's *Human Ethology* in its second edition, all published in 1975. George Barlow's (1991) candidates for competing syntheses were Jerram Brown's book and Michael Ghiselin's *The Economy of Nature and the Evolution of Sex* (1974). Others believed that Robert Hinde's *Biological Bases of Human Social Behavior*, published just a year before Wilson, received much less attention than it deserved. For instance, van der Steen and Voorzanger (1983) argued that 'Hinde's approach includes what should be termed "sociobiology", but he did not use the label'. In their view, Hinde had explained the relevance of biology for the study of man in a very lucid and broad perspective, but they found that his work was 'completely disregarded in many sociobiological texts'.

Much, of course, depends on what people perceive as the scientific meaning of 'sociobiology'. 'What . . . is this cluster of ideas, this bundle of concepts that have become linked in people's minds both with each other and with the name sociobiology?' asked Dawkins in 1979. His answer was: 'kin selection, parental investment, reciprocal altruism, evolutionarily stable strategy'. But, according to Dawkins, 'Wilson's *Sociobiology* can hardly be the common denominator, for, although these concepts are mostly mentioned there, so is everything else. As benefits his own definition, Wilson rightly devotes more space to the comparative study of social systems and their correlation with environmental variables, important topics which seem to be absent from the mysterious cluster. . .' (Dawkins, 1979a).[5] After this, Dawkins went on to suggest that 'sociobiology is the branch of ethology inspired by W. D. Hamilton'.

Maynard Smith, in his Introduction to *Current Problems in Sociobiology* (King's College Sociobiology Group, 1982), noted that two main concepts had dominated the study of the evolution of social behavior during the last fifteen years. The first, 'tracing back primarily to the work of John Crook, is that social systems should be seen as ecological adaptations'. The second dominant concept, 'which we owe mainly to W. D. Hamilton, is that the evolution of behaviour is influenced by the fact that the genes of relatives may be identical' (Maynard Smith, 1982e, p. 1). (He added that the interest in kinship, however, may have blinded evolutionists to a third important idea— mutualism—'two animals may cooperate because it pays both of them to do so', also present in the sociobiological discussion and recently becoming more prominent; p. 2.) Later, in an article entitled 'The Birth of Sociobiology', he described Wilson's *Sociobiology* as 'a valuable summary', but 'not . . . the origin of the ideas that have revolutionized our knowledge of social evolution' (Maynard Smith, 1985). What were these new ideas? Maynard Smith's list included the following three: 1) the idea that societies usually consist of relatives; 2) the idea that both partners in a co-operative interaction may benefit; 3) the concept of evolutionary stability in cases where the best action for an individual depends on what other individuals are doing.

Let us consult Hamilton. What did he regard as important synthetic attempts? Hamilton recognized three main independent efforts in the early 1970s to pull together the different facts and theories that had accumulated: Wilson's *Sociobiology*, Dawkins' *The Selfish Gene*, and Robin Fox's *Biosocial Anthropology* (1975) (based on the 'Biosocial Anthropology' conference convened in 1973 in Oxford). About the last meeting he said:

> The new ideas underlying the papers of the meeting were . . . largely the same as underlay the offending chapters of Wilson's massive work. Like Wilson, Robin Fox had noticed the rapid accumulation of changes both in the facts and the theories in the area; he wanted a meeting to pull various new lines together and to help establish a new perspective. Thus Fox and Wilson went at their tasks in complete independence but drew on much the same material. Simultaneously, and even more independently, Richard Dawkins was working on his book *The Selfish Gene*, destined to come out in 1976. Our book was a very small brother to the other two yet, nevertheless, it was another mark of rapidly changing times and the emergence of a new view of evolution and ourselves (Hamilton, 1996, p. 316).

Unlike Wilson's, Fox's book did not generate much criticism. What was the reason? Hamilton pointed out that neither the meeting nor the book's intention was to 'assert sweeping changes in the world of social science'. It was rather to record the steady but rapid extension of an existing paradigm. Had the conference been arranged one year later, the topic of the meeting might really have been 'human sociobiology', he mused (Hamilton, 1996, p. 316).

But clearly what created the scandal was not only Wilson's threat to forcibly scientize the social sciences, it was also the political storm around the book. And this, of course, many observers have noted. For instance, Maynard Smith doubted that without the last chapter and the inclusion of humans 'the book would have achieved the fame—or the sales—that it did' (1985c). But there is an additional conspiracy scenario. According to this, *Sociobiology*, through a well-orchestrated campaign of pre-publication articles, full-page advertisements, and an attractive price, was able to effectively *overshadow* other contemporary efforts of a similar kind (Mazur, 1981).[6] Moreover (this scenario suggested), a whiff of scandal and danger was deliberately made to surround the book a month before it was published. Accordingly, Boyce Rensberger's front-page article in *The New York Times* on 28 May 1975 was actually designed to *plant* the idea of opposition by stating that Wilson's last chapter about humans was controversial and would surely meet objections (Mazur, 1981). In other words, on this conspiracy view, the action by the Sociobiology Study Group was nothing but the outcome of a self-fulfilling prophecy—*somebody* was expected to react *somehow*. (It also implies that we ought to see Wilson's ferocious critics as mere lap dogs, falling into predesigned roles devised by master strategists! An interesting thought experiment, indeed.) The basic suggestion, however, is that with these marketing ploys, Wilson got an unfair advantage over others.

But, of course, there were not only books summarizing and discussing the new ideas; various seminal articles also appeared. One such article was Richard Alexander's long 1974 contribution 'The Evolution of Social Behavior' in *Annual Review of Ecology and Systematics*; there were others by, for instance, West-Eberhard (1976), and Maynard Smith (1976a). Together, this makes for quite a concentration of intellectual, synthetic effort in the mid-1970s.

Now we get to an interesting issue, which might be called 'Hamilton's lag'. Hamilton's 1964 two-part paper was little cited before the mid-1970s. But in the mid-1970s, there started what Dawkins called an 'epidemy of quotations' of Hamilton's 1964 paper, rising to a peak in 1981 (Dawkins, 1989, p. 325). One explanation for this phenomenon is that Hamilton was finally 'discovered' through these various summarizing books and articles, which for the first time introduced and explicated Hamilton's ideas to a broader readership.

In this context, *Sociobiology* may have taken on a special role. Jon Seger and Paul Harvey (1980) suggested that Wilson's *Sociobiology* was probably instrumental in boosting Hamilton's fame. In fact, they believed they had evidence to show that people who referred to Hamilton had actually done it 'through' Wilson's *Sociobiology*. Their indicator was that, in 1978, a 'mutant' title for Hamilton's 1964 paper made up 80 per cent of the total citations in the Science Citation Index. The correct title of Hamilton's paper 'The Genetical evolution of Social Behavior' had been replaced by the mutant title 'The Genetical theory of Social Behavior'. And the same mutant version could also be found in the references to Wilson's *Sociobiology*! It could also be found in *The Selfish Gene*.

Dawkins, however, commented that the mutant title did not necessarily have to derive from Wilson's book, or from his own, for that matter—it could have come about quite independently, since the mistake was a natural one to make. The title of Hamilton's article might be easily confused with the title of Fisher's famous book *The Genetical Theory of Natural Selection*. (Dawkins noted that he himself had misquoted the title of Hamilton's paper back in 1970 in a bibliography distributed to students; Dawkins, 1989a, p. 328.) So, if Wilson and Dawkins had already independently made the mistake, how many more might not have done so? Dawkins also pointed out that the upturn in citations started *before* the publication of *Sociobiology*, in 1973–4. This is why he firmly dismissed the idea that *Sociobiology* and *The Selfish Gene* were responsible for the initial upsurge of interest in kin selection as merely a 'memic myth' (Dawkins, 1989a, p. 326).

If we concentrate on the period 1975–6, however, a good explanation may still be that whatever their *original* source of Hamiltonian inspiration, when looking up the exact *reference* people simply chose to consult the biggest book around—Wilson's *Sociobiology*—or the handiest one—Dawkins' *The Selfish Gene*—instead of going to the library! Clearly, then, both Wilson and Dawkins can be suspected of having substantially contributed to the upswing in Hamilton's citation pattern. Looking at the text of the two books, however, it appears that it was rather Dawkins than Wilson who explicitly boosted Hamilton. Of course, Wilson indirectly supported Hamilton by the mere fact that he declared altruism to be the central problem of sociobiology and focused on the gene as the agent in evolution—Hamilton's fundamental points. (In fact, because of Wilson's formulations in his first chaper, some believed that Wilson, too, represented a 'selfish gene' approach of the Dawkins type—which he didn't.) And later, the subsequent scandal around the book could only have helped highlight the idea of genes 'for' altruism.

But if we look closely at *Sociobiology*, we find it does not mention Hamilton's inclusive fitness theory until Chapter 5. That chapter is entitled 'Group Selection and Altruism', and here *altruism* is the focus. Hamilton's idea of inclusive fitness represents only one of many competing theories of altruism. Wilson clearly explicates Hamilton's basic ideas (including an eye-catching diagram on p. 119), cites his published papers, and calls the Hamilton models 'beguiling in part because of their transparency and heuristic value' (1975a, p. 119). Still, he concludes:

> But the Hamilton viewpoint is also unstructured. The conventional parameters of
> population genetics, allele frequencies, mutation rates, epistasis, migration, group size, and
> so forth, are mostly omitted from the equations. As a result, Hamilton's mode of reasoning
> can be only loosely coupled with the remainder of genetic theory, and the number of
> predictions it can make is unnecessarily limited (1975a, p. 120).

On the other hand, Wilson made Hamilton's explanation for haplodiploidy in Hymenoptera his first example of 'phylogenetic inertia', one of his two 'prime movers of social evolution'—the other is 'ecological pressure'—discussed in Chapter 3 of his book. According to Wilson, 'social evolution is the outcome of the genetic response of populations to ecological pressure within the constraints imposed by phylogenetic inertia' (p. 32). He cites Hamilton as having 'argued with substantial logic and docu- mentation' in his 1964 paper that the peculiarity of eusociality in Hymenoptera is related to the haplodiploid mode of sex determination in these insects.

Hamilton himself noted the odd fact that his 1964 paper, which was supposedly expressing a universal formula, for a long time was cited mainly by scientists interested in social insects! They seem to have regarded his paper as a study of altruism in Hymenoptera. This was particularly ironical because the Hymenoptera part had been added later as an illustrative *example* in Part II of the paper (Hamilton, 1996, p. 20). However, there is an explanation. This particular interpretation of Hamilton's message might well be traced back to Wilson and his *The Insect Societies*, published in 1971, Wilson's first attempt at integrated sociobiology, before he ventured into vertebrates. As we saw, Wilson by his own account seems to have read Hamilton in 1965 largely as an explanation of the mystery of caste in Hymenoptera.[7]

And look what else we find in *The Insect Societies*: the title of Chapter 17 is 'The Genetic Theory of Social Behavior'—the possible origin of Wilson's own mutant reference in *Sociobiology* (he has the correct reference to Hamilton's paper in his 1971 book). This chapter introduces Hamilton in the following way: 'Hamilton (1964) has created an audacious genetic theory of the origin of sociality which assigns the central role to haplodiploidy in a wholly different way' (p. 328). After describing the idea, Wilson goes on to say: 'This idea is so simple and starkly mechanical that my own first reaction was to reject it out of hand. But the implications, once the proposition is made the basis of evolutionary models, are so extensive and intricate that I soon became absorbed in its possibilities' (ibid.). Thereafter, Wilson goes on to evaluate the consequences of the theory in detail and suggest directions that further research might take. Hamilton's theory was an obvious boon for students of insect societies. Indeed, as Wilson later remarked, 'a sizable research industry has been built upon this single paper' (Wilson, 1994, p. 316).[8]

But what about Hamilton himself? Is it not possible that Hamilton largely launched *himself*, later boosted by Wilson, Dawkins, and others? After 1964 Hamilton continued publishing, including one article in *Science* (1967) and one in *Nature* (1970). The 1967 article contained the germ of many important ideas, including the 'unbeatable strategy' (Hamilton, 1996, p. 133).[9] The *Nature* article 'Selfish and Spiteful Behaviour in an Evolutionary Model', again captured Hamilton's ideas in only three pages. Obviously, being published in *Nature* 'legitimated' Hamilton as an important name in the field. And there was one more article in 1971, 'Geometry for the Selfish Herd', which later became a citation classic (Hamilton, 1971a). This was Hamilton's most popularly written paper (he had originally written it for Martin Gardner's mathematical puzzle column in *Scientific American*). And, of course, Hamilton had been invited to the important Man and Beast conference in 1969, the proceedings of which were published in 1971 (Hamilton, 1971b). Finally, we have Trivers' (1971, 1974) very visible contributions highlighting Hamilton's work, and Trivers' and Hare's (1976) article in *Science* providing what appeared to be convincing evidence for the Hamiltonian model (Parker, 1978).

Indeed, there is support for this interpretation, too. Using a logarithmic scale, Dawkins demonstrated that the spread of Hamilton's idea has the form of a 'gathering epidemic', 'a single slow-burning explosion of interest, running right through from 1967 to the late 1980s' (Dawkins, 1989a, p. 326). During this period, 'individual books and papers should be seen both as symptoms and causes of [a] long-term trend', Dawkins emphasizes. In other words, the mid-1970s books themselves should be seen as a *reflection* of a bandwagon effect rather than its cause. In Dawkins' opinion, they expressed an idea which was 'in the air', and there was a process of mutual reinforcement taking place (p. 326).

And if we take a closer look at these influences, they have an interesting transatlantic flavor. In the first place, we have Fisher, Haldane, and Sewall Wright, two British and one American, the background architects of gene-selectionist thinking. Bill Hamilton can make Britain proud, but his close collaborator, George Price, was an American, who had come to live in England. Later, Maynard Smith collaborated with Price on the ESS. Hamilton, again, partly traces his thinking to an early paper of George Williams (and D. C. Williams), in yet another transatlantic influence.[10] Williams (1966), in turn, was crucial for Dawkins (and seemingly for Wilson, too), but Williams himself got activated by reading Wynne-Edwards.[11] Trivers' early papers were an important inspiration for Dawkins (Dawkins, 1989a, p. 298); Dawkins, together with Wilson, became vehicles for spreading Trivers' and Hamilton's ideas (Dawkins also promoted the notion of an ESS). And these ideas, again, had a complex relationship with ethology—partly originating from ideas in this field, partly influencing them, and partly being influenced by them in turn.

I believe that the emergence of sociobiology can be described as largely a collective effort. We can see the surge of enthusiasm around certain books and conferences, the intricate pattern of paths crossing, of people inspiring one another and their students with exciting new ideas. And as we saw in the previous chapter, an important role in the process of articulating sociobiological theory was played by 'facilitators'—individuals who could spot, nurture, and promote the genius of others. My best examples are Hamilton and Maynard Smith 'discovering' and encouraging Price, and De Vore and Wilson supporting Trivers, who, in turn, had an impact on Wilson's *Sociobiology* and helped promote and explicate Hamilton's ideas. And so on and on, in a pattern of as yet unknown connections and reinforcements. It is tempting, then, to see the emergence and articulation of sociobiology as a beautiful example of mutual aid.

The Man and Beast conference: a catalytic event

There is one particular event that may well have had a catalytic effect for the development of sociobiology. That was the 1969 Man and Beast conference in Washington, DC. In May 1969, a large conference was called at the Smithsonian Institution, arranged by the then secretary of the Smithsonian, S. Dillon Ripley, an eminent ornithologist. The subtitle of the resulting book with the same name, edited by John Eisenberg and Wilton S. Dillon in 1971, was 'Comparative Social Behavior'. As it turned out, the conference had a much broader scope.

What was the aim of this conference? Why was all this money spent, and why were biologists invited? Bill Hamilton, one of the invitees, describes it as a grandiose operation, involving lavish receptions in various big Washington hotels, with speeches by Nobel laureates and eminent politicians (personal communication, and Hamilton, 1996, p. 187):

> I recall talking to senators who seemed proportioned in size to the halls where they held court. More vividly still I recall a more European-sized wife of one senator pinning me at once with her chin and her fierce eyes as she asked me how my theory could help to reduce violence and crime in America. . . . I recall scientists of every type but most of them larger both physically and, seemingly, in spirit than those I knew in England. Here were the laureates, the pompous, the hirsute, the fantastical, the unbelievably industrious, the funny, pugilistic, queer . . . ; Tolstoyans like Alexander, Rabelaisians like Chagnon. Perhaps I would have been less amazed and less entertained if I had been to a scientific meeting in England, but this was my first (Hamilton, 1996, p. 187).

Ripley had asked the conference participants to address four questions: what are the physiological and behavioral mechanisms underlying social behavior? Is man unique?

Are creatures similar, and can man endure? (Sebeok, 1991). Why was this perceived as such an urgent topic at the time? Hamilton had the impression that the conference was called to invite biologists to formulate solutions to current social ills. Indeed, it was 1969. In America, the Great Society was being threatened by erupting violence. There had been the Little Rock riots and the turmoil during the Chicago democratic convention in 1968; inner city trouble was at its height. And, of course, there was the Vietnam war.

There is no doubt that Lorenz' *On Aggression* had particularly stirred the hope that biologists might have something to contribute. Read in the right spirit, Lorenz' book could be seen as an impassioned appeal to do something about aggression (in contrast to many critics who thought he argued that aggression was innate and therefore ineradicable). Ripley himself was very concerned about aggression (Robinson and Tiger, 1991). In his Preface to *Man and Beast*, Ripley wrote: 'Should the study of man be based on man alone? . . . do genes control how we hunt, protect our young, affiliate, cooperate, fight or claim territory . . . The study of the inheritance of traits which affect culture is much needed' (Ripley 1969, quoted in Robinson and Tiger, 1991). And there were other relevant books by ethologists and biosocial anthropologists. Just before the symposium, Tinbergen's student Desmond Morris had published *The Naked Ape*, and in the same month as the symposium Tiger published *Men in Groups* (Tiger and Robinson, 1991). Indeed, the participants did feel called upon to do something:

> There was a general sense of excitement and of impending discovery and even of the promise of clarity. As well, there was an innocence about all this, a cheerful assumption that the world was waiting for the announcements of scientists about the nature of nature and of human nature. Who could object? (Tiger and Robinson, 1991.)

Lorenz' book had also refueled the intellectual debate concerning instinctive vs learned behavior. Was there any reasonable compromise in sight? One of the results of the conference was Tiger and Fox's idea of a behavioral 'biogrammar'—an offshoot of the Chomskyan idea of an innate universal linguistic capability in humans, with the recognition of a great variety of specific cultural expressions.

One of the people directly affected by the conference was Wilson. As he himself indicated some two decades later at the follow-up conference 'Man and Beast Revisited', that 1969 conference 'was an early milestone in the development of sociobiology', in that it *brought together scholars from different fields and showed that a common language was possible*. He reported that he 'was personally encouraged by the event, and . . . made friendships that have persisted through the years' (Wilson, 1991, italics added). One of the people he met (again) was Bill Hamilton.

Both Wilson and Hamilton had taken the conference's invitation very seriously and prepared papers addressing questions about the relationship between culture and evolution. Wilson here presented a model of how human evolution could be speeded up (Wilson, 1971c). Hamilton felt that he was invited especially to try to apply the new kin selection ideas to humans (Hamilton, 1971d).

While Wilson saw the conference as an opportunity to argue for an alternative to the

Lorenzian view of aggression (see the next section), Hamilton was not happy with what he felt he had to say. He described his thoughts as 'painful', and realized that they went counter to a current moral world view. Still, what he felt he had been invited to discuss was the nature of 'the beast within'. He believed he would have to discuss the evolution of xenophobia and human warlike inclinations, even if he would have to 'endure the tortures of Orestes' for communicating such a heresy (1996, p. 189). But Aeschylus had also told the hounded Orestes: 'Then fly and do not weaken', and this is what Hamilton took as his personal advice (1996, p. 191).

Hamilton was certain in 1969 that 'reliance on human nature as currently evolved, the instincts of a supposed "noble savage", is no answer to the Prisoner's Dilemma or to Malthus'. (His own Prisoner's Dilemma model involved a multilevel sequence of escalating warfare, 1996, p. 191.) In Hamilton's opinion, 'we may have good reason to consider some aspects of human character inappropriate in the modern world and to wish certain traits would disappear. If we decide we need policy for assisting the disappearance, it will be well to understand how human nature was constructed' (ibid.).

And at this Washington conference there was no doubt about the political import given to biology. For instance, Senator J. William Fulbright is quoted as saying the following:

> What is important to those of us who happen to be in the Senate, in the Congress, is to feel that it is possible, or even probable, that we can influence the decisions which affect the future of this country. . . . If we assume that men generally are inherently aggressive in their tendency, . . . if this is inherent and man cannot be educated away from it, it certainly makes a great deal of difference in one's attitude toward current problems. . . . If we are inherently committed by nature to this aggressive tendency to fight, well then, I certainly would not be bothering about all this business of arms limitations or talks with the Russians (Fulbright, quoted in Eisenberg and Dillon, 1971, p. 373, editor's note).

Statements like these indicate that the critics of sociobiology some years later were not so far off the mark in their assumptions about the kind of reasoning that might be typical for policy makers in Washington.

Thus, the 1969 Man and Beast conference might be seen as having a motivating effect on many later efforts to apply biological insights to the study of human society, as well as a serious beginning of a common move toward a sociobiological type of thought, later expressed in individual books and papers emerging in the mid-1970s. This collective effort was stimulated by the urgency of the conference's subject matter, the participants perceiving themselves as capable of making a difference, the general buzz, and last but not least, perhaps, the presence of Hamilton, the representative of a bold new way of thinking about social behavior.

But at the follow-up conference twenty years later, one of the two conveners, self-described 'old guard', Oxford trained ethologist Michael Robinson, put his foot down. He pointed out that *ethologists* ought to get much more recognition for the development of sociobiology than they were usually given:

the essential basis of sociobiology was in the work of Niko Tinbergen, Lorenz, and their colleagues and students who with such productivity studied animals in environments as natural as possible. They were thus able to add to the results of psychologists working in labs their observations about the broad social lives of animals, the animals' links to environment, and . . . how the life cycle affected long-term developments in social structure (Tiger and Robinson, 1991, p. xx, italics added).

And, indeed, the ethologists may have good reason for seeing the roots of sociobiology not in kin selection theory but rather in ethology; i.e. in the tradition of field study of animal behavior. George Barlow (1989) noted that large parts of *Sociobiology* could as well have been found in a traditional ethology book and he had a hard time distinguishing what was what.

Let us take a quick look at the rather complex relationship between ethology and sociobiology (in Chapter 16 this will be discussed again). The ethologists *were*, arguably, recognized from the very beginning, and by some influential 'sociobiologists'. Note, for instance, that Dawkins in 1976 presented Hamilton's 1964 paper as *part of ethology*:

His two papers of 1964 are among the most important contributions to *social ethology* ever written, and I have never been able to understand why they have been so neglected by ethologists (his name does not even appear in the index of two major text-books of ethology, both published in 1970) (Dawkins, 1976a, p. 97, italics added).

Wilson, however, in *Sociobiology*, had a dual stance toward ethology. On one hand, he briefly gave credit to ethology, writing that 'Konrad Lorenz and his fellow biologists . . . convinced us that behavior and social structure, like all other biological phenomena, can be studied as "organs", extensions of the genes that exist because of their superior adaptive value' (Wilson, 1975a, pp. 21–2). On the other, he spoke about 'the ad hoc terminology, crude models, and curve fitting that characterize most of contemporary ethology and comparative psychology' (1975a, p. 6).

David Barash, in his popular *Sociobiology and Behavior* (1977)—with a Preface by Wilson—presented ethology as having made a major contribution. The field had an evolutionary orientation from the start, and emphasized species-specific and genetically mediated behaviors (in America, partly as a protest against the extreme environmental determinism of early American psychology). The evolutionary approach stressed the need to look at each behavior in its entirety within the environment in which it evolved. Still, Barash contrasted ethology's view of evolution with that of sociobiology, describing the former as historic or static; there was not much *explanation* in ethology (Barash, 1977, p. 6). Sociobiology, on the other hand, 'emerged from the recognition that behavior, even complex social behavior, has evolved and is adaptive' (p. 8).

Barash may have exaggerated here the gap between ethology and sociobiology. Tinbergen's students would surely protest, pointing to Tinbergen's famous four questions, that is, four equally important ways of *explaining* a behavioral mechanism (its function, evolution, development, and control; Tinbergen, 1963). Incidentally, the ethological community's initial lack of interest in Hamilton, which puzzled Dawkins in

1976, may be simply explained in that most ethologists—unlike the functional ethologist-turned Dawkins—resisted having to restrict themselves to only *one* type of explanation: the function or adaptiveness of behavior.

Unfortunately for the ethologists, however, sociobiology happened to strike just when their own field was at an exciting point in its development, but had not crystallized enough to resist the lure of the new genetic thinking (Bateson and Klopfer, 1989). One example of the broad integrative effort in the 1970s was, for instance, Bateson and Hinde's insightful *Growing Points in Ethology* (1976). But with the advent of sociobiology, many ethologists and behavioral ecologists started focusing almost exclusively on adaptive explanations—so much so that it raised the question of whether ethology was really destined to follow the so-called 'dumbbell' or 'bubble gum' model at the beginning of Wilson's book, where ethology was to be swallowed up by sociobiology by the year 2000 (Bateson and Klopfer, 1989).

At the end of the 1980s, the ethologists' answer was no. Sociobiology had rather *stimulated* ethology. George Barlow (1989), for instance, saw ethology and sociobiology as interdependent and mutually reinforcing. He suggested that sociobiology had given ethology a healthy 'kick in the pants' and that the new emphasis on genetic explanation had helped move the field from a static to a process view of evolution.[12]

Wilsonian sociobiology: a synthesis for a purpose

Wilson opens his chapter in *Man and Beast* by forcefully rebutting the ideas that aggression could be an instinct of some sort. He particularly takes issue with popular ethologists, such as Robert Ardrey, who argue that competition is inevitable, and that humans are stuck with a nasty Pleistocene nature, as well as Raymond Dart (1953) with his bloody reconstruction of the history of Man. The main point of Wilson's chapter is to demonstrate that aggression is most probably an *adaptive* trait also in man, that is, a trait under evolution. In other words, we are no longer whatever we were in a Stone Age existence—which in any case we have no information about, Wilson adds. Whatever our nature may have been like, Wilson argues, there has been ample time for us to have changed our nature over and over again. He cites a number of animal studies that show that evolution can be speeded up; he says he believes that, for humans, a significant change can happen in ten generations, or 200–300 years.

Wilson goes as far as suggesting that aggression may even be a *recently acquired* trait in humans, during, say, the last 300 years. This would have happened through 'genetic assimilation', whereby a learned behavior is later 'tracked' genetically. Here, then, we may have the proto-statement of his famous pronunciation that 'the genes hold culture on a leash'—this time run in the *opposite* direction, however, that is: culture holding the *genes* on a leash, or the genes tracking culture! This is Wilson in his social planning mode. (And, in fact, he briefly mentions the importance of his points for social planning.) 'Man makes himself genetically', was what Wilson concluded in 1969. (Over time, of course, Wilson developed both sides of the story, genes holding culture on a leash and culture holding genes on a leash. Finally, Wilson and Lumsden were to unite the two sides in *Genes, Mind and Culture* and *Promethean Fire*; see Chapters 8 and 18.)

Here, then, we have the reason why Wilson was emphasizing the *adaptiveness* of aggression, something over which the Sociobiology Study Group, and Lewontin particularly, gave him so much trouble. It is not that he wanted to harp on about aggression as a trait; rather, he saw the adaptiveness of aggression as a *counterargument* to the (Lorenzian) perception of aggression as innate. For Wilson, this also meant that aggression was a trait which would be typically expressed under particular, known circumstances, such as overpopulation—circumstances to avoid if we wanted to diminish it. In other words, aggresssion was a density-dependent trait.

In his chapter, Wilson also totally rebutted Robert Ardrey's suggestion that competition between individuals was necessary for natural selection. Interestingly, it turns out that Ardrey's book *The Social Contract* (1970) was, in fact, partly an attack on *Wilson*. Ardrey had read Wilson's chapter in *Man and Beast* in pre-print form when he wrote his book, and Wilson now had what he called the 'unusual privilege' of responding to Ardrey in the very same chapter. Wilson's basic position was that Ardrey did not know evolutionary theory. It is competition between *alleles* that matters, Wilson pointed out. And he went on to answer 'yes' to Ardrey's query as to whether evolution could take place through other processes than competition: 'I can only repeat my generalization: theory predicts that competition is not an essential property of species, and data from empirical studies . . . show that *competition is in fact very far from being universal*' (Wilson, 1971c, p. 211, italics added).

Here, then, we have Wilson speaking *against* a nasty vision of humans, *against* a vision of innate aggressiveness in animals and aggression as a ubiquitous trait, and *against* over-emphasis on the importance of competition in nature or as a force of evolution. And this was also what a sea of senators and Washington people heard, as Wilson presented this chapter at the Man and Beast conference. There is no doubt that in the contemporary climate Wilson saw himself—and was most probably seen—as a *liberal*, acting against any deterministic view. At the same time, of course, he represented a particular type of liberal, a '*scientific*' liberal if you will, which distanced him from what he himself called 'humanistic liberals'—Montagu (1965) and Leach (1968).

And his particular liberal stance meant that Wilson, upfront, took issue with the other extreme: the over-emphasis on culture. He said he believed that it was

> much too early to attempt to make a judgment on the matter, as Dobzhansky (1963a) has done with the following statement: 'Culture is not inherited through genes, it is acquired by learning from other human beings . . . In a sense, human genes have surrendered their primacy in human evolution to an entirely new, nonbiological or superorganic agent, culture. However, it should not be forgotten that this agent is entirely dependent on the human genotype'. Obviously human genes have surrendered a great deal, but perhaps they have kept a little of their old heritability and responsiveness to selection. This amount should be measured, because it is crucial to the planning of future society (Wilson, 1971c, p. 208).

The key to Wilson's relative optimism in the face of the situation of mankind was that human evolution might in principle be speeded up so as to match the progress of cultural evolution: mankind was not doomed to be the victim of its own cultural creations. The necessary conditions were all there for rapid behavioral evolution in humans. 'By rapid I mean significant alteration in, say, emotional and intellectual traits within no more than ten generations—or about three hundred years' (p. 207). Wilson concluded: 'Man therefore has the genetic *capacity* to track some of the dominant features of particular cultures. Whether he does so—and to what degree—remains an open question.'[13] As we see, in many ways the fundamental agenda for *Sociobiology* (and later works) is set out in this early paper, at least with regard to Wilson's long-range plan for mankind.[14]

Compare this with Hamilton, who did not have an obvious solution when asked by the Senator's wife what biologists could do.[15] As noted earlier, he saw himself as a messenger of unavoidable bad news, which he gave to the audience both in Washington in 1968 and at the Biosocial Anthropology conference in Oxford in 1973 (see Chapter 7). The reason for this was Hamilton's straightforward application of his ideas to humans; unlike Wilson, he did not factor in the intervention of culture. For Hamilton, life on Earth was a seamless continuity, with man just one species among many. In his autobiographical notes (1996), it becomes clear that Hamilton has an almost super-naturalistic identification of himself with living things—including flowers, bugs, and even, at one point, an intestinal parasite! Of course Hamilton did not disregard cultural influences, but he did not see them as strongly affecting or modifying genetic influences —and this was what later got him into trouble with anthropologists (see Chapter 7).

While Hamilton might be classified as a 'Darwinian anthropologist', to use current terminology (Symons, 1992), Wilson already appears in 1969 as something of a gene-culture interactionist. However, at that point he had not yet factored in the human mind, as he (and the evolutionary psychologists) would do later. 'Man makes himself genetically' was Wilson's provocative slogan, in clear opposition to the culturalist view later to be taken by the opponents of sociobiology, namely that 'man makes himself'— period.

Wilson's ambitions were even more wide-ranging than this. Wilson wanted to establish his claim that aggression was not an innate trait by undertaking a broad comparative analysis across species. Such an analysis would show that aggression as a trait varied widely, that its expression required particular ecological and other conditions; moreover, aggression was only one way among many to deal with problems of existence. This would have to be argued against the background of a general overview of variation in animal social behaviors, all seen as subject to adaptation by natural selection. For this purpose Wilson needed empirical studies of different species' social behavior in different ecologies, and a theory which made it plausible that social behavior was, in fact, adaptive in this way.

But Wilson had all this—and within reach—in Washington! At the same conference was John Crook, the acknowledged leader in comparative ecological studies of social behavior, presenting a nice inventory of empirical studies of variations in social behavior across animal societies (Crook, 1971). (Wilson had already started an inventory, largely of variation of aggression in insects, which he also presented in his paper.) For the requisite mathematical population genetic theory, again, there was Bill Hamilton, whom Wilson had, of course already 'discovered' in 1965, but now had an opportunity to hear and meet again. (Wilson quoted Hamilton, 1964, in support of his own point that a reduction in inclusive fitness would work against aggressive behavior; p. 199.) And there were Tiger and Fox, the biosocial anthropologists. And finally, there was his Harvard colleague Irven DeVore discussing the evolution of human society (DeVore, 1971). The two of them could later at close range sustain the excitement engendered by the conference.

So, we may say that, in a sense, *Sociobiology* was not 'just' a synthesis of empirical studies and theoretical developments over the last thirty years. It was a synthesis for a purpose. It had the aim of demonstrating the adaptiveness of social behavior in animals under various demographic and ecological constraints, and this in the new language of population genetics. In this way, for instance, aggression might be exactly expressed as varying with ecology and population pressure and across animal populations. It may very well have been Wilson's initial preoccupation with *aggression* rather than with altruism that originally led him to his own broad 'Wilsonian' synthesis, instead of a more limited provision of genetic formulas for altruistic behavior in animals.[16] Or, more precisely, Wilson's leading concepts originally may have been two: aggression and co-operation, both seen as dependent on ecological circumstances as well as considerations of genetic relatedness. The new theories of Hamilton, on the other hand, only concentrated on altruism/co-operation because of genetic relatedness. This was too limited for Wilson's purpose, although the mathematics were impressive. Later, however, Wilson did declare altruism the central problem of sociobiology.

What's in a name? The connotations of 'sociobiology'

What about the name 'sociobiology' itself? This is what Wilson said in 1978 at the AAAS Symposium in Washington, DC, still wet from the ice-water poured down his neck:

> Sociobiology is defined as the systematic study of the biological basis of social behavior and the organization of societies in all kinds of organisms, including human beings. Its novelty comes from the current reconsideration of social phenomena with reference to the principles of population ecology and population genetics, many of the most relevant of which are comparatively new. Only within the last several years has this synthesis achieved a large enough aggregate of self-sufficient ideas to qualify as a distinct discipline of biology, but the logic of demarcating such a discipline was apparent many years earlier (Wilson, 1980b).

He went on to mention that in 1950 J. P. Scott, the Secretary of the Committee for the Study of Animal Behavior, had suggested sociobiology as the word for the 'interdisciplinary science which lies between the fields of biology (particularly ecology and physiology) and psychology and sociology'. Later, the term acquired a quasi-official status: there was a Section on Animal Behavior and Sociobiology of the Ecological Society of America (later the Animal Behavior Society), and 'sociobiology' was sometimes used in technical papers (together with 'biosociology' and 'animal sociology'). Wilson continued:

> When I wrote the final chapter of *The Insect Societies* (1971), which was entitled 'The prospect for a unified sociobiology,' and *Sociobiology* (1975), I chose the word sociobiology rather than some other, novel expression because I knew it would already be familiar to most students of animal behavior and hence more likely to be accepted (Wilson, 1980b).

Wilson obviously had good grounds for using a concept known to his closest scientific colleagues. But there were those who thought that 'sociobiology' was not a good choice at all. For them, the obvious association was with 'social biology', which in turn brought the thinking to *Sozialbiologie* and its Nazi connections (see, for example, Chorover, 1979). And because of these connotations and the political storm created around *Sociobiology*, many started feeling acute discomfort using 'sociobiology' at all. Describing their own activity as 'sociobiology' after the scandal around Wilson's book would indicate tacit acceptance of its purported political goals. Barlow (1991) noted that the critics' 'creation of an image of sociobiology as an evil doctrine . . . extended to those studying animal behavior. That image cost the field, and precipitated a scramble to call oneself a behavioral ecologist'. He went on to observe:

> During and after the sociobiology tumult I traveled to a number of meetings and universities. Old colleagues, not reading the primary literature nor working the field of behavior, responded to the mention of sociobiology as anathema. When asked about the workings of the field, they had no understanding whatsoever. They knew it had to do with animal behavior, and that it was bad, it was sexist and racist or something like that, but little more (Barlow, 1991, p. 293).

But there was also a strategical reason, or the matter of academic politics. At least for behavioral ecologists and ethologists, it was hard to willingly relabel themselves under a term which was no longer loosely applied to animal social behavior, but had now been usurped by Wilson to militantly emphasize the importance of evolutionary aspects of behavior above all other (and, in fact, go as far as promising a takeover of these fields by 'sociobiology' by the year 2000; Wilson, 1975a, pp. 5–6).

No wonder that many of the British students of animal behavior did not wish to be called sociobiologists, as I found out during interviews in 1981. Other British researchers, again, resisted the label 'sociobiologist' because they felt that Wilson's view of 'sociobiology', which embraced group selection, clashed with their own newer gene-selectionist view.

This political charge of the term 'sociobiology' was news for Patrick Bateson, when in 1976 he suggested changing the name of a project at the Research Centre of King's College, Cambridge, to 'Sociobiology' instead of 'Behavioral Ecology'.[17] The reason for this was that they 'wanted to include functional studies of social behaviour which were not necessarily ecological in character' (Bateson, 1982a, p. x). Bateson saw no problem with that. In fact, as we see, his explanation parallels Wilson's own. That was before

Bateson knew about the connotations, and before the sociobiology controversy had been 'imported' to Britain (interview):

> The term 'Sociobiology' had been in use since the late 1940s; indeed, the present-day Animal Behavior Society had grown out of a section of the Ecological Society of America and the American Society of Zoologists called 'Animal Behavior and Sociobiology'. However, we should, perhaps, have been quicker to realize how much opinion would be polarized by the recent attempts to inject a particular brand of biology into the social sciences. The lacerations resulting from the ensuing ideological conflict have not yet healed, and in many places 'Sociobiology' is either a battlecry or a term of abuse (Bateson, 1982a, p. x).

The reason the King's College Sociobiology project could remain unaffected by these developments, Bateson explained, was because of the participants' strong commitment to empirical research. Indeed, one of the worst accusations of the critics of sociobiology had been that sociobiologists were telling just-so stories and carelessly extrapolating from animals to humans. This, however, was not the case with the Fellows of his project, Bateson emphasized: 'Nobody who knew their work could accuse them of doing bad science. Furthermore, they would tolerate neither sloppy argument nor extravagant generalizations from studies of animals to humans' (Bateson, 1982a, p. x).

During its four years' lifetime, the project proceeded well, including a well-attended weekly seminar and a final conference resulting in the book *Current Problems in Sociobiology*. Still, when it came to the name for the group behind the book, the old problem re-emerged. Considering the political connotations, was it really advisable for them to call themselves the King's College Sociobiology Group, in print? According to Maynard Smith, the question of the name 'sociobiology' did cause considerable stir and many participants felt strongly that another name should be used. At this point, however, Mary West Eberhard spoke up. She asked the group whether they stood behind the ideas of sociobiology or not. If they did, they ought to use the name, too! That impressed the members of the group. They now decided that in the present situation, it was more important to show support for the new name than to register their differences with the way the name was used (Maynard Smith, personal communication).

This is the only incident I know of a deliberate decision to use the term 'sociobiology' in the face of its political connotations. Instead, what has been typical has been various types of *avoidance maneuvers* by Wilson's colleagues and a certain inventiveness when it comes to alternatives to 'sociobiology', which, in turn, Wilson has not taken lightly (see Chapter 16). Some colleagues, however, accepted the label (such as Daniel Freedman, 1979). Dawkins, too, despite stubborn persistence in calling himself and Hamilton 'ethologists', in 1985 finally classified himself as a sociobiologist—for strategic reasons, he wanted to counterattack on behalf of himself and others against the allegations in Lewontin, Rose, and Kamin's *Not in Our Genes* (see Chapter 9). And Hamilton notes, perhaps slightly ironically, in his autobiographical writings that 'sociobiologists' is what they 'came to be called'.

CHAPTER 6

Assault on adaptationism—a delayed scientific critique

What's wrong with adaptationism?

It was not until some years after the beginning of the *Sociobiology* controversy that the attack on 'the adaptationist program' became more concerted. Most elements of the scientific criticism of Wilson, mixed with moral and political criticism, were already inherent in the early publications of the Sociobiology Study Group. A detailed scientific criticism had in fact already been spelled out by Lewontin in 1976 in a paper read to the Philosophy of Science Association, but this reached only a limited audience. Thus, it was not until 1978–9 that the biological community got a clear view of Wilson's main critics' basic *scientific* objections to sociobiology.

The relevant papers are specifically Lewontin's 1978 and 1979 papers on adaptation, especially 'Sociobiology as an Adaptationist Program' (1979a), and Gould and Lewontin's 'The Spandrels of San Marco and the Panglossian Paradigm' paper read to the Royal Society in 1978 (Gould and Lewontin, 1979). As mentioned already, both Ernst Mayr and Wilson considered Lewontin's 1979 paper 'good criticism' and both wished that the attack on sociobiology had been presented originally in this form, without the political overtones. Mayr was especially vehement about the missed opportunity for effective scientific criticism. He wished that Gould and Lewontin had been 'honest' at the beginning so that their perfectly well-taken points about adaptation would have been received more seriously. According to Mayr, now people got the impression that the critics' data base must be poor: 'Dishonest methods are bad if you have a good case', said Mayr.

But it was not really easy for Gould and Lewontin to disconnect the scientific from the moral/political aspects, because for them, these were deeply intertwined. Lewontin's 1976 and 1979 papers, however, did show an effort at producing 'clean' scientific criticism of adaptationism. The best place to find such criticism is in Lewontin's reviews of Maynard Smith's work. We shall examine Lewontin's critique of *Evolution and the Theory of Games* (Maynard Smith, 1982d) for this purpose.

I will first discuss Lewontin's general objections to the adaptationist program and his identification of adaptation with optimization. After that we will see how (and why) ESS passed through the eye of Lewontin's needle. Then we consider one of the fundamental claims of the adaptationist program—to be found as early as 1964: that the aim of optimizers is to demonstrate evolutionary perfection. This, in turn, invites a check on Wilson to see what kind of optimizer he is, and speculation as to why Lewontin himself abandoned optimization theory, after which we will invite Maynard Smith to tell Lewontin that he is wrong about the motivations of optimizers. But Maynard Smith's rebuttal goes unheard, because the same year (1978) and the next are exactly the years of Lewontin's and Gould's anti-adaptationist papers. The high point of the story is the 'Spandrels' talk at the Royal Society and its aftermath.

What is now the adaptationist program? In 1979 Lewontin stated:

> I call that approach to evolutionary studies which assumes without further discussion that all aspects of the morphology, physiology and behavior of organisms are adaptive optimal solutions to problems *the adaptationist program*. It is not a contingent theory of evolution or hypothesis to be tested since adaptation and optimality are *a priori* assumptions. Rather, it is a program of explanation and exemplification in which the purpose is to demonstrate *how* organisms solve problems optimally, not to test *if* they do. In this sense, such studies are much more akin to engineering than they are to physics (Lewontin, 1979a, p. 6).

As we see, Lewontin succeeded in making it sound lightly conspiratorial to regard the organism as an optimizer, although at the same time he admitted that this was a reasonable approach for evolutionary biologists, who in vain had been seeking a formal optimality principle flowing from the kinetic equations of population biology, something like the least energy principle in physics (p. 5).

Later, Lewontin complained that the assumption of optimality had come to permeate evolutionary thinking. Here he included his own game theory approach (1961), where he conceived evolution as a 'game against nature' and tried to determine the optimal strategy for the species; Levins' (1968) 'fitness sets' for the optimal strategy in changing environments; and Maynard Smith's ESS for optimal behavioral strategy when fitness is frequency-dependent (that is, the best strategy is dependent on what strategies other animals employ). (He does not mention Oster and Wilson, 1978.) Lewontin is as hard on himself as he is on others:

> Another attempt to make evolutionary predictions on the cheap was my introduction in 1961 of the apparatus of game theory into evolutionary biology. I had hoped that by drawing analogies—a population to the player, and the population's genetic structure and parameter values to a strategy—the entire apparatus of game theory could be used to make evolutionary predictions. But this attempt foundered on precisely the same rock as optimization theory: there is no guarantee that the actual kinetic process of gene frequency change will carry an evolving population to one of the so-called 'solutions' in the game-theoretic problem. That is, evolutionary equilibria are not necessarily the same as game-theoretic equilibria (Lewontin, 1982a).

Lewontin here admits that his own game-theoretical approach failed for the same reasons as optimization theory: the problem of *correct description of reality*.

At the same time, however, this statement can be interpreted as a priority claim. Lewontin seems to be saying that it was he who introduced game theory into evolutionary biology. This is interesting, because there are other candidates. For instance, in 1996

Hamilton stated that his 1967 paper on unusual sex ratios, the paper he was 'most proud of', among other things involved 'the initiation of game theoretic ideas in evolutionary biology' (Hamilton, 1996, p. 133).[1] Maynard Smith, too, tells us that while visiting the department of theoretical biology at Chicago, he 'decided to spend the visit learning something about the theory of games, with a view to developing Price's idea in a more general form . . . While at Chicago, I developed the formal definition of an evolutionarily stable strategy . . . I also realized the similarity between these ideas and the work of Hamilton (and also MacArthur) on the sex ratio' (Maynard Smith, 1976b/1989, p. 205). (This was the origin of Maynard Smith, 1972, Maynard Smith and Price, 1973, and Maynard Smith, 1974; the visit to Chicago occurred in 1970.)

Judging from this, it appears that Lewontin could, indeed, lay claim to priority. But of course there was a way to give priority legitimately to Britain instead. In his review of *Evolution and the Theory of Games* (1983), Dawkins pointed out the very different conceptions of 'game' in Lewontin's 1961 article and Maynard Smith's book, despite the identical titles.[2] Even better: he could cite Maynard Smith's observation that R. A. Fisher had already used the principle (although not the name) of ESS in at least three different places in *his The Genetical Theory of Natural Selection*! Indeed, 'Fisher himself (1958) explicitly proposed the application of the mathematical theory of games to biology three years before Lewontin did'. After quickly noting 'other pioneers', H. Kalmus and W. D. Hamilton, Dawkins concluded that 'it was not until G. R. Price stimulated Maynard Smith into a vision of the great possibilities of game theory for evolutionary biology that the subject really took off'. Still, as we see from Maynard Smith's statement, and also in Maynard Smith and Price (1973), Hamilton's 1967 paper on the idea of an 'unbeatable sex ratio' as a 'strategy' appears to have been an equally important, even earlier inspiration than Price's.

Returning to our topic, the critique of the adaptationist program, why did the critics consider this program wrong in principle? This was Lewontin's answer in 1979:

> In order for a trait to evolve by natural selection, it is necessary that there be genetic variation in a population for such a trait . . . Not only is the qualitative possibility of adaptive evolution constrained by available genetic variation, but the relative rates of evolution of different characters are proportional to the amount of genetic variance for each. These considerations make both retrospective and prospective statements about adaptive evolution extremely uncertain unless there is evidence about genetic variation . . . Knowledge of the relative amounts of genetic variance for different traits is essential *if evolutionary arguments are to be correct rather than simply plausible* (Lewontin, 1979a, pp. 9–10, italics added).

When it comes to animal populations, prospective studies of additive genetic variance for different traits are possible for animals with different degrees of relationship. But what about knowledge of actual genetic variance of existing human traits? According to Lewontin, 'there is no way in human populations to break the correlation between genetic similarity and environmental similarity, except by randomized adoptions'. But such adoptions do not exist. Ergo, 'we have no way of estimating genetic variances in human populations except for single-gene traits in which environmental variation is trivial, e.g., blood groups' (Lewontin 1979a, pp. 9–10).

In other words, we can never be sure that our adaptationist explanation of a phenomenon is a correct account of the evolutionary process. Neither can we prove that an observed trait of a species is optimal. Of course, Lewontin somewhat sneeringly notes, it is always possible to find a satisfactory fit between the measured traits and a postulated optimal solution, by using a method of 'progressive ad hoc optimization' or 'imaginative reconstruction'. Still, in neither case do we have experimental testability (Lewontin, 1979a, pp. 11–13). And when it comes to retrospective studies, the problem is that 'evolution by natural selection destroys the genetic variation on which it feeds . . . There is no conceivable observation that could disprove the contention of past evolution of the trait.'

Although Lewontin was in general against game theory, he was still favorable toward Maynard Smith's ESS. What were the reasons for that? Finding out why Maynard Smith was acceptable but other game theorists were not can give us a clue to Lewontin's general attitude to optimization theory.

In his review of Maynard Smith's 1982 book he commends the author for 'keeping it clean', that is, keeping the theory totally within the standard kinetic structure of population genetics ('that is the secret to its success') and making 'very explicit what the set of alternatives are that are being considered'. What Maynard Smith does, according to Lewontin, is to cut through the thicket of problems plaguing prediction in population genetics, especially the problem of a 'fitness set' (that is, a genotype may have several different phenotypes) and of frequency-dependent fitness (that is, the phenotype displayed may depend on the phenotype of other organisms). These problems make it difficult to compute the 'average fitness' of the various genotypes in the population, and this computation is basic for theoretical population genetics (Lewontin, 1974a). But the ESS theory faces up to these problems, particularly the fact that 'an animal may sometimes act in one way and sometimes in another, while the fitness value of these actions will depend upon what other animals are doing'. The solution is to concentrate not on individual animals but on the entire pattern of animal behavior. Thus ESS theory attempts to define the pattern among a set of alternative ones that, if established in a population, will be 'evolutionarily stable', that is, resist replacement by an alternative pattern.

In fact, Lewontin makes quite explicit why he approves of ESS, but not of the 'adaptationist programs': ESS makes explicit the alternatives that are being considered, unlike 'vague optimization theories'; ESS can be shown to be a *real* phenomenon in nature, applicable to a wide range of animal behavior; and finally, while ESS predictions are difficult to falsify because of the large standard error involved, they are 'not more unfalsifiable than anything else in population genetics'.

On the other hand—and here Lewontin waves a warning finger even at his friend Maynard Smith—even if ESS has *predictive* power, it does not have *explanatory* power, *post hoc*: 'We simply cannot say that a species is at an ESS because we do not know what set of alternatives were available.' And of course, Lewontin reminds the reader, ESS requires the conditions to be right, so that the mixture of genotypes forming the basis of behavioral phenotypes can indeed stably create an ESS. This is Lewontin in high form. But now Lewontin's critical persona gets the better of him. It would have been better to use a more modest name than ESS, he admonishes Maynard Smith:

> [T]he very words 'Evolutionarily Stable Strategy' have a kind of puffery about them that invites the same sort of over-generalization as the not-so-Fundamental Theorem of Natural Selection. After all, evolution has been going on for three billion years, and if some strategy is evolutionarily stable, why surely that must mean that it is here to stay. The letters ESS now rival DNA as the most fashionable acronym in biology, and we may expect that many vulgarizers both outside and within evolutionary biology will simply not appreciate the contingency of the method. . . . *we are still not free to ignore the material particularities that underlie phenomena.* When all is said and done, 'God is in the details.' (Lewontin, 1982a, italics added)

This very clearly illustrates Lewontin's general scientific attitude, congruent with his main critique of sociobiology: 1) arguments should be correct rather than simply plausible; 2) correctness is more likely to be obtained by the experimental method than any other process; 3) speculation about past evolution can be at the most plausible, never proven; therefore it is not scientifically fruitful; 4) big generalizations are almost sure to be incorrect because of the complexities involved in evolutionary processes; 5) therefore, the most scientifically sound thing to do is to concentrate on prediction, use the experimental method, and ask restricted questions. We also see Lewontin's distaste for unnecessary 'puffery' with words and acronyms (incidentally, shared with Peter Medawar: see, for example, Medawar, 1981b).

Nobody is perfect

Another important aspect of Lewontin's anti-adaptionist program was the allegation that people using optimization theory believed that animals were optimally adapted, or on an 'adaptive peak'. Now at least since 1964 Lewontin had consistently stressed Sewall Wright's point that there could exist multiple adaptive peaks in a population, and that therefore a population need not end up at the absolute optimum:

> So, two populations under *identical* selective forces may climb two different adaptive peaks. This is not '*le meilleur des mondes possibles*' and so natural selection may move the population to a point of maximum that is lower than the greatest possible maximum . . . (the average fitness) may be, but is not necessarily a measure of how successful the population is *as a population* . . . We see, then, that the principle of maximization of fitness must be stated as follows. The population will change its gene frequency in a way that leads the population to *one* of the many local maxima of fitness (Lewontin, 1964, p. 307).

In 1964, however, Lewontin's position on adaptive peaks was connected to his view of the motive force of evolution as a competition between inter- and intrademe selection, that is, between selective forces at different levels (Lewontin, 1964, p. 310). In other words, Lewontin's early opposition to the adaptationist program was based on a commitment to the reality of group selection as a modifier of individual selection. This was not spelled out, however, in his later attacks on the adaptationist program. Instead, Lewontin kept accumulating more arguments as to why this program had serious flaws. To non-testability and 'tautological' selection (later on subsumed under 'allometry') Lewontin added genetic linkage, and pleiotropy (for example, Lewontin, 1979a).

What, then, of Wilson's oh-so-incorrect view of adaptation? Throughout the controversy, Wilson was criticized for neglecting other than adaptive processes. But Wilson *did* discuss adaptation in regard to other forces in great detail. It was all there in *Sociobiology*: linkage, pleiotropy, multiple adaptive peaks, and more. Perhaps the criticism should be understood as a *moral* one: Wilson did not do enough! Wilson ought to have constantly stressed the non-ubiquitousness of adaptation so as not to make the reader draw adaptationist conclusions about human society, too. (This line of reasoning becomes more evident as we follow the development of the anti-adaptationist program.) And what was the evidence that Wilson had some kind of perfection in mind? Wilson stated straight out in *Sociobiology*: 'No organism is ever perfectly adapted' (Wilson, 1975a, p. 144). On the contrary, for Wilson, organisms, including humans, were undergoing constant evolution, in the spirit of Dobzhansky's 'balance' hypothesis.[3] On the other hand, he clearly found the assumption helpful that much of animal behavior could be described by optimization models. *Optimization theory, in fact, provided Wilson's longed-for heuristic for an integrated sociobiology*. In order to be able to develop an integrated sociobiology at all, Wilson needed the heuristic assumption that social behaviors represented evolutionary optima.

Therefore, when Wilson in his text described social behaviors as located on adaptive peaks, this might be interpreted as *implicit argument for the validity of optimization analysis* rather than reflecting deep ontological convictions. But as the controversy proceeded, Wilson became very well aware of the need to demonstrate that optimization analysis really worked. I remember a visit to his lab in the early 1980s when he excitedly pointed to a two-part recent paper (Wilson, 1980c). There ant behavior could indeed be shown to be exactly at the adaptive peak predicted from theoretical models. Wilson regarded this as a triumph, and as a suitable response to Lewontin in particular.

Thus, it was Wilson's goal of mathematical modeling rather than his belief in perfection that informed his statements (and overstatements). Least of all did he have a view of a 'great chain of being' type of human perfection, something which Gould, for instance, seemed to want to pin on him (Gould, 1981c). In interview, Wilson himself also strongly rebutted this kind of allegation.

Wilson thus went on pursuing his initial agenda from the 1960s and continued using optimization theory. It is interesting to note that Lewontin, too, was still an optimizer in the late 1960s. Dawkins unearthed his statement: 'That is one point which I think all evolutionists are agreed upon, that it is virtually impossible to do a better job than an organism is doing in its own environment' (Lewontin, 1967; Dawkins, 1982, p. 30).

What made Lewontin change his mind? A guess is that it was partially his own research that convinced him that all was not well with natural selection as a process which leads to the optimal phenotype in the existing environment. In fact, his own discovery (Lewontin and Hubby, 1966) of unexpected but widespread genetic polymorphisms, first in fruit flies and later in human blood groups, came to stir up the triumphant program of mathematical population genetics. It turned out that the genetic variability in natural populations was much greater than evolutionists had believed possible, basing themselves on the simple assumption of 'mutational equilibria' where a small reservoir of genetic variation was created by mutation and then tested by natural selection. Additionally, sometimes this variability served no obvious function with regard to biological fitness (see, for example, Wilson, 1975a, p. 71; Lewontin, 1972a and 1977a). Of course, in the late 1960s Lewontin also started looking at the social implications of concepts such as optimization and adaptation, and from having been an exclusively scientific critic he now also became a social critic of science.

In any case Lewontin's most basic objections to optimization and the adaptationist program were based on his view that such approaches incorrectly depicted the true nature of reality. For him science had to be as correct as possible, because mistaken scientific theories lent themselves to political abuse. It is in this light that one has to see Lewontin's objection to Wilson's type of human sociobiology. It was not the project *per se* to which Lewontin objected, but the way in which Wilson incorporated various types of fundamental scientific 'errors' into his models.

But Maynard Smith, in his 1978 review article on optimization models in evolution, thought Lewontin was mistaken in his assumption that evolutionists used optimization models in order to demonstrate that organisms optimize.[4] Rather, these models were 'an attempt to understand the diversity of life' (Maynard Smith, 1978b, p. 52). Moreover,

> *The hypothesis of adaptation is not under test.* What is under test is the specific set of
> hypotheses in the particular model . . . I think he is mistaken in supposing that the aim of
> optimization theories is to confirm a general concept of optimization (Maynard Smith,
> 1978b, pp. 39–40, italics added).

And as a response to Lewontin's complaint that adaptive explanations were non-testable, Maynard Smith presented several ways in which functional explanations *could* be tested—including optimization models, 'which sometimes make fairly precise quantitative predictions'. A model could be tested, for instance, by a direct test of its assumptions, or by comparing its predictions with observations, he pointed out. Maynard Smith again reminded readers that we are *not* testing the general proposition that nature optimizes; instead we are testing specific hypotheses about constraints, optimization criteria, and heredity (p. 35). And taking it one step further, he went on to encourage fellow researchers not to give up on their models too early, even when contradicted by observations. Often, the solution is to modify the model by adding hypotheses, he noted (pp. 52–3).

The scoundrels of San Marco: Gould and Lewontin baffle the Royal Society

Adaptation had been made to sound like a sociobiological conspiracy from the very beginning. In their first letter, the Sociobiology Study Group charged that 'for Wilson, what exists is adaptive, what is adaptive is good, therefore what exists is good', and 'It is a deeply conservative politics, not an understanding of modern evolutionary theory that leads one to see the wonderful operation of adaptation in every feature of human social organization' (Allen *et al.*, 1975).

In their 'The Spandrels of San Marco and the Panglossian Paradigm: A Critique of the Adaptationist Programme', Gould and Lewontin (1979) spelled out this allegation in greater detail. According to them, 'the new Panglossians' believed that every trait of an organism, including its behavior, was perfectly adapted. Consequently, in this paper the authors took considerable pains to collect and list the many different reasons why we should *not* assume that the phenotypes we see are perfectly adapted, that is, located at evolutionary optima. In support of their argument Gould and Lewontin brought up such things as allometry, genetic linkage, and pleiotropy, already to be found in earlier papers (such as Lewontin, 1978, 1979a, and even 1976a). What was scientifically new was particularly the idea of developmental constraints with reference to the European-inspired idea of the Bauplan (fundamental patterns of structure in organisms), championed by Rupert Riedl and others. This was the first time that the scientific arguments against sociobiology had been forcefully presented to a predominantly British audience.

The paper was delivered at a two-day Royal Society symposium: 'The Evolution of Adaptation by Natural Selection' in December 1978, arranged by Fellows John Maynard Smith and Robin Holliday. It was also Maynard Smith who had invited Lewontin as a useful critic. No doubt Maynard Smith was keen on having a continued discussion about optimization theory and evolutionary game theory. It would also be useful for his colleagues to hear and react to Lewontin's criticism.[5] But this was not to be. What the audience got, instead of Lewontin debating the fine points of optimization theory, was Stephen J. Gould attacking pan-adaptationism with the help of architecture.

Gould opened his talk with a slide presentation, showing his audience how the four 'spandrels' in the ceiling of the cathedral of San Marco, beautifully adorned with the four evangelists, might indeed make the visitor believe that the purpose of the architecture had been expressly to accommodate the evangelists. (Gould referred to the tapering triangular spaces created in the upper corners when a dome is mounted on arches.) 'But that would invert the proper path of analysis', Gould pointed out. 'The system begins with an architectural constraint: the necessary four spandrels . . . they set the quadripartite symmetry of the dome above' (Gould and Lewontin, 1979, p. 148). So spandrels were byproducts of architecture, they had no function as such; they were just necessary spaces which had later been decorated.

And it was just the same with the Tudor roses and portcullises in the ceiling of King's College chapel, Gould continued: these were cleverly put as ornamentation in open spaces left along the midline of the fan-vaulted ceiling, but they were not necessary parts of the architecture. And now came the charge:

> Anyone who tried to argue that the structure exists because the alternation of rose and
> portcullis makes so much sense in a Tudor chapel would be inviting the same ridicule that

Voltaire heaped on Dr. Pangloss: 'Things cannot be other than they are . . . Everything is made for the best purpose' . . . Yet evolutionary biologists, in their tendency to focus exclusively on immediate adaptation to local conditions, do tend to ignore architectural constraints and perform just such an inversion of explanation' (Gould and Lewontin, 1979, p. 149).[6]

After Candide and Dr Pangloss followed a quick excursion into anthropology—and cannibalism. Here the authors wielded a recent *Science* report as a weapon to criticize E. O. Wilson's acceptance of Aztec cannibalism as a response to protein deficiency.

What, if anything, did all this have to do with adaptation? Gould and Lewontin were obviously using all kinds of analogies from outside science as ammunition for their attack on pan-selectionism, the belief that every part of every organism—and in the case of sociobiology, every behavior—was perfectly adapted. Did they offer any alternative? Yes, they argued for an alternative view of 'pluralism' (attributing such a view to Darwin himself), and for a return of the *organism* to evolutionary theory:

Under the adaptationist programme, the great historic themes of developmental morphology and Bauplan were largely abandoned; for if selection can break any correlation and optimize parts separately, then an organism's integration counts for little. Too often, the adaptationist programme gave us an evolutionary biology of parts and genes, but not of organisms. It assumed that all transitions could occur step by step and underrated the importance of integrated developmental blocks and pervasive constraints of history and architecture. A pluralistic view could put organisms, with all their recalcitrant, yet intelligible, complexity, back into evolutionary biology (Gould and Lewontin, 1979, p. 163).

Now for some background to this paper. How was it that *Lewontin* had been invited but *Gould* showed up? Gould himself explained that Lewontin hated to fly and that he, Gould, wanted to go to England anyway. The scientific ideas were mostly Lewontin's, Gould explained, but the framework was his (Gould's), and it was he who, in fact, ended up writing most of the paper, drawing on discussions with Lewontin. So, it was Gould who singlehandedly invented and delivered spandrels, Candide, and cannibalism. We have this from the horse's mouth (Gould, 1993b).

The Gould–Lewontin paper was the last one presented at the two-day symposium. There were ten papers in all, and one final commentary.[7] Again, there was an unexpected twist of events. The moderator had been Arthur Cain, and it was also he who presented the final comments. But Gould reacted strongly to Cain's words. This is how he explained his emotion: 'Arthur Cain and I are old friends and fellow workers on land snails, but he overstepped the accepted bounds . . . and I got angry'. According to Gould, Cain 'devoted almost his entire time to "Spandrels" and argued, basically, that Lewontin and I had consciously betrayed the norms of science and intellectual decency by *denying something that we knew to be true* (adaptationism) because we so disliked the political implications of an argument (sociobiology) based upon it' (Gould, 1993b, italics added). Gould also noted that the published version of Cain's talk (Cain, 1979) was a 'very tame' version of his oral remarks.

But Cain had every reason to be upset. Here stood Gould in the heart of the Royal

Society in 'a nation with a three-hundred-year-old commitment to adaptation' (as Gould himself had pointed out, 1993b, p. 316), attacking adaptation. Even more pointedly: the Spandrels paper could indeed be seen as a direct attack on *Cain's* particular vision of adaptation, in his famous 1964 paper 'The Perfection of Animals'. (One of that paper's main points is that often features which have been regarded as non-adaptive have later been discovered to be adaptive, after all.) Moreover, Cain had an old score to settle with Lewontin. Lewontin (1972a) had characterized the British interest in naturalism and adaptation as a typically 'genteel' activity. In his response Cain now pointed to his own less-than-genteel background to demonstrate Lewontin's error. But Cain went further, into a discussion of emotional responses vs objective responses, noting that an emotion-based response might be adaptive in the young of the species. Still, a more mature approach required serious consideration of available scientific knowledge as a basis for wise decisions. Cain here appeared to be using an adaptationist argument to 'explain' Gould's and Lewontin's anti-adaptationist behavior!

And it was not only Cain who believed that the Spandrels paper was a politically motivated attack on sociobiology. For instance, Queller (1995) later argued that

> In the case of Spandrels, the context was the attempted intellectual lynching of a young science, sociobiology, which at its most uppity claimed to account for human nature in ways that were distasteful to many, not the least those with Marxist inclinations. The lynching failed and the discipline still thrives, though many sociobiologists have been forced underground, traveling under disciplinary pseudonyms.

So was the Spandrels paper, then, predominantly a critique of sociobiology? Let us see what Gould himself says about his and Lewontin's reasons for writing this paper. In 1993, looking back at this episode, Gould explained that sociobiology was, indeed, an impetus for the Spandrels paper. Still, the paper was not written specifically to attack sociobiology:

> [T]he order of concern must not be inverted. Lewontin and I did not write 'Spandrels' as a *roman à clef* about a greater concern with sociobiology. Wilsonian sociobiology was an important part of the context—and we did not try to hide this concern, what with our early reference to Wilson's support for the adaptive value of Aztec cannibalism, and our later choice of Barash, author of the leading popular text on sociobiology . . . *But sociobiology is only a miniature or microcosm of the larger issue*—one of the grandest themes in all biology, with a pedigree of argument far antedating evolutionary theory itself: *the conflict between functional (adaptationist) and formalist approaches to the interpretation of morphology, physiology, and behavior. We had our eye on these higher stakes* (Gould, 1993b, p. 316, italics added).

Gould gives us a broad historical contextualization for a better understanding of this issue. Within the 150-year history of Darwinism, 'hardliners have seen selection as a nearly exclusive mechanism and have therefore interpreted all but the most trivial or secondary structures as adaptations'. And he goes on to say: 'This is the position that we characterize as the "Panglossian paradigm"—not a statement about abstract perfection or optimality, for no one . . . could be such a foolish Pollyanna'. Gould also tells us that pluralists have in fact allowed adaptation a major role 'but have honored constraints of development and history, and strictures of organic integrity, as coequal in importance, not as bothersome epiphenomena upon the primacy of adaptation' (Gould, 1993b, p. 311).

So, Gould conjures up an image of prevailing pluralism, which was temporarily suppressed when in the 1950s the Modern Synthesis 'hardened' into a belief in the pervasive power of adaptation through natural selection. Ernst Mayr's *Animal Species and Evolution* is now presented as the Bible of the 'hardline' version. Gould offers us the following Mayr statement:

> Every species is the product of a long history of selection and is thus well adapted to the environment in which it lives. There is no doubt that the phenotype as a whole, including its physical properties, is adaptive and is produced by a genotype that is the result of natural selection. This is not contradicted by the fact that an occasional component of the phenotype is adaptively irrelevant (Gould, 1993b, pp. 314–15, quoting Mayr, 1963, p. 60).

In turn, according to Gould, in the 1960s and 1970s, this hardline version met resistance both from 'below' (molecular genetics) and 'above' (paleontology). There was Kimura's theory of neutralism, which suggested that randomness was a factor in evolutionary change, and there were the theories of punctuated equilibria (Eldredge and Gould, 1972; Gould and Eldredge, 1977) and mass extinction (Alvarez *et al.*, 1980), which 'suggested that extrapolation of gradual and imperceptible change through time might not encompass all of evolution at grander scales' (Gould, 1993b, p. 315).

But then, says Gould, just in the middle of all these promising new developments, sociobiology appeared, 'launching its founding document' with Wilson's *Sociobiology*! Sociobiology now '*reasserted the Panglossian form of adaptationism just at a time when much of the excitement in evolutionary theory was breeding departure from this former orthodoxy*' (italics added). Some see sociobiology as a kind of revolution, but it simply does not fit the picture, says Gould. Rather, sociobiology should be seen as 'a *counterreformation* of sorts' (Gould, 1993b, p. 315).

This was an excursion into a broader contextualization of the ambition of Gould and Lewontin, and a refutation of Cain's and others' claims that he and Lewontin attacked adaptationism *in order to* attack sociobiology. I will now turn to Gould's invited response to Cain's comments—and one more memorable performance at this memorable Royal Society meeting. (Gould is usually well prepared for almost any occurrence, and he did not disappoint his audience this time. He had done his homework for an effective *riposte*.)

Gould describes the scene quite dramatically himself. When he stepped forward to reply, he asked Holliday to step aside, which seemed an unusual request. But he wished to point to the motto of the Royal Society. *Nullius in verba*. Now Gould could take a certain pleasure in being able to point out to the assembly that *Nullius in verba* did not at all mean what current members of the Royal Society believed it meant—something along the lines of 'Not by words' (meaning: you have to do the experiment). No, it was in fact a shorthand reference to the beginning of a famous poem by Horace, known to every member of the Royal Society in the seventeenth century and all educated men at the time, Gould told his readers in 1933. That famous beginning reads:

> *Nullius addictus iurare in verba magistri*
> *quo me cumque rapit tempestas, deferor hospes.*

> (I am not bound to swear allegience to the words of any master;
> Where the storm carries me, I go ashore and make myself at home.)

So Gould reports he told the assembly both of the correct translation and the standard mistranslation based on the belief that 'nullius' is nominative, while it is really genitive. More specifically, he 'made the obvious point, directly to Arthur Cain', that his talk (Gould's) 'had merely tried to follow the venerable motto of the sponsoring society —by questioning a dogma and trying to expand the realm of alternatives—and had not been an exercise in political restriction' (Gould, 1993b, pp. 317–18).

One can hardly be more effective than that. Interestingly, Gould in his 1993 retrospective on this incident apparently believed that Maynard Smith had hated his whole performance and had developed some sort of long-term program of punishing him. How else shall we interpret Gould's claim that Maynard Smith 'is still royally put out by "Spandrels" and recently devoted almost an entire article in *The New York Review of Books*, ostensibly on the disparate subject of dinosaurs, to a critique of my views of adaptation' (Gould, 1993b, p. 316; referring to Maynard Smith, 1991). But that was well over a *decade* after the Royal Society symposium! It seems to me that Maynard Smith is not one to hold grudges of this sort. Is it not possible that Maynard Smith, as Gould's anti-adaptationist program progressed, simply *continued* disliking it, and *continued* saying so? (I believe this is the case, and we shall see more examples later.) There is, indeed, an almost moving vulnerability among some of the harshest critics of socio-biology when they themselves feel mistreated (in Chapter 3 we saw Lewontin complaining about Boyce Rensberger, and in Chapter 9, we will meet Steven Rose complaining about Dawkins).

I had not read this particular Gould comment when I talked to Maynard Smith, but I brought up the Royal Society meeting in our discussion for another reason. I had heard from one evolutionist that several of his colleagues had expected there to be something really important in Lewontin and Gould's criticism, something that they would have had to take into account in their work. After seeing the result, they concluded that there was nothing to it, and they could proceed as normal. Maynard Smith, however, thought the whole thing had gone 'rather well', and that Gould's response had been 'rather good'. He remarked that Cain had not been the original choice as commentator; he was replacing Peter Medawar, who at the last minute had been prevented from attending.

Reactions to Spandrels

Did Gould and Lewontin succeed in their criticism of adaptationism? In Gould's own view, they did. According to him, Spandrels did 'provide a focus and a terminology, and thereby helped to coordinate a disparate body of information and ideas' (1993b, p. 331). Moreover, Gould was convinced that the actual success of Spandrels came from its *rhetoric and its humanistic imagery*, which 'caught our colleagues unawares and won attention for "Spandrels"' (p. 333). Scientists are easily taken in by rhetoric, because 'scientists, for the most part, simply do not acknowledge that the form and language of an argument (as opposed to its logic and empirical content) could have anything to do with its effectiveness'. But, 'since good and honorable rhetoric works . . . an addition of an element of surprise—in this case, a surprise never revealed—boosts utility enormously' (p. 323).[8]

The context of this comment should be clear, however. Gould is here responding to the participants in a symposium on the Spandrels paper arranged by students of rhetoric and literary criticism. This resulted in a book (Selzer, 1993) with various textual analyses and a final piece by Gould telling us about the backgound to the paper (it is this I have been quoting from up to now). And these humanists were rather perceptive in their analyses of the various techniques used in the paper. For instance, in 'Intellectual Self-Fashioning: Gould and Lewontin's Representations of the Literature', Gould and Lewontin are seen as trying to '*control the communal memory* and thereby the framework of knowledge' by both their presentation and citation strategies. According to the author, '[i]f Gould and Lewontin can construct the history of evolutionary discourse as a struggle between foolish adaptationism and a wiser pluralism, they can knock the communal underpinnings out from sociobiology, which they consider morally, politically, and intellectually repellent' (Bazerman, 1982, p. 37).

Gould may have believed that the rhetoric worked, but there is of course the question of how the paper was actually read by scientists. Scientists typically read selectively and purposively, focusing on such things as theory, methods, or data; few read whole articles, or from beginning to end (Bazerman, 1988; Charney, 1993). One study of Spandrels showed that experienced scientists typically did not read the paper as a whole from beginning to end—they previewed and they skimmed. So, the fine points of Gould and Lewontin's argument may not have been noticed by such scientists (Charney, 1993, p. 214).

Of course, scientists may have been convinced, nevertheless. What other evidence do we have? Gould made much of the fact that his friend David Raup, ten years later, told him 'we have all been spandrelized'. This Gould took as a sign that his word had now become a term in the language, like 'Kleenex' or 'Jell-O'. Based on this, Gould declared victory. 'When your example becomes both generic and a different part of speech, you have won' (Gould, 1993b, p. 325).[9] Another indicator for Gould was the fact that in 1990 the Spandrels article had become the most cited among all his articles. That year it even superseded his and Eldredge's 1972 article on punctuated equilibria (p. 330). (Meanwhile, Gould lamented that nobody seemed to be interested in the much more time-consuming and painstaking researches he had done on landsnails.)

There is also, of course, the question of how his paper was cited. Citation analysis is an interesting genre and it is by no means clear that citation of a paper means that the paper is actually used as a building block in an article (see, for example, Gilbert, 1977).

One study of a sample of papers citing Spandrels found that many of them actually used the idea of Panglossianism to *distance* their own 'sensible' adaptationist approach from Gould's and Lewontin's caricature (Winsor, 1993). In other words, some of the quotes may be 'routine' quotes, in the style of 'I am not a Panglossian'. Even Gould admitted that some of the references might be of a 'knee-jerk' variety, but argued that even this indicated that the Spandrels paper had become a point of reference for a particular point of view (Gould, 1993b, p. 331).

There is the possibility, too, that rather than convince people of an 'alternative' way, the Spandrels paper actually *fortified* the adaptationist program. Dawkins (1982) is perhaps the best example of how the Spandrels paper may have stimulated general reflection and creative counterargument. His Chapter 3 in *The Extended Phenotype* ('Constraints on Perfection') can be seen as an excruciatingly thorough answer to Gould and Lewontin. Noting that 'history seems to be on the side of the adaptationists' (p. 31), Dawkins presents a dizzying array of rejoinders to the various types of anti-adaptationist criticisms mobilized in the literature up till then. After dismissing three more prominent ones as 'less persuasive', he adds and discusses six more of his own: time lags, historical contraints, available genetic variation, constraints on costs and materials, imperfections at one level due to selection at another level, and mistakes due to environmental unpredictability or 'malevolence' (Dawkins, 1993, pp. 35–54).

Dawkins starts by declaring neutral mutation 'irrelevant' to the argument, because neutralism will have no phenotypic effect (p. 32). The two other dismissed arguments deal with allometry and pleiotropy. Dawkins agrees with Lewontin that the allometric constant is a parameter of embryonic development (large deer have proportionally larger antlers); still, it may be subject to genetic variation and therefore change over evolutionary time. Meanwhile, Dawkins sees no real disagreement with Lewontin's statement that 'many changes in characters are the result of pleiotropic gene action' (1979). Why stop there? Dawkins complicates the issue by suggesting that the phenotypic effect of one mutation may be modified by another; selection, for instance, may favor modifier genes. In fact, Dawkins ends up admonishing Lewontin: 'As in the case of allometry, Lewontin took too static a view on gene action, treating pleiotropy as if it was a property of the gene rather than of the *interaction* between the gene and its (modifiable) embryological context' (p. 35, italics added). Lewontin ignoring interaction? That was not a nice thing to say.

But Dawkins also came to the direct defense of adaptationism. He invoked Cain's 'trenchant and elegant' paper of 1964, which argued for the functional interpretation of purportedly 'ancestral' characters and seemingly 'trivial' ornaments—having one or two bands *did* matter to a particular snail, and a purported 'ornament' in reality turned out to be the pivot of the animal's life (Dawkins, 1982, p. 31). Adaptationism as a *working hypothesis*, 'almost a faith', had inspired many important discoveries over the years, Dawkins observed (p. 31); moreover, adaptationism had stimulated testable hypotheses in physiology (p. 32). So, adaptationism had virtues as well as faults. And, finally, '*[t]here is indeed much more agreement than the polemical tone of recent critiques would suggest*', Dawkins emphasized (italics added). He pointed out that his own criticism of naïve adaptationism had 'much in common with those of Lewontin and Cain, and those of Maynard Smith (1978b), Oster and Wilson (1978), Williams (1966), Curio (1973) and others' (Dawkins, 1982, p. 35).

What other indicators might there be? Queller (1995) suggested that a real test of the effect of the Spandrels paper would be to see if Bauplan explanations had increased after the paper. According to one study, they had not (Winsor, 1993). But there were other signs of increasing interest in constraints on adaptation, whether or not due to the Spandrels paper.[10] Gould himself admits that, even without the Spandrels paper, the 'hardline' version of adaptationism would have been abandoned. Still, he added that '"Spandrels" did provide a focus and a terminology, and thereby helped to coordinate a disparate body of information' (p. 331). He went on to declare that the paper's real measure of success 'must lie in its future utility in advancing fruitful work of a field'. And here he cited his own work stimulated by Spandrels: the coining of the 'missing term' 'exaptation' (a structure now used for a particular role, but in fact developed for another function) (Gould and Vrba, 1982), and his focus on historical contingency as expressed in *Wonderful Life* (1989): 'What happens makes sense but life's history could have cascaded down millions of other equally sensible alternative paths, none (or preciously few) of which would have led to the evolution of self-conscious intelligence' (Gould, 1993b, p. 332).

In one of the studies of Spandrels, scientists were invited to add their own spontaneous comments and reactions to the paper as they read it aloud. This produced interesting remarks (some almost too spontaneous). How did scientists handle, say, the argument about constraints? It turned out that some just dismissed it as 'old news'. One scientist commented that the ideas of developmental morphology and Bauplan had been tried, but abandoned 'simply because they didn't pan out in terms of evidence' (Charney, 1993, p. 221). Another claimed that sophisticated adaptationists in America had always thought about constraints, 'these things were already being talked about as long ago as the early sixties'. This scientist went on to say: 'he's like a knight in shining armor trying to reintroduce, and against everybody else . . . something that he's not aware that everybody else has developed' (Charney, 1993, p. 222).[11] While Gould and Lewontin were seen as trying to strengthen their own arguments and weaken those of the opponents (Winsor, 1993), the counterstrategy of many participants in the symposium was simply 'refusing to accept the division of *us* and *them* that . . . opponents have drawn' (Myers, 1993).

Spandrels' blurring of boundaries between science and literature appears to have worked the other way, too, stimulating evolutionists to exercise their literary talents. Spandrels might have had a liberating effect on the community, because we find two light-hearted pieces in a relatively serious journal (*Quarterly Review of Biology*), one entitled 'The Scandals of San Marco' (Borgia, 1994) and the other, mysteriously called 'The Spaniels of St. Marx' (Queller, 1995). Spaniels? The mystery was cleared up when the author explained that Gould and Lewontin could be likened to dogs listening attentively to their master's voice, the master being Marx. (This was a play on a subheading in the Spandrels paper, 'The Master's Voice Re-Examined', the Master being

Darwin.) Spandrels even inspired new lyrics to Gilbert and Sullivan. Guess who is cast as the Major General:

> I am the very model of a science intellectual,
> I've information lexical, political, and cultural,
> I know the themes of Voltaire, and I quote the sites historical,
> From San Marco to Mexico in order allegorical . . . (Queller, 1995).

An even more esoteric spin-off was probably Gould's 'friendly' architectural debate with Pat Bateson about the ceiling of King's College, Cambridge. The matter was resolved by both of them taking a walk up there and looking for themselves! (A glorious example of *Nullius in verba*—mistranslated version.) At stake was specifically the status of the bosses with roses and portcullis in the openings created by the fan vaults in the middle of the ceiling. Were they necessary, or were they merely decorative, as Gould had argued in the Spandrels paper? Lo and behold, it seemed they had indeed been put in afterward, that is, they were not part of the original structure. At this point Bateson developed a new argument, suggesting that the weight of these hanging decorations may in fact have constituted a needed counterforce to the tensions created by the vaults. Gould, however, rebutted this by referring to other ceilings of other chapels without such extra hanging decorations (Gould, 1993b, p. 334). (Clearly, this dialogue can continue.) Incredibly, the discussion about adaptation was on the verge of turning into a discussion of architecture.

And it did. It took some time until there was an architectural critique of Spandrels. But when it came, it looked like a rather serious blow to the Spandrels argument. Daniel Dennett (1995a) started his critique by pointing out that 'spandrels' was a misnomer: the proper term ought to be 'pendentives'.[12] Worse, Dennett turned the Gould and Lewontin argument upside down, suggesting that spandrels were not necessary at all, but actually *optional*: 'You have to put something there to hold up the dome—some shape or other, you decide which.' Dennett argued that other options, 'brackets' or even 'squinches', might have been chosen instead of pendentives. One of the reasons why pendentives were chosen, according to Dennett, was that they produced a surface ideal for mosaics—and it was these mosaics that were the *raison d'être* for San Marco (according to an authority on the cathedral's mosaics). In other words, the aim of the pendentives *was*, after all, to accommodate evangelists!

But a professor of civil engineering and architecture did not let Dennett get away with this. According to this academic, Dennett did get the point with 'pendentives' right, but he was quite wrong about their being chosen for esthetic reasons. Neither brackets nor squinches would have been able to support such a large and heavy structure. This was something that had already been concluded, without scientific stress analysis, in the sixth century. Since then, pendentives had become the element of choice for large buildings. And since pre-scientific builders usually stuck with proven approaches, it was 'unlikely that the designers of St. Mark's would have considered other systems'. So, concluded this architect, 'Dennett's critique of the architectural basis of the analogy goes . . . astray because he slights the *technical rationale* of the architectural elements in question' (Mark, 1996; italics added). So 'spandrels' again became a *necessity*, not a choice—this time for historically constrained structural reasons. After a rather amazing excursion, the Spandrels argument had now come full circle.[13]

Confessions of a former adaptationist

According to Gould, Cain had 'got the causal pathway backward' when it came to the reasons for his (Gould's) attack on adaptationism. Gould said that he had started having doubts about adaptationism long before sociobiology, but admitted that the publication of Wilson's *Sociobiology* 'helped cement my doubts' (1993b, p. 319):

> I considered the basic argument of sociobiology as flawed, and I was bothered by the political implications of its genetic determinism. One encounters flawed arguments by the score every day. A decision to grant special scrutiny and attention to such an argument may then be influenced by other factors—including dislike of its implications. . . . When I located adaptationism as the central intellectual flaw of sociobiology, I gained more insight into the scope of misuse and came to regard the subject as sufficiently important for attention and ink. . . . In short, I did not attack adaptationism because I disdained sociobiology; I disliked sociobiology because I regarded its central premise as fatally flawed (and regretted the social implications falsely drawn therefrom) (Gould, 1993b, pp. 319–20).

We get more personal thoughts from Gould, including a 'confession'. It turns out that Gould is, in fact, a former adaptationist himself.[14] And, indeed, with a glimpse of self-reflection he says: 'Show me a zealot for the banning of cigarettes . . . and I'll show you a former smoker. . . . The "zeal of the convert" is a cardinal phenomenon of sociobiology and will certainly help explain my own participation in "Spandrels"' (Gould, 1993, p. 318). So, while others converted from group selection to kin selection, Gould instead converted from adaptationism to anti-adaptationism! When did that take place, and how?

Gould did his graduate work at Columbia University from 1963–7 (Gould, 1993b, p. 354). He characterized this as 'the strongest bastion of the hardline synthesis', with Theodosius Dobzhansky, Ernst Mayr, and George Gaylord Simpson—the leaders of the Modern Synthesis—on the faculty. 'I emerged as a philosophically committed adaptationist', he admitted, '. . . hoping to supply the quantitative rigor that adaptationist tales in the "story-telling" mode had lacked.' He explained that his first papers on allometry, 'a traditional bastion of nonadaptationist thinking', were in fact an attempt to 'win these cases for adaptationism'. But now Gould said he was embarrassed to see himself in print with such statements as 'I acknowledge a nearly complete bias for seeking causes framed in terms of adaptation' (this he did in Gould, 1964, p. 588) (Gould, 1993b, p. 318).[15]

What made him change his mind? Gould himself refers to his reading of German evolutionary theory in the preparation for his book *Ontogeny and Phylogeny* (1977a) (Gould, 1993b, p. 319). He also refers to his collaborative work with Tom Schopf, David Raup, and Daniel Simberloff, known among their colleagues as 'the gang of four' for their self-conscious effort 'to buck tradition in paleontology and see how far purely random models could be pushed to encompass the observed order of the fossil record'. They could, to a surprising degree (Raup *et al.*, 1973; Gould *et al.*, 1977). Meanwhile, this apparent order had always been taken as *prima facie* evidence for adaptation. Gould concluded that there was a need for a methodological reassessment of claims for adaptation (Gould, 1993b, p. 319).

But *Ontogeny and Phylogeny* is not a clearly anti-adaptationist book; Gould seems not to have been an anti-adaptationist when he wrote it. Assuming a lag time of a couple of years for a book to get into print, it appears that it was right around the time of the sociobiology controversy that Gould started having his most serious doubts and undergoing his real 'conversion' experience ('The publication of Wilson's *Sociobiology* . . . did help to cement my doubts'). In fact, at a retrospective meeting on the motives for the sociobiology controversy arranged by Science for the People at Harvard in the spring of 1984, Gould stated—turning appreciatively toward Lewontin—that it was, in fact, Lewontin who 'saw much more clearly than me that the issue lay in adaptation; I was trained as an adaptationist'. If that was so, then Lewontin hardly had much opportunity to influence Gould before he himself came to Harvard—not long before the sociobiology controversy.

In any case, according to Gould, when the invitation came to the Royal Society, he 'had come to regard adaptationism as a conceptual impediment to evolutionary biology in several important domains'. Moreover, he believed he 'had a positive alternative to suggest' (Gould, 1993b, p. 320). Gould may have seen the Royal Society occasion as a welcome opportunity to 'synthesize' his own opposition to adaptationism. Until then, he had written on adaptationism only in conjunction with sociobiology in popular journals, mostly shortly before this symposium (for example, Gould, 1976, 1978b, 1978c). In 1978 *Ever Since Darwin* had also been issued in paperback (Gould, 1978d).

The sociobiology controversy as a Trojan horse

Gould felt that he had to resort to a unusual approach in order to break through the resistance from his colleagues, he said in 1993. This was why he deliberately involved esthetics and emotion in the Spandrels presentation.[16] It seems he was rather proud of his achievement:

> We faced a special and unusual sort of problem in gaining attention and understanding for alternatives to adaptation. . . . How can you challenge something if most people simply regard it as true and therefore haven't even conceptualized the possibility of another reading? *You can't initiate this sort of reform from within.*
>
> I didn't think I had a chance of success if I tried to raise the argument head-on by labelling a set of biological structures as potential spandrels. Too many colleagues would have turned off right there—either by putting all their ingenuity to finding a proper adaptationist explanation for the examples, or, much worse, by failing to understand the point because, after all, we know that all well-designed parts of organisms are adaptations; what else could they be? But, by using a 'neutral' architectural example, I could make an end run around these prejudices and compel attention. . . . The Spandrels example worked beautifully (Gould, 1993b, p. 325, italics added).

Of course, there was the problem of how to get to biology from architecture, but Gould explains that for this he used an approach of 'continuity in graded sequences', going first to architecture in nearby Cambridge, then to literature (Dr. Pangloss), then to anthropology (Aztec cannibalism), and finally back home. Gould admitted that the Spandrel paper was, indeed, unusual as a scientific paper, but he defended it as an 'opinion piece'—a third recognized scientific genre in a field like evolutionary biology after data papers and review articles—although not acceptable to most standard journals (Gould, 1993b, p. 321).

Still, for its scientific credibility the Spandrels paper was dependent on references to other papers. But these earlier papers were published in places like *Scientific American*, *Behavioral Science*, and *New Scientist*—which gave them something of 'opinion paper' status themselves rather than constituting serious contributions to the field. The reason these papers generated general interest—and were granted precious journal space—was their connection with the critique of sociobiology and the ongoing controversy. In other words, the adaptationist critique was intimately tied to the critique of socio-biology, which in turn generated publishable opinion papers because of the ongoing controversy. But what if there had existed no controversy? Would the anti-adaptationist approach *then* have been taken seriously? Gould's own explanations of the particular strategy needed to convey the message of the Spandrels paper indicates that it might not.

We have then two scenarios. Some believe that Gould and Lewontin attacked adapta-tionism in order to get at sociobiology. Gould himself declares that anti-adaptationism existed before sociobiology, but was 'cemented' when he found adaptationism to be the root of the problem with sociobiology. But there is a final piece of information that does shed some light on the relationship between anti-adaptationism and sociobiology. I refer again to the spring meeting arranged by Science for the People at Harvard in 1984, with the sociobiology controversy as its main focus. (It was also just around the time of the publication of Lewontin, Rose, and Kamin's book *Not In Our Genes*.) At this meeting Gould explained to the audience 'why we have won the debate' even though 'we made some mistakes'. And how did they win the debate? This is what Gould said at the meeting:

> We opened up the debate by taking a strong position. We took a definitive stand in order to open up the debate to scientific criticism. Until there is some legitimacy for expressing contrary opinions, scientists will shut up. A scientist will reason: 'If I say this, they will accuse me of something unbiological' (Gould, spoken comment in 1984).

What I take Gould to be saying here is that the controversy around Wilson's *Socio-biology* was, in fact, a *vehicle* for the real scientific controversy about adaptation! Far, then, from 'dragging politics into it', or being 'dishonest' as Mayr accused Gould and Lewontin of being, their political involvement would have been instead a *deliberate maneuver* to gain a later hearing for their fundamentally scientific argument about adaptation. What Gould seems to have been saying here is that the scientific con-troversy about adaptation could not have been started without the political controversy about sociobiology. Lewontin at the same meeting observed that 'the brouhaha about sociobiology has had good effect in biology' and 'the debate had helped evolutionary biology'.

What emerges, then, is a sort of *two-step* or *Trojan-horse approach* to breaking down the resistance to a new scientific idea and creating legitimacy. First, draw attention to the new scientific idea by any means; for instance, by making it 'interesting' to scientists through its moral/political connotations. Then, use the newly created interest in the issue to gain journal space. Finally, at the right moment, eliminate the moral/political cocoon, and what emerges is the original argument—in this case anti-adaptationism—which could not have been considered in an unsupported form, because it would have been originally dismissed as too far outside prevailing orthodoxy. (In the meantime, more scientific arguments would have been assembled to lend plausibility to the critique of adaptationism.)

But as we saw, Gould at least believed that the second step, too—the presentation of the real scientific argument hidden within the extrascientific shell—required extra-scientific props, esthetic, moral, and so on, in order to be effective (this was why he mobilized spandrels, Candide, and cannibals). Perhaps what we need, then, is a kind of Russian-doll Trojan-horse approach. (And there may still be more Trojan horses inside, as I shall argue in later chapters.)

So, were Gould and Lewontin some kind of buccaneers, deliberately breaking the rules in order to break into the biological discussion at the time? Or were they defenders of the 'real' truth, fighting the 'counterreformation' of sociobiology by any means? Or were they simply defending their own scientific interests in launching and promoting the anti-adaptationist program? Was the whole sociobiology controversy skillfully engineered by the two pair-hunting raptors, Gould and Lewontin, for the singular purpose of boosting a scientifically vulnerable anti-adaptationist view? On this view, for Gould and Lewontin, the whole political upheaval by the Sociobiology Study Group and its later association with Science for the People would have largely fallen into the odd category of *science by political means*.

For the members of Science for the People, too, the opposition to sociobiology was clearly a focus for organizing the movement. The majority of the opponents to socio-biology were not trained in evolutionary biology and had little idea exactly what the scientific dispute was about. Here they had to trust Gould and Lewontin. What they did know, though—or thought they knew—was that sociobiology in its emphasis on behavioral genes was just as bad as IQ research, at least in its foreseeable social con-sequences. For Science for the People, therefore, the storm around sociobiology was largely *politics by scientific means*.

I do not wish to make too much of the differences between the sub-goals of the different factions within the Sociobiology Study Group. In Chapter 10, I will show that there was no contradiction with regard to the group members' central vision: their moral/political conviction about the ideological nature, scientific untenability, and bad social consequences of sociobiology, and it was this that formed the taken-for-granted bond of solidarity between them.

As we saw, some regarded Wilson himself and the publicity campaign around his book as instrumental in creating controversy. Also, some biologists I interviewed in 1981 believed that 'Wilson wanted to make a splash', which might be interpreted along the same lines. The question is the nature of this 'splash'. Was Wilson, too, doing science by political means? Wilson himself has steadfastly denied knowledge and consideration of political consequences of sociobiology; he says that he wanted to provoke the social sciences into taking biology seriously (see, for example, Wilson, 1991a, 1994). Still, the fact remains that he did put the last chapter into the book at a time when it was still likely to create scandal; the aggression debate around Konrad Lorenz and the critique of the early 1970s' popular books was still fresh in the memory. The immediate scientific aim of a political scandal would, obviously, have been to spread the important message of Wilson's book. So, on this view, just like Gould and Lewontin, Wilson, too, employed a Russian-doll approach. And he also had a second doll inside: there was a moral message within (or coupled to) his scientific socio-biological program.

If both characterizations are valid, we have an extraordinary situation of synergy between the critics of sociobiology and the target himself colluding in creating a highly visible political scandal, each in the hope of having their (widely disparate) *scientific* arguments taken seriously! Do I believe this? Not really. There are still more Russian dolls.

Let us take a sneak preview into the inner one of Gould's Trojan horses, the case of a scientific truth (anti-adaptationism) which contains inside itself a moral/political truth. Gould's charge was not only that evolutionists believed in the best of all possible worlds. Between the lines—and sometimes on the lines—there was a moral charge of a different nature: that the adaptationist program's aim was to demonstrate that nature optimizes. Why were purported adaptationists not simply criticized on scientific grounds, but charged with ridicule and diffuse moral guilt as well?[17] What was their sin? For the critics, the adaptationist program, because it did not consider alternatives, prevented the whole truth from being revealed. In this way, inferences about human society, too, became misleading. Indeed, it seems that often, even though they discussed adaptation in general, the critics had the implications for human society in mind.

Dawkins (1982, p. 50) surely spoke for many when he stated that he considered it 'unfair' to equate modern adaptationism with naïve perfectionism, in the style of Dr Pangloss. This is because, despite the claims of Gould and Lewontin (1979), 'there are many kinds of adaptive, indeed Panglossian, explanations which would be ruled out by the modern adaptationists'. But the argument was never really about science from the point of view of a practicing scientist; adaptationism was primarily interpreted as repre-senting a *metaphysical* belief with dangerous consequences. While many adaptationist researchers used the assumption of adaptation or optimization as a heuristic device, the critics refused to even consider such a possibility. Their opposition to adaptationism was at the same time scientific and moral. 'Vulgar adaptationism' had to be avoided so that 'bad science' would not obscure the truth, and give laymen wrong ideas about every-thing in society being for the best: biological Panglossianism would be easily interpreted as a support for the social status quo as the best of all possible worlds. The following passage beautifully captures Lewontin's anti-adaptationist moral-cum-scientific belief. It is hard to believe he is here talking strictly biology:

> The truth is that evolution has taken and is taking place and that it is often direct natural selection for particular character states that is responsible for differences between species. But it is also true that *some significant fraction of evolutionary change has occurred without creating the best of all possible worlds*. It is true that 'many are called but few are chosen', but it is equally true that 'the race is not to the swift nor the battle to the strong nor yet bread to the wise . . . but time and chance happeneth to them all' (Lewontin, 1981d, italics added).

The question, of course, is how large this 'significant fraction' *is*. Gould, especially, has later taken a variety of positions, sometimes appearing to go much further than Lewontin. It is interesting that Gould should later have become even more of an anti-adaptationist than Lewontin, but that can probably be partly attributed to his more recent 'convert' status. And of course, unlike Lewontin, Gould did have an alternative theory to promote, the theory of punctuated equilibria, to which we will now turn.

Puncturing punctuationism

> I think I can see what is breaking down in evolutionary theory—the strict construction of the modern synthesis with its belief in pervasive adaptation, gradualism and extrapolation by smooth continuity from causes of change in local populations to major trends and transitions in the history of life.
>
> A new and general evolutionary theory will embody this notion of hierarchy and stress a variety of themes either ignored or explicitly rejected by the modern synthesis (Gould, 1980b).

These two quotations from Gould's article in *Paleobiology* formed the backdrop of Maynard Smith's critical articles in the early 1980s concerning the new claims of the so-called punctuativists, republished in his *Did Darwin Get It Right?* (1989). The question was: was a new paradigm really emerging in evolutionary biology, mortally threatening neo-Darwinism? Or was the claim exaggerated, so that, for instance, the purported new paradigm was not really new, not empirically viable, or not a serious alternative to the leading paradigm of evolution by natural selection? This was Maynard Smith's verdict:

> The latest attempt to dethrone Darwinism as the central theory of biology is the 'Punctuationist' theory of Gould, Eldredge and Stanley. It has some positive features, most notably . . . that it emphasizes the role that paleontology can play in evolutionary theory. Nevertheless, I believe it to be largely mistaken . . . There have always been schools critical of Darwin, partly because there is always fame to be won in science by killing the king and partly for . . . ideological reasons (Maynard Smith, 1981a/1989a, p. 123).

Maynard Smith distinguished between two different claims among the punctuativists, the 'minor' and the 'major' claim. The minor, or minimum, claim was the empirical claim that species often showed millions of years of stasis punctuated by relatively brief periods of evolutionary change. These punctuations were seen to involve speciation—the split of a single species into two species. But there was also the major, or maximum, claim, that large-scale change in evolution did not take place according to the Modern Synthesis—that is, through accumulation of changes in populations and geographical speciation—but through some other processes. If true, that claim, going contrary to Darwin's own and contemporary Darwinist belief, would indeed represent a major upheaval in evolutionary thinking. However, Maynard Smith continued, it was perfectly possible to agree with the first part of the punctuationist thesis without having to accept the second. And this was exactly what he proceeded to do himself.

Maynard Smith showed his willingness to accept the minor thesis by quoting a study by Williamson (1981) of the fresh-water molluscs of the Lake Turkana basin in Africa over five million years. This he saw as 'a clear example of stasis and punctuation'. Still, he immediately noted that this study did not support the more radical claim of evolution by some other process than natural selection, because it clearly showed the existence of intermediate populations. Anyway, why should there exist stasis in time, he asked, when there is no stasis in space? Species are not uniform in space, and are often linked by a series of forms, of which the extreme ones may behave like separate species. The simplest explanation of stasis was that it reflected an environment that had remained constant, Maynard Smith concluded (1981b/1989a, p. 152).

What were the alternative processes suggested by the punctuativists, intended to explain the occurrence of stasis? There were basically two. The first was the existence of developmental constraints within each species. The other had to do with the idea of genetic barriers to evolutionary change; according to that, evolutionary change could take place only in small, isolated populations (1983/1989a, p. 142). The punctuativists now upheld these two processes as serious alternatives to the traditional population geneticist explanation for stasis: the idea of 'normalizing selection' (selection that favors the norm and eliminates the extreme phenotypes) (1983/1989a, p. 126).

Maynard Smith said he had no problem with developmental constraints, that is, the idea that the form of a species cannot be easily changed through selection. In fact he had already discussed these things in his first book, published in 1958. H. J. Muller had pointed out that '[t]he organism cannot be considered as infinitely plastic in all directions, since the directions which the effects of mutations can take are, of course, conditioned by the entire development and physiological system resulting from the action of all the other genes already present' (Maynard Smith, 1983/1989a, pp. 142–3). There was no doubt, then, that developmental constraints *existed*; the question was whether they could explain stasis. Maynard Smith believed they could not. 'They limit the *kinds* of change that can occur, but they do not rule out all change' (Maynard Smith, 1983/1989a, p. 142). A further extension of the idea of developmental constraints was that of Bauplan, major patterns of organization. Again, the existence of these were not at issue, Maynard Smith pointed out, but the question was, how did they arise? Darwin had written about 'unity of type', explained by 'unity of descent'—former adaptations were inherited. The alternative, which Maynard Smith believed was mistaken, was any suggestion that there existed laws of form or development which would permit only certain combinations and forbid others (1981b/1989a, p. 156).

What about the argument concerning the existence of genetic barriers to evolutionary change, and that evolutionary change could occur only in small, isolated populations? Maynard Smith noted that although there were no barriers to change in big populations in principle, there was one kind of change that could not take place in big populations: 'the passage from one adaptive peak to another through a selectively inferior intermediate' (1983/1989a, p. 143). In a small population, however, that change could occur. Still, the question was how *important* was this in overall evolutionary change? Here, Maynard Smith noted, we run into a classical disagreement between the founders of population genetics. Sewall Wright thought it was important; Ronald Fisher didn't. 'As a student of Haldane I take an impartial view', Maynard Smith quipped.

However, Maynard Smith's next point makes it less attractive for the punctuativists to claim Wright on their side. He informs us that Wright's model 'in its later form' was really 'a model of phyletic evolution of a *whole species* that, because of its demic structure, is able to cross adaptive valleys that would be impossible to a large panmictic population' (italics added). The model is really about the evolution of species with large numbers, *not* about small populations. The model simply makes an improbable event—the crossing of an adaptive valley (going from one adaptive peak to another through an intermediate of lower fitness)—more likely by dividing a species into a large number of smaller demes, any of which might do the crossing. Plausible or not, the model involves the evolution of a whole species, and thus does not support the punctuativist claim.

Maynard Smith discussed another possibility, however: Ernst Mayr's idea of a 'genetic revolution' happening through genetic drift and the isolation of a small population from the parent species. In this way, a new species might, indeed, arise through a process that might be called 'species selection' (p. 146). Still, Maynard Smith doubted that Mayr believed that these changes that occurred by chance would give rise to a complex new adaptation, since he had elsewhere said that the idea of a systemic mutation in a single step giving rise to a well-adapted individual (Goldschmidt's hopeful monster) was 'equivalent to a belief in miracles' (Maynard Smith, 1981a/1989a, p. 146).

There was no reason to rule out the idea of hopeful monsters a priori, said Maynard Smith. 'It seems certain that gradual changes in genetic constitution can lead to discontinuous changes in phenotype' (1983/1989a, p. 136). But how often were large changes really incorporated and not eliminated? The evidence showed that a difference in some morphological feature between related species was not of this hopeful monster type, but caused by small effects of a number of genes—quite in line with Darwin's conviction that an adaptation required a large number of selective events (1983/1989a, pp. 153, 136).

Species selection is the idea that when a new species arises by splitting, it undergoes change in characteristics, which is not caused by within-population selection. Moreover, the direction of change is random. But because the new species will have different likelihoods of extinction and/or undergoing new speciation, depending on its particular characteristics, the result will be selection between species, which will create trends in species characteristics, explained Maynard Smith (1983/1989a, p. 137). Still, he found it hard to regard species selection as an important evolutionary force. There was the seeming quantitative difficulty of achieving all the independent changes in character states actually observed solely through extinction and speciation events. Another difficulty was the fact that many characteristics affecting survival were related to effects on *individuals*, not species, although he admitted that there might also exist emergent species-level traits, such as capacity to evolve rapidly (influenced by, for instance, sexual selection) and likelihood of speciation (influenced by, for instance, dispersal behavior). Certain conditions needed to be fulfilled, however, for one to be able to call it species selection: 'The concept applies only if new species arise suddenly, with new characteristics, and are at once isolated reproductively from the ancestral species. Only if this is true does the concept have any meaning' (1983/1989a, p. 141).

Maynard Smith additionally observed that the whole idea of species selection came from a *typological* view of species. Just as the laws of physics admit only certain kinds of atom and therefore rule out certain intermediaries in chemistry, equivalent principles in biology might involve such things as developmental constraints and the argument that evolutionary change can take place only in small and isolated populations (1983/1989a, p. 142).

In addition to the real disagreements, however, there were also exaggerations in the debate, Maynard Smith found. He accused the proponents of speaking and writing 'as if the orthodox view is that evolution occurs at a rate which is not only "gradual" but "*uniform*"' (italics added). But, he noted, 'it has never been part of the Modern Synthesis that evolutionary rates are uniform'; G. G. Simpson himself explained that in his *Tempo and Mode in Evolution* (Maynard Smith, 1981a/1989a, p. 151). And Simpson, one of the main architects of the Modern Synthesis, had in fact demonstrated the compatibility between the facts of paleontology and the Modern Synthesis. So was the dispute, then, perhaps purely semantic? According to J. S. Jones, for instance, 'one man's punctuation is another man's gradualism' (Jones, quoted in Maynard Smith 1984a/1989a, p. 126). 'A change taking 50,000 years is sudden to a paleontologist but gradual to a population geneticist', Maynard Smith remarked, and went on to say: 'My guess is that there is not much more to the argument than that. However, the debate shows no signs of going away' (1981a/1989a, p. 151).

Others, too, found the whole thing exaggerated. For instance, there were protests against the 'sensationalist' reporting from the macroevolution conference in Chicago 1980 (Lewin, 1980). And here, interestingly, Lewontin was one of the signers of a letter in *Science* criticizing the dramatic headings and subheadings, 'Evolutionary Theory Under Fire', 'An Historic Conference in Chicago Challenges the Four-Decade Dominance of the Modern Synthesis' (Futuyama *et al.*, 1981).[18] The letter writers accused Lewin of partisan reporting: 'the saltationist view is represented by numerous quotes from Gould, Vrba, and others. But proponents of the synthetic view appear in quotes rarely, and then only as complainers. We never hear them explaining their views.'[19] In general, charged the signatories, the article's advocacy encouraged widespread misunderstanding:

> Lewin's article gives the impression that skepticism concerning these claims was expressed by a minority of the participants. In fact many (perhaps most) of those present remained

skeptical, and the proportion of doubters within evolutionary biology as a whole is almost certainly higher than that seen at the conference (Futuyuma *et al.*, 1981).

Maynard Smith also attended the conference and is quoted as saying: 'You are in danger of preventing understanding by suggesting that there is intellectual antagonism where none exists' (Lewin, 1980). He put his finger on the reason why the punctuativists failed to convince the rest:

> Perhaps the greatest weakness of the punctuationists is their *failure to suggest a plausible alternative mechanism*. The nearest they have come is the hypothesis of 'species selection' . . . In 'species selection' as compared to classical individual selection, the species replaces the individual organism, extinction replaces death, the splitting of species into two replaces birth, and mutation is replaced by punctuational changes at the time of splitting (Maynard Smith, 1981a/1989a, p. 154, italics added).

Although '[s]ome such process must take place', this was a weak force compared to typical Darwinian between-individual selection, Maynard Smith continued. Gould was right to complain of some of the more fanciful adaptive explanations that had been offered; still, 'the residue of genuine adaptive fit between structure and function is orders of magnitude too great to be explained by species selection' (p. 154). Maynard Smith may have spoken for many when after the conference he declared that the punctuationist view represented 'a ripple rather than a revolution' in the history of ideas, and that the attempt to uncouple macroevolution from micro-evolution had failed.

And it was not only Maynard Smith who showed displeasure with the idea of punctuated equilibria in its various versions (Eldredge and Gould, 1972; Gould and Eldredge, 1977; Gould, 1977, 1980 a,b, 1982). Among evolutionists there followed a serious reaction, including criticisms by Mayr (1981), Simpson, (1981), Levinton (1982), Stebbins and Ayala (1986) (and also later Wilson, 1992, 1994). Gould was typically criticized mainly for two things: exaggerating the problem, and restating what others had already said. (However, in the next chapter we will meet a valiant defender of Gould and other advocates of macroevolution, Niles Eldredge.) We will now turn to the other major scientific bone of contention in the sociobiology controversy: the question of the unit of selection.

CHAPTER 7

The unit of selection and the connection with culture

Truth and error in the unit of selection dispute

The sociobiology controversy soon became a forum for the continuing debate about the true unit of selection as well. In this dispute, strongly held convictions made evolutionists very critical of colleagues with different views, and the literature abounded with people accusing each other of scientific 'error'. Let us take a quick tour through this early period of the sociobiology debate. I will start with an overview of some of the most blatant disagreements affecting the sociobiology controversy up to the early 1980s. 'Errors' abound. From the selfish gene perspective, talk about *individual* fitnesses was 'erroneous'. Here we have Dawkins criticizing Richard Alexander in *The Selfish Gene*:

> Alexander's argument . . . erred through looking at things from the point of view of an individual . . . I believe this kind of error is all too easy to make when we use the technical term 'fitness'. This is why I have avoided using the term in this book. There is really only one entity whose point of view matters in evolution, and that entity is the selfish gene (Dawkins, 1976a, p. 147).

Meanwhile, the selfish gene perspective met severe resistance in many quarters, including Harvard's biology department. Ernst Mayr was one of those who put his foot down. For him, what existed was only the genotype, not 'genes'. He was quite vehement about this in my interview with him in 1981. When I dared use the careless expression 'genes' he immediately interrupted me, saying: 'Now you are making a big mistake!' In fact, Mayr was of the opinion that had Dawkins only called his book The Selfish Genotype much of the criticism would have disappeared! Wilson, too, was sensitive about this matter. When, in 1981, I showed him an article (King, 1980) which claimed that sociobiologists thought in terms of the selection of single genes, and asked if this was true for him, he not only told me that the allegation was completely wrong, but added that he 'did not make the same mistake as Dawkins'.

Lewontin, too, was concerned with the reality of genotypes, not genes. According to him, Dawkins had made 'an epistemological error which comes from the lack of understanding of population genetics'.

Lewontin himself, of course, had proposed the genome as the unit of selection (the title of a chapter in his 1974 book), a claim which, in turn, invited criticism from others:

> 'The genome as the unit of selection' is an interesting proposition, but it should never have been stated as a fact. Such a statement is particularly hazardous when we know that detecting the direct effects of natural selection on individual loci is not only possible but has often been accomplished (Clarke, 1974).

Interestingly, in his interview with me seven years later, Wilson defended Lewontin's position as correct at the time. But he pointed out that, since then, the original models of population genetics had been regaining respect—and Lewontin had better pay attention:

> A lot of geneticists around 1970 felt that the standard genetic models were pretty far removed from reality, even if those people still conceded that these were useful in model building. Lewontin correctly stressed this viewpoint in 1974. But since then the evidence has built up considerably by population geneticists working explicitly in this field. It has been found that major genes of the kinds used in the elementary models are common, and that even when you have multiple loci operating to influence the trait, it is frequently the fact, it may usually be the case, that no more than half a dozen loci may be involved. Therefore the original model of population genetics . . . is closer to the mark than may have been thought ten years ago . . . There is rapid progress. On pages 198–99 of our book [*Genes, Mind and Culture*] we deal with this, we mention Lewontin and say: 'However, current research suggests that the problem may not be nearly so formidable as the more naïve arithmetic exercises suggest!' Incidentally, Lewontin in his criticism of our book [Lewontin, 1981a] did not dispute this—*I think he has to come around to this or be separated from his fellow population geneticists* (Wilson, 1981, interview).

Wilson, then, took an intermediate position. While he recognized the reality of linkage and interaction in the genome, he still did not think that the only solution was to consider the whole genome a unit.

How, then, did Dawkins handle such things as interaction and linkage? At first blush, these phenomena might have seemed as a deadly blow to 'picturing genes as hard, discrete units', one critic's description of (what he believed to be) the typical thinking of sociobiologists (King, 1980). No problem! For Dawkins, 'gene' was not a concrete unit, it was an abstract *concept*. 'Gene' actually meant 'genetic replicator' or 'replicator'. (This became clearer with his next book, *The Extended Phenotype*, 1982; see, for example, p. 85). Therefore, *any portion of the chromosome could be regarded as a potential candidate for 'replicator'* (Dawkins, 1982, p. 87, italics added). It was a purely practical matter how large or how small a portion of the chromosome it would be useful to consider in any particular case:

> Natural selection is the process by which replicators change in frequency in the population relative to their alleles. If the replicator under consideration is so large that it is probably unique, it cannot be said to have a 'frequency' to change. We must choose our arbitrary portion of chromosome so that it is small enough to last, at least potentially, for many generations before being split by crossing-over; small enough to have a 'frequency' that is changed by natural selection (Dawkins, 1982, p. 89).

In this scenario, then, if the linkage ('linkage disequilibrium') was strong, it simply meant that a larger chunk of the genome would have to be considered (p. 89).

Indeed, the reactions to *The Selfish Gene* had made Dawkins particularly concerned to emphasize the purely *logical* nature of a 'replicator'. For him, the basic question that needed answering was: 'What qualities should we require in a successful replicator?' His answer was the French Revolution-type slogan 'Longevity, Fecundity, Fidelity'. Replicators needed to be able to last long enough to produce additional replicators which retained their structure largely intact (Dawkins, 1982, p. 84).

The logical nature of the replicator also meant that Dawkins had no difficulty replying to various molecular biologists who had registered protest with his view of 'the gene'. One of the most vehement was Gunther Stent, who called Dawkins' 1976 definition of the gene 'a heinous terminological sin' (Stent, 1977). (Stent was really arguing with George Williams, who had first introduced the conceptual notion of a gene similar to Dawkins' in his 1966 book.) In Stent's view, a gene was 'unambiguously' that unit of genetic material which encoded the amino acid sequence of a particular protein (a cistron). To this kind of terminological 'monopoly', the philosopher of biology David Hull perceptively remarked: 'Memory is short. Mendelian geneticists raised exactly the same objections to the perverse redefinitions of the gene being urged upon them a generation ago by such molecular biologists as Stent' (Hull, 1981a/1984 p. 157). Indeed, the development of terminology was quite rapid—for instance, a few years later it seemed that the names 'gene' and 'allele' had lost their meaning (Lewin, 1981b). It was also noted that 'geneticists continue to employ different definitions of the gene for different purposes' (Keeton, 1980).

And it did not take long until the selfish gene itself—or rather, selfish DNA—entered the terminology in molecular biology (Orgel and Crick, 1980; Doolittle and Sapienza, 1980). In *The Selfish Gene* Dawkins had discussed the phenomenon of 'surplus DNA', the large part of DNA that is never translated into protein. The general mystery had been what this seemingly non-functional DNA was doing. Dawkins had suggested that since, from the selfish gene perspective, DNA's 'purpose' was simply to survive, it didn't have to be 'doing' anything: the simplest way to explain surplus DNA was to suggest that it was merely 'hitching a ride in the survival machines created by the other DNA' (Dawkins, 1976a, p. 47).

What, then, of the individual organism? Gould was one of the first to point out what he considered to be Dawkins' serious mistake (Gould, 1977b). He pointed out that in Darwinism the *individual* is the unit of selection: the struggle for existence is between individuals. But he also noted that during the last fifteen years this notion had been challenged 'from above' and 'from below': on the one hand by Wynne-Edwards' idea of group selection, and on the other by Dawkins' claim that the genes were the true units of selection, and individuals merely their temporary receptacles. But, protested Gould, selection cannot 'see' genes, it can only see individual bodies!

But Dawkins had the answer ready. Again, he characterized the dispute as philosophical, not factual. He, Dawkins, was addressing the fundamental question of what we ought to mean when we talk about a unit of natural selection. Should we mean a 'vehicle' such as an individual body? Or should we mean a 'replicator'—something of which copies are made? Again, because this was a *philosophical* question, not a *factual* one, for him, the unit of selection dispute was not about what was the 'real' unit of selection in a hierarchy going from gene to organism and to higher level units. He was interested in a philosophical discussion about the characteristics required of anything that was to *count* as a unit (and here his position was that the unit had also to be able to function as a replicator). However, he recognized that, at the same time, there was, indeed, another, factual dispute going on about the actual *vehicles* for these replicators. That dispute concerned the question as to whether these vehicles were organisms, or groups of organisms. But that was not the debate he was himself engaged in, Dawkins emphasized (Dawkins, 1982, p. 82).

Dawkins further noted that the replicator's survival interest often did coincide with the organism's. Still, the replicator's survival might equally be dependent on *other* bodies containing copies of itself. For this purpose Dawkins formulated the new way of looking at this, 'the gene's eye view' (or rather, 'replicator's eye view') as follows:

> A replicator may be said to benefit from anything that increases the number of its descendant ('germ-line') copies. To the extent that active germ-line replicators benefit from the survival of the bodies in which they sit, we may expect to see adaptations that can be interpreted as for bodily survival. A large number of adaptations are of this type. To the extent that active germ-line replicators benefit from the survival of bodies other than those in which they sit, we may expect to see 'altruism', parental care, etc. To the extent that active germ-line replicators benefit from the survival of the group of the individuals in which they sit, over and above the two effects just mentioned, we may expect to see adaptations for the preservation of the group. But all these adaptations will exist, fundamentally, through differential replicator survival. The basic beneficiary of any adaptation is the active germ-line replicator, the optimon (Dawkins, 1982, pp. 84–5).

So, from a logical point of view, Dawkins may have solved the problem to his own and many others' satisfaction. But many of his colleagues were primarily interested in the real world, not in philosophical questions. A 'realist' reading of Dawkins obviously quickly led to misunderstandings of Dawkins' true position. For instance, Mayr, Wilson, Lewontin, and Gould were all opposed to thinking of the gene as the unit of selection. They probably believed that Dawkins had in mind a physical gene.

What did Dawkins have to say to Gould's point that selection acts on bodies, not directly on genes? This is what Gould had written:

> Selection cannot see genes and pick among them directly. It must use bodies as an intermediary. A gene is a bit of DNA hidden within a cell. Selection views bodies. . . . If, in favoring a stronger body, selection acted directly upon a gene for strength, then Dawkins might be vindicated. [But] bodies cannot be atomized into parts, each constructed by an individual gene. Hundreds of genes contribute to the building of most body parts and their action is channeled through a kaleidoscopic series of environmental influences: embryonic and postnatal, internal and external (Gould, 1977b, quoted in Dawkins 1982, p. 116).

Dawkins' response was that Gould was making a mistake: he failed to distinguish genetics from embryology.

> The argument . . . is a valid argument against particulate embryology and in favour of blending embryology . . . Genes do indeed blend, as far as their effects on developing phenotypes are concerned. But, as I have already emphasized sufficiently, *they do not blend as they replicate and recombine down the generations* (Dawkins, 1982, p. 117, italics added).

Thus, Dawkins said he had due appreciation for embryology, but that was not what the selfish gene approach was about. One field in biology was the study of development, another was the study of natural selection. This is also what he told one of his etho-logical colleagues, Patrick Bateson, a specialist on development. Bateson had early on worried that Dawkins was 'giving special status back to the gene as a programmer' (Bateson, 1978). Dawkins dismissed this as simply a misunderstanding between embryology and evolution:

> An embryologist rightly sees no fundamental distinction between genetic and environmental causal factors, and he correctly regards each as necessary but not sufficient. Bateson was putting the embryologist's point of view . . . But I was not talking about embryology . . . I was talking about replicators surviving in evolutionary time (p. 99).

(As it turns out, however, the matter went beyond a mere misunderstanding; see for example, Bateson, 1986.)

Gould had also criticized Dawkins in another way: Dawkins' description did not correspond to known facts. According to Gould, Dawkins' view of 'individual genes plotting the course of their own survival bears little relationship to developmental genetics as we understand it'. Therefore, in order to satisfy the reality criterion, Dawkins would have to use another metaphor of 'genes caucusing, forming alliances . . . gauging environments'. But, said Gould, 'when you amalgamate so many genes and tie them together in hierarchical chains of action mediated by environments, we call the resulting object a *body*' (Gould, 1977b, italics added).

At first blush, that may have sounded like a blow to the selfish gene idea. But Dawkins responded by agreeing. He said he just wanted to put the matter more subtly than Gould: 'Selection favours those genes which succeed *in the presence of other genes, which in turn succeed in the presence of them.* Therefore mutually compatible genes arise in gene pools. This is more subtle and more useful than to say that "we call the resultant object a body"' (1982, p. 117). In other words, Dawkins' philosophical selfish gene approach could easily accommodate this type of criticism, too. In fact, Dawkins ended his second book with a chapter called 'Rediscovering the Organism'. He described a multicellular organism as 'a phenomenon which has emerged as a result of natural selection on primitively independent selfish replicators. It has paid replicators to behave gregari-ously' (Dawkins, 1982, p. 264). Meanwhile, '*[t]o regard an organism as a replicator . . . is tantamount to a violation of the "central dogma" of the non-inheritance of acquired characteristics.*' Anything that happens to a body but not its genome is not passed on to the next generation (p. 97, italics added).

So here we have it: Gould accusing Dawkins of lack of realism, and Dawkins accusing Gould of deviating from the straight and narrow path of Darwinian logic. This was only to be the opening of more than two decades of surprisingly predictable exchange between these two evolutionary biologists.

Obviously we are not yet through with the dispute over unit of selection. Typically, those who had adopted 'selfish gene' thinking tended to discard *group selection* as an 'error' or to consider it disproven (for example Krebs and Davies, 1978, p. 8; Dawkins, 1976a, p. 2; Daly and Wilson, 1980, p. 326). But those who emphasized gene selectionist thinking were opposed by some biologists who considered group selection a reality. And here we had not only Wynne-Edwards, who persisted in his own views, but also such people as Michael Wade (1978) who suggested that kin selection could be subsumed under group selection, and most vehement of all, David Sloan Wilson.

D. S. Wilson is described in a 1996 *New York Times* profile as someone who in the late 1960s walked into George Williams' office and told him that he would persuade him about group selection (Berreby, 1996). He didn't succeed. Williams, of course, had just published his famous book *Adaptation and Natural Selection*, advocating that no higher level of selection ought to be invoked than was necessary. In practice, this was seen as a critique of group selection, and many drew inspiration from this book for a 'gene's eye's view'. In 1971 Williams edited *Group Selection*, a collection of recent contributions and polemics on this matter. However, D. S. Wilson's 1980 book seemed to give new hope to those who were still holding out for group selection despite Williams' and Maynard Smith's (1964, 1976a) demolition attempts. Wynne-Edwards in particular got a new boost from Wilson's work (interview in 1981). But when I presented D. S. Wilson's 1981 challenge to Maynard Smith, he dismissed D. S. Wilson's models of 'trait group' selection as not 'true' group selection and as actually describing a type of individual selection (interview in 1981).

In 1983, Maynard Smith tried to sort out the confusion that had arisen because of the dual use of group selection. 'Evolution by natural selection requires that there be entities with the properties of multiplication, variation, and heredity. Given these properties, entities will evolve characteristics ensuring their survival and reproduction ("adaptations"). Individual organisms have these properties. Wynne-Edwards proposed that groups of organisms might also have them, and hence might acquire adaptations ensuring group survival (for example, epideictic displays).' And it was just this type of group selection that he and others had criticized as unlikely. On the other hand, D. S. Wilson's groups were not reproductively isolated, like Wynne-Edwards' groups. Maynard Smith's suggestion was to stop the confusion by dropping the term 'group selection' and use instead 'interdemic' and 'species' selection for the Wynne-Edwards type of group selection (Maynard Smith, 1984b).

But there were those who did consider ('true') group selection a real phenomenon at a time when many had abandoned the idea. One of these was E. O. Wilson, and he told me so in interview. It is not hard to guess at least one source of Wilson's group selection interest: his 'mentor' W. M. Wheeler, a believer in Kropotkin's idea of mutual aid. Lewontin, meanwhile, told me in interview that he believed group selection was possible, but unlikely. Lewontin had himself been a group selectionist—his and Dunn's 1960 research on *t*-alleles in mice was considered one of the few cases of real group selection in nature—he had now come to accept the mounting criticism. But Dick Levins, just like Wilson, told me he did believe in group selection as a real phenomenon in nature. With Wynne-Edwards' strong vision of a connection between group selection and moral values (interview, 1981) and Levins admitting to me that there was, indeed, something politically appealing in group selection, it is hard to get away from the suggestion that some kind of *moral interest* was driving group selectionists—particularly those who persisted even in the face of the new, fashionable, kin selection paradigm.

For Wilson, altruism was the central problem of sociobiology, and kin selection and group selection represented but two of many alternative models for the evolution of altruism in *Sociobiology* Chapter 5. For Dawkins, however, Wilson's classification of kin selection as a type of group selection was an error, something to be counted among his 'Twelve Misunderstandings of Kin Selection' (Dawkins, 1979b; see also Dawkins, 1976a, p. 146). But Wilson never bought into kin selection in a wholehearted way. Although in his first chapter he wrote about the morality of the gene, he did not in fact systematically adopt a gene's eye's perspective in *Sociobiology*. On the contrary, unlike Hamilton and Dawkins who were taking it as their basis, Wilson in fact criticized George Williams' single gene selection model, at the same time as he criticized Wynne-Edwards' group selection model (1975a, p. 110, p. 30). Wilson, then, positioned himself somewhere in the middle of a hypothetical hierarchy of units of selection, just as Gould did in his 1977 critique of Dawkins (cf. Dawkins, 1982, p. 82).

Finally, let us bring in Hamilton. It turns out that he was not interested in making such a sharp distinction between kin and group selection as, for instance, Maynard Smith, or Dawkins. In 1975, Hamilton employed Price's general covariance formulae and derived again his model of inclusive fitness, now in a more 'elegant' form. He concluded that the model for positive selection of altruism $(FK - k) > 0$ was general and independent of group size; the important point was that the benefits of altruism should fall on individuals more likely to be altruists than random members of the population. In general, Hamilton wanted to point out that *'inclusive fitness' was a much more general concept than 'group selection', 'kin selection', or 'reciprocal altruism'*; this meant that it could be used even in cases of ungrouped, 'viscous' populations (1975/1996, pp. 336–7).

Unfortunately, there existed some typical misunderstandings of the concept of inclusive fitness, Hamilton continued. One was the identification of inclusive fitness with kin selection, which was then presented as an alternative to 'group selection' as a way for altruistic behavior to evolve by natural selection. (He traced this interpretation to the way Maynard Smith had originally explained the concept in 1964.) But, Hamilton pointed out, kinship is only *one* way of getting the benefits of altruism to fall on individuals who are likely to be altruists. The altruists can be true relatives, but they do not have to be. Altruists may settle with altruists because they have never parted (an individual's neighbors tend to be his kin) or because they recognize fellow altruists, or because of some pleiotropic effect of the gene on habitat preference. In conclusion:

> [I]t seems on the whole preferable to retain a more flexible use of terms; to use group selection where groups are clearly in evidence and to qualify with the mention of 'kin' (as in the 'kin-group' selection mentioned by Brown), 'relatedness' or 'low migration '. . . or else, 'assortation' as appropriate (Hamilton, 1975/1996, p. 337).

It appears, then, that Hamilton's own definition was in fact so general as to actually encompass not only group selection, kin selection, and reciprocal altruism, but also 'trait group' selection *à la* D. S. Wilson. Also—on second thought—was E. O. Wilson's Chapter 5 in *Sociobiology* perhaps not a 'misunderstanding' at all, but on the contrary, an intuitive *understanding* of the actual meaning of 'inclusive fitness'?

Harvard holism vs British beanbag genetics

The general division between those who accepted thinking in terms of single genes and those who did not appears to have to do largely with the scientific tradition in which they operated. In principle one can perceive a division between a *Harvard 'holist' tradition* with Mayr, Lewontin, Levins, Gould, and Wilson against the *'beanbag* genetics' tradition inspired by Fisher in Britain, represented by Maynard Smith, Dawkins, and others. And one thing which united the Harvard 'holists' in the sociobiology controversy was their common view that Dawkins' views were in error.

The reason for that, again, was an ontological commitment they all shared, to the reality of 'the unity of the genotype', Mayr's famous formulation of 1963. In 1975, Mayr stated this view as follows:

> Free variability is found only in a limited portion of the genotype. *Most genes are tied together into balanced complexes that resist change.* The fitness of genes tied up in these complexes is determined far more by the fitness of the complex as a whole than by any functional qualities of individual genes (Mayr, 1975, in Mayr, 1984, p. 71, italics added).

According to Mayr, now putting on the hat of the historian of science, there have been various swings of the pendulum between two extreme attitudes to the genotype. The pre-Mendelian breeders were blinded by the idea of the essence of a species as an indivisible whole; for them, asking questions about individual genetic factors made no sense. But after the rediscovery of Mendel, the pendulum swung to the other extreme, toward an entirely atomistic approach, where each gene was treated as if it were totally independent of other genes. Despite the subsequent discovery of such phenomena as linkage, epistasis, pleiotropy, and polygeny, Mayr complained, 'only lip service was paid to these complications. Evolution, as recently as the 1950's, was defined as a change in gene frequencies; the replacement of one allele by another; thus it was treated as a purely additive phenomenon' (1975/1984, p. 70). Why was there resistance? According to Mayr, people wanted to avoid 'the stultifying concept of holism', and thought that emphasis on gene interaction would make 'meaningful analysis' impossible. On the other hand, Mayr continued, a small minority of authors did stress the integration of the genotype, for example, Chetverikov (1926), with his concept of the 'genetic milieu'. Mayr singles out 1954 as the year 'signaling a new interest in the interactions of the genotype', with a book by Lerner (1954) and an article by Mayr (1954) (Mayr, 1975/1984, pp. 70–1).

Apparently, Mayr in 1975 was envisioning the beginning of a new era, The Era of the Genotype. What he got instead was the opposite: a new surge of 'beanbag genetics' with

Dawkins' *The Selfish Gene*. In fact, he ended his 1975 article with a summary which looks very similar to the position that Gould and Lewontin later took in their struggle against Dawkins particularly, and which also indicates the origin of the later disputes about speciation and macroevolution. It is probably fair to regard Gould and Lewontin as 'executors' of Mayr's profound objections to gene selectionism—pun intended. Here is Mayr's summary:

> The genes are not the units of evolution, nor are they, as such, the targets of natural selection. Rather, genes are tied together in balanced adaptive complexes, the integrity of which is favored by natural selection. . . .
>   It is important to understand this cohesion of the genotype, because it permits the explanation of many previously puzzling phenomena of speciation and macroevolution (Mayr, 1975/1984, p. 82).

Where did Mayr get his views from, and what was the connection between Mayr and Gould and Lewontin? Why did they share this kind of holistic view, unusual among American evolutionists at the time? In his conception of interaction and integration, Mayr represented the fiercely anti-atomistic Continental tradition in biology (with Hegelian overtones), and it would not be surprising if he imparted this view of biology to his student Stephen J. Gould, too. Gould's view may have been additionally fortified with a Marxist philosophical orientation, but this was certainly true of Lewontin, who had learnt his dialectical approach from the truly holistic Richard Levins, and Lewontin later tutored Gould, at least in regard to criticism of adaptationism. Mayr's way of thinking seems to have fitted Lewontin as hand in glove; his 1974 'the genome as the unit of selection' was an extension of Mayr's thesis of 'the unity of the genotype'. We can now see a good reason why Mayr helped Wilson get Lewontin to Harvard from Chicago. Perhaps he hoped, just like Wilson, to collaborate with Lewontin; at the very least, he may have wished to gather the scattered holists in one place. (Sure enough, Levins was later brought in, too.)

Among his Harvard colleagues, Wilson could best be called a 'pragmatic holist'. As we saw in Chapter 3, he had redefined his holistic interests in the language of genetic reductionism. For his moral-cum-scientific program to work, he was dependent on available predictive models based on frequencies of single genes. As we saw, he had also come to believe that new findings supported the viability of single gene models. Lewontin and Mayr, on the other hand, were more skeptical. In interviews, it turned out that they did not find the new evidence as compelling as Wilson. (Of course, unlike Wilson, they were not dependent on these models and could perhaps afford a more critical stance.)

What, then, was Dawkins' response to criticisms of gene selectionism coming from the champions of the unity of the genotype? Mayr was certainly sticking by his original position. Sewall Wright, in his nineties, had in 1980 published an article in *Evolution*, 'On Genic and Organismic Selection' which was widely regarded as repudiating gene selection. (For instance, Gould later invoked Wright's article against selfish genery.) But Dawkins said he found no disagreement at all with those of the Old Guard who had criticized him. On the contrary, Dawkins claimed he was only presenting 'a truer and clearer expression' of Mayr and Wrights's own views (Dawkins, 1982, p. 238)! He was *not* advocating a naively atomistic and reductionistic view of 'genic selection'—that was a sheer straw man. Because, said Dawkins,

> if genes are correctly understood as being selected *for their capacity to cooperate*, we arrive at a theory of genic selection which Wright and Mayr will recognize as fully compatible with their own views (Dawkins, 1982, p. 239).

What is more, Dawkins had found an apparently devastating quote from Peter Medawar, who once characterized Sewall Wright as 'a principal innovator' when it came to 'the new conception that a population that was deemed to undergo evolution could be best thought of as a population of fundamental replicating units—of genes— rather than as a population of individual animals or of cells' (Medawar, 1981a; in Dawkins, 1982, p. 239). In this scenario, then, Sewall Wright, upheld by the critics against gene selectionism, would be a gene selectionist himself.

I will bring in Maynard Smith to sort things out. In his review of Ernst Mayr's *The Growth of Biological Thought* (1982), he observed that Mayr, although he recognized the contributions of the mathematical geneticists who showed the compatibility between Darwinism and Mendelian inheritance, missed the important role that mathematics later played when it came to analyzing social behavior. And, according to Maynard Smith, 'natural history without mathematics is muddled'. He went on:

> The issue is best illustrated by Mayr's attitude to what he has called 'beanbag genetics'. . . . Mayr objects that selection acts on individuals, not on genes, and that individuals are the product not of one gene, but of complex sets of 'co-adapted' genes. This seems to me both true and largely irrelevant. A particular gene will increase in frequency, or not, depending on the effects it has on individual fitness, against the background of all the other genes present and the environments experienced. It has to be a good 'mixer'. . . .
>
> There are, however, two points of view, which one could almost call the 'English' view, deriving from Fisher, and the 'American' view, deriving from Wright. To oversimplify matters somewhat, Fisher thought that each substitution of one gene for another in evolution occurred because it was beneficial, on its own, and that the role of chance events (other than mutation) was slight. Wright thinks that, often, several gene substitutions would be beneficial if they occurred simultaneously, but that each by itself would be harmful. If so, the only way the change can take place is by chance in a small, local population. *In effect, the English think that evolution is a hill-climbing process, and the Americans that it also involves jumping across valleys.*
>
> As a student of Haldane's, I take an impartial view. However, both views are essentially reductionist, and both were first formulated mathematically. There *is* only beanbag genetics (Maynard Smith, 1982g/1989a, p. 11).

Of course, this is not the way the holists viewed things at all. We will continue to follow their different attempts to emphasize the existence of *other* than gene-selectionist processes in evolution, including the presence of constraints on natural selection. Here Gould had emerged as the activist, arguing much along the lines of his teacher Ernst Mayr, and supported by his buddy from graduate school, Niles Eldredge at the Museum of Natural History in New York. Meanwhile, the British side could be seen as fortifying its position with books such as Dawkins' *Climbing Mount Improbable* (1996), demonstrating just how adaptation by natural selection could work over time to achieve apparently surprising results. Yet how much was the matter a question of emphasis, how much one of a genuine clash of convictions about evolution? And what about those British evolutionists who had never subscribed to a strictly genetic explanation but from the beginning had taken a 'holistic', or at least complex, view—I have here in mind particularly many ethologists? We saw the ethologists' protest in the last chapter. The protest continues throughout this book (see especially Chapter 16).

Over time, however, there has been more appreciation of the possibility of constraints among the purported beanbag geneticists. Maynard Smith later discussed constraints in several articles (for example, Maynard Smith, 1986a; Maynard Smith *et al.*, 1987). Also Dawkins' (1989b) concept of 'the evolution of evolvability' can be seen as one step toward recognizing constraints (see Chapter 16).

We will now move to an ontological *cri de coeur* about gene selectionism, and how it misrepresents the 'true' evolutionary process, perceived to be a multi-level one. The protester is Niles Eldredge, Gould's 'brother' and fellow graduate student (Gould, 1995).

The levels of selection: an ontological protest

How true is the depiction of the gene as the unit of selection? Dawkins' 'selfish gene' approach particularly bothered those who believed that the complexity of the evolutionary process was best characterized by a nested hierarchy of levels of selection, an idea elaborated particularly by Niles Eldredge in his *The Unfinished Synthesis* (1985). The idea of multi-level selection as such was not new; it had been discussed already by Lewontin (1970b), for instance. Wilson, too, in his group selection chapter in *Sociobiology*, emphasized the different levels at which selection can take place.

But with whom exactly was Eldredge arguing, considering that even Dawkins, in his second book, *The Extended Phenotype*, *acknowledged* the idea of a nested hierarchy? According to Dawkins, 'there is a hierarchy of entities embedded in larger entities, and in theory the concept of vehicle might be applied to any level of the hierarchy' (1982, p. 112).[1] Dawkins also admitted that '[n]atural selection will . . . at least to some extent, favour replicators that cause their vehicles to resist being destroyed. In principle this could apply to groups of organisms as well as to single organisms . . .' (p. 114). He even discussed what it would mean to have 'reproduction' at the group and higher levels (ibid.).

Obviously, the problem did not really concern hierarchies, if even Dawkins recognized the existence of an evolutionary hierarchy. What, then, was all this about? The point is that when Dawkins talked about the unit of selection, he was not interested in vehicles, only in replicators. Dawkins' chief concern was *proper explanation*. He saw himself as self-consciously advocating a 'neo-Weissmannist view of life', with the genetic replicator as the basic unit of explanation (1982, p. 113). In fact, he explicitly said that his main purpose was 'to draw attention to the weakness of the whole vehicle concept, whether the vehicle is an individual organism or a group' (Dawkins, 1982, p. 114).

For Niles Eldredge, too, it was *vehicles* that mattered. Although he said he found it 'difficult to disagree with much of what Dawkins says' in discussing replicators, vehicles and a nested hierarchy, Eldredge pointed out that the emphasis on replicators 'leads us to throw out the baby with the bathwater' (1985, p. 6). Eldredge declared that he, in contrast to Dawkins, found the vehicle concept 'far more compelling'. Dawkins was concerned with *replication fidelity*, and this decreases as we go up the scale of entities. But if one focuses on another vital aspect of the entities, their *longevity* or permanence, the inverse is true, he pointed out. Longevity increases: genes live shorter lives than demes, and, in turn, species are shorter lived than monophyletic taxa of higher rank (Eldredge, 1985, p. 7).

Eldredge went on to argue that species were in fact repositories of information:

> It is the survival of that *information* (instructions for products; information about the environment in the broadest sense) that the evolutionary game seems to be all about, at least from a genealogical perspective. *Species might simply be stable entities, packages of information,* maintained albeit in a more dilute form (but for longer periods of time) than in exact replicants (p. 7, italics added).

And here Eldredge noted that both Williams and Dawkins 'for all their talk of the potential immortality of genes, have always quietly acknowledged that it is the information, not the genes themselves, that is potentially immortal' (ibid.).

Eldredge envisioned a nested hierarchy where all of the different entities did in fact reproduce but in a different way from Dawkins' replicators.[2] 'They do not necessarily make more of *themselves*; they make additional entities of *like* kind, the sine qua non for a genealogical hierarchy. Ascending the scale from genes through species, resemblance between parent and offspring becomes progressively less faithful', he observed (p. 6). Moreover, Eldredge argued, species have births (speciation) and deaths (extinction), and so do all the other levels in the hierarchy, although the birth and death processes they go through are all vastly different biologically (Vrba and Eldredge, 1984, p. 177).

Why was Eldredge doing all this? He wanted to develop a *revised ontology* of evolutionary entities, which would help in a larger project: a basic restructuring of evolutionary theory. For Eldredge, the problem with the Modern Synthesis was that it limited its attention to only a few of the biological entities that seemed to exist in the world and to be involved in the evolutionary process (pp. 6–7). Much of this had to do with the way the synthesis had been recently interpreted, for instance as stated in Ernst Mayr's much-quoted 'one two' punch summary, said Eldredge. This was the way Mayr formulated it:

> The term 'evolutionary synthesis' was introduced by Julian Huxley in *Evolution: The Modern Synthesis* (1942) to designate the general acceptance of two conclusions: gradual evolution can be explained in terms of small genetic changes ('mutations') and recombinations, and the ordering of this variation by natural selection; and the observed evolutionary

phenomena, particularly macroevolutionary processes and speciation, can be explained in a manner that is consistent with the known genetic mechanisms (Mayr, 1980, p. 1; Eldredge, 1985, p. 5).

The problem, said Eldredge, was that this was not merely taken to mean that natural selection was the major cause of organic change and that the patterns recorded by geneticists, systematists, and paleontologists were *consistent* with the idea of selection. Instead, it had been interpreted as 'the stronger notion that such change was, at base, *the direct production of a selection process*' (p. 5, italics added). As a result, what had happened was 'the removal of most biological disciplines except population genetics from the active ranks of investigation into the evolutionary process' (pp. 6–7). Currently, only '[g]enes . . . , organisms, demes (to some degree), and species are explicitly addressed . . . ; monophyletic taxa are but dimly perceived: and ecological entities . . . are not even addressed' (p. 7).

And the way in which the 'levels of selection' problem had been typically resolved was in favor of a reductionist, single-level point of view, Eldredge observed. But this was effectively 'removing some of the main issues that (primarily) Dobzhansky saw as crucial in the early days of the synthesis. *Why* do we have species? *Why* are some species . . . relatively broad-niched, and others (closely related) relatively narrow-niched?' (p. 108, italics added). Although these questions had not been completely abandoned, Eldredge noted, 'the turn to the genetics of populations and ultimately to the dynamics of genes themselves . . . took the attention of evolutionary geneticists away from such matters' (ibid.).

But there had been serious disagreements among the architects of the Modern Synthesis themselves about just these matters, he continued. For instance, Dobzhansky had said about Fisher that 'problems were created by the tendency of some biologists to equate *adaptation* with *evolution* (Dobzhansky, 1937, quoted in Eldredge, p. 106). It was just this trend that Williams and Dawkins had later continued.[3] In other words, Eldredge showed that the opposition between the more holistically oriented biologists and the 'beanbag' ones went back to the time of the Modern Synthesis itself; the current struggle was but a 'second generation' manifestation of the original battle.

What bothered Eldredge most, it seemed, was the 'deeper' ontological commitment that he perceived in Dawkins and Williams. Williams had questioned the effectiveness of group selection 'for almost any group of organisms' (Williams, 1966, p. 114; Eldredge, 1985, p. 107).[4] Dawkins saw both individuals and groups as 'dust storms in the desert', as temporary aggregations. And populations, because they blended with other populations, were seen as constantly losing their identity (Dawkins, 1976a, p. 36). In Dawkins' conception, 'the gene is all', Eldredge complained. '[O]rganisms, demes, species and so forth, *as unstable packages of genetic information*, become, almost progressively, relatively unimportant items for consideration of the evolutionary process' (Eldredge, 1985, p. 107). In addition to the ontological problem, Eldredge had identified one piece that was clearly missing from the synthesis altogether: There was 'no formal effective integration of *ecology* with the entities *usually* construed as evolutionary —entities that form the "genealogical hierarchy" ' (p. 118, first italics added).

It was for these kinds of reasons, Eldredge explained, that he and some of his colleagues had recently criticized the Modern Synthesis. But their criticism should not be misunderstood:

> There has been an undue amount of confusion in recent years about the proposals of some of us who see less than an utterly complete theory in the synthesis (e.g., Gould, 1980b, 1982). In particular, it is often perceived that a hierarchically based evolutionary theory—a theory that sees ontologically based hierarchies of evolutionary entities—constitutes a strict and total *alternative* to the synthesis. For example, Thompson (1983, p. 450) writes that 'Gould, Stanley and Eldredge [must] provide an alternative theory of heredity' . . . According to Thompson . . . we are producing an 'irreducible evolutionary hierarchy' (Eldredge, 1985, p. 118, italics added, reference notation adjusted).

Eldredge presented this as an 'egregious misunderstanding', emphasizing that he, together with Gould, Vrba, Salthe, Damuth, Stanley, and others had 'no intention of junking the synthesis' (p. 118).

> Specifically, *no one denies that there is design in nature*—design called adaptation. Adaptations in this conventional sense are attributes of organisms—anatomical, behavioral, physiological phenotypic features . . . We have a theory—natural selection which is highly corroborated in field, experimental, and mathematical inductive examination . . . Tautological problems aside, removing natural selection as a force in evolutionary theory is as easy—and as desirable—as taking the gin out of a martini (p. 119, italics added).

If this was so, what on earth was all the hoopla about? 'It is the second part of Mayr's statement—the "extrapolationist" segment—which alone is under challenge', Eldredge explained. Stating that the core paradigm of neo-Darwinism was *consistent* with all other known evolutionary phenomena did not mean that it was *sufficient* for explaining them. According to Eldredge, the challenge was partly epistemological (the synthesis limited direct testing of evolutionary hypotheses to data that could be expressed in terms of gene frequencies) and partly ontological (in order to use the neo-Darwinist paradigm we are forced to ignore some biological entities, which are historically as real and coherent as organisms). Still, Eldredge wanted to make clear exactly what he was arguing for:

> It is this natural hierarchy . . . that dictates the necessity of adopting a hierarchical structure of evolutionary theory, at least if that theory is to embrace all evolutionarily relevant processes. *It is not the demonstration . . . of hierarchically arrayed processes* that forces us to consider a hierarchically structured evolutionary theory . Such matters of process remain contentious and highly debatable. There is no ineluctable demonstration, for example, of any form of group selection as a general phenomenon . . . Thus, *the fundamental issue is indeed ontology*' (pp. 119–20, italics added).

Here is Eldredge's formulation of the new ontology that would be needed to 'finish' the 'unfinished' synthesis:

> This revised ontology, I will argue, automatically forces us to consider an alternative
> approach to the very structure of evolutionary theory—simply because it presents us with
> an alternative description of the organization of biological nature. That structure is
> *hierarchical*. Genes, organisms. demes, species, and monophyletic taxa form one nested
> hierarchical system of individuals that is concerned with the development, retention, and
> modification of *information* ensconded, at base, in the genome. But there is at the same time
> a parallel hierarchy of nested *ecological* individuals—proteins, organisms, populations,
> communities, and regional biotal systems, that reflects the *economic* organization and
> integration of living systems. The processes within each of these two process hierarchies,
> plus the interactions between these two hierarchies, seems to me to produce the events and
> patterns that we call evolution (Eldredge, 1985, p. 7).

Eldredge has here surely produced a complex metaphysical description of what evolution may look like, taking into account a number of relevant aspects now disregarded in one form or another by the more limited metaphysics of current theory. His statement about how things are is a more comprehensive and potentially 'truer' (more descriptively correct) one than the 'hard' version of the Modern Synthesis. Also, it is possible that the focus on changes in gene frequencies as the most important mechanism for evolutionary change invites and perpetuates a limited ontology of evolutionary processes. But surely the architects of the Modern Synthesis must have considered these kinds of issues themselves? And still they settled on the synthesis. For them, there were obviously other, more important things than making sure that the theory's ontology was correct.

What might those reasons have been? One could have been the sheer expediency of having a clear statement about evolution, in order to be able to integrate and organize research in a variety of fields. Moreover, the synthesis had heuristic power: the focus on gene frequencies was a clear guide to empirical research. This does not preclude the possibility that the synthesis was motivated also by various 'extrascientific' concerns; say, a belief that substituting typological thinking with 'population thinking' might contribute to the fight against racism (particularly in the case of Mayr and Dobzhansky). The main point I am making here is that the Modern Synthesis—just as with other theoretical breakthroughs—was probably not primarily oriented toward *correct ontology*: the primary objective was to have a promising framework in place when it came to *generating new scientific research*. At the same time, we might say that the architects had built into the Modern Synthesis its own defense mechanism against invasion or extinction. To be taken seriously by practicing scientists, any serious alternative or modification would have to provide an obviously better promise for empirical research—and quantitative at that.

The problem of culture

What most of the critics of sociobiology saw as an insurmountable problem for an integrated sociobiology—also some of those who were generally supportive of the idea—was the special status of the human species. The strongest opponents to human sociobiology maintained the separateness of humans from other animals because of language and culture. Human culture was seen as totally uncoupled from biological evolution. Wilson called this 'the extreme orthodox view of environmentalism', formulated by Dobzhansky (1963) (Wilson, 1975a, p. 550).[5] We have seen that the members of the Sociobiological Study Group collectively took this position: their original letter stated that the biological functions of humans typically boiled down to 'sleeping, eating and excreting' (Allen et al., 1975). It was just this attitude that Wilson, in turn, called 'tabula rasa environmentalism', with 'Marxist' sometimes thrown in for effect.

However, later statements by group members indicated that the group was in fact not supportive of a blank-slate idea. The critics of sociobiology were against any kind of determinism, environmental as well as biological. Humans should be seen as free agents, having choices (see, for example, Larry Miller, 1978, speaking for the group). The emphasis was on the lack of biological constraints on the development of human culture. In this vein we have, for instance, Gould writing on biological potentiality vs biological determinism (1976), and Lewontin pointing out that culture (for example, airplanes) can be used to overcome biological limitations (for example, lack of wings) (Lewontin, 1981a; Levins and Lewontin, 1985).[6]

The critics' position on the uniqueness of humans was largely connected to the idea of the human capability for language. The strict separation between culture and nature was based on Chomsky's idea of an innate language capability. Chomsky himself had not really discussed the origin of this language capability, but it was seen as a unique thing having happened in human evolution. Later, Gould would explicitly champion a 'spandrel' type of argument for language: language was a byproduct of something else, like walking upright, but certainly not an adaptation (see, for example, Gould, 1993b).[7]

Early on in the debate, social anthropologists also joined this kind of critique, emphasizing the uniqueness of humans and the crucial role of language and convention. There was no doubt that sociobiology presented a continuing threat to the very raison d'être of social or cultural anthropology. In Sociobiology, Wilson had called for a new genetic anthropology; in 1977 he declared anthropology and sociology the 'anti-disciplines' of sociobiology (the task of an anti-discipline would be to reduce explanations in a 'higher' field in a scientific hierarchy to explanations in the field immediately 'beneath') (Wilson, 1977c).

The issue of sociobiology had been on the agenda at the annual meeting of the American Anthropological Association as early as 1976. According to Wilson, the members of the Association

> considered a motion to censure sociobiology formally and to ban two symposia on the subject scheduled earlier. The arguments of the proposers were mostly moral and political. During the debate on the matter, Margaret Mead rose indignantly, great walking stick in hand, to challenge the very idea of adjudicating a theory. She condemned the motion as a 'book-burning proposal'. Soon afterward the motion was defeated—but not by an impressive margin (Wilson, 1994, p. 331).

Lionel Tiger, again, described the atmosphere of such meetings as follows:

> Throughout the 1970s and early '80s, the opposition to the biosocial—or sociobiological—
> enterprise grew more heated. I felt a sense of almost physical apprehension, knowing how
> easily I could become the object of censure. At meetings of the American Anthropological
> Association, conversation would stop and people would stare when I entered an elevator
> and they saw my name tag (Tiger, 1996).

Tiger noted that he 'wasn't alone', referring to Wilson and the ice-water incident at
AAAS in 1978. How does, then, Tiger's own career as a defender of the truth compare
with Wilson's? Let's take a look at Tiger's list:

> In addition to slander and calumny . . . I have received bomb threats at lectures in
> Vancouver and Montreal and the promise of a 'kneecapping' at the New School of Social
> Research in New York. I have been the object of a demonstration of angry male transvestites
> at the Royal Institution in London, and I have seen one of the books I co-authored, *The
> Imperial Animal*, compared to *Mein Kampf*! (Tiger, 1996)

Angry transvestites and threat of knee-capping? Not bad, as credentials go in this field.

Social anthropology, of course, was the stronghold of the culturalist paradigm, with
Margaret Mead as its foremost messenger. Also, this field had had enormous social
impact as a source of liberalizing ideology. There was not only Mead's book on
adolescent life in Samoa, but also the view of cultural relativism, fostering understanding and respect for other cultures, and in this sense having an anti-racist social
function. Patterns of other cultures could be held up as a mirror to existing industrial-
ized (American) society. During this period, the tendency was to emphasize the
uniqueness and differences of other cultures from the Western one (cf. Brown, 1991;
Barkow *et al.*, 1992).

Marshall Sahlins was the social anthropologist who took immediate issue with
sociobiology in his book *The Use and Abuse of Biology* (1976). An engaging lecturer, he
had considerable impact. He mobilized three arguments in particular against sociobiology: kin selection presumed that animals could count and calculate, which was
ridiculous; actual behavior toward kin in human societies did not follow the sociobiological calculus; and sociobiology was just the reading of society into nature.
Dawkins, however, made the requirement for animals—or humans—to count and
calculate his 'misunderstanding number 3' in his 'Twelve Misunderstandings of Kin
Selection' (1979b): 'The idea of animals behaving *as if* calculating odds without really
doing so is fundamental to an understanding of the whole of sociobiology' (Dawkins,
1979b/1981a, p. 568). (Maynard Smith (1984a/1989a, p. 192) invented the shorter term
'Sahlins's fallacy'.) Dawkins' colleague John Krebs, however, described Sahlins (and
Harris) as just operating 'at a different level' (interview, 1981).[8]

Marvin Harris, an exponent of 'cultural materialism', was also critical of Wilsonian
sociobiology, although he admitted that in some respects the fields were natural allies.[9]
His main objection was that 'the reductionist principles of sociobiology' could explain
'only an insignificant portion of human sociocultural differences and similarities'
(Harris, 1979; see also Wilson and Harris, 1978). According to Harris, 'sociobiologists

overlook or minimize the genetic trait that by their own criteria ought to be emphasized above all others. That trait is *language*' (Harris, 1979, italics added). Edmund Leach, the Cambridge social anthropologist, already critical in 1978 (Leach, 1978), in 1981 wrote a strongly negative review in *Nature* of *Genes, Mind and Culture*. We will return to Leach in Chapter 8.

Interestingly, some social anthropologists were not as opposed to sociobiology as one might have expected. According to Wilson, Margaret Mead in fact *liked* sociobiology, and over dinner had told him that she, too, had written on the biological basis of human behavior. (Wilson, 1994, p. 348).[10] He also believed that when Claude Lévi-Strauss said that 'sociobiology is 90 per cent correct', it meant that Lévi-Strauss found *Sociobiology* 'true through the chimpanzees but not a line further' (Wilson, 1994, p. 328).[11]

But it was not only social anthropologists that were alarmed. Among early critics of sociobiology could also be found physical anthropologists. For instance, Vernon Reynolds, himself an author of *The Biology of Human Action* (1976, 1980), was very critical of sociobiology. He believed it was important to examine the relationship between culture and human nature, but not at the genetic level. Rather, he recommended that we study such things as the *physiological* pressures that modern society put on its members as a guide to finding less stressful life forms. The Australian anthropologist Derek Freeman, too, like Harris felt that Wilson was making too little of the biological facts he *himself* emphasized as a unique part of the human genetic endowment. Wilson said such things as 'human social evolution is more cultural than genetic' (1976, p. 343); he described human spoken language as an extremely efficient means for generating new information (1975a, p. 555), and declared the emergence of human speech a 'quantum jump in evolution comparable to the assembly of the eucaryotic cell' (1975a, p. 556). Wilson seemed to pay a lot of attention to culture: he described the existence of animal 'traditions' passed on from generation to generation by learning (1975a, p. 168), and discussed the potential role of learned behavior as 'an evolutionary pacemaker' (p. 171).

Still, Freeman noted, Wilson seemed unwilling to totally uncouple genetic and cultural evolution. Wilson kept saying such things as 'the genes keep culture on a leash', or postulated a limited number of trajectories for the evolution of human cultures (Wilson, 1978, p. 207, p. 167). This Freeman took as an indication that Wilson wanted to *reduce culture to genes*, cultural evolution to genetic evolution. But, Freeman pointed out, 'we clearly have the empirical evidence to make a general distinction between these two codes, and to argue that their co-existence, during several million years of history, has, in the singular case of the human species, resulted in the emergence of *two separate, though very closely interacting, evolutionary systems*' (Freeman, 1980, p. 205, italics added). Freeman also approvingly quoted Tinbergen's statement that culture had taken off on the top of organic evolution, although organic evolution still continues in humans (Tinbergen, 1978).

Freeman went on to speculate that Wilson's sense that culture was subjected to genetic constraints might derive from an epistemological bias of evolutionary biologists: their exaggerated preoccupation with 'the blind decision-making process of natural selection' (Wilson, 1978a, p. 197). He also quoted Dawkins' admission that evolutionists easily tended to forget other types of evolution than natural selection (Dawkins, 1976, p. 208; Freeman, 1980, p. 212). Freeman worried that sociobiologists might not even *see* the problem with open behavior programs, learning, and exogenetic codes because '*there is a persistent feeling that the range of observed behavior is kept within bounds by natural selection and that any observed behavior is almost certainly adaptive*' (Freeman, 1980, p. 212, italics added).[12]

Still, Freeman insisted, 'it has long been apparent to most anthropologists and many biologists' that two different systems exist: exogenetic or Lamarckian evolution and genetic evolution.[13] The social transmission of ideas is a fundamentally new and different type of evolution (see, for example, Dobzhansky, 1963; Tinbergen, 1978), in which information is not only accumulated in a Lamarckian fashion but also subjected to conscious human *choice* (Monod, 1969; Freeman 1980, p. 211). Freeman could simply not see how sociobiological theory might take into account the fundamentally exogenetic nature of culture (p. 212). He went on to criticize Barash (1977) for not including in his discussion of human sociobiology 'any specification of the *mechanisms* by which cultural practices, in general, could conceivably be genetically determined' (Freeman, p. 213, italics added). But, Freeman warned, 'when natural selection, operating "to maximize the inclusive fitness of individuals", is evoked as a general explanation of "cultural factors", sociobiology becomes an actively unscientific doctrine' (p. 213). What was needed instead was 'informed study of the way in which the interaction of cultural and genetic processes has produced the human brain and language and made possible the unique character of human history' (p. 212).

Freeman's criticism of Wilson is one of the most detailed I have seen. While emphasizing at the very beginning that he both accepted scientific materialism and believed that 'the modern theory of evolution is basic to an authentic science of anthropology' (p. 199), he did point out difficulties with the 'straight' application of sociobiology to culture. The question is, of course, whether Wilson was a 'straight' sociobiologist, subsuming cultural processes under genetic ones, or whether Wilson, rather, had some *implicit mechanism* in mind whereby genes would somehow be connected to culture (I believe the latter). Freeman himself appeared to oscillate between recognizing that Wilson was not quite this first kind of sociobiologist, and accusing him of being one (perhaps this was why Freeman resorted to attacking Barash?).

What is clear, however, is that in their different ways the anthropological critics did put their finger on important problems of human sociobiology, particularly when they were willing to follow Wilson's presentation in a close but critical way. As we shall see in the next chapter, Wilson seems to have taken to heart this anthropological criticism and tried to respond to it. (In interview, however, I remember Wilson dismissing Freeman's criticism of sociobiology. Wilson told me that Freeman had first 'tried to criticize sociobiology', but when that did not succeed, he had moved on to attacking Margaret Mead instead.)[14]

Jerome Barkow, an anthropologist at Dalhousie University sympathetic to biological explanation, emphasized the fact that there were many more explanations valid for human behavior than an evolutionary one; in fact, proximate factors were much more important than ultimate ones in human behavior (Barkow, 1980). However, this kind of criticism did not have any impact on Wilson's further development of human sociobiology.

Moving now to the sympathizers, we can note that the biosocial anthropologists had already approved of sociobiology, and Wilson had duly quoted Tiger and Fox's idea of a bio-grammar early on in *Sociobiology*. Biosocial anthropologists typically postulated tensions between our Stone Age human nature and modern culture. In 1979, Napoleon Chagnon and Irons edited *Evolutionary Biology and Human Social Behavior: an Anthropological Perspective*, bringing an evolutionary explanatory framework to anthropology. Some of the biosocially or sociobiogically inspired anthropologists would later open up new branches of the enterprise on their own. Here we have particularly John Tooby, who with Leda Cosmides, a psychologist, and with the general encouragement of Irven DeVore, started developing the new field of evolutionary psychology.

But there were also sociobiologically inclined anthopologists who felt perfectly comfortable applying sociobiological concepts directly to human culture. A collection of early research in this genre can be found in Betzig (1997) (see Chapter 14). The editor Laura Betzig herself stated: '[E]verything we think, feel, and do might be better understood as a means to the spread of our own—or of our ancestors'—genes' (p. 2), and 'I, personally, find culture unnecessary' (p. 17). (It is sociobiologists of this sort that would have made a better target for Freeman's attack, it seems.) But there was the one sociobiologist who from the very beginning had clearly suggested separating genetic from cultural evolution: Richard Dawkins—whom, incidentally, Freeman cited with approval (Freeman, 1980, p. 212).

Interestingly, such 'direct' attempts met opposition from ethologists and others oriented to complex interactions between cultural and genetic factors. For instance, Robert Hinde called Chagnon and Irons' approach 'simplistic' (interview, 1981). And John Krebs (with Axel Kacelnik) would later write *contra* Betzig: 'We, personally, find culture necessary' (Kacelnik and Krebs, 1997, p. 27).[15]

There was, however, one notable early attempt to make sense of the fact that humans have culture, while still connecting culture to biological evolution. That was William Durham's co-evolutionary theory of human biology and culture. According to Durham, 'this theory can explain the biocultural evolution of human attributes *without* presuming a genetic basis or predisposition for all adaptive forms. To the extent that humans do behave in ways that maximize their individual inclusive fitnesses, this would suggest that it is generally for both cultural and biological reasons' (Durham, 1978, pp. 444–5, italics added). In other words, the operation of a mechanism of 'cultural selection' may sometimes *replace* the operation of natural selection.[16] Still, Durham warned that 'although a coevolutionary theory can potentially contribute to an understanding of the adaptive significance of cultural attributes, it is not necessarily the key to understanding the *meaning* and symbolic significance people may give to those attributes' (p. 430, italics added).

Durham's theory (also published in Chagnon and Irons, 1979) may have contributed to the further development of human sociobiology, in the sense that it helped convince Wilson of the necessity of a co-evolutionary process and the need for making such a process explicit. In the next chapter, accordingly, we will meet 'Sociobiology II': a mutant type which did take culture into account.

Hamilton's 'racist' paper

The attempt to apply kin selection theory directly to humans met with vehement protest at least on one public occasion. That was the Biosocial Anthropology conference in Oxford in 1973 and its aftermath—all this before the upheaval around Wilson's *Sociobiology*. Hamilton tells us that some 'hot coals' fell on him at that conference, in the form of Sherwood Washburn's critique of his invited paper. Washburn's criticism totally baffled Hamilton. The conference was, at Fox's suggestion, dedicated to Washburn and Tinbergen. And Hamilton, a great admirer of Washburn, had used a quotation from Washburn to introduce his own paper. The quote was about learning not being a generalized ability, but related to the evolutionary significance of *particular* skills and attitudes for a species.[17] (Hamilton later mused that perhaps it was exactly this that Washburn hated—namely, seeing his own ideas extended further than he wished; Hamilton, 1996, p. 317.) But Washburn (1976), in an *Anthropology Newsletter*, had declared Hamilton's paper 'racist, reductionist and ridiculous'. Even Trivers had later in conversation referred to it as Hamilton's 'racist' paper (Hamilton, personal communication).

What was it that Hamilton had said in his presentation? Washburn had singled out the following as the offending passage:

> The incursions of barbaric pastoralists seem to do civilizations less harm in the long run than one might expect. Indeed, two dark ages and renaissances in Europe suggest a recurring pattern in which a renaissance follows an incursion by about 800 years. It may even be suggested that certain genes or traditions of the pastoralists revitalize the conquered people with an ingredient of progress which tends to die out in a large panmictic population for reasons already discussed. I have in mind altruism itself or the part of altruism which is perhaps better described as self-sacrificial daring. By the time of the renaissance, it may be that the mixing of genes and cultures (or cultures alone, if these are the only vehicles, which I doubt) has continued long enough to bring the old mercantile thoughtfulness and the infused daring into conjunction in a few individuals who then find courage for all kinds of inventive innovation against the resistance of established thought and practice. Often, however, the cost in fitness of such altruism and sublimated pugnacity to the individuals concerned is by no means metaphorical, and the benefits to fitness, such as they are, go to a mass of individuals whose genetic correlation with the innovator must be slight indeed. Thus civilization probably slowly reduces its altruism of all kinds, including the kinds needed for cultural creativity (Hamilton, 1975; also quoted in Washburn, 1978a).

But looking back on this in 1996, Hamilton was unrepentant:

> All I allow is that the matter is, of course, speculative, and I add the thought that I could, and perhaps should, have left out one word, 'genetic', from the sentence preceding [the last]... I

had indicated earlier that the effects I had been talking about could be partly cultural and there was no good reason only to mention the genetic possibility when referring to the same idea below. However, I have never seen any evidence that a genetic interpretation or a genetic component is out of court and the idea in general continues to be justified in my mind. I do not believe that it poses any threat or insult to any races; multiracial mixture almost throughout our species is involved in the pattern I suggested . . . In general, I think it would be sad to have to accept a culturist's conclusion that current minority and traditional cultures have nothing that they can usefully contribute genetically to the systems that dominate them (Hamilton, 1996, p. 317).

He then went on to say that critics should support their criticisms with facts, and this Washburn did not do, according to Hamilton.

In fact Washburn did, although not in that particular *Newsletter*. In at least two longer articles he explained in rather patient detail his exact objections (Washburn, 1978a, 1978b/1980). According to Washburn, Hamilton's passage 'precisely repeats the errors of the early evolutionists who thought that their facts were so powerful that they could just be arranged in order without doing the necessary research. Stone tools were arranged in evolutionary orders without archaeological information. The orders proved to be wrong' (1978a, p. 55). Of course, Washburn admitted, now the general theory of evolution is correct, 'but a theory does not give conclusions—it directs the nature of the research, but *each application of the theory demands careful research*' (p. 56, italics added). Take human evolution. What we know is that just before the development of agriculture the conditions that had dominated human evolution for millions of years changed drastically. Everything indicates that that change was the result of *learning*. Washburn's overall assessment was that 'there has been no important change in human abilities in the last 30000 years'; and for instance, the rapid increase in population in the last 200 years is clearly the result of technological innovation, not changing gene frequencies (pp. 56–7).

Consequently, Washburn's verdict on Hamilton's claim that 'civilization probably slowly reduces its altruism of all kinds, including the kinds needed for cultural creativity' was the following: 'The absurd conclusion is a correct deduction from evolutionary theory. *It simply proves that the theory is useless* when applied to the interpretation of learned behaviors and recent human history. *There is no evidence that civilization reduces altruism*—quite the contrary—and there is every evidence that cultural creativity is greatly increased' (italics added). Washburn attributed Hamilton's reasoning to 'overconfidence in evolutionary theory', and noted that such overconfidence had been seen before (Washburn, 1978b/1980, p. 270). Sociobiologists made practically no effort to understand human behavior, he complained. Meanwhile, 'the application of the genetic theory of natural selection requires research' (p. 276).

But Hamilton had said much more in his presentation—in fact, he had mentioned many of the very same things for which Wilson got into trouble. For instance, he suggested that human cultures were somehow genetically constrained, and further, that he hoped to produce evidence that some phenomena that are usually seen as purely cultural—such as racial discrimination—had actually deep roots in our animal past.

For instance, we may have been prepared by selection to develop xenophobia (Hamilton, 1975, p. 330).

It seems that Washburn responded equally strongly to this aspect of Hamilton's talk. In his other writings, Washburn elaborated on the *'racism' inherent in sociobiology's fundamental calculus*, based on the genetic resemblance between relatives.

> The sociobiological calculus is necessarily racist because geographical distance was a major factor in determining the formation of races [here he quoted Barash, 1977, p. 311]. In general, the further that two populations were apart at the time when races were forming, the greater the genetic difference; *hence the less ethical responsibility people should have for members of the other group.* The contrary argument is that most genes are shared and that gene frequencies in which races differ are behaviorally unimportant (with some exceptions, such as sickle-cell disease) (Washburn, 1978b/1980, p. 276, italics added).

And Vernon Reynolds, the Oxford anthropologist, noted the same thing. Reynolds' interpretation of the meaning of Hamilton's model was the following:

> The genetic aspect indicates that as human groups become spatially further apart, as their gene pools become less closely related, so they will be less co-operative and more competitive. Hamilton makes this perfectly clear in his chapter . . . He postulates an evolutionary model of small hominid/human groups that will inevitably, because of kin selection and reciprocal altruism, tend to select for co-operation between neighbouring groups and correspondingly to select for aggression and hostility to more distant, unrelated individuals and groups. *Xenophobia and racial hostility come as no surprise on this hypothesis; indeed, the rigid application of sociobiological genetics shows that logically they must occur* (Reynolds, 1980, p. 39, italics added).

Even George Price, whose formula Hamilton in this paper had successfully applied to group selection, had reacted to an earlier draft of the paper. According to Hamilton, Price approved the formal part of the paper (which he had helped inspire), but was guarded as to the rest: 'There's a lot I wasn't expecting—interesting, but I must read it again,' he told Hamilton. In Hamilton's opinion it was almost as if Price were trying to 'conceal his formula's full significance' (Hamilton, 1996, p. 318). It is not hard to see that if Price's had the type of absolutist mind which took evolutionary theory as directly applicable to humans as well as animals, at the same time as he recognized no forces other than evolutionary ones affecting human behavior, he would easily have ended up exactly with the 'racist' conclusions of Washburn and Reynolds. (Hamilton, we saw earlier, called his own thoughts 'painful' and seems to have envisioned no obvious solution, except the existence of 'pockets of altruism in viscous populations', as he hinted in his 1996 book.)

Scientifically, Hamilton regarded this paper as fundamentally paying tribute to Price and exploring the possibility of the evolution of altruism in a new way by extending Price's group selection model. He was happy to be able to derive a more elegant model for inclusive fitness than that in his original 1964 paper. 'I was told to apply kin selection theory to culture for this conference, so I did', he told me, somewhat defiantly (personal communication). Hamilton even mentioned that he sometimes amuses himself thinking about the conflict people may experience when choosing between quoting his 1975 paper because of its scientific value, and not quoting it because of its 'racist' implications (Hamilton, 1996, p. 324).

It is hard to tell whether Washburn was more offended with Hamilton on moral/ political or scientific grounds. Probably it was a combination. He described sociobiology as continuing 'a history of scientific error. When applied to human behavior, it renews the mistakes of social Darwinism, early evolutionism, eugenics, and racial interpretations of history' (Washburn 1978b/1980, p. 256). Moreover, as a social scientist, he found errors of yet another kind. For humans, it was *social organization*, not sex, that was the most important adaptive mechanism (p. 260). Here Washburn went on to quote Alexander's (1974) point that '*human social groups represent an almost ideal model for potent selection at the group level*' (italics added). Humans adapt through knowledge and organization, both of which depend on speech. In turn, knowledge and organization are properties of groups, transmitted by *learning* to the next generation (p. 266, italics added). '*The laws of genetics are not the laws of learning*,' said Washburn, 'and as long as sociobiologists confuse these radically different mechanisms, sociobiology will only obstruct the understanding of human social behaviors' (Washburn 1978b/1980, p. 278, italics his).

We see here how close to Washburn's heart the idea of learning was, and how he emphasized the role of group selection for humans. No wonder, then, that Hamilton succeeded in offending him—first by introducing his article with a quotation from Washburn presenting learning as genetically constrained, and second by simply being who he was: the developer of the theory of kin selection, the official competitor with group selection. It is now easier to see how Irven DeVore and Washburn could really have a falling-out over the issue of kin selection vs group selection—something that DeVore had told me with great sadness. For Washburn, it seems that kin selection implied genes but group selection did not. Therefore, to him it must have seemed that introducing genetic notions of individual fitness instead of cultural group-level properties in human affairs would be the beginning of the end. Washburn may not have realized that DeVore, despite his professed enthusiasm for kin selection, really did not think of it in terms of genes *either*.[18]

This brings us to a question lingering in the back of many people's minds during the sociobiology controversy, but one which was seldom made explicit. That was: can you have sociobiology without genes?

Are genes necessary?

Evolutionary Biology and Human Social Behavior: An Anthropological Perspective (1979) offered what seemed to be a solution to the sticky problem of cultural inheritance. The idea, originally conceived by Bill Durham, and developed in the three introductory chapters by Irons, Durham, and Alexander, was this:

> Cultural adaptation is expected to fit biological theory because of two evolutionary effects, neither of which selects directly for particular behaviour patterns. First, humans are

supposed to have evolved the capacity to estimate subconsciously or consciously the probable fitness effects of employing alternative behaviour patterns. Second, they are supposed to have evolved the will to choose whichever pattern maximizes probable inclusive fitness ... By this view *the frequency and distribution of behavioural traits is merely the result of a series of individual choices* (Wrangham, 1980, p. 174, italics added).[19]

It was Richard Wrangham, an anthropologist at the time working with the King's College Sociobiology Project and also closely with DeVore, who saw this approach as a possible solution to the problem of human sociobiology. The novelty with this idea was that it emphasized *decision-making*, a better notion than the 'potential for learning' typically used for explaining non-genetic adaptation. It provided a simple mechanism by which different behavior shown by different individuals was not dependent on *genetic* differences. The idea of choice separated the question of the origin of behavior patterns from the question of how or why they were used. With the help of the idea of choice, the study of adaptation could be divorced from theories of genetic determinism, Wrangham observed. He even believed that the idea of choice might help bridge the social and biological sciences (Wrangham, 1980, p. 175). The problem of applying sociobiology to culture was now solved with the help of a combination of choice and inclusive fitness theory:

> Anthropologists have long recognized that cultural practices change as a result of individual acceptance or rejection of particular traits. ... Previous theories have suggested that individuals choose so as to get rich, get protein, get children, or by other criteria. The inclusive fitness theory has the advantage of allowing such criteria to apply in particular cases, while also being capable of explaining why different societies should have different criteria (Wrangham, 1980, p. 175).

According to Wrangham, '*the inclusive fitness theory emerges looking healthy*' (my italics) in Chagnon and Irons' book, where it is applied to a variety of social practices. But the book had raised a further question. Could one apply the same thesis to *biology*, too? Clearly this could not become part of 'classical' sociobiology, Wrangham admitted, noting that 'the concept of animals making decisions about unprogrammed behaviour patterns is unrecognizable as part of formal sociobiological theory' (p. 175). Wrangham knew full well that in Krebs and Davies' *Behavioural Ecology*, for instance, animals were only described as shifting between alternative 'strategies'; that is, they were choosing between alternative fitness-maximizing behavioral options or genetically coded programs, and that this, in turn, was following Hamilton's 1964 theory, which described behavioral evolution as due to genetic mutation, not individual choice (Wrangham, 1980, p. 175).

Still, was the underlying *premise* of the Chagnon and Irons volume wrong, or could it in principle be used to inform biology, asked Wrangham? Existing models were deterministic, they identified the conditions under which an altruistic gene would spread at the expense of its alternative alleles. But, argued Wrangham, 'the logic which grants these models a universal role is surely wrong'. He warned that continued focus exclusively on genetic mutation might in fact prevent further progress in the field.

Mutations are only one source of genetic change; another source of new phenotypes is a reorganization of the genome. If a particular trait can come about through many pathways, this may produce a more rapid response than the appearance of a mutant, Wrangham observed.

He went on to point out that behavioral mutants could arise and spread in a population even without genetic change. The best example here was the cultural transmission among great tits who have learnt to open milk bottles. The behavioral mutation did not need to be genetic, said Wrangham; one might regard the tits as making the decision to adopt or not adopt the new behavior. (The tit example appeared to be something of a British exemplar; I had also heard it from Hinde himself—he had discovered the behavior—and from Krebs. Tits opening milk bottles had become the British equivalent of macaques washing sweet potatoes.)

There were other examples of how behavioral change in animals might well be dependent on ecological non-genetic change. For instance, Wrangham (consulting Brian Bertram) pointed out that lionesses often help their sisters and their offspring—they let their nieces suckle them—and this could well have a non-genetic cause. Perhaps lionesses could judge the probable effect on their daughters' fitness of having a hunting companion, which is what suckling a niece would produce (Wrangham, 1980, p. 176). And there was a more general point in support of the idea that learned behaviors involved choice: 'Shouldn't any animal which can learn also be capable of adaptive choice of behavioural options? Otherwise the learned behaviours would be of little use', Wrangham argued (ibid.).

All this was testable, Wrangham emphasized. Considering that individuals may express new behavioral patterns even without genetic change, one might experimentally assess 'how far animals are ecologically rather than genetically predisposed to certain types of social relationships'. At the same time, this would be a way to combat genetic determinism.

> Genetic questions will then be referred away from particular acts toward more complex characteristics such as those concerned with motivation, emotion, learning abilities and insight. And as this happens the grip of genetic determinism will be relaxed, and sociobiologists will feel freer to pay attention to individuals and their private minds (Wrangham, 1980, p. 176).

Jon Seger, a biologist working at Harvard's Biological Laboratories at the time, also wondered whether sociobiology really insisted on a strict connection between genes and behavior. He had observed that at least the critics of sociobiology seemed to believe that any variation that had a 'biological' explanation was necessarily heritable. But what about the sociobiologists themselves? Did they believe that there had to be genes 'for' every behavior? Seger answered this question differently from Wrangham. Interestingly, he saw sociobiologists as much more open-minded:

> Sociobiology does, in part, attempt to explain behavioural variation. But does it really argue for the *heritability* of such variation? Those who think that sociobiological theory derives from traditional behavioral genetics say 'yes'; this group includes [many critics] but very

few sociobiologists. Those who identify sociobiology with the newer work on sex ratios, sexual dimorphism, kin-directed altruism, life-history strategies and the like, say 'no'; this group includes most sociobiologists . . . (Seger, 1981).

Seger went on to cite the anthropologist Jerome Barkow's point, that 'Evolutionary biology does not require . . . a direct link . . . between a particular gene and a particular behavior, even if careless reading (and writing) of sociobiology may occasionally permit that impression', and that selection may often favor behavioural flexibility 'mediated by *learning* preferences', both for humans and animals (Barkow, 1980). This kind of flexibility, in turn, allows an individual 'to recognize and seize unique opportunities'. Seger's conclusion was the following: 'If sociobiology is really about the evolution of learning and other environmentally mediated developmental processes, then . . . [i]ndividual differences map onto differences of *environment*, not of genotype . . .' (italics added).[20]

That was Seger's and Barkow's view of sociobiology, while Wrangham seems to have concentrated on the strict (Hamiltonian) sociobiological position. Still, this kind of flexibility of sociobiology was clearly not apparent to most readers of Wilson's *Sociobiology*. So, could sociobiology be rescued from the charges of genetic determinism after all? In my interview with Lewontin, I brought up Seger's attempt to 'save' sociobiology by emphasizing learning and flexibility. But Lewontin did not think it was possible to do sociobiology without genes for behavioral traits. Seger was a very good biologist, he said, but you have got to have *genes*!

And Dawkins agreed. According to him, objections to the 'unnecessary geneticizing' of the language of functional ethology just demonstrated a fundamental failure to face up to Darwinian selection. (We see Dawkins persisting in not calling the field sociobiology.) He complained that people kept asking him why he 'had to drag genes in' to their perfectly nice-sounding explanations. You *have* to drag genes in, protested Dawkins, otherwise you cannot use a theory that involves Darwinian selection! (1982, p. 28.) As we see, then, Dawkins and Lewontin were equally adamant about the need to involve genes in a proper sociobiological explanation.

But others did what they could to avoid mentioning—or even thinking about—the dreaded four-letter word 'gene'. Dawkins tells us a story about an anthropology seminar he attended, where a presenter had tried to use kin selectionist theory to predict the conditions under which one would expect to find the mating system of polyandry. In particular, he wanted to show that his polyandrous tribes lived under the special conditions required by Maynard Smith and Ridpath's (1972) model for polyandry in Tasmanian native hens—that is, the sex ratio in the population needed to be male biased and the partners close kin. Now look what happened at this peaceful seminar with the 'bad boy' Dawkins present:

> I tried to warn him of some difficulties in his hypothesis. I pointed out that the theory of kin selection is fundamentally a *genetic* theory. . . . Had his polyandrous tribes been living . . . under their current peculiar conditions for long enough—enough generations—for the necessary genetic replacement to have taken place? Was there, indeed, any reason to believe that variations in human mating systems are under genetic control at all?

The speaker, supported by many of his anthropological colleagues in the seminar, objected to my dragging genes into the discussion. He was not talking about genes, he said, but about a social behaviour pattern. Some of his colleagues seemed uncomfortable with the very mention of the four-letter word 'gene'. I tried to persuade him that it was he who had 'dragged genes in' to the discussion although, to be sure, he had not mentioned the word gene in his talk. . . . By even *speculating* about kin selection as an explanation of differences in tribal mating systems, my anthropologist friend was implicitly dragging genes into the discussion (Dawkins, 1982, pp. 27–8, first and last italics added).

Dawkins commented on the irony of this whole thing. Although it was in fact he who had suggested the *least* 'genetic determinist' view of polyandry, it was he who was seen as the 'typical genetic determinist' among those present. At the same time, the only thing he had done was to make *explicit* the fact that you cannot invoke kin selection without discussing genes.

So, holding the banner of logic high, Dawkins concluded that people like him had been unfairly accused of being obsessed with genes just because they had tried to make their reasoning *explicit* in order to avoid errors. He added: 'Of course, individual sociobiologists may or may not be genetic determinists. They may be Rastafarians, Shakers or Marxists. But *their private opinions on genetic determinism*, like their private opinions on religion, *have nothing to do with the fact that they use the language of "genes for behaviour"* when talking about natural selection' (Dawkins, 1982, pp. 28–9, italics added).

The communication between Dawkins and DeVore may or may not have suffered somewhat because of Dawkins' insistence on genes and DeVore's wish to avoid them. In 1981 Dawkins told me that he was not clear about DeVore's actual stance on sociobiology—did he think all our behaviour served to propogate our genes? He related with great bafflement how DeVore once during an evening at a conference had kept telling him how being the author of a book would help him 'get women'. DeVore had gone on and on about this. Dawkins seriously wondered about the evolutionary logic of this. Probably, for Dawkins, only two models existed: either genetic or cultural transmission. Meanwhile, DeVore may have been following the 'Durham' logic, a type of co-evolutionary reasoning process. (As we saw, DeVore's friend Wrangham was very enthusiastic about this approach. In fact, it was DeVore who originally alerted me to Wrangham's article and kindly gave me a xerox of it.) If the assumption was that women in general wanted men of high status, in the particular academic subculture this would have translated among other things into fame coming from book authorship. (This kind of reasoning was later to become part of evolutionary psychology; see, for example, Buss, 1994.)

DeVore did not like genes. He was certainly disturbed over what he considered Wilson's overemphasis on genes (which he thought unnecessarily connected sociobiology to the upheaval about IQ). In this sense, he did act just like one of those seminar anthropologists that Dawkins mentioned (perhaps the seminar *was* DeVore's?). This means that DeVore fell into an unusual category of people who had been converted to kin selection without really believing that you 'had to have genes'. But as we saw, ironically, colleagues he met at conferences believed he was a Wilsonian sociobiologist, and Washburn that he was an avid kin selectionist.

One biologist who believed that one *could* have adaptation without genes was Paul Sherman, the student of ground squirrels and mole rats. In fact, he felt that sociobiology overemphasized genes. He suggested that one reason might be that ants were Wilson's primary species (interview, 1982). This, of course, did not prevent Sherman from having a nice collegial relationship with Wilson.

What should we call these two types of sociobiologists, then, one who believes that you have to have genes, and the other allowing such things as animal decision-making in the picture? Perhaps it is the opposition between a 'Hamiltonian' sociobiological and a more ethologically oriented approach. (For ethologists, 'adaptation' can also be adaptation during the lifespan, or/and it can be adaptation through learning and culture.) Or perhaps we should call it 'narrow' and 'broad' sociobiology, where 'narrow' would employ exclusively gene-theoretical explanatory models, and 'broad' would cover also ecological, life-history, and other factors. The opposition between these two kinds of 'sociobiology' would continue throughout the sociobiology controversy. Recently the 'broad' approach has started having more influence. (In the latest edition of *Behavioural Ecology*, the field has been redefined as broader than before and has begun to include more considerations from ethology; Krebs and Davies, 1997a. We will return to this in Chapter 16.)

So, when the Sociobiology Study Group and other critics kept saying things like 'you cannot do sociobiology without genes, the whole enterprise is meaningless without them', they were not necessarily being facetious. They were merely stating an important *fact*—at least from a hardline sociobiological point of view.

CHAPTER 8

Sociobiology adapts to criticism: *Genes, Mind and Culture*

Sociobiology reinvents itself—or does it?

After *Sociobiology: The New Synthesis*, Wilson expanded his final chapter dealing with *Homo sapiens* into a full-length work, *On Human Nature* (Wilson, 1978a). But, although Wilson took the opportunity to respond to some of the criticism of *Sociobiology*, it was essentially a development of earlier ideas. Wilson's next significant conceptual move came through collaboration with Charles Lumsden, who had joined Wilson's lab as a post-doctoral student. In thus working with someone who had considerable mathematical talents, the naturalist Wilson followed a familiar pattern, for he had previously worked with similarly formally gifted thinkers (MacArthur on biogeography and George Oster on caste in the Hymenoptera).

Although it may have seemed to some that Wilson was desperately looking for mathematical talent to help him model human sociobiology, this was not the case. Lumsden originally came to Wilson's lab as a post-doctoral student to model *ants*, not humans. To complicate the matter further for conspiracy theorists, Lumsden was turned down at first, but he persisted, and was finally accepted. Once at Harvard, it was Lumsden's interest in cognitive studies that made him and Wilson abandon their original plan and 'opportunistically' (Wilson's description) collaborate on the human end of the sociobiological enterprise (Wilson, interview; Lumsden, interview). Wilson was pleased with the collaboration; in interview he enthusiastically compared himself and Lumsden to Watson and Crick. (When I mentioned this to Lumsden, he dryly commented that he sometimes wondered who was Watson and who was Crick.)

Genes, Mind and Culture, the major fruit of the Wilson/Lumsden partnership, draws on highly abstract mathematical models (developed in physics) and attempts to put human sociobiology on the firm theoretical, quantitative basis that the critics had found lacking in Wilson's earlier work. In particular, the authors met head-on a criticism often made by Lewontin and others:

> Population genetics makes quantitative predictions about the rates of change of genetic composition with time and also provides actual data on the quantitative genetic differences

in gene frequencies in present-day human groups. Both kinds of numbers are too small to fit sociobiological theory. Only 100 generations have passed since the Roman Republic and this time span is far too short for there to have been any major change in gene frequencies. Yet human social institutions have undergone an extraordinary change in those few generations. In a mere 30 generations, Islam rose from nothing to be the greatest culture of the Western World and then declined again into powerlessness. How can one compare the social institutions of the modern British with the political, social and economic institutions of Roman Britain? Moreover, at least 85 per cent of known human genetic variation exists, at present, within any local national population and at least 95 per cent within any modern major race. How are we to explain, on a genetic basis, the immense cultural differences between present day populations? The sociobiologists have the answer. It is the 'multiplier effect' (Lewontin, 1976a).

Using ideas introduced in Wilson's earlier works, Lumsden and Wilson argued that even small genetic differences and changes could explode up into significant cultural differences and changes; that there could be feedback, from cultural change to genetic change. Whereas in previous works this had been little more than an unsubstantiated suggestion (and criticized by Lewontin and others), now the claim was that the 'multiplier effect' had been made fully scientifically respectable.

It cannot be denied that, in some respects, *Genes, Mind and Culture* was something of a rush job. Wilson admitted this himself; he and Lumsden were pressed for time, knowing about other possibly competing workers, particularly Cavalli-Sforza and Feldman and their simultaneous effort to produce models of cultural change (Cavalli-Sforza and Feldman, 1981) (Wilson, interview). On the other hand, Wilson was in 1981 very proud of his and Lumsden's achievement and believed that *Genes, Mind and Culture* had won the race:

> We produced the first theory! We are the only game in town! We are the only ones who have a theory which takes what is known about cognitive psychology, development, and so on, and ties this together in a series of models and conceptual schemes (Wilson, interview).

At the very outset of *Genes, Mind and Culture*, Lumsden and Wilson were quite explicit about how they differed from earlier views on human sociobiology :

> For mankind at least, these postulates are radically incorrect. Behavior is not explicit in the genes, and mind cannot be treated as a mere replica of behavioral traits. In this book we propose a very different view in which the genes prescribe a set of biological processes, which we call epigenetic rules, that direct the assembly of the mind. . .[C]ulture is the translation of the epigenetic rules into mass patterns of mental activity and behavior . . . Genes are indeed linked to culture, but in a deep and subtle manner (Lumsden and Wilson, 1981, p. 2).

Here we have, then, a realization of Wilson's basic moral-cum-scientific agenda. He had now found a way of integrating social and natural science by applying evolutionary biology to the most central concerns of the social sciences. He was doing this by demonstrating that it was indeed possible to also derive patterns of cultural diversity from what he called 'biological ground rules'.

At the same time, *Genes, Mind and Culture* was the final explication of the 'multiplier effect' and a demonstration of how it was possible, after all, for the genes to hold culture (read: religion) on a leash. In fact, the authors themselves stated in the Introduction to their book:

> The epigenetic rules will . . . tend to channel cognitive development toward certain culturgens as opposed to others. We refer to this relation informally as the 'leash principle' in order to make it metaphorically more vivid: genetic natural selection operates in such a way as to keep culture on a leash (1981, p. 13).

Thus, Wilson believed that finally he had theoretically demonstrated that religion could indeed be kept on a leash. He was now closer to satisfying his metaphysical urge to supersede traditional theology by a view based on materialism and evolution, particularly since his new models also took into account the human mind.

Wilson had already been quite explicit about the need to also address the human mind in a talk to a Star Island symposium on science and religion in 1979. Although in *On Human Nature* he had made such statements as '[t]he scientist's devotion to parsimony in explanation excludes the divine spirit and other extraneous agents' (Wilson, 1978a, p. 192), this was apparently not good enough. He warned the symposium participants that '[a]nother possible refugium of divine influence is in the deep recesses of the mind' (Wilson, 1980a, p. 425). For Wilson, the new task, therefore, was to explain divine revelation. For this, he would need to somehow scientifically account for exactly those 'deep recesses of the mind'.

The reason why Wilson felt he was approaching his goal in *Genes, Mind and Culture* was tied in with his epistemological conviction that *something has been explained if we have been able to create a model of it*. Wilson had already expressed such a conviction in 1971 in *The Insect Societies*, where he attempted a 'cybernetic translation' of the old superorganism metaphor into the new language of communication theory (see Chapter 5). (For earlier steps in this 'translation' of the superorganism concept, see Ghiselin, 1974). This is the way Donna Haraway described the cybernetic ambition of Wilsonian sociobiology:

> For Wilson, concepts like superorganism were archaic verbal play, not explanation. Explanation in the new biology was the fruit of an experimental, quantitative program that dis-assembled and re-assembled in vitro the biological system at hand into different sorts of natural-technical objects. These objects were pre-eminently code-structures and control elements. Animal behavior was in this respect no different from molecular biology—and both drew from technological communications systems theories in enforcing such an experimental, quantitative program. Other kinds of explanations just no longer 'counted' (Haraway, 1981–2).

And this is how Wilson in his 1971 book formulated his idea of explanation as an *in vitro* reconstruction:

> [I]n time all the piecemeal analyses will permit the reconstruction of the full system in vitro. In this case *an in vitro reconstruction would mean the full explanation of social behavior* by means of integrative mechanisms experimentally demonstrated and the proof of that

explanation by the artificial induction of the complete repertory of social responses on the part of the isolated members of insect colonies (Wilson, 1971a, p. 319; quoted in Ghiselin, 1974, p. 227, italics added).

It was this same conception of explanation as modeling that Wilson used for his larger goal to explain religion. At the Star Island symposium, he admitted that God was still 'a viable hypothesis' (Wilson, 1980a). On the other hand, if God was a hypothesis, God could be subjected to testing. How would one go about this? Following his earlier approach, Wilson again suggested an *in vitro* reconstruction. This time the task would be achieved through 'the creation of varieties of *synthetic biological gods*':

> This . . . could be accomplished by models of brain action, utilizing computer simulations and working progressively away from the cellular mechanisms of human cognition. One would then test, in the sociobiological mode, whether the peculiarities of the human perception match the exigencies of the particular environment in which the evolution of the human brain is inferred to have taken place. *If such matching does exist, then the mind harbors a species god, which can be parsimoniously explained as a biological adaptation instead of an independent, transbiological force.* The species god is perhaps more potent than a tribal god but unlikely to be the reflection of a universal deity (Wilson, 1980a, p. 427, italics added).

Thus, Wilson here seemed to suggest that the creation of a synthetic god would constitute the ultimate refutation of God as a hypothesis. Speaking for 'the materialists', he told the Star Island symposium how the biological god in the future would disappear:

> For their part, the materialists are convinced that . . . *[e]very nuance of mental action will prove not only to have a physical basis, but also to represent idiosyncratic adaptations to the special circumstances in which the brain evolved.* When these Darwinian isomorphisms include also what has hitherto been explained as divine revelation, the biological god will disappear and the concept of a personal deity will revert to the category of blind faith (Wilson, 1980a, p. 426, italics added).

I asked Wilson in interview whether he really believed that 'every nuance of mental action will prove . . . to have a physical basis'. He answered in the affirmative. Pointing to the book *Between Science and Values* (Graham, 1980) lying on his desk, Wilson explained that he classified himself as an 'expansionist' in the Loren Graham sense, that is, as someone who saw no limits to science:

> I just believe, to put it as simply as possible, that science should be able to go in a relatively few decades to the point of producing a humanoid robot which would walk through that door. The first robot would think and talk like a Southern Baptist minister, and the second robot would talk like John Rawls. In other words, *somehow I believe that we can reconstitute, recreate, the most mysterious features of human mental activity*. That's an article of faith but it has to do with expansionism. That's expansionism! (Wilson, interview)

I have tried to reconstruct the deep metaphysical motives driving Wilson in *Genes, Mind and Culture*. But let us now return to the area of interest to fellow scientists, such as Lewontin, and study their reactions to the book. Obviously, whatever his private metaphysical motives may have been, Wilson (with Lumsden's help) had written a book which he conceived of as a *scientific* contribution, and wanted to be evaluated as such by his peers.

One of the chief scientific criticisms of sociobiology had been that it was not testable, or deliberately unfalsifiable. For instance, this was the way Lewontin formulated it early on in the controversy:

> I am not a Popperian and I do not believe that strict falsifiability is necessary for a valid scientific theory. There is, however, a more elementary demand. Even if a theory has no potential falsifier it must at least have the potential of failure of confirmation. It must be possible to construct an experiment or observation which would fail to confirm the theory in that instance. We must reject out of hand any theory so built that every observation is a necessary confirmation of the theory. But sociobiological theory has precisely such a structure, carefully built up to isolate it from any disagreement with the contingent word (Lewontin, 1976a).

Wilson, with Lumsden's help, had now made a deliberate attempt to put the socio-biology argument into explicit mathematical form. How was testability now related to the models in *Genes, Mind and Culture*? In interview, Wilson rejected the accusation that the sociobiology of *Genes, Mind and Culture* was non-testable:

> I believe that what most people mean when they say: . . . 'sociobiology is all-explanatory and therefore explains nothing', is: they are referring specifically to natural selection hypotheses concerning *human* behavior, and even that is completely wrong, because there are again in the explanation of human behavior with the aid of sociobiology a whole range of *specific* explanatory schemes dealing with different phenomena from brother–sister incest to territorial behavior, the shaping of color vocabulary among cultures . . . and if those sets of explanations fail, then the general conception of evolution by natural selection and sociobiology would be in trouble . . .
>
> *There are plenty of ways to put it into trouble* . . . if human societies were known in which the brother–sister incest taboo were negated or reversed, it would be in trouble; if situations were found in which special unilateral care of closest relatives were abrogated in favor of more distant related people at cousin level, or even more, of strangers—and so on down the list of virtually every one of the main entries and modes of analysis . . .
>
> Furthermore, now that we are entering cognition and incorporating that into theory . . . we are no longer talking about *general tendencies* such as incest, territorial behavior and the like, we are talking about *cultural patterns*, and so . . . we expect certain patterns of cultural diversity to originate and not others, and that would put in jeopardy a whole range of the theory (Wilson, interview).

In other words, Wilson was convinced that, methodologically, sociobiology was now (with *Genes, Mind and Culture*) on safe ground. Wilson had thus gone ahead with his program, answered his critics, and created explicit testable mathematical models for his claims. More specifically, he had dealt with the criticism of the mysterious 'multiplier effect', which had been under suspicion ever since the critics' first letter in *The New York Review of Books*. As we saw earlier, Lewontin had already, in his presentation to the Philosophy of Science Association (1976a), considered the 'multiplier effect' one of the chief problems of Wilson's sociobiological program. What, then, was Lewontin's reaction to Wilson's efforts in 1981?

In his review of *Genes, Mind and Culture* (entitled 'Sleight of Hand') in *The Sciences* (Lewontin, 1981a), Lewontin, far from being appeased, delivered his heaviest blow so far to the efforts of his colleague. He called Lumsden and Wilson's central claim 'absurd', their model equally 'absurd', their assumptions of the nature of mind and culture 'vulgar reductionist', and their mathematical models based on some 'curious choices'. Lewontin's bottom line was that the authors had tried to 'save' sociobiology by demonstrating that the multiplier effect worked, after all. Thus, far from redeeming himself in Lewontin's eyes for having made a legitimate (if flawed) attempt to put human sociobiology on a proper foundation and for having offered a more plausible account of the operation of the multiplier effect, Wilson was almost explicitly accused of a conspiracy:

> The argument is now complete. A small difference in natural selection will cause a small change in gene frequencies, the small change in gene frequencies will cause a small change in 'epigenetic rules,' and a small change in epigenetic rules will lead to a huge change in the culturgen frequency in different populations. So, the multiplier effect works after all, and sociobiology is saved. The only trouble is that each step of the model-building process is carefully designed to achieve that end. The authors have tried to cover their tracks by dusting their path with epsilons and deltas, but the plan is clear (Lewontin, 1981a).

Maynard Smith checks the mathematics

To understand why Lewontin's review had a systematically negative tone, we have to go back to his long-range moral-cum-scientific agenda and see how *Genes, Mind and Culture* in fact became antithetical to some of his most deeply felt convictions.

But it is instructive first to discuss other reviews of this book, especially a review that a serious critic *might* have written. Such a review is the one by the English biologist John Maynard Smith and anthropologist Neil Warren in *Evolution* in 1982. While some of the initial reviews of *Genes, Mind and Culture* were positive, many were very negative. For instance, Peter Medawar in his *New York Review of Books* review entitled 'Stretch Genes' (Medawar, 1981b) accused Lumsden and Wilson of such things as 'mathematical puffery' and neologisms. The anthropologist Edmund Leach wrote a particularly slashing review in *Nature* ('Biology and Social Science: Wedding or Rape?'), suggesting the book came very close to a parody (Leach, 1981a). A common feature of some of the negative reviews was also that they regarded it as an error to use a particularistic view of mind and culture.

But none of the initial reviews, including a whole set of peer reviews in *The Behavioral and Brain Sciences* (in response to the Précis, Lumsden and Wilson, 1981b), dealt seriously with the mathematics involved. At the same time the central claims of the book were supposedly derived precisely from its mathematical models. If this was indeed the case, then criticism of other aspects of the book could be seen as reactions having to do with more extraneous things, such as, for instance, a critic's personal taste.

The problem was that no one seemed willing to deal with the mathematics in the detail necessary to either substantiate or refute the authors' claims.

As it happens, while commending Wilson for spelling out in clear mathematical form the different models and thus improving the testability of sociobiological hypotheses, Maynard Smith and Warren ended up taking a rather negative view of *Genes, Mind and Culture*. But what is interesting is the background to this review. In July 1981 when I interviewed Maynard Smith, he was just in the process of reading the Lumsden and Wilson book in order to review it for *Evolution*. He explained that it was very frustrating reading and that it was going to take a month or more of his life, but that he felt that someone who was competent in mathematics simply *had* to examine the models and their assumptions. Exactly because of the anticipated labor, he had consistently refused to review this book. However, after seeing other reviews (especially the one by Leach in *Nature*), he felt that the book had to be 'properly' criticized and that would mean going to the most fundamental models in the book to see if they were sound. At the time of the interview, he said that he had absolutely no idea how the review would come out, because everything depended on the mathematics. To clarify obscure points, he engaged in a lengthy correspondence with Charles Lumsden, asking him for explanations, especially regarding the mathematics involved in the derivation of the 'counter-intuitive' result that culture speeds up genetic change (see Maynard Smith and Warren, 1982, p. 626).

For Maynard Smith and Warren, then, it was crucial to study the mathematics involved in Lumsden and Wilson's models in order to assess the book correctly. Why was this, when the authors themselves repeatedly say that the book can be read without the mathematics? The answer can best be seen in relation to another book on models simultaneously reviewed: Luigi Cavalli-Sforza's and Marc Feldman's *Cultural Transmission and Evolution* (1981). According to Maynard Smith and Warren:

> The crucial difference between CF and LW, therefore, is that the former present a *logical structure*, the conclusions from which depend on empirical data which the authors consider to be still largely lacking, whereas the latter are making important *assertions* about the nature of man and society. For this reason, it was clear to us before we tackled the models in LW that we must decide whether the models do in fact justify the assertions made. Further, since the models will inevitably be opaque to many readers, we ask whether the predictions of the models are in any sense counter-intuitive, or whether they are of a kind which can readily be understood without elaborate mathematical calculations (Maynard Smith and Warren, 1982, p. 622, italics added).

What was the conclusion of Maynard Smith and Warren after their lengthy work? (It took several months, not only one.) Like many reviewers of the book (and, indeed, Lumsden and Wilson themselves, 1981a, p. 296), they considered it one of the central claims that the 'thousand year rule', according to which the genetic basis of human cultural behavior is likely to change in the order of one thousand years, was deducible from the model. If this conclusion held, then the criticism of someone like Lewontin, objecting to sociobiology (as science) on the grounds of the speed of cultural change, would be answered. Maynard Smith and Warren said this about the rule:

> There is no sense in which the thousand year rule follows from the model. It follows from the assumptions of strong selection and high heritability . . . Our conclusion, then, is that little that is not self-evident emerges from the models, and that the results which LW regard as important, like the 'thousand year rule', do not depend on the cultural components of the model. Our complaint is not that genetic and cultural processes have not interacted during human evolution, but that the models in LW do not do much to illuminate the interaction (Maynard Smith and Warren, 1982, pp. 624–5).

Maynard Smith and Warren also noted Lumsden and Wilson's dismissal of models like those of Piaget, Lévi-Strauss, and Chomsky with the argument that these were not experimentally based, but commented that strict requirements for experimental design would simultaneously disqualify nearly all the evidence Lumsden and Wilson themselves considered (ibid.). Additionally, the reviewers observed omissions and 'cavalierly sampled' data.

We must not assume simply that the reviewers were set against any attempt at putting human sociobiology on a firm basis. Indeed, it is important in this context that Maynard Smith considered human sociobiology quite *legitimate*, and in my interview said that the anthropologist Mildred Dickemann especially had convinced him about the applicability of sociobiological models to humans (Maynard Smith, interview; e.g. Dickemann 1979, 1981). Furthermore, the reviewers took a strong public stance against other critics like Leach: 'Ridicule is not an alternative to criticism.' And as to criticisms that the book's models were reductionist, they retorted: 'It is not *obviously* true that an atomistic analysis of society is doomed to failure.' Finally, Maynard Smith, while a friend of Lewontin's, had systematically been defending Wilson's work in public against political accusations (Maynard Smith, 1975, 1978a), and at an early point in the controversy had written a letter to Wilson saying that he disagreed with the critics' approach (interview with Wilson). Thus, there are good reasons to consider Maynard Smith and Warren's review a 'serious' review of *Genes, Mind and Culture*. Note, finally, that Maynard Smith invited the anthropologist Neil Warren as a co-reviewer exactly to counterbalance any possible bias that he himself might have (Maynard Smith, interview; see Chapter 12 for his views on Wilson and sociobiology).

The central concern here is not the negative verdict of Maynard Smith and Warren. The importance of their review lies not so much in the conclusions themselves, but in the way the review throws light on the opposition between Wilson and Lewontin. On the one hand, as already noted, the review is undoubtedly a model of what might have been expected from serious critics of *Genes, Mind and Culture*, and thus serves as a foil for Lewontin's review, to be discussed next. On the other hand, the review surely underlines the powerful extra-scientific factors which drive Wilson into areas where his fellows will not follow.

Lewontin feels disdain

Turning now to Lewontin's reaction to *Genes, Mind and Culture*, we encounter an altogether different tone and approach. As we saw, Wilson and Lumsden are almost explicitly accused of bad faith, at least of very sharp practice.

Was the attempt of Lumsden and Wilson to mathematically justify the multiplier effect in itself a 'crime' of some sort from Lewontin's point of view? No, said Lewontin, this was something that any scientist, including himself, would have done: after all, both he and others had repeatedly criticized Wilson and said that sociobiology must be able to explain the big difference between human cultures:

> And that is a very, very serious criticism of this theory, and that has to be met. And so, my assertion is that *Genes, Mind and Culture* is a concrete attempt to develop a model which will meet that criticism. It's a perfectly valid thing to do. I mean, if I make a theory and people say: yes, but, ah, the theory has a hole in it!, what do I do next? I sit down and patch the hole, showing that it is plausible that even under my theory these things will happen. So there is nothing *bad*, or *evil* (laugh), or *dishonest* about trying to create a model which patches a hole in a theory! . . . What was nasty in my review was that given that the book was written for that purpose it was written dishonestly—I said that.
> Q: You did?
> A: Well, I didn't use the word 'dishonest', but I used all kinds of nasty kinds of words . . . 'covering the tracks with epsilons and deltas'. . .
> Q: So you were aware that it sounded nasty?
> A: I *meant* it to sound nasty! I meant the review to be a nasty review! The one thing that *wasn't* nasty—I am just trying to be very careful here: The review was a nasty review, and I meant it to be a nasty review—it is a nasty book!—but the one thing that is *not* nasty in the review is the assertion that the reason the book is written is to cover a previous hole in the theory! (Lewontin, interview)

Why, then, was the review written in a nasty tone, if Lewontin thought that Lumsden and Wilson's behavior was indeed scientifically defensible? Lewontin's answer was:

> I don't really think we are engaged primarily in an intellectual issue. I do not think that what he has been doing for the last ten years has been primarily motivated by a genuine desire to find out something true about the world, and therefore I don't think it is serious. One of the reasons my book review of Lumsden and Wilson had a kind of sneering tone is that it is the way I genuinely feel about the project, namely that it is not a serious, intellectual project. Because I have only two possibilities open to me. Either it is a serious intellectual project, and Ed Wilson can't think, or he can think, but it is not a serious project and therefore he is making all the mistakes he can—he does. If it is a really deep serious project, then he simply lowers himself in my opinion as an intellectual . . . It is a question of what kind of intellectual work you have to do to meet a certain intellectual pretension to explanation about the world. If I am going to sit down and write a theory about how all of human culture is explained by biology, I have a lot of epistemological groundwork to learn, I mean, a fantastic amount . . . I mean, these guys have just jumped feet first into a kind of naïve and vulgar kind of biological explanation of the world, and the consequence is a failure. It is a

failure as a system of explanation because they haven't done their homework. . . . I have to
honestly say that my chief feeling—I'll be honest about my chief feeling when I consider all
this stuff—it's one of disdain. I don't know what to say, I mean, it's cheap! (Lewontin,
interview)

So Lewontin saw Wilson as spurred primarily by career or other base ambitions, and as
'not doing his homework'.

The meta-scientific level of Lewontin's critique is strongly highlighted by the indignant response of Wilson to this charge. According to Wilson in interview, in-depth
preparation was exactly what he *had* done, because he believed that he had correctly
presented both the newest developments and the consensus in the different fields on
which he relied in *Genes, Mind and Culture*:

> Even in cognitive psychology, which is not my field, we checked a lot of the recent literature
> and consulted with a couple of cognitive psychologists about what is the latest . . .
> Q: Does this mean you would claim that you are on top of the *consensus* in cognitive
> psychology?
> A: Precisely! Of course, everyone trying to cover such a broad field is subject to criticism, but
> I would suggest we are less than most, because we put in an enormous amount of work. You
> see all those boxes [points to a room-length of file boxes]—those are *primary* references . . .
> that's what I do! Note that in the field of population genetics where we present a consensus
> we were not opposed by anyone of the population geneticists, not Lewontin, not Hartl,
> not Maynard Smith—none of them said that we had misrepresented in any way the latest
> views . . . that is true about Dawkins, but that is not true about us (Wilson, interview).

The same view was reflected in an unpublished letter written by Wilson and Lumsden
to the editors of *Nature* in response to Leach's (1981) slashing review of the book:

> In his May 21 review of our book *Genes, Mind and Culture*, Edmund Leach presents himself
> as a professional anthropologist and us as amateurs whose statements in the field are
> sufficiently error-filled to be dismissible. But in the examples cited it is he who is in error.
> He appears not to have analyzed the recent relevant literature of anthropology, whereas we
> made a conscientious attempt to do so in preparing our monograph.

Thus, 'homework' for Wilson meant taking primary references at face value, while
homework for Lewontin meant critical scrutiny of the various elements going into
larger model-building. Their views about homework were obviously linked to their
views about scientific progress. This can be seen in Wilson's answer to the question of
whether Lewontin's main criticism might not have derived from his view of science as
based on certified knowledge:

> A: He might believe it himself, but if he does, he is overlooking most of the history of
> science, which shows that the boldest advances are often due to those conceptual leaps—
> Q: Which were not proven at the time?
> A: Yes, that's right! (Wilson, interview)

Here it becomes clear that Wilson had a dual approach to modeling. He admitted that he
was telling a story but he also believed that it would eventually be proven true (Wilson,
interview). He was expecting other scientists to fill in the missing conceptual links

following the developments in different relevant fields. This in turn was based on his view of science as proceeding in bold leaps and his view of the 'tractability' of an area.

Asked whether he perceived the danger that the models might have nothing to do with reality (Lewontin's main point, in his 1974 book), Wilson answered:

> It has happened in some fields, such as population genetics; it makes this field arid. On the other hand, because of the ebullience of scientific research and creativity, whenever conceptual expansion is possible in addition to mathematical modeling, experiments and so on, it gets done. Increasing aridity in a field—as everyone agrees happened in theoretical population genetics—is usually not so much the capture of the field by the mathematicians or the ossification of the thinking of a few key individuals, although this contributes; it is usually because the area turns out to be less tractable than they thought. Whenever an area is even moderately tractable, approachable, doable, it gets done! (Wilson, interview)

There is no question, then, that for Wilson modeling was the key to scientific progress.

We have seen that, in the 1960s, Wilson and Lewontin had a common interest in creating new models in evolutionary biology and shared many convictions about the evolutionary process. Indeed, Lewontin himself (for example, Lewontin, 1961) tried to create game-theoretical models, which would give strong predictive results. But Lewontin's point was later that that was 'evolutionary theory on the cheap' and that 'God is in the details' (cf. Lewontin, 1982a). In interview he even mentioned that he sometimes blushes when he thinks about his former large-scale attempts. Thus, at one level, it is probably enough to explain the tone of Lewontin's review of *Genes, Mind and Culture* on the basis that, according to him, Wilson had produced evolutionary theory 'on the cheap'. But considering that Lewontin had abandoned large-scale modeling himself for philosophical reasons, he was not really in direct competition with Wilson in the sense of who had the better theory. Hence, the conflict concerned rather the nature of good science in general and biological theory in particular, that is, it was of a meta-scientific nature. We could say that *Wilson and Lewontin were involved in a tacit struggle for scientific and moral authority in regard to the meaning of 'good science'*.

But there is another reason why *Genes, Mind and Culture* drove Wilson's and Lewontin's different conceptions of scientific modeling to a head-on collision: this was the first time that Wilson attempted to model not ecological systems but human beings and human societies. From Lewontin's point of view, Wilson's assumptions about individuals and society were both methodologically and ontologically erroneous. In his 1976 philosophical statement Lewontin had already declared that sociobiology rested on a confusion between materialism and reductionism:

> It is sure that we are material beings and that our social institutions are the products of our material beings, just as thought is the product of a material process. But the content and meaning of human social organization cannot be understood by a total knowledge of biology any more than by a total knowledge of quantum theory. War is not the sum total of individual aggressive feelings and society cannot be described if we know the DNA sequence of every individual in it. The naive reductionist program of sociobiology has long been understood to be a fundamental philosophical error. Meaning cannot be found in the movement of molecules (Lewontin, 1976a).

What is more, in *Genes, Mind and Culture* Wilson was not only engaging himself in 'incorrect' modeling of human beings, he was also trying to sell his reductionist program to the social sciences, thus undermining their struggling efforts toward 'correct' holistic theory formation.

The dispute cut still more deeply, and just as we had to refer back to explain Wilson's efforts, so we must also refer back to explain Lewontin's critique. From Lewontin's point of view as a moral/political actor, it was blatantly obvious that if the overall thesis of *Genes, Mind and Culture* was granted or not opposed, then this was a further driving in of the wedge of 'biological determinism' that was first inserted by *Sociobiology: The New Synthesis* (and, immediately before that by the arguments of such people as Jensen and Herrnstein). Thus, the controversy about *Genes, Mind and Culture* should be seen as a culmination of the conflict between Wilson's and Lewontin's total moral-cum-scientific agendas.

In this context, two factors in particular should be emphasized. First, *Genes, Mind and Culture* was the point at which Wilson, with Lumsden's help, most explicitly used population genetics, Lewontin's field, to suit his own purposes (that is, to prove that it was at least theoretically possible for genes to hold culture on a leash). Second, there was an even more irritating matter. For the multiplier effect to operate, Wilson needed at least some genetic variation between groups. What was his evidence for this? None other than the small genetic differences between human groups that Lewontin discovered using molecular techniques. As we have seen, these differences are slight—only 15 per cent of the variation within human blood types exists between groups, whereas 85 per cent of the variation is shared across groups. Wilson argued nevertheless that this small amount was enough for the multiplier effect to take action. Thus, Wilson turned on their head those very differences which had become the basis for the liberal and left-wing argument against racism!

Lewontin was therefore put in the uncomfortable situation of having produced research that might be used, after the fashion of *Genes, Mind and Culture*, to support the argument for 'innate cultural differences'. At the same time he was well aware that on the left the 'multiplier effect' from the very beginning had been considered politically suspect, and that groups such as CAR had consistently attacked Wilson as racist, on this ground, among others. But this, then, would mean that Lewontin himself had in fact indirectly contributed to the abuse of biological theory, quite contrary to his intentions to provide 'good modern science' as against 'bad old science' (as he said, for example, in the Nova program in 1975)! Lewontin's deliberate scientific effort to dispel racism had thus been cast in dubious light by Wilson and Lumsden. The *Genes, Mind and Culture* theory 'had to' be wrong, because otherwise Lewontin was in trouble.

This may be part of the reason why Lewontin in his review presented Wilson's model-building not only as scientifically unacceptable but as suspect *overall*, and as having ulterior (though unspecified) motives. There was a moral question at issue here, with Wilson's work threatening Lewontin's own integrity as an ideologically unimpeachable Marxist in the eyes of his left-wing audience. The readers that Lewontin cared about surely knew what he meant when he began and ended his review with the statement: 'Nothing makes sense except in the light of history' (a Marxist spin on Dobzhansky's dictum that nothing makes sense except in the light of evolution).

It is ironical that in the case where Lewontin most clearly spelled out his epistemological, methodological, and ontological objections to modeling of the Wilson and Lumsden type, his 'coupled' agenda, with its obligatory conspiracy set-up and occasional Marxist puns, prevented him from reaching Wilson at the desired meta-scientific level. What happened instead was that Wilson could choose to be offended by his tone and refuse to take him seriously. Thus, in their reply to Lewontin's attack (Lumsden and Wilson, 1981b), the authors of *Genes, Mind and Culture* turned his criticism to their own advantage, stating that Lewontin had not addressed the 'issue', which for them was the content of their book and the factual evidence, not an issue of a meta-scientific nature.

This reply also produced Wilson's first direct attack on Lewontin as a Marxist: Wilson defined Lewontin's opposition to sociobiology as 'political, not scientific', and presented him as in principle opposed to 'the very idea of an analytical program of research on human society'. Thus, far from being rebutted at the level of his serious meta-scientific intent, Lewontin was simply told by the authors to 'fish or cut bait'. Once more, the controversy between Wilson and Lewontin had been reconfirmed in the public realm as a personal one with a political basis, and once more the possibility of a serious meta-scientific communication between Lewontin and Wilson was short-circuited.

But by now it would be naïve to believe that we had simply a case of cognitive differences, depending on two different moral-cum-scientific agendas. Once the sociobiology controversy began, strategical interests came into play on both sides. As the debate evolved, it was in neither party's interest to straighten out misunderstandings; instead, the point became to develop one's own position while dismissing the opponent's as 'extrascientifically' motivated. This way Lewontin let Wilson graduate to being a leader, first of the 'adaptationist' and later of the 'reductionist' program, while Wilson chose to retain Lewontin as a useful straw man for 'tabula rasa', 'Marxist' environmentalism. Thus, what Lewontin and Wilson were really doing, while strategically defending their own new moves in the sociobiology debate and in each case making the opponent a caricature of positions they wanted to attack, was using the sociobiology controversy to further their long-range moral-cum-scientific agendas. Wilson became a grateful target for Lewontin's expanding 'critical' program while Lewontin's political objections served Wilson well in his ambition to promote his own 'positive' program as beyond serious scientific criticism.

Thus, paradoxically, one could describe the situation between these two opponents in the sociobiology controversy as really one of symbiosis. It was in both parties' interests to keep the controversy going, not to clear up misunderstandings, and not to examine too closely where the real differences lay. This shows that the terms of a scientific debate, while set by the protagonists, may not be a true representation of what the conflict is, in fact, about.

Edmund Leach prefers ethology

The conception of culture that Wilson was trying to combat was later to be explicated as 'the Standard Social Science Model (SSSM)' (Cosmides and Tooby, 1992). The following passage was written by Wilson much later, but I believe it reflects the way he was already thinking in *Genes, Mind and Culture*—he just did not have a name then for what he was objecting to:

> The SSSM views culture as a complex system of symbols and meanings that mold individual minds and social institutions. That much is obviously true. But the SSSM also sees culture as an independent phenomenon irreducible to elements of biology and psychology, thus the product of environment and historical antecedents.
>
>   In purest form *the Standard Social Science Model turns the intuitively obvious sequence of causation upside down. Human minds do not create culture but are themselves the product of culture.* This reasoning is based, once again, on the slighting or outright denial of a biologically based human nature. Its polar opposite is the doctrine of genetic determinism, the belief that human behavior is fixed in the genes, and that its most destructive properties, such as racism, war, and class division, are consequently inevitable. Genetic determinism, proponents of the strong form of the SSSM say, must be resisted not only because it is factually incorrect but because it is morally wrong.
>
>   To be fair, I have never met a biologist who believes in genetic determinism as just defined. Conversely, although the extreme form of the SSSM was widely held among serious scholars in the social sciences twenty years ago, today it is rare (Wilson, 1998a, p. 188, italics added).

As we see, in this passage Wilson asserts that the social sciences' focus on learning and culture due to 'fear of genetic determinism'. This is of course a possible explanation, but is it the most plausible one? In the social sciences the focus of interest is obviously on social or cultural aspects of human behavior, rather than on our hardware for acquiring culture. *Of course* biologically constructed human minds (what else?) must originally have created culture, and continue to create culture. Nobody disputes that. The point that Wilson *may* have wanted to make in this somewhat elliptic passage could have been that adherents of the Standard Social Science Model typically resist the very thought that there might be constraints on the *kinds* of cultures that can be created, whereas biologists, say, would be more willing to do so. This was one of the big objections of various critics to Wilsonian sociobiology. I believe that Wilson, with the 'SSSM', may here in fact more particularly mean 'the environmentalist paradigm' established by Franz Boas and his anthropological school in the 1930s. One of the motivations of this school was clearly 'fear of genetic determinism'—and for good reason (see Chapter 2). Or Wilson may have simply used an unscientific-seeming extreme to implicitly argue for the scientific reasonableness of his own co-evolutionary model.[1]

  It will be illuminating to bring in more detailed anthropological reasoning about Lumsden and Wilson's own genes-mind-and-culture model to show that the issues regarding culture are more complex. My guest is anthropologist Edmund Leach, interviewed in 1981. Interestingly, we will find that Leach fulfills Wilson's two criteria: he *does* think that the mind creates culture, and he *does* recognize a biologically determined human nature, but still disagrees with Wilson and Lumsden. At the same time he demonstrates in his own way that cultural anthropologists can, in fact, find common ground with evolutionary biologists—it just has to be the right ground. For Leach, the genes–mind–culture approach won't do. (Leach, of course, has his own idiosyncracies, and his views, in turn, can be criticized by others.) To show that at issue may, in fact, be Wilson and Lumsden's *particular* conception of the relationship between genes, minds, and culture, rather than an opposition as such between the social sciences and biology, I will conclude by bringing in some 'internal' critics from the biological camp.

From Leach's *Nature* review of *Genes, Mind and Culture* it seemed that he somehow considered a statistical treatment of social behavior wrong. What exactly did he dislike about the attempts to join sociobiology and anthropology, and why was the title of his review: 'Biology and Social Science: Wedding or Rape?' (Leach, 1981a)? A couple of months after the publication of the review, I set out to find out from Leach himself. Before meeting Leach, two friendly 'native informers' on British academic culture, Jon Hodge and John Turner at the University of Leeds, had suggested to me that Leach's resistance to sociobiology most probably reflected a more general British academic phenomenon. According to them, everybody wanted their discipline to be as close to *philosophy* as possible, because philosophy was the queen. Leach's specialty, structural anthropology, had done rather well in this respect—and now Wilson with his statistics was dragging the discipline down. Horror!

I checked Leach's review again. It began: 'This book comes so close to being a parody that I have difficulty in believing it is not an academic hoax.' Later it mentioned 'a massive battery of diagrams, graphs, and sophisticated-looking algebraic equations'. But, according to Leach

> this whole elaborate apparatus is devoid of meaning because it assumes that human culture can be broken down into clusters of traits (which the authors call 'culturgens') which can then be counted and subjected to statistical analysis . . . the whole argument presupposes that culturgens are readily identifiable entities. With very few exceptions, contemporary social and cultural anthropologists are unanimous in holding that human culture cannot be broken down into units of this or any other kind (Leach, 1981a).

All the authors' examples of 'gene–culture translation' were defective, Leach continued. For instance, they claimed that there was 'a nearly universal avoidance of marriage and full sexual relations between full brothers and sisters. The epigenetic rule appears well established: a deep sexual inhibition develops between those who live in close domestic contact during the first six years of life'. But no such rule had been 'well established', Leach maintained.

Leach had sounded very ill-tempered in his review, but the Leach I met just kept on *laughing*! He didn't seem particularly angry with sociobiology; he just thought Lumsden and Wilson had got their facts so completely wrong. Leach was a most convivial interviewee and seemed quite happy to let me grill him. We had finished lunch in the cafeteria of King's College and were now comfortably settled in his office. The time had come for a little anthropology lesson for me.

Leach started off saying that he was perfectly willing to admit that humans are a species whose peculiar characteristics are genetically based, and that within the species exist groups with special characteristics, such as skin color—a result of adaptations in the past. But he was not willing to say that these racial adaptations corresponded to cultural differences, or, say, modes of subsistence, such as agriculture or pastoralism: 'Cultural differences have no relationship at all to genetic differences. I can't see how they could. The populations that are culturally peculiar are not closed populations in any sense.' Cultural anthropologists have also shown that in a single generation the culture can change totally, Leach pointed out. So, Leach concluded, in so far as this was what sociobiologists claimed, they were talking nonsense, 'they don't use "culture" in a sense I know at all'.

There were other problems with the sociobiological attempt to deal with culture. Leach laughingly declared Wilson and Lumsden 'totally innocent—they don't know how varied human cultures are', or 'they just don't know the facts'. He gave an example: 'Sociobiologists are interested in succession, who mates with whom. They are interested in genetic convergence or a rule that says no marriage at all. But there is no uniformity at all! . . . As far as cousin marriage goes, for instance, there is every possible combination of rules!' Leach went on to criticize the sociobiological idea of individual investment in the next generation, 'this curious idea that by and large individuals can somehow *choose* their mates! In most of the world they can't! Their love affairs are different from their marriages. Their marriages are arranged by their seniors for political reasons.'

Leach went on to dismiss as 'nonsense' the idea of a rule of sexual inhibition between people who live in close contact during the first years of life ('he has picked up some stuff from Robin Fox', he said about Wilson). According to Leach there was hard evidence, census records, which had survived. Marriage had to do with things such as consolidation of land ownership. One example he gave was the situation in southern India today: 'you marry your sister's daughter, it is a principle'. And he thought of an even better example: adopted children in south-east Africa. Parents adopt a young female child who later becomes the wife of the son. 'This way the boy is married off to a cheap girl—ordinary brides are expensive!' This is a very widespread custom, Leach told me, in Taiwan, Hong Kong, Burma, Thailand—and very advantageous from the *parents'* point of view. At this point I ventured the counterpoint that Maynard Smith had been impressed when he had read the stories about the Israeli kibbutzim (that children avoid mating with those they grew up with). 'Childish!', said Leach, 'European, Marxist ideas!'

I asked about the Yanomamö. 'Most unconvincing', answered Leach. He told me about a sociobiology research group the previous year, led by Tim Clutton-Brock, with Napoleon Chagnon as a visitor.[2] 'They missed all the sociological points', said Leach. 'It was so apparent that the Yanomamö do have a system of endogamous patrilineage, a rather unusual system, comparable to semitic culture,' he noted. Now I ventured that sociobiological anthropologist John Hartung, in a 1981 *Nature* article, had connected the sister's son/brother inheritance pattern to the prevalence of extramarital sex for women; he argued it was linked to the certainty of paternity. Leach declared this 'absolute rubbish' and went on to describe the societies in which he had worked. In one society, for instance, they were supposed to marry their mother's brother's daughter. 'All their affairs were with girls they were not supposed to marry!', said Leach, and giggled.

Did he then think, that cultural systems were totally arbitrary, or did they have some kind of relation, say, to the environment? 'The principle of adaptation is a pseudo-Marxist one', said Leach. 'There is always adaptation to the environment. When the environment changes, the culture changes very fast!' I decided to push the idea of constraints further and asked him about the idea of a 'human biogram'. Leach dismissed it as 'absolute nonsense'. He gave the example of the north African pastoralists who, he said, are capable of living anywhere; they are not adapted to a special habitat at all. 'Language gives extraordinary power of adapting to the environment. I am always baffled at how skillful they are; their marvelous clothing, marvelous adaptation.'

And now we got to the crucial point: language. For Leach, human language was the biggest obstacle to the genes–mind–culture idea. Any child could learn any language. You can put a child with Bushmen and she would learn to speak their language. 'Clearly Wilson has not thought about this idea at all', said Leach. 'My daughter-in-law is genetically full-blooded Chinese—she was brought up speaking English. She has no Chinese characteristics!' Leach thought that the co-evolutionary theory had to go together with the idea that humans are divided into endogenous groups. But even our elementary knowledge of human blood groups shows that there are no closed populations—already the Australian aborigines have scores of different groups, he said.[3]

The question of language clearly presented a challenge to the Lumsden–Wilson theory, and I had been wondering about the matter myself, too. Later, I asked Wilson exactly how language fitted in with the theory. Should not the co-evolutionary circuit give rise to a tendency for one to learn the language of one's own culture better than others? But at the same time we know that any child can learn any language. 'It is not proven!', Wilson quickly replied. Rather surprised, I went to try my luck with Lumsden instead. (Lumsden was still at Harvard in the early 1980s.) He told me the same thing! Neither seemed to wish to discuss this, and I did not persist.

Returning to Leach, he was not critical only of the Lumsden–Wilson notion of culture; he was equally unhappy with the way culture was generally conceived by social anthropologists. According to him, the anthropologists, particularly the American ones, were too influenced by people such as Leslie White, who believed that only *humans* had culture. But, according to Leach, 'you will find that all animals have culture—all social animals anyway.' This started sounding interesting: Leach the social anthropologist relating to animals?

He now told me about a great breakthrough in his own thinking that had happened in the early 1960s. He had been invited to a Royal Society symposium which involved a debate about ritual. The anthropologists had introduced what they meant by ritual, as against the ethologists' conception of ritual. Out of this grew a seminar and a symposium on nonverbal communication arranged by Hinde (Hinde, 1972). 'Various anthropologists tended to drop out', observed Leach, but he did not. 'It was at this level I got to talk to the ethologists', he explained. 'I understood what they were talking about!' He had now discovered the possible meeting point of anthropology and other fields:

> Anthropologists emphasize language. We don't invent a language, we acquire what we learn in a communication that already exists. It is this, a cultural phenomenon, an interaction system out there, that makes you a member of this intercommunicating group (Leach, interview 1981).

Patrick Bateson in particular appeared to have been the ethologist responsible for opening Leach's eyes. At the seminar, Bateson had been criticizing the notion of imprinting. 'The chick the moment it is born really has very little behavior—the way it pecks, etcetera, is taught to it by its mother', Leach informed me. He could relate to that, he said.

But there was a profound difference between humans and animals, Leach continued. 'A lot of creatures are cultural—they alter the world, they don't accept the world as it is. Humans are quite peculiar—we alter the world more than other creatures, but also in another way.' Leach described how humans all over the world produce very simple patterns and shapes—for instance, rectangular lines. But nature does not have rectangular lines. The reason for these patterns, repeated again and again, is that our minds are organized around the binary code ('I am a structuralist', Leach added). Leach contrasted the simple forms generated by the mind with the typical forms produced by Darwinian selection. Genetics did *not* seem to be very good at producing simple forms, he said. Darwinian selection was driving toward specialization.

For Leach, it was pure arrogance and naïveté to believe that humans were just another species—the existence of language made a difference. He went on to make an epistemological point. Whatever view you have of human beings is going to be limited by the fact that you are yourself a human being, he said. In principle, there could be a cat sociobiology and a dog sociobiology, he laughed. 'This argument has two parts', he continued on a more serious note. 'We can only understand the things we make; a carpenter can understand things that he has made. We didn't make the natural world. But we can understand society—we made it', said Leach.

Finally we got to the political objections to sociobiology. Leach remembered his first confrontation with *Sociobiology*. He had been at Johns Hopkins in 1975 and out of the blue received a highly agitated telephone call from Toronto: 'Have you seen this awful book? Can you do something about this book?', somebody had asked him. 'I didn't even know this darned thing *existed*', laughed Leach, 'even less what I could do about it!' Again the matter became more serious. 'Politically, I am to the left of center', explained Leach. 'I have a gut feeling that sociobiologists are caught in a political trap they don't fully realize', he said, adding that they may in fact be helping support feelings of racial superiority. This was not true of all biologists, however. And Leach added immediately:

> I wouldn't for a moment want to accuse Wilson of being consciously political. . . . All I am saying is that there is a kind of consistency between the arguments he is presenting and the views that are held by racialists.

And when we discussed the critics of Wilson, he noted: 'I am perfectly aware that you cannot separate your scientific position from your political position.' He gave an example of his own behavior: he was 'extremely hostile' to a particular government in one of the countries he was studying, and this was consistent with things he objected to, such as genocide.

As we saw, Maynard Smith had not been satisfied with Leach's review in *Nature*, because it did not touch on the mathematics of the book. Does this mean that, when Leach criticized what he called Wilson and Lumsden's 'phoney mathematical apparatus', he was acting in the same manner as Peter Medawar's professor friend, who 'hummed' through statistical formulae to get on with the reading of a text (Medawar, 1981b)? Not quite. Leach was, in fact, a rather competent reader of mathematical formulae. Before his career as an anthropologist he had obtained a BA in engineering and mathematics at Cambridge. As an anthropologist, however, he had found plenty to criticize without having to go into the mathematics. And was Leach just exhibiting a social-science knee-jerk response to the 'biologizing' of culture? Not at all. In his review he had emphasized that '*the findings of biology and social science need to be compatible if either are to rate as science*' (italics added). But he also asked for a marriage of mutual respect, not a takeover bid.

What Leach may not have grasped—and here he was in good company with many others—was the nature of the epigenetic rules as being another way of talking about persistent biases in human judgment, apparently deriving from some kind of 'default settings' of the human mind. (This is particularly the realm of social psychology and, most recently, evolutionary psychology.) Indeed, during our interview Leach himself had invoked something that, with hindsight, looked like an epigenetic rule: the tendency for humans to see and reproduce a set of simple forms. Leach may have been closer than he thought to Wilson and Lumsden in this respect. And as to the rule not to mate with individuals familiar from early life, his ethological friends, again, might have told him that this rule was 'well established' at least among animals (Bateson, 1986), although Leach's own human data did not confirm the rule. Perhaps it was Leach's additional conception of the genes–mind–culture model as exploitable for racist purposes that motivated him to too quickly dismiss all of it as 'just bunk'.

Why did Leach find ethology but not sociobiology compatible with his ideas? For this, we may go to Leach's 'guru', Patrick Bateson, who of course represented a novel type of ethology, not the older Lorenzian kind. With Bateson, we get an explanation for his own and other ethologists' resistance to Wilsonian sociobiology (both the original and the genes–mind–culture type). Here is Bateson a few years later commenting on Wilsonian sociobiology and explicitly contrasting it with the thinking of British ethologists (or 'sociobiologists'). Bateson's position had remained the same for a long time, and it was presumably this kind of ethological view he had also imparted to Leach:

> E. O. Wilson believed that he could treat development of the individual merely as a complex process by which genes were decoded. It was this belief that enabled him to blend evolutionary and developmental arguments, and it is this that made him a genetic determinist.

The generation of talented whole-animal biologists and biological anthropologists that was set on fire by the evolutionary ideas soon began to realize that Wilson was wrong. Just how behavior develops in individuals should have been left as an open question. Whether or not behavior involves some instruction from a normally stable feature of the environment, or whether it would be changed by altering the prevailing social and physical environment, cannot be deduced from even the most plausible evolutionary argument. The issues of evolution, development, and current function are not the same. The majority of the scientists who now call themselves sociobiologists know this and say so (Bateson, 1985).

In my interview with Robert Hinde, Bateson's Cambridge colleague, he had also pointed out that Wilson was wrong. All Tinbergen's levels were interrelated, said Hinde, one could not just study ultimate explanations. He brought in the example of great tits opening milk bottles as a demonstration of the importance of learning and culture in animals. When I interviewed him he had not read *Genes, Mind and Culture*, however, and could not comment on the book.

But John Krebs, Dawkins' colleague at Oxford, was familiar with the book. He belonged to the handful of ethologists I met who thought that the idea of genes–mind–culture was plausible. He told me that although Wilson and Lumsden's book had been much criticized, he found their basic theme quite reasonable: 'I don't see why people object so much', he said. There is a genetic variation in propensity to learn different things; those who are better at learning will improve their reproductive success, and that will feed back. 'That seems to me to be a very elegant and simple way to tie together learning and genetic transmission', Krebs observed.

What, then, about the so-called thousand-year rule? Krebs thought it was plausible at the animal level, in fact implicit in the idea that there is feedback. Evolution might be proceeding fast. But Krebs did not want to speculate as to what extent it could be applied to human culture. What? It became clear that when Krebs found the approach to be 'reasonable', he was not thinking of the model as applied to humans at all. He had been talking about *animal* culture all the time! This was a totally new approach to *Genes, Mind and Culture*—using Wilson and Lumsden's model developed for humans to boost ethological reasoning about the interaction of genes, mind and culture in animals. How subversive!

This chapter has dealt with the serious scientific attempt of Wilson and Lumsden to model human sociobiology, and the various criticisms—scientific and political—that were launched against it. In the next chapter, we will again pick up the specifically political thread of the sociobiology controversy, and follow its different strands through the mid-1980s.

CHAPTER 9

The moral/political conflict continues

Emerging trends

In the last three chapters, I have focused on many of the serious scientific issues involved in the sociobiology controversy, issues that emerged only as the debate evolved. As we saw, it was not until the end of the 1970s that there was a decent discussion regarding adaptation, the unit of selection, and the like. Also, in conjunction with the criticism of *Genes, Mind and Culture*, important issues in regard to scientific models and their assumptions were debated—at least indirectly. This indirectness was typical of the whole unfolding controversy; it was still difficult to keep the scientific issues separate from the political and moral ones. There were, however, exceptions: an admirable example of 'pure' scientific criticism is the Dahlem conference (Markl, 1980), and an example of 'pure' scientific discussion at this time is the edited scientific collection *Current Problems in Sociobiology*, published by the King's College Sociobiology Group (1982).

As the sociobiology controversy continued, the strategies of the critics became more diverse. Most of the critics of sociobiology continued the critical agenda, with statements ranging from direct accusations of racism to moral fingerpointing at sociobiologists for lending themselves to racist interpretations, to more sophisticated political-cum-scientific critique, to (almost) 'pure' meta-scientific critique of sociobiological epistemology, methodology, language use, and the like. (As it turned out, it was rather difficult for most critics to keep themselves from inserting political or moral comments even in their most scientifically intended critiques.)

This was also the time of anthologies of essays and reviews critical of sociobiology; a good example is Ashley Montagu's 1980 *Sociobiology Examined* (in 1968 Montagu had done a similar job collecting essays and reviews critical of Lorenz and Ardrey, see Chapter 2). Other anthologies attempted a more balanced picture, such as Gregory *et al.* (1978) *Sociobiology and Human Nature*. And there was, of course, the often scientifically oriented volume produced by the organizers of the 1978 AAAS conference *Sociobiology, Beyond Nature–Nurture* (Barlow and Silverberg, 1980). Also, a whole issue of *Philosophical Forum* (1981–2) was devoted to the sociobiology debate.

While the critical attack arguably reached its height with Lewontin, Rose, and Kamin's *Not In Our Genes* (1984) and Gould's continuing stream of anti-sociobiological essays in his *Natural History* column, later collected as books (perhaps particularly *An Urchin in the Storm*, 1987), an interesting parallel development was taking place with the 'positive' critical agenda championed by some of the most adamant opponents of sociobiology. Among these we find again Lewontin—this time in a more analytical than accusatory mode—in the book he wrote with Richard Levins in 1985: *The Dialectical Biologist*.

What were the leading sociobiologists doing during this time? Wilson, after writing his two books with Charles Lumsden in 1981 and 1983, *Genes, Mind and Culture* and *Promethean Fire*, retreated from the battlefield of human sociobiology to his favorite place: the rainforest. (Indeed, he had said in interview in 1982 that that is what he wanted to do, and so he did.) The result was his *Biophilia*, published in 1984, according to which humans have innate preferences for living nature (as well as innate phobias). A later collection co-edited with Stephen Kellert, *The Biophilia Hypothesis* (Wilson and Kellert, 1993), continued along the same lines, with examples drawn from a wide variety of fields, including fairy tales. But Wilson was later to follow up this rather meditative phase with a new militancy. Toward the end of the 1980s he was already onto his next major project: to save the world's biological diversity. We will return to the further adventures of Wilson in Part III.

The relative withdrawal of Wilson from the sociobiology controversy in the 1980s also meant that the critics of sociobiology could not find a sparring partner in him; there were no more indignant responses to Lewontin's and Gould's continued highly critical reviews in places such as *The New York Review of Books*. After the early 1980s, there was little visible interchange between Wilson and his original critics. The person who picked up the battle-ax instead was Wilson's transatlantic comrade-in-arms, Richard Dawkins.

Dawkins' *The Extended Phenotype*, published in 1982, was partly devoted to a thorough response to the critics of sociobiology; he took on Gould in particular and the latter's critique in *Ever Since Darwin* (1978a). This was the beginning of a new overt opposition between Gould and Dawkins; Gould supported in the background by Lewontin, and Dawkins defended particularly by John Maynard Smith. It was now Gould and Dawkins, rather than Wilson and Lewontin, who slowly emerged as the new 'public' scientists in the sociobiology controversy. At the same time, the controversy was beginning to circle around important issues in evolutionary theory itself (see Chapters 6, 7, and 16).

Wilson may have refrained from counterattack, electing instead to continue with his broader interest—life on Earth—but this did not mean that Lewontin and Gould remained scot-free. Toward the end of the 1970s, a strong ally of Wilson had emerged among his Harvard colleagues—Bernard Davis, a medical doctor and microbiologist from Harvard Medical School. It was Davis, rather than Wilson, who went out on the war path when Gould published his *The Mismeasure of Man* in 1981 (Davis, 1983) and against Lewontin, Rose, and Kamin's collective opus *Not In Our Genes* (1984) (Davis, 1985b). Note, however, that in his many writings and editorials Davis did not necessarily 'represent' Wilson—he did have an agenda of his own. We will return to Davis and Gould in Chapter 11.

'Racist' allegations and rebuttals

From the very beginning, the critics of sociobiology had worried about possible misuse of sociobiological theory. And as the controversy proceeded, political references to sociobiology did indeed emerge. In 1979 a heading in *Nature* announced: 'Sociobiology Critics Claim Fears Come True' (Dickson, 1979).[1] This gave the critics of sociobiology something new to focus on. Jon Beckwith provided a thorough documentation of political use of sociobiology and related claims (Beckwith, 1981–2). An article reprinted in *Sociobiology Examined* informed readers about intricate use of Wilsonian sociobiology by the conservative Club d'Horloge in France. After that, the author went on to establish the most seemingly compromising links possible between sociobiology and the circle around *Mankind Quarterly*, including Arthur Jensen and Hans Eysenck (Sheehan, 1980). Here we see one more example of the totally taken-for-granted connection between the IQ and sociobiology controversies in most critics' minds.

Finding such direct expressions of political abuse was no doubt a triumph for the critics, but even the potentiality of abuse was quite enough to invite censure. Thus, for instance, the fact that Wilson in 1980 gave an interview to *Le Figaro*, and there stated what he believed to be the current status of IQ studies, was already seen as incriminating. This is what political-abuse watchdog and Science for the People leader Jon Beckwith said about Wilson's reckless behavior:

> In the interview, Wilson states, without qualifications: 'It has clearly been established that intelligence is, for the most part, inherited'. This statement is, in a scientific sense, meaningless, since the evidence on heritability of intelligence has been discredited. Further, by implication, it suggests a fixity to the quality of intelligence (whatever that is) which is at odds with genetic theory . . . However, the interview is not meaningless in a political sense. By granting such an interview to a group whose political goals are so close to the Nazis, and in the context of an article which claims scientific justification for its ideology, Wilson, unwittingly or not, has lent his prestige to this movement (Beckwith, 1981–2, p. 318).

This is quite an allegation. Wilson's crime here is not only that he is making a 'false' scientific statement about a socially important issue, but also the very fact that he gave an interview to a conservative magazine. (It certainly did not help the case that the article was entitled 'Confirmation: l'intelligence est hereditaire'.) I asked Wilson to comment on this particular charge shortly after it had been launched. Wilson responded that he gave an interview to the liberal *Le Monde* as well—but this was evidently not recorded by the critics. He said that he did wish that the critics would register his 'good' deeds as well as his 'bad' ones. As an example of the latter, he told me that, at the very beginning of the controversy, he had spoken up against racism at a town meeting. Nobody had given him credit for that.

It is true that any popular appearance on Wilson's part was seen as highly suspect. His interviews in popular magazines were taken as part of a political crusade. And when, at an early point in the controversy, Wilson gave a radio interview, and Paul Bensaquin, the talk-show host, without Wilson's knowledge presented that interview in a context of theories of racial conflict, this was seen as one more expression of Wilson's own true beliefs. What if Wilson had refused to talk? It is unlikely it would have helped much. For instance, the fact that Wilson did not want to appear on a panel debate with the Science for the People after the first interchange of polemics was seen as 'an attempt to stop criticism'. But was it even a fact? Doubts arise when we learn from Tiger (1996) that he and others, as part of a series of seminars at the University of Chicago in the mid-1970s, had 'tried to invite Wilson and his colleague Richard Lewontin to discuss their differences over sociobiology. But Lewontin refused to be in the same room with the man who had been among those responsible for Harvard's hiring him in the first place.'

A triumph for the political critics of sociobiology was undoubtedly the National Front's appropriation of sociobiology. In 1981, Steven Rose, 'Britain's Lewontin', wrote a letter to *Nature* asking leading sociobiologists to respond to the fact that the journal of this right-wing organization, *New Nation*, had recently published articles entitled 'Nationalism, racialism: products of our selfish genes' and 'Science is championing our creed of Social Nationalism'. The journal had cited Dawkins, Wilson, Maynard Smith, and 'one Travers' in support of the view that

> our genes do not permit us to live in a Marxist-Rousseauesque egalitarian communist utopian World State of universal altruism. It was an inevitable result of the way evolution works that our genes would not permit us to so live (quoted in Rose, 1981a).

In his letter Rose challenged Maynard Smith and Dawkins to actively 'disassociate' themselves from the use of their names in support of this kind of 'neo-Nazi balderdash'. The implication was that if they did not, people might believe that these scientists in fact *approved* of the political use of their theories.

Rose's challenge was immediately met. Maynard Smith provided a typical curt response, saying that 'there is nothing in modern evolutionary biology which leads to that conclusion' [that racial integration is impossible] (Maynard Smith, 1981b). Dawkins was also quick to deny that there was any justification of racism in the study of the biology of human behavior. Unlike Maynard Smith, Dawkins chose a painstakingly pedagogical approach, pointing out the various fallacies reflected in *New Nation*'s reasoning. He took particular issue with the belief that genetically inherited traits were by definition unmodifiable:

> What is really wrong with the National Front quotation is not the suggestion that natural selection favoured the evolution of a tendency to be selfish and even racist. What I object to is the suggestion that if such tendencies had evolved they would be *inevitable* and *ineradicable*; the suggestion that we are stuck with our biological nature and can't change it (Dawkins, 1981b, italics added).

To make his own position absolutely clear, Dawkins invoked his own final sentence in *The Selfish Gene*: 'We, alone on earth, can rebel against the tyranny of the selfish replicators.' After that, it was time for a countermove. Dawkins wondered how it was that Rose and the National Front thought so much alike about genes as destiny?

> How Steven Rose and the spokesmen of the National Front came to share their fatalistic views on the inevitability of genetic determination I cannot guess, unless it has something to

do with the fact that 'historical inevitability' is as dear to the Marxist heart as the related concept of 'destiny' is to the Nazi one. In their biological manifestations, the two concepts are as fatuous as each other (Dawkins, 1981b).

Now, seemingly emerging from nowhere, there appeared a response from E. O. Wilson! Wilson found it 'curious' that Rose had not invited him to respond, although his name had also been mentioned by the National Front. After this, Wilson went on to say that he wanted to 'keep the record straight' and point out that 'there was no justification for racism to be found in the truly scientific study of the biological basis of social behavior'. He continued:

> If there is a possible hereditary tendency to acquire xenophobia and nationalist feelings, it is a *non sequitur* to interpret such a hypothesis as an argument in favor of racist ideology. It is more reasonable to assume that a knowledge of such a hereditary basis can lead to circumvention of destructive behavior such as racism, just as a knowledge of the haemoglobin chemistry and insulin production can lead to amelioration of their pathological variants (Wilson, 1981a).

If Wilson had hoped for an apology, or even some kind of acknowledgement from Rose, he was mistaken. Rose kept it British. He duly recognized Maynard Smith's and Dawkins' replies—then simply proceeded with his critique of sociobiology. This time he pulled out a new card against Dawkins, the question of free will. How was it possible for us to be at the same time genetically programmed DNA survival machines and have the capability to transcend this programming, he asked?

> Free will, intentions and wishes (or Dawkins' memes), like the US cavalry, come galloping over the horizon in the nick of time to rescue us from our genes . . . But *where* does our free will etcetera come from? (Rose, 1981b)

(As we shall see, this question of genes and free will was to become the subject of the next *Nature* correspondent, too—the mysterious Isadore Nabi, who caused a minor, interesting epicycle in the debate, to be studied in the next section.)

The group that most relentlessly pursued their political goal in regard to sociobiology was CAR, the Committee Against Racism. Typically, CAR handed out flyers in Harvard Square and on campus. In 1977, one such CAR flyer had said:

> Sociobiology, by encouraging biological and genetic explanations for racism, war and genocide, exonerates and protects the groups and individuals who have carried out and benefited from these monstrous crimes (CAR flyer, excerpt from Rosenthal, 1977).

In 1982, CAR's tactics had not changed. 'Picket E.O. Wilson's lecture—fight racist lies!' said the heading of a flyer handed out to people waiting for entrance to Wilson's public lecture on *Genes, Mind and Culture* in Harvard's Science Center on 10 February. The flyer linked Wilson to Harvard's earlier 'racist' record:

> [T]o give a 'respectable' cloak to racism, certain scribblers at Harvard are working overtime . . . A short list of Harvard's 'master race' ideologues: D. Moynihan (1965, blamed racist oppression of blacks on their so-called matriarchal family structure); A. Jensen (1969, *Harvard Ed Review* published his ravings about black 'genetic inferiority'); E. Banfield (1970,

The Unheavenly City: 'poor people like to live in slums'). But in 1975, E. O. Wilson laid claim to the title of chief of this group, when in *Sociobiology* he postulated genes for all social life, including war, business success, male supremacy and racism.

The second page reproduced an excerpt from the above-mentioned pamphlet distributed by the National Front in Britain. The pamphlet was described as paying tribute to '"sociobiologists", led by Harvard zoologist E. O. Wilson', while linking social inequality to biological differences. The CAR flyer concluded on the following rousing note: 'Militant action, not merely academic debate, is needed to crush Wilson's fascist theories.'

But there was a clear and rather embarrassing discrepancy between the militant flyer and the actual picketing effort. This became obvious to the audience waiting to get in to hear Wilson speak. Finally, the crowd got inside and settled down. Wilson himself was in top form. He started his lecture in a calm and good-humored way, simply noting that CAR had misunderstood his book. In 1982, it did not take more than that to discredit CAR's attempt in front of a popular/academic audience. The protest subsided and Wilson delivered his lecture unchallenged.

In contrast to CAR, convinced of the racism of sociobiology, from the beginning there had been some disagreement among the members of the Sociobiology Study Group as to whether or not sociobiology was inherently racist. Some of Wilson's colleagues at Harvard had stated that they did not think sociobiology was a racist doctrine (particularly Lewontin, 1975c). Even so, as Wilson himself dryly noted in interview, the critics did not seem to mind being quoted in CAR's anti-racist pamphlets. Wilson himself, when attacked, had persistently done his best to combat racist implications and emphasize the universalistic aspects of sociobiology (for example, Wilson, 1976a). He had even in writing clearly distanced himself from 'the notorious racist' (Wilson's expression) William Shockley (Wilson, 1976c).

Still, there remained some ambiguity among the critics. To quote a leading member of Science for the People, Joe Alper:

> The early statements of the Sociobiology Study Group of Science for the People (SSG) were interpreted to mean that sociobiology was a racist theory equivalent to Social Darwinism, and some members in the group felt the need to state publicly that SSG did not believe that sociobiologists are racists. SSG believes that sociobiology is not racist in the usual sense of the term. However, *built into the theory is the biological inevitability of intergroup conflict.* Given the history of our country and recent political realities, such a theory can be easily used to support doctrines of discrimination. *We believe that sociobiologists cannot divorce themselves from the racial implications of their theory* (Alper, 1978; italics added).

After this Alper himself went on to demonstrate in detail how, despite all, sociobiology did carry a racist message. To do this he invoked—surprisingly—group selection theory rather than kin selection theory, and then proceeded to identify 'group' with 'race' (which is something that Wilson, for instance, would not have done). After this, Alper was able to extract the 'true' message of Wilson's sociobiology: '*War is the natural outcome of the struggle of one group against another.*' (For more detailed appreciation of the steps in this exercise, I refer the reader to the original, Alper, 1978.)

In addition, Alper and many others in the Sociobiology Study Group saw a 'deeper connection between sociobiology and racism'. What alarmed them was Wilson's suggestion that 'variation in the rules of human cultures, no matter how slight, might provide clues to underlying genetic differences' (Wilson, 1975a, p. 500). Alper did not fail to cast suspicion on the project by pointing out that Wilson's ambition was a *scientifically strange* one: 'Given the number of important unsolved problems in biology, it seems peculiar to worry about 'slight' genetic differences and to postulate unprovable biological explanations for social phenomena which might arise from these differences.' It may seem surprising that in presenting sociobiology as suspect science, Alper, a chemist, felt comfortable judging what counted as acceptable interests for evolutionary biologists! But this was not the way he himself, nor the other critics, saw it. In fact, Alper's suspicion that sociobiology was not based on a 'true' scientific interest echoed the views of many other members of the Sociobiology Study Group, including Lewontin.

Compare Alper's view of racism with that of Gould. Gould seemed to reason that there was no way to avoid racism in science: science is necessarily part of the social context, and therefore a racist society automatically does racist science (Gould, 1981a). But Chomsky's view of racism beat them all. For him, the sheer *discussion* about group differences—arguing for them *or* denying them—would indirectly only serve to promote racism. This was, in fact, one of the reasons why he stayed away from the sociobiology controversy, as he told me in interview in 1982!

Thus, among the academic left at the time, there existed a spectrum of different attitudes to the relationship between science and racism. Still, it often seemed that critics wished to make the strongest possible case for the connection between sociobiology and racism. Alper was one of the most persistent in trying to pin down Wilson as a racist. In a 1982 book review in *Science for the People*, he appeared more determined than ever. The book under discussion was Allan Chase's (1977) *The Legacy of Malthus: The Social Cost of the New Academic Racism*. Alper found it expedient to inform his readers that the 'scientific racists' of the past 'were not the ancestors of the Ku Klux Klan or the Birchers but of E. O. Wilson, the most prominent of the human sociobiologists, who is a Professor of Zoology at Harvard, and of Arthur Jensen, Professor of Psychology at the University of California'. Alper went on to warn the readers about the danger of criticizing the theories of scientific racists as pseudoscience. That would only 'play[s] into the hands of a Wilson, who claims that his theories are the first which deserve to be termed scientific' (Alper, 1982). Here Alper clearly deviated from the position of someone like Lewontin, for whom sociobiology was *obviously* a pseudoscience. Lewontin tended to have differences of this kind with people like Alper and Beckwith, the leading members of Science for the People, and the result was that he parted ways with this organization rather soon. (In interview, Lewontin briefly referred to 'political disagreements' between SftP and himself.)

The diverse, dedicated, and sometimes desperate attempts to connect sociobiology with racism ever since the beginning of the sociobiology debate suggest that more was at stake than mere concern with the political underpinnings of biological theories. From the mid-1970s to mid-1980s, sociobiology appears to have been vitally important as an *organizing factor* for the academic left-wing movement, mostly in the US, but to some small extent also in the UK. Sustaining the image of sociobiology as racist was important, because in this way sociobiology could be connected to an important political issue, and further identified with a long tradition of 'academic racism'. Wilson (or, rather, 'Wilson') in particular filled a clearly defined political function in this respect, and became the sociobiologist everybody loved to hate.

The Nabi episode: manners and morals in science

Just as the 'genes and race' interchange in *Nature* may have indicated to readers the seriousness with which the critics of sociobiology took their political mission, so the 'Nabi' episode that followed could have easily given the impression that the critics were rather a bunch of prankish schoolboys. The Nabi episode was one of those incidents in the course of the sociobiology controversy which was seen very differently from different Harvard offices. For Lewontin and Levins it was hysterically funny. For Wilson and Davis, it was not funny at all.

Who was Nabi? That was exactly the question asked by the readers of *Nature* in the spring and fall of 1981. A month after Dawkins' response to Rose, a letter appeared by an Isadore Nabi, who gave as his address Museum of Comparative Zoology, Harvard University. Nabi said he was 'confused' by Dawkins' answer. In *The Selfish Gene*, Dawkins had said that we are 'robot vehicles blindly programmed to preserve the selfish molecules known as genes', but now he told us that we may have to fight against our genetic tendencies:

> It really is very vexing. Just as I had learned to accept myself as a genetic robot and, indeed, felt relieved that I was not responsible for my moral imperfections, Dr Dawkins tells me that I am not as manipulated as I thought. This is a problem I keep having in my attempt to understand human nature. Professor Wilson, in his book on sociobiology, assured me that neurobiology was going to provide me with a 'genetically accurate and hence completely fair code of ethics' (p. 575). I was euphoric at the prospect that my moral dilemmas at last had a real prospect of resolution, when suddenly my hopes were dashed by an article in which Professor Wilson warned me against the naturalistic fallacy (*New York Times* 12 October, 1975). You can imagine my perplexity. I do wish I knew what to believe (Nabi, 1981a).

It was in response to this that Wilson's letter 'Who is Nabi?' appeared. In that letter Wilson (1981b) told *Nature*'s readers not only that Nabi has misrepresented his (Wilson's) true position on sociobiology and ethics, but also that the name Nabi was fictitious. Appended to Wilson's letter was a note by the editor that read: 'Isadore Nabi is believed to be the pseudonym of Professor R. C. Lewontin of Harvard University.'

Not so!, responded Lewontin. In a letter headed 'Credit Due to Nabi', he said: 'Let me state categorically that any assertion that Isadore Nabi is none other than R. C. Lewontin is incorrect' (Lewontin, 1981d). Among the 'corroborative details' Lewontin offered in order to clear up the matter was an excerpt from *American Men and Women of Science*, containing Nabi's biographical data. As he pointed out, the reader could clearly see that for a start Nabi's age and bachelor's degree from Cochabamba University did not coincide at all with Lewontin's own biography. Lewontin further pointed out that Nabi was listed as the editor of the journal *Evolutionary Theory*. Why would the managing editor of *Evolutionary Theory*, Professor Leigh Van Valen, list Lewontin on the editorial board of that journal if he (Lewontin) was already the editor? Finally, noted Lewontin, Isadore Nabi was the author of several important works, such as the seminal 'An Evolutionary Interpretation of the English Sonnet'. Which, he was 'sorry to say, are not at all of my creation'. And, gloriously compounding the confusion, Lewontin ended by reporting that recently Van Valen himself had been identified as the Nabi who wrote the letter—'an assertion which he denies' (Lewontin, 1981e).

Indeed, some three weeks before there had appeared in *Nature* a letter by an *Isidore* Nabi from the University of Chicago. Referring to the original Nabi letter, this gentleman protested: 'My acquaintances all seem to think that I wrote that letter, so I wish to state publicly that this is not the case. His first name is spelled "Isadore".' (Isidore Nabi, 1981).

In the early fall of 1981 a *Nature* editorial seemingly put an end to the fun and games around Nabi. It read: 'Isidore Nabi, RIP' (*Nature*, 3 September 1981). What did this killjoy editorial have to say? This is what *Nature's* readers were told:

> There has been a great confusion in the scientific literature because of a jape that began at the University of Chicago some years ago. A non-existent scientist, Dr Isidore Nabi (whose first name is sometimes spelled Isadore), was blessed with a biography in *American Men and Women of Science* by a group of scientists including Professor Leigh Van Valen (still at the University of Chicago), Dr Richard Lester (now at the Harvard School of Public Health) ...
>
> Unfortunately, the joke has gone too far. Apparently Nabi's three creators have been in the habit of using his fake existence as a means of concealing their own identity. Earlier this year, for example, a letter supposed to be from Nabi was published in *Nature* (290, 183; 1981) making an otherwise plausible point about the controversy over the Natural History Museum. . . . The objection to this use of Nabi's fictional identity as a pseudonym in the scientific literature is twofold. First, it is a deception. Second, it allows people with known opinions on important controversial matters to give a false impression that their opinions are more weighty than truth would allow (*Nature*, 293, 2; 1981).

But the Nabi controversy was not over yet. Who was Richard Lester at the Harvard School of Public Health? There was no such person, as far as anyone knew. Still, perhaps Richard Lester existed, after all, because he responded as follows to the editorial:

> I was taken aback to discover that I was referred to in your editorial of 3 September (p. 2) as one of the creators or co-authors of the works of Isadore (Isidore) Nabi. This is completely untrue.
>
> I am shocked that you make this allegation without checking with the people concerned, presumably on the basis of claims by some third party who prefers to hide behind the anonymity of a *Nature* editor. The error in relation to my own role causes me to doubt the accuracy of the rest of the claims in the editorial, including those about Professor Nabi (Lester, 1981).

Appended to Lester's letter was once again an editorial comment. It read: 'Richard Lester is believed to be a pseudonym of Richard Levins, one of the true culprits.' That letter published at the end of October marked the chronological end of the Nabi controversy.

But the Nabi mystery had, in essence, already been resolved earlier that month. It was Leigh Van Valen who got the last word. In a letter to *Nature* he said he wanted to make some corrections and additions regarding Isadore Nabi. In effect, he gave away the show:

> The committee called Nabi was formed in the early 1960s, with a programme analogous to, but much less ambitious than, that of the French mathematician Nicholas Bourbaki. Nabi's initial consultants were Richard Levins (not Lester), then at the University of Puerto Rico, Richard Lewontin, then at the University of Rochester, the late Robert MacArthur, then at the University of Pennsylvania, and myself, then at the American Museum of Natural History. Three of us moved to the University of Chicago, which had no role initially. I believe that Edward O. Wilson, then as now at Harvard University, became peripherally associated for a while.
>
> While scientific work can ordinarily stand on its own, I agree that political statements such as those recently published in Nabi's name should be evaluated with knowledge of their author. Indeed, Nabi's consultants are politically diverse. While I am not a sociobiologist, my political opinions do not resemble those of Levins and Lewontin; neither did MacArthur's. However, this did not affect our collaborations.
>
> Our consultation with Nabi was scientific, intended to further an analytic and unified approach to evolutionary biology, an approach which was then very unfashionable. Nabi's book, however, was only partly written when circumstances caused its abortion (Van Valen, 1981).

It is a different vision of Nabi we get here—a fictional person created originally for the *scientific* purpose of promoting an unfashionable biological program, rather than a pseudonym invented for satirical scholarship. In fact, Nabi sounds very much the kind of name that might have been adopted by the little group of 1960s biological 'revolutionaries' described by Wilson in Chapter 3 of this book, a group to which Wilson himself belonged. And voila—this is exactly what Levins and Lewontin (1985) tell us. Or almost:

> Isadore (Isidore) Nabi first became known to us when he made his appearance at a working meeting in Vermont that at first included only Robert MacArthur, Leigh Van Valen, and the two of us (Levins and Lewontin, 1985, p. 127).

But where was Wilson in this story? (As we saw, Van Valen also believed that Wilson became associated with Nabi for some time.) And what is the relationship between Isadore Nabi and a certain George Maximin? According to Wilson, seemingly describing a similar meeting at MacArthur's place in Marlboro, Vermont, a pseudonym 'George Maximin' was conceived in imitation of Bourbaki: 'Maximin was named . . . after the point of greatest minimum in optimization theory; George was an arbitrary first name added. With Maximin we thought we could achieve the twin goals of anonymity, with its freedom from ego and authorial jealousy, while acquiring licence to be as audacious and speculative as the group decided' (Wilson, 1994, p. 254). But, Wilson continued, Maximin 'died an early death', because the group was drifting apart, and several members had misgivings about using the pseudonym.

But Nabi seems to have survived.[2] Indeed, one can find references to Nabi in the scientific literature, for instance in a paper by Simberloff (1980a). The much celebrated paper 'On the Tendencies of Motion' (Nabi, 1981b) was for a long time part of the samizdat literature in evolutionary biology, and 'everybody' knew that the paper's true authors were Levins and Lewontin. In that paper, Nabi (1981b) tries to calculate the gravity constant g by making a number of measurements on different types of falling bodies, including apples, putting it all into a complex multiple regression analysis of simulated motion.

There still remain some unanswered questions. For instance, was it or was it not Lewontin who wrote the first Nabi letter? And who, if anybody, was behind the editorial for *Nature*? Was it perhaps a prank by the editors, signalling that they were actually in on the joke? (Because, as anyone could see, the editorial contained *two* misstatements, one about Lester and another about the content of the original Nabi letter—it had nothing to do with the controversy about the British Museum also going on in *Nature* around that time.)

I asked Lewontin about his role in all this. He cheerfully admitted that it was indeed he who wrote the first Nabi letter. But he said he had in fact given the American editors of *Nature* the option of using *either* Nabi *or* his own name. It was the editors that had chosen to use Nabi! In other words, the whole controversy was at least partly created by the editors of *Nature*. And the problem was compounded by the fact that *Nature*'s editors, unlike many evolutionary biologists, were not in on the joke of using the pseudonym Nabi for collective scientific criticisms in evolutionary biology, Lewontin chuckled.

So what about Wilson? Why did he choose to ask 'Who is Nabi?' if he, just like most evolutionary biologists—or even more—was in on the joke? I asked him about this shortly afterwards. Wilson gave me the following reason: he felt that the opposition to sociobiology had been given an unfair advantage. Working under the cover of a pseudonym, the critics had suggested that there was widespread resistance to sociobiology! Wilson said he fully agreed with *Nature*'s editorial on this matter.

And this brings us to the next question. Who was really behind that *Nature* editorial, 'Isidore Nabi RIP', which discouraged the use of pseudonyms? The answer is: none other than Wilson's ally, Bernard Davis! This I did not learn from Wilson, but from Davis himself. He told me that he had written a letter to *Nature* about the 'true identity' of Nabi. It was his letter that had later been turned into the *Nature* editorial of September 3.

There was no doubt that Wilson regarded that editorial as a personal victory over 'the opposition'. Wilson had prepared xeroxed copies of it, and triumphantly handed one of them to me to read. It was clear that Wilson was extremely serious about the whole Nabi affair. He told me he believed the Nabi incident to be 'a direct blemish on Lewontin's reputation'.

Here we have, then, Wilson and Davis both taking a very grave view of the act of using a pseudonym for criticism, while Lewontin and his friends considered the whole Nabi incident hilariously funny. (Van Valen, however, may on the whole have found the Nabi incident somewhat less funny than Lewontin and Levins. When I asked him about the Nabi story, he told me—smilingly—that Lewontin had not consulted him when using the Nabi name for the original *Nature* letter.)

We see an interesting irony in this drama of mistaken identities: it began with a letter by a critic of sociobiology masquerading as a pseudonym, and ended with a letter by a supporter of sociobiology, masquerading as a *Nature* editor. At bottom, this was a controversy about manners and morals in science, a sideshow to the sociobiology controversy. But it was also a situation where the full authority of *Nature* was mobilized against the questionable authority of a scientific pseudonym.

The critics develop a positive program

Initially, the critics' main interest was to prove their targets—sociobiologists, psychometricians, and other purported biological determinists or 'reductionists'—to be 'bad' both scientifically and morally/politically. Later on, they embarked on a parallel course: developing their own 'good' anti-agenda, which would systematically connect 'correct' scientific to 'correct' political belief. This meant proposing such things as an 'emancipatory' science, or a 'dialectical biology'. The hope was that science executed in the desirable epistemological-cum-political spirit would by that very fact produce truer—more empirically adequate—results than the existing one.

One attempt to construct an emancipatory science was an interdisciplinary symposium in Bressanone in 1981, arranged by Hilary and Steven Rose. That conference resulted in two volumes: *Against Biological Determinism* and *Toward a Liberatory Biology* (Rose, 1982a, b). This was the rather tall order for an emancipatory science:

> The tasks of an emancipatory science are defined by the critique of contemporary bourgeois reductionist science. It must overcome and transcend: 1) the subjectivity/objectivity split; and 2) the domination of the natural and human worlds by instrumental rationality. And it must achieve: 1) the democratization of science; and 2) a dialectical view of nature, including human nature, as neither static nor infinitely plastic; that is, a materialist view (Rose and Rose, 1982).

This kind of description sounded good to Lewontin, among others, who wrote an enthusiastic review in *The New York Review of Books*, alluding to the 'funeral of reductionism' (Lewontin, 1983). Patrick Bateson, however, who had attended the conference himself, felt that the participants were exaggerating their case (Bateson, 1982c; see further, Chapter 12).

Soon, Lewontin himself came up with what could be called a 'positive' contribution. Perhaps as a response to people like Wilson and Lumsden, who were growing irritated with his persistent criticism and had told him to either 'fish or cut bait' (Lumsden and Wilson, 1981), in 1985 Lewontin, together with Levins, issued *The Dialectical Biologist*. There they presented what they saw as a deliberately Marxist alternative to 'the reductionist program'—the umbrella term for the type of science they disliked. The book was partly a collection of earlier published papers, such as 'Evolution and Theory and Ideology', 'The Organism as Subject and Object of Evolution', and 'The Problems of

Lysenkoism', with some new material such as 'The Political Economy of Agricultural Research' and 'Applied Biology in the Third World: The Struggle for Revolutionary Science', as well as an introduction and a conclusion. One highlight in the book is undoubtedly Isadore Nabi's 'On the Tendencies of Motion'.

Indeed, Levins and Lewontin regarded their book as a direct response to a manifesto issued by the Dialectics of Biology Group at the Bressanone conference. According to the authors, that conference 'left for the future the constructive application of a dialectical viewpoint to particular problems and, indeed, an explicit statement of what the dialectical method comprises' (Levins and Lewontin, 1985, p. viii).

What is interesting about this book is Levins and Lewontin's particular brand of Marxism, which can be said to be one up on Friedrich Engels' philosophical classic, *The Dialectics of Nature. The Dialectical Biologist* aimed at a synthesis of dialectical and historical materialism, or, rather, at demonstrating the inherent connection between them. As the authors themselves say: 'Indeed, it is a sign of the Marxist dialectic with which we align ourselves that scientific and political questions are inextricably inter-connected—dialectically related' (Levins and Lewontin, p. viii). Incidentally, an interesting consequence of this new approach was that it seemed to shift the focus of analysis away from the postulated political convictions of individual scientists. The new culprit was more abstract: it was the political ideology of the society that gave birth to modern science itself. Let us take a quick look at the gist of the reasoning involved.

According to Levins and Lewontin, the physical world view taken for granted by contemporary Western science in reality reflects basic conceptions of bourgeois society. In the bourgeois view the individual was central as a social actor, and the actors were seen as social atoms colliding in the market. This is why in today's reductionist science the taken-for-granted world view is one where 'parts are separated from wholes and reified as things in themselves, causes separated from effects, subjects separated from objects' (pp. 269–70). And why are reductionists so fond of assuming that stability and equilibrium is the natural state of a system? There is an ideological explanation:

> Legitimation of bourgeois society meant denial of the need for fundamental change, or even the possibility of it. Stability, balance, equilibrium and continuity became positive virtues in society and therefore also the objects of intellectual interest' (Levins and Lewontin, 1985, p. 275).

But, according to the authors, a dialectical view of the world is more correct than this kind of 'alienated' reductionist view. Why is that? The dialectical view focuses on wholeness, change, and interaction, which are *true* characteristics of the world. It turns out that Levins and Lewontin are interested in no less than '*the complex set of interacting causes of all events in the world*' and an understanding of objects in all their complexity (p. 221). Moreover, their quest is not only an epistemological one, representing a kind of dialectical materialist philosophy. The authors' surprising twist at this point is to also bring in a historical materialist perspective and link up dialectical and historical materialism with each other. They are able to do this since, for them, 'the complex set of interacting causes of all events in the world' is not limited to natural phenomena. It especially applies to the domination of the capitalist system of all aspects of society, including science. Thus, for Levins and Lewontin—unlike Engels (and Marx, and Lenin), for whom natural science was largely exempt from social forces—science is in a very fundamental way connected to the social order.

In looking for a new post-Cartesian epistemology, Levins and Lewontin's intent appears very similar to that of some other authors, who around the same time diagnosed the ills of present-day science and epistemology and traced their roots to the conditions of the emerging bourgeois society. Here we have, for instance, Morris Berman's (1981) *The Reenchantment of the World*, and Fritjof Capra's (1982) *The Turning Point*. These authors were looking for possible new scientific epistemologies which would be able to transcend the subject–object distinction, or bridge the gap between facts and values, and they, too, discussed various connections between science and politics. In *The Dialectical Biologist*, however, Levins and Lewontin went one step further. They seemed to regard getting rid of capitalism as a pre-condition for the development of a new type of science. Currently, the capitalist system was preventing a better and truer 'dialectical' scientific epistemology from prevailing (1985, p. 287).

Enough! say the sociobiologists

Levins and Lewontin's ambitions to develop a 'total' Marxist world view did not mean that they abandoned their criticism of research in the biology of human behavior. We need only look at the publication dates of *The Dialectical Biologist* and *Not In Our Genes*, which more or less coincided. I will now turn to an interesting incident involving *Not In Our Genes* (Lewontin, Rose, and Kamin, 1984).

A striking feature of what we have seen so far has been the imbalance of the whole situation. The burden of proof was on sociobiologists and IQ researchers to prove their innocence, not on their accusers to prove the formers' guilt. Sociobiologists were declared guilty until proven innocent. (In fact, it is hard to see what might ever have constituted evidence of innocence, since it seems that no protestations of innocence were registered anyway.) Meanwhile, the sociobiologists were under constant scrutiny by their ever-vigilant critics, who did not fail to find ever new political and scientific errors in the former's work. Most galling for the sociobiologists as scientists was perhaps the persistence with which any statement about genetic effects was immediately equated with genetic determinism and seen as supporting the idea of a necessary social order.

Dawkins had suffered his fair share of allegations of this kind. One of the more irritating published examples was probably Steven Rose's last sentence in the 1981 'genes and race' interchange in *Nature*. That included the statement: 'I challenge anyone to read *The Selfish Gene* and come away without a clear impression of Dawkins' view of what biology has to say about the Welfare State, sexual mores or microeconomics' (Rose, 1981b). And Lewontin had written a very negative review of *The Selfish Gene* in *Nature* (Lewontin, 1977a; we will return to the review in Chapter 13).

In 1982 Dawkins tried to clarify matters with the help of logic. The critics have got it wrong, he argued. The issue did not concern genetic determinism but *genetic selectionism*:

> Gene selectionism, which is a way of talking about *evolution*, is mistaken for genetic determinism, which is a point of view about *development*. People like me are constantly postulating genes 'for' this and genes for that. We give the impression of being obsessed with genes and with 'genetically programmed' behaviour. . . .
>
> Why, then, do functional ethologists talk about genes so much? Because we are interested in natural selection, and natural selection is differential survival of genes. If we are to so much as discuss the *possibility* of a behaviour pattern's evolving by natural selection, we have to postulate genetic variation with respect to the tendency or capacity to perform that behaviour pattern (Dawkins, 1982, p. 19, italics added).

Of course the behavior pattern might not be a Darwinian adaptation at all, and in that case the argument did not apply, Dawkins added.

So when Lewontin criticized Wilson's *Sociobiology* in the following way: 'Genes for conformity, xenophobia, and aggressiveness are simply postulated for humans because they are needed for the theory, not because any evidence for them exists (Lewontin, 1979)', this was not very damning (p. 19). Dawkins calmly continued: 'Apart from possible political repercussions . . . there is nothing wrong with cautiously speculating about a possible Darwinian survival value of xenophobia or any other trait.' After all, it was Lewontin himself who had emphasized that '[i]n order for a trait to evolve by natural selection it is necessary that there be genetic variation in the population for such a trait' (Lewontin, 1979a). And talking about 'genetic variation for' a trait X was only a more elaborate way of talking about the shorthand notion 'a gene for' X (Dawkins, 1982, p. 20).

Still, even Dawkins came to a point where he had simply had enough. The publication of *Not In Our Genes* may have been the last straw. It was time for the sociobiologists to strike back against the unfair political allegations of their critics. A review of the book gave Dawkins an opportunity to finally confront directly one of the favorite claims of the opponents of sociobiology:

> Sociobiology is a reductionist, biological determinist explanation of human existence. Its adherents claim, first, that the details of present and past social arrangements are the inevitable manifestations of the specific actions of genes (Lewontin, Rose, and Kamin, 1984, p. 236).

To this Dawkins retorted:

> Rose *et al.* cannot substantiate their allegation about sociobiologists believing in inevitable genetic determination, because *the allegation is a simple lie*. The myth of the 'inevitability' of genetic effects has nothing whatever to do with sociobiology, and has everything to do with Rose *et al*'s paranoic and demonological theology of science (Dawkins, 1985, p. 59, italics added).

Did the authors of *Not In Our Genes* let this pass as an understandable protest by a sociobiologist finding himself and his colleagues misunderstood one more time? Not at all. Incredibly, Rose threatened to sue Dawkins for libel! (Patrick Bateson and Richard

Dawkins, personal communication.) Although, in the end, nothing came of this threat, there was quite a flurry of activity at the time to protect Dawkins. Bill Hamilton, reportedly, approached Wilson about a copy of my dissertation, which, it was hoped, might contain some material that could be used in a possible defense. Dawkins himself wrote me a letter in 1985 asking me whether I could find a single political message in the writings of sociobiologists! It was not hard to respond to that request (I took it as a request—perhaps the question was rhetorical). Putting on the critics' hat, I sent Dawkins a list of passages in Wilson's *On Human Nature* which I knew either had been or easily could be interpreted as purported political statements.

As mentioned earlier, the British 'sociobiologists' did not want to be called that at all. They would have preferred to be called behavioral ecologists, or functional ethologists —anything but 'sociobiologists'. But in his review, Dawkins decided to take the bull by the horns. He said that 'much as I have always disliked the name, this book finally provokes me to stand up and be counted' (Dawkins, 1985). There is another interesting aspect to Dawkins' review, which may have contributed to Rose's ire. Originally the *New Scientist*, which commissioned the reviews, had expected Patrick Bateson to write a positive and Dawkins a negative review, side by side in the same issue (Dawkins, personal communication). But as it happened, Bateson's review, too, turned out quite negative! (This may have been particularly disappointing for Rose, a friend of Bateson's.)

In his review, Bateson, after first being impressed with the authors' methodological critique of IQ and schizophrenia research, had found serious flaws in their treatment of sociobiology. Even worse, he had encountered 'deterministic thinking of the type they revile elsewhere'. And this, he said, led him to reconsider the whole book:

> Sloppy scholarship and bad argument, even when casually introduced, seriously devalue the whole enterprise. I was predisposed to be sympathetic to their general approach, but, altered by their peccadillos in my own field, I began to wonder about the chapters I much admired, such as those on IQ and schizophrenia. Had they done their homework properly? Or had they selected and distorted the evidence in order to make a good story? This may be unfair, and it is unlikely that they all took an equal amount of trouble over each chapter. Nonetheless, in a book with such a strongly moralizing thrust, they would have been wise to have maintained scrupulous standards throughout (Bateson, 1985).

This is one of the few times in the sociobiology controversy that sociobiologists went on clear counter-offensive against their detractors. At the same time, it underlines the imbalance in the sociobiology debate: 'politically correct' academics felt that they could require sociobiologists and others to be careful in their actions and choice of words, while they did not see the need to censor their own language when they accused the former of political intent. Sociobiologists were held to high standards, while the critics of sociobiology felt they could get by with easy dismissals of sociobiological theorizing (for instance, Bateson identified reasoning that he called 'ill-informed and silly'). Anti-sociobiologists were allowed to see all sorts of links between sociobiology and unsavory politics, but the sociobiologists were not allowed to respond that sociobiology's alleged political intent was a 'lie' (or 'simple lie').

What does this mean? The anti-sociobiologists were in fact behaving as if there were already an academic or social *norm* established, whereby a scientist not only would have to do research but also foresee all kinds of possible political abuses of this research. One can only say that the critics were sanctioning a so-far nonexistent norm. Or, perhaps they, through their very activities, were trying to bring such a norm into existence? We will return to this in Chapters 15 and 19.

Whose fault is it?

Whose fault is it when people draw moral and political conclusions from socio-biological theory? That question was raised and answered by leading sociobiologists and their critics at the height of the sociobiology controversy.

There had already been the question of who 'started' the sociobiology controversy. Many academics thought it obvious that it was the Sociobiology Study Group with their letter in *The New York Review of Books*. But several members of that group with whom I spoke insistently pointed to the publication of *Sociobiology* and its announcement as an event on the first page of *The New York Times* as the thing which 'started it all'.[3] We also remember the critics' worries about the impressions that the 'innocent layman' would get from sociobiological writings: the layman might easily come to believe that this was the best of all possible worlds, that inequality, racism, sexism, and the like were natural and 'in our genes'. Ironically, Wilson himself thought he was bringing a hopeful message to mankind: we have gone astray on the wrong path of environmental deter-minism, but there is still time to mend our ways and get back on the right path with the help of scientific knowledge. In 1975, he gave us a hundred years.

Another thing Wilson thought he was doing right, and which would benefit the layman, was pointing out the genetic components of human behavior. In his view, Freudianism had too strongly informed popular thinking and early childhood educa-tion and in this way created an enormous burden of guilt for innocent parents. He thought an emphasis on the genetic components of personality would help diminish guilt feelings in parents, making them realize that the eventual outcome is a product of both their upbringing and the child's own genetic endowment. This he told me in interview in 1982. (At present, there is much more support for such a view than there was in the 1970s, not the least because of the researches of Wilson's psychology colleague Jerome Kagan; Kagan *et al.*, 1994.)

But it was the critics' seemingly unending harping on the inevitability of genetic effects that made Dawkins' blood boil. In his response to Rose's (1981a) letter about the National Front and its 'neo-Nazi balderdash', Dawkins declared that 'the real balder-dash' was the idea that we are stuck with our biological nature and cannot change it. And who was responsible for this, asked Dawkins: ['B]ut where on earth did the myth of the inevitability of genetic effects come from? Is it just a layman's fallacy, or are there influential professional biologists putting it about?' (Dawkins, 1981b).

Dawkins also dismissed Rose's attempt to connect the new theory of kin selection to Thatcherism. Rose had described the rise of kin selectionist theory as 'part of the tide which has rolled the Thatcherites and their concept of a fixed, nineteenth century competitive and xenophobic human nature into power'. For Dawkins it was 'annoying to find this elegant and important theory being dragged down to the ephemeral level of human politics, and parochial British politics at that'. But who was it that was connecting sociobiology to politics? 'It seems that the National Front are not alone responsible for this', Dawkins observed (Dawkins, 1981b).

In his (uninvited) response letter to Rose, Wilson, too, made a similar point. Like Maynard Smith, Wilson noted that there could be no justification for racism in the biological study of human behavior. He continued:

> I now call on Professor Rose to consider these and similar arguments raised in my writings. It is my hope that he will not confine himself, as he has in the past, to arguments that link sociobiology to racism and thus to continue to abet the very misuse which he piously claims to deplore (Wilson, 1981a).

We know that Rose did not heed Wilson's advice. If anything, it is probably Rose who throughout the sociobiology controversy has most actively portrayed Wilson and Dawkins as politically 'bad' sociobiologists—sometimes even desperately so. But what is more interesting is the response that Dawkins and Wilson in turn triggered in Rose— and Nabi. It was Nabi who first turned the sociobiologists' weapon on themselves. After documenting seemingly different positions taken by Dawkins on the role of genetics in human behavior, he ended his letter in the following way:

> But I see that Dr Dawkins himself is uncertain. I can only echo the question he asks in his letter. 'Where on earth did the myth of the inevitability of genetic effects come from? Is it just a layman's fallacy, or are there influential professional biologists putting it about?' (Nabi, 1981a).[4]

And Rose, a couple of weeks later, wrote:

> If sociobiologists want to avoid the charge that they believe that biology is destiny, they should beware of telling magazines that they know 'why we do what we do' or entitling their book The Selfish Gene, The Inevitability of Patriarchy or On Human Nature. The trouble is they want to have their cake and eat it. They imperialize the human sciences (vide the first paragraph of Sociobiology, The New Synthesis) and are embarrassed by the outcome.
>
> When Dawkins disdains the ephemera of mere 'human politics', or accuses his critics of being as guilty as the Nazis of dragging the elegant purity of his neo-Darwinism into the litter of the city streets, he does so at the peril of a repetition of the tragedies of the 1930s (Rose, 1981b).

So, for Nabi and Rose it was the sociobiologists who were the original sinners, and they should not try to pin the guilt on their critics.

Finally, there was another important question. Who was responsible for the creationists' use of the controversy in evolutionary theory to argue for the truth of their own position? Here we have the following very interesting piece of reasoning by Lewontin in an editorial in BioScience (Lewontin, 1981d). First he points out that creationists have used published statements in the controversies about evolution 'dishonestly', trying to suggest that there is doubt about the fact of evolution. He then calls on students of the evolutionary process, 'especially those who have been misquoted and used by the creationists' to state clearly that evolution is *fact*, not theory, and what is taking place is a minor quibble about the relative importance of different forces molding evolution. But now comes the point: whose fault is it that the creationists misquote evolutionists in this way? *It is the fault of vulgar Darwinism*, Lewontin asserts:

> A major cause of much of the present controversy—and the rich opportunity it affords creationists to find out-of-context quotations—is the growth of a vulgar Darwinism that sees direct adaptation in every feature of life. By making claims for natural selection that are as tortured as the absurd claims of the 19th century evolutionists who saw God's wisdom in everything, the vulgar adaptationists seriously weaken the power of evolutionary explanation. When called to account, they declare those who dispute them to be anti-Darwinians and even anti-evolutionists. And all the while creationists smile and take notes (Lewontin, 1981c).

A remarkable statement—including the worry about out-of-context quotations.

There is even the question as to who is the persecutor and who is the victim in the sociobiology controversy. Interestingly, both sides have attempted to present themselves as victims. The sociobiologists obviously had immediate cause to see themselves persecuted. For instance, at the founding meeting of the Human Behavior and Evolution Society in Evanston in 1989, Bill Hamilton, the Society's first president, gave an address in which he described scholars interested in the evolutionary basis of human behavior as a small, besieged group, almost like a secret society. He urged the members to bravely persist in the face of difficulties. What the critics of sociobiology considered dangerous political individuals, Hamilton saw as a small, besieged group.

In their victim mode, too, the critics were bringing up racism and the Nazi horrors and even, on occasion, the McCarthy era. For instance, when as part of an ongoing *Nature* debate about a new cladistic exhibit at the British Museum of Natural History, L. B. Halstead connected punctuated equilibrium theory to Marxism, Gould's response included the following plea: 'May we avoid red-baiting; it may not always be harmless' (Gould, 1981b). At this point evolutionary biologist John Turner stepped in, telling Gould not to try to play victim:

> Although Gould would like us to believe that he is the potential victim this, in view of recent history, is a piece of *chutzpah*. Within the academic community, it is those scientists whose theories could be conveniently labelled 'racist' or 'right-wing' who have been subjected to unofficial but nonetheless unpleasant persecution (the assault on Eysenck) (Turner, 1981).

As we see, who was the persecutor and who was the victim was in the eye of the beholder. What was obvious to one side was not obvious to the other. What is clear, however, is that both sides believed that they were defending a noble cause in the face of adversity and potential danger, a sentiment which helped create a sense of camaraderie within each besieged camp of truth seekers.

Clearly, the sociobiologists were not about to give up their science. Still, as decent fellows disturbed about the critics' allegations, they often tried to disconnect themselves from the purported political implications of their research. On occasion, they even struck back, as in the case of Dawkins rebutting Rose, sometimes charging that the critics were engaged in 'demonology'. But why was it so difficult for the critics to give up their cherished interpretation of the 'true meaning' of sociobiological statements, despite the persistent protests and rebuttals from sociobiologists? The reasons are explored in Part II.

PART TWO

Making sense of the sociobiology debate

CHAPTER 10

Inside the mind of the critics

Coupled logic and the quest for certainty

When Wilson was interviewed in *The Harvard Gazette* shortly after the critics' letter in *The New York Review of Books*, his reaction was the following: 'Every important point they make is wrong and represents either a false statement or a distortion . . . In most issues they refer to I have said or implied the opposite' (Wilson, 1976b). However, the critics persisted in their claim that they had not misrepresented Wilson at all. This can be clearly seen from their reaction to an early article on the sociobiology controversy written for *Science* by science journalist Nicholas Wade (Wade, 1976). Wade's article supported Wilson's view that the Sociobiology Study Group 'had utterly misrepresented the spirit and content' of his book, that they had 'seriously' and 'systematically' distorted his position, and that they were engaged in a 'personal vendetta' and 'in an unwarranted political attack against a work of objective scholarship'. The critics responded by inviting the readers to check for themselves:

> Readers of *Science* can only judge the truth of these accusations by reading Wilson's book and our critique for themselves. We strongly urge everyone to do so. We agree with Wade that we previously failed to recognize that Wilson was 'hedging' in his statement about the existences of 'conformer genes', and we apologize to him for implying that he asserted their existence as a matter of fact. *But we can find no other instance in which we misquoted or otherwise misrepresented his position.* We have no interest in cutting off debate. We contend that a careful reading of *Sociobiology* will suffice to rebut the charge of distortion and will confirm that the 'new synthesis' contains numerous inconsistencies and transparent political messages. Although Wade's superficial and uncritical reading ignores it and Wilson's own statements disclaim it, *there is politics aplenty in Sociobiology and those of us who are its critics did not put it there* (Alper *et al.*, 1976, italics added).

It is now exactly this kind of checking that can give us an insight into the *critics'* reasoning and their strategies for making their case. Let us examine some of these strategies.

It seems that the critics took for granted that their targets made assumptions, constructed models, or employed formulas for expressly *political* reasons. This meant, on the one hand, that everything these scientists did was to be scrutinized for underlying political motives, and, on the other hand, that no explanations other than political ones were acceptable. Thus, the critics discounted the possibility that the choices made by scientists in these fields might be motivated by *other* than political concerns, for instance, be theoretically supported or based on various types of *heuristic* considerations. The obvious task for the critics of sociobiology, IQ research, and the like was therefore to show the innocent layman just how political ideology inevitably led to false science. In the following, I will give examples of how the critics' analytical machinery worked in practice.

As we saw, in their 1975 letter the Sociobiology Study Group formulated their criticism of *Sociobiology* as if Wilson was necessarily both a politically and scientifically 'bad' scientist. This is, they did not limit themselves to criticizing the extension of sociobiological theorizing to the human species, they also depicted Wilson's *general* scientific views on evolutionary biology as erroneous and outdated (particularly regarding the role of adaptation in evolution and the nature of genes). It did not seem to matter that Wilson himself in his overview in *Sociobiology*, of contending perspectives on evolutionary theory, had approvingly discussed Lewontin's view of the genome as an interacting whole and *explicitly* recognized the limitations of current heritability formulas based on single-locus genetics. It did not help, either, that Wilson then *explicitly* stated his own heuristic decision: he was going to use the existing formulas provisionally, waiting for better ones to be developed (Wilson, 1975a, p. 70). In order to fit the critics' logic-in-operation, Wilson had to be dismissed as an overall 'bad' scientist.

If general sociobiology was bad, human sociobiology was worse. It was inconceivable for the critics that a view on any aspect of the biology of human behavior could be held on any other than political grounds. This was particularly the case with tentative findings in the field of human behavioral genetics. Here Wilson (like many other respected members of the scientific community, including many biologists) was of the opinion that the results were relatively well established, despite the well-known methodological difficulties of twin studies (which he also discussed in *Sociobiology*). As I argued in Chapter 3, Wilson needed for *practical* reasons to postulate behavioral genes in humans, since the larger population genetic formulas he wished to develop for the 'trajectory of mankind' were based on the idea of an available genetic variation in human behavioral traits.

How does one demonstrate, for the benefit of the 'innocent layman' and others, that it is a scientist's political bias that is the cause of 'bad' science, at least in fields that have serious sociopolitical implications? The critics seem to have believed that this was an easy match if one just examined closely the texts of 'bad' scientists, since such texts were bound to exhibit both *political ideology* and *scientific error*. The general strategy used by the critics in conjunction both with the IQ and sociobiology controversies was already spelled out in Lewontin's criticism of Arthur Jensen in 1970, where he explained that he would show 'how the structure of his argument is designed to make his point and to reveal what appear to be deeply embedded assumptions derived from a particular world view, leading him to erroneous conclusions' (see Chapter 3). We saw how Lewontin later expanded his critique to the entire area of research in cognitive abilities—according to him, the students of IQ 'could not' be motivated by a genuine scientific desire, since 'the only truly scientifically interesting questions about cognitive traits can be asked at the molecular level' (Lewontin, 1975a). Therefore, he reasoned, it 'must' be their underlying sociopolitical bias that was driving these researchers to bad science.

The same type of reasoning, connecting bad science to ideological bias, was evident in the Sociobiology Study Group's letter. According to the critics, Wilson's basic point with *Sociobiology* was to prove that human social behavior could be analyzed in the same terms as the social behavior of other species:

> In his attempt to graft speculation about human behavior onto a biological core, Wilson uses a number of strategies and sleights of hand which dispel any claim for logical or factual continuity . . . . Wilson places 500 pages of double column biology between his first chapter on 'The Morality of the Gene' and the last chapter, 'From Sociobiology to Sociology.' But *Wilson's claim for objectivity rests entirely upon the extent to which this chapter follows logically and inevitably* from the fact and theory that come before (Allen *et al.*, 1975; italics added).

Thus, according to the group's 'sandwich model' of *Sociobiology*, Wilson tried to persuade the innocent reader of a logical continuity between human and animal behavior. By identifying Wilson's intent in this way, the critics indirectly defined their own mission as well: to show that 'Wilson's claim to continuity fails'. The critics saw their own task as being to reveal Wilson's different attempts to 'confirm selectively certain contemporary behavior as adaptive and "natural" and thereby justify the present social order' (Allen *et al.*, 1975).

Just as in Lewontin's (1970a) criticism of Jensen, the innocent reader was being helped to see the light and not to be persuaded by speculative arguments. And in the case of both Jensen and Wilson, what the author himself intended to be a scientific *plausibility* argument, the critics treated as a *logical* statement instead and targeted for demolition. By revealing Wilson's various claims as scientifically or logically ill-founded, the Sociobiology Study Group would unmask Wilson's attempts to distort science for political ends and triumphantly stand up for the truth.

We see, then, that the critics took a particular attitude to plausibility arguments and speculative elements in science. These were not assessed as to their reasonableness on scientific grounds, but treated as *a priori scientifically unjustifiable*. An example of the critics' attitude was their attack on 'the multiplier effect'. They contended that '[a] crucial point in Wilson's explanation remains purely speculative', and that 'nowhere does Wilson present any basis for introducing the multiplier' (Allen *et al.*, 1975).

The question here is what the critics meant by 'basis'. It seems that they had something other in mind than the various types of scientific arguments that a scientist might use to back up a claim. Let us see what 'basis' Wilson himself believed that he was providing. In the first chapter of *Sociobiology* (pp. 11–14) Wilson quoted several examples as to how the multiplier effect worked among insects and then primates; that is, he tried to demonstrate 'how a small evolutionary change in the behavior patterns of individuals can be amplified into a major social effect by the expanding upward distribution of the effect into multiple facets of social life' (p. 11). He also showed how 'socialization appears to amplify phenotypic differences among primate species', even though 'the evidence is still largely inferential' (pp. 12–13). Furthermore, he suggested that 'socialization can also amplify genetic variation of individual behavior within troops', so that 'the initial differences in developmental tendencies will be amplified into the striking divergences in status and roles that provide much of the social structure, assuming there is at least some degree of heritability in traits for dominance—especially among primate mothers raising their offspring to become dominant males' (p. 13). Finally, he referred to the sixth edition of Darwin's *Origin* for the general idea that 'when evolution involves both structure and behavior, behavior should change first and then structure' (p. 13). In sum,

> The multiplier effect, whether purely genetic in basis or reinforced by socialization and other forms of learning, makes *behavior* the part of the phenotype most likely to change in response to long-term learning (Wilson, 1975a, p. 13, italics added).

It is hard to see how this would not constitute a possible 'basis' for the reasoning of a biologist. Another question is whether this basis was firm or weak, acceptable or unacceptable to Wilson's fellow biologists. However, Wilson's real problem here was to argue for the plausibility of such a multiplier effect operating also in the human species. For such an effect to work, he had to postulate the availability of genetic variation for behavioral traits in human societies. This he did by quoting none other than Lewontin on the existing, although very small, genetic variation between populations in regard to blood factors, and arguing that there was no particular reason to believe that this gene distribution was much different from 'other, less accessible systems affecting behavior'. And to show that the idea of human behavioral traits was at least reasonable, he cited results from existing studies in human behavioral genetics on the heritability of some personality traits believed to affect behavior.

Thus, Wilson was here relying on a chain of *plausibility arguments*, while the critics alleged that Wilson was trying to demonstrate a *logical* and *factual* continuity between animal and human behavior. In this spirit, they also alleged that Wilson 'relies on the unproven assumption that genes for behavior exist' (Allen *et al.*, 1975). But such is the nature of assumptions! Thus, the critics blatantly dismissed the legitimacy of plausibility arguments and hypothetical constructs in scientific reasoning. Speaking in the name of science, but taking a very strict view as to what could and could not be legitimately stated, the critics were able to depict Wilson as someone who simply pulled speculations out of a hat *without* any scientific basis, and who therefore 'must' have other, sinister motives.

It is important to notice that there was a connection between the critics' moral-cum-scientific criticism and their conception that 'bad', and only 'bad', science would be socially abused. It was this latter cognitive link which is the reason why the critics were so much against various tentative approaches to account for human behavior. If it was 'bad' (or even 'unproven' or 'unprovable'—usually treated as synonyms) science that got abused, then it was *morally wrong for a scientist to produce anything else than absolutely certain knowledge.*

The best example of the critics' overall position in regard to science is probably Lewontin's formulation in an interview in *The Harvard Gazette* (3 November 1975):

> At present our ignorance on this question is so enormous, our investigatory techniques so primitive and weak, our theoretical concepts so unformed, that it is unimaginable to me that lasting, serious truths about human nature are possible. On the other hand the need of the socially powerful to exonerate their institutions of responsibility for the problems they have created is extremely strong. Under these circumstances any investigations into the genetic control of human behaviors is bound to produce a pseudo-science that will inevitably be misused (Lewontin, 1975c).

This statement represents in a nutshell the general moral-cum-scientific spirit characteristic of the Sociobiology Study Group: 1) in principle they had faith in the progress of science (cf. 'at present'), but 2) solid foundations were needed before we could make any 'serious' statements about humans, which meant that 3) current theories about human behavior were only based on plausibility statements, not on 'hard' data, and *were therefore not part of science.*

It seems that in their zeal to combat 'biological determinism', the opponents of sociobiology typically took a very absolutist, not to say unrealistic, view of science. For these critics, scientists were not allowed to operate with data or methods that these scientists *themselves* considered acceptable! The critics acknowledged no gray area of knowledge, where different 'expert opinions' might legitimately prevail: the situation could only be black and white. There were good and bad scientists, and these had correct vs incorrect, modern vs old-fashioned views. And this seemed to directly translate to the scientist, either emphasizing or de-emphasizing the role of biology for human behavior.

In the following, I now want to cast doubt on the whole idea that there is an *obvious* link between a scientist's scientific views and political convictions—one of the taken-for-granted assumptions of the critics. I call such a belief 'coupled reasoning'. But this was not only a tendency of the Sociobiology Study Group. In the next few chapters, we will examine the emergence of two larger camps in this controversy and additional taken-for-granted assumptions of both the critics and their targets. We will see how the proponents and opponents of sociobiology did seem to live in quite different worlds.

Chomsky's challenge

Since the main target of the critics was those scientists who supposedly promoted 'biological determinism' and thereby helped sustain the social status quo, the obvious implication was that an environmentalist (that is, culturalist) position would be politically acceptable. In fact, the attack on the idea of a genetic basis for human behavior as politically conservative or worse was evident in the writings of the critics of IQ and sociobiology from the very beginning.

But it is, of course, neither logically necessary nor historically true that a 'hereditarian' position should be associated with conservatism and an 'environmentalist' one with progressive thought, even though the critics never brought up this fact. Many hereditarians were actually socialist reformers, among others the left-wing biologists in

Britain in the 1930s (see, for example, Werskey, 1978) and the early eugenicists in Germany and the Soviet Union (Graham, 1977). Wilson (1975b), in his response to his critics, pointed out the interest of such left-wing intellectuals as Noam Chomsky and Herbert Marcuse in the biological basis of human nature. From their point of view, there were good *political* reasons for arguing for a relatively fixed human nature, since postulating an endlessly malleable human nature would legitimize any oppressive social regime (Chomsky, 1975; Marcuse, 1955).

For a left-wing academic, there are thus two alternative routes to take, a hereditarian and an environmentalist one, and it does not seem obvious which is the more politically desirable or correct, particularly since the perspectives may also correspond to long-term vs short-term political strategies. In an encounter that may be termed 'historical' in its nature, Noam Chomsky and Richard Lewontin found out that, prominent left-wing academics though they were, they had in fact quite divergent views on the nature of human nature and its political meaning.

This historic encounter occurred in May 1976 during one of the monthly meetings of the Sociobiology Study Group, to which Noam Chomsky had been invited; I was present as an observer. The group had been hoping that Chomsky would agree to write a devastating critique of sociobiology and thus help the cause. Not only was Chomsky well-known as a political activist and for his linguistic theories, he was also widely celebrated for his 'definitive' critique of B. F. Skinner's behaviorist theory of language learning (Chomsky, 1959). Thus, there were great expectations that he would now write a similar brilliant critique of sociobiology. The meeting was well attended and there was something of awe in the air when the special guest was introduced and the reason for inviting him explained. But Chomsky unexpectedly suggested that he and the group members first have a discussion to find out where they stood on various issues. It was quickly decided that Lewontin would represent the Sociobiology Study Group's position. He and Chomsky pulled up chairs for what was to become a two-person panel discussion.

Obviously, Chomsky was particularly interested in the Group's objections to Wilson, and the discussion from the outset turned to Wilson's last chapter and the group's critique of his attempt to establish a biologically based human nature. The audience now found Chomsky and Lewontin both giving brief, almost formal-sounding lectures on the nature of human nature. It became obvious, and rather embarrassing, that while Chomsky and Lewontin both invoked Marx as the authority on human nature, each had in mind a *different* Marx—which meant that they had diametrically opposite views of the nature of human nature! Chomsky's Marx turned out to be the young Marx with his idea of an unchanging human 'species nature', while Lewontin quoted the old Marx and his idea of socially shaped and historically changing human needs. Lewontin had apparently taken it for granted that 'everybody' in the progressive academic camp would have the same view as himself of a historically changing human nature, and was visibly taken aback at this unexpected disagreement. What was worse, Chomsky could not just be dismissed—his radical credentials were impeccable, and he had been a left-wing activist longer than most people present.

Adding salt to the wound, Chomsky even stated that he thought it *important* for political radicals to postulate a relatively fixed human nature in order to be able to struggle for a better society. We need a clear view of human needs in order to know what kind of society we want, Chomsky proclaimed. Not surprisingly, under these conditions, no Chomsky critique of sociobiology emerged.

The considerable consternation caused by Chomsky's cameo appearance at the Group meeting later led to a well-mannered correspondence between Chomsky and Lewontin. Was it or was it not possible to be a political activist without postulating a particular view of human nature, that is, arguing for a set of needs which would have to be satisfied by a socialist society? Lewontin maintained that it was indeed possible to fight for a better society without postulating an unchanging human essence—as an activist, one could always choose to fight against what was *not* acceptable, the kind of society one didn't want. Chomsky, in his response, politely recognized that this was indeed a *possible* position, but he maintained his original position on the importance of knowing about human nature (Lewontin and Chomsky, private correspondence in 1976).

In my interview with Chomsky in 1982, I asked him about his non-involvement in the sociobiology controversy. The main reason was indeed that he disagreed with the critics of Wilson, who seemed to think that it was wrong to even try to find out about the nature of human nature. For Chomsky, finding out about human nature constituted the most interesting challenge there was. Surprisingly, however, he said that he doubted that *science* would be able to say much about it—he suggested that we might rather try to find the answer to human nature in literature. (Unlike Wilson, Chomsky did not put much hope in the progress of cognitive science. According to him, many earlier enthusiasts, such as Francis Crick, had become less optimistic about the possibilities in this field.) Where Chomsky agreed with Wilson's critics was that Wilson should have made clearer to his readers what was fact and what was speculation. Here we have, then, a member of the academic left in the Boston area who took a view different from the Sociobiology Study Group concerning the legitimacy of the Wilsonian enterprise. (In Chapter 12, we will meet another left-wing activist, Salvador Luria, who also decided not to get involved.)

Other aspects of the taken-for-granted view of the Sociobiology Study Group could also be challenged. Political scientist Roger Masters (1982), for instance, pointed out that it was a mistake to automatically identify sociobiology with conservative political thought. He looked at the underlying assumptions of sociobiological theory. In his view, sociobiological thinking and its central idea of inclusive fitness theory was clearly part of the individualistic tradition in Western thought, but this tradition might be used for both conservative and radical purposes. According to Masters, the reason why sociobiology had been treated as a politically conservative ideology when applied to humans was that the critics had collapsed two parallel distinctions in the Western theoretical tradition. *On the one hand*, there was the distinction between individualistic cost-benefit or social-contract theories and systemic theories; *on the other hand* there was the distinction between political right and left. It seemed to Rogers that the critics had totally ignored that many systemic theories had been conservative (for instance, Durkheim's) and many individualistic theories radical (for instance, Rousseau's).

One obvious way to assess the correctness of the critics' assumptions about their targets' political motivations would be to see whether these hold up *empirically*. This leads directly to questioning the political orientation of modern sociobiologists. From the beginning of the sociobiology controversy, because of their presumed biological determinist positions, these scientists were grouped together with various unsavory right-wing political movements and linked up particularly with Nazism and racism. But the connection between right-wing political interests and sociobiology, however suggestive and politically useful, may not have been well-supported in practice. As Pierre van den Berghe pointed out during the heat of the controversy, one might as well have made just the *opposite* political case:

> Actually, a review of the politics of leading sociobiologists would lend more credence to the contention that *sociobiology is a Communist conspiracy*: J. B. S. Haldane, who is generally credited for having first hit on the notion of kin selection—a theoretical cornerstone of sociobiology—was a leading member of the British Communist Party; so was John Maynard Smith. E. O. Wilson and most other leading sociobiologists are left-of-center liberals or social democrats. 'Racist' Trivers is even married to a Jamaican and is heavily involved in radical black politics' (van den Berghe, 1980; italics added).

The least one can say, then, is that it should have been considered an *empirical* question exactly where a specific biologically oriented scientist stood politically. But that was not the kind of investigation that was typically of interest to members of the academic left. They preferred their own method of inquiry, which involved scrutinizing their targets' statements or theories for underlying ideological assumptions. If empirical facts went against the results of critical studies, so much worse for the facts![1]

'Plato's big lie': the clue to the critics' reasoning

We are now getting to the core of the matter: the particular assumptions shared by the members of the Sociobiology Study Group. Wilson, for one, was puzzled about the 'strange logic' he perceived in some of the critics' arguments (for example, Wilson, 1978b). However, as I hope to demonstrate here, the 'logic' in question was not the typical logic of scientific argumentation: it was rather a logic of a moral–legalistic kind applied to science. It was this type of reasoning that constituted the basis for the shared interpretive framework of Wilson's critics and made them agree so unproblematically on his moral guilt. The criticisms shared a common feature: Wilson's statements were given their true meaning only when transformed into examples of maximally undesirable social views.

In their analysis of their targets' texts, the critics used a method I call *moral reading*. The basic idea behind moral reading was to imagine the worst possible political consequences of a scientific claim. In this way, maximum moral guilt might be attributed to the perpetrator of this claim.

I will now examine one such attempt, the most glaring one I have found. At the same time, it contains what I believe to be the core assumption of the critics. In his book *From Genesis to Genocide* (1979), Sociobiology Study Group member Stephen Chorover, gave 'sociobiology' a broader meaning than the one in Wilson's book. It was no longer a scientific discipline dealing with the exploration of all aspects of social behavior, but became identified instead with a 'family of sociobiological ideas about human inequality and a specific class of political inferences drawn from Darwinism' (p. 9). After this, Chorover proceeded to connect sociobiological scholarship to Nazism. But if he had in this way already tainted sociobiology with the gravest possible crime, what more could conceivably be said? Not to worry. Chorover had found a brand new angle from which to attack sociobiology. He was a psychologist, and he set out to make a link between sociobiology and behavioral control, the basic theme of his book.

The concept he used to sustain the link between sociobiology and behavioral control was his notion of 'Plato's big lie' about the different worth of different members of society:

> Plato's big lie was not that human diversity exists or that it is innately determined, but that it is *inherently definable according to a scale of social value*. That is, he established a conjunction between his proposed social value of political inequality and the fact of human diversity by calling the latter a God-given or 'natural' value hierarchy, using the analogy of more or less precious metals from which people were forged (Chorover, 1979, p. 25).

It is a notion which is the clue to most of the 'strange logic' exhibited by Wilson's critics. Plato's big lie was, in fact, their collective guiding concept. It also defined their mission: one of search and destroy when it came to examples of Plato's big lie in science.

We can now see why there was a persistent tendency for the critics to 'translate' scientific statements about individual differences into (hypothetical) statements about *group* differences instead. The critics appeared to assume that there existed some kind of mental process whereby data on individuals would be automatically mapped onto a hypothetical construct: a 'natural' value hierarchy postulated to exist in (some?) people's heads. This explains why the critics of Wilson and Jensen felt justified in calling IQ research on *individuals* 'racist'. (The ironical feature in all this, of course, was that the presumed value hierarchy was as hypothetical a construct as IQ.) Among the critics, it was probably Chorover who at an early stage most clearly expressed what was going on in the minds of the critics.

Gould came in second when it came to introducing 'Plato's big lie'. But he compensated by invoking it on the second page of the Introduction to his *The Mismeasure of Man* (Gould, 1981a):

> This book is about the scientific version of Plato's tale. The general argument may be called *biological determinism*. It holds that shared behavioral norms, and the social and economic differences between human groups—primarily races, classes, and sexes—arise from inherited, inborn distinctions and that society, in this sense, is an accurate reflection of biology. This book discusses, in historical perspective, a principal theme within biological determinism: the claim that worth can be assigned to individuals and groups by *measuring*

intelligence as a single quantity. Two major sources of data have supported this theme: craniometry (or measurements of the skull) and certain styles of psychological testing (Gould, 1981a, p. 20).

And, according to Gould, for the last two centuries, science had taken over the earlier role of the Church as the primary agent for validating Plato's myth, and genes had taken over the function of Plato's metals (p. 20).

But although the Sociobiology Study Group may have implicitly agreed on a particular 'Plato', there were other possible Plato interpretations. Here is Dobzhansky's version of Plato's tale:

> Genetic diversity on the one hand, and equality or inequality on the other, are *independent in principle.* And yet they are by no means mutually irrelevant. The rationale of human equality is not to make everybody physically or psychologically alike, or engaged in the same work or occupation. On the contrary, *the purpose is to derive from the available diversity of humans the greatest possible benefits to the society, as well as to the individuals concerned.* Plato, in *The Republic* apprehended that, since different persons have different abilities, they achieve their own greatest well-being, and also make greatest contributions to the common good, when they develop their particular skills to the fullest extent . . .
>
>   The way to make sure to the fullest extent of the available pool of genetic talents and abilities is acceptance of meritocracy and equality of opportunity. Anybody should be entitled to aspire to any position or role in the society. . . .
>
>   Ideally, every person would elect the occupation or career for which he or she is most qualified genetically. The idea is far from always realized, but mistakes are correctable if discovered early enough (Dobzhansky, 1973b, italics added).

In other words, while Chorover and the others chose an interpretation where the idea of social hierarchy became the central concern, Dobzhansky derived support from Plato for his idea of matching innate talent with the needs of society.

For the critics, however, demonstrating that Wilson was a perpetuator of Plato's big lie did not come easy. A detailed analysis of Chorover's moral reading of Wilson shows that considerable *work* had to take place before Wilson could meet Chorover's requirements for a modern behavior-control technologist of his particular 'Plato' kind. Part of the problem here was that Wilson himself was an adherent of the *other* version of Plato: the Dobzhansky interpretation! But this was merely an obstacle to be overcome. I will now examine how Chorover was able to make Wilson an example of the concept he was launching.

The truth will out: massaging texts through moral reading

According to Chorover, instead of explaining the existence of classes and roles by analyzing institutional patterns of race and sex discrimination, sociobiology asserts 'that all societies are naturally stratified in a hierarchical fashion' and 'that individuals generally come to rest in the point in the hierarchy they inherently deserve to occupy' (p. 198). In fact, according to the author, the main point of sociobiological reasoning is to show that it is impossible to establish a society where human equality exists. It is not for scientific reasons that sociobiologists have developed a large number of different arguments, Chorover tells us; instead, each argument

> is intended to show (as did Plato's big lie) that in one way or another, social inequality merely reflects the natural and inherent inequality of different individuals, races, sexes, ethnic groups, economic classes and so on.

This was quite a charge. Chorover tries to demonstrate that sociobiologists really believe this by mobilizing Wilson's description of !Kung society:

> Even in the simplest societies individuals differ greatly. Within a small tribe of !Kung Bushmen can be found individuals who are acknowledged as the 'best people'. . . !Kung men, no less than men in advanced industrial societies, generally establish themselves by their mid-thirties or else accept a lesser status for life. There are some who never try to make it, live in rundown huts and show little pride in themselves or their work. The ability to slip into such roles, shaping one's personality to fit, may itself be adaptive. Human societies are organized by high intelligence, and each member is faced by a mixture of social challenges that taxes all of his ingenuity. . . (Wilson, 1975, p. 549, quoted by Chorover, p. 108).

For Chorover, this clinches his argument, and he wryly notes: 'Thus it would appear that Plato's lie was really a premature scientific truth' (p. 108).

But let us see how he succeeded in arriving at this particular interpretation. Chorover starts by claiming that Wilson defines 'success' in a particular way, 'not simply an indicator of intelligence but as a form of intelligence itself'. This is why, 'Wilson is able to contend that the *possession of high status is itself evidence of a natural right to it*, an argument reminiscent of Aristotle's defense of slavery' (p. 108, italics added). And how does Chorover make Wilson take the next step, argue that success is in our genes (and that the !Kung are merely legitimizing natural inequality)? This is what Wilson *ought* to be saying in order to fit the Plato bill. No problem. Chorover now brings in two other quotations from Wilson to lend support to his 'Plato' interpretation:

> If a single gene appears that is responsible for success and an upward shift in status, it can be rapidly concentrated in the upper socioeconomic classes (Wilson, 1975a, p. 554).

> The hereditary factors of human success are strongly polygenetic and form a long list, only a few of which have been measured. IQ constitutes only one subset of the components of intelligence. Less tangible but equally important equalities [sic] are creativity, entrepreneurship, drive, and mental stamina (ibid., p. 555).

These statements are now Chorover's evidence for the fact that Wilson indeed believes in a genetic basis for success. Q.E.D.

So, this just goes to show that sociobiology is part of a long tradition of justifying discrimination. We are back to where Chorover wants to be: Plato's big lie and its horrendous social consequences:

> From the very beginning of recorded political discourse, efforts to justify social inequality have been predicated on sociobiological falsehoods . . . Once people have been ranked in a way that permits comparison along an arbitrary scale, the attributes on which individuals or groups differ become more easily amenable to measurement and control, and an

atmosphere of scientific 'objectivity' comes to surround discussion in which human beings are regarded as so much raw material to be manufactured, manipulated, marketed, or (if powerful interests desire it) discounted, discarded, or destroyed.

In the last analysis, it was sociobiological scholarship, claiming to be scientifically objective, morally neutral, and ethically value free, that provided the conceptual framework by which eugenic theory was transformed into genocidal practice.... (p. 109).

It appears, then, that sociobiology is guilty almost of original sin. But is it really sociobiology that should be blamed? At the very end of his analysis, Chorover makes an interesting admission: sociobiology may not be guilty alone—it has been in the service of (yes!) Plato's big lie, now presented as representing a particular tradition of political thought.

Chorover's representation of Wilson's purported reasoning is a typical example of what I have called moral reading. For Wilson himself, and for many other readers of Wilson's text, Chorover's quotations would be seen as completely misrepresenting Wilson's true position.[2] However, Chorover 'knows' what sociobiological theories are necessarily about, so he 'helps' the reader by teasing out of Wilson's formulations the 'true' messages underlying his work. The time has come for us to appreciate the obstacles this valiant worker had to overcome in his efforts to guide the reader to the truth.

This guided reading starts with the necessary assumption that Wilson has a political point to prove—in this case, that all societies are stratified and that individuals' social positions are based on their genetic endowment. (The reader needs to keep this in mind in order to read the text 'right'.) Second, all non-pertinent quotations are ignored, and only the ones that bring out Wilson's 'true' meaning presented. Chorover does not mention that Wilson, after discussing the possibility of a genetic predisposition for classes and roles, himself explicitly rejected the idea of 'genes for success'.[3] By contrast Wilson makes the point that human roles are in fact extremely *flexible*: 'Human societies have effloresced to levels of extreme complexity because their members have the intelligence and flexibility to play roles of virtually any degree of specification, and to switch them as occasion demands' (Wilson, 1975, p. 554).

So Wilson himself explicitly *rejected* the very Plato version that Chorover was trying to pin on him. What is going on here? A closer look at the initial context of the two quotations that Chorover extracted from Wilson—the one about a single gene for success and the other about polygenic factors for success—shows that Wilson actually used the second quote about multiple polygenetic traits to *refute* the first quote (including the idea of IQ as the main basis of success)! Wilson is here making exactly the opposite point to the one he is accused of making. Against the idea of IQ, he emphasized the 'less tangible, but equally important qualities for human success'. Wilson was *playing down IQ*, as much as he could. Even more importantly—and again contrary to Chorover's particular allegation—Wilson emphasized that *success is hardly hereditary*:

Let us assume that the genes contributing to these qualities are scattered over many chromosomes. Assume further that some of the traits are uncorrelated. Under these circumstances only the most intensive form of disruptive selection could result in the formation of stable ensembles of genes. A much more likely circumstance is the one that apparently prevails: the maintenance of a large amount of genetic diversity within societies and the loose correlation of some of the genetically determined traits with success. This scrambling process is accelerated by the continuous shift in the fortunes of individual families from one generation to the next (p. 554).

One could hardly imagine a more liberal-sounding scenario—that is, if one first accepts Wilson's basic assumption that it is likely that biologically based behavioral traits exist. It seems truly unbelievable that Chorover could have missed what Wilson actually said about genes and success, considering that this was on the exact page from which he was quoting other things. In fact, Wilson was one of the very few persons—unlike, for example, the Sociobiology Study Group—who in the heated matter of IQ actually *played down* its social importance, and, even more blatantly, *played down* any strong link between genetic traits and success. (Here he was in direct opposition to such people as his Harvard colleague Richard Herrnstein; Herrnstein, 1971, 1973). It was probably the fact that Wilson talked about heritable traits *at all* that in the critics' eye made him an automatic supporter of 'genetic determinism', which they in turn identified with 'Plato's big lie'.

He *said* it! The power of the word

How could the critics, individually and as a collective, feel justified in doing such a terrible hatchet job on Wilson's text? Wilson himself often protested that he had been taken out of context, and he appears to have been right. One clue to the members' mindset might be the following interview that I conducted with one of the active critics from Science for the People, the physicist Bob Lange. I asked Lange whether the Sociobiology Study Group in their criticism hadn't really taken Wilson out of context. His answer was surprising: 'Context, context, people always talk about context. He *said* certain things, for instance the thing about sex roles and the division of labor, which none of us would have ever *said*!'

What was it that Wilson had said that was so awful? Lange referred to a particular statement about sex roles in an article in *The New York Times Magazine*:

> In hunter-gatherer societies, men hunt and women stay at home. This strong bias persists in most agricultural and industrial societies and, on that ground alone, appears to have a genetic origin . . . My own guess is that genetic bias is intense enough to cause a substantial division of labor even in the most free and egalitarian of future societies . . . Even with identical education and equal access to all professions, men are likely to continue to play a disproportionate role in political life, business and science (Wilson, 1975b).

This is the quote that the critics treasured and held up as evidence (for instance, Gould, 1976). Meanwhile, they felt free to ignore the fact that Wilson, immediately after stating his belief in slight sex differences, indicated that he was just guessing, and *dismissed* the idea that the potential evidence for differences had obvious implications for career counseling and social policy: 'But that is only a guess and, even if correct, could not be used to argue for anything less than sex-blind admission and free personal choice.'

Later, in *On Human Nature*, Wilson sorted this out in more detail. He pointed out that this was an empirical question, and that whatever the case, there existed a number of different social policy options: through education, for instance, society might decide to deliberately *counteract* sex-role bias. Incidentally, these kinds of views were not unusual for biologists to hold; for instance, in his review of *On Human Nature*, Maynard Smith (1978a) supported the idea that 'the twig is already bent a little at birth'. And there was the awkward fact that Wilson considered himself a *feminist*, as I gleaned from an interview with him in *Harvard Magazine* in 1982 and in personal communication.

But it is also true that in their interpretation of the true meaning of the sex-role statement, the critics were not alone. In the academic liberal climate of the time, where the 'default' position was environmentalist, statements such as the one above about possible innate differences between the sexes were absolutely unacceptable, because seen as automatically signaling a conservative stance. Among people who regarded themselves as academic liberals, this Wilson statement on sex roles later appears to have become *the* piece of evidence for Wilson's political motives, quoted and requoted. We find this not only among feminist critics of sociobiology, but also in various books on science (for example, Grove, 1989, p. 114; Wilkie, 1993, p. 180). It seems to me that this quotation took on a life of its own: followed by a proper condemnation, it became a sort of *signal* that left-liberal academics used to communicate their true belief to one another.

But how can we explain the critics' astounding disregard for the original context of their citations, particularly in cases where they cut and pasted so as to make Wilson say the opposite of what his original text said? From the interview with Lange we get a hint. Perhaps the critics felt justified in processing a text in any way they wanted—including cutting and pasting—*as long as they were dealing with passages that could indeed be found somewhere in the text*. Just like other scientists, the critics knew they were not free to invent 'data', but, just like other scientists, they may have felt free to 'massage' existing data to make the result come out more clearly. (Substitute 'data' here for socio-biological text.) In fact, one might describe the critics' data selection process as a rather blatant case of what Charles Babbage in his *The Decline of Science in England* (written in 1830!) famously called 'cooking', that is, selecting only those pieces which (in his words) 'will do for serving up'.[4]

A possible interpretation, then, which could explain why the critics may have felt justified in subjecting Wilson's text to various treatments, is that they also extended their scientific habits of data inclusion and exclusion to their analysis of sociobiological texts. Perhaps they regarded only the pertinent parts of the text as 'data' and dismissed the rest as 'noise'? Indeed, many of the leading critics did come from the experi-mentalist tradition in science (see further Chapters 13 and 14).

There is also another possibility, which points to a possible fundamentalist streak in the critics. They seemed unduly concerned about texts and exact words ('He *said* it'). Their reasoning here might have been that, as soon as there were written words, these could become candidates for *textual truth*. Therefore, in order to make sure that a text would not be able to lend itself to political misinterpretations, it had better not mention certain things at all!

Of course it was not only a matter of interpreting the true meaning of a text. A moral reading clearly served other functions also. Chorover was employing Wilson's book as *pedagogical material*. He was the teacher, showing the 'innocent reader' just how sociobiological explanations were cleverly constructed to support a particular political point. He was teaching the reader to read in the right spirit. In this way, the reader would learn to recognize such arguments in other material as well (Chorover, 1979, p. 107). We can now see yet another reason why Wilson's text had to be 'treated' when it did not say clearly enough what it 'ought to'. In their original form, sociobiological texts were sometimes simply not good enough to serve their purpose as political exemplars!

CHAPTER 11

Planters and weeders in the garden of science

Traditional and critical views of science in society

Another common characteristic of the members of the Sociobiology Study Group was their particular conception of the social responsibility of the scientist, different from that of the scientific mainstream. These critics might best be described as belonging to a rather unusual group of scientific 'weeders', working in direct opposition to the established majority of scientific 'planters'—in fact, trying to weed out exactly what some of these planters plant! What I call planters are mainstream scientists with an unproblematic belief in the pursuit of knowledge and the integrity and social usefulness of scientific knowledge products. Planters basically want to go on with their research. Weeders, on the other hand, believe that *'bad' science has to be identified and exposed before it can do social harm.* Therefore, they see it as their mission to be on constant lookout for dangerous messages embedded in scientific texts, new or old. Here is a particularly vivid description of the plight of weeders:

> Critics of biological determinism are like members of a fire brigade, constantly being called out in the middle of the night to put out the latest conflagration, always responding to immediate emergencies, but never with the leisure to draw up plans for a truly fireproof building. Now it is IQ and race, now criminal genes, now the biological inferiority of women, now the genetic fixity of human nature. All of these deterministic fires need to be doused with the cold water of reason before the entire neighborhood is in flames. Critics of determinism, then, seem to be doomed to constant nay-saying, while readers, audiences and students react with impatience to the perpetual negativity. . . In the words of Lumsden and Wilson, defending their *Genes, Mind and Culture* against those who accuse it of extreme determinist reductionism, critics should 'fish or cut bait' (Lewontin, Rose, and Kamin, 1984, p. 266).

Let us look at the planter side. The best examples here are undoubtedly Wilson and his older Harvard colleague, microbiologist Bernard Davis. These two got to know each other in conjunction with the sociobiology controversy, became closer over the years, and spoke with almost one voice when it came to the freedom of scientific inquiry and the possibility of scientific objectivity. The following quote from 1979 is typical of Davis' tireless fight for a traditional conception of science, a cause which he defended until his death in 1994. Davis here upholds the social system of science as a guarantor of reliable knowledge:

> I believe we will also need a restoration of trust in the scientific community. For scientists have a remarkable record of professional honesty and responsibility—not because they are inherently more virtuous than other citizens, but because neither they nor the world gain from their research unless their actions and findings are made public, subjected to minute scrutiny by their peers, and found to be verifiable. Moreover, as an intensely communal, critical activity, science has developed finely honed mechanisms for evaluating controversies dispassionately, and with emphasis on evidence and logic rather than on rhetorical skill and public stature. It is difficult for the public to make such distinctions . . . Of late, perhaps because of guilt over the charge of elitism and the ills of technology, some scientists appear to be losing confidence in the objectivity of scientific knowledge and in the ability or the right of their community to speak with any authority. But while there is no room for absolute authority in science, there is also no room for extreme intellectual relativism. In the areas of its expertise the scientific community has the authority, and the obligation, to help the public to discriminate between rational and irrational views (Davis, 1979/1986, pp. 245–6).

Thus, Davis drew a sharp distinction between scientific experts and the general public, and argued that there was good reason to trust scientific experts. Wilson, too, emphasized the role of objective scientific expertise (Wilson, 1977b; see his response to Peter Medawar in the next chapter). For Wilson and Davis, then, the social responsibility of a scientist consisted in acting as an objective and rational authority for the public. With regard to decision-making, Davis championed a two-step process whereby scientific experts would first have a rational discussion among themselves and only then would the issues be brought up to public debate. (Davis had here some experience from the public involvement with the recombinant DNA controversy around Harvard and MIT in Cambridge, Mass. According to him, the conclusion was that the scientists had acted responsibly in regard to laboratory safety; Davis, 1979/1986, p. 240.)

Davis' position was as far as one could get from the critics' view of the ideological underpinnings of sociobiology and behavioral genetics, or from Lewontin's suggestion that scientists sometimes 'lied'. Indeed, when it came to the moral/political aspect of science, it was Davis, rather than Wilson, who was Lewontin's foremost adversary. Although Wilson agreed with Davis, and later increasingly took upon himself a similar active statesmanlike role (see Part III of this book), it was Davis rather than Wilson who during the sociobiology controversy led the campaign against what he perceived as the enemies of science within science itself. Davis, in short, became 'Wilson's bulldog'. He penned a stream of guest editorials and articles emphasizing the values of traditionalist science and denouncing the critics' position. In this endeavor, Davis undoubtedly had the advantage of being close friends with Daniel Koshland, the then editor of *Science*, and personally connected to much of the scientific leadership through his membership in such organizations as the National Academy of Science and the American Academy of Arts and Sciences.

Lewontin had expressed his quite sinister view of experts already in the Nova program on Public Television in February 1975. I quote Lewontin's transcript on this:

> Professors in general believe themselves to be superior to other people. They are part of a political and social elite in America. They are called to Washington. Their voices are heard ... And they don't have to think explicitly about it to know on which side they stand. They say, well, I'm an expert and you must believe me as an expert, that indeed you are doomed to your position in life because of your bad genes. Now, the one thing that the misuse of biology tells us is that you mustn't believe any experts. I suppose that means you mustn't believe in me either, since in some sense I pose as an expert. But it is important to realize that expertise is misused as much by experts as by those who have direct political power and direct political responsibilities. That *experts are servants of power*, by and large, and that they must be viewed always as servants of power. One must always ask when told some facts solemnly by an expert, who does it serve? Whose good is served? (Lewontin, 1975b, italics added)

Thus, Lewontin and his fellow-weeders saw themselves as guardians of the innocent laymen against bad science; they wanted to warn the public not to trust experts ('experts are servants of power, by and large'), while the proto-typical planters, Wilson and Davis, encouraged the public to trust the neutrality of scientific expertise.

Where did the critics' negative view of science come from, and how did they reconcile it with the fact that they themselves were also practicing scientists? We can explain the differences between planters and weeders if we regard the members of the planter camp as traditional 'positivist' scientists, who saw a clear division between science and politics, and the weeders as representing a later generation of radical thought in academia, which saw the political values of the dominant class as permeating all realms of society, including science. Since planters believed in rational decision-making and a division of labor between politicians and scientists, they typically trusted the democratic process to make responsible social policy decisions informed by the best available scientific knowledge. Weeders, on the other hand, fundamentally distrusted the political system of liberal democracy and its ability, or political will, to work for a more just society. In many ways, the beliefs of weeders coincided with the political tenets of the 1960s' American student movement and the broader peace movement of that time.

In his early study of European and American radicals in the late 1960s, David Bouchier (1977) observed the following differences between the prevailing left-wing ideology in Europe and America. He noted that while the American radical ideology was changing from a general anti-war attitude to an eventually Marxist position, it did not originally rely on Marxist *theory* like the European one. Rather, it was based on its members' more 'personal' knowledge of alienation, war, racism, and poverty. Unlike the European left-wing movements with their traditional Marxist class analysis, the theories adopted by American movements (such as SDS, Students for a Democratic Society) were inspired instead by modern critics of mass society, such as Herbert Marcuse and other members of the Critical School. These critical theorists helped convince American radicals of a *power-élite* manipulating the atomized citizens of a mass society. Moreover, Bouchier tells us, this conviction typically went together with the view that 'not only were things worse than they seemed, but there was very little to be done about it'. This kind of ideology might best be called 'radical idealism', he suggested.

This description seems to fit the group of critics around Wilson and Jensen very well. In the critics' writings, we did indeed see attempts to connect Wilson and Jensen with the interests of a power-elite. And perhaps it was partly the pessimism connected with such a power-elite and mass society analysis that made the critics so set on *morally* condemning their targets for their scientific pronouncements. Here we have, then, a possible explanation for the surprisingly *personal* nature of the American scientific activists' political attacks on fellow scientists. A European-style Marxist perspective would presumably have produced a more abstract and theoretical political critique. (On the other hand, such a critique may not have been very efficient in the United States.)

The difference between American and European radicalism can also explain another puzzling feature of the behavior of the critics. While vigorously attacking individual scientists for scientific claims which purportedly upheld the status quo, they did not seem interested in arguing for a radically different type of society. This may have been due to a different conception of 'equality' among American and European left-wing radicals at the time. As Daniel Bell had already noted in 1972, the European socialist radicals were fighting for the *equality of result*, while the American radicals were largely promoting the *equality of opportunity* (Bell, 1972; see also Bouchier, 1977, p. 35).

Thus, at least initially, instead of arguing for a real alternative to the present social order, that is, a society not based on equal opportunity and meritocracy, the critics instead attacked scientists whose theories seemingly supported the inequalities in the present system. This lack of an alternative vision, their own location within academia rather than on the barricades, and their particular perception of the social responsibility of scientists, may explain the relentlessness with which the critics were denouncing dangerous-sounding scientific claims—just in the way Lewontin, Rose, and Kamin described it in their fire-brigade metaphor.

Some of the American critics of sociobiology may have been relative newcomers to academic activism. Indeed, in my interviews with scientists I heard scattered remarks about some of the members of the Sociobiology Study Group, who reportedly had been regular 'jacket-and-tie' types before becoming radicalized. Interestingly, this exact expression was used both for Richard Lewontin and Robert Lange. Lewontin was also reported as coming from a well-to-do family, but as having been radicalized in the 1960s by his own son, and as having later sought the Marxist tutelage of Richard Levins. (I learnt none of this from Lewontin himself. I merely asked if he had always been a radical, and to this he just responded with a curt 'yes'.)

We might even regard the Sociobiology Study Group's collective opposition to IQ research and sociobiology as a kind of radical collective 'work in progress'. While collectively reacting as one body to new moves by the 'enemy', individual academic activists were able to develop their own personal critical styles (see, for instance, Chapter 10). But during this time, the radical academic discourse itself was changing. What was taken for granted as 'correct' radical belief at the beginning of the 1970s was rapidly giving way to new interpretations. With the introduction of Affirmative Action, the earlier individual-centered view of equal opportunity was steadily becoming replaced by a different, group-centered one, which at the same time implied a new definition of equality. We will return to this in the last section of this chapter.

We have, then, the planters who believed that they were unproblematically producing useful knowledge and who were willing to leave it to the democratic process to decide about the eventual use of this knowledge, and the weeders, who distrusted the democratic process and therefore took it upon themselves to weed out 'bad' science from the very beginning, *before* it could do social harm. The scientists from the weeder camp saw it as their political task to prevent the power holders from abusing 'bad' science for political purposes. And since bad science was produced within the scientific society itself, by people who were *bona fide* scientists, the primary task for weeders was to identify and debunk 'bad scientists'.

What about Wilson, the presumed perpetrator of dangerous claims? Did not Wilson see any danger in the new scientific powers—was he not afraid, like the critics, that scientific results would be politically misused? I asked him exactly this in interview in 1981. Wilson answered as follows:

> I think that we now after hours of conversation have hit on the main difference between me and my critics! I trust the common man. These ideologues, even if they talk about fighting for the masses—they don't trust *anybody*. They don't trust democracy, they don't trust the judgment of educated citizens—they really are *élitists*! They think there will always be an elitist control of society and that we must not provide the instruments by which the elite can control it. But I am really an avid believer in democracy!

Wilson also explicitly stated that he saw only benefits, not dangers, in the new scientific developments. In this interview, we had been talking about the Harvard molecular biologist Matthew Meselson's recent Bicentennial Address at the American Academy of Arts and Sciences, where Meselson had discussed the new biotechnology and warned about possible dangers (Meselson, 1981). Wilson, without hesitation, declared that he was only looking forward to the possibility of 'having more control over our individual lives' with the help of a new genetic technology combined with a new philosophy provided by sociobiology.

Thus, planters such as Wilson and Davis were not worrying about the possible negative aspects of new scientific developments. (Davis, 1980a, addressed exactly this question in his article 'Three Specters: Dangerous Products, Powers, or Ideas'.) No wonder, then, that Davis early on took issue with the Sociobiology Study Group, and criticized them for exaggeration. According to him, this group was underestimating the possibility of human morality to adjust itself in the light of new scientific findings. He argued that we should allow future generations to think for themselves (Davis, 1976a, 1978). His belief in liberal democracy and the democratic process of decision-making was so strong that he even criticized *Wilson* for failing to pay enough attention to it in his sociobiological scheme. According to Davis, Wilson seemed to believe that we could unproblematically predict *social* developments on the basis of information about *individuals.* But Wilson did not take into account the intervening *political process*, on whose basis social decisions are negotiated, and consciously taken (Davis, 1980b and interview). Thus, while the critics were typically criticizing Wilson for ignoring culture, Davis more specifically put his finger on Wilson's neglect of social interaction and the bargaining involved in the political process itself.

This was an interesting criticism, considering that Wilson himself had emphasized such things as the particular human propensity for social contracts. Perhaps we have here an illustration of the fact that Wilson did not naturally think of politics as a *process*, or as a resolution of a conflict of social interests. Unlike the British sociobiologists, Wilson appears not to have been at all interested in game theory, where the outcome of an interaction is dependent on the perceptions and actions of two or more parties. Wilson fundamentally may be what a social scientist would call a 'consensus theorist'. He may simply not have had use for game theory in his larger theory-building attempts. And this may explain why Maynard Smith's Evolutionarily Stable Strategy is missing in *Sociobiology*—something that puzzled many, including Dawkins (1981a) and Hamilton (1977a). The book also shows no trace of the various evolutionary strategies developed by contemporary behavioral ecologists—at least, they are not identified by this name. It was rather Dawkins who made his contemporary book a display of these kinds of new game-theoretical developments. That was one reason why *The Selfish Gene* was such a different book from *Sociobiology*—something that the American critics of sociobiology almost totally ignored.

What is to be done? The responsibility of the scientist

Wilson was right about his critics. The group members did not trust the usual mechanisms to take care of things, but appointed themselves policemen of 'bad science'. For them, the political struggle *within* science was important. To get a sense of the complex subjective situation for a scientific radical, let us see how Jonathan Beckwith, an eminent scientist and something of a veteran of scientific controversy, formulated the task at a conference in 1976: 'There is no escape from the burden of the scientist . . . You cannot escape by quitting science, even if a radical scientist sees that he cannot contribute to radical change in any major way through his science' (Beckwith, 1976). According to Beckwith, the scientist's task might be:

1) to inform the public about the dangers of runaway technology—scientific progress is not inherently for the better;

2) to lend his expertise to groups working for social change;

3) to bring science to the people, educate the public, and 'respond to the distorted use of scientific methods to support racism and discrimination against women', and,

4) to operate within his place of work on the same principles which he wishes to prevail in the outside world, that is, 'by working to destroy the hierarchical structure of labs . . . and to attempt to influence the role of one's institution in the outside world'. He added: 'Hopefully it is from beginnings like this on a small scale that the greater changes in society will arise' (Beckwith, 1976).

What about the other members of the initial group of Wilson's critics? Many of the most active members of the Sociobiology Study Group confined their political activity to strictly scientific issues, while some lent their expertise to the outside world, or engaged in general 'enlightenment'. Lewontin and Gould were especially active as speakers on different occasions, and wrote for the general public. Also, together with Levins, Lewontin was involved in the World Agricultural Research Project operating from Harvard, which did research and provided information on agriculture and health (cf. Lewontin, 1979b). Unlike many of his radical scientific colleagues, Beckwith was active as a political organizer outside academia, too ('a darned good politician', according to Salvador Luria, a left-wing activist-cum-Nobel laureate, whom we will meet in the next chapter).

The Sociobiology Study Group, like many other activist movements, had a 'total' democratic ambition as the ideal. For instance, there were attempts to 'democratize' science at the laboratory level. Lewontin, who tried it, concluded by 1979 that it is difficult to create democratic collectives within a hierarchical system, where the professors by definition have access to the funds and the power (Lewontin, 1979b). Another approach was to give critical courses at the university. For instance, in 1981 Lewontin and Gould, together with Richard Levins and Ruth Hubbard, organized an undergraduate student seminar at Harvard on the social implications of biology. The contradiction inherent in being a politically concerned person but still remaining within science was acutely felt by some, for instance Stephen Chorover, who told me so in interview. Others solved the problem by regarding scientific criticism of dangerous-seeming theories as 'political action in one's own workplace'. This was, for instance, Lewontin's solution (Lewontin, interview). These differences within the group of critics when it came to reconciling science with the political struggle led to internal tensions. As Lewontin told me in interview in 1981, it was 'political disagreements' between himself and the leadership of Science for the People (presumably Beckwith and Alper) that made him later disassociate himself from that group.

Interestingly, many critics of sociobiology did not perceive as a problem the fact that they were not familiar with evolutionary biology. They seemed to regard it as merely an obstacle to overcome; and so they did, by learning it sufficiently well to be able to criticize it. For instance, the chemist Joseph Alper at the University of Massachusetts, the physicist Robert Lange at Brandeis, and David Layzer, an astrophysicist and epistemologist at Harvard, all learnt the basics of population genetics in order to be up-to-date with the latest controversies (Layzer, interview; Lange, interview). The result of this self-education was, for instance, Alper and Lange's criticism of *Genes, Mind and Culture* in *Proceedings of the National Academy of Sciences* (*PNAS*) (Alper and Lange, 1981) and Layzer's review of the same book (1981). We will return to the Alper and Lange critique in Chapters 12 and 15.

An obvious problem for any democratic collective working for a specific intellectual goal is the fact that some members are more knowledgeable than others. This was also one of the problems of the Sociobiology Study Group, which included biologists such as Lewontin and Beckwith, leaders in the attack on sociobiology. Although Beckwith had isolated the first gene, the lac-operon, in 1969 (and, according to Davis, who had imported him to Harvard Medical School, was of 'Nobel laureate quality'), it was Lewontin, because of his training in evolutionary biology, who was the clear critical expert in these matters. This can be seen from the fact that he was entrusted with the authorship of the Group's longer collective statement in 1976 (see Chapter 2). Finally, it is difficult to imagine that Lewontin's Harvard location one floor below Wilson did not matter for the perception of him as leader—particularly since the paper was distributed from a box in his office. Lewontin was the *de facto* leader for the overall attack on sociobiology, whatever he may have said or wished himself. (In his interviews with me, Lewontin often complained about the fact that people saw him as Wilson's chief opponent.) Gould, again, was less visible as an activist. Instead, he spoke and wrote critically about sociobiology in *Natural History*, *The New York Review of Books*, and other popular places. Meanwhile, his *Natural History* columns were being collected and published in paperbacks.

Was it perhaps worthwhile to sacrifice critical expertise in order to satisfy democratic ideals within the group itself? This is an inherent problem in any political movement, and it became a real question at one of the meetings of the Sociobiology Study Group in the winter of 1976, at which I was present as an observer. At this meeting, a couple of women in the group (among others Jon Beckwith's wife Barbara Beckwith, a teacher) accused Lewontin and other leading males of 'sexism' and 'elitism'—they complained that these males were too much in charge! This was a small meeting, and we were all sitting on the floor close to one another. Under these conditions, the charge took on a very direct quality, and Lewontin appeared to feel very uncomfortable. There was not much he could say, except that this had not been his intent, and that he encouraged others to continue with the criticism. The implicit ideal of the group was indeed a collectivist one; this is why, for instance, Elizabeth Allen, a student, became the famous first signatory of the infamous 1975 Letter to *The New York Review of Books*.

Fear of facts?

As we have seen, many radical scientists seemed to take for granted that science with socially undesirable implications—morally/politically bad science, 'must' also be *scientifically* bad. This is why the critics were not only interested in unraveling hidden political assumptions, but also in documenting various types of scientific *errors*. What counted, then, as error? The errors ranged from reference mistakes to 'erroneous' conceptions of genes and 'philosophical errors' in thinking about human behavior, society, and human nature. Methodological problems peculiar to the fields of IQ studies and sociobiology, or even specific problems of biological language, were also attacked. In this process genuine differences in scientific views as well as structural problems of science were routinely and unproblematically turned into errors of individual scientists.[1]

Judging by the critics' reactions, they seem to have considered it a *moral* offense to make a *scientific* error. It was also a moral offense for the culprits to state their own scientific beliefs if, from the *critics'* point of view, these beliefs were erroneous!

But weeders could be even more dedicated as error-finders. As we saw in the last chapter, in order to weed out 'bad' science, they would first undertake a 'moral reading' of their chosen textual object. One might, of course, claim that in doing so, weeders were simply in agreement with Gould's (1981a) view of debunking as a positive science (p. 321). But the mere notions of debunking and error-finding cannot account for all activities of these ardent gardeners. As we saw, they did not mind doing some pruning and grafting work, too, when their culprits were not saying clearly enough what they 'ought to'.

The critics' fundamental conception of the role of the scientist as a weeder of bad science was hard for planters to understand or accept. Bernard Davis, the most vehement defender of the freedom of research—and behavioral genetics and sociobiology in particular—was convinced that the criticism of sociobiology and IQ research was exclusively *politically* motivated. Since for him there was only *one* possible attitude to science (and note here that he counted IQ research as part of *natural* science; Davis, 1983, pp. 45, 55), he could not recognize the legitimacy of an alternative critical conception of science or the role of the scientist (Davis, interview).

In 1978, Davis coined the expression 'the moralistic fallacy' for what he perceived as the view of the opponents. In his opinion, the critics of sociobiology were confusing the normative with the empirical, and were therefore 'scared of facts' (Davis, 1978). Wilson, too, suggested that there was a 'fear of facts' among the critics (Wilson, 1978a,b). But was this really the case? In 1982, I asked a couple of members of the Sociobiology Study Group, Jon Beckwith and Bob Lange, exactly this question. Beckwith told me that it was not impossible that there existed genes for such things as depression. So far, however, in his view, the evidence was not in (Beckwith, interview). This came as a relative surprise to me; at this point I was still trying to figure out the real differences between Wilson and Davis and their critics when it came to scientific belief. I had actually expected Beckwith, as a member of the Sociobiology Study Group, to deny the existence of such genes.

But the real surprise came in my subsequent interview with Bob Lange. As we saw in the previous chapter, Lange had severely criticized Wilson for making that famous statement about the possible biological basis of sex roles. When I pointed out the total context of the statement, he had simply declared that no member of the Sociobiology Study Group would ever have said such a thing. Lange seemed to be a good person for the question I really wanted an answer to: what would he do if incontrovertible facts about sex roles or, even worse, racial differences, really were to emerge?

If Davis was right that there existed this 'fear of facts' among the critics, then someone like Lange ought to have denied the existence of race differences, or the very possibility of finding out about such differences, or something along these lines. But Lange instead quite spontaneously answered my question as follows: 'Then I would evidently have to become a racist, because I would have to believe in the facts!' But he went on to cheerfully add that, so far, there were no such facts! (Lange, interview.)

So Davis appears to have been wrong about the critics' fear of facts. How can we explain their attitude, then? The answer may be the following: the critics did not deny facts as such, but they did not think that any results that existed so far *counted* as facts, since they were not products of 'serious' science. In a sense, Davis was right, after all. The critics were indeed afraid of 'facts', that is, *purported* facts produced by what they considered 'bad science'. Again, the reason here was their concern that such 'facts' would be inevitably prone to political abuse. Davis and Wilson had good reason to believe that the critics' stance did reflect a 'fear of facts'. As we have seen, in their attacks, the critics usually did not limit themselves to pointing to our relative scientific ignorance, or even to making clear exactly what they would count as facts. Instead, they went on to find hidden ideological motives in those who took a more generous view of the scientific acceptability of current results in fields such as behavioral genetics and mental testing.

The morality of science

But, we may ask, if they were really so politically concerned, why were the members of the Sociobiology Study Group not fighting on the barricades? It seems that one reason why these radical scientists remained in science was its inherently *moral* appeal: science as the pursuit of truth. Statements to this effect can in fact be found in the critics' writings. Thus, for instance, Gould wrote that he did not reject biological determinism because he disliked its political usage: '*Scientific truth*, as we understand it, *must be our primary criterion*. We live with several unpleasant biological truths, death being the most undeniable and ineluctable. If genetic determinism is true, we will learn to live with it as well' (Gould, 1976/1978, p. 349, italics added). But such a general attitude was surely true of Wilson and Davis as well—if anything, they probably emphasized truth even more than the critics.

How could different scientists, all pursuing truth for its moral value, have been so opposed to each other's views? One reason seems to have been that Wilson's and Davis' traditional 'positivist' view of science went hand in hand with a belief in the moral imperative of the so-called 'ethos of science'—Robert Merton's set of norms that supposedly characterized science as an institute (Merton, 1942). For them, *the morality of science coincided by definition with current practice*. For the critics, on the contrary, scientific practice was not guaranteed to be *inherently* moral, since it was demonstrably capable of giving rise to bad science! Morality had to do with the *use* to which science would be put.

In his defense of science, Davis went far beyond his own field, microbiology. In fact, in parallel with his scientific activity he increasingly started taking upon himself the role of a statesman of science, reinforced by such distinctions as membership in the National Academy of Sciences and his earlier role as president of the influential American Society for Microbiology. He once proudly mentioned to me that the doyen of sociology of science, Robert Merton himself, had told him that he (Davis) was the scientist who best represented the 'ethos of science'. (This was put more curtly by Luria: 'Davis has an overstrong commitment to the integrity of science', Luria, interview, 1982.) Indeed, Davis systematically took action whenever he perceived some distortion of truth or threat to academic freedom, or even an over-emphasis on dangers of science (for example, Davis, 1976a, 1978 and 1979). Later, he extended his position to arguing also for such things as the promise of biotechnology and genetic engineering (for example, Davis, 1991); however, he was an early opponent of the Human Genome Project (Davis et al., 1992).[2]

It may have been their view of science as an inherently moral endeavor that made Davis and Wilson also concerned with *perceived deviations from the tacit rules of scientific conduct or etiquette*. Examples of this abound in the sociobiology controversy. Davis complained of bad manners among the critics, particularly Lewontin's. On several occasions Lewontin had refused to even talk to him outside the contest of an organized panel debate. Also, it irked Davis that Lewontin had not had the civility to even respond to Davis' invitation to participate in the Darwin Centennial Conference arranged by the American Academy of Arts and Sciences in 1982. Davis had a much better opinion of someone like Beckwith, despite Beckwith's political activism (Davis, interview).

It is clear that 'bad manners' are not just something that can be easily brushed off— they take an emotional toll on the one who is being treated badly. Wilson, too, was obviously sensitive to bad manners, and not only among his sociobiology critics. It is interesting to observe that Wilson in his autobiography duly noted the bad manners of his earlier adversary Jim Watson (with whom Wilson was involved in 'the molecular wars'—a struggle between molecular and evolutionary biology in the biology department at Harvard; Wilson, 1994). According to Wilson, Watson simply acted as if he did not see Wilson in corridors, and in general behaved in a very arrogant fashion (no wonder Wilson's nickname for him was Caligula).[3] This, in turn, spurred Wilson into action (see Chapter 14).

The sociobiology controversy sometimes gave the impression of a 'total' war. Both sides paid close attention to the opponents' moves and registered even minute details of scientific conduct and manners. This practice of close, almost petty, checking came to the surface particularly in interviews and in contexts such as Davis' semi-autobiographical essay collection *Storm Over Biology* (1986) or Wilson's retrospective *Naturalist* (1994). We have already seen one such example of attention to conduct in the exchange between Steven Rose and Richard Dawkins in Chapter 9, where Rose—rather unbelievably—threatened to sue Dawkins for libel. The case that best illustrates the different conceptions of the morality of scientific conduct among the traditionalists and the radicals, however, was perhaps the 'Nabi' episode, which might, indeed, be regarded as an almost purely *moral* offshoot of the larger sociobiology controversy. The Nabi episode showed that what the critics considered harmless fun, Davis and Wilson took as serious, underhanded action. It motivated Wilson to write a letter to, and Davis an (anonymous) editorial in, *Nature*, condemning the use of pseudonyms in science. The best indication of the gravity with which Wilson regarded Lewontin's behavior in the Nabi affair was perhaps his view that this had seriously hurt Lewontin's reputation.

Thus, the issues involved in recent controversies might be classified as much *moral* as political. While Wilson appeared to believe that all his radical opponents were 'Marxists' (maintaining this may also have been strategically useful), from a European

Marxist point of view, the critics represented concerns rather typical of American radicalism. It was, then, the *lack* of a coherent Marxist framework rather than a rigid adherence to Marxist theory that left room for the surprisingly individualistic and moralistic side of the critics' analysis. But how does all this fit the fact that Lewontin, Levins, and Gould all regarded themselves as Marxists? The answer will have to wait till Chapter 14.

The battle around behavioral genetics

A question that resurfaced around the time of the IQ and sociobiology controversies was whether there were certain kinds of research that should not be conducted; certain kinds of knowledge that were too dangerous. In 1974, just before the sociobiology controversy, there had been the Asilomar conference, where scientists collectively decided to proceed cautiously with the new technique of recombinant DNA. (These restrictions were later waived, because of failure to demonstrate serious dangers; for a brief account see, for example, Davis, 1979.) And such questions have come up again and again: a decade later there were similar questions raised around the release of genetically engineered micro-organisms (see, for example, Segerstråle, 1990b). Most recently, such problems have resurfaced in conjunction with the Human Genome Project (see for example, Wilkie, 1993; Kevles and Hood, 1992).

How did the two camps of planters and weeders relate to the issue of moratoria on dangerous knowledge? In the early days of the sociobiology controversy, there were seeds of conflict in this respect between the would-be larger scientific camps. Some members of Science for the People, particularly Jonathan Beckwith, successfully fought an ongoing research project at Harvard involving a program for detection of the so-called 'criminal' XYY gene in newborn males. Meanwhile, his colleague Bernard Davis was actively campaigning for freedom of research and wrote an eloquent essay dismissing the perceived dangers (Davis, 1976a). Davis also went on direct counterattack. In an article in the alumni journal *Harvard Magazine*, after first describing the history of the XYY controversy, he continued:

> Why, then, should an activist political group make such an issue of XYY, with all its scientific and ethical ambiguities and with so few 'victims' involved, when much larger and more indefensible medical problems abound?
>
> The key, I suggest, is not primarily concern for the innocent children, though that is surely present. It is the conviction that any attention to genetic factors in behavior will have reactionary social consequences, just as Social Darwinism and the eugenics movements of the nineteenth century did. In a letter published last year, members of Science for the People stated that attention to genetic factors in behavior 'only serves to propagate the damaging mythology of the genetic origins of "antisocial" behavior,' and so it interferes with the job of eliminating the social and economic factors involved in such behavior.
>
> ....
>
> [W]e must recognize that we are dealing not simply with legitimate dissent. *Just as Lysenko destroyed all of genetics in the Soviet Union from 1935 to 1969, Science for the People*

aims to destroy the field of human behavioral genetics. And we would be naive not to recognize that an opposition to certain ideas underlies its attack on allegedly harmful research activities (Davis, 1976b, italics added).

Thus, Davis here drew a direct parallel between Lysenko and Science for the People.

In 1978 Wilson wrote an article in the *Journal of General Education* entitled: 'The attempt to suppress behavioral genetics' in which he interpreted the current attack on biological studies of human behavior as a misguided attempt to forbid such research. In this article, Wilson once more reiterated some of the points he had made in his response to the Sociobiology Study Group, such as the political dangers of *tabula rasa* assumptions about human nature. But this time he used an additional weapon: he reminded his readers of the attempts to suppress science in conjunction with the Lysenko affair. Why was Wilson so concerned about behavioral genetics, not his particular scientific field? The answer is at least twofold. As already noted, Wilson needed even the tentative results obtained so far in behavioral genetics for his sociobiological modeling efforts— you cannot do population genetics without genes. It is also likely that he was encouraged to do this by his older colleague, Bernard Davis, who had by then become something of a brother-in-arms, and for whom behavioral genetics and IQ research was a central issue.

It is no wonder that by this time Wilson and Davis were already forming a united front. Around the beginning of the sociobiology controversy, Davis, too, had been attacked by many of the same critics as Wilson, although for different reasons. Also he had had the unenviable first-hand experience of being attacked by Lewontin. Davis told me the story about his nastiest experience in this respect. Lewontin had invited him to participate in an AAAS panel on IQ research, which had been rigged so that Davis was the only pro-IQ scientist on the whole panel. As a result, Davis had had to single-handedly defend the legitimacy of mental testing against a number of detractors. Davis recalled that the first thing he had said to Lewontin was 'Is this fair?' Still, he reckoned that he did a decent job on the panel, despite the set-up. He even had a picture to prove that his performance had had at least some effect on Lewontin. The text of the photograph said something along the lines of 'Lewontin and Davis discussing intelligence testing'. The picture showed Lewontin with his back turned to Davis.

Soon after this episode, Davis was labelled a 'racist' by Beckwith and other members of Science for the People. The occasion was a talk he had given at the Cambridge Forum on the importance of learning about the genetic basis for human diversity (Davis, 1976b). This became the subject matter of a special issue of *The Present Illness*, a Harvard Medical School bulletin. Davis was very upset over this. He did not consider himself a racist—for instance, he prided himself on having brought the first black faculty member to Harvard Medical School. (Ironically, as I learnt in this interview, it was also Davis who was responsible for bringing in Beckwith. Here we have an obvious parallel with Wilson, who had also imported his own nemesis, Lewontin.) Under some pressure, Davis finally admitted to being an elitist or a meritocrat. But he was *not* a racist, he insisted—that black doctor was excellent! (Davis, interview.)

Davis' medical colleagues also testified to his general liberal stance in a special issue of the *Harvard Alumni Newsletter*. This became necessary after another scandal erupted. A *New York Times* editorial quoted Davis' worry that Affirmative Action lowered standards in medical schools (Davis 1976e, 1986b; Kogan 1976). This was said in his support:

> Davis's own credentials . . . indicate a consistent concern with social justice; he was the organizer of antiwar demonstrations in the 1960s, the first department chairman in the history of Harvard to preside over the appointment of a black man to a tenured post, and for many years a member of the advisory board of the Civil Liberties Union of Massachusetts. As a teacher of genetics to undergraduates . . . Dr. Davis is seen by *The Harvard Crimson* as providing a 'strictly objective discussion of biology and genetics, laying the foundation for an analysis of the implications of recent advances in these fields for philosophy and ethics (Richardson, 1976).

Still, it was clear that Davis' position was of relevance for racial minorities, since he not only spoke about genetic factors in intelligence, but also pointed to the probability of statistical but overlapping differences between racial groups in this respect (echoing Jensen's stance). Although his policy recommendation was that we should use these facts to maximize the opportunity for development in each individual, regardless of race, he also warned that we should not try to 'legislate the facts of nature'. And here his traditional-liberal, meritocratic vision of racial color blindness went directly against the newer, radical-liberal conception that drastic measures were needed to restore the social balance.

If anything, then, Davis had been even more strongly attacked by Lewontin than Wilson (perhaps not a surprise, considering Davis' explicit pronouncements in a very sensitive area). With such parallel experiences and both feeling themselves generally misunderstood by fellow academics and attacked by common Harvard colleagues, no wonder that Davis and Wilson over the years became something of brothers-in-arms. Another contributing factor may have been that Davis was already on friendly terms with Wilson's older colleague, Ernst Mayr. And in this process of mutual support against common enemies, Davis taught himself evolutionary biology (see, for example, Davis, 1982, 1985a), while Wilson became more alert to the larger political battles in academia. It was probably through Davis that Wilson became acquainted with academic politics and the full repertory of pro-science arguments in the planter camp.

Neo-Lysenkoism in American academia?

The Lysenko affair has become something of an exemplar referred to by academics to emphasize the importance of freedom of science, or as an example of what happens when scientific objectivity is abandoned for political reasons.[4] It seems that the Lysenko affair is as routinely invoked by scientific traditionalists as the notorious sterilization laws or Immigration Act are invoked by radical scientists. Ironically, both sides use their chosen precedents in order to demonstrate the *same* thing: the dangers of politically influenced science. As we saw, Davis had invoked Lysenko in 1976 in the context of the

Science for the People protest against the XYY study. That study was indeed stopped, although it is arguable whether the various considerations involved in the Harvard Medical School decision can be readily compared to a Lysenko-like total political ban.

A decade later, Davis made a surprise come-back. In a brief new introduction to one of the articles collected in his *Storm over Biology*, he made a direct connection between the behavior of Science for the People in the XYY controversy and the behavior of the Sociobiology Study Group in the sociobiology controversy. This time he singled out Gould and Lewontin (Davis, 1986, p. 141). According to Davis, in both controversies the aim was the same: to stop research for political reasons. But how well did the Lysenkoist label really fit Gould and Lewontin?

Starting with Lewontin, it seems that he did not question the *legitimacy* of certain types of research that he otherwise criticized. For instance, he is rather surprisingly on record in 1976 saying that he had nothing in principle against human sociobiology (Lewontin, 1976a).[5] But Lewontin wanted 'good science', and this for him could only be arrived at by the extension of safely established knowledge. Also, Lewontin's views concerning the genetics of IQ in 1975 (Lewontin, 1975a) indicated that he, at least at that point, was *not against research in intelligence as such*. What was it, then, that he objected to, and what was it that made him speak up against 'racist' research and sign the 1973 Resolution against Racism in *The New York Times* (a fact which Wilson duly noted in his 1978 article)?

The answer is somewhat complicated. According to Lewontin, there was no way at present that we could enumerate human genotypes and characterize the norm of reaction for each one of these (for a similar position, see, for example, Hirsch, 1969; Bodmer and Cavalli-Sforza, 1970; Dobzhansky, 1973a). Therefore we were not yet able to answer scientifically such a question as 'How much can we boost IQ and scholastic achievement?', which meant that *the very posing of such a question was already unscientific* (Lewontin, 1970a). In other words, already from the outset IQ research of the Jensen kind was 'bad science'. And, as we saw in *The Harvard Gazette* quote, bad science was morally bad and socially dangerous. Still, we may wonder what avenues for 'legitimate' scientific research were left open in this kind of scenario. One answer can be found in Chapter 14.

Turning now to Gould as a candidate for Neo-Lysenkoism, one of the odder episodes in the sociobiology controversy is surely the exchange between Davis and Gould in the journal *The Public Interest*. There, in an article, 'Neo-Lysenkoism, IQ, and the Press' (Davis, 1983), Davis launched a frontal attack on Gould and his *The Mismeasure of Man*, which had received the National Book Critics' Circle Award. Davis' article analyzed not only Gould's book, but also the various reactions to it. He pointed out that the book had been enthusiastically received by the general press, but that the reviews in leading scientific journals had been consistently critical.

What was it that Gould had done in his book that so upset Davis? Starting with craniology, going through sociobiology, and ending with Jensen and IQ research, Gould had documented how presumably objective scientists, one after the other, had turned out to be mistaken about race and sex differences in cognitive ability. (What

Davis would have *liked* Gould to do, I found out in interview, was to state that the science of mental testing had indeed made some mistakes in the past, but that it had now cleared up its errors and become a reliable, modern science.) Davis was absolutely furious that Gould associated today's sophisticated methods of mental testing with old-fashioned and outdated craniology. In this way he gave the general public a totally wrong idea about the reliability of current IQ research! (Davis, 1983, and interview.)

But making this kind of association may, of course, have been exactly Gould's point. Just as modern IQ testers were at the forefront of their science, so craniology at some point was state-of-the art. And just as no one then questioned the craniologists' conclusions, because they conformed to prevailing social belief, people today, too, might believe in mental testing, because its results supported current social conceptions. In other words, for Gould, the science of measuring cognitive ability had not necessarily eliminated its errors. Therefore, what Gould may have wanted to do in the book was exactly to question some of today's taken-for-granted scientific knowledge, with regard to both its ideological underpinnings and its basic scientific assumptions. (Moreover, because of actions such as this, future historians would not be able to say of our time, at least, that 'everybody' believed in IQ measurement!)

Just like the other members of the Sociobiology Study Group, Gould seems to have assumed that IQ testing, a science with potentially dangerous sociopolitical consequences, 'must' also be bad science. This meant he was expecting and looking for some kind of error in IQ research. Although today's sophisticated methods make it harder to find errors of the same sort as in earlier skull measurements, one can criticize mental testing in other ways: one might question what it is that intelligence testing really measures, whether something called 'general intelligence' really exists, and whether it can be represented by a single factor *g*. This is exactly what Gould did.

And it was just this that upset Davis. Davis noted that, unlike earlier critics of Jensen, Gould was not content with merely criticizing the methodology of IQ research, but was now trying to demonstrate that the very *concept* of general intelligence, *g*, had no meaning. In this way, speaking about its *heritability*, too, would be meaningless, Davis continued. Here, then, was Gould's attempt to deliver the *coup de grâce* to all further controversy about the heritability of IQ, fumed Davis! (Davis, 1986, pp. 114–115.)

Davis' (1983) article is now a good illustration of 'coupled reasoning', of the very same kind that we earlier encountered among the members of the Sociobiology Study Group. Here we have a scientist (Davis) reasoning about another scientist's (Gould's) purported 'error' (his treatment of the concept of general intelligence, *g*). Just like the critics of sociobiology, Davis had clear conceptions as to what 'could' and 'could not' lie behind his target's position. For Davis, there could be no good reason why Gould came to the conclusion he did in *Mismeasure*, other than the fact that he was blinded by Marxist ideology! To support this, Davis tried to show first that Gould was affected by political ideology, and second that Gould was a bad scientist.

The first task was relatively easy. Davis decided to focus on Gould's 'main scientific contribution', his and Eldredge's theory of punctuated equilibria (Gould and Eldredge,

1977). For Davis, the politically incriminating evidence was that Gould, in a Dialectics Workshop talk, had drawn a parallel between this theory and Marxist philosophy (Gould, 1979). To prove his second point, that Gould did bad science, Davis invoked the fact that '[h]is claim to have disproved the widely-accepted, "gradualist" view of evolution has had great appeal for science reporters but it has been subjected to intense criticism by his professional colleagues' (Davis, 1983, p. 57).

Davis, usually so judicious in his editorials and commentaries, here seems to have been carried away by holy indignation combined with the typical tendency of scientists to attribute other scientists' errors to 'extrascientific' causes (cf. Mulkay and Gilbert, 1982). For Davis, the reason for Gould's straying from the shining path of truth was purely political, and Davis believed that he was making a serious and convincing point. What he didn't consider were alternative possibilities—for instance, the possibility that Gould's (and Eldredge's) theory about punctuated equilibria might be right or wrong *independently* of ideological influences (and anyway, Eldredge was not a Marxist), or that, even if Davis was empirically correct in his impression of a predominantly negative scientific response, the immediate reception of a theory did not necessarily reflect its truth or falsity. (As we saw in Chapter 6, the theory had, indeed, been criticized.)

Indeed, after first suggesting the connection, Davis himself seems to have realized he was going too far and slightly backed off, stating that 'it would not be appropriate here to judge Gould's stature as a scientist'. Yet he continued, now focusing on similarities between Gould the scientist and Gould the popularizer:

> It is pertinent, however, to note features of his professional writing remarkably similar to those I have criticized in *The Mismeasure of Man*. In both contexts, he focuses primarily on older approaches to problems in which genetics is now central; he picks his history; and he handles key concepts in an ambiguous manner. Moreover, he is fond of artificial dichotomies that oversimplify complex issues: evolution by leaps versus evolution by gradual steps; biological determinists versus environmentalists; general intelligence versus specialized intelligence (Davis, 1983, p. 57).

But surely there existed better candidates than Stephen J. Gould, if Davis by 'neo-Lysenkoism' meant the attempt to prevent certain kinds of research! Although Davis did not fail to mention that Gould was a member of Science for the People (Davis, 1983, p. 56), unlike Beckwith and others, Gould had not been involved in direct actions or advocated the shut-down of any project. What he had done was to *criticize* a number of scientists—including Jensen and Wilson—all of whom he bunched together as 'mis-measurers of man'. I read an early draft of Davis' paper and, as often happened in our discussions, found myself in wild disagreement with the author. It was unclear to me how the charge of 'neo-Lysenkoism' could be applied to Gould in particular, and to many of the other critics of sociobiology as well. Moreover, it appeared unnecessary to try to demonstrate a link between Gould's ideological beliefs and his status as a scientist, since it was so obviously possible to be a Marxist and an eminent scientist at the same time (J. D. Bernal, J. B. S. Haldane, Salvador Luria, for example). I tried to probe Davis' reasoning in this matter.

Was the case, perhaps, that Davis was a scientific purist of some sort, upset with Gould's tendency to popularize science? Did he believe that popularizers cannot be good scientists? This might indeed have been the case to some extent; during my interview Davis emotionally pointed to the cover of *Newsweek*, featuring Gould and a dinosaur, and asked: 'Why is Gould so popular?' But popularity does not preclude good science, or otherwise Davis would have had to use the same criterion for his friend Wilson. (Incidentally, I did get Davis to admit that Gould was doing good and important work as a popularizer of evolutionary biology.)[6]

What the Davis–Gould dispute admirably demonstrates is two different views of 'good science' in conflict. Just like Wilson and other traditionalists, Davis believed in the inherent objectivity of science and the tendency of scientific error to be eliminated in the long run. Gould, on the other hand, explicitly tried to establish the principle of *debunking as good science* (1981a, p. 321). Thus, he was arguing for *the legitimacy of a type of 'quality control' in science.*

For Gould, debunking was not the same as forbidding research. (It is not surprising that Gould, in an indignant response to Davis' charges, asked: 'Who has donned Lysenko's mantle?'; Gould, 1984.) But this was what Gould's critique of the idea of general intelligence *g* meant to Davis. And for him, since IQ research was well-established, serious science, Gould 'could' have no legitimate *scientific* reason for his critique, and 'must' therefore be operating solely on *political* grounds. But here, Davis was in fact mistaken, as we shall see in Chapter 14.

We thus had a situation where, from each side's perspective, the *other* side's position clearly looked ideologically biased. While Davis believed that scientific objectivity was unproblematic, because science was inherently moral, or would at least correct itself in the long run, for Gould and his critical colleagues, scientific objectivity was not given, but would have to be fought for. But *contra* Davis, this did not mean that Gould or his colleagues believed that truth was unattainable, or that they were 'anti-science', an epithet typically launched by scientific traditionalists against radical critics (for example, Page, 1972; Shils in his Foreword to Davis, 1986). For Davis, however, there was no doubt that Gould's position epitomized an anti-scientific position:

> [H]owever much the findings in some areas of science may be relevant to our social judgments, they are obtained by a method designed to separate objective analysis of nature from subjective value judgements. Long experience has shown that when these findings are well-verified, they have an exceedingly high probability of being universal, cumulative, and value-free. Gould, however, treats the history of science like political history, with which his readers are most familiar: a history in which human motives and errors from the past will inevitably recur. He thus skillfully promotes a doubt that the biological roots of human behavior can ever be explored scientifically (Davis, 1983, p. 56).

Where did Davis get his strong emphasis on scientific objectivity from? In interview, it emerged that, for Davis, *the idea of objectivity was a political ideal*. Indeed, Davis quite emotionally spoke of the need to proclaim objectivity—for him, this was the only defense against ideologically biased science of any kind. And like the members of the Sociobiology Study Group, he held up the warning example of Nazi science. He pointed out that he and other critics had equally good reason to abhor the Nazis, and that he thought it was sad that the Sociobiology Study Group and he should find themselves on opposite sides. He explained this division of opinion by the fact that he and the leading critics belonged to different generations of Jewish intellectuals. (Davis was some fifteen years older than Lewontin and over twenty years older than many other critics.)

For the Sociobiology Study Group, too, it was exactly *objective-sounding* biological claims about humans which would be abused by conservative politicians, including Nazi types. This is why they saw it as their task to reveal the ideological underpinnings of objective-sounding theories.

Paradoxically, then, for planters or weeders, emphasizing or de-emphasizing objectivity were really alternative strategies for reaching the same goal of *keeping science pure*. While the critics wanted to unveil and debunk IQ research as 'bad' science, this was exactly what Davis wanted to preserve, in the conviction that it was 'good' science. And just as for the critics of sociobiology the danger of bad science was tied to its potential social misuse, so for Davis, the promise of good science was connected to its potential social usefulness. According to Davis:

> if we refuse to recognize the importance of genes for human behavioral diversity, and if we reject the use of science to help us understand and build on that diversity, our society will lose more than it will gain (Davis, 1986, p. 114).

He noted that the same thing had already been said a decade ago, and more eloquently, by Theodosius Dobzhansky, in the latter's *Genetic Diversity and Human Equality* (1973a). Davis continued connecting Dobzhansky's position to that of Jensen:

> This view obviously did not prevail. The next decade saw an extraordinarily widespread denial of the pertinence of genetic differences, however obvious, for various educational and social problems, while virtually all those persons who disagreed were silent lest they be accused of racism. Arthur Jensen, a very able and responsible educational psychologist, collected massive evidence for the importance of genetic factors in intelligence, and for the high probability of statistical, but overlapping, differences between racial groups; and he predicted great harm to our educational system if we ignore that reality and attempt to legislate the facts of nature, instead of using those facts to help us maximize the opportunity for development in each individual, regardless of race. He was vilified as a racist, though his writings repeatedly emphasize that any differences between mean group values must not be used to justify discrimination against individuals (Davis, 1986, p. 114).

Davis was not alone in his continuing, stubborn emphasis on the *individual*, despite the shift of the liberal discourse toward an emphasis on the rights of groups. Indeed, his belief was shared by many other influential academics, such as Harvard sociologist Nathan Glazer, the then editor of *The Public Interest*. For Davis, however, his liberal individualism was tied to a strong belief in scientific knowledge as a guideline for social decision-making. And one of the sciences he championed for its social utility was IQ testing. It was simply inconceivable to him that there could be serious scientific disagreement about this respectable field and its well-established results.

But he was wrong. There was indeed a profound disagreement among the very 'experts' Davis liked to quote. The disagreement concerned particularly the meaning of that 15-point difference in mean IQ scores between the white and black population in the United States. These differences, in turn, often reflected different assumptions about behavioral genetics held by geneticists and educational psychologists. In fact, among those who disapproved of Jensen was none other than Davis' foremost authority, Theodosius Dobzhansky himself. In the very book, *Genetic Diversity and Human Equality*, which Davis quoted in support of his own position, Dobzhansky himself had declared that he remained 'unconvinced' by Jensen's argumentation, and that based on the evidence '[o]ne can only conclude that the degree to which differences in the IQ arrays between races are genetically conditioned is at present an unsolved problem' (Dobzhansky, 1973a, pp. 21, 91).

In the next chapter we will take a rest from the attempts to couple science and politics, and focus instead on a few scientists who were actively trying to keep science and politics *apart*.

CHAPTER 12

To be or not to be—in the sociobiology controversy

The thankless task of uncouplers: Peter Medawar

'Coupled' thinking—that is, a belief that a scientific position different from one's own must be politically motivated—was prominent among the protagonists in the 1970s and 1980s conflicts about genes and behavior. It is therefore informative to examine a case where 'couplers' from *both* sides in the sociobiology controversy admonished the same 'uncoupler' for not seeing the light. The case involves two letters in *The New York Review of Books* in 1977, one from Wilson, and another from two of Wilson's critics, Larry Miller and Jonathan Beckwith. Wilson, Miller, and Beckwith all felt prompted to respond to the same article by Peter Medawar. This article, entitled 'Unnatural Science', was a book review of Block and Dworkin's *The IQ Debate* (1976) and Leon Kamin's *The Science and Politics of IQ* (1974).

Medawar criticized attempts by various 'soft' sciences to mimic the natural sciences by using such things as statistics and mathematics in order to look more rigorous. Meanwhile, he praised those scientists who tried to point out methodological flaws in such 'unnatural' sciences. For Medawar, IQ research was a case in point, and he commended the critical efforts in the books he was reviewing.

But Wilson, in a letter to the journal, felt that Medawar played down the role of political ideology in all this:

> P. B. Medawar correctly observes that the subject of IQ heritability is 'bedeviled more than any other by the tendency of disputants to spring into political postures which allow them no freedom of movement.'... The doctrinaire Marxists are next dismissed along with the politically motivated hereditarians; the merit of objectivity in science is reaffirmed; the intricacies of the subject and the great difficulty of assessing the evidence are stressed.
>
> Then Professor Medawar falls into a trap. He notes that several leading geneticists are sceptical of the existence of any substantial heritability of IQ. Why, he asks, do they lean to the extreme environmentalist view? Because 'at a time of deeply troubled race relations... these geneticists feel an urgent desire to put the record straight'.
>
> This, I submit, is pure rhetoric... Professor Medawar gives the appearance of coming down on one side of the argument—it doesn't really matter which side—on the basis of political considerations. I would like to recommend a different attitude... *we should distinguish between those who wish to politicize human behavorial genetics and those who wish to depoliticize it*... The analysis should be judged by experts who are not committed to an ideology that requires one outcome as opposed to another (Wilson, 1977b, italics added).

Thus, Wilson suggested that it was for *political* reasons that Medawar supported the books' methodological critique. We know that Wilson at this time was heavily involved in the sociobiology controversy and attacked from all angles, including being labeled a racist. He had particularly suffered the allegations of the Sociobiology Study Group and its implicit leader, Lewontin. It is not surprising that Wilson was convinced that Medawar had made a mistake about the motives of the geneticists he commended (Michael Lerner, Walter Bodmer, John Thoday—and Richard Lewontin).

Medawar's answer was indignant. He said that Wilson had not grasped the gist of his article: the point of the article was *not* that differences in IQ were not to any degree heritable. Rather, it said that *bad science* should not be allowed to endanger race relations or put the underprivileged at a still greater disadvantage. And as to the leading geneticists mentioned in the article, Medawar stated: 'I believe it libellous to the point of being actionable to impute political motives to them' (Medawar, 1977b).

What happened here? It seems that Wilson took Medawar's general criticism of IQ studies—a criticism which Medawar himself said he had 'inherited' from J. B. S. Haldane and Lancelot Hogben—as proof that he basically leaned towards an environmentalist stand. Meanwhile, Medawar was genuinely of the opinion that IQ research was methodologically unsound, since in his view intelligence could not be separated into a genetic and an environmental component. Here, Medawar took a stronger position than many others, who believed that such a separation was possible in principle, with the help of correct and careful psychometric techniques.

It is useful here to survey briefly the main issues under debate with regard to IQ at this time. There were at least three sub-disputes involved in the general discussion about IQ.

1) Is the heritability of IQ in white Caucasian populations really 'quite high' (up to 0.8), or is a high estimate an artifact of some assumptions and/or of methodology? This was being addressed, for instance, by Cavalli-Sforza and Feldman (1981). (See also their letter to Herrnstein in 1982; and Feldman and Lewontin, 1975.)

2) Can an exact number be assigned to the heritability of IQ and can one talk about the 'genetic' and the 'environmental' component in any serious way? Jensen, Herrnstein, and other IQ measurers believed so; Wilson, Davis, and Maynard Smith (1973), too, and, it appears, even Lewontin, in his earlier days, while others, such as Medawar and Jerry Hirsch argued that this could not be done (often referring to Haldane). Gould and Luria (and Lewontin later) declared that IQ did not exist as a physical reality and could thus not be meaningfully measured (see Chapter 14).

3) Is the heritability of IQ in the white population at all relevant for the estimation of the heritability of IQ in other populations? Jensen argued from plausibility that a 15-point difference in IQ scores between the white and black populations might reflect genetic differences, while Lewontin, Maynard Smith, Hirsch, Thoday, Bodmer, Cavalli-Sforza and others concerned with 'the norm of reaction' (the fact that the same gene is expressed differently in different environments) considered such a speculation an 'error in genetics'. They argued that comparison is legitimate only if the environments of whites and blacks can be said to be the 'same', which is obviously not the case in reality. All parties agreed, however, that there was no direct evidence one way or the other about genetic differences in intelligence between populations.

Thus, Medawar's main point in his article was *methodological*, as his title already indicated; moreover, his methodological position was a scientifically possible one. Further, in his article, Medawar can be described as having tried to *uncouple* science from politics, by pointing out what he considered to be some real methodological weaknesses of IQ research. He seemed to believe, with many other scientists, that bad science was likely to cause social harm. But it was exactly the *uncoupling* attempt with which Wilson took issue. The passage that particularly prompted Wilson's reaction came at the very end of Medawar's article:

> Why, then, is it that some of the world's most prominent geneticists—among them Michael Lerner, Richard Lewontin, Walter Bodmer and John Thoday—remain so deeply unconvinced by the hereditarian argument of such as Jensen and Eysenck? *We need not resort to murky ideological explanations to find the reason*. It is more likely, I suggest, that . . . these geneticists feel an imperatively urgent desire to put the scientific record straight (p. 18, italics added).

Thus, as we see, Medawar himself did not care for 'ideological explanations' for what he regarded as methodological positions. In fact, in this dislike of ideology, he sounded as if he were on the same side as Wilson and Davis. As an example of an ideological explanation, Medawar particularly singled out Kamin's 'conspiracy theory of heritability', which, according to Medawar, tried to demonstrate that the whole project of IQ psychology is a rationalization to save the public conscience as well as the public purse. This Medawar dismissed as 'Olympian glibness'. What is more, he valiantly *defended* human geneticists against the 'malevolent intentions' imputed to them by 'disputants claiming to speak . . . for "the people"'. He even classified the present climate for liberals as one in which 'those whose views conflict with the dogma of equality are vilified, shouted down, and rebutted by calumnies' (p. 13). Importantly (and bravely, considering the 'climate') he *defended* the IQ testers against suggestions of malevolence and held up 'the inherent failings of IQ testing itself' as the main reason for 'the socially disruptive inferences that have been drawn from them' (p. 16). He even tried to explain Cyril Burt's notorious twin data not as fraud but rather as an error deriving from Burt's strong conviction that he was right (Burt was compared to Mendel, whose 'too good' ratios have been questioned, p. 17).

This, if anything, seemed like an attempt to be fair to all parties in the hot discussions about IQ, while steering a clear methodological course. What was it, then, that made Wilson believe that Medawar himself, and, more importantly, the geneticists he quoted, were 'leaning toward an environmentalist view' in the face of the fact that Medawar explicitly *criticized* such a view ('Kamin goes too far')? I suggest that Wilson while reading the article had simultaneously been on the lookout for some kind of *indicators* as to where Medawar 'really' stood. Having found the tell-tale signs, Wilson was convinced that, somehow, Medawar 'must' be supportive of the environmentalists, after all.

One such indicator for Wilson was style. Wilson was language-conscious and viewed himself as a 'story-teller'. But his story-telling was of an affirmative nature. He did not enjoy 'good criticism'—a feature which is shared by most writers and readers of *The*

New York Review of Books. Or rather, he did not enjoy criticism as an abstract art, in the way that Medawar evidently did. An example of Medawar's attitude in this respect was the fact that, in his article, despite his disagreement with Kamin's main conclusion and allegations, Medawar still called certain passages in Kamin's book 'fine polemical writing' (Medawar, p. 16). He also commented on Lewontin's 'grave, learned and witty investigation' of Jensenism (p. 18). For Wilson, on the other hand, praise of *style* meant automatic agreement with the author. Wilson may have been particularly sensitive on this point, since he had been the target of so much criticism himself. (Not surprisingly, Wilson had declared different 'witty' criticisms of his own work *ad hominem* attacks, and as not dealing with the issue; for example, Lewontin, 1981a; Leach, 1981a; and Medawar, 1981b.)

Thus, while Wilson allowed himself to get carried away occasionally in his own writing, he expected criticism to follow certain strict rules of objective language. Conversely, while some critics felt free to create any critical scenarios they liked, they expected Wilson to restrict himself in his writings to a strictly objective and dry language so as not to mislead 'the innocent layman'. Among the American participants in the controversy, there seemed to be an overall *fundamentalist* attitude to language, selectively applied to friends and foes.

Still, it was probably Medawar's mention of Lewontin that for Wilson constituted the dead giveaway. Wilson had not only suffered at the hand of his critics, but he also saw their position as one of '*tabula rasa* Marxism'. For Wilson, anyone who questioned the heritability of IQ could not have *scientific* reasons, only ideological ones. One wonders what more Medawar himself could have done to indicate that he was really concerned with methodological, not ideological, questions in IQ research. That he was not an ideological sympathizer with Marxists should at least have been obvious, since he in his article also clearly attacked 'doctrinaire Marxists'.

An alternative interpretation is that Wilson did not really misunderstand Medawar, but used his response to Medawar's article as a vehicle for emphasizing one of his own important themes: the scientific objectivity of studies in behavioral genetics and the possibility of scientific expertise as such. Again, one wonders why Wilson here was so adamant about behavioral genetics and the heritability of IQ—not his particular interest, except for the usefulness of existing results in behavioral genetics as an argument for the possibility of building population genetical models. As we saw in Chapter 10, Wilson in fact went out of his way to play down the importance of IQ in the last chapter of *Sociobiology* and instead emphasized other bases for social success. Also, at this time Medawar had not said anything unfriendly about sociobiology (he reviewed *Genes, Mind and Culture* only in 1981), so there was no 'obvious' reason for Wilson to attack Medawar. But someone close to Wilson did care very much about IQ research and had been consistently fighting the battle for the non-zero heritability of IQ, and that was Bernard Davis.

Thus, just as in Wilson's 1978 article, I perceive here Davis' encouragement behind Wilson's unexpected letter in *The New York Review of Books*. But if he was so outraged at Medawar's article, why did Davis not write a critical response to Medawar himself? The reason may have been that a couple of years earlier Davis himself had had a letter on the topic of IQ rejected by this journal. That letter had been an attempt to enter into the polemics around an article by Salvador Luria (Luria, 1974a,b), which among other things dismissed IQ research as scientifically and socially useless. Davis was rather proud of his letter, and was disappointed that it had been rejected (Davis, interview). (We shall return to Luria's article in the last part of this chapter.)

But Medawar had to fight another front at the same time. Ironically, exactly because Medawar addressed left-wing beliefs, he got into trouble with two members of Science for the People as well. In his article, Medawar charged that Marxists believed that truth is 'a bourgeois superstition' and that the great crime committed by human geneticists in the XYY controversy was to provide evidence of inborn human inequality (Medawar, p. 14). It was these statements that provoked a response from Larry Miller and Jon Beckwith. Beckwith had been heavily involved in the 'criminal' XYY gene issue at Harvard Medical School and instrumental in the discontinuation of a research project involving counseling for parents with XYY sons (see Chapter 11). These left-wing critics liked Medawar's position as little as Wilson:

> Medawar, while penetrating the myths surrounding IQ research has fallen prey to similar myths and misinterpretations in the field of XYY research. The IQ and XYY issues have unfortunate parallels. In both cases, responsible and eminent scientists with little knowledge of the field have made sweeping public pronouncements, which in turn have helped perpetuate a scientific myth. We believe that a crucial part of science 'for the people' will involve critical attention to scientific research on the part of both scientists and the public. Scientists must take the lead in encouraging such criticism and informed discussion, rather than using the banner 'freedom of inquiry' to stifle discussion (Miller and Beckwith, 1977).

Just as in his response to Wilson, Medawar in his answer to Miller and Beckwith took issue with the very foundation of their criticism, in this case their conception of the ideological bias of scientific research. Medawar called their argument concerning hidden influences on scientific research and the need to reveal these through criticism 'simple-minded historicism'. What is more, Medawar classified their suggestion of a special 'science for the people', different from usual science, as leaning toward Lysenkoism (Medawar, 1977c). Thus, Medawar strongly upheld the banner for 'good science' and truth and showed his clear dislike for any suggestions that science might be ideologically biased one way or the other. He thus saw a clear analytical division between science and ideology. This was a position that he shared with the other scientists featured in this chapter.

The discussion above has served to demonstrate both Wilson's own and (two of) his critics' refusal to accept that someone could have convictions about 'good science' on sheer methodological or epistemological grounds. This was shown by the fact that both parties felt the need to correct Medawar's purported misconceptions about scientific matters. For both sides, a balanced stance taken by a liberal like Medawar was untenable. To Wilson, Medawar appeared to have 'bought' the environmentalists' myths, while Miller and Beckwith thought he had been duped by the XYY myths. What this means is that both sides claimed higher authority than Medawar as to the 'real truth' in this scientific matter—rather amazingly, considering the latter's career both as a scientist and a commentator on science.

But it was also possible to interpret the responses not as directed at Medawar himself but rather as contributions in their own right to the general discussion concerning science and society, using the polemics against Medawar as a *vehicle*. In this way, Wilson got in one more point about 'the environmentalists', and Miller and Beckwith one more point about the infiltration of society's values into scientific research. This could explain Wilson's surprising sacrifice of exactitude when he put Lewontin together with, for example, such an 'obvious' hereditarian as John Thoday (who did, however, share Medawar's views concerning both the scientific and ethical importance of *correct methodology*). This, then, would be an example of how polemics about a particular issue might serve to further larger agendas of scientists.

Finally, we might see Medawar's article as an illustration of his activity as a deliberate uncoupler. Medawar had a long-term interest in tracking down various 'isms' which he saw as distorting the objectivity of science. Such 'isms' were, among others, 'geneticism', 'historicism' (see, for example, Medawar and Medawar, 1977), and 'poetism' (Medawar, 1982). Here, geneticism was the belief that there 'must' be genes underlying every aspect of human behavior and culture; historicism was the basically Popperian criticism of vulgar Marxism, and poetism was the tendency in science to see significant relations between unconnected phenomena. These concepts were the filters through which Medawar put the material he read and he usually succeeded in coming up with at least one 'ism', because these are common ways of looking at the world for anyone, including scientists. In his review of Lumsden and Wilson, for instance, Medawar criticized the book for both geneticism and historicism (Medawar, 1981b), and his book *Pluto's Republic* (1982) is full of inhabitants of the 'scientific underworld' committing various 'isms'. The indicators employed by Medawar, again, were such things as neologisms and complicated-looking statistical formulas—anything that could be classified as unnecessary 'puffery'.

One foot in each camp: the mediating efforts of John Maynard Smith and Patrick Bateson

Another uncoupler in the sociobiology debate was John Maynard Smith. Maynard Smith showed a remarkable ability to keep an intermediate position while trying to explain the views of both sides in the sociobiology controversy to each other, and to the general public. He was in the unusual position of being able to identify with both the sociobiologists and their critics. But this was not an easy task. In an interview in 1981 he explained that he perceived a conflict between his 'gut feelings' and his scientific desire for fairness, and that *Sociobiology* presented him with a real challenge:

> I have a lot of the gut reactions of my age of being horrified and scared of the application of biology to the social sciences—I can see . . . race theories, Nazism, anti-semitism and the

whole of that. So that my initial gut reaction to Wilson's *Sociobiology* was one of considerable annoyance and distress . . .

Q: Because of the last chapter?

A: Because of the last chapter—it seemed to me half-baked, silly . . . We had a good branch of science—why . . . And it was also absolutely obvious to me—I cannot believe Wilson didn't know—that this was going to provoke great hostility from American Marxists and Marxists everywhere . . .

Q: I think he was more out to provoke some kind of loose social theorizing than to provoke any Marxists out there . . .

A: Yes, I think he was. I think it is the difference between a European and an American. No European with his degree of culture and general education [would have been unaware of the political implications] . . . *My immediate reaction was one of great hostility—to the book as a whole—I wrote quite a polite review of it*, I thought the book had great merits—but I was horrified—possibly over-horrified, my gut reactions are probably far too strong . . . *On the other hand, I am equally disturbed, made angry by what I think is the unreasonableness of much of the criticism that has been made of Wilson*. And I find that if I talk to Dick Lewontin or Steve Gould for an hour or two, I become a real sociobiologist, and if I talk to someone like Wilson or Trivers for an hour or two, I become wildly hostile to it—I mean, this must have something to do with feelings! . . . (laugh) (Maynard Smith, interview, my emphasis).

Thus, Maynard Smith was in the interesting position of being able to empathize both with Wilson and with the critics, especially Lewontin. Unlike the opponents to socio-biology, however, he made a clear analytic distinction between science and moral/political concerns. This was not always so, he explained: being a Marxist in the early decades of this century meant to be a Marxist in scientific thinking as well as in political concerns. What made him choose to finally separate the realm of science from the realm of political interest were two things. One was that an experiment he attempted in the Lamarckian spirit, and which he 'would have liked to be true', failed dismally. The other was his witnessing of the whole Lysenkoist affair, where he saw 'scientists who should have known better' put their political commitment before their scientific judgment. This made him decide to try to keep the realm of science away from his political gut feelings. He continued his story about his chosen position in regard to both science and politics as follows:

> I think that if I had to choose, ultimately, that *science has to come first*, and that may be unusual . . .
>
> Look, I really think one has to make an order of priorities in this world and it is not an easy one to do. I believe that purely personal things come first: one's loyalty to one's family and to one's friends, no matter who they are . . . but if one then considers loyalty to more abstract goals like science or politics or something, I think differently now than what I did when I . . . that's why I no longer think of myself as a Marxist; I am too interested in other types of commitments (Maynard Smith, interview).

Thus, in Maynard Smith's case, his reaction to *Sociobiology* and *On Human Nature* ought to be seen as a product of his scientific rather than his political mode. This is quite clear from his reviews of these books (Maynard Smith, 1975, 1978a). Also, he made a special point of telling Wilson in person at an early stage in the controversy that he did not share the Sociobiology Study Group's interpretation of *Sociobiology* (Wilson told me this in one of my interviews). In his review of *Sociobiology*, and against the Sociobiology Study Group, Maynard Smith was concerned to point out the following:

> Attempts to import biological theories into sociology, from social Darwinism of the 19th century to the race theories of the 20th, have a justifiably bad reputation. Readers may therefore approach a book entitled *Sociobiology*, with a certain trepidation. They should not be put off. Dr. Wilson's book is an important contribution to science . . . This is not another Territorial Imperative, or Naked Ape, or Descent of Woman, in which one aspect of human evolution is pressed into service to explain everything. It is true that Wilson does make big claims for the relevance of biology to sociology. For reasons I will return to, I think that these are exaggerated or unjustifiable. But they do not detract from the major contribution this book makes to our understanding of animal societies (Maynard Smith, 1975).

What we see in the above quotation are two things. One is Maynard Smith's ability to distinguish his gut reaction from his scientific analysis, and thus to be able to do two types of different 'reading' of a text at the same time. The other is his willingness to act as a communicator between the potential critics of *Sociobiology* and its author, trying to make known Wilson's 'real' intentions. Finally, yet another factor which helped Maynard Smith keep the first and last chapter apart from the rest of the material in the book, despite the fact that he initially reacted negatively to the book as a whole, was his naturalist's interest in animal behavior, which, after all, formed the bulk of the book. We will return to the importance of this naturalist interest in the next chapter.

Maynard Smith's review of *On Human Nature* was also eminently decent. He found some of Wilson's speculations about early human history 'careful' and 'plausible', and hoped that the book would evoke discussion rather than be needlessly misunderstood. (For instance, he approved of Wilson's idea of human nature having been formed as a product of both individual and group selection in early tribal societies.) In that review, Maynard Smith also indicated that Wilson had now cleared up the initial confusion in *Sociobiology*, which had led many, including himself, to wonder whether Wilson was in fact condoning the present state of human affairs. However, he did criticize Wilson for unnecessarily dramatic use of language, especially concerning sensitive subjects such as aggression.

Maynard Smith was thus fundamentally concerned with good communication and with clearing up misunderstandings. This could also be seen in his attempts to 'explain' Dawkins to the latter's critics. In his review of *The Extended Phenotype*, he emphasized that Dawkins's book was a book about *evolution*, not about morals, or politics, or anything else, and that those who were looking for these kinds of messages were 'only going to be needlessly angry' (Maynard Smith, 1982a).

He tried to intervene in other controversies as well, for instance in the one concerning punctuated equilibria (see Chapter 6). There, as we saw, he pointed out that those who stressed this as a controversy in evolutionary biology were 'guilty of overemphasizing conflict where none exists'; in general, he regarded the dispute as one over semantics. (Later, however, Maynard Smith took a more critical view of punctuated equilibria and appears to have become increasingly irritated with Gould. We will return to this in Chapter 16.)

Another one of his concerns was to try to open up the discussion between molecular and evolutionary biologists. He saw some problems, though, among other things because he perceived some group selectionist thinking lingering among molecular biologists (Maynard Smith, interview; see also Lewin, 1981b). A final example of Maynard Smith's strong commitment to both fairness and communication was perhaps the review of Lumsden and Wilson discussed earlier. As he indicated himself, he wrote it together with the anthropologist Neil Warren exactly to make sure that his own gut feelings would not take over. It seems that he wanted to give the mathematics a chance to speak to him. It turned out, however, that he was not persuaded of the correctness of the model (also, he thought the mathematics had some errors in it), and his review on the whole was negative (see Chapter 8).[1]

Finally Maynard Smith took up—unwittingly—the position of a mediator between Lewontin and Wilson and their graduate students. He recalled that during one of his Harvard visits, he found himself having to sort out fine points of population genetics for students. During his seminar, he complained, these students just kept raising questions and nobody seemed interested in what he really had to say—but soon enough, they came privately asking him for help, one by one. They obviously felt they could not ask their mentors (interview in 1998).

There were, indeed, rather few scientists well-positioned to be communicators or 'arbiters' between the sociobiologists and their critics, because few scientists understood both sides. And, even if they had, it is not clear that people would have believed it worth their time and energy to increase communication between the warring camps. Another one of these unusual scientists was Patrick Bateson.

In his role as a developmental biologist, Bateson admonished the sociobiologists 'from the inside' for 'bad language habits'. He thought these had contributed to misunderstandings and belief in 'genetic determinism' (Bateson, 1981).

> If anything got sociobiology a bad name it was the way in which evolutionary theories were used to justify a naïve form of genetic determinism in the development of individuals . . . *I think that a great deal of miscommunication between the sociobiologists and their critics has arisen from sloppy use of language and not from any commitment to genetic determinism on the part of the sociobiologists* . . . [M]uch of the language used by contemporary sociobiology is preformationist in character and implies that a behavioural trait spreading through a population . . . is somehow represented in miniature form in the relevant gene. The effect is that critics and naive disciples alike believe that the developmental process has been dismissed as being altogether trivial and uninteresting . . .
>
> I believe, then, that the 'gene for a character' language should not be used even as a shorthand . . . The introduction of 'innate behaviour' or 'innate rules' into the vocabulary simply compounds the difficulties . . . In any event, 'innateness' is unnecessary to an evolutionary argument. *If we accept that natural selection acts on phenotypic characters the precise way in which a character develops is irrelevant.* It does not matter to the evolutionary argument that normal development may depend on instruction from a stable or reliable feature of the environment (Bateson, 1981, italics added).

In the same article, Bateson was thus able to criticize both sociobiologists such as Wilson (who uses the term 'innate') and critics such as Gould, who in his criticism of Dawkins invoked developmental factors (Gould, 1977b; see also Dawkins, 1982, p. 116).

But Bateson proceeded further in his role as mediator. For instance, he participated in the 'anti-reductionism' conference in Brezzanone in 1980, arranged by Steven and Hilary Rose (see Chapter 9). There he suggested ways in which development and learning might be regarded as interacting with genetic processes in a 'dialectical' sense. At the same time he asked the critics of sociobiology and reductionism to clean up their act, too:

> Such approaches to development do, I believe, represent a synthesis of seemingly opposed views. But they do require acceptance that there is a considerable intrinsic control over what happens. While that is not a deterministic view in that it does not imply that internal influences are all that matters, it may still be unpalatable to many people who feel that even going this far is selling out to the 'enemy'. However, *loyalty to allies and to previously held positions should not be subordinated to intellectual honesty*. Such loyalty is not likely to liberate anybody and in the long run will merely be stultifying and oppressive. If the dialectical approach is going to achieve anything in biology it must mean that from time to time we abandon old and much loved positions (Bateson, 1982, italics added).

It is significant for this active communicator that, at around the same time that he was contributing to *Toward a Liberatory Biology*, one of the two books emerging from the conference, he was actively involved in publishing the King's College Sociobiology Group's collected efforts in the book *Current Problems in Sociobiology* (see Chapter 5). And as we saw in Chapters 8 and 9, in his review of *Not in Our Genes* Bateson at the same time criticized both the critics and Wilson for their approaches to sociobiology: Lewontin, Rose, and Kamin for scientific errors in their representation of facts, and Wilson for initially creating a 'muddle' by taking a too genetic–determinist view of development in *Sociobiology*.

I have here singled out Maynard Smith and Bateson because of their unusual position, having 'one foot in each camp' both scientifically and morally/politically, and for their persistent efforts to identify problems in the reasoning of both sides. Of course, throughout this book we are also meeting Richard Dawkins, a supreme clarifier of scientific issues. The reason I do not classify him as a mediator in this chapter is that he clearly does *not* have a foot in the critical camp in the same sense as the former.

There are other scientists who have tried to sort out particular intellectual matters and in that way mediate between different scientific camps in the sociobiology controversy, for instance Wrangham (1980), Freeman (1980), and Seger (1981) (see Chapter 7). And even before the sociobiology controversy, there were those who tried to address the question of the biological basis of behavior across disciplines. Here we have Robert Hinde, at an early point mediating between ethology and comparative psychology (see Barlow, 1991, and Chapter 5), and later working on further integration between ethology and the social sciences; child ethologist Nick Blurton Jones and anthropologist Vernon Reynolds mediating between biologists, anthropologists, and psychologists, trying to identify fundamental questions that needed asking and answering (Blurton

Jones and Reynolds, 1978; Blurton Jones, 1976; Reynolds, 1976, and interviews). In behavioral genetics, it seems that John Thoday occupied a role similar to that of Maynard Smith and Bateson in sociobiology: a concern to set the record straight, while being aware of the positions on both sides (see, for example, Thoday, 1972, 1981).

But these scientists were clear exceptions. It is safe to say that, in controversies in general, there is only a limited number of scientists who have ties to both the opposing camps. And fewer still regard it as their task to enter the controversy in order to increase mutual understanding between parties in a polarized situation. It seems that most scientists are content with taking a passive stance, from which they watch the show while they get on with their *own* research. And those who do get involved presumably do so because of the relevance of the issues to their own scientific and moral goals, a motivation which is not conducive to understanding the opponent's position.

Notes from a leftist non-participant: Salvador Luria

In this section we will examine the views of a scientist strongly associated with left-wing political activism, but who was visibly absent from the sociobiology debate, even though he participated in the earlier IQ debate. That is Salvador Luria, a molecular biologist and Nobel laureate at Massachusetts Institute of Technology. To be precise, Luria made an indirect appearance in the sociobiology controversy in 1981 as a sponsor of Alper and Lange's review of *Genes, Mind and Culture* in the *Proceedings of the National Academy of Science* (scientists who are not members of the National Academy of Sciences need sponsoring to get published in the *PNAS*), but he did not himself sign the initial letter of the Sociobiology Study Group, nor write anything on sociobiology.

Here we have a scientist who, since he was a socialist activist, 'should' have been involved, but was not. Again, the fact that Luria chose to stay away illustrates my earlier point that the position of the Sociobiology Study Group was not the only obvious one even for their fellow left-wing scientists—although it may well have been obvious to the members of that group. Since the interview with Luria (in February 1982) is such a useful one for our purposes, I will quote from it at length. Here we get an insight into yet another standpoint regarding the relationship between science and politics. We can contrast Luria's position with the reasoning of both the members of the Sociobiology Study Group and scientific traditionalists such as Davis and Wilson. Yet we will also see that, in the end, it was not easy to totally disconnect science from politics, even for this scientist, who clearly wished to do so.

Let us start with Luria's assessment of the sociobiology debate, the political implications of *Sociobiology*, and the criticism of Wilson. Luria thought that the Sociobiology Study Group may have been mistaken about Wilson's political intent:

> I believe that at least in the case of somebody like Wilson—whom I never met—that, very likely, the intention in writing *Sociobiology* was possibly not to start anything controversial, but simply to draw conclusions in the sphere of human affairs based on his observations in the field of animal communities. Whether this was justified or not I cannot say, because I never read the book.

Thus, unlike most of his left-wing colleagues, Luria did not automatically assume a political motive in the last chapter of *Sociobiology*. But the main reason why he did not get involved appears to have been the fact that sociobiology was not a good enough political issue to get excited about:

> I don't know . . . I would find it questionable whether it would pay, for example, for me to accept the argument that sociobiology can be abused in society on the part of the people in power and so on, and therefore I should fight not only the abuses but also sociobiology itself. Well, *I find it difficult to believe that this is an important enough issue*. I think that if nobody had ever raised it, nobody would ever had read Wilson's book in the first place, outside of a few zoologists!
>
> On the other hand, when it comes to Jensen, it is different. Jensen started an article in the *Harvard Educational Review* by saying that compensatory education had been tested and it had failed. That was not so, and I fought. I was involved . . . in *The New York Review of Books* [Luria, 1974a, b], in the arguments and polemics there, because that was a political, a straight political issue, white vs black . . . *In the other one, the implications had to be created.* And people who are going to use it are likely to exist anyway . . . (italics added).

To illustrate his point, that power-holders are able to pick and choose whatever scientific findings they like, Luria gave the 'classic' example from Allan Chase's book, *The Legacy of Malthus* (1977), involving two groups of scientists studying the cause of pellagra in the southern United States in the 1920s. Here Davenport's report, stating that pellagra was a genetic disease of poor southerners, was preferred over the study by Goldberger, which said that pellagra was due to a vitamin deficiency. (In his report, Davenport cited Goldberger's research only in a footnote, without mentioning his name.) In view of this, Luria did not think that the content of any specific book mattered politically. The battle was not academic but social:

> It is not really the book by one or another that is going to foster these kinds of things. *The prejudice in society is there, and can be fought only by political means.* But, if people care to fight it at the level of scientific dispute, they are welcome . . . I don't consider it negative; rather than doing nothing, it is better that people spend their time fighting against potential misapplications of science . . . I prefer to protest in Washington about military aid to El Salvador—I think it is much more important to protest about it than sociobiology!

Also strategically, for Luria, sociobiology was not worth serious involvement—it was simply not a good issue to become the basis of organized political action:

> Now clearly, these scientific items are not good for organizing. You can use the anti-Jensen campaign, for Jensen's was a definitive political action, and you can get the blacks to complain. But a few scientists who are divided on sociobiology are not going to make any big difference. . . .
>
> Now I don't believe that in our society the split between capitalism and the working class, or conservatism and liberalism, is such that the opinion of some conservative biologists, if such exist—I assume they exist because of all the polemics—or the opinion of some progressive biologists, is going make much difference.

Luria contrasted the political situation surrounding sociobiology with situations where a political action by a small group *could* be effective: in cases where there was already a constituency that was ready to function, then a push by a small group could help. He had an illustration close at hand: 'It was true, for example, when right here from MIT and Harvard we helped defeat the whole program for civil defense shelters, because that was an issue on which the Congress was split and the administration was split, and the strong forceful action from MIT and Harvard helped.'

What might be the reason, then, why other radical scientists were so much involved in fighting sociobiology? Luria gave me the following assessment of the critics of sociobiology:

> There are people for whom the political commitment is strong, but at the same time it also demands to be used within the same field of expertise. And, therefore, it becomes really very concentrated; there is a large amount of effort. Anybody who has spent time reading all the writings of Wilson must put lots of time in it, and thinking about it, and calculating, and so on. But after having done that, you can very well imagine that they are going to want to get something out of this involvement politically—I mean, say, to make a case out of it . . .
> Really, it is a matter of the geometric mean among many interacting commitments: politics, professionalism, safety, whatever . . .

But why did the critics feel that their political and scientific commitments had to meet in science? Was it perhaps because they believed so much in the importance of science and scientific data? In part, that was so, Luria agreed. This question prompted him to express his own view of the importance of science:

> I believe in the *integrity* of science—I don't believe in the *importance* of science. There is no question that music or literature are more important . . . I am not terribly interested in what scientists have to say, since I am convinced that, when it comes to matters of social importance, it is not sociology, and possibly not even psychology, but it is *politics* that matters. I prefer to have a poet interested in Marxism than a great scientist interested in sociobiology!
>
> It seems to me that *the problems of humanity are the problems of choice and not the problems of knowledge*—somehow one has to make a commitment in absence of significant knowledge. But this is a rather unusual position, I know, because I am rather uninterested in knowledge. I prefer any day to get my feelings out by reading Ferlinghetti, or Wallace Stevens or T. S. Eliot—ranging from the *left* [Ferlinghetti] to the *right* [Eliot] in poets—than reading *Nature* or *Science* . . .
>
> I must say that there are separate areas of activity. . . and most areas of activity are not such in which one can be sure. Therefore, if one wants to be functional *one has to make commitments*—what the scientist calls working hypotheses—and if one begins to concern oneself that they all be consistent with one another I think one gets into trouble . . . *The ideal is to have a commitment to society and to try to make it progressive, in whatever direction one wants, without compromising what I call the intellectual experience* (italics added).

So Luria did not, then, see any necessary link between his science and the fact that he was a socialist?

> I don't try to force them, no, certainly not . . . As a molecular biologist, as a scientist, I am really interested only in the things that can be pared down to the ultimate level of reductionism.

Luria himself, as a molecular biologist, might be able to be a reductionist, but what about scientists working with complex questions in biology, or in fields having to do with human beings—would it be a necessity for them to become non-reductionistic dialectical materialists in order to do good science? Here I mentioned the example of Lewontin and Levins. Luria did not believe one had to become a dialectical materialist:

> No, I don't think I'd say it is so much a necessity. I'd simply say that it seems to me that it would be desirable if scientists, like everybody else, were to think more in terms of dialectics of society, rather than of the static analysis of society in terms of, let's say, biological givens. But I don't see any reason why other people should be forced into the same point of view.

Here we obviously had a different type of left-wing scientist than, say, Levins and Lewontin. What was, then, Luria's exact position on the relationship between science and politics, I asked, and if he was a Marxist, what kind of Marxist was he? Luria explained his own position on science and politics in the following terms:

> I am committed to the rationalism of Diderot and D'Alembert. And I am at the same time committed to an existentialist form of Marxism, believing that even if there is no ultimate progress, there are certain things one should work for in society.

Luria now got back to what he himself regarded as the central theme: the idea of different commitments balancing each other. He also strongly stated his belief in *the integrity of science*:

> For example, my commitment to the scientific enterprise is one that would make it very difficult for me to do what some of my young colleagues did in the 1960s—to attack science as such, at first as a tool of capitalism, and then even worse, this thing *à la* Theodore Roszak or something—attacking science as an intellectual activity, as an intrinsically damaging intellectual activity.

He told me that, as a scientist, he had taken a position different from some of his colleagues at Harvard regarding the recombinant DNA controversy—exactly because he could not see the dangers.[2] Also, he thought it was a 'bad political issue' anyway. On the other hand, Luria admitted, when matters were really truly political, he tended to see things much more from the left. But that involved areas where he himself could claim no scientific expertise:

> In matters like social behavior, or behavior in general, not being an expert, I am biased. I am bound to be limited only to my political choices, which are not necessarily intellectual or scientific choices. I mean, I am a socialist, and *as a socialist I am more sympathetic in an argument, even if I don't know the facts, to my fellow socialists* (italics added).

This explains, then, why Luria sponsored Alper and Lange's review of *Genes, Mind and Culture* in the *PNAS*: he trusted his 'fellow socialists'' view that it was important to criticize Wilson and Lumsden's new book, even if he had not looked into the issue himself (and, as he said himself, did not even think that Wilson's motives were political). Thus, the scientist Luria supported his fellow socialists' *scientific* article for *political* reasons, even though neither he nor they were formal experts in the field they were criticizing—Alper and Lange were a chemist and a physicist, respectively, who had taught themselves population biology. (On the other hand, as Lange told me in interview, Lewontin had taken a look at their review, so it had indeed been subjected to a very informal type of peer review.)

So far we had discussed sociobiology and general issues of science and politics. What was Luria's view concerning the allegation by Davis, Wilson, and others that the criticism of IQ research was politically motivated? (I mentioned particularly the disagreements surrounding Gould's *The Mismeasure of Man*; see Chapter 11.) Luria's immediate response was that this was not the case; it was a matter of *scientific evidence*:

> No, *it is not a matter of political commitment*! If one wanted to be conciliatory—the most conciliatory position that I would take is the fact that the total of the IQ data are a reasonable predictor for a certain proportion of people, how they are going to function in a certain type of school. That is a fact, because that has been arranged. Beyond that, that IQ has any relation to anything, either intrinsic genetically or intrinsic from the point of view of success in other ways, I would say it cannot be denied, but there is zero evidence. Here I read a little bit more: there is zero evidence to me. . . . I think Steve is perfectly right there, that *there is no evidence for intelligence*. I think, personally, that if we could afford it, having expert teachers interview children we would get much more information than in IQ tests. . . .
>
> Anyway—without being nearly as much an expert as he is, on the matter of IQ I think he is right. I think it is a very important thing to realize that *those tests could not be anything more than what they are devised for, they are not based on any scientific background*. You see, it has something in common with Creation science. You say something, and then you insist it may be so because somebody said it in a book! (italics added)

According to Luria, 'the only evidence of the inheritance of general abilities to function one way or another' was 'the fact that you can trace remarkable abilities, for instance musical ability in the Bach family for several generations, independent of opportunities'. But he considered this evidence 'too soft' to be used for generalizations about the whole of society.[3]

In the light of this, I was interested in how Luria explained the fact that among scientists there appeared to exist two absolutely different views in regard to the heritability of IQ. Luria's immediate response was that most scientists had not thought about it, or did not care. But, I pressed him: what about scientists who had thought about it? Luria's answer was instructive. Unhesitatingly, he now employed a straight political interpretation:

> Look, let's come down to fundamentals. *In society there is a line. The line is between the right and the left. Whether people know it or not, whether they consider themselves liberal or not liberal.* There are people who are committed to the right and people who are committed to the left, and people who are committed to nothing. And as soon as that commitment comes, it makes people interpret all the things they have according to the portion which is applicable to the political realm. Somebody like—let's say you put them in order all the people you have mentioned—somebody like Dick Lewontin is maybe farthest to the left. Bernard Davis fairly to the right (italics added).

I observed that many scientists, like Davis and Wilson, truly believed it had been clearly established that intelligence could be measured, and that it was largely heritable.

To this Luria just exclaimed: 'But that's opinion! *Opinion* counts from where they stand with respect to that imaginary line. That's the point!' Obviously, then, Luria did not share Davis' view of the existence of objective scientific expertise, or Wilson's view of the possibility of distinguishing between 'those who wish to politicize human behavioral genetics and those who wish to depoliticize it' (Wilson, 1977b).

Luria went on to declare claims about a high heritability of IQ 'nonsense'. He seemed to believe that *even if IQ tests were scientifically impeccable, they would still be useless*. Here, he referred to an article he had written in 1974 in *The New York Review of Books*, entitled 'What Can Biologists Solve?', in which he had made a strong case that biologists should resist the lure of research on nonbiological social problems. For instance, according to Luria, crime was a product of poverty and not of the expression of a few genes or chromosomes. Likewise, the question of how to get the most out of each person according to his or her ability was not a biological problem. These were all 'socio-political traps' beyond the scope of science.

Obviously, then, Luria did not share Wilson's and Davis' conviction that science could at least be helpful in providing answers to social problems. Indeed, he took the diametrically opposite view, as his title indicated. In his article, he formulated the rationale for his position as follows:

> If scientists are lured into claiming that they have the know-how to solve what are really social crises they will share the responsibility for the fact that these crises remain unsolved. They actually aid and abet those who are responsible for generating and maintaining the crises. Physicians are well aware of comparable attempts to use medicine as a cover in order not to attack the real roots of a variety of social problems, from drug addiction to malnutrition (Luria, 1974a).

It is interesting to note that such a position might well have served as an indirect critique of the *critics* of sociobiology and IQ as well. We did not see the members of the Sociobiology Study Group worry about scientists not having the know-how to solve social problems. Instead, they kept talking about 'good' and 'bad' science, and telling people to be suspicious of experts in the service of social power-holders. If anything, they kept the discussion a matter of science rather than a matter outside science. Thus, whatever their real intentions, through their own stance, which systematically connected scientific knowledge to social policy implications, the critics in fact helped sustain the impression that biologists *could* indeed solve social problems—exactly the position Luria had warned about!

Luria, however, did not present this as a criticism of the Sociobiology Study Group. He had other things to say. He believed there had been some 'misunderstandings' in the sociobiology debate. According to him, Wilson's guilt had been constructed. He even thought that some of Wilson's critics from Science for the People had gone too far and had 'lost some credibility'. To illustrate what he meant, Luria analyzed what he regarded as a parallel case, involving the controversial Whitehead Institute at MIT.[4] In that case, a young man with a 'perfectly sensible argument' had formulated it in such a 'nonsensical' manner that no one had paid any attention to him. 'It is the *manner*, you see', said

Luria. He was of the opinion that Lewontin especially, but sometimes also Beckwith, had made mistakes in their approach. (Still, Luria quickly added that he considered Beckwith 'a darn good political person; he has been working hard in the black communities and all that'. While Beckwith was 'sometimes right, sometimes wrong', he was 'actively interested in good politics'—for Luria, a redeeming factor.) Thus, Luria's criticism of the critics of Wilson had primarily to do with their specific *approach*. But as we saw, he did not see sociobiology as a politically worthwhile issue in the first place.

The most interesting insight from this interview was probably Luria's balancing act when it came to science and politics. As we saw, Luria originally said that he regarded 'the integrity of the intellectual enterprise' and his personal political commitment as separate. But later he declared that there was 'a line' dividing scientists when it came to views on IQ and other sociopolitically relevant scientific issues. Thus, it seems that in regard to IQ, he excluded the possibility that a scientist's position concerning IQ might have a purely *scientific* rationale.

With regard to IQ, Luria had gone even further in 1974, something which Bernard Davis had brought to my attention in an interview. In follow-up polemics to his 1974 article in *The New York Review of Books,* Luria had said:

> Scientists claim the freedom of doing research and of criticizing other people's research— both the results and the subject matter —so long as others have the same freedoms. It is this process of criticism that keeps research reasonably honest and meaningful. A common *misunderstanding among the uninformed is to assume that all undertakings labelled as 'research' are equally legitimate* and that only their methodology should come under critical scrutiny (Luria, 1974b, italics added).

But what did this statement mean? For Luria, was the important thing to keep *criticism* as open as possible, so that he wished to *include* even the (seemingly unavoidable) political biases (Luria's 'opinions'), in the scientific discussion itself? Or did Luria here show his colors as a would-be weeder, even at the funding stage of scientific projects: all aspects of a project, including *the social legitimacy of the research topic itself,* should be subject to scientific criticism? The answer can be found in his preceding paragraph. There Luria referred to the 1972 petition in the *American Psychologist,* signed by supporters of IQ research and several Nobel laureates (Page, 1972) (see Chapter 2). This was his version of what had taken place:

> In 1972 about fifty people, including some eminent and reputable biologists and psychologists, were coopted or 'conned' into signing an apparently innocent letter to the editor of the *American Psychologist.* The letter querulously appealed for freedom of research for individuals concerned with genetics of intelligence, and implied that such freedom was threatened in various ways. That letter was, in my opinion, an insidious effort to block criticism of what I consider a controversial field of research (Luria, 1974b).

As we see, here Luria interpreted *the very claim for freedom of research as an effort to block criticism,* that is, as having a political or other non-scientific intent, rather than as constituting support for 'the integrity of the scientific enterprise'.[5]

I asked Luria directly what he meant by this statement. He only reiterated what he had said in 1974: according to him, there was no real threat to the freedom for research in IQ at the time, and the purported appeal to the freedom of research was in fact hidden support for the controversial studies by Jensen and others! We see, then, that Luria's 'invisible line' was pushed back one step further. In practice, Luria had already drawn his line when it came to 'correct' and 'incorrect' interpretation of the *prevailing attitude* to IQ research at the time!

Davis believed that Luria had badly misrepresented the situation and had tried to respond.[6] But his letter to *The New York Review of Books* had been rejected (Davis, 1974). He had tried to point out that there *did* exist a threat to freedom of inquiry at the time. His evidence was the Resolution against Racism published as an advertisement in *The New York Times* in 1973, which had collected over 1000 signatures (see Chapter 2). That petition had explicitly asked scientists to 'urge professional organizations and societies, academic departments, and editors of scholarly journals to condemn and refuse to disseminate racist research'. Moreover, the term 'racist' 'clearly included any research concerned with possible group differences in the distribution of intelligence'. And Luria himself was one of the signers of that petition, Davis noted (this was, indeed, the case).

Davis showed me the reason why his letter had been rejected: a letter Luria had written to the editor of *The New York Review of Books* declaring that he had neither time nor desire to respond to Davis (Davis had received a carbon copy). Luria saw all the recent talk about freedom of research as nothing but an attempt to stop Affirmative Action:

> There is, I believe, a group of elitist academicians out to destroy the Affirmative Action program. Whether Professor Davis belongs to that group or not, I prefer to spend time trying to make the program work at MIT rather than arguing on what racism is or is not. Traditionally, the word has had different meanings to different people depending on where they stand.

Luria's stance on IQ, then, was not only a matter of 'evidence' but also intimately connected to a political issue, Affirmative Action—just as Davis' position seems to have been, too (see Chapters 2 and 11). Luria wanted Affirmative Action to work. Davis, in turn, was not against the idea in its original form—he supported the idea of picking out *individual* talent—but he was afraid that if the program was to be implemented at the group level (for instance, quotas applied), this would lower academic standards.

What happened, then, to Luria's suggested process of inter-scientific criticism, so important for keeping science honest? There appears to be little room for it in the present scenario—unless we extend the critical process in science to include *also* various types of *public* petitions![7] Obviously, even for Luria, science and politics could not be so easily kept apart, after all—at least not when it came to IQ research.

I have discussed Luria's views at length, because of his willingness to explain himself in detail, and because his reasoning illustrates the dilemma faced by left-wing scientists with regard to research in human behavioral traits—particularly one who would have liked to keep what he called 'the integrity of science' and his own political convictions as much apart as possible. We saw that, for Luria, this desire in practice led to some kind of contradiction, or at least to a seemingly unusual interpretation of standard termin-ology, such as the meaning of 'criticism' in science. What is of particular interest to us is that Luria, unlike the Sociobiology Study Group, gave Wilson and sociobiology the benefit of the doubt when it came to political intent. However, with regard to IQ, Luria's conviction was as strong as those of the members of the Group: scientists who supported IQ research 'could not' be motivated by scientific reasons but 'must' be driven by political concerns. We will return to this issue in Chapter 14.

CHAPTER 13

A clash of traditions

Communicative naturalists and critical experimentalists

The controversy about sociobiology can at least be partially explained as a conflict between the taken-for-granted attitudes to research held by practitioners trained in two different scientific traditions: naturalists and experimentalists. Indeed, one might say that, as scientists, naturalists and experimentalists live in partly different worlds. For the Sociobiology Study Group, a factor that contributed to their hostility to sociobiology and made its members from the very beginning read sociobiological contributions in the 'wrong' spirit was their *lack of a shared naturalist interest*, the wish to know and understand nature for its own sake, typical of an older tradition in evolutionary biology.

Many of the most vociferous critics came from the experimentalist tradition in science, from fields such as genetics, molecular biology, physics, and chemistry. But these fields do not only lack the naturalist spirit, they also train their practitioners in a hard-nosed and critical attitude to research. It seems that in these exact fields, there is little room for tentative statements and little tolerance for error—in fact, error-finding is encouraged, and students are trained early on in close and critical reading of scientific texts. This is how Jon Beckwith described the critical capabilities developed among graduate students in his own field, molecular genetics:

> During the semester I occasionally hand out journal articles whose conclusions are wrong and ask the students to find the errors. I also include a paper that is generally accepted to be correct, but tell the students that the paper is also wrong. They return to the next class having demolished this paper, finding holes in the reasoning, missing controls, and unfounded assumptions (Beckwith, 1987).

Beckwith went on to say that almost anything may turn to dust under the onslaught of enthusiastic critics. In the light of this, it becomes more understandable that, for scientists trained in an exact experimentalist tradition, the plausibility arguments and 'adaptive stories' typical of the writings of naturalistically oriented evolutionary biologists may easily violate their sense of 'good science'.

But before they got involved in the sociobiology debate, the 'hard science' critics of sociobiology had probably paid little attention to the writings of naturalists. Not so Lewontin. He was in the unusual position of representing the experimentalist attitude in a field traditionally dominated by naturalists. Lewontin's location within the field of evolutionary biology can be traced back to the Modern Synthesis, according to which evolutionary theory could be expressed in terms of population genetics, and which thus brought laboratory scientists and field naturalists together within the new field of evolutionary biology. I will now explore Lewontin's lack of a 'naturalist spirit' as an important contributing factor to his opposition to Wilson and Dawkins.

The potential opposition between naturalists and experimentalists within biology itself was well formulated by Maynard Smith (1982b). He pointed out that even though evolutionary biology had been traditionally linked to natural history and had its very roots in natural history, not all biologists saw this connection as important:

> 'Natural history' is seen by some professional biologists as hardly deserving to be regarded as a part of science. Compared to the experimental sophistication of molecular biology, and the apparent generality of its conclusions, natural history is no more than a collection of particular facts of little theoretical or practical import. There are two reasons why one should dissent from this judgment. The first is that the task of biology is to explain the living world, and that world is irreducibly complex. . . . The second reason for taking natural history seriously is that the central theoretical idea in biology is that of evolution by natural selection, and this idea was formulated by men who were naturalists first and evolutionists second (Maynard Smith, 1982b).

What Maynard Smith says here applies very well to the differences between Dobzhansky and his student Lewontin. A reviewer once described Dobzhansky as follows: 'To him, as to Emerson, life is rather a subject of wonder than of didactics' (Carson, 1977). This was not the way Lewontin saw it. Before the sociobiology controversy, Lewontin had already showed his taste in this matter. In a book review in 1972, for instance, he launched a broadside against the British naturalist tradition (Lewontin, 1972a). He described this school as carrying on 'the genteel upper-middle class tradition of fascination with snails and butterflies'. He noted that the book under review (a Festschrift for E. B. Ford, 'the social and scientific quintessence of that tradition') was appropriately 'replete with primroses, snails, ladybirds and the Pale Brindled Beauty Moth'. Lewontin thus showed little patience with what he called the British pastime devoted to the demonstration of natural selection.

Why was Lewontin so dismissive of the naturalist tradition? Maynard Smith, who belongs to the naturalist tradition in principle, even if his best-known contributions are in population genetics, explained the difference between Lewontin and the naturalists in the following way:

> I remember my friend Dick Lewontin giving a seminar on 'causal and historical explanations in science'. To illustrate his point, he raised the question: why are there no penguins in the Arctic? It might be (causal explanation), that some features of the Arctic make the penguin way of life ill-adapted. Alternatively (historical explanation), it might be that penguins evolved in the Antarctic, and have never been able to cross the tropics to invade the Arctic. After discussing the question for some time, he asserted that the wise biologist would answer that there are penguins in the Arctic, only we call them auks (e.g., puffins, guillemots). *In other words, we should not bother with the fine distinctions* between armadillos and pangolins, *but should content ourselves with understanding the features common to different ecosystems* (Maynard Smith, 1982b, italics added).

As for his own stance, he said:

> I share with Dick Lewontin a wish to find general rules, I mean, I would *like* there to be
> general rules underlying evolution, but I think I differ from him in that I am deeply moved
> by natural history—I share that with Darwin and all the great naturalists, I am just
> fascinated by animals and plants, by the sheer diversity (Maynard Smith, interview).

He added that he could easily spend six months of his life trying to understand the evolution of a specific phenomenon in certain plants, and simply *knowing* it as a fact, while Lewontin would not be content with the sheer knowledge of it, but would want to *explain* it by a law.

Thus, there appears to exist a true difference in motivation in what leads a biologist to study the complexity of the living world. While Lewontin was explicitly concerned with variation, as can be seen in the introductory statements in his 1974 book, for instance, his own writings lent support to the view that he was really not interested in the existing variation in nature *per se*, but rather in trying to *explain* this variation.

It seems that this lack of naturalist spirit was at least partly responsible for Lewontin's attitude to sociobiology, too. Lewontin's review of Dawkins' *The Selfish Gene* (1977a) clearly illustrates this. In his review, he examined the book from a stern philosophical and methodological point of view and profoundly disliked what he saw. Indeed, the tone in this review was as fierce as in many of his writings concerning Wilson's *Sociobiology*. The criticism proceeded on a dual track. Lewontin singled out the two main causes for error in Dawkins' and other sociobiologists' reasoning: 'the adaptationist program' and the 'confusion between materialism and reductionism'. He called Dawkins' book a popular manifestation of a 'new caricature of Darwinism'. And it was not only Dawkins that came under attack here: Lewontin took a shot at the whole genre. According to him, the scientific manifestation of this caricature of Darwinism could be seen not only in the school of sociobiology but also in journals such as *The American Naturalist*, which he saw as permeated by the language of game theory (Lewontin, 1977a). It seems, then, that for Lewontin there existed a '*true*' Darwinism, which had been compromised by sociobiology.

For Lewontin, the universal message of *The Selfish Gene* was 'the theme of our passive manipulation by our gene captors'. He argued that it was the 'old error that *all* describable behavior must be the direct product of natural selection' and 'the form of reasoning linked to this view [that is, the invention of plausible adaptive stories], leads Dawkins . . . to this view of gene and organism. Thus, Lewontin believed that Dawkins was making an erroneous assumption about the world. Furthermore, apparently 'clever game playing' and invention of adaptive stories *offended* Lewontin's conception of true science. As he put it himself: 'it is not clear whether we are dealing with science or with high-table wit'. Indeed, Lewontin so disliked *The Selfish Gene* that, according to one of his colleagues, it was extremely difficult for him to make himself read Dawkins' book; he had to stop after a few pages. (We must assume, however, that Lewontin as a conscientious critic did read the book. In 1981 I witnessed an interesting presentation in an undergraduate seminar at Harvard, where Lewontin first gave a fair overview of

Dawkins' book, whereupon he immediately proceeded to demolish its argument as erroneous.)

Conversely, a good illustration of the opposite point, that *having* a naturalist background helps a scientist read a sociobiological book in the 'right' spirit, is Bill Hamilton's protest against Lewontin's review. In a letter to *Nature*, Hamilton called it a 'disgrace'. He continued:

> It fails to meet any of the standards of informative value, objectivity and fairness to the views of others that are part of the code of science. . . . [A] reader unacquainted with the controversy which is its background may well be left with the impression that, even setting aside the obvious unpleasantness in the review, the book itself probably is unsound and not worth reading. This is a great pity, since in fact the book is not only the best existing outsider's introduction to a new paradigm . . . but . . . is itself a significant contribution to this field.
>
> For its intellectual worth, and seemingly in motivation as well, Lewontin's outline of the book is on a par with Bishop Wilberforce's notorious attack on Darwin and Huxley at the British Association meeting of 1860 (Hamilton, 1977).

Hamilton proceeded to dismiss as scientifically uninteresting one of the major 'errors' that Lewontin had identified as typical of Dawkins and sociobiological thought in his review: a belief that human beings could be understood on the basis of their genes, and societies on the basis of the properties of their members. To this Hamilton said:

> Whether the literature of sociobiology reflects an ignorance of the difference between 'properties of sets and properties of their members' or confusion between materialism and reductionism are matters about which I feel little concerned. On the other hand, I feel a warmth very far from indifference when I encounter in much of the literature in question *signs of a spirit which I share and which I have always assumed is the same as that which motivates scientific enquiry in all its branches. I can most simply express this spirit by calling it a desire to understand and communicate the nature of the world.* I find it present in full measure in *The Selfish Gene* and totally absent in Lewontin's review (Hamilton, 1977, italics added).

Thus, we see that Hamilton regards the 'communicative' spirit of the naturalists as the 'true' scientific attitude in general and seems to consider Lewontin quite *unusual* in his scientific quest. As we shall see in Chapter 14, however, Lewontin is in good company. There I will more closely examine the larger epistemological and even ontological divide between the proponents and opponents of sociobiology and IQ research.

Maynard Smith also disagreed with Lewontin's critique of Dawkins. While Lewontin claimed that it was a 'fallacious view of human society' (that is, an atomistic conception) that lay behind both Dawkins' selfish gene and meme ideas (Lewontin, 1977a), Maynard Smith retorted that the error which Lewontin identified here was not a *logical* error (Maynard Smith, interview in 1981). He later found an opportunity to make this explicit point in his review of *The Extended Phenotype*, Dawkins' second book. There he said, obviously responding to Lewontin:

> Dawkins' meme concept has been criticized on the ground that an atomic theory of culture is necessarily wrong. This may well prove to be correct, although I am astonished at the confidence with which it is sometimes asserted. Animal bodies show a far higher degree of coherence and functional interrelationship than do human societies, and yet an essentially atomic theory of genetics has had a lot to say about the evolution of animal bodies. However, that is not the defence which, in *The Extended Phenotype*, Dawkins makes of memes. Instead, he defends himself by saying that he was trying to make a logical point . . . he is trying to explain to us the mode of existence of replicators (Maynard Smith, 1982a).

Indeed, throughout the controversy, Maynard Smith consistently defended the view that it was not *obviously* wrong to have an atomic theory of animal bodies or human societies. This was apparent also in his and Warren's review of Wilson and Lumsden's *Genes, Mind and Culture* (1981), a book he severely criticized for other reasons, especially problems with the mathematics (see Chapter 8).

What about Gould in this respect? According to Maynard Smith, Gould shared with Lewontin this preference for universal explanations over naturalistic detail (Maynard Smith, interview). What he apparently had in mind here was Gould's opposition to 'the adaptationist program' (see, for example, Gould and Lewontin, 1979) and Gould and Eldredge's attempt to explain macroevolution through punctuated equilibria (1977), and, of course, Gould's Marxism. Interestingly, in 1981 Maynard Smith's picture of Gould as a universalist appeared undisturbed by Gould's prolific writings on natural history themes. The reason may have been that Maynard Smith's discussions with Gould had consistently been at the level of universalist theory, where they were in disagreement, rather than at the level of specifics about the natural world—exactly because Maynard Smith and Gould had different positions on adaptationism. As Maynard Smith said, talking to Gould or Lewontin for an hour tended to make him into an ardent sociobiologist!

It was, rather, Dawkins who wondered about the seeming contradiction between Gould's naturalist and political interests, which he did not fail to bring up in his review of Gould's *Ever Since Darwin*, a book critical of Dawkins and sociobiology. The review was wittily entitled: 'Rejoicing in Multifarious Nature'. In the book, Dawkins had found the following gem: 'I will rejoice in the multifariousness of nature and leave the chimera of certainty to politicians and preachers.' (Gould, 1978a, p. 269.) This led Dawkins to wonder:

> How can a mind capable of such rejoicing, open enough to contemplate the shifting splendour of three thousand million years, moved by the ancient poetry written in the rocks, how can such a mind not be bored by the driveling ephemera of juvenile pamphleteers and the cold preaching of spiteful hardliners? (Dawkins, 1978b)

There is perhaps an answer to this mystery. Gould was not rejoicing all the time. The naturalist spirit was in Gould's case not free-standing, able to be mobilized independently of other concerns: it was kept in check by Gould's overriding critical spirit, which as we have seen was directed toward both scientific and moral/political matters. The two types of critical concerns were most pointedly combined in the anti-adaptationist stance that Gould shared with Lewontin. Anti-adaptationism was at the same time a scientifically and morally/politically critical program, linked to a dismissal of an optimum state of affairs, whether in nature or society. For Gould, nature might be described, but this ought not to be an invitation for drawing conservative political lessons out of such descriptions—which is why nature could *not* be described as well-adapted.

In *Ever Since Darwin* Gould also made the (seemingly obligatory) critical point that it was Dawkins' fundamental belief in the adaptationist program that was responsible for his 'ultimate atomism' (Gould, 1978, p. 269). This, however, Dawkins dismissed as follows:

> (I)t [the gene selection idea] has nothing to do with 'supreme confidence in universal adaptation' (p. 269), which is as likely to be found among devotees of 'individual selection' or 'species selection' (Dawkins, 1978b).

Thus, like Maynard Smith, Dawkins rejected the purported *necessary* connection between the belief in adaptation on the one hand, and an atomistic world view on the other. This was the belief that Lewontin had earlier tried to pin on Dawkins.

The prevalence of a common natural-history spirit among the initial readers and reviewers of *Sociobiology* can also explain why Wilson encountered no real opposition before the critics' letter (cf., for example, Rensberger, 1975b). Most reviewers were biologists, sharing that spirit, mentioned by Hamilton, of attempting to understand and communicate the nature of the world. Furthermore, Wilson was considered to have rendered the biological community a tremendous service with his synthetic effort, which had taken several years.[1] Even those biologists who objected to Wilson's terminology (the name 'sociobiology' itself, 'overstrong' claims for sociobiology, the naturalistic fallacy, and the like), and those biologists who did perceive the political danger inherent in overstatements about human society, generally agreed that Wilson's book was completely within the spirit of the best tradition in biology.

But, obviously, Wilson was not only writing in the naturalist mode. His aim with *Sociobiology*, as already stated in the last chapter in his earlier *The Insect Societies* and in an article derived from this (Wilson, 1971a, 1971b), was to provide a fundamental theory for all social behavior, including human social behavior. This means that in *Sociobiology* he was also, and even primarily, operating in a *universalist* mode: he aimed for a total scientific explanation. And it was in this universalist realm that he clashed head-on with Lewontin and other critical universalists. As discussed in Chapter 3, Wilson regarded the mathematical formulas of population genetics as the 'hardest' ground on which to base his universalist claims, while his ultimate goal lay beyond population genetics. What counted for Wilson was the predictive power (or 'fit'), of models, not their 'true description' of reality. For Lewontin, however, models had to 'correctly' describe reality. His whole 1974 book was an attempt to raise fundamental questions in population genetics actualized by recent findings and to *specify the requirements for evolutionary genetic theory*. No wonder, then, that Lewontin saw *Sociobiology*, full of heuristic decisions as to how to proceed with modeling (despite all his warnings), as a clear violation of his own much more stringent criteria for 'good science'.

The clash between Wilson and Lewontin thus took place at the universalist level, and there was no shared naturalist spirit—or critical spirit, for that matter—to provide any basis for mutual understanding. (Arguably, the confrontation became even harder because Lewontin had explicitly abandoned exactly the kind of modeling efforts that Wilson embraced in his book.) In this controversy, however, when two scientists who disagreed on some theoretical point had a shared background tradition of some kind, there was a good possibility of balanced criticism and communication. This was the case, for instance, with Lewontin and Maynard Smith. Their criticisms of each other were moderated by the fact that they had critical concerns in common—furthermore, of both a scientific and moral/political kind (see examples in Chapters 6 and 12). Finally, having a foot in both quarreling camps—that is, being a naturalist while also sharing some of the critics' concerns—made for a possible role as a mediator between opponents in nature–nurture controversies. In the last chapter we discussed two such mediators, John Maynard Smith and Patrick Bateson.

The presence or lack of a shared naturalist spirit can also account for the initial reactions to Dawkins' *The Selfish Gene*. While for people like Lewontin and Gould uncritical use of Fisher's single gene genetics was both incorrect and socially potentially dangerous, in Britain Fisher's theory was the natural basis for the development of sociobiology. Also, in Britain, interest in genetics had old roots in *left-wing* political associations, which went back to the early decades of this century and scientists such as J. B. S. Haldane (see Werskey, 1978). Finally, we may have been dealing with important stylistic differences in British and American biology. In Britain, there was a tradition of conjuring up imaginative scenarios to convey a basic *logical* point. To readers used to this tradition, it would not occur to take such scenarios *literally*. However, for readers of a more 'fundamentalist' bent—such as Dawkins' experimentally trained American critics—this kind of biological prose may have been shocking reading indeed.

The shared naturalist spirit among British biologists, and the lack of a clear negative social connotation for 'gene thinking' there, can explain why academics in Britain on the whole read Dawkins 'right', as someone genuinely attempting to convey the logic of natural selection in terms of kin selection, Evolutionarily Stable Strategies, and other new ideas, in an easily accessible form. As an ethologist and a student of Tinbergen's, Dawkins obviously had the 'right' naturalist training, and was, therefore, despite his gene-oriented sociobiological message, able simultaneously to convey enthusiasm for explaining the natural world. Thus, even those who criticized Dawkins' approach understood his naturalist ambition and were able to read him in the right spirit. For instance, it was possible for Patrick Bateson to regard Dawkins' 'gene's eye view' as at least heuristically useful, even if he disagreed with the very idea of the gene as the unit of selection, and his own work primarily involved behavioral development (Bateson, 1978, 1981, and interview). The ones who got irritated with Dawkins in England tended to be geneticists, again a demonstration that a lack of common naturalist interest changes the focus of the reading of a text. Additionally, for geneticists there was the question of the 'legitimacy' of the sociobiological conception of 'gene', a matter that we will return to in the next chapter.[2]

Thus, it is not surprising that in 1981 there appeared to be almost a consensus among biologists in Britain that the sociobiology controversy had no real basis there, but 'had to be imported'. Perhaps more importantly, in Britain the discussion about Dawkins' book was seen as quite separate from the discussion of Wilson's *Sociobiology*. It was, rather, the members of the Sociobiology Study Group in the United States, Lewontin's close British colleague, Steven Rose, and the group calling itself Science as Ideology Group of the British Society for Social Responsibility in Science who *combined* Wilson and Dawkins under the common umbrella of 'genetic determinism' (for more on the British critique, including the philosophical critique, see Chapters 4 and 9).

If there was a sociobiology controversy in Britain, it was of a scientific rather than a political nature. At the outset, there were protests from the animal research group in Madingley, Cambridge. Having been trained to consider all of Tinbergen's famous 'four questions' about animal behavior (questions at the phylogenetic, ontogenetic, physio- logical, and functional levels) equally important and legitimate, these ethologists and behavioral ecologists were understandably opposed to a take-over bid by sociobiologists —if this meant that developmental and interaction effects were to be considered less important than purported 'ultimate' evolutionary explanations. However, again the shared naturalist spirit kept the disputes between proponents and critics of socio- biological reasoning in check. For instance, in order to find out about their differences, members of both groups participated in a King's College sociobiology seminar in Cambridge, arranged by Bateson (King's College Sociobiology Group, 1982). Earlier, in 1979, Maynard Smith had convened a conference at the Royal Society, featuring representatives of a variety of traditions in evolutionary biology (and for critical spicing, also Gould and Lewontin; see Chapter 6). The shared naturalist background of Wynne- Edwards and Maynard Smith, may explain why the basic controversy about group and kin selection never got very heated between them (see Chapter 4).

There may be more to the unity of the naturalists, however, than just a shared scientific orientation and background training. There is the deeper historical con- nection between the naturalist spirit and natural theology—traditionally, the naturalist spirit is connected to the idea of finding revelations of God's design in nature. For earlier Christian naturalists, God's law was not only to be found in the Bible but also in the Book of Nature.[3] And elements of this lingered on in later generations; for instance, for Wilson's scientific 'grandfather', Wheeler, the social insects still epitomized the moral virtue of hard work and co-operation and were upheld as a model also for human society.

There seems indeed to exist something of this stronger link among modern natural- ists, too, including those whom we are encountering in and around the sociobiology controversy. The clearest example is obviously Wilson, who goes as far as looking for a natural moral order. A good second is probably Wynne-Edwards, whose writings on group selection are permeated with religious parallels and who gives the impression of belonging to the 'old-fashioned' type of naturalist school (Wynne-Edwards, interview). The list goes on; for instance, Theodosius Dobzhansky was a devout Russian Orthodox and an ardent naturalist and evolutionary theorist. Interestingly, similar parallels have been drawn by the sociobiologists themselves. Harvard's Irven DeVore suggested that there was a close connection between interest in sociobiology and Christian faith (he himself was a former Methodist minister; DeVore, interview). Maynard Smith recently remarked on the connection between his own religious upbringing and his naturalist interests, and pointed out that this was true for a large number of other contemporary sociobiologists, too (Maynard Smith, 1995). And Richard Alexander, author of *The Biology of Moral Systems* (1987), the mentor of many practitioners of sociobiological research, and the past president of the Human Behavior and Evolution Society (a society for researchers in sociobiology and related fields), believed there was a clear connection between the things he heard as a child in (a Methodist) church and his becoming an evolutionary biologist (Alexander, 1996). Sociobiological anthropologist Sara Hrdy, too, recently told me: 'Count me in.'[4]

Thus, we may argue that for naturalistically oriented scientists, the *truth is literally 'out there'*, waiting to be found by curious naturalists. This means that the truth of deepest interest to these scientists is not found 'in there', in the controlled conditions of the laboratory or by different kinds of textual exegesis.

Many have commented on a basic opposition between what they called an 'urban' and a 'country' type of scientist in the sociobiology controversy. The first one who implicitly suggested this was Luria. While he believed Wilson innocent of serious political intent in *Sociobiology*, he at the same time somewhat disparagingly called Wilson 'a country boy', which for him explained Wilson's relative lack of sophistication in political matters (Luria, interview, 1982). Later, evolutionary biologists Larry Slobodkin and Jeffrey Levinton at the State University of New York, Stony Brook, told me that they thought the sociobiology controversy was basically a conflict between 'urban' and 'country' type scientists (interviews, 1984). And recently, Maynard Smith is quoted as having made a similar observation, drawing a contrast between urban intellectuals and more politically innocent 'country' naturalists (Maynard Smith, quoted in Lewin, 1992, p. 43).[5]

The text and the truth

The opposition between a naturalist and an experimentalist approach can now explain why the sociobiologists' scientific work was subjected to such severe scrutiny by the critics. The 'adaptive stories' suggested by sociobiologists as a matter of course 'could not' from the critics' 'hard data' point of view be intended as serious science, and were therefore immediately suspected as being motivated by extrascientific, political concerns.[6] Thus, for the critics, what evolutionary biologists did as a matter of course—that is, argue on the basis of tentative knowledge—now became a sanctionable moral/ political error. As we saw in Chapter 10, the members of the Sociobiology Study Group were so sure of their case that they even invited the readers of *Science* to check for themselves the truth of their claim that 'the "new synthesis" contains numerous inconsistencies and transparent political messages'. Although a superficial reading of *Sociobiology* might not capture these political messages, the critics observed, thorough, critical scrutiny would bring them out (Alpen *et al.*, 1976). We saw some examples of such critical readings and noted that, in order for the hidden political truth to clearly emerge, the initial text often needed to be 'massaged' in some way. What was not in doubt was that the underlying truth could, in fact, be extracted.

But were the critics totally unjustified in their claims, especially their more general one that Wilson 'wanted a genetic explanation', or that he made a 'leap of faith'? The answer is no. A close textual analysis shows that they did have a point. The disputed last chapter of *Sociobiology* contained, for instance, the following strong formulation:

> Although the genes have given away most of their sovereignty, they maintain a certain amount of influence in at least the behavioral qualities that underlie variations between cultures.

This statement was immediately followed by the sentence:

> Even a small proportion of this variation might predispose societies toward cultural differences.

There is no doubt that the first sentence appears to be a statement of fact, while the second one is clearly a speculative or hypothetical statement. One of the critics' charges was that Wilson had 'stated as fact that genetical differences underlie variations between cultures' (Sociobiology Study Group of Science for the People, 1976a). This Wilson in turn rejected, saying that the co-signers had misrepresented him, as usual. According to Wilson himself, what he really had said was that 'Even a small portion . . . *might* pre- dispose societies toward cultural differences' (Wilson, 1976b). But Wilson did talk, in a factual-sounding way, about genetic influences on 'the behavioral qualities that under- lie variations between cultures', which on the face of it does sound like a statement about a genetic basis for cultural differences.

I believe, however, that what Wilson was really doing here was referring in an elliptic way to his multiplier effect and the genetic variation within and between populations. Left implicit in the first statement above was the fact that that there did indeed exist small differences between populations (documented for bloodgroups by Lewontin) and Wilson's argument that, by analogy, the same thing might be said to hold for other traits as well. Lewontin himself would have subscribed to the reasoning up to this point (for example, Lewontin 1974, 1982b). But he (and the other members of the Socio- biology Study Group) would not have agreed with Wilson's next step, his further suggestion (also left implicit here), that the same reasoning was applicable to 'other, less tractable traits guiding *behavior*'. Lewontin and the other critics did not believe that there *existed* any genetically influenced behavioral traits; consequently, for them there did not exist either any genetic variation for such traits whether within or between populations. This was why one could not meaningfully talk about any 'small proportion of this variation' between populations, on which a postulated multiplier effect might work, and 'predispose societies toward cultural differences'.

A more unambiguous example of Wilson's oscillating style was his treatment of the 'Dahlberg gene' for social success. (Incidentally, as Lewontin pointed out with some glee, the Dahlberg gene really came from a textbook example in mathematical population genetics and was not a real model at all, Lewontin, 1981a. But that was a later discovery.) What the critics (read: Lewontin) objected to in their 1976 longer critique was Wilson's presentation style. They accused him of first postulating genes 'left and right' and then going on to argue as if these genes were demonstrated facts.

> An instance of the technique is on pages 554–555 of Wilson's book: 'Dahlberg showed that *if* a single gene appears which is responsible for social success and upward shift in status . . .' and 'Furthermore, there *are* many Dahlberg genes' (our emphases throughout).

Wilson had here undoubtedly made a leap from the hypothetical to the real, *in terms of style*, but did this reflect an inherent *belief* in the reality of Dahlberg genes? Looking more closely at the context, it appears that, on the contrary, it was exactly Wilson's eagerness to argue *against* the idea of a single 'gene for social success' that made him not only dismiss this idea in general, but additionally remark that such a gene would not be single anyway (see the discussion of this in conjunction with my analysis of Chorover, Chapter 10, part 2). Still, the critics' general observation is correct (Wilson, judiciously, did not respond to this particular criticism in his 1976 reply to the critics).

Thus, the critics correctly picked up the hesitations in Wilson's style, and then proceeded to make these into a moral issue. By ignoring the context, they were able to read Wilson in a way opposite to what he intended. The immediate context in both the cases cited was one of cautious speculation (and in the Dahlberg case, Wilson used this stylistic move, if anything, to persuade the reader that intelligence was not the only trait responsible for social success). Thus, Wilson was 'right' about his *intended* meaning, but the critics were 'right' as to what he 'actually said'—at least according to a plausible *prima facie* interpretation. And this was sufficient justification for the critics to take action.

As we saw in Chapter 10, the mere fact that Wilson *said* something was enough—in the critics' fundamentalist-style conception, *certain statements should simply not be made* if there was the possibility that they might be interpreted as a biological legitimation of the social status quo. The strongest statement from the critics in this respect was SftP member Bob Lange's explicit point that *context did not matter* (see Chapter 10). According to him, Wilson's culpability was already obvious, because he had said certain things which none of Wilson's critics would ever have said. This shows the extreme attention paid to the exact words used, typical of the close and critical reading style of Wilson's leading opponents, and encouraged by both their scientific training and moral/political interest in 'ideology criticism'.

But what was it that made Wilson write in this particular style in the first place? According to a friendly critic, Bernard Davis, Wilson was tired and rushed with the last chapter (Davis, interview). Others have suggested that Wilson was just politically naïve (for example, Maynard Smith, interview; Mayr, interview). These explanations may well be true, but considering Wilson's larger moral-cum-scientific agenda (see Chapter 3), it is hard to get away from the idea that Wilson's intent *was* exactly to persuade, and that this was also directly reflected in his style. In this respect, then, the critics got him right.

But the critics were mistaken in believing that Wilson's motivation was political. Wilson's particular style was, rather, based on his self-perception as a moral and scientific visionary with concern for mankind's future. As we saw, Wilson thought it important to be able to 'move people with language'—his heritage from the evangelist preachers—and it was just this basically religious presentation style which was later carried over to contexts where Wilson wanted his message to come across. Part of Wilson's ambition as a preacher was to make a reluctant reader at least *consider* the possibility of a genetic basis for behavior. Thus, Wilson was indeed moving between what is and what might be, at least in this respect.

An insightful article dealing with style in academic writing discussed the fundamentally different stylistic requirements for 'hard' science and 'soft' science when it came to persuasive prose (Bazerman, 1981). As an example of hard science, the author examined the original Watson and Crick paper in *Nature*, while he chose Robert Merton's sociological paper on the 'ambivalence of scientists' as an example of the predicament of writers in soft science fields. In the Watson and Crick paper, the tone could be low key; the paper was presented almost as a challenge to readers to check for themselves. The paper's provocative and relatively laconic style was possible because of the state of knowledge in the field at the time, the practitioners' shared perception of reality, and the possibility of direct proof or disproof based on 'hard' evidence and agreed-upon methods. In glaring contrast to this, Merton was dealing with a topic which was not so far recognized among the audience—in fact, he was trying to launch a new concept (the ambivalence of scientists). Therefore, Merton had to accomplish two things at the same time: 1) persuade the reader of the sociological legitimacy of the paper's subject, that is, present his new concept as part of a shared tradition, and 2) argue for the correctness of his paper's specific claims in regard to this concept.

This double trouble might now explain the special strategy chosen by Merton in his paper. His technique was to immediately draw the reader into a certain 'we-spirit': 'This technique bears similarity to the way Hemingway opens *To Have and Have Not* ... The reader is drafted into a club, and only gradually is he filled in on the experience he presumable shared from the beginning' (Bazerman, 1981, p. 371). Merton needed to employ such a drafting maneuver because his concept was totally based on metaphor. He had no hard data to point to, so the only way the new concept could be given a certain stability was through the hope that the metaphor, 'when combined with other underconstrained terms and contextual clues, may create a web of approximate meanings surrounding the actual thing, such that a meaning develops adequate to the situation' (ibid.). In other words, Merton could only hope that the reader would read him 'in the right spirit', and bear with him long enough for him to get a chance to prove his case!

I believe that this kind of analysis is eminently applicable to Wilson. His style appears to have resulted from a mixing of the Watson-and-Crick and the Merton strategies. The Watson-and-Crick-type hard science position is where Wilson wanted to go, but his original position was the dilemma of Merton. Wilson's specific tool for developing the required 'web of approximate meanings' was the introduction of various types of plausibility arguments and neologisms. (I am not referring here to the inherent problems in anthropomorphic zoological language; these he shared with all biologists.)

Wilson was uncertain of just who his audience was and what could therefore be taken for granted. He knew that biologists were used to regarding human beings as an animal species and would thus be sure to read him in the intended spirit, but he also knew that social scientists would be hostile. His resulting stylistic compromise was therefore a precarious balance between what he believed was true and what he knew was not yet proven. In his 'evangelist' mode he attempted to make the readers see things from his point of view: he transported them to the promised kingdom of sociobiology. In his Watson-and-Crick mode, again, he was interested in hard evidence. This oscillation 'between the rash and cautious' was observed by several reviewers of Wilson's books (for example, Mackintosh, 1979; Maynard Smith, 1978a). It is also a style which is easily perceived and resisted by anyone not willing to be drafted into the sociobiological club spirit.

However, it is not difficult to point to cases where there was a similar stylistic oscillation in the *critics'* writings. For instance, it may have been the lack of clarity about the exact audience for the Sociobiology Study Group's position paper in 1976 that inspired some of its particular style. The paper contained such categorical statements as 'It cannot be done' in regard to the possibility of separating learned from genetic elements in behavior. This statement was surprising, since in 1975, in a different context, the chief author of this paper had been quite prepared to recognize the 'considerable technical difficulties' involved in such studies, without stating that it was impossible in principle to sort out environmental from genetic elements (Lewontin, 1975a).

An even more mysterious statement was the following:

> The earlier forms of determinism in the current wave have now been pretty well discredited. The claims that there is a high heritability of IQ, *which implies both the unchangeability of IQ and a genetic difference between races or between social classes*, have now been thoroughly debunked (Sociobiology Study Group of Science for the People, 1976a, p. 182; italics added).

It seems that the group members (read: Lewontin) were here putting themselves in the position of an innocent reader who was somehow assumed to believe that high heritability of IQ implied both unchangeability of IQ and genetic differences between races or social classes. But why would a reader assume this, *if* properly educated about some basic principles of genetics? A statement such as this transported the reader to a hypothetical worst scenario—which is exactly where the critics wanted to go. The critics conjured up not the kingdom of a sociobiological heaven, but instead the hell of social discrimination. But, just like Wilson, they also ended up conflating two perspectives. Read as a scientific statement, the above quotation becomes quite absurd. Even a highly heritable trait can be environmentally manipulated (for example, the standard PKU or myopia examples), and Lewontin himself in his critique of Jensen had pointed out that it was a scientific mistake to draw conclusions about between-group differences in IQ from knowledge about within-group heritabilities (Lewontin, 1970a).

But considering that they, too, had to persuade their readers, it is not surprising that the critics also oscillated between what is and what might be—that is, between what

Wilson's text said and what they would have *wanted* it to say. We have seen examples of this in Chapter 10. It looks as if the critics were also attempting to draft the reader into a 'club spirit'—a critical one this time. One of the important premises of the critical club spirit was that 'genetic determinists' could have no good scientific grounds for their scientific claims, and that these invariably hid ideological motives, which just needed unveiling. And just like Wilson, the critics were also busy creating a web of approximate meanings and associations—political ones this time—to stabilize *their* interpretation of the real meaning of sociobiological statements.

Interestingly, in the sociobiology controversy, such drafting attempts could also be seen in the real world, not only in literary exercises. For instance, some of the same affirmative and 'evangelist' spirit that could be found in Wilson's writings was also evident in his enthusiastic response to telephone calls during my interviews with him in his office in 1981–2. Wilson, as a matter of course, seemed to be drafting anyone asking for information or calling him for other purposes into the club of sociobiological we-spirit, informing the caller about the latest victories on the sociobiological front. I found Wilson reporting in an upbeat fashion that 'the Marxists' were on the retreat. I asked him about that. One of Wilson's indicators was that he had learnt that Lewontin was then getting deeply involved in an agricultural project, whose relevance to sociobiology was 'not obvious'. (Wilson also told me that Alper and Lange's critique of his and Lumsden's book demonstrated that the critics had now 'surrendered their ace card' and met him and Lumsden on their own ground.)

In the same way, I saw live drafting in the critical camp, not least in the public meetings, where it was always tacitly assumed that the audience shared the premises of the critical speakers. In Chapter 2, I mentioned one meeting where this taken-for-granted atmosphere was for a moment broken by Irven DeVore. In Chapter 10, we saw how Chomsky resisted being drafted into the critical club.

I know of one other case where the critical assumptions were challenged by the audience. In 1981, there was an undergraduate seminar on biological determinism at Harvard, arranged by Lewontin, Gould, Ruth Hubbard, and others, with invited guest speakers covering such things as Nazi biology (Robert Proctor). Again, I was generously allowed the status of observer. At the end of the term, an interesting thing occurred within an open evaluation of the course itself. A student pointed out that since the seminar had been so critical about the ideological assumptions in other scientists' theories, he would have liked Lewontin, Gould, Hubbard, and the other seminar leaders to have stated *their* value assumptions. There was some mumbling assent to this from the other students. This complaint was rather unexpected and visibly baffling to the seminar leaders, who had until then operated quite unchallenged within the critical club spirit. Valiantly, they recognized the student's point.

The divided academy and its two worlds of truth

Throughout this book we have seen that, in their analyses, the members of the Socio-biology Study Group always ended up with the same result: that Wilson (and Jensen before him) was morally guilty. This conviction was so strong that different elaborate schemes were developed to show just how Wilson apparently thought, and how in this way ideology infiltrated science. Indeed, within the critical camp there appeared to exist an attitude of 'anything goes' in regard to criticism of sociobiology—a lack of internal controls as to what could conceivably be said; (see Chapter 10 for representative examples). Despite their internal disparity, these different interpretations were seen as supporting one another in the common endeavor of proving the moral guilt of selected targets. Paradoxically, while the critics of sociobiology attacked the evolutionary biologists for their 'adaptive stories', they were themselves indulging in the same game of 'just-so' story telling—in their case, *critical story telling*.

Criticism can indeed be fun. The upbeat spirit and laughter during my interviews suggest that many critics derived great pleasure from efficient fault-finding, witty commentary, and the creation of persuasive critical packages. For instance, Lewontin reported that his friends found the whole 'Nabi' incident endlessly amusing, and described with some pride how he had cleverly formulated a letter to *Nature* saying that he and Nabi were not the same person (see Chapter 9). And one of the most entertaining pieces produced within the critical camp was undoubtedly Isadore Nabi's satire 'On the Tendencies of Motion', an attempt to model gravity by averaging results derived from experiments with falling bodies, including apples (Nabi, 1981a), in fair competition with 'A Sociobiological Explanation of the Evolution of the English Sonnet', (Nabi, 1980). Lewontin's lab looked like a fun lab—and self-ironical at that. Among the journals could be found the *Journal for Irreproducible Results*, and on the blackboard I once read the following encouraging statement: 'Rabbi [some name or other] says you are not obliged to succeed, but you are obliged to try!'

Why was it, then, the serious side of the critics that came out in polemics? One reason why controversies in science easily become acrimonious could be that they serve as emotional outlets for scientists, who are not only under constant performance pressure but are also expected to adhere to a rigidly 'scientific' writing style. (This need for emotional outlets for scientists was suggested by Stephen Chorover in interview. Like the other critics, Chorover was reflective and charming in person, but relentless in his written attacks on sociobiology.) Looking at the difference in scientific training of the vocal critics of sociobiology and their targets, there may even be a corollary: the *less* one is allowed to play freely in one's own field of science (that is, the 'harder' it is), the *more* pent-up emotion goes into participation in scientific controversy. Perhaps, then, the opponents to sociobiology, whose criteria for 'good' science were so stringent that they recognized no tentative or plausibility arguments, had surreptitiously transferred the play element in science to the level of *criticism* instead—critical story telling—while denying it legitimacy in science proper? Controversy may thus be a place to play for fun-starved scientific purists, while they keep their own science clean.

But we are not concerned here merely with different attitudes to play and 'serious' science. There were broader differences in the taken-for-granted worlds of proponents and opponents. In fact, the sociobiology controversy illustrates a polarization of the scientific community into two larger camps, with different but co-existing interpretations of reality. Members of these two communities drew on *different* stocks of knowledge, or, alternatively, interpreted the same facts differently, because of their different logics-in-use. Both parties collected 'facts' and arguments, and both saw their primary mission as a *moral* one: either to protect the freedom of inquiry, or to warn about dangerous science. In this process, both sides also turned to the general public for support. In such a situation, every move by one side was subjected to scrutiny by the other, and each side saw the other as blinded by ideology, and therefore incapable of seeing the truth. Let us take a look at these parallel meaning universes or taken-for-granted worlds.

For traditionalist scientists, the common stock of knowledge included such things as existing tentative results in behavioral genetics and intelligence research. It also included a set of shared opinions and judgments. Let us look at some elements of these taken-for-granted views, which continue today.

1. IQ testing is a well-established branch of science with reliable results. The heritability of IQ among whites is relatively well established. (A list of recent such 'well-established' beliefs in regard to the status of IQ research can be found in the *Wall Street Journal* in mid-December 1994 in an 'expert' response to widespread critique of Herrnstein and Murray's much-debated *The Bell Curve*, 1994.) A corollary of this belief is that critics of IQ 'cannot' have legitimate scientific reasons for objecting to existing results, but 'must' be wanting to stop scientific inquiry as such. Here, the charge of Lysenkoism comes in handy (Davis, 1976d, 1983; Herrnstein, 1973; Wilson, 1978b).

2. A further belief, held by, for instance, Jensen, Herrnstein, and Davis, but not Wilson, is that, although this cannot be formally proven, it is 'likely' that the white–black difference in IQ has a genetic component (Jensen, 1972; Herrnstein, 1973; Davis, 1986).

3. In response to the other camp's allegations that educational psychologists and other scientists were responsible for the passing of the Immigration Law in 1924 (see below), the traditionalist camp has been collecting counter-intelligence about the circumstances around the passing of this law. According to this camp, early IQ testers, such as Goddard, in fact aimed at making the selection of immigrants at Ellis Island more scientific, and therefore *fairer*. Furthermore, they corrected their methods after getting obviously outrageous results (Davis, 1983). Psychologists should not be held responsible for the Immigration Law and the quotas that were established for eastern and southern European immigrants—this was rather the doing of the *public*, who were inundating Congress with letters (Snyderman and and Herrnstein, 1983), and of 'a far-flung coalition of forces', including the labor unions in a national situation of severe unemployment (Samelson, 1979, p. 135). (The conflict about the true background story in regard to these laws regularly manifested itself. For instance, it flared up between Davis and Beckwith at a meeting of the New York Academy of Sciences in 1976).

4. IQ testing is alive and well despite the Cyril Burt affair, that is, the contention that Burt, who developed the methodology used in current mental testing, was himself guilty of fraud in his twin studies (Gillie, 1974; Kamin, 1974; Hearnshaw, 1981). From the very beginning, the Burt story was an embarrassment to the intelligence testing movement, but Jensen himself had raised doubts about Burt at an early stage. However, from having earlier accepted Burt's fraud as a fact, Jensen later changed his position to

'not proven' (Jensen, 1991). Here he relied on two recent re-evaluations of the Burt case (Joynston, 1989; Fletcher, 1991).

Among the critics, too, we have the following examples of common arguments and beliefs, which were constantly drawn upon in their writings.

1. IQ studies have been thoroughly debunked (Allen *et al.*, 1975; Sociobiology Group for Science for the People, 1976a). Because of this, the prudent view is to assume zero-heritability (Kamin, 1974; Lewontin, 1976c; Layzer, 1981). More recently, the specter of the IQ debate was raised again in conjunction with *The Bell Curve* debate, this time in a political climate where there was explicit support for cutting programs for the dis-advantaged. (The current responses to this book are not only critical reviews, for example, Fraser, 1995, but also a volume, *Inequality by Design*, written by sociologists; Fischer *et al.*, 1996).

2. Jensen *asserted* that the differences in IQ between blacks and whites are genetic (see, for example, Gould, 1981a).

3. It was mainly due to the actions of psychologists and geneticists that the Immigration Act of 1924 was passed, which in turn resulted in the turning back of many Jews to Europe (see, for example, Kamin, 1974; Chorover, 1979; Gould, 1981a). Inter-estingly, Lewontin (1975b) accuses these scientists of *inaction* instead—they were quiet when 'lies' were being told. In this particular case, the 'facts' even include the exact quotation concerning the high percentages of different ethnic groups that were rated as 'feebleminded' in Goddard's early study (83 per cent of the Jews, 80 per cent of the Hungarians, 79 per cent of the Italians, and 87 per cent of the Russians). These statistics are repeated over and over again in the radical literature, usually giving Kamin, 1974 as a source (for example, Chorover, 1979; Lewontin, 1975b). (Incidentally and ironically, this much-quoted Kamin reference happens to refer to the *wrong* Goddard article—a fact enthusiastically noted by Herrnstein in interview, 1982.)

4. Because Cyril Burt's twin data were demonstrated to have been fraudulent, the whole field of IQ testing is on shaky ground (see, for example, Lewontin, 1981b). A later version of this argument addresses Joynson's and Fletcher's attempts to defend Burt. (Here the radical camp's counterevidence is Samelson's (1992) article, which argues that these authors' attempts to exonerate Burt are not convincing.)

5. One more often-quoted fact on the left was Allan Chase's historical (1977) study of the opposition to Goldberger's findings, showing that pellagra was not a genetic disease among poor people, but was instead associated with bad nutrition (Chorover, 1979; Alper, 1982; Luria, interview). (Here, surprisingly, since the critics do not care for correlations—see Chapter 12—the critics chide Goldberger's opponents for not taking his correlation analysis seriously.)

The validity of IQ testing was undoubtedly one of the sorest issues dividing the camps. As we saw in Chapter 11, Davis complained that Gould and other critics represented IQ testing as scientifically unsound and did not give credit to recent developments in this field. Herrnstein (in interview in 1982) was bitter that Gould's exposition of old errors and the Cyril Burt case were given enormous attention, while the fact that the Burt revelations did not rock the boat of IQ testing as such was systematically suppressed. No one mentioned that there were *other* twin studies beside Burt's which yielded the same conclusion of high heritability, and that therefore the field was alive and well despite Burt. (Herrnstein was not alone in this view. This was also the assessment of Thoday, 1981, a methodological critic of IQ research.)

Even before the sociobiology controversy, the larger camps had completely different assessments about the nature of the prevailing academic climate. The position of the traditionalist camp can be seen in the 1972 'Resolution on Scientific Freedom Regarding Human Behavior and Heredity' (Page, 1972). It was invested with a lot of authority: signed by 50 eminent academics from different fields, including Jensen, Herrnstein, Hans Eysenck, and other psychologists, and five Nobel laureates, among them Francis Crick, Jacques Monod, and John Kendrew. The resolution spoke of a climate of 'suppression, punishment, and defamation of scientists who emphasized the role of heredity in human behavior' and called on 'liberal academics' to protect 'any qualified faculty members who responsibly teach, research or publish' in this area. Not only did the statement depict researchers in heredity and behavior as comparable with other martyrs for truth in the history of science, but it also suggested that opponents to such research were typically not *scientists*; they were described as taken in by 'anti-science', and emotion instead of reason.

This resolution aroused some critical responses, most notably a statement by a Commission appointed in New York by the Society for the Psychological Study of Social Issues, one of the members of which was Ethel Tobach, a comparative psychologist and well-known as an anti-racist. This Commission 'on the new assault on equality' questioned the purported 'facts' in the petition; for instance, whether there were really 'any instances in which a "hereditarian" viewpoint has been the basis on which a scientist had lost a position in an academic institution, was prevented from teaching, was prevented from doing research, or was not allowed to publish in appropriate scientific journals' (Proshansky *et al.*, 1973). Another commentator questioned the point of the resolution, since the issue causing controversy was not heredity and behavior, but rather *race* and behavior (Stagner, 1973). Still another correspondent suggested that when the signatories declared that they 'have investigated much evidence concerning the possible role of inheritance in human abilities', they could not have investigated the evidence presented by Jensen, since in that case they could not have 'failed to notice the deficiencies, the contradictions, and the outright misrepresentations' (Vetta, 1973).

But the crucial document of the critical camp is the Resolution Against Racism published in 1973 in *The New York Times*, signed by over a thousand American academics from identified institutions. It declared race differences in intelligence non-existent, and research aimed at establishing such differences both scientifically invalid and socially pernicious, linking this research to 'master-race' and Nazi theories. It dismissed appeals to scientific freedom for 'racist' researchers as 'subterfuge'. Just like the 1972 Resolution, this one called on academics—but this time to actively *resist* the use of academia for 'racist' attempts. It was signed by several members of the Sociobiology Study Group, including Lewontin and Beckwith, (and also Luria). Already before *Sociobiology*, then, a deep political divide had emerged.

It was not only the academic climate that was differently perceived by members of the two camps. They also had different conceptions as to who controlled the media. The Sociobiology Study Group and the Science for the People saw the media as manipulated by social power-holders aiming at reinforcing the status quo (see, for example, Alper, Beckwith and Miller, 1978). In contrast, Herrnstein believed there existed a liberal conspiracy which prevented certain truths from being published (Herrnstein, 1983). Davis saw a popular press preference for polemical critique and was particularly appalled at the popular acclaim for Gould's *The Mismeasure of Man* (Davis, 1983).

Both Jensen (1972a) and Herrnstein (1973, 1982) were concerned that the media seemed to regard only certain facts as 'news' while they suppressed others. Herrnstein was especially bitter that the Burt story was told over and over again, while it was not considered news when one of the central and celebrated environmentalists, Heber, with his much-quoted 'IQ-increasing' program for ghetto children (Heber, 1968; even quoted by Dobzhansky, 1973a, p. 14) was revealed as a fraud (Herrnstein, interview, and Herrnstein, 1982). Herrnstein also complained about 'distortions', rejected attempts at clarification, etc. (cf. the first chapter in his 1973 book).

Thus, we can say that the two academic camps that had formed on the basis of the IQ and sociobiology controversies effectively came to live in two different worlds of factual knowledge, taken-for-granted assumptions, and attitudes toward such things as the media. Basic social psychological theory can make some predictions as to what will typically happen in a case of such pre-existing interpretative frameworks. Any incoming information will be accommodated in line with existing convictions; various well-known cognitive defense mechanisms will be operating to effectively protect the members of each camp from serious challenges to their existing 'knowledge'; and within each camp, members will reinforce one another's beliefs. This seems also to have happened in the sociobiology controversy, as it transformed itself into other academic debates, while the initial camps remained largely the same. We will return to this in Part III.

CHAPTER 14

Conflicting views of the nature of science

'True causality' vs models and measurement

In this chapter I will demonstrate that what united the critics was not only their political concerns with the implications of sociobiological and IQ research, but also a shared epistemological belief. It will become clear that the critics' convictions about the nature of 'good science' were fundamentally different from the views of people like Jensen or Wilson. Indeed, it was partly because of the existence of such a larger, shared scientific world view that many critics perceived their criticism of sociobiology as a direct and logical *continuation* of their criticism of Jensen and IQ research. The very perception of such a connection has puzzled many, not the least Wilson himself, who in the last chapter of *Sociobiology* actively sought to avoid the IQ trap. Over the years, the criticisms of sociobiology and IQ have converged into a broader attack on 'reductionism', one of the central themes of this chapter.

Interestingly, in the sociobiology controversy, neither party seems to have explicitly recognized the fundamental differences in their conceptions of 'good science'. At least in written polemics, both sides tended to routinely connect the opponent's purportedly 'erroneous' scientific opinion to political factors. I will now examine more closely the nature of the two scientific world views that came into conflict in these recent controversies. We saw some of this in Chapter 3, with Wilson and Lewontin epitomizing these contrasting meta-scientific conceptions. Here I will bring in additional representatives in order to illustrate the depth of the epistemological divide.

What united the researchers in IQ and sociobiology was the common need for workers in these fields to use hypothetical constructs, statistical methods and probabilistic 'systems thinking' for the mapping of unknown territory. The critics of IQ research and sociobiology, on the other hand, were deeply concerned with the establishment of *true* causality, that is, getting to the 'hidden reality' itself. Therefore they did not accept the established heuristics in these fields. Needless to say, this was obviously not the way the critics formulated their objections. Instead, they had a tendency to discuss the heuristics of IQ testing and sociobiology as if *methodological* decisions automatically implied also (unacceptable) *ontological* commitments to an either 'unreal' or 'reified' world.

In the sociobiology controversy this was already obvious in the critics' letter in *The*

New York Review of Books, and the longer critique, in which Wilson was accused of discussing genes 'for' behavioral traits. The complaint was that such genes were not only hypothetical, but also that they broke 'the totality of human social phenomena into arbitrary units'. But these early manifestos are not useful documents for examining the critics' scientific position more deeply, because they attacked sociobiology from so many different angles simultaneously and coupled scientific and moral/political concerns. In order to clarify the exact locus of the epistemological disagreement, it is necessary to go to a variety of other contexts. Here the IQ controversy provides some important insights into the critics' reasoning about good science in general.

Let us first examine the idea of *true causality* and 'correct' representation of reality. Lewontin, in his 1970 criticism of Jensen, had suggested in passing that the 'general intelligence' factor *g*, which can be identified through factor analysis of IQ test scores, did not correspond to a real object, but was a construct, and that, like all products of factor analysis, it was based on arbitrary decisions by the analyst. He did not take this point further at the time. This is not surprising, since Lewontin until the time of the sociobiology controversy had been primarily involved in *technical* criticism of IQ, not criticism of the possibility of measuring IQ as such (see especially Lewontin, 1975a). In his general writings, however, he was becoming increasingly preoccupied with a broader theme: the 'unreality' of statistical correlations. It bothered Lewontin that these did not have a real basis in nature, or presumed a stochastic universe without proper causal laws. Consequently, it was along these lines that Lewontin criticized the analysis of variance (Lewontin, 1974b), the calculation of average genetic fitness by followers of the Fisher school in population genetics (for example, Lewontin, 1977a), and stochastic models in ecology (Levins and Lewontin, 1980). Maynard Smith aptly summed up Lewontin's position as follows: 'Dick likes there to be decent causes for things' (Maynard Smith, interview).

Lewontin may have been on the right track, but it was rather Gould who became the champion of the idea of the 'reification' of IQ. That was his leading argument in his criticisms of Jensen in 1980 and 1981. In *The Mismeasure of Man*, Gould threw IQ measurements together with craniology and other older methods in the dustbin of failed attempts to find 'real' physical sites for mental characteristics. (He even managed to include sociobiology among such efforts.) Lewontin soon caught up with the reification line of attack. Certainly by 1981 he had abandoned his earlier methodological criticism of IQ and was, just like Gould, now arguing against the 'reality' of IQ measurements. In fact, in his *New York Review of Books* review of *Mismeasure* (Lewontin, 1981b), he formulated himself so mysteriously about this matter that two philosophers, Tomkow and Martin, asked him what he meant.

Lewontin's answer gives us his position as clearly as can be desired:

> Tomkow and Martin have thoroughly muddled 'intelligence' with notions about intelligence. IQ tests do pick out people whom teachers and psychologists think are intelligent. Unfortunately, that fact has confused even our philosophers into thinking that the test picks out people who have a physical, heritable, internal property, 'intelligence', that stands apart from socially determined mental constructs . . . It is not simply our 'judgments

of intelligence' but the very idea of intelligence that is a historically contingent mental construct.

It is important to point out that the distinction between mental constructs and natural attributes is more than a philosophical quibble, even when those constructs are based on physical measurements. *Averages are not inherited; they are not subject to natural selection; they are not physical causes of any events.* There are no 'genes for handsomeness' or 'genes for intelligence' any more than there are 'genes for saintliness'. *To assert that there are such genes is a conceptual, not a factual error* and one that has major consequences for scientific practice and social analysis (Lewontin, 1982c, italics added).

Lewontin appears to have come a long way since his 1975 review of the genetics of intelligence, where he used 'intelligence' and 'IQ' interchangeably, and seriously discussed the methodological problems involved in assessing the heritability of intelligence. Had Lewontin now radically changed his position on intelligence, so that he currently believed that one could not, after all, talk about heritability? His statement that there are no genes for intelligence may well have created such an impression. But Lewontin's central point was really that *averages* are not inherited.

It was just because Lewontin was strongly opposed to the idea of averages that he was also opposed to Dawkins' idea of the selfish gene. This is how he formulated his criticism in 1981:

I mean, it is absolutely the case that one can calculate an average fitness of a gene, one can always calculate it, but it turns out that the fitness constantly changes with the frequency of the genotypes when the population changes: it is nothing but a calculation. And his error—I think it is an error of reification—is to think that *because he can assign a number to a thing that that thing somehow is real and causal*. It is exactly the same error as saying: Look, I can calculate the average height of a population. But *the average height is not a natural attribute of any natural object . . .* it is a statistical construct! (Lewontin, interview, emphasis added.)

Lewontin went one step further and labelled Dawkins' attitude 'an epistemological error', which, according to him, came from 'a lack of understanding of population genetics'. But, as we saw, Maynard Smith—clearly addressing Dawkins' critics—explicitly emphasized that neither *The Extended Phenotype* nor *The Selfish Gene* contained any logical errors. He also emphasized that an atomic theory of genetics, or even of human culture, was not *obviously* wrong (Maynard Smith, 1982a; Maynard Smith and Warren, 1982).

For our current purposes, it is actually more interesting to look at Lewontin's suggestion that Dawkins (or anyone else) tended to believe that as soon as you can calculate something, that thing is real. This seems a clear case of overkill. Obviously one does not have to *believe* in 'reified' average fitnesses in order to find them *useful* in models! Nor does one have to swear to the reality of average height (or IQ) in order to use such a number as a standard for comparison. Thus, it does not seem necessary to assume with the critics that methodological reductionists were automatically ontological reductionists of this odd kind, believing in the reality of averages.

Moreover, even though sociobiologists, IQ researchers, and the like used models and formulas involving hypothetical genes, this did not mean that they did not believe that the material, molecular basis for postulated behavioral or cognitive traits would *eventually* be found. Wilson was quite clear about this in *Sociobiology*, and this also seems to have been the belief behind, for instance, Jensen's continuous insistence on a factor *g* for 'general intelligence' (Jensen, 1979, 1985). For these researchers, modeling, statistics, and the like were a provisional way of getting to the ultimate goal. Measurement was an indirect way of approaching the real phenomenon. For the critics, however, it was only experimental science that held the secret to scientific success, *not* models based on 'unrealistic' assumptions and statistical formulas. The critics wanted *real*, not hypothetical genes. In their view, therefore, statistical analysis could not substitute for a real understanding of phenomena, which was, after all, the aim of science (see, for example, Layzer, 1972).

For those scientists who were used to indirect methods because of the nature of their subject matter, this was at the very least puzzling. Early on in the IQ controversy, Jensen tried to explain the scientific rationale behind IQ research:

> Disagreements and arguments can perhaps be forestalled if we take an operational stance. First of all, this means that probably the most important factor about intelligence is that we can measure it. Intelligence, like electricity, is easier to measure than to define. And if the measurements bear some systematic relationships to other data, it means that we can make meaningful statements about the phenomenon we are measuring. *There is no point in arguing the question to which there is really no answer, the question of what intelligence really is.* The best we can do is obtain measurements of certain kinds of behavior and look at their relationships to other phenomena and see if these relationships make any kind of sense and order. It is from these orderly relationships that we gain some understanding of the phenomena (Jensen, 1969, p. 4, quoted in Layzer, 1972, p. 272, italics added).

This approach to science was strongly rebutted by David Layzer, an astrophysicist at Harvard. Layzer was one of the leading critics of Jensen in 1971, and later continued with sporadic criticism of sociobiology (such as a review of *Genes, Mind and Culture* in 1981). According to Layzer, the idea of an 'operational stance' was based on a profound misunderstanding of what physicists really do. According to him, the first and crucial step in natural scientific research is not measurement, but the decision of what to examine. This means that there has to be a *theory* to guide the investigation and it is only on the basis of hypotheses derived from this that measurements are made, in order to compare prediction with empirical data (Layzer, 1972).

Later on, Gould took a different tack in the collective effort to criticize Jensen, with his argument that Jensen's 'real error' was his 'reification' of *g*, a statistical construct (Gould, 1981a). According to Gould, the problem with *g* was that it reduced intelligence, obviously a multidimensional concept, to a single dimension, and further, because it was an artifact, it obviously did not represent an underlying physical reality. Gould particularly disliked 'the practice of assuming that the mere existence of a factor, in itself, provides a licence for causal speculation' (Gould, 1981a, p. 268). Against such criticism, Jensen again attempted to scientifically justify his approach. This time he said:

> In fact, what Gould has mistaken for 'reification' is neither more nor less than *the common practice in every science of hypothesizing explanatory models or theories to account for the*

observed relationships within a given domain. Well known examples include the heliocentric theory of planetary motion, the Bohr atom, the electromagnetic field, the kinetic theory of gases, gravitation, quarks, Mendelian genes, mass, velocity, etc. . . . The *g* factor, and theories attempting to explain *g* in terms of models independent of factor analysis itself, are essentially no different from the other constructs of science listed above . . . Would Gould then deny psychology the common right of every science to the use of hypothetical constructs or any theoretical speculation concerning causal explanations of its observable phenomena? (Jensen, 1982; italics added.)

I have used these two quotations from Jensen to illustrate on the one hand the similarity between the positions of IQ research and sociobiology as sciences, and on the other hand the clear common opposition of critics like Layzer, Gould, and Lewontin to science of the Jensen or Wilson type. In the latter type, there is a need to use hypothetical constructs, statistical methods, and other means for the mapping of unknown territory. But for the critics, it seems that the important thing was to establish '*true*' causality, and this could not be achieved through correlational analysis.

The legitimacy of 'correct' intelligence research

The best demonstration that the opposition to IQ research was not purely political is probably the unexpected fact that *the critics were not opposed to research in intelligence as such.* The problem was only that the research was now of the 'wrong' kind. As Lewontin had said already:

> All research on the genetics of normal human intelligence has been of a *statistical* nature, using the techniques of biometrical genetics to estimate genetic and environmental sources of variation in specific populations. There has not been, and in the present state of developmental and neural biology cannot be, any attempt to analyze cellular and developmental mechanisms of gene action in influencing *cognitive traits* (Lewontin, 1975a, italics added).

But, as we learnt, it was exactly at this level, Lewontin believed, that the only scientifically interesting questions about human intelligence could be asked. Note also that the other critics who kept criticizing and questioning the 'reality' of IQ measurements did not deny the existence of heritability for *cognitive traits.* There are quite explicit statements to this effect, for instance by Stephen Chorover (1979), and David Layzer (1978). Even Gould, by himself (1981a) and in a biology textbook that he co-authored with Singer and Luria, subscribed to the idea of *genetically controlled cognitive traits as a legitimate object of research* (Luria, Gould, and Singer, 1981, p. 308). Thus, it seems clear that for this group of critics of Jensen and Wilson, evidence at the molecular level was acceptable, but the methodological approach typical of sociobiology and IQ research was not.

What is going on here? How is it that on the one hand human intelligence is an acceptable object of research, but that on the other hand current IQ research is unacceptable? Why is it that, despite the fact that scientists like Wilson and Jensen obviously were *also* hoping for the real molecular level to be found eventually (in *Sociobiology* Wilson was particularly putting his hope on neurophysiology), and thus seemed to have *prima facie* the same basic goal for science as their critics, they were being attacked as 'bad' scientists?

I am not here addressing the fact that the critics found errors or 'errors' of various kinds in Jensen and Wilson (error-finding in Jensen, especially, appears to have been quite a lucrative industry in psychology; for instance, Leon Kamin is said to have got tenure at Princeton for his 1974 book-length critique of Jensen). I am instead asking what was basically wrong with models and statistical methods when it came to humans, *if* the critics considered the aim of investigating possible genetic foundations for human cognitive traits defensible as such?

My guess is that a largely implicit *political* consideration entered here. The great distrust of statistics among the critics might not have only been epistemologically or ontologically based, but also combined with a suspicion that statistical methods and other approaches involving measurement would invariably lead to 'mismeasurement' of various kinds. Obviously, one of the problems with statistics is that it makes it easy to calculate averages, which could conceivably lead to treating individuals as statistical averages of their respective groups, thus inviting stereotyping and discrimination. We had a glimpse of this type of reasoning in Chapter 10, with the discussion of 'Plato's big lie'.

Perhaps it was this kind of worry that animated Gould in *The Mismeasure of Man*, and caused puzzlement among some of his reviewers (Ravitch, 1982; Samelson, 1982). These reviewers could not see what exactly Gould was opposed to, particularly since he seemed to recognize the importance and legitimacy of testing, for instance in diagnosing learning disabilities at the individual level (he even wrote about his own son's learning disability). The reviewers further noted that Gould chastised early IQ testers for being 'bad' scientists and implied that it was they who were responsible for the discriminatory measures taken against US immigrants early in this century. Still, he seemed to admit that the results of current IQ tests were valid in the sense that they could be used as predictors of social success—without, however, telling us anything about the nature of intelligence as such (Gould, 1981a, p. 315).

Perhaps the simple rule for understanding Gould, at least, would be that for him individual testing was acceptable, but group testing was not acceptable, because *any* measurement that could be used for comparison between two groups might further be used as a tool for ranking and discrimination. Or it may be that for Gould the assessment of a multitude of individual 'factors' for intelligence was acceptable, but the idea of a general factor was not, again because a general factor would be easier to use for ranking. (Still, it is not clear how this would solve the problem, since if one *insisted* on creating devices for ranking, one could quite easily obtain an average from the test scores for these individual factors, too, or alternatively, decide that one of these factors was the most socially valuable.) But here we might well ask if it was really IQ testing as such or, rather, a more fundamental interest in *the measurement of performance*, typical of such societies as the American one, that should be ultimately criticized?[1]

Thus we can see that what unified the critics of sociobiology and IQ research was an opposition to calculation and measurement, or any indirect methods in science, while their opponents considered these scientifically legitimate and typical. What I have tried to show so far in this chapter is that *in addition* to the political considerations involved, the critics had basic objections of a meta-scientific, more closely of an *ontological*, nature.

Sociobiology and IQ research as 'unnatural science'

Even though one might argue that the critics had unrealistically strict standards for science, they did represent a *possible* position with regard to 'good science'—one might call this the 'hardline' position. And this position was not particularly 'Marxist'. To demonstrate this, let us return to Peter Medawar and his methodological critique of scientific fields which regularly rely on statistics. In Chapter 12 we encountered Medawar involved in polemics with both Wilson and two members of Science for the People (and ending up being misunderstood by both sides). We also saw that Medawar was critical of Marxist ideology in science as well as the idea of a special 'science for the people', and believed that IQ research could be criticized on purely methodological grounds.

One of the first things Medawar did, when I interviewed him in 1981 to get his opinion on the sociobiology controversy, was indeed to refer to his *New York Review of Books* article, 'Unnatural Science'. For Medawar, this represented a good formulation of exactly what he also objected to in sociobiology. That article, of course, was written in 1977 as a review of two books critical of IQ research and apparently had nothing to do with sociobiology. What united IQ research and sociobiology in Medawar's mind was that for him they were both examples of 'unnatural science'.

What, then, is unnatural science? According to the author, unnatural sciences typically use mathematics or statistical models in order to lend themselves an aura of respectability. Unnatural sciences are such fields as meteorology and earth science— and also IQ testing. There are three features that are typical for practitioners of such fields:

> 1) the belief in measurement and numeration as intrinsically praiseworthy activities, 2) the whole discredited farrago of inductivism, especially the belief that *facts* are prior to ideas and that a sufficiently voluminous compilation of facts can be processed by a calculus of discovery in such a way as to yield general principles and natural-seeming laws; . . .[and] 3) their faith in the efficacy of statistical formulas, particularly when processed by a computer—the use of which is itself interpreted as a mark of scientific manhood (Medawar, 1977a).

According to Medawar, all these beliefs about the characteristics of natural science were quite mistaken.

We see that Medawar had a hardline vision of 'good science' quite similar to the critics of IQ testing and sociobiology. And for Medawar, the problem with sociobiology was just the same as with other unnatural sciences. Indeed, in his later critique of *Genes, Mind and Culture*, 'Stretch Genes' (Medawar, 1981b), he reiterated some of his earlier points, and added some new, rather devastating ones, such as the suggestion that the reader might want to 'hum' through the statistical formulas in the book and get on with the text.

If we now compare some aspects of David Layzer's critique of Jensen with Medawar's putdown of 'unnatural scientists', we see that Layzer's critique appeared simply to spell out Medawar's basic objections more clearly. According to Layzer, Jensen treated systematic errors in a way that 'real' natural scientists do not; he indiscriminately collected the data from all available studies of correlations for mental traits between relatives, threw them into a computer and obtained a general number. But this is not correct procedure, Layzer contended: what would such a number mean? In contrast to this, Layzer approved of 'the careful procedure of Jencks (1971), who in his reanalysis of Jensen's data considered both the type and the quality of the various studies and came up with *ranges* of variation for IQ within different types of family relationships'. (Kamin, 1974, later produced a similar criticism of Jensen, which was hailed by Lewontin, 1976c.)

Thus, from the point of view of Layzer or Medawar, the problem did not primarily have to do with lacking *objectivity* (for instance, obtaining a number with the help of a computer is a quite 'objective' procedure), but with a 'misapprehension of the criteria for scientific inquiry' as such, in both an epistemological and a methodological sense. Layzer, in an exceptionally clear way, spelled out the fundamental difference between the two major scientific camps in the IQ and sociobiology controversies—that is, from a scientific hardliner's point of view.

As we saw, Lewontin, like Medawar, did not single out mental testing as a particularly 'unnatural' science, but regarded this field as having the same difficulties as any other science which used statistics as its main tool. In a charitable mood, Lewontin once even reflected on the problems shared by *all* current science, including IQ research:

> The reification of intelligence by mental testers may be an error, but it is deeply built into
> the atomistic system of Cartesian explanation that characterizes all of our natural science. It
> is not easy, given the analytical mode of science, to replace the clockwork mind with
> something less silly . . . Imprisoned by our Cartesianism, we do not know how to think
> about thinking (Lewontin, 1981c).

We have, then, a basic opposition regarding the nature of science between on the one hand the members of the Sociobiology Study Group, and on the other what Layzer called 'Baconians' and Medawar 'unnatural scientists'—that is, fact-driven and measurement-driven scientists. The differences in these two groups' conceptions of science appeared to exist at many different levels, going all the way from basic epistemological, methodological, and ontological differences, to tacit rules of scientific judgment, to the very attitude to data and numbers.

The foremost opposition here existed between what could be called a causal and a correlational approach, or perhaps 'realism' and 'instrumentalism'. More specific questions involved such things as the very possibility of partitioning IQ into genetic and environmental components. As noted in Chapter 12, Medawar belonged to those who believed that one cannot meaningfully do so. While Wilson appeared to believe that

Medawar's position was a political one, for Medawar, his own view simply reflected a *methodological* conviction 'inherited from Haldane' (Medawar 1974 and 1977a).

Another point of contention in the IQ controversy was the question of whether it was scientifically meaningful to compare the mean IQ scores from two populations, white and black, whose 'environment' in reality could not be said to be the same. Here not only Lewontin (1970) and Layzer (1972), but also, for instance, Maynard Smith (1973) all contended that the existing environmental differences between the black and the white populations could not be simply 'eliminated' by artificial means through calculation, as Jensen seemed to assume, and that therefore the formula he used was incorrect. However, representatives of the other camp, such as Jensen, Herrnstein (1973), and Davis (1986), all argued that the reasoning here merely had to do with the '*likelihood*' that the between-group heritability was greater than zero (cf. Jensen, 1972b, 1973a, note p. 162).

And finally, there was the question of the heritability of IQ as such. Here Maynard Smith, despite his opposition to a comparison between black and white populations, still accepted the heritability of IQ *within* the white population as fairly well-established. Lewontin, too, earlier appeared to have accepted some medium-to-high estimate of heritability (0.4 to 0.8, to go by his attack on Jensen; Lewontin, 1970), but later declared that this was not so.[2] In any case, his new approach was to favorably quote Kamin's (1974) conclusion that there was currently 'insufficient evidence to assign any non-zero heritability to IQ in any population' (Lewontin, 1976d, note p. 87). Layzer (1975), too, in his review of Kamin's book in *Scientific American*, accepted the latter's conclusion that until better studies could be conducted, one could not reject the null-hypothesis that IQ was totally environmentally determined, that is, had *zero* heritability.

Bernard Davis considered such a reasoning totally wrong (Davis, interview). He was rather agitated about this and in fact spontaneously brought it up as a good example of politically influenced reasoning among the critics of IQ. But this was not only Davis' view; it was shared by some methodological critics. For instance, geneticists McGuire and Hirsch (1977) pointed out the untenability of assuming zero heritability. Also, in their own contribution to *The IQ Controversy*, Block and Dworkin took a similar stance. They did not

> agree with Kamin's conclusion that the data are insufficient to lead a prudent man to reject the 'null hypothesis' that H is zero. *The hypothesis that H is zero has no more claim to be regarded as the null hypothesis than the hypothesis that H is any other number.* When data are worthless, one should conclude that no estimate can be made (Block and Dworkin, 1976, note 12, italics added).

This same example shows that we might also characterize the conflict as a dispute about the *tacit rules* accepted by participants in the controversy. Tacit rules deal with such things as what counts as 'sufficient' evidence, or what passes for a 'plausible' argument. These rules typically involve field-specific traditions. As the zero-heritability example shows, these rules may also have to do with such things as the level of scientific certainty desired for moral/political reasons.

Finally, Medawar's choice of the epithet 'unnatural' about a specific group of sciences seemed to suggest that unnatural scientists were actually acting in bad faith. Like many critics of IQ research, Medawar deplored the ease with which data could be compiled as averages of a large number of cases. Meanwhile, there seemed to exist no clear guidelines or critical reflection regarding the criteria for inclusion or exclusion of specific cases. Medawar also ruthlessly criticized the 'unnatural' sciences for attempting to use *numbers as rhetoric*. Unlike the critics of sociobiology, however, Medawar did not seem at all concerned with ontological questions about statistical relationships or the problem of 'reification'. When, in our interview, he disparagingly joked about 'the Marxist boys', he obviously did not have Lewontin or Gould in mind.

The basic difference, then, between the opponents of sociobiology and IQ and critics like Medawar, was that, unlike Medawar, the former *did not confine their criticism to a methodological level*. They regarded their targets' different conception of science as a scientific error, which they attributed to political motives and condemned on moral grounds.

Holism, reductionism, and Marxism

In conjunction with the debates about sociobiology, behavioral genetics, IQ research, and the like; the reductionist–anti-reductionist debate in science has again come to the fore. As a methodological strategy in science in general, reductionism entails that 'systems at one level are analyzed into their component parts and the behavior of these higher level systems are explained in terms of properties, behaviors and arrangements of these parts' (Hull, 1974. p. 4). Traditionally, criticism of reductionism has typically been of an epistemological, methodological, or ontological nature. An example of a formulation that seems to capture all these objections simultaneously is Polanyi's: 'no theory which deals with highly structured entities can be reduced to lower-level theories because these entities cannot be explained by these lower-level theories' (Polanyi, 1968, paraphrased in Hull, 1981b).

For the last three decades or so, the academic world has seen an increasing attack on reductionism also because of its perceived *political* consequences. The interesting thing is that the critics in these debates have given 'reductionism' a partially new meaning: they identified it with *biological determinism* as an ideology (see, for example, Lewontin, Rose, and Kamin, 1984; Lewontin, 1983; Gould, 1978a; Rose, 1982a, b). One formulation is as follows:

> Biological determinism is, then, a reductionist explanation of human life in which the arrows of causality run from genes to humans and from humans to humanity. But that is more than mere explanation: It is politics. For if human social organization, including the inequalities of status, wealth, and power, are a direct consequence of our biologies, then, except for some gigantic program of genetic engineering, no practice can make a significant alteration of social structure or of the position of individuals or groups within it (Lewontin, Rose, and Kamin, 1984, p. 18).

I have already discussed the scientific and political convictions of the critics. They now seemed to come together in this redefinition of 'reductionism'. In practice, 'reduction-ism' became an umbrella term for the critics: it became a convenient universal tool for attacking a variety of scientific targets. At the same time, it set the 'anti-reductionists' own scientific and political agenda.

The main reason for the critics' attack on modelers was that they believed that their own approach was somehow 'truer' scientifically. Obviously, this can hardly be proven by any external adjudication, since the two approaches presuppose fundamentally different conceptions of science. As Maynard Smith pointed out, it is not *obviously* true that a reductionist strategy is wrong. But why did the critics believe that a 'reductionist' approach to science was necessarily incorrect? This was the reason given by Levins and Lewontin:

> The error of reductionism as a general point of view is that it supposes the higher-dimensional object is somehow 'composed' of its lower-dimensional projections, which have ontological primacy and which exist in isolation, the 'natural' parts of which the whole is composed (Levins and Lewontin, 1980, 1985).

Interestingly, Levins and Lewontin seemed convinced that because of this *implied* ontological commitment in modern science, real practicing scientists were also automatically ontological reductionists. But, obviously, commitment to a reductionist *methodology* does not necessarily imply a reductionist *metaphysics*. That is an empirical question. Dawkins observed a similar problem in *Not in Our Genes*:

> Why do Rose *et al.* find it necessary to *reduce* a perfectly sensible belief (that complex wholes should be explained *in terms of* their parts) to an idiotic travesty (that the properties of a complex whole are simply the *sum* of those same properties in the parts)? 'In terms of' covers a multitude of highly sophisticated causal interactions, and mathematical relations of which summation is only the simplest. Reductionism, in the 'sum of the parts' sense is obviously daft, and is nowhere to be found in the writings of real biologists. Reductionism, in the 'in terms of' sense, is, in the words of the Medawars, 'the most successful research stratagem ever devised' (*Aristotle to Zoos*, 1984) (Dawkins, 1985).

It may, indeed, be easier to attack an implicit metaphysical assumption than to give examples of a truly non-reductionist approach in scientific research. When it comes to convincing practicing scientists about the need to abandon reductionism, the problem is that it is hard to find examples of non-reductionist approaches in science that are not, after all, construable as reductionist ones. The best example here is perhaps Levins' and Lewontin's claim in 1976 that they had tried to develop an alternative, non-reductionist approach to science, and that using this approach they were hoping to better capture those interaction phenomena that reductionist methodology was unable to cope with. This is the way they described their efforts: 'As working scientists in the field of evolutionary genetics and ecology, we have been attempting with some success to guide our own research by a conscious application of Marxist philosophy' (Levins and Lewontin, 1976, p. 35).

This statement was brought to my attention by none other than Levins' and

Lewontin's purportedly 'reductionist' colleague, E. O. Wilson, who declared that their claim was 'quite false'. Now, according to Wilson, the example that Levins and Lewontin presented here was nothing else than the theory of community ecology, which emphasizes the community matrix and species interactions. Wilson pointed to another passage in the text where the authors assert that this theory 'derives, in part, from a conscious application of a Marxist world view'. This he dismissed as nothing other than the theory that Levins had developed in his 1968 book *Evolution in Changing Environments*, where he was simply deriving community properties from pairwise interactions in a very standard way. What on earth was Marxist about that, asked Wilson? He was quite agitated at this point. And, Wilson added, if *that* was Marxist, then he was more Marxist than Levins and Lewontin!

This may seem a surprising outburst on Wilson's part, since he has so far emerged in our story as somebody who was opposed to Marxism. But the reality is more complex. What he seemed to dislike about his 'Marxist' opponents was their political and activist side. Meanwhile, he was genuinely interested in the philosophical side of Marxism and even once told me in interview that he read *Science and Nature*, a self-consciously Marxist scientific journal (whose first issue appeared in 1979). How are we to understand this? The answer is Wilson's enormous admiration for Levins as a theorist and as a person.

Wilson made the following comparison between his earlier colleagues and 'fellow-revolutionaries' in shaping the field of evolutionary biology in the early 1960s:

> In retrospect, MacArthur was the genius. Levins was potentially a genius—he did some extraordinary things in the 1960s. Everybody expected him to do great things . . . He was the meteor going through the skies, but then he suddenly snuffed out in the 1970s . . . I have always had the highest respect for him, because I felt that, unlike Lewontin, he was rigorously intellectually honest. You don't get the feeling with Levins of anything like jealousies, rivalries, overarching ambition, territorialities. I think he is a fanatic . . . there is a pure fire burning within him. That is what must have attracted Lewontin to Marxism . . . He [Levins] was extraordinarily original and visionary, but it was very difficult in many ways to make any connections between what he was thinking and the real world.

Thus, at an earlier point Wilson's, Levins', and Lewontin's interests in community ecology were practically identical and they were all attempting to develop models in this field (Wilson, 1971b and Chapter 3 in this book). Wilson admired Levins' (1968) book *Evolution in Changing Environments* and also endorsed it in *Sociobiology*. In fact, he informed me that he had made major efforts to encourage Levins to develop his models, both in 1968 and later, and even gone so far as to try to 'clean up' some problems and launch Levins' models as one of the major approaches of group selection in *Sociobiology* (Wilson, interview). For Wilson, who had been searching for mathematical models that would capture the 'holistic' nature of community ecology as faithfully as possible, it must have appeared strange to give Marxist thinking credit for what he himself perceived as good standard science. But it also became clear from the interview that Wilson was not only indignant about what he thought was a misrepresentation; he was also *disappointed*, since he would really have been interested in seeing a Marxist model of ecology (Wilson, interview).

In my subsequent interview with Levins, I asked him to reply to Wilson's challenge. In what sense was his model Marxist? Levins' answer was rather surprising: 'It is the *intent* that is Marxist!' This example indicates how difficult it is even for the most anti-reductionistically minded to establish a truly non-reductionist science in practice.

It is interesting to note that both Wilson (1975a, p. 7) and Lewontin and Levins (1976, p. 33) were explicitly against 'obscurant holism'. If obscurant holism was out, what was then a better approach for a holist? Wilson chose his 'new holism' inspired by cybernetic theory as a heuristic. His Marxist colleagues, by contrast, believed that the solution rather lay in *making theory more complex* (Levins and Lewontin, 1980).[3] The problem with such a suggestion, however, was that it was not clear how to integrate it with existing scientific practice. For instance, the ecologist Daniel Simberloff pointed out that their suggested approach would only bring with itself new problems, such as the problem of realism, and perhaps even require an abandonment of the criterion of prediction (Simberloff, 1980b).

I also discussed the question of Marxism and reductionism with Maynard Smith. He was the perfect person to turn to, because of his own Marxist background. What was even more valuable from a comparative point of view was that he as a Marxist had adopted a 'total' dialectic materialist view; as he said in interview in 1981, he compared his own scientific approach then to the current one of Richard Levins. According to Maynard Smith, Levins was a 'real Marxist', in the sense of also philosophically being a Marxist. I asked him how he thought that a Marxist philosophy might be implemented in science. The answer was interesting. While he believed that a Marxist in science could take a lot of different positions, he saw the need for 'some kind of substitute for Hegelian dialectics . . . some kind of concept that in dynamical systems there are going to be sudden breaks and thresholds and transformations, and so on'. He added that, in his opinion, 'today we really do have a mathematics for thinking about complex systems and things which undergo transformation from quantity into quality'. Here he saw Hopf bifurcations and catastrophe theory as really nothing other than a change of quantity into quality in a dialectical sense (Maynard Smith, interview).

These were, then, possible candidates for a Marxist science, coming, as it were, 'from the horse's mouth'—at least one of the horses. I could not resist asking Richard Levins later what he thought about Maynard Smith's suggestions. Did we here have an answer to the problem of Marxist science? No, said Levins. He just brushed aside Maynard Smith's ideas as 'reductionist' and 'not typically Marxist' (Levins, interview). Perhaps, then, the dialectical approach is still waiting for its true realization? Meanwhile, this quest for perfection could easily have a paralyzing effect on Marxist scientists.

Reductionism as a definition game, or how the pot could call the kettle black

The time has now come to tackle one particular matter head-on. There was the nagging feeling all along that something was not quite right with the critics' pronouncements about reductionism. How anti-reductionistically minded were the anti-reductionists really? We have dealt with the critics' supposedly Marxist-inspired epistemology. But as we saw earlier, at least Lewontin's Marxist position seemed to be *some kind of extension of a more profound ontological commitment to the molecular level and to 'true' causes*. We have also seen that scientists from such fields as physics, chemistry, and molecular biology could typically be found in the group of vocal critics of sociobiology. But now it is high time to finally ask the question: are not these fields exactly 'reductionist' in the traditional sense? We have seen Lewontin unproblematically identify 'good' science with either 'modern' (reductionist?!) laboratory science or science that does not use models, formulas, or statistics but deals with the 'real' (reductionist?!) molecular level instead. We are faced with the strange circumstance of *reductionist scientists (in the traditional sense) attacking 'reductionism' (in their own newly defined sense)!* Here we see how shifting terminology may allow some critics of 'reductionism', apparently, both to have their cake and to eat it.

Indeed, there was a paradoxical feature particularly in Lewontin's position. While he was ferociously attacking the 'Cartesian program', which he, in turn, linked to 'bourgeois science', his own research interests involved an ever-more detailed understanding of the molecular basis of genetic change—interests which were about as 'reductionist' as it is possible to be. I turned again to Maynard Smith for clarification:

> Q: I have tried to find these things [scientific Marxist approaches] in Lewontin, but he is harder to pinpoint, because he is actually dealing with a kind of reductionistic—
> A: [interrupts] Dick Lewontin is an old-fashioned mechanistic reductionist, who was brought up that way!
> Q: But he would like to be a Marxist.
> A: That's right!
> Q: So what does one do?
> A: Well—when he goes to heaven he can be a Marxist! (laugh) Dick started trying to be a Marxist too late, really, to internalize that way of thinking, I think, and while he has undoubtedly learnt something from Marxism, his classical—I don't know what one calls it—'Western science' kind of approach was so deep in his thinking by the time he was forty, that his thinking is still fundamentally that when he is thinking about science (Maynard Smith, interview).

Maynard Smith was quick to point out, however, that this judgment held only for Lewontin's *scientific* Marxist ambitions, not his political ones. But in the political area, we have also seen that Lewontin's criticism often sounded as if it was motivated rather by individualistic (bourgeois?) moral concerns than a more abstract Marxist analysis.

Incidentally, Maynard Smith's comment is said to have caused a minor ideological identity crisis for Lewontin. In 1986, Maynard Smith's own written assessment of Lewontin's Marxism appeared in a review in *The London Review of Books* (Maynard Smith, 1986a). Thus, the (for academic radicals) scandalous secret was out that, deep down, Lewontin was perhaps not quite a Marxist after all. Lewontin is reputed to have said to close colleagues at Harvard, 'If I am not a Marxist, what am I?', or something along these lines. After a week or so, however, he reportedly snapped back to his usual self and—perhaps to cheer himself up—gave a talk on this subject.

To underscore my point that the critics use 'reductionist' as an epithet in a rather idiosyncratic way, let us once more return to Medawar, our prototypical traditional scientific reductionist. Medawar, like the critics from the Sociobiology Study Group, had little sympathy for either IQ research of the Jensen type, or sociobiological modeling of the Wilson type (the latter was clear from his review of *Genes, Mind and Culture*, Medawar, 1981b). But when I asked him whether he agreed with the critics that sociobiology was reductionist, I got an unexpected answer. For Medawar, the problem with sociobiology was not that it was reductionist—it was that it was *not reductionist enough*! There were no *facts* yet, he told me.

So, obviously, characterizing the critics' approach as an attack on 'reductionism' is really a terrible misnomer, since, as we have seen, the reasoning of supposed anti-reductionists is about as reductionist as one can get in one's attitude to science! How can this contradiction be explained? The clue seems to lie in the redefinition of reductionism to mean biological determinism. This redefinition may have created a seeming paradox in the following way: in the critics' view, those scientists who were researching the biology of human behavior were also automatically biological determinists. Now, in sociobiological and behavioral genetic reasoning, 'behavior' is linked to the existence of hypothetical genes. In turn, these genes are for *heuristic* reasons in models and formulas treated as if they were 'beans in a bag'. The critics now felt free to draw the conclusion that *behind such a reductionist methodology must lie also a reductionist metaphysics*: they believed that they had identified real *ontological reductionists* in the scientists involved with IQ testing, behavioral genetics, and sociobiology. That is why we had the odd situation of the pot seemingly calling the kettle black.

There is, of course, another explanation: 'reductionism' may simply have meant the attempt to reduce sociocultural phenomena to biologically tractable ones. While this interpretation is undoubtedly correct, it cannot be the whole explanation, since it cannot account for those critics who disliked modeling and statistics *as such*, even when these models had nothing to do with humans.

What was, then, the critics' supposed message for 'reductionists'? Obviously, if practicing sociobiologists and researchers in human intelligence took the critics' conception of 'good science' seriously, they might as well give up entirely. (Robert Trivers reflected on this: 'They are just wasting our time!'. Trivers, personal communication.) Of course, in practice, the attacked scientists just seemed to get on with their work. In doing so, they were at the same time following *their* conviction about how scientific progress is actually made.

One could, indeed, characterize the critics' metaphysical interest in science and emphasis on true causes as a sort of *déjà vu* of an earlier period in the history of science. In their book *Leviathan and the Air-Pump* (1985), Shapin and Schaffer gave an account of Hobbes' and Boyle's debate about the 'correct' epistemology for the new science in Restoration England. Hobbes objected to Boyle's experimentalist approach exactly because it did not involve the search for 'true causes'. For Hobbes, it was inconceivable that one could just bracket the question of the nature of air, and limit oneself to its measurement. However, one might argue exactly the opposite: that it was only when scientists *abandoned* the search for ultimate causes, or 'why' questions, and instead concentrated on proximate ones, or 'how' questions, that scientific progress could be made at all (see, for example, Shapere, 1980). Whatever the historical reason (there are many competing accounts), the experimentalists 'won' the epistemological battle, and it is undeniable that scientific progress has been made. And just as Boyle did not need to know the nature of air in order to measure it, so it appears that evolutionary phenomena can be described without knowing details at the molecular level. It is therefore remarkable that the critics would seemingly require fellow scientists to return to the question of underlying causes, a question which was declared scientifically unfruitful centuries ago.

There could, of course, be another explanation. Just as Hobbes' larger moral-cum-scientific agenda was being undermined by the existence of vacuum—Hobbes was a plenist and a Cartesian—so the larger program of the critics, their desire to combine moral/political and scientific truth in their opposition to 'Plato's big lie', was being undermined by re-emerging scientific claims about genetic differences. And just as one might characterize Hobbes' requirement for underlying causes as a type of obstruction strategy, so perhaps might we interpret the critics' unusually strict criteria for 'good science' as an attempt to hold back potentially undesirable results. As we have seen, the critics' criteria for 'good science' did not seem invented for this purpose, but reflected, rather, their deep commitment to a 'molecular' kind of truth.

The exception was Richard Levins, who did indeed come as close to dialectical thinking as it was possible—with the relative handicap it seemed to confer on anyone attempting empirical research. Perhaps Levins perceived some of the irony in the fact that the critics were attacking the holistically oriented Wilson for reductionism. I always wondered what he meant when in one of our discussions about the sociobiology controversy he brushed off a question about reductionism by declaring it a red herring.

The critics seem, indeed, to have been barking up the wrong tree. It can hardly have been 'reductionism' *per se* that was the problem with Wilson's scientific standpoint, since many respected scientists were using reductionist approaches for admirable scientific or moral-cum-scientific causes. Here we have for instance, Maynard Smith's game-theoretical analyses, Cavalli-Sforza and Feldman's attempt to measure the amount of environmental influence on traits (Cavalli-Sforza and Feldman, 1983), and Goldberger's oft-cited statistical demonstration that pellagra was due to a vitamin deficiency, not to 'poverty' (Chase, 1977).

But there is no doubt that Wilson did have some *other*, rather unusual views. Wilson really believed that neurophysiology would give us also the *content* of thought, a belief he shared perhaps with the most avid proponents of artificial intelligence, but not necessarily with most practicing scientists (including his friend Bernard Davis; Davis, 1982, and interview; see also Chapter 8). Around the time of *Genes, Mind and Culture*, Wilson was already putting enormous hope in the development of cognitive science. Others, such as Noam Chomsky, Walter Rosenblieth (interviews in 1981), and Francis

Crick (according to Luria, interview 1982) doubted that this field would live up to the exaggerated expectations.

The other belief that Wilson, but few others, entertained was that we could and should derive moral values from knowledge of evolutionary biology. Although he hesitated on this around the time of *Sociobiology* (Wilson, 1975b), he later reasserted his belief. For instance, in 1982 he said: 'To put the matter as succinctly as possible, I do not think that the is/ought distinction is necessary. I believe that we should work to eliminate it as soon as possible!' (Wilson, 1982.) He also returned to this in his papers co-authored with Michael Ruse (Ruse and Wilson, 1985, 1986). And in his newest book, *Consilience*, Wilson restated his view with full force. I will return to a discussion of the relationship between science and values in Chapter 19.

Why Wilson is not Watson

In his review of Wilson's *Naturalist*, Steven Rose registered the fact that Wilson described Jim Watson as 'the most unpleasant human being I had ever met'. This description referred to an early stage in Wilson's career, when he and the new Nobel laureate were both assistant professors at Harvard, and it seemed that the molecular geneticists, led by young, arrogant Watson, were out to take over the whole world of biology, including Harvard's biology department. According to Rose:

> What is odd about Wilson's commitment to reductionism is the hostility he displays towards those one might expect to be his natural allies: the molecular biologists. Molecular biologists share with Wilson a gene's-eye view of the world; for them, reductionism is not second but first nature . . . Yet, one of the more surprising passages is Wilson's account of the arrival at Harvard in 1956 of James Watson . . . (Rose, 1995).

Rose presents it as self-evident that Wilson is a Watson-type reductionist, while he rather surprisingly describes Watson as someone who takes a gene's-eye view of the world. This does not quite seem to capture Watson, who would presumably be more interested in the *building blocks* of genes. After this, Rose continues on a didactic note, telling the reader (supposedly *contra* his newly construed Wilson/Watson), that 'each level of complexity of living systems requires study in its own terms—nothing is elucidated by collapsing "higher" into "lower"', and that such things as the self-organizing properties of a cell, the beat of a heart, or the dynamic ecosystems of coral reefs cannot 'be explained merely in terms of atoms or genes'.

But why this little lecture? Wilson would obviously agree. The beginning of Wilson's second chapter in *Sociobiology*, 'Elementary Concepts of Sociobiology', started with the statement that 'the higher properties of life are emergent'. He then went on to argue how, from the cell to organisms to societies, higher level phenomena cannot be described solely on knowledge of the properties of their composite components. And in the next paragraph he said: 'In the sections to follow we will examine several of the properties of societies that are emergent and hence deserving of a special language and treatment.'

What Rose has picked up as concrete evidence for Watson-type reductionism in *Naturalist* is a sentence in which Wilson accounts for his early wish to provide a scientific explanation of religion: 'There must be a scientific explanation . . . Religion had to be explained as a material process, from the bottom up, atoms to genes to the human spirit.' Rose comments as follows: 'Reductionism of this sort has characterized his life's work ever since.' I believe that Rose is mistaken here. This quote is not an example of Wilson's purported reductionism, it is rather an example of Wilson's materialism and *inductive approach as a scientist*; as we just saw, he is willing to acknowledge emergent properties. Wilson could probably best be described as some kind of 'cumulativist'. However, this particular statement does reflect another thing: Wilson's rather unusual belief that cognitive science will finally be able to explain also the content of thought and feeling. This Wilson himself acknowledged, was a statement of faith (see Chapter 8).

So why don't we take a closer look at what Wilson himself says about his relationship to Watson? Even if Watson may have acted like the Caligula of biology ('He was given licence to say anything that came to his mind and expect to be taken seriously. And unfortunately he did so, with a casual and brutal offhandedness', Wilson, 1994, p. 219), Wilson acknowledged the tremendous importance of Watson and Crick's discovery and the great inspiration that the solution of the structure of DNA provided for himself and his generation:

> In 1953 Watson and Crick showed that pairing in the double helix exists and is consistent with Mendelian heredity. Soon it was learned that the nucleotide pairs form a code so simple that it can be read off by a child. The implication of these and other revelations rippled into organismic and evolutionary biology, at least among the younger and more entrepreneurial researchers. If heredity can be reduced to a chain of four molecular letters—granted, billions of such letters to describe a whole organism—would it not also be *possible to reduce and accelerate the analysis of ecosystems and complex animal behavior*? I was among the Harvard graduate students most excited by the early advances of molecular biology. Watson was a boy's hero of the natural sciences, the fast young gun who rode into town. I was never able to suppress my admiration for the man. He had pulled off his achievement with courage and panache. He and other molecular biologists conveyed to his generation *a new faith in the reductionist method* of the natural sciences. *A triumph of naturalism*, it was part of the motivation for my own attempt in the 1970s to bring biology into the social sciences through a systematization of the new science of sociobiology (Wilson, 1994, pp. 224–5, italics added).

What we see here is that Wilson was inspired by the obvious triumph of the reductionist method even in such a seemingly complex and intractable field as heredity, and even more so, because of its apparent compatibility with Mendelian notions. For Wilson, therefore, Watson and Crick's feat was not only an achievement in molecular biology, but also demonstrated the *potential compatibility between reductionist analysis and naturalist observation* in general. As we see, Wilson went as far as provocatively calling their discovery 'a triumph of naturalism'!

There is, thus, not a trace here of any purported belief that organisms can be reduced to their genes, or that ecosystems can be reduced to individuals; the emphasis is on *method*. Wilson was interested in capturing and structuring uncharted fields, and wanted to put metaphysical-sounding notions on a solid, workable basis; he wanted to make evolutionary biology tractable. Wilson was a holist, but a practical one: he wanted to do *science*, not philosophy. Incidentally, on this point Wilson made an interesting comparison between himself and his early collaborator in evolutionary biology, Larry Slobodkin, whom he greatly admired, but with whom his collaboration eventually fizzled out. The reason? 'Slobodkin was in fact a *philosopher*. I came to think of him as progressing through a scientific career to a destiny somewhere in the philosophy of science, where he would become a guru, a rabbi, and an interpreter of the scripture of natural history', (Wilson, 1994, p. 235, italics added).

In any case, to a sympathetic reader, Wilson's holistic interests should have been already apparent in 1975, since on p. 7 of *Sociobiology* he said:

> The recognition and study of emergent properties is holism, once a burning subject for philosophical discussion by such scientists as Lloyd Morgan (1922) and W. M. Wheeler (1927), but later, in the 1940's and 1950's *temporarily eclipsed by the triumphant reductionism of molecular biology. The new holism is much more quantitative in nature*, supplanting the unaided intuition of the old theories with mathematical models (Wilson, 1975a, italics added).

Also, from reading Wilson's own description of what he called his 'molecular wars' with Watson, it is clear that he was basically engaged in a fight for the legitimacy of 'classical' biology. He describes how he took the lead in trying to save this field from the onslaught of the molecular biologists, and how in this process the field got its new name: 'evolutionary biology'. We also learn how some of Wilson's own immediate colleagues at different stages of this battle disappointed him by siding with the enemy. George Wald, for instance, declared: 'There is only one biology, and it is molecular biology', while Donald Griffin stated: 'We are all evolutionary biologists, are we not? Doesn't what we learn at every level contribute to the understanding of evolution?' (Wilson, 1994, pp. 222, 228–9.) If Wilson had really been a Watson-type biologist, why all this battle and sense of disappointment with some of his colleagues?

Wilson saw himself primarily as a naturalist, and he could become a militant one. If the molecularists had won the battle of the definition of 'biology' and let evolutionary biology survive at all, he noted, they would surely have turned it into something else, 'working upward from the molecule to the cell to the organism'. But this was something that Wilson was determined would not happen:

> The evolutionary biologists were not to step aside for a group of test-tube jockeys who could not tell a red-eyed vireo from a mole cricket. *It was foolish, we argued, to ignore principles and methodologies distinctive to the organism, population, and ecosystem*, while waiting for a still formless and unproved molecular future (Wilson, 1994, p. 228, italics added).

The problem was that while molecular biology had its double helix, there was no comparable great progress in evolutionary biology, no clear advance that could be upheld to emphasize this field's importance. But it was exactly this lack that now spurred

Wilson to action: 'I wanted a revolution in the ranks of the young evolutionary biologists . . . I felt driven to go beyond the old guard of the Modern Synthesis and help to start something new' (1994, p. 232). He started looking around for like-minded younger biologists, in the hope of better structuring the field. One of them was Larry Slobodkin, who was working on mathematical models in ecology:

> He argued that such complex phenomena as growth, age structure, and competition could be broken apart with minimalist reasoning, leading to experiments devised in the postulational-deductive method of traditional science. He went further: the hypotheses and experimental results could be greatly enriched by explanations from evolution by natural selection. . . . It dawned on me that ecology had never before been incorporated in evolutionary biology . . . He also posed . . . the means by which ecology could be linked to genetics and biogeography. Genetics, I say, because evolution is a change in the heredity of populations . . . Genetic change and interaction determine which species will survive and which will disappear. In order to understand evolution, then, it is necessary to include the dynamics of populations (Wilson, 1994, p. 233).

This indicates Wilson's interest in using the reductionist method to tackle complex phenomena—but again, *his goal was ultimately to broaden the range and explanatory power of evolutionary biology*. Needless to say, 'genetics' here for Wilson is not Watsonian molecular genetics, but *population* genetics, one of the great achievements of the Modern Synthesis; a combination of the principles of Darwinian evolution and Mendelian genetics. It may be that for the molecular-minded, left-wing critics of Wilson, there was only one 'real' genetics. Different conceptions of the 'gene' can account for at least some of the tenacity of the sociobiology controversy.

CHAPTER 15

Capitalizing on controversy

Moral recognition as symbolic capital

In the sociobiology controversy, some thought that the critics of Wilson were wasting their time. Wilson early on declared that '[t]he members of the Science for the People have achieved a limiting chilling effect only at the price of large expenditures of their own time and energy' (Wilson, 1978b). But, I asked Wilson in interview, is it not possible that Lewontin and the other group members, after all, get some kind of scientific recognition for their critical efforts? Wilson didn't think so. According to him, criticism as such is not rewarded in science. And this is something that one often hears from scientists: there is no merit in merely pointing out errors in someone else's research, *unless* you at the same time provide a positive solution yourself (see, for example, Segerstråle, 1993).

As we saw in Chapter 12, Salvador Luria, too, was concerned that the critics' activities had taken a lot of time away from valuable research. With all that investment of time and energy in the scrutiny of Wilson's book, he told me, 'they must be getting something out of it'. For busy scientists, time is a precious commodity and should not be wasted *unless* there is something to be gained. George Wald, a Nobel laureate and left-wing biologist at Harvard, was much more critical than Luria. He saw the sociobiology controversy as a terrible waste of time for scientific activists and seemed very displeased with the Sociobiology Study Group. For Wald, the real issue was the threat of nuclear war (interview, 1981). In this chapter I will now pick up on Luria's hunch. In fact, I will show—*contra* Wilson and Wald—that in the sociobiology controversy the critics were actually not wasting their time, and that they *did* get something for their efforts. That something was moral recognition. In fact, the sociobiology controversy can be regarded as a moral capital-making machine.

So far we have been dealing with different types of scientific and moral/political convictions on both sides in the sociobiology controversy. But the world of science is obviously characterized by fierce competition as well. One way of seeing scientists is to regard them as quasi-economic actors striving to increase their 'symbolic capital'—the recognition they get from their peers for their scientific contributions. According to this kind of reasoning, the time (and risk) that a particular scientist is willing to invest in a particular idea or project always depends on its estimated recognition-capital in the scientific community at the time (Bourdieu, 1975). If we now expand this model to scientific controversies which touch value-sensitive issues, such as nature–nurture debates, an interesting new phenomenon emerges: the regular scientific competition expands into the moral/political realm. And just as scientific recognition is given for scientific contributions, moral recognition is awarded for contributions in the moral/political realm. Scientists involved in nature–nurture controversies soon become interested in accumulating *moral capital*, a new type of symbolic capital, on top of or instead of their regular scientific quest.[1]

The quest for moral credit can help explain some puzzling features in the sociobiology debate. It makes it easier to understand why the critics kept accusing sociobiologists of 'genetic determinism', even though the latter shared with all modern scientists the basic textbook view of gene–environment *interaction*. Indeed, one reason why the critics were so hectically construing Wilson as a racist, sexist, IQ meritocrat—*anything* maximally undesirable—was that this would increase the prize awarded the revealer of such miscreants. No wonder 'the worse the better' seemed to be the motto. (One way to achieve this was to present any plausibility arguments as representing hard, factual claims. This prepared the ground for subsequent 'moral reading'; see Chapter 10.)

Another mystery, too, may be solved: if the critics were so concerned about the 'innocent layman', why did they not from the very beginning make greater efforts to *educate* this innocent layman about the modern interactionist view of genetics? Would this not have helped combat false notions about nature vs nurture still lingering in the mind of the general public (and academia as well)? But no—through their own writings, the critics seemed to only be *perpetuating* the false and outdated gene–environment dichotomy. However, if their aim was not to educate the innocent layman, but rather to collect moral brownie points for unmasking 'genetic determinists', then there was obviously no point in providing updated information and thereby undermining their own chance for profit.

Of course, it is not only the critics of sociobiology that can be analyzed for attempts to collect moral brownie points. Like the critics, the defenders of traditionalist science, such as Davis and Wilson, in principle had vast opportunities to derive moral credit as the controversy evolved. Their audience consisted of that part of the larger scientific and lay community who held traditional beliefs about science (the mainstream 'planters' seen in Chapter 11). Ironically, perhaps, people like Davis and Wilson did not even have to *do* very much: it was enough that they held up the textbook truth of gene–environment interaction against extreme environmentalist claims, or defended academic freedom and objective science against purported 'neo-Lysenkoist' proscription. It is clear that words like 'neo-Lysenkoist' and 'Marxist' (and later, 'postmodernist', or 'anti-science', see Chapter 17) would earn traditionalist scientists easy moral credit from the academic mainstream.

It was also possible for both camps to obtain moral recognition for more abstract arguments about science and its social consequences. As we saw in Chapters 11 and 13, there appeared to be two main standpoints within the scientific community with regard to 'socially dangerous knowledge'. The traditionalists supported freedom of inquiry, arguing that dangers and benefits were not inherent in a scientific product and that benefits would far outweigh dangers. The critics, in turn, considered the moral risks of 'bad science' too grave, and encouraged restriction of research in controversial areas (at least until more reliable methods and data were available): these were typically the contrasting views of planters and weeders, respectively. Fellow scientists, too, depending on their own stance, might be willing to grant moral recognition to either type of defender of the truth: those who fought for the objectivity of science, *or* those who warned about the dangers of 'bad science'.[2] Finally, both camps were appealing to the general public as well. Much of the controversy was, indeed, *public* in nature and conducted and reported on in places such as *The New York Review of Books* and popular media.

Yet another mystery may be explained. As an argument against the other side, each side tended to uphold the *same* textbook orthodoxies: studies of phenylketonuria (PKU), showing how a genetically based disease might be environmentally interfered with; Dobzhansky's 'norm of reaction' argument, according to which genes are differently expressed in different environments (for instance, Japanese-Americans are on average taller than Japanese born in Japan); and the 1972 blood factor studies by Lewontin and others showing the relative smallness of genetic variation between populations (races) compared to the large variation within a population (race). Bateson (1985) pointed out that the authors of *Not in Our Genes*, after lambasting genetic determinism and other evils throughout the book, ended up invoking a surprisingly tame and conventional interactionist model.[3] And in his review of the book, Dawkins (1985) discovered that when Lewontin, Rose, and Kamin presented their supposed alternative to 'genetic determinism'—dialectical biology—they in fact resorted to the very same 'cake' metaphor that he himself had used in 1981! The cake metaphor (which, Dawkins noted, was originally Bateson's) argues that there is no one-to-one mapping between recipe and resulting cake; the whole recipe maps on to the whole cake.

But how could the critics credibly go on criticizing targets who apparently *shared* their scientific views? That was, indeed, a problem and it often forced the critics to somewhat desperate maneuvering. This could be seen not only in their construction of 'genetic determinists', but particularly in their fabrication of 'racists'. Take, for instance, the critics' treatment of Bernard Davis. They systematically 'translated' Davis' statements about *individual* differences into *racist-sounding* statements. Meanwhile, Davis' own emphasis on the role of population genetics for obliterating typological conceptions of race was systematically ignored.[4] The critics appeared to follow a clear strategy. Having first got rid of a *competitor for moral credit* (Davis) by rendering his position morally suspect (making him a racist), the critics were now free to hold up the very *same* argument themselves (that is, populational as against typological thinking) against a group of 'racist geneticists'—one of which they had just helped construct! In this way the critics pulled off the remarkable feat of using textbook science as a source of moral capital.

'Racist', of course, was (and is) one of the strongest stigmata that could be attached to anyone in the US, and those who appeared as exposers of racist beliefs could count on moral credit not only from the academic community but also a large liberal consensus as well. The critics' obvious task, therefore, was to demonstrate that the research they attacked was, indeed, 'racist'. But this was not such a terrible challenge. Because of the social sensitivity of this issue, people could not afford to be very technical about the 'true' definition of racism—even to discuss it would seem racist! No wonder then that academics here tended to err on the side of caution, which in practice meant that almost any allegation was accepted at face value. Thus, as we have seen, the critics over time broadened the definition of 'racist' research to mean research into any group difference, or even research into genetic differences between individuals, without being clearly challenged by anybody.

The fuzziness in definition of racism and the general sensitivity of this issue may have served Lewontin well in his review of *Genes, Mind and Culture*, where he once again attacked Wilson's ever-suspect 'multiplier effect' (see Chapter 8). In his critique, Lewontin did not have to suggest that Wilson was a racist (which he did not believe anyway); by merely vehemently attacking the multiplier effect on *scientific* grounds, he would be able to extract automatic *moral* recognition as well. This was achieved by the *tone* of the critique, which suggested a conspiracy of sorts (Lewontin himself admitted it was a nasty review). So, although Lewontin in private did not think that Lumsden and Wilson were doing anything unusual in trying to patch up their theory, in public, by using a particular tone, he ensured a moral point as well from all those who were deeply suspicious of the effect because of its perceived racist implications.

The quest for moral recognition might, perhaps, explain the perplexing difference between Lewontin's private and public statements concerning Wilson and sociobiology. Lewontin's tone in his public statements about Wilson was in stark contrast with his view in private, where I could find not a trace of a political verdict concerning Wilson. Lewontin in private appeared to see Wilson as mainly pursuing career ambitions. (This corresponds with the view of many biologists who often used the phrase 'Wilson wanted to make a splash'.) At the same time, there was no doubt that Lewontin's own deeply felt convictions about 'good science' had been profoundly challenged.

Also with regard to Dawkins, despite his scathing review of *The Selfish Gene* (see Chapter 13), Lewontin had no political or other objections in private. For him *The Selfish Gene* was a popular book based on a fundamental technical error:

> *The Selfish Gene* is not a book that says anything substantive about science, it is a popular book to popularize a notion that some people have about genes but it is wrong in my opinion, because it misunderstands the meaning of fitness and why the gene is not the unit of selection. Of course, we can talk about evolution as if genes were selfish. It is a metaphor . . . It is a *technical* error, it is not a *moral* error, it is a pure out and out technical error in understanding of genes and organisms and statistics and so on. He has made a common mistake, and that is he believes that if you can calculate something, it is real (Lewontin, interview, 1981).

If we now compare these private statements with, for instance, the 1976 position paper of the Sociobiology Study Group (written by Lewontin), and Lewontin's *Nature* review of Dawkins (Lewontin, 1977a), we may perceive a certain pattern. It appears that Lewontin sometimes simply added a moral or political insinuation to a more fundamental scientific or epistemological critique. Unlike the members of the Sociobiology Study Group, who appeared to almost automatically connect perceived scientific error with moral/political error (see Chapter 10), Lewontin did seem *in principle* capable of occasional 'uncoupling' of scientific and moral/political matters (see, for example, Lewontin, 1976a; Lewontin, 1979a). However, *in practice* this happened extremely rarely, and certainly not when he collaborated with (or wrote for) the Sociobiology Study Group.

Interestingly, *both sides* typically ended up invoking the *same* traditional liberal view of the need for the realization of every individual's fullest potential. But how did the critics often end up sounding so much like their targets? Should the two camps not have been saying quite *different* things, if they were supposedly political opponents?! The reason may be that the critics of Jensen and Wilson were not *radical enough*. They were heirs to American 1960s activism, rather than really 'serious' Marxists or even serious advocates of an alternative society.[5] As already discussed in Chapter 11, the 1960s movement in the US has been characterized as a reaction to social injustice, but as lacking both theoretical analysis and an alternative social vision, and as not having taken the ultimate step—arguing not for the equality of opportunity, but for the equality of *results*. This could explain why the social vision of the different camps in these controversies was essentially the same: a liberal quest for equal opportunity and meritocracy. In other words—paradoxically—the critics and their targets were competing for moral credit for upholding the *same* socially acceptable belief in the American Dream! (Only later, in *Not in Our Genes*, did there appear an explicit statement that some of them wanted a socialist society.)

The battle over 'the issue' in the sociobiology debate

Let us abandon the discussion about moral recognition for a moment and look at another aspect of controversy in science. A scientific controversy is always at the same time a second-order controversy: it is a conflict about the game rules of science as well, about *what counts as 'good science'*. And this has important consequences for a scientist's accumulated recognition capital. The situation has been succinctly depicted as follows (it is one of my favorite formulations):

> The definition of what is at stake in the scientific struggle is thus one of the issues at stake in the scientific struggle, and the dominant are those who manage to impose the definition of science which says that the most accomplished realization of science consists in having, being and doing what they have, are or do (Bourdieu, 1975).

Expanding this idea now to encompass also the moral realm—that is, broadening the meaning of 'good science'—we can see that it was in each side's interest to define the 'issue' under debate in a way that benefitted their own side, so that they themselves would be seen as being correct and the opponents wrong.

Addressing first the matter of 'the issue', it is interesting how different Wilson's and his critics' conceptions were of what was really the issue in the sociobiology controversy. One of Wilson's standard rebuttals of his critics was that they had not addressed 'the issue' (see his and Lumsden's replies to both Medawar's and Lewontin's reviews of *Genes, Mind and Culture*, Lumsden and Wilson, 1981a, b, and Wilson, interview). 'The issue' for Wilson was the *content* of his own specific sociobiological claims, *not* the scientific justifiability of his approach. Wilson was discussing on the basis of *evidence and plausible inferences from evidence*. He had a naturalist's unproblematic outlook on fact-gathering, model-making, and matching models with observations—an inductivist approach. In polemics, he consistently refused to discuss epistemological or methodological questions in the abstract (although he discussed such matters in his own terms in his writings). He even appeared to sometimes consider his critics' insistence on *methodological* discussion politically suspect (see, for instance, Wilson's response to Medawar in Chapter 12; Wilson 1977b).

The critics, on the other hand, saw 'the issue' as having less to do with the *content* than with the *structure* or logic of the argument and with the moral and social implications of presenting tentative (in their view erroneous) findings as serious science—a deductivist form of reasoning. Therefore the critics struggled to keep 'the issue' at this level. In both cases, it was in the contestants' interest to define the discussion as being 'about' the issue which would help them accumulate most symbolic capital, or best protect former investments. But it was also a battle where the final victors would be able to claim credit for all their capital accumulated up to that point and, in retrospect, make the opponents' science seem erroneous and morally reprehensible by the *new* standards for 'correct' scientific and moral belief.

Continuing with the economic metaphor, we are dealing here with the question of protecting investments and accumulated capital. In order to protect their investments in the sociobiology controversy, both camps should be working for a *future* definition of 'good science' which would correspond to the positions they had already taken in this controversy. It was obviously in the strategical interest of both sides to continue presenting their own epistemological, methodological, and moral conceptions of 'good science' as the only acceptable ones. We see that this spread as far as scientific etiquette in the 'Nabi' controversy (see Chapter 9).

For the critics, the long-term struggle would seem to entail making moral recognition, too, a legitimate type of scientific recognition —that is, working for an *expansion of the scientific reward system* to accommodate recognition for criticism of 'bad science'.[6] Needless to say, this was never spelled out, but the critics did act *as if* they had such a goal in mind. Throughout the IQ and sociobiology controversies, they behaved as if there were already a scientific norm in place, according to which scientists must carefully consider the political consequences of their research before being allowed to go public with their scientific findings. They were collectively working for a new taken-for-granted picture of scientific behavior in scientific fields impinging on human values. Had they had their way, it seems that they would have wished for a change in the game rules of science so that 'mere criticism' of another scientist (behavior many scientists, including Wilson, believed was currently not rewarded) would, after all, get peer recognition, in the form of moral recognition. One step in this direction was Gould's explicit attempt to make 'debunking' into a positive science (Gould, 1981a).

This may be the place to question a general belief about scientific controversy. We often hear complaints that opponents in controversies debate strawmen, insist on unrealistic scenarios (for example, Midgley's description of the sociobiology debate as involving 'rival fatalisms'), that they 'talk through each other' (Kuhn's incommensurable paradigms), or miss obvious opportunities to settle issues (for example, Sutherland, 1981, on a debate between Eysenck and Kamin). These are based on the belief that scientists in controversy *wish* to communicate and settle their differences. What has not been observed is that parties in controversy may be literally going out of their way to *avoid* communication. There are good reasons why it may not be in the objective interest of protagonists to ever stop or settle a controversy. I have suggested two. One is the need to continue in order to change the game rules of science, another is the continuous chance for accumulating moral capital that a controversy may offer.[7] Interestingly, unlike science, it seems that when it comes to the moral realm, a contribution does not have to be *new* to receive recognition.

Thus, far from engaging in a futile dispute, or as Lewis Thomas characterized it: 'debating the unknowable' (Thomas, 1981), both parties in the sociobiology controversy may have been interested in keeping the controversy going because of the chances for short-term and long-term profit it offered when it came to symbolic capital. This capital could be both scientific and moral, and for some of the participants it was, indeed, both.[8]

The scientist as optimizer

Prior to this chapter, I have emphasized the major differences in conceptions about 'good science' between the two camps. I have presented the participants in the sociobiology debate as driven by both intellectual and moral commitments. In this chapter, on the other hand, I have depicted the participants as involved in competition for peer recognition, pursuing recognition-capital in both the scientific and moral realms. If both these things are going on, how might one distinguish scientists' *genuine convictions* from their *strategical interests* in increasing their symbolic capital? The answer is that it may not be necessary to do so.

I believe it is most useful to describe scientists is as *optimization strategists*. How does optimization work? For bench scientists, optimization entails working in 'hot' areas, making contributions which can be used by scientists in a large number of fields, or opening up new work opportunities for others. Such optimization strategies were also clearly evident in the sociobiology controversy. Here we have, for instance, Wilson's self-conscious move into a broad sociobiological synthesis, and his 'opportunistic' (his own expression) shift to human sociobiology at a point when there was increasing interest in that field and Lumsden was around to help with mathematical models. The desire to work in a hot area was also evidenced by the general flurry of research triggered by kin selection and other sociobiological models.[9]

Wilson provided yet another example himself. After *Genes, Mind and Culture*, he told me, there was an influx of scientists from other fields into sociobiology, from mathematical model-builders to psychoanalysts. Wilson suggested that the first group was searching for some new material to tinker with, the second for some post-Freudian theory with which to fight the drug-oriented psychiatrists (Wilson, interview in 1981). This type of opportunistic spirit was also alluded to by a Harvard anthropologist, whom I interviewed around this time. We discussed Napoleon Chagnon's much-quoted Yanomamö Indian data and how these had been used in *Genes, Mind and Culture*. According to the anthropologist (who thought the models did not do justice to the Yanomamö), this was a mutually beneficial arrangement: 'Chagnon has a lot of data, but no theory. The sociobiologists have theories but no data. They *need* each other!'

For morally committed scientists, such as those involved in the sociobiology controversy, another type of optimization strategy was evident. As we have seen, these scientists were naturally attracted to *scientific issues of a socially relevant nature*, and in some cases were even self-consciously pursuing moral-cum-scientific agendas. From a strategical perspective, this meant that by following their natural taste, they could obtain recognition in both the scientific and the moral realm for a particular scientific effort.

Scientists, then, may be described *as if* they were following unconscious optimization strategies. But these strategies may not even be unconscious—at least the following statements suggest that optimization strategies may be quite deliberate. Lewontin told me in one of my interviews that he could not fight all the bad science in existence, nor all politically dangerous statements, but that when these two coincided, 'then I strike'.[10] Wilson, in turn, said he considered it *scientifically* profitable to go into areas that were *socially* taboo. As he told an undergraduate class at Harvard (autumn 1980), and later me in interview, 'when you walk on the edge of a volcano, there are few others competing with you, and you have great chances for important discoveries.' Or, as he wrote in 1978, seemingly speaking about sociobiology and himself:

> Can political ideology destroy a field of science in a democratic society? I think not. Where free speech is guaranteed and the laws of libel are upheld, a fair share of adventurous and creative individuals in each generation will always be drawn to subjects considered to be forbidden or dangerous. They are the taboo breakers who enjoy the whiff of grapeshot and the crackle of thin ice (Wilson, 1978b, pp. 282–3).

And this was true for the critics, too. Sociobiology Study Group member Bob Lange told me quite seriously that he regarded it as a smart move *scientifically* to focus on 'obviously' ideologically motivated theories. He said he could be sure to find errors in them, and thus relatively easily write a critical review—that is, secure one more publication! Lange seemed very pleased about this. Indeed, this had been the exact reasoning behind his and Joe Alper's review of *Genes Mind and Culture* in the *Proceedings of the National Academy of Science* (Alper and Lange, 1981), Lange told me, and there they certainly had found plenty of errors.[11]

The other members of the Sociobiology Study Group also appear as clear optimization strategists. We noted how the political activity of these critics was systematically concerned with *scientific* topics, not with general political topics, such as nuclear disarmament, matters of concern to such left-wing scientists as Luria, Wald, and Chomsky, who chose not to participate in the sociobiology debate.[12] In Chapter 11 I linked this to the political heritage from the 1960s, particularly the idea of university activism. I also suggested that the members of the Sociobiology Study Group were attracted to science as a pursuit of truth. Still, it may have been their desire to optimize that oriented the critics toward issues having to do with science, rather than political issues in the real world. As long as they operated within academia, they could kill two birds with one stone: their critical efforts would bring them both scientific and moral recognition at the same time.

We also now have an explanation for why the various criticisms of sociobiology often appeared rather contrived: in order to ensure the best return for their critical investment, it was important for the critics to keep the discussion *closely to their own respective fields of expertise*. We can now understand Chorover's rather tortured attempt to classify sociobiology as part of social control technology in his *From Genesis to Genocide*—such an area falls under psychology, and here he was the expert. Gould, too, in his *The Mismeasure of Man* chose to link a disparate string of 'mismeasurements' to one another, starting with craniology and paleontology, going all the way to IQ testing and sociobiology. As we saw, Davis was furious with Gould for connecting obviously wrong old science to modern IQ research; Wilson was puzzled over the 'odd' inclusion of sociobiology (Wilson, interview); even Lewontin (1981b) thought there was too much about old science in the book. Why, then, was Gould doing all this? I maintain that the seemingly 'unnecessary' moves on Gould's part fall nicely into place if we explain the book as the outcome of an optimization strategy. By including the hot topics of IQ testing and sociobiology and connecting them to earlier craniological attempts, Gould was brilliantly turning his own somewhat dusty scientific specialty, paleontology, into an exciting and relevant field of contemporary academic controversy!

Attributing extreme views to a perceived opponent in order to promote one's own favorite theory is common in science, and so it was in the IQ and sociobiology debates. Here, those who stood to gain the most were scientists who could promote their own scientific theories as both scientifically and morally/politically superior by proving another scientist both scientifically and morally wrong. This was most easily achieved by ascribing scientifically and morally untenable views to suitable opponents, 'revealing' the errors, and then presenting one's own position as the obvious solution.

A mild version of the strawman strategy is exemplified by Wilson, who early on in the debate persisted in his criticism of *tabula rasa* environmentalism. By demonstrating the scientific and political untenability of an extreme environmentalist stance, Wilson was directly or indirectly arguing for the reasonableness of his own sociobiological position. Meanwhile, such a *tabula rasa* position was held by nobody at the time, not even by Skinner himself (Skinner, interview, and Skinner, 1981).

Gould, however, is a stronger case in point. The scientific connection between Gould's persistent anti-adaptationist crusade and his promotion of the theory of punctuated equilibria appears obvious. The more adaptationism could be debunked, the more power would presumably go to punctuated equilibria. But Gould's anti-adaptationism did not only have to do with increasing his symbolic capital in the scientific realm.

Indeed, among the actors in the sociobiology debate Gould is my tentative candidate for the Optimization Award. It is hard to imagine a more efficient way of simultaneously promoting one's moral and scientific interests than by employing the punctuated equilibria theory to criticize adaptation as a scientific approach, while hinting that adaptation implies a morally unacceptable support for the social status quo as the best of all possible worlds. Lewontin's anti-adaptationism, although ferocious, lacked this ultimate self-promoting twist, since Lewontin did not propose an alternative scientific theory.

This chapter has dealt with the competitive element in science. How much attention did the participants themselves pay to scientific competition? In his autobiography, Wilson readily admitted that he was driven by a competitive spirit (Chapter 14). The critics, on the other hand, systematically ignored the fact that they as scientists were automatically engaged in a competitive enterprise. In interviews and writings, I was surprised to find no mention of competition as a fact of scientific life. An exception was Lewontin, who suggested to me that *Wilson* was driven by an overarching ambition!

But the critics could not escape the scientific struggle just by ignoring it. As I have tried to show, for them the struggle was in fact so pervasive that it surreptitiously spread to the moral realm as well. And it was probably just *because* they were unaware of the objective conditions for their own activity (the scientific quest for recognition) that the critics did not guard themselves against the temptation of easy profit. Instead of using the criticism of sociobiology to illustrate what they believed to be dangers of biological reasoning in general, they attacked *individual* villains in science for purported crimes. In other words, the quest for credit often came to undermine their larger critical ambition: to enlighten the innocent layman and to demonstrate the inherent link between science and values.

PART THREE

The cultural meaning of the battle for science

CHAPTER 16

The sociobiologists and their enemies: taking stock after 25 years

The rise of the evolutionary paradigm

In the academic climate of the 1970s and early 1980s, it was clearly still too soon for biologists to speculate about human nature without triggering an avalanche of counter-literature from fellow academics. The climate of opinion was so strongly pro-'culturalist' (a better term today than 'pro-environmentalist') that it was simply not possible for Wilson to 'counter-define' his political critics' interpretation of *Sociobiology* and convince people that this book was not meant as a political contribution. Wilson was simply outdefined by the critics.

Toward the end of the 1980s, a notable climate change was already apparent, effected by both scientific and sociohistorical developments. The post-Second World War taboo on biological explanation of human behavior appeared to be broken. New developments in many fields indicated accumulating evidence for the importance of biological factors. But perhaps most importantly, the development of biotechnology and particularly the enormous Human Genome Project had made genetics into a household word. Scientific journals and popular magazines alike soon started reporting a gene 'for' now this, now that behavior, including such things as a gene for 'thrill seeking'. 'Genetics' and 'behavior' were no longer seen as incompatible when it came to humans.

At the same time, there was a relative weakening in the cultural resistance to implicating biological constraints in the explanation of human behavior. Anthropology had earlier provided evidence for a tremendous diversity among human cultures, but recent analysis now questioned some of the earlier results and focused on human universals instead (Brown, 1991; Barkow *et al.*, 1992). And, of course, there were some highly visible challenges to a totally culturalist type of explanation of human behavior, most conspicuously Derek Freeman's attacks on Margaret Mead's studies of life in Samoa (Mead, 1928; Freeman, 1983, 1998). At least for the time being, the long-term struggle between culturalists and universalists when it came to behavioral patterns seemed to have been resolved in favor of the universalist position.

And recently even language—the major cultural stronghold of the opposition to sociobiology—has been rocked on its pedestal. A long-defended citadel is being besieged: Chomsky's conception of language as innate and the product of a unique process in human evolution has been re-examined as an adaptive feature instead (Pinker, 1994). Other developments, too, are currently serving to question the idea of a unique human capability for language. New research presents animals as much more sophisticated than before, more 'similar to us'. Here we have such things as research on animal proto-language (for example, Cheney and Seyfarth, 1990; Evans and Marler, 1997), and popular books and films on chimp language, a field where research has resumed after the controversies in the 1970s and early 1980s (Savage-Rumbaugh *et al.*, 1993; Lewin and Savage-Rumbaugh, 1994).

Still another front has opened up against those who emphasize language as the linchpin of humanity. Nonverbal communication and emotions are gaining increasing force in the investigation of human behavior—we are seen more as feeling and empathizing organisms than as rational calculating machines. In fact, nonverbal communication can be regarded as a fundamental link between nature and nurture (Segerstråle and Molnar, 1997).

Animal analogies, too, are becoming popular once again. Unlike the popular ethological books of the 1960s, which created so much uproar among the academic liberal-left, what is now emphasized is not our aggressive nature or our origin as hunters. Now we are *moral* animals instead! An indicator of the intense public interest in animal stories of this kind is the fact that Robert Wright's *The Moral Animal* (1994) was on *The New York Times*' bestseller list for two years. Frans De Waal's *Good-Natured* (1996) was also well received. If animals are nice rather than nasty, it obviously makes the comparison between us and them more comfortable.

And it is not only scientific developments that have helped strengthen the argument from biology. Certain historic events, too, may have served to undermine the critics' position. Since 1989 the Marxist position of some of the leading critics may have become more politically vulnerable—even though Marxism is still alive and well on university campuses—and this could be exploited by those who had used 'Marxist' as a convenient label to discredit the opponents of sociobiology. A worse blow for the critics, however, may have been the 1980s' unexpected shift of interest among the academic left away from those issues that the critics of sociobiology held dear: questions about good and bad science, science and ideology, and truth. The new 'cultural left' in academia, uninterested in such traditional left-wing concerns, instead focused their energy on postmodernist theory and 'standpoint' epistemologies. Indeed, in the light of a younger generation's new postmodern concerns, the radical critics of sociobiology were now at risk of being dismissed as old-fashioned defenders of the truth! (I will return to this in Chapter 17.)

Thus, during the last three decades or so the idea of a biological foundation for human behavior has become more acceptable on both scientific and intellectual grounds. At the same time, the social and political climate is quite in tune with this overall rise of the acceptability of biological explanation. Politically, the ideas of the Great Society and Affirmative Action are being slowly dismantled. In 1994, the timely and well-managed publication of Richard Herrnstein and Charles Murray's *The Bell*

Curve argued for a strong correlation between cognitive ability and social success, both for the elite and the socially disadvantaged. For many, this book did indeed vividly demonstrate the use of biological claims for legitimizing a social state of affairs—just what the critics had (unfairly) accused Wilson of twenty years earlier. And, as might be expected, that 800-page tome met political opposition in academia similar to that of *Sociobiology*, and involved some of the same critics (see, for example, Fraser, 1995; for professional social science criticism, see Fischer *et al.*, 1996).

While, in the United States at least, *The Bell Curve* seemed to indicate that biological explanations were considered as useful as ever in political life, there was another development: an upswing in religious fundamentalism. This put the critics of socio-biology in an interesting dilemma. On the one hand, evolutionary explanation was badly needed in the intellectual fight against creationism; on the other hand, the critics would not wish the biological nature of *humans* to be emphasized in this way—or at least not in the 'wrong' way. It may be this tension that has informed some of the typically 'American' developments in evolutionary theory (I will return to this in Chapters 19 and 20).

Wilson's evolution in a changing environment

By the end of the 1980s, Wilson had seemingly transformed himself from Wilson I, the politically incorrect sociobiologist, to Wilson II, the politically correct environmentalist. How did this happen?

After *Genes, Mind and Culture* and *Promethean Fire*, Wilson wanted to go back to the rainforest, the place where he felt himself to be happiest (as he revealed in interview at the time). And that was exactly what he did. His next book, *Biophilia*, published in 1984, can be seen as a transition into the next stage of his exploration of life on Earth. The book dealt with a particular postulated 'epigenetic rule'—that of biophilia, our love of nature. At the same time, the book emphasized the human need for nature, and therefore, the need to preserve it.

The decision to focus on the protection of the environment and the defense of the world's biodiversity was deliberate on Wilson's part. According to a friend who spent some time at Harvard during a sabbatical at this time, Wilson did not really want to get involved in a political crusade of this kind, but he felt that it had to be done. And, we may observe, when Wilson sets his mind to something, he does it well. There is no doubt that Wilson's writings had a major impact on people's perception of the need to sustain the word's biodiversity. The book that followed, *The Diversity of Life* (1992), beautifully argued for the importance of saving the species-rich rainforest, and was enthusiastically quoted among others by the Sierra Club's magazine.

The model Wilson used to demonstrate the rate of destruction was the one he had used in his earlier island biogeography (Oster and Wilson, 1978). He wanted to point to the interrelation between all the different ecosystems and how the destruction of even a limited area had unforeseen repercussions for a much wider area. Considering the number of insects (particularly ants) populating the rainforest, it was not hard to point to a hair-raising number of species becoming extinct every day. In a special issue of *Science* devoted to biodiversity, Wilson estimated that one quarter of the now extant 100 million species could be eliminated within 50 years (Ehrlich and Wilson, 1991).

Still, not everybody agreed with Wilson's application of his island biogeography model to the rainforest. A minority of scientific critics suggested that deforestation and extinction were entirely different things; for the model to apply, certain assumptions had to be made about the rate of habitat loss, the species–area curve, and the absolute number of species—all wide open to question (Mann, 1991). They accused people like Wilson and Ehrlich of 'bio-dogma' and asked for better data about extinction rates. But these things could not easily be stated publicly. One prominent conservationist, demanding anonymity, noted that 'they'll kill me for saying this' and another reported that he 'almost got eaten alive' when he pointed out at the National Forum on Biodiversity in 1986 that cut virgin tropical forest actually turns into secondary forest, not wasteland (wasteland was the equivalent of water in the biogeography model). In response to criticisms, Wilson agreed that of course more data were needed but added that the imminence of the extinction of species—above all in tropical forests—was 'absolutely undeniable' (Mann, 1991).

In general, though, Wilson's work was very well received. Wilson had seemingly completely reinvented himself. So in the 1990s, a new generation of university students and environmental activists were learning about Wilson II, the 'good' environmentalist, rather than Wilson I, the 'bad' sociobiologist. Moreover, Wilson's new focus on the future of life on Earth as a whole may even have made his critics' human concerns seem limited, even 'speciesist'. Why worry about politics when the fate of the world was at stake?

What did all this mean? By turning into a defender of the environment, had Wilson now finally 'repented' and changed course, going from a genetically focused sociobiology to a seemingly opposite concern for the external environment? Had he now abandoned genes for nature? Not at all! Rather, by emphasizing our need for nature and the interdependence of all ecosystems, Wilson had created the emotional and intellectual platform from which it now seemed logical and legitimate to argue for the existence of an evolutionarily adapted human nature. What Wilson had been doing during all his years of seeming exile in the rainforest was quietly bringing sociobiology back in—through the side door of environmental concerns.

But there was another development as well. In the mid-1990s, Wilson joined the league of pro-science activists—scientists like Gross and Levitt (1994)—who were speaking up for science and truth against postmodernist and constructivist 'anti-science' in the so-called Science Wars (see Chapter 17). In fact, in his autobiography Wilson attempted to interpret the criticism of sociobiology, too, as an early manifestation of postmodernism. In the ever-present quest for academic recognition, Wilson was asking the larger academic community for nothing less than retroactive moral credit for the sociobiology controversy (see Chapter 15)! And Wilson kept changing the game. An even later move was his book *Consilience, The Unity of Knowledge* (1998a). This book was a quest for the ultimate synthesis, but also a timely response to the seeming divide between the Two Cultures (see Chapter 18).

Moral victors in the sociobiology debate

A quarter of a century after the beginning of the sociobiology controversy, we might ask: who won the sociobiology debate, the sociobiologists or their critics? In regard to the early political allegations against sociobiology, the question can be answered. It is becoming increasingly difficult to uphold the original political interpretation—the 'sandwich' model of *Sociobiology*, in which 25 animal chapters were simply regarded as the filling between two all-important human chapters—which now appears plain wrong. It is becoming clear that Wilson's motives, though complex, were certainly not 'political', at least not in the way attributed to him in an early phase of the conflict. (A different question is the extent to which evolutionary biologists ought to be held responsible for the popular interpretation of their theories; I will return to this in Chapter 19.) Thus, the critics were wrong about Wilson, and in this moral respect, Wilson emerges as a winner.

Indeed, one way of looking at the sociobiology controversy is to see it as a twenty-odd-year-long morality play with an interesting twist. Wilson, the villain in the first act, here seen as a supporter of conservative political interests, becomes the hero in the last act, now seen as saving the world. Meanwhile, Lewontin, the hero in the first act, here seen as leading the chase and brilliantly unmasking the villain's evil schemes, in the last act appears as a mere nay-sayer in the wings, asserting that biology is ideology and that various biological projects won't work. Contributing to this is a shift in the academic climate and a turnover of generations. Meanwhile, Wilson's agenda remains largely the same.

Again, if we are to look for a moral winner of the transatlantic version of the socio-biology debate, that is Richard Dawkins, without a doubt. Receiving such a hostile review by Lewontin in *Nature* that Hamilton was moved to write a letter of protest, and threatened with a lawsuit by Steven Rose for his review of *Not in Our Genes*, Dawkins has come a long way, indeed. Not only has he continued writing books explaining the theory of evolution, but recently an endowed chair at Oxford was created for him. Since 1995, he has been the Charles Simonyi Professor for the Public Understanding of Science. Dawkins sees his role as trying to explain science as clearly as possible to the layman. In this spirit, he has produced new popular books, such as *River Out of Eden* (1995a), *Climbing Mount Improbable* (1996), and *Unweaving the Rainbow* (1998a). The criticism of Dawkins simply did not work. Dawkins was just as difficult to stop as Wilson.

I have looked here at Wilson and Dawkins as *moral* victors in the sense that the critics were simply wrong about their motives, and that their fame and popularity have only increased. In Wilson's case his new project of saving the Earth from extinction appears 'politically correct'. Note that I am not here discussing the status of their *scientific* claims. This I will leave for later in the chapter.

Still, it may be a hasty conclusion to say that the sociobiology controversy in a moral/political sense is 'over'. In principle, at least, there are indeed comeback possibilities for the anti-sociobiologists. To 'win' a controversy might mean simply to be able to mobilize the general opinion in one's own favor, while casting unfavorable light on one's opponent. The important point is that your side should be seen as being with the angels. Whether this is possible or not at a particular time may largely depend on the prevailing intellectual and sociohistorical climate. It is clear that the critics of sociobiology (and IQ research) capitalized heavily on the post-war taboo on biological explanation, just as the present proponents of biological factors in human behavior may be buoyed by the current larger receptivity to biological explanation.

How would this translate into general strategies for winning and losing? For the critics, it might mean, for instance, sticking to their larger story of genetic determinism, keeping sociobiology as part of that story, and using whatever new academic disputes may come along to combat the purported message of genetic determinism (or some even more inclusive term). Indeed, this is exactly what Gould has done in the expanded edition of *The Mismeasure of Man* (1996a), which now contains also his fierce criticism of the *The Bell Curve*. What should sociobiologists do? Of course, they can continue defending themselves and patiently demonstrate that their critics are wrong (Dawkins' and Maynard Smith's early strategies). Or, they might make a frontal attack on the critics, as Dawkins, Maynard Smith, Wilson, and others have done more recently. (In Chapter 19, I will explore other possibilities for both sides.)

But moral victory in the sociobiology controversy is a funny thing, because victory for one person does not necessarily mean defeat for another. Rather, it seems that almost everybody wins and gets prizes! Thus, it is certainly not possible to claim, for instance, that Wilson or Dawkins, for all their current popularity, have 'won' over Gould, because Gould remains as popular as ever, expanding his original agenda. Obviously there is an enormous audience out there for popular books about evolutionary biology, and several different 'messages' are simultaneously appreciated. Indeed, perhaps the real victor of the sociobiology controversy is evolutionary biology itself.

What has Gould been up to? Gould has been operating on two fronts. He has continued his columns in the *American Naturalist*, turning them into a stream of popular paperbacks. In fact, Gould told an interviewer that he receives so many invitations to speak that he has had to develop a polite form letter to decline invitations (Shermer, 1996a). Like Wilson, Gould also often appears on American Public Television. Here Wilson is the icon for saving the rainforest, while Gould is usually fighting creationism —when he is not questioning the millennium. Gould has been busy promoting a series of theories: (different versions of) punctuated equilibria, the idea of 'exaptation' (Gould and Vrba, 1982), the idea of contingency in evolution (for example, Gould, 1987, 1989), and the emphasis on bacteria as the most important species in biodiversity (for example, Gould, 1996b). For the last few years he has been working on a major history of evolutionary theory which will present alternative explanations to Darwinism (see Shermer, 1996b). And in 1999, he became the president of the American Association for the Advancement of Science.

In the meantime, Gould has become ever more popular among humanists and social scientists, and also among anti-adaptationist biologists (for example, in France; Pierre Jaisson, personal communication). I was told that Gould is immensely popular in

England, too, by, as it so happened, the curator of Darwin's Down House, Dr. Solene Morris.

What happened to Lewontin, Wilson's original nemesis? Lewontin has continued his general critical agenda, for instance in *Science as Ideology* (1991) and critical articles on such things as the Human Genome Project, DNA fingerprinting, and sex research. His popular lectures on biological determinism have been largely directed to humanists. For instance, in the spring of 1993 he gave a seminar at the University of Michigan, which Richard Alexander described as 'nineteenth-century biology' (personal communication), and in 1996 he participated in a panel about racism at the American Historical Association's annual meeting in Atlanta. He wrote the Preface to Richard Lerner's *Final Solutions* (1992), a book which (I am sorry to say, because of its moving Introduction and the sympathy the author induces), misrepresents and misquotes Wilson and Dawkins, seemingly in order to fit them into a larger, nasty, biological–determinist framework. Lewontin has also produced the slim trade book *Human Diversity* (1996), and a book written with Michel Schiff from CNRS on educational testing, *Education and Class: The Irrelevance of IQ Studies* (1986).

Wilson appears to have concluded that Lewontin's scientific productivity had slackened off. Some years ago Wilson commented on Lewontin's performance in an informal group discussion after a public lecture: 'What has he *done* recently?!' (Wilson himself at that point had just published his autobiography and was onto a new grand project, which turned out to be *Consilience*.) From Wilson's tone, it was clear that he thought Lewontin was totally wasting his time. I mentioned this to Maynard Smith, who saw the situation quite differently:

> When there is someone who has an interesting idea in evolutionary biology, you can almost be sure that that person has been through Lewontin's lab. *That* is what he has done all these years—he has been educating students! (Maynard Smith, interview, 1998)

Maynard Smith shifted the question of Lewontin's scientific activity to one regarding his overall scientific impact instead. And, indeed, how should we count impact in science? Is it to be measured as the number of publications and books, the actual influence on the thinking of other scientists, as the establishment of an intellectual lineage through the training of students, or how? Wilson himself, for instance, has had few direct graduate disciples in sociobiology; it is, rather, Richard Alexander who has been training graduate students. So, 'what has he done?' is actually a rather complex question, with no obvious answer.

These were some preliminary notes on the protagonists. We will soon look at the various scientific issues that continue dividing the sociobiologists and their enemies. First, however, I want to examine the situation of Wilsonian sociobiology.

Wilsonian sociobiology—an assessment

Taking stock of the situation in 1989, Lionel Tiger and Michael Robinson declared that '[a]ggression, instinct and sociobiology have passed to the *passé* as far as current fashions in science go' (Tiger and Robinson, 1991, p. xxi). What had at this point entered center stage in biological thinking instead was 'at last, biology itself'. They saw a shift toward 'such stimulating issues' as the problems raised by Dawkins in *The Selfish Gene* and *The Blind Watchmaker*. At the same time, in their view, the idea about punctuated equilibria 'takes theory back to James Hutton and uniformitarianism' (Tiger and Robinson, 1991, p. xxi). This may be seen as a relatively authoritative assessment, coming from the editors of the book from the 1989 Washington conference Man and Beast Revisited, and from other people who had been closely following the developments over the last two decades.

Sociobiology *passé*? Had they not listened to Wilson's own presentation at the same conference, where he stated that sociobiology was making strong progress: five journals had been launched since the original Man and Beast conference in 1969, and research and teaching in the field had spread on an international basis, including socialist countries (Wilson, 1991a)?

Indeed, a look into one of the many existing databases—it happened to be the combined Wilson Index (no connection to E. O.)—brought up over 13 000 entries under 'sociobiology'. A closer examination showed that 'sociobiology' covered an extremely broad range of efforts to link social—often human—behavior to evolutionary theory, spanning a number of academic fields. There is no doubt that 'sociobiology' has become established as a name. (Dawkins might say that 'sociobiology' turned out to be a good meme.) And Wilson might indeed wish to regard all these as his intellectual offspring. However, what was the contribution of Wilsonian sociobiology to the empirical study of social behavior?

Wilson modestly presented himself as a synthesizer of recent theories and empirical findings; he wanted *Sociobiology* to be an 'encyclopaedia' (Wilson, 1994). And there are those who see the book as just that, a collection of information—although awesome in scope—and who believe that the credit, strictly speaking, should go to the original theorists of 'sociobiological' thinking, such as Hamilton, Trivers, and Maynard Smith and Price. According to them, 'Wilson did not do anything new'. But these people perhaps fail to recognize the particular *kind* of contribution Wilson made: he created a field by demonstrating to its potential members that it existed—partially by co-opting them as contributors to his project!

In 1985 John Krebs assessed the impact of Wilson's *Sociobiology*. According to him, although the book 'was by no means the start of sociobiology and behavioural ecology' (two names which Krebs, interestingly, regarded as interchangeable), the book was important for three reasons: 'It was published at just the right moment, coinciding with, and acting as a focus for, the surge of interest in the subject; it defined in a thorough way the range of possible contents of the discipline and it gave a name to a field of study that had not before seen itself as a single, unified enterprise' (Krebs, 1985). Mayr (1991) also described Wilson as creating a field and giving it a name.

These are no mean contributions, and it seems to me that this is what Wilson himself primarily was striving for. The philosopher of biology David Hull has suggested that the growth of science often depends on the existence of specific individuals and books which can become the foci of new fields. The scientists themselves do not have to be great scientists, and the books do not have to be great books, but there needs to be *some* man and *some* book (Hull, 1980). Hull's own example is Schrödinger's slim book *What Is Life*, functioning as a sort of reference point for the physicists creating the field of molecular biology.

While this observation may be particularly true when it comes to the question of the coalescence of a field vs a field not coming together at all, it can only help the case if 'the book' is of an encyclopaedic nature *and* well written, and if 'the man' is an eminent scientist at a top institution! And might it not help further if the promoter of the new field is an unbeatable enthusiast, and sees himself as a visionary and revolutionary, who 'enjoys the whiff of grapeshot and the crackle of thin ice' (Wilson, 1978b)?

Still, sociobiology was not only the broader discipline; Wilson also developed a particular brand of sociobiology, or actually two: one involving gene frequencies and population parameters, sketched in *Sociobiology*, and the other developed in *Genes, Mind and Culture*. How did these fare?

In 1989, at the Man and Beast Revisited conference, Wilson told his audience that the political conflict about sociobiology had now faded. The controversy was now largely over the relevance of evolutionary biology to the social sciences, he said:

> Does culture really have a biological basis in any sense that can be expressed in the language of present-day biology? Incest avoidance and color vocabularies can be explained in part with existing biological models, but is the same possible for ten-year economic cycles and military coups? In my opinion one of the great unsolved problems of science is the relation between biological and cultural evolution or gene–culture coevolution (Wilson, 1991a).

It is clear from this that, for Wilson, 'sociobiology' was no longer the earlier type of sociobiology, the direct influence of genes on behavioral traits, but rather the newer type explicated in *Genes, Mind and Culture*. For Wilson, the situation had been brought back to what he so boldly sketched in the first chapter of *Sociobiology*: a dispute between biology and the social sciences. (It was this conflict that he would later try to resolve in *Consilience*.)

Thus, Wilson clearly believed that the idea of gene–culture co-evolution was a key achievement. In 1994 he reflected on the fact that *Genes, Mind and Culture* had not been as well-received as he had hoped. He referred to the unfavorable reviews the book had received in 'key journals' (Wilson mentioned Leach in *Nature*, Medawar in *The New York Review of Books*, and Lewontin in *The Sciences*) and continued:

> The subject of gene–culture coevolution simply languished, mostly ignored by biologists and social scientists alike. I was worried, and puzzled. *The critics really hadn't said much of substance*. Had we nevertheless failed at some deep level they saw but we failed to grasp? (Wilson, 1994, p. 353, italics added.)

Well, they *had*—at least Maynard Smith and Warren (1982) had, in their review in *Evolution*, arguably the most 'key' of key journals. No doubt Wilson was right about the apparently cavalier reviews by Leach, Medawar, and Lewontin, but Maynard Smith and Warren had painstakingly examined the very core assumptions of the mathematical models, and found them to be rather dubious (see Chapter 10). Of course, Maynard Smith and Warren's negative verdict may not have been the actual reason for what Wilson described as a lack of enthusiasm about gene–culture co-evolution. Wilson noted that others, too, who had tackled the link betweeen genes and culture in their own ways, such as Kenichi Aoki, Robert Boyd, Luigi Cavalli-Sforza, William Durham, Marcus Feldman, Motoo Kimura, and Peter Richerson, had 'met with only limited success, at least as measured by the spread and advance of the total theoretical enterprise' (Wilson, 1994, p. 353). Perhaps one reason was simply the complexity of the endeavor and the relative intractability of the field, or at least lack of promise for quick empirical prospecting?

The harshest critic of sociobiology was surely the philosopher Philip Kitcher in his 1985 book *Vaulting Ambition*. There he distinguished between 'pop' sociobiology (Wilsonian) and other sociobiology (presumably 'serious'). He likened Wilson's sociobiology to a ladder 'rotten at every rung'. In fact, as some observers noted, Kitcher's verdict on sociobiology in general, even 'serious' sociobiology, was so harsh that very few studies would have passed muster at all. 'This is strong stuff!', said none other than seasoned Science for the People leader Jon Beckwith in his own review of Kitcher's book (Beckwith, 1987).

The philosopher Alexander Rosenberg, in contrast, thought that Kitcher's criticism was exaggerated and something of an overkill. He emphasized the importance of new, stimulating ideas in science and the point that scientists do not have to be *right* for their ideas to be important (Rosenberg, 1987). Still, some sociobiologists recognized that some of Kitcher's criticisms of 'serious' sociobiology were to the point and took notice. Maynard Smith—ever the critical analyst—characterized Kitcher's book as 'admirable' (Maynard Smith, 1985b). Indeed, *Vaulting Ambition* is a treasure trove for all conceivable kinds of criticisms of sociobiology, and as such may have significantly contributed to strengthening the sociobiological enterprise.

Still, others wondered if Kitcher's critique had been affected by the fact that he was under Lewontin's influence when he wrote it, having temporarily relocated to Harvard. They spotted a kind of sneering attitude in the book—or was it a sneering-plus-political attitude? What surprised some was particularly Kitcher's seeming non-sequitur introduction, where he made an explicit connection between IQ testing and sociobiology and even brought in his young British cousin who a long time ago had failed an 11+ test originally designed by the posthumously notorious Cyril Burt. It turns out that Kitcher had particular moral/political reasons for making this connection; he was concerned about the social consequences of insufficiently established scientific claims—in other words, he did share the concerns of the critics of sociobiology as I have characterized them.

Coming to terms with human sociobiology

'Onward sociobiology!', said the militant-looking ant in Wilson's Harvard office around the time of the publication of *Genes, Mind and Culture*. And there is no doubt that sociobiology has marched on. Wilson had been one of the pioneers in storming the culturalist bulwark. But as he moved on to the new challenges of protecting the world's biodiversity, an opportunity opened up for the next wave of biological explanation of human behavior: evolutionary psychology. This was a field promoted particularly by younger scientists such as Harvard-trained anthropologist John Tooby and psychologist Leda Cosmides. These, in turn, joined forces with older biologically oriented anthropologists, many of whom had been attacked during the critical heydays of the 1970s, such as Lionel Tiger and Robin Fox, Napoleon Chagnon, Bill Irons, and Donald Symons, who brought Tooby and Cosmides to Santa Barbara and helped found the Center for Research in Evolutionary Psychology. (Irven DeVore, meanwhile, was the ever-supportive godfather in the background.)

Evolutionary psychology tried to actively distance itself from sociobiology. Its proponents emphasized that this new field explicitly dealt with universal features of the human *mind*, evolved to solve problems in the Environment of Evolutionary Adaptation (EEA). The programmatic book of this new field was *The Adapted Mind* (Barkow, Cosmides, and Tooby, 1992), particularly its manifesto-like Chapter 1.

With its emphasis on the human mind, evolutionary psychology appeared to be more palatable than the earlier sociobiological discussions about genes and behavior. Now it was evolutionary psychology's turn to make the cover of *Time* magazine (28 August 1995), just as sociobiology had in 1977. A stream of popular books in this new genre followed, such as David Buss' *The Evolution of Desire* (1994), William Allman's *The Stone Age Present* (1995), and Robert Wright's *The Moral Animal* (1994).

For many, it may have seemed as though evolutionary biology was a truly alternative paradigm to sociobiological explanation, with the latter's relentless focus on genes. Wilson, however, from the very beginning insisted that evolutionary psychology was the *same* as human sociobiology. This was, for instance, his position at the founding meeting of the Human Behavior and Evolution Society in Evanston, 1989. He was, in fact, rather incensed that the society did not call itself the Society for Human Sociobiology—its *obvious* name, according to him (personal communication). Wilson simply refused to consider the point that 'sociobiology' was still not a politically wise name to use in 1989, something that was eminently obvious to the founders of this society (personal communication). And, ever since, Wilson has maintained, in writing and informal discussion, that evolutionary psychology is the *same* thing as sociobiology (for example, Wilson, 1998b; Miele, 1998). Wilson had his own explanation as to why evolutionary psychologists insisted on keeping their field separate from sociobiology: they did it for professional reasons. The reason was simply that they needed to get their academic credit *within* their own field of psychology (Miele, 1998)!

Now, what Wilson meant when he said that evolutionary psychology was 'the same' as sociobiology was probably not his position in *Sociobiology* (Sociobiology I) but rather his revised view in *Genes, Mind and Culture* (Sociobiology II). In the latter book the epigenetic rules figured prominently, and these epigenetic rules were indeed described as rules that guided the development of mind: the focus of evolutionary psychology. Another explanation is that, from the standpoint of Wilson's all-encompassing view of sociobiology, *any* attempt to describe human behavior as subjected to biological constraints at all—be it directly through genes and development, or taking the route through the mind—would be part of the 'same' genre.

However, two things can be said in defense of the evolutionary psychologists' position that their field is a different one. First, Wilson may have later changed his mind, but 'sociobiology' had already acquired its connotations early in the controversy and become firmly associated with the idea of gene-driven behavior. Therefore, his and Lumsden's later idea of intervening epigenetic rules is not *typically* regarded as being at the core of the sociobiological enterprise; sociobiology is not seen as primarily a science of the *mind*. (This is, in fact, what I recently said to anthropologist Sarah Hrdy in conversation. Hrdy, in essence, was defending Wilson's notion that evolutionary psychology was just a branch of sociobiology, pointing out the broad range of positions that can be taken under the name of 'sociobiology', all the way from Mary West Eberhard's rather environmental approach to the most hard-nosed of genetic views.) The other difference, however (and I believe I got Hrdy to agree with this), was that evolutionary psychologists concentrate on the features of our *evolved* architecture of the mind—that is, they do not emphasise the mind's future genetic evolution—while Wilson focuses on *continuing human evolution*, with its resultant genes–mind–culture feedback process.

In 1996 an exchange in *Science* highlighted the awkwardness still surrounding the label 'sociobiology' in academic circles, and the wish for many academics to distance themselves from it. A news notice carried the following heading: '"Sociobiology" to History's Dustbin?' (*Science*, 273, 19 July 1996, p. 315). This notice reported that the Human Behavior and Evolution Society's journal was changing name from *Ethology and Sociobiology* to *Evolution and Human Behavior*, based on a vote by its own members. The note observed that 'HBES members cite a variety of reasons for changing the journal name, explaining that the new moniker more accurately reflects the breadth of HBES's concerns. But UCLA anthropologist Nicholas Blurton-Jones, an associate editor, admits that "sociobiology" raised too many hackles and got us into too much trouble.' The report produced an outcry from a number of people who regarded themselves as exactly practicing sociobiologists. In a letter of protest, the signatories pointed out a number of significant recent contributions to the field (Hrdy *et al.*, 1996).

But the matter goes beyond political connotations. Some intellectual tensions between the different schools of sociobiological thought have indeed developed over the last twenty-odd years. Evolutionary psychology is only one branching-off attempt from sociobiology, or rather human sociobiology. Other branches of human sociobiology are represented by Richard Alexander and his students at the University of Michigan. It was, in fact, Alexander rather than Wilson who published early books explicitly on human sociobiology, and also Alexander, rather than Wilson, who over the years trained a new generation of human sociobiologists (although they would not call themselves that). It was from Alexander's 'shop', too, that the Human Behavior and Evolution Society originally emerged.

The type of sociobiology pursued by the Michigan group was exactly the type of research in human sociobiology that had come under the sharpest criticism from the

Sociobiology Study Group and Science for the People. These hardline Darwinians applied sociobiological models directly to human affairs, to such things as marriage arrangements, inheritance patterns, and abuse of foster children vs biological children, usually employing a kin-selectionist approach. Many of these researchers were and are anthropologists, and very active in the Human Behavior and Evolution Society, where they later joined forces with the evolutionary psychologists. An interesting collection of early papers of this branch is *Human Nature* edited by Laura Betzig. In the Introduction, we read the following: 'It's happened. We have finally figured out where we come from, why we're here and who we are' (Betzig, 1997, xi). How did it happen?, the editor continues. And here is the answer: Patrick Matthew, Alfred Russell Wallace, and Charles Darwin, followed by the next batch: Ronald Fisher, William Hamilton, Robert Trivers, and George Williams. Then it is on to the event which was 'the beginning of the end for every pre-1859 answer to the question, what are we doing and why?' What was that? According to Betzig, that was when Duxbury Press published Chagnon and Irons' *Evolutionary Biology and Human Social Behavior: An Anthropological Perspective* in 1979. Betzig's book, which she calls 'a record of that revolution', tells a story that is almost E. O. Wilson-free. In the whole book, his name is referred to in parentheses in two footnotes, and in the text he is officially cited only for having said that sociobiology would cannibalize other fields (p. xiv). There is one lone acknowledgement by John Hartung, who thanks Wilson for teaching him evolutionary biology.[1]

This is in glaring contrast to another retrospective book, representing yet another branch of human sociobiology, the Festschrift for the University of Chicago's Daniel Freedman (Segal, Weisfeld and Weisfeld, 1997). Freedman himself pays ample tribute to Wilson, describing how he was inspired by Wilson's *Sociobiology* and decided to devote his seminar in 1975 to the discussion of it (Freedman, 1997). Freedman himself is the author of *Human Sociobiology: A Holistic Approach* (1979), a book which documents his research on infants in different cultures, reporting slight differences in temperament. His research combines an evolutionary approach with consideration of cultural factors such as child-rearing practices. The book has an appreciative Preface by Eibl-Eibesfeldt.

In addition to these clearly defined schools, 'sociobiology' today covers a very broad range of approaches, including rather speculative attempts to connect various fields of human endeavor to evolutionary theory. Examples of the use of 'sociobiological'—that is, evolutionary biological—explanation in a variety of disciplines, from law to arts, can be found in Mary Maxwell's *The Sociobiological Imagination* (1990), and in the series of edited conference proceedings published by the European Sociobiological Society (ESS), ranging from topics on conflict to creativity (for example, Falger *et al.*, 1998).

The ESS, founded by the late Dutch medical doctor Jan Wind (an enthusiastic founder also of the Language Origins Society), has retained Wilson's sense of sociobiology as a very broad and inclusive field of research into possible evolutionary origins of social behavior. Unlike HBES, ESS is a less technically oriented society, and with a broad interdisciplinary and international membership.[2] Other societies with similar very broad interests in the evolutionary basis of behavior, but which do not use the term 'sociobiology' and do not call themselves 'sociobiologists', are the International Society for Human Ethology and the Association for Politics and the Life Sciences (APLS), associated with the American Political Science Association. The ethologists maintain their distance from sociobiology, and the evolutionarily oriented political scientists sometimes refer to 'biopolitics' (see Wiegele, 1979; White, 1981 for early positions). Still, many are members of all or most of these societies, since the areas of interest tend to overlap.

Of course, most 'sociobiologists' are not at all interested in humans—their concern is the study of *animals* from dungflies to deer. The bulk of practicing evolutionary biologists in the United Kingdom, in particular, from the very beginning wished to be called not 'sociobiologists' but 'behavioral ecologists' or 'functional ethologists'. After 'sociobiology' became identified with *Wilson's* particular synthetic effort and its political connotations there was no 'innocent' sociobiology any longer—not even for dungflies.

Shooting past each other: Gould's and Dawkins' drawn-out duel

Over the years, the sociobiology debate has taken on an increasingly transatlantic flavor. At the same time, it has become more abstract in nature—which, of course, does not exclude the occasional potshot or political insinuation, particularly in book reviews. After all, we are dealing mainly with the same cast of characters, take or leave a few. For some time, the most visible gladiators in the sociobiology wars have been Dawkins and Gould: at one point they even met in person to debate in front of an audience at Oxford's famous Sheldonian Theatre—an occasion which was so popular that it was sold out well in advance. Considering that Wilson and Lewontin never debated their differences face to face in public, but rather engaged in formal polemics (and avoidance behavior in the corridors of Harvard), it satisfies the dramatic imagination that at least Gould and Dawkins recognized the performative potential of the debate.

Gould and Dawkins had their polemics going ever since Gould's early comments on selfish genes (Gould, 1977b) and Dawkins' spirited riposte in his review of *Ever Since Darwin* (Dawkins, 1978b) and *The Extended Phenotype* (1982). What was at issue was especially the need to take into account developmental processes in evolutionary models. Gould emphasized developmental constraints, while Dawkins tried to point out that these did not affect the *logic* of population genetics, which operates with end results rather than processes. Later on, the conflict moved to another level, with Gould trying to undermine and Dawkins defend the adaptationist program. In fact, Dawkins' *The Blind Watchmaker* (1987) can be seen at least in part as an answer to Gould's ideas of 'punctuated equilibria' and developmental constraints, his main challenges to adaptationism at the time. To make his point even more forcefully, Dawkins provided a computer model to show how random changes could, indeed, produce what seemed like meaningful design. Dawkins has continued emphasizing these themes in later books, too.

What, then, is the prevailing explanatory approach in evolutionary biology? Many take it for granted today that it is the neo-Darwinian gene-selectionist approach (for instance Maynard Smith, personal communication). And it may be hard to argue with the empirical evidence. According to one observer, '[t]he theoretical work of Williams,

Hamilton, and Trivers has inspired a truly monumental array of empirical evidence on individual and kin-group adaptations, running to tens of thousands of publications' (Smith, 1994). It is also hard to ignore the fact that the promoters of the gene-selectionist approach have been internationally recognized and awarded prestigious prizes.

Gould, however, totally disagrees with the view that the selfish gene idea has had a major impact:

> Not many people take this view seriously. A lot of people like it as a metaphor for explanation. But I think that very few people in the profession take it seriously, because it's logically and empirically wrong, as many people, both philosophers and biologists have shown—from Elliott Sober to Richard Lewontin to Peter Godfrey Smith (Gould, 1995, p. 62).

And Lewontin chimes in:

> Dawkins' vulgarizations of Darwinism speak of nothing in evolution but an inexorable ascendancy of genes that are selectively superior, while the entire body of technical advance in experimental and theoretical evolutionary genetics of the last fifty years has moved in the direction of emphasizing non-selective forces in evolution (Lewontin, 1997a).

One criterion for practicing scientists might be how useful Dawkins' vs Gould's approaches have been for them. But here we also get two types of answer. Genetics professor Steve Jones saw Dawkins as someone whose 'metaphor has been extra-ordinarily productive and useful, because it gives you all kinds of ideas about how to test it'. This did not mean that the selfish gene idea was necessarily *correct*, he added, but it had generated a lot of interesting work. For someone like Jones, science is essentially *data-driven*, not *theory-driven*. In contrast to Dawkins, Jones felt that Gould and Lewontin, although their Spandrels argument might contain some truth, effectively told biologists the following: 'Abandon hope, go home, and become a liberal-arts graduate.' Still, what happened because of Spandrels, asked Jones? His answer was: 'Not much' (Jones, 1995, p. 117). Niles Eldredge, too, described Dawkins as 'enormously good for the profession'. Gene selectionism started a 'kitchen industry' and 'gave lots of people a lot of work' (Eldredge, 1995b, p. 91).

Still, others have found the Spandrels critique useful. For instance Francisco Varela, the proponent of self-organizing systems (autopoiesis), stated that he learned a lot from the critique of the adaptationist program. He added that 'with regard to the Dawkins–Gould debate, if I wanted to be brutal I would say that Gould is right, Dawkins is wrong' (1995, p. 67).

Many have wondered at Gould's (1992a) particularly ill-tempered review of Helena Cronin's *The Ant and the Peacock* in *The New York Review of Books* (for instance, Maynard Smith, 1993). The book, a *New York Times* bestseller, is a history of the Darwin–Wallace debate about sexual selection and a lucid exposition of how various puzzles have been recently resolved in the light of a gene's-eye Dawkinsian 'sociobiology', most import-antly, the questions of altruism ('the ant') and sexual selection ('the peacock'). Gould found several things to disagree with, in addition to Cronin's 'fundamental error' of upholding the gene-selectionist approach in the first place (for instance, her attempt to explain human altruism as natural). Fair enough, but why did he accuse Cronin not only of errors and omissions, but also of tricks, falsities, and rhetorical flourishes—all purportedly needed so that she could make her point? My guess is that it was probably the book's more general message that galled Gould: Cronin presented the gene-selectionist view as the new *consensus* in evolutionary biology.

Gould fought back. In his review he informs us that several of his colleagues 'toyed with gene selectionism in the '70s', but that the majority of them now agree that it is a 'marginal position'. Since the 1970s, gene selectionism has been 'devastatingly criticized', we learn further (Gould refers to the books by Elliott Sober, 1984, and Elisabeth Lloyd, 1988, and to articles by Lewontin and Sober, and Godfrey-Smith and Lewontin in *Philosophy of Science*). Moreover, Gould reports that even Dawkins himself 'backed away' in *The Extended Phenotype*! This is why, according to Gould,

> the main excitement in evolutionary theory in the last twenty years has *not* been—as Cronin would have us believe—the shoring up of Darwinism in its limited realm (by gene selectionism or any other patching device), but rather the documentation of the reasons why Darwin's crucial requirement for extrapolation has *failed*. Selectionism is *not* a general model for evolutionary change at most levels' (Gould, 1992a, p. 53, italics added).

And in 1995 Gould had not changed his mind: 'If you read the British philosopher Helena Cronin's book *The Ant and the Peacock*, she argues that the whole profession has been transformed by this idea', he said, and continued: 'Whatever my personal point of view might be, *her claim is sociologically wrong in a purely factual or Gallup Poll sense*' (Gould, 1995, p. 62, italics added).

But this gave rise to an interesting sideshow. Gould's public attack on Cronin succeeded in bringing out no less than *two* knights in shining armor. Who were the defenders of Cronin's honor? One was Maynard Smith. The more unexpected appearance was that of a new player on the sociobiological team, the philosopher Daniel Dennett. Dennett called Gould's attack on Cronin 'desperate'. Moreover, he had no trouble rebutting Gould by citing other philosophers, who had indeed found Dawkins' idea of the gene as the unit of selection commendable (such as Sterelny and Kitcher, 1988).[3]

Later, with *Darwin's Dangerous Idea*, Dennett emerged as one of Gould's most vehement critics. According to Dennett, in his protest against adaptationism, Gould 'hankers after skyhooks':

> What Darwin discovered, I claim, is that evolution is ultimately an algorithmic process—a blind but amazingly effective sorting process that gradually produces all the wonders of nature. This view is reductionist only in the sense that it says there are no miracles. No skyhooks. All the lifting done by evolution over the eons has been done by nonmiraculous, local lifting devices—cranes. Steve still hankers after skyhooks. He's always on the lookout for a skyhook—a phenomenon that's inexplicable from the point of view of what he calls ultra-Darwinism or hyper-Darwinism. Over the years, the two themes he has most often mentioned are 'gradualism' and 'pervasive adaptation'. He sees these as tied to the idea of progress—the idea that evolution is a process that inexorably makes the world of nature globally and locally better, by some uniform measure (Dennett, 1995b, p. 72).

Dennett further noted that Gould always tried to keep the three themes of progress, gradualism, and adaptation together—that is, in his criticisms, he usually accused people of all three at the same time (pp. 72–3). But, according to Dennett, Gould 'is a gradualist himself; he has to be. He toyed briefly with true nongradualism—the hopeful monsters of saltationism. He tried it on, he tried it pretty hard, and when it didn't sell he backed off. There's nothing wrong with gradualism' (p. 73). According to Dennett, Gould 'wants to see himself as a revolutionary', but he is not. In fact, there is nothing original or revolutionary in Gould. But the public gets the impression that Darwinism is on its deathbed 'as Stephen Jay Gould has shown us' (Dennett, 1995b, p. 72, citation marks in the original).

But there was also support for Gould—and among important evolutionists. For instance, George Williams admitted that Gould had 'done a great job' of explaining chance in macroevolution (Williams, 1995, p. 71). Still, he wondered why Gould wished so much to minimize the impact of natural selection in general (p. 70). And Ernst Mayr has often supported Gould's points, many of them being derived from something he had already said (for instance, punctuated equilibria from peripatric speciation; Mayr, 1991, p. 153). (On the other hand, Mayr has also criticized Gould for misrepresentations; for example, 1991, p. 142.)

Many may have felt that Dennett's book was welcome: it was high time that someone came to Dawkins' defense, considering Gould's remorseless and persistent criticism of Dawkins over the years. In 1995, for instance, Gould presented Dawkins as a 'strict Darwinian zealot',

> who's convinced that everything out there is adaptive and a function of genes struggling. That's just plain wrong, for a whole variety of complex reasons. There's gene-level selection, but there's also organism-level and species-level . . . I'd question Richard on the issue of gene-level selectionism and why he thinks that the issue of organized adaptive complexity is the only thing that matters. I am actually fairly Darwinian when it comes to the issue of organized adaptive complexity, but there's so much more to the world out there. Why does he think that adaptation in that sense is responsible for everything in the history of life? Why does he insist on trying to render large-scale paleontological patterns as if they were just grandiose Darwinian competitions? They aren't. He has this blinkered view in which the classic Darwinian question of adaptation is somehow becoming coextensive with all of evolutionary theory (Gould, 1995, p. 63).[4]

And Dawkins responded in the same style:

> Stephen Jay Gould argues against progress in evolution. We all agree that there's no progress. If we ask ourselves why some major groups go extinct and others don't, why the Burgess Shale fauna no longer exist, I'm sure the answer is 'Bad luck'. Whoever thought otherwise? There's nothing new about that. On the other hand, the short-term evolution within a group towards improved adaptation—predators having arms races against prey, parasites having arms races against hosts—that *is* progressive, but only for a short time. . . .
>
> *The 'pluralist' view of evolution is a misunderstanding of the distinction I make between replicators and vehicles.* . . . There's a hierarchy in levels of selection as long as you are talking

about vehicles. But if you are talking about replicators, there isn't. There's only one
replicator we know of, unless you count memes.

Steve doesn't understand this. He keeps going on about hierarchies as though the gene is
at the bottom level in the hierarchy. The gene has nothing to do with the bottom level in the
hierarchy. It's out to one side (Dawkins, 1995b, p. 84, italics added).

And these are just two examples from a larger pattern established between the two.
Dawkins may try to explain himself blue in the face, but Gould does not pay any
attention to Dawkins' explanations. Each new option from Dawkins is reacted to by
Gould—and, we should note, vice versa. Just as Gould, in almost each new book, makes
some observation on sociobiology or Dawkins, so does Dawkins not fail to explain
exactly how Gould is wrong!

What, then, was the reaction of their colleagues to Gould and Dawkins' transatlantic
tiffs? Dennett defended Dawkins as 'oversimplifying' but doing it deliberately (1995b,
p. 93). At the same time, he admitted that 'Gould is even somewhat right'. Life and
evolution are more complex than Dawkins presents them as being. So, concluded
Dennett, Dawkins could actually say: 'Thanks, Steve, I needed that!' (p. 94). But Nick
Humphrey commented: 'Some of what Richard Dawkins and Steve Gould go on about
in their debate is old-hat, and they ought to stop it. New things have come up since the
Selfish Gene and since Gould's earlier writings. We are into new territory now'
(Humphrey, 1995).[5]

Is all this really a matter of one scientist misunderstanding another? Of course, we
are dealing with deep-seated scientific convictions, and both scientists probably feel
they have good grounds for sticking to their guns. No doubt it is also an intellectual
challenge, and both may be enjoying the sheer sport of it. We have a sort of duel going
on. Still, could the point of this drawn-out battle between Gould and Dawkins—
seemingly going nowhere—be that Gould and Dawkins might not really *wish* to resolve
their differences? Is it rather that Dawkins and Gould are using each other as sparring
partners to generate new points and counterpoints in their best-selling books? The
reason why they do not 'stop', as Humphrey wished, may well be that they need each
other. Each new attack by Gould is an opportunity for Dawkins to explain just *how*
Gould is wrong, and each new explanation is a fresh chance for Gould to point out just
why Dawkins is mistaken about how things really are. The general public expects more
of the same, and more of the same they get! At least the Natural Science Book Club has
already seen it as convenient to sell Dawkins and Gould *together* as the choice of the
month.[6]

And of course both are aware of the fact that they are best-selling antagonists. In the
same breath as he criticizes Dawkins as a zealot, Gould compliments him as being 'the
best living explainer of the essence of what Darwinism is all about' (Gould, 1995b,
p. 63). And Dawkins reports that he finds Gould 'wrong but interesting' and that Gould
feels the same about him (Dawkins, 1989a, p. 275). In Chapter 3 I described Wilson and
Lewontin as involved in a kind of symbiosis. Here we have an even better example of the
fact that controversy pays, and that it takes two to tango.

Defenders of the Modern Synthesis: the why and the how of evolution

One of the more recent strategies of the anti-sociobiologists has been to divide the Darwinists into two camps when it comes to who is the truer follower of the Master. The sociobiologists are faulted for living in a world of single genes and not recognizing macroevolutionary forces at all. Gould has divided the Darwinians into 'strict' or 'ultra-darwinians' on the one hand and 'pluralists' on the other. The first group is said to believe that evolution can be explained exclusively through adaptation and competition between genes, while the second group accepts the existence of multiple forces in evolution and selection at different levels (Gould, 1995). Niles Eldredge, too, distinguishes between 'the naturalists' (Gould and himself) and the 'ultra-Darwinians' (Maynard Smith, George Williams, and Richard Dawkins) (Eldredge, 1995b, pp. 122–3). He admits that they 'all agree on the rudiments of evolutionary change: adaptive modification through natural selection'. But, according to Eldredge, the ultra-Darwinians try to explain the structure and history of large-scale systems purely in terms of relative gene frequencies. He even muses that the ultra-Darwinians have a kind of 'physics envy'. Having a model of genes competing with each other may seem more like physics to them. Like Gould, Eldredge is disappointed that the ultra-Darwinians do not pay more attention to macroevolution:

> In a sense, I think it's intellectually incomplete rather than dishonest. . . . I feel like I spend a lot of time learning how to sing these guys' song. I don't see them turning around and learning the song that Steve and I and Elisabeth Vrba and Steven Stanley have been singing. I think they're so wrapped up in their own gene-centered world that they have an *incomplete ontology of biological nature* (Eldredge, 1995b, p. 123, italics added).

Eldredge's criticism is somewhat different from Gould's. He complains that Maynard Smith, Williams, and Dawkins concentrate too much on *mechanism*. For instance, in *The Blind Watchmaker*, Dawkins explains 'in loving detail' *how* natural selection shapes organismic adaptation. But there is nothing there about the context of adaptive change; *why* adaptive change occurs. It is just an 'in principle' argument. In contrast, according to Eldredge, what the naturalists are saying is that '*natural selection seems to produce adaptive change mainly in conjunction with true speciation*—the sundering of an ancestral reproductive community ('species') into two or more descendant species' (Eldredge, 1995, p. 124, italics added).

What is all this about? It seems to me that we here encounter a really profound opposition between so-called ultra-Darwinians and so-called pluralists or naturalists. Eldredge and Gould are looking for a *correct ontology*. This is why they describe themselves as pluralists and naturalists; a *correct* explanation of evolution will have to take into account all the forces and all the levels involved. And since adaptation through natural selection is only *one* such force, it obviously cannot be sufficient, and any explanation based only on this approach is therefore false. 'Theirs is an incomplete description of biotic nature, rendering their theory simplistic and incomplete', says

Eldredge, pointing a finger at the ultra-Darwinians (1995b, p. 122). This means that the pluralists/naturalists, in their quest for total, ontological truth, see no merit in a description of a plausible mechanism, however excellent, for what they know is a *limited* aspect of evolution. They want the whole truth and nothing but the truth.

We have, therefore, an opposition between what we might more appropriately call *metaphysicians* or ontological truth-seekers and—well, what should we call the other group? The others are concerned with the mechanism of natural selection, and with 'in principle' arguments. I will call this group *logicians* or mechanism-oriented truth-seekers. It is not really a matter, then, of profoundly different beliefs in the true forces of evolution; it is rather a difference in attitude to 'good science'. As we can see, this represents a continuation of the discussion in Chapter 14, where the division was made between 'realists' and 'modelers'. We have a profound distinction between those who believe that evolutionary biology should answer Why? questions and those who think that this science should limit itself to How? questions—an opposition between 'philosophers' and 'scientists' in evolutionary biology.[7]

Obviously, not all critics of sociobiology were craving correct ontology. Philip Kitcher's criticism of both Wilsonian and general sociobiology in 1985 was fundamentally methodological. Indeed, a sign of Dawkins' relative success is that Kitcher in fact *approved* of Dawkins' gene-selectionist approach (Sterelny and Kitcher, 1988). That meant, too, that here Kitcher was parting ways with Lewontin, who had argued against Dawkins' gene selectionism and kept on doing so (Sober and Lewontin, 1982; Lewontin, 1997b, 1998a). Sober and Lewontin's main objection in 1982 had been that 'the computational adequacy of genetic models leaves open the question of whether they also correctly identify the causes of evolution'. Against Dawkins, they invoked Ernst Mayr and his 'The Unity of the Genotype' (Mayr, 1963, Chapter 10). Clearly their objection was ontological, because they argued that '[g]enic selection is not impossible, but the biological constraints on its operation are extremely demanding' (Sober and Lewontin, 1982).[8]

It is in the area of the unit of selection that the most obvious opposition exists between the metaphysicians and the logicians. In 1995 we have Eldredge stating: 'Ultra-Darwinians are reductionists, but only down to the genes-within-populations level. *They are afraid of still lower levels* . . . What we're saying is that there are more levels, both higher and lower, than in the traditional bailiwick of population genetics' (1995b, p. 123, italics added). It is rather surprising still to see this kind of statement in 1995. The difference between the Gould–Eldredge and the gene-selectionist position should have been obvious by the end of the 1980s and early 1990s—considering that clear-minded philosophers of biology had been helping sort out misunderstandings between the gene as a physical and logical unit of selection (for example, Lloyd, 1988; Hull, 1981, 1984)— if not by 1982 with Dawkins' own extensive explanations in *The Extended Phenotype* of the distinction between vehicle and replicator.[9]

George Williams put yet another twist on the discussion. In *Natural Selection* (1992), he made it clear that one should distinguish between the gene as an *informational* unit and the gene as a *physical* unit. This, in fact, together with sexual selection, he saw as the thing that 'he will be remembered for' (rather than the gene-selectionist approach, which he believes that someone else would have come up with anyway; Williams, 1995, p. 45). Williams specified this further. According to him, what was being transmitted was basically *information*. He believed that because Dawkins had been emphasizing the gene as an object, and the importance of replication, he had had trouble convincing people. 'Until you have made the distinction between information and matter, discussions of levels of selection will be muddled' (Williams, 1995, p. 44). Interestingly, Williams said it was Dawkins' meme concept that had influenced his development of this idea (p. 43).[10]

But Eldredge was not happy. He raised an ontological objection: he saw it as 'disturbing' that Williams 'goes out of his way to stress that species are no special category of biological entity'. Still, Eldredge did reflect on the reason for population geneticists' relative neglect of species: 'The data they handle aren't at the intraspecies level. They're not used to thinking about these problems' (Eldredge, 1995b, p. 122).

And now we get to the central point. The real question may be: *who are the true defenders of the faith* when it comes to the Modern Synthesis: the 'naturalists' or the ultra-Darwinians? Eldredge described the first group as representing an earlier tradition in evolutionary biology; more specifically, a tradition that recognized nature as *discontinuous* rather than *continuous*:

> Punctuated equilibria reasserts the importance of discontinuity in evolutionary discourse. Though it's usually the ultra-Darwinians who are cast in the role of *defensores fidei*, it was actually Mayr and Dobzhansky, as founders of the 'modern synthesis', who originally managed to inject an element of discontinuity into the evolutionary discourse. *So it's actually we naturalists who are defending a corner of orthodoxy here.* As Dobzhansky said, Darwin established the validity of natural selection, and natural selection generates a spectrum of continuous variation. But nature is *discontinuous*. It's discontinuous (as Dobzhansky said in 1937) at the gene level and again at the species level (Eldredge, 1995b, p. 122, italics added).

Of course, 'the faith' that is being defended by evolutionists in the footsteps of Mayr and Dobzhansky has to do with much more than discontinuity. It relates to 'the way Nature "really" is'. And this has been a theme throughout this book. We have, for instance, seen Lewontin (1974) emphasize such things as the real variation observed in nature, nature's real 'suture lines' for adaptive traits, and the need for capturing reality in all its complexity. More recently, Lewontin has discussed the attitude to evolution conveyed in the Modern Synthesis. According to Lewontin, *The Modern Synthesis* (1942), edited by Julian Huxley, which brought together the leading evolutionists at the time, 'was filled with the consciousness of *historical contingency*' (Lewontin, 1998a, italics added). 'While some argued that the differences between species were direct consequences of natural selection, others argued that reasonably often "the race is not to the swift, nor the battle to the strong, nor riches to the wise man, but time and chance happeneth to them all"', Lewontin pointed out, using his favorite all-purpose quote.

In other words, just like Eldredge (1985 and later) and Gould (1993b), Lewontin argued that the architects of the Modern Synthesis had a far more pluralistic view of the forces involved in evolution than the latter-day neo-Darwinists. In contrast to these, Lewontin characterized current evolutionists as Panglossians, believing in optimality and viewing evolution as an always successful mountain-climbing process, with no accidents and no failures.

But this was not enough for Lewontin. He had to add his verdict. There *could not* exist a scientific reason for this, Lewontin maintained:

> This change has not occurred because a mass of new facts has forced us to a new vision of reality. On the contrary, the development of very sophisticated statistical methods has been required to detect any signal of natural selection over the din of random DNA variation observed by modern molecular evolutionists. Where does the faith in optimality come from? Certainly not from inside science' (Lewontin, 1998).

Aha! After proving in this 'external' way that optimality assumptions 'must' be ideological (without recognizing the need to examine how those who use optimality assumptions *themselves* account for their particular choice), Lewontin provided a quick sociohistorical explanation to account for the difference between earlier and later evolutionary theory: the earlier interpretation of evolutionary theory, with its sense of historical contingency, reflected the relative pessimism after the First World War and the Great Depression. By contrast, the current optimistic idea of genes competing with each other is a direct reflection of the 'exuberant expanding' capitalism of the last fifty years.

Are scientists really hapless beings reflecting the *Zeitgeist* in this almost over-transparent way? Looking at the history of science, I think we can find as many countercases as supportive cases for this kind of direct mirror theory. I think Lewontin has to give scientists—as he gives organisms—more credit as *actors* who construct their own environment (Lewontin, 1981e). Scientists want something to *do*. Might it not be the case that gene-selectionist and optimization models turned out to be unusually *yielding* for scientific research, forming an understandable basis for a new scientific industry, while the alternatives appeared less promising?

If anything, from all these dichotomies and classifications it appears that the urge to divide the world into Us and Them is almost endemic among the critics of sociobiology. Eldredge's *Reinventing Darwin* (1995a) identified what he saw as a deep division between the (sensible) naturalists and the (unreasonable) ultra-Darwinians. Gould, however, soon realized that something new was called for. So we have Gould calling his critics the worst name he can think of: 'Darwinian fundamentalists' (Gould, 1997a). The arch-fundamentalist Darwinist is, of course, Richard Dawkins; others are Maynard Smith and Dennett (Gould is still miffed with them after what they said about him in 1995).[11] Evolutionary psychology, too, gets a kick, and the 'Darwinian fundamentalists' are contrasted with Darwin himself, who is praised for his sensible belief that natural selection is not the only force (Gould, 1997b). For those who have followed Gould's argumentation over the years, this part appears very much *déjà vu*. There is, however, a special new touch: we now learn that the ultra-Darwinians are all also '*constructivists*'— the most awful label imaginable for a scientist in the light of the recent Science Wars![12]

But there are those who see all kinds of dichotomies as artificial and illusory. Sooner or later, they tell us, the apparent contrast between the two camps will dissolve and a new synthesis emerge, embracing both. Or both sides will be modifying each other. Dennett, for instance, noted that, historically, many so-called revolutions within Darwinism later actually turned out to support Darwinism. He uses an example given by John Maynard Smith: '[T]he early Mendelians . . . at first thought of themselves as anti-Darwinians. They thought of Mendelism as a way to nip Darwinism in the bud. They didn't see that in fact it was the salvation of Darwinism. It's roughly half the Modern Synthesis' (Dennett, 1995b, p. 72). And he went on to a more recent example: Stuart Kauffman, with his ideas of complexity. Kauffman started off believing he was anti-Darwinian, but ended up in fact offering an improvement to some part of Darwinism (ibid.).

And they may be right. For instance, all the talk about constraints and higher-level selection may well have helped inspire Dawkins' recent interpretation of the idea of 'the evolution of evolvability' or 'kaleidoscopic embryology' (Dawkins, 1998b). According to Dawkins, some organisms may just be better at evolving than others: 'There can be a kind of higher-level selection for embryologies that lend themselves to evolution: a selection in favour of evolvability. This kind of selection may even be cumulative and therefore progressive, in ways that group selection is not' (Dawkins, 1998a, p. 269). Dawkins said he discovered this by using his own computer program, The Blind Watchmaker (cf. Dawkins, 1995b, p. 83).[13]

Finally, of course, there are those who will have none of the above. Here we have Lynn Margulis, the celebrated discoverer of the endosymbiotic origin of the eukaryotic cell from prokaryotic cells (Margulis, 1981). In 1995 she had a message for *both* the neo-Darwinists and their critics. According to her, Dawkins, Maynard Smith, Williams, Lewontin, Eldredge, and Gould all dealt with 'a data set some three billion years out of date'. The problem is that they focused on animals and people, but 'they miss four out of the five kingdoms of life', she complained (the other kingdoms are bacteria, protista, fungi, and plants). Margulis went on to say that animals, give us 'little real insight into the major sources of evolution's creativity'. Although Margulis was somewhat more positive about Gould, Eldredge, and Lewontin than about Dawkins and Maynard Smith, she had some strong words reserved for neo-Darwinism as a whole. She dismissed it as pseudoscience:

> Both Dawkins and Lewontin, who consider themselves far apart from each other in many respects, belong to this tradition. . . . *The neo-Darwinist population-genetics tradition is reminiscent of phrenology,* I think, and is a kind of science that can expect exactly the same fate. It will look ridiculous in retrospect, because it is ridiculous. I have always felt that way, even as a more-than-adequate student of population genetics with a superb teacher—James F. Crow, at the University of Wisconsin, Madison (Margulis, 1995, pp. 132–3, italics added).

The main problem, Margulis charged, was that the algebra and arithmetic of neo-Darwinist formality is inappropriate for biology. The language of life is *chemistry*, not mathematics. 'The practicing neo-Darwinists lack relevant knowledge in, for example, microbiology, cell biology, biochemistry, molecular biology, and cytoplasmic genetics.

They avoid biochemical cytology and microbial ecology. This is comparable to attempting a critical analysis of Shakespeare's Elizabethan phraseology and idiomatic expression in Chinese, while ignoring the relevance of the English language!', she erupted (pp. 133–4).[14]

But we can hardly leave the chapter in Margulis' hands. Let us end on a positive note. It does seem that various challenges to neo-Darwinist theory are being taken into account and new aspects explored. Research is continuing—after all, this is what science is all about. For instance, a recent editorial in *Science*, entitled 'The Revolution in Evolution' observed:

> On another front, the classical Darwinian model of natural selection has given way to a
> more complex view; selection of the 'selfish' gene affects organizations at all levels, giving
> rise to parent-offspring, male-female, and intragenomic conflicts of interest. A new wave of
> advances is promised by experimental evolutionary biology, as theories are tested from
> direct observations of evolution in the laboratory, and results are assessed at the phenotypic,
> genetic, molecular, and structural levels.
>
> Notwithstanding this recent metamorphosis, many mysteries in the field remain to
> challenge us. . . . One fundamental challenge is to understand the extent to which the
> mechanisms that account for microevolution can explain the elaboration of forms in
> macroevolution (Bull, 1998).

Recently, part of the discussion has moved to the level of the genome. One question is whether the relatively newly discovered processes, such as genomic imprinting and other intragenomic conflicts (see, for example, Haig, 1997), are compatible with existing theory or not. And this is one place where the sociobiology controversy continues. Bob Trivers (1997), for one, had no problem seeing genomic imprinting as simply an extension of selfish gene thinking (according to genomic imprinting, genes inherited from the father and the mother are responsible for different traits, and may be in objective conflict). The battle for truth continues within the genome. 'I will get Lewontin at the molecular level!', Trivers told me in 1993. Lewontin, of course, in the Mayr tradition of an integrated genome, had suggested in 1974 that the genome was the unit of selection. But at the same time, there seems to be support also for the Mayr–Lewontin kind of interpretation, or at least for the notion that genes, *despite* seeming to be in conflict, together form an evolutionarily stable genome after all (Haig, 1997).[15] Intellectually, then, it seems that in the recent developments of evolutionary biology we may well be witnessing relatively rapid sequences of theses, antitheses, and syntheses in a dialectical Hegelian movement—toward Truth, one would hope. Or, less dramatically, we may here have a good illustration of the typical pattern of intellectual conflict, as studied by the sociologist Randall Collins (1998) on a world–historic scale.

Toward an integrated study of behavior?

There are further signs of convergence. In the fourth edition of their *Behavioural Ecology* (1997a), John Krebs and Nick Davies assess the current relationship between ethology and sociobiology in the following way:

In 1975, Wilson predicted the demise of ethology, with mechanisms becoming the domain of neurobiology, and function and evolution the domain of sociobiology. This prediction was fulfilled until recent years, when there has been a welcome renewed interest in linking mechanism and function. We have marked this change by devoting the first section of this volume to this fruitful interchange (Krebs and Davies, 1997b, p. 5).

The authors go on to introduce, on the one hand, studies on foraging behavior which have stimulated new questions about learning and memory mechanisms (Giraldeu, 1997), and on the other hand, studies on the functional significance of recognition mechanisms of kin, mates, and predators (Sherman *et al.*, 1997).

Although Tinbergen's four questions equally emphasized function, causation, development, and evolutionary history of a particular behavior, Krebs and Davies comment, there was an early tendency to focus exclusively on function and ignore the other three questions. In the 1930s, some studies regarded animals as little machines following fixed action patterns. In the 1970s, again, in the early days of sociobiology and behavioral ecology, there was a shift to the opposite extreme. Now animals were seen as scheming strategists instead, always assessing the costs and benefits of their actions, and always choosing the best alternative. Currently, researchers take an intermediate position: 'While we expect selection to favour mechanisms that maximize an individual's fitness, we must recognize that mechanisms both constrain and serve behavioural outcomes' (Krebs and Davies, 1997b, p. 4).

The present position of Krebs and Davies is that *studies of mechanism and function must go hand in hand*. It is often, in fact, the mechanisms, the learning rules, which determine the actual costs and benefits. For instance, a bird's rejection or acceptance of cuckoo eggs may have to do with whether the cuckoo egg was already in its nest when a general learning rule developed about the typical pattern of its eggs, later leading it to reject strange-looking eggs. On the other hand, cuckoo chicks are never rejected. The cost would be too high: an initially parasitized bird would, paradoxically, end up rejecting its own chicks. Accordingly, no learning rule exists as to the typical pattern of chicks—better have a general rule stating 'accept all chicks in your nest'. Krebs and Davies use this example to illustrate their general point: discussing the evolution of a behavior, in this case, 'rejection', without taking into account the actual mechanisms involved is unfruitful (Krebs and Davies, 1997b, p. 5).

Krebs and Davies also respond to the criticisms of the last twenty years, particularly accusations of genetic determinism. They acknowledge that behavioral ecologists have paid too little attention to behavioral development. However, they assert with Dawkins (1982) that expressions such as a 'gene for' a trait 'is never used to imply genetic *determinism*, but rather as a shorthand for '. . . genetic differences between individuals that are potentially or actually subject to selection' (p. 10, italics added); in other words it implies gene selectionism not genetic determinism.

As to the criticism of 'Panglossianism', the view that every single detail of an animal's behavior, anatomy, and so on can be explained by natural selection, they note that Gould's critique has changed over time. Earlier, his criticism was that behavior is never perfectly adapted, it is always constrained by such things as interactions between genes, developmental constraints, and accidental factors. Gould's 1989 criticism, however, was that evolution is a historical process, influenced by chance, so that if the tape of life were played all over again, the outcome might be quite different. Therefore, according to Gould, there may be no logic underlying the differences between species and phyla— they may just be a chance outcome. In Krebs and Davies' view, 'these criticisms do not undermine the value of a Darwinian framework'; still, taking Gould's critique into consideration, they have now 'included greater emphasis on the analysis of historical events in evolution, increasingly possible because of new phylogenetic data, and on the constraints that limit adaptation here and now' (pp. 10–11).[16]

And in the last paragraph of the Introduction, Krebs and Davies do not fail to repeat their message: Wilson's 1975 prediction that ethology will split into a functional and causal approach *is not happening*! Instead, 'what is now emerging is a new form of integrated study of behaviour. In order for this to flourish, one of the keys will be to embrace the powerful armory of techniques from gene splicing to magnetic resonance that have transformed other areas of biology' (p. 12).

Does this mean that the original Wilsonian type of sociobiology and behavioral ecology are diverging further from one another, or will the new approach complement Wilson's original vision? It remains to be seen. Wilson has always been primarily concerned with ultimate causes, but he has of course recognized other factors, although he in practice treated them as some kind of 'noise', which led to protests from many ethologists. It seems to me that Wilson is too good a naturalist not to recognize that his colleagues were right. But while launching sociobiology, Wilson had to exaggerate his stance in order to carve out a niche for sociobiology as different from ethology. Now the behavioral ecologists, temporarily drawn to functionalist explanations because of their obvious tractability, have started incorporating the ethologists' objections into their thinking, and increasingly, too, the criticism of sociobiology. With the sociobiologists approaching the ethologists and keeping a critical window open, the discussion is increasingly moving to the level of the genome.

Ernst Mayr, too, in his recent book *This Is Biology* (1997), emphasized the importance of considering both proximate and ultimate factors in regard to behavior. Moreover, according to Mayr, it was exactly the need to consider *both* proximate and ultimate factors that was the reason why biology could not be reduced to physics. In this respect, then, Mayr was in clear agreement with the behavioral ecologists and ethologists. Mayr, of course, had had these views about the nature of biological explanation for a long time (for example, Mayr, 1963). Still, it is possible to see Mayr's *This Is Biology* as a kind of 'counterbook' to Wilson's *Consilience* (see Chapter 18), because Mayr implicitly *discouraged* the idea of the unity of science in the style of Wilson.[17]

CHAPTER 17

Truth by dispute? The sociobiology debate and the Science Wars

Defenders of science on the warpath against 'anti-science'

'Anti-science' is a label that has recently been applied to a wide variety of criticisms of science. The 'manifesto' of this new expression of pro-science activism by scientists in the United States was Paul Gross and Norman Levitt's *Higher Superstition: The Academic Left and Its Quarrels with Science* (1994). The ground had already been prepared by Gerald Holton's *Science and Anti-Science* (1993). On the other side of the Atlantic, Lewis Wolpert's *The Unnatural Nature of Science* (1992) was an early British statement. Later books with pro-science themes were, for instance, Richard Dawkins' *River out of Eden* (1995a) and Robin Dunbar's *The Trouble with Science* (1995). And even later there emerged E. O. Wilson's *Consilience* (1998a), a new bid in the continuing dispute about science, and Wilson's own answer to the so-called Science Wars.

It is interesting that among the scientists who have recently been particularly active in taking up the defense of science are several biologists: Gross (a developmental biologist), Wolpert (an embryologist), and among the evolutionary biologists Wilson, Dawkins, and Dunbar. Popular pro-science journals, such as *The Skeptical Inquirer* and *The Skeptic* have recently contained articles written by Gross and Levitt, and the latter has also published interviews with Dawkins and Wilson, among others. The involvement of Wilson and Dawkins would indicate that there are some connections between the sociobiology controversy and the Science Wars, something I will explore in this chapter. In fact, the sociobiology controversy can in several respects be seen as a stepping stone on the way to the Science Wars.

In *Higher Superstition*, Gross and Levitt led the charge against the recent challenges to science coming from some parts of the social sciences and humanities. The book was a fierce attack on what they called the 'academic' or 'cultural' left, largely the promoters of various 'postmodern' trends in the humanities, and constructivist and relativist sociologists of science. Gross and Levitt felt free to bunch these separate academic endeavors together because they perceived a common goal among this new 'cultural' left: a challenge to science's ability to produce knowledge which was in any sense 'truer' than other types of knowledge.

In *Higher Superstition* Gross and Levitt did not mince their words, a fact that was quickly picked up by the media. For instance, in the autumn of 1994, the American academic weekly *The Chronicle of Higher Education* dramatically quoted the authors as dismissing 'the relativism of the social constructivists, the sophomoric skepticism of the postmodernists, the incipient Lysenkoism of feminist critics, the millenialism [*sic*] of the radical environmentalists, the radical chauvinism of the Afrocentrists' as 'unscientific and antiscientific nonsense' and as a 'bizarre war against scientific thought and practice being waged by the various ideological strands of the academic left' (Cordes, 1994; Gross and Levitt, 1994, pp. 252–3). In a later article entitled 'Antiscience in Academia—Knocking Science for Fun and Profit', Gross and Levitt charged that the new post-modern critique of science was popular with lazy academics, because it did not require mastery of the content of science. Their serious charge, however, was that the academic left's deep hostility to science was undermining the general public's trust in this enterprise.

When these two pro-science warriors launched their attack, most scientists had paid little attention to what some of their fellow academics in humanities and social science departments were doing. (Incidentally, even Gross and Levitt themselves had been quite unaware, until they happened to be around cultural critics of science and started learning about the new types of analysis.) Therefore, at least for some scientists, *Higher Superstition* was a wake-up call. Others, again, felt that the book's message was exaggerated, and that Gross and Levitt were by no means speaking for all scientists when they described the threat to science from the academic left.

But Gross and Levitt went further. They pointed out that the real danger of the 'hostility' to science from the new academic left was not to science itself, but rather to the larger culture as a whole. In this way Gross and Levitt appealed not only to scientists, but also to academics who had already been alerted to the issues in the earlier 'Culture Wars' on American university campuses. In fact, the extension of the 'postmodern' type of radical cultural analysis to science was only to be expected, if we are to believe the philosopher John Searle (1990). According to him, the new wave of humanists no longer saw themselves as upholders of Western cultural values, but rather as political radicalizers of a new generation of students. The political initiative on campus was now with the humanities, he noted.

The guiding star of the new radical humanists was French poststructuralist and postmodernist theory. Texts were now under suspicion: Michel Foucault had equated knowledge with power, and Jaques Derrida had shown how to 'deconstruct' texts in order to unmask hidden power dimensions. Anything could be treated as a text, and therefore deconstructed—including science. (As it turns out, the American post-modern exercises pale compared to the creativity of their French counterparts, at least judging by the controversial analysis by Sokal and Bricmont, 1997, 1998, reviewed by among others, Callon, 1999, Dawkins 1998.) What was more, from the perspective of various newly developed 'standpoint epistemologies', different political groupings (such as various kinds of feminists) could now develop their own particular truths, or 'ways of knowing'. In this decentered situation, science had no privileged position; it represented only *one* way of knowing—when it was not directly identified with social power, masculine oppression, or Western domination.

But even before the postmodernists were pursuing their textual analyses, various types of 'social constructivist' and 'relativist' approaches to science had already been developed in the new field of Social Studies of Science, or Science and Technology Studies (STS). These new research programs emphasized the social foundation of all knowledge claims, including scientific ones. The leaders here were the so-called 'sociologists of scientific knowledge', an umbrella term for the different social constructivist and relativist schools that emerged in the early 1970s. Ironically, the leading constructivist school, sporting the so-called 'Strong Programme', emerged from the Edinburgh Science Studies Unit, a unit initially established for the purpose of 'humanizing' scientists and engineers. Many such science and technology studies programs had been established in technologically oriented universities around 1970, both in the United States and the United Kingdom. As it turned out, however, the research in some of these—notably the Edinburgh unit—later became increasingly epistemological and lost the orientation toward science–society relations which had been part of the original idea (for perspectives on the Science Wars, see Segerstråle, 2000).

Thus ensued the Science Wars, one more of those polarizations so typical in contemporary academia, with loose coalitions on both sides. One one side were the pro-science activists joined by academic traditionalists from different fields, on the other the different groups that Gross and Levitt collectively accused of 'anti-science', and loosely united under umbrella terms such as 'cultural constructivism' or 'postmodernism'. Although Gross and Levitt in this way connected the postmodern humanists with the social constructivists, the intellectual roots of these groups were completely different, and they had little to do with each other. (Incidentally, the expression 'Science Wars' was coined by Andrew Ross, the editor of a special issue of *Social Text* dedicated to criticism of Gross and Levitt's book, later published as *The Science Wars*, 1996.)

The annus horribilis was 1994, the year when the pro-science warriors struck out against what they presented as irrational forces of 'anti-science'. This was the year of the publication of *Higher Superstition*, a broadside against all kinds of current critics of science, most blatantly postmodern humanists, and constructivist sociologists. This was also the year of the first of two conferences arranged by The National Association of Scholars, an academic organization originally dedicated to traditionalism in the university curriculum, now trying to create a united front against a purported anti-science threat. The first of these well-publicized events, 'Objectivity and Truth in the Natural Sciences, the Social Sciences, and the Humanities', was held in Boston, Mass., and included the Nobel laureate, physicist Steven Weinberg, E. O. Wilson, and Gerald Holton as speakers.

This was also the year of the famous 'showdown' between sociologist Harry Collins and biologist Lewis Wolpert at the meeting of the British Association for the Advancement of Science (BAAS) in Loughborough, England (see, for example, H. Rose, 1996). At that conference, it appeared that constructivists and scientists had difficulties even speaking to one another. This initial exchange of views between the scientist and constructivist camps was later followed up in the pages of *The Times Higher Education Supplement* (30 September 1994). A conference in Durham (England) in December was arranged in the hope of bringing scientists and social scientists together. That conference's focus on case studies, however, may have only widened the gap. The scientists present could not agree with the social scientists' analyses (Fuller, 1995).

Where did this new 'constructivist' approach to the sociological analysis of science come from, and why was it so difficult for scientists to swallow the results of the new case studies? According to one spokesman for the new 'sociology of scientific knowledge', the motivation for the leaders of this effort, the Strong Programmers of the Edinburgh School, was their dissatisfaction with existing explanatory paradigms in their field: on the one hand the framework developed by Robert K. Merton in 1942 (science as exemplifying a particular normative system), on the other, the prevailing rationalist philosophy of science (e.g. Collins, 1983). The sociology of scientific knowledge now exploded a long-standing taboo: making the *content* of science an object of sociological study. Until the early 1970s, the content of science had been off-limits for students of sociology of science, and its sister field, the sociology of knowledge, as well. In fact, the father of sociology of knowledge, Karl Mannheim, had early on exempted natural science from the postulated class determination of all cognitive interests. (He also exempted 'the freely suspended intelligentsia', the intellectuals.)

What prompted the change? The new sociologists of scientific knowledge had been inspired particularly by Thomas Kuhn's famous *The Structure of Scientific Revolutions* (1962, 1970). For many, Kuhn was seen as sending a liberating message. If science was not a paragon of rationality after all, there would be a place for 'extra-scientific' factors. And they now saw the chance to introduce a *sociological* rather than philosophical explanation of scientific knowledge. What took place, in fact, could be described as a deliberate paradigm change effected in the field of the sociology of science itself.[1]

Like scientists, sociologists are obviously attracted to new approaches in their field which promise to open up fresh avenues for empirical research. The new paradigm was to yield a lucrative new academic industry for some twenty-five years to come. No wonder many welcomed the new prospecting opportunities opened by the Strong Programme, the Empirical Program of Relativism, championed by Harry Collins (then) at the University of Bath, or the French sociologist Bruno Latour's Machiavellian 'actor–network' theory, according to which actors 'enlist' other actors—and machines —in strategical schemes for winning the scientific game. New laboratory studies emerged, with novel methodology. Scientists were now studied 'ethnographically', that is, externally or behavioristically—which also meant that the analysts' description came to override the scientists' own interpretation of what was going on (see, for example, Latour and Woolgar, 1979).

The new approach was surely radical-sounding, but what did the social constructivists actually mean when they said that scientific facts were socially constructed? Did they *mean* that there existed no scientific facts? Or did it mean that what came to be *counted* as 'facts' were really more a matter of convention or contextual factors than of inherent scientific necessity? Or was this perhaps a strategical or methodological claim ('as a sociologist, act as if the only factors that count are social factors')? This seemed never to be satisfactorily resolved, even in open disputes at conferences. In any case the challenge was to demonstrate the fundamentally *social* reasons behind the most abstract-looking scientific ideas, and to show how scientific convictions could in fact be reduced to social and political interests. The most self-consciously radical contribution in this respect was David Bloor's *Knowledge and Social Interests* (1970), arguing for the fundamental social grounding of mathematics and logic.

Many scientists—once they got to know about it—were baffled by the notion of social constructivism. Still, it seems that many of them would have *liked* to have a strong, challenging case to grapple with, in fact. Therefore a common complaint was that 'strong' constructivists, when challenged, typically regressed toward the harmless-sounding assertion that science was influenced by social factors, a 'weak' constructivism of sorts. This certainly showed a game spirit among scientists! Still, when the scientists came across explicit statements along 'strong' constructivist lines, they found these hard to take, because they seemed so absurd. At a session that I organized about the Science Wars at the 1995 Annual Meeting of the Society for Social Studies of Science, a scientist in the audience reported that he had attended a seminar where a constructivist asserted that it was in principle possible for there to exist a chemical element between hydrogen and helium in the periodic table. This scientist could hardly contain his emotion when he stated that he could not see how anyone could seriously hold such a belief. As the chair of the session, I called on the only identifiable constructivist present, Trevor Pinch, to sort this out. He did not answer that question, but informed us instead that scientists at Cornell, after a week-long seminar, were still puzzled by his own and Collins' book *The Golem: What Everybody Should Know About Science* (1993). His conclusion: more seminars with scientists were needed!

Another example comes from Richard Dawkins. He once asked a social scientist the following question:

> Suppose there is a tribe which believes that the moon is an old calabash tossed just above the treetops. Are you saying that this tribe's belief is just as true as our scientific belief that the moon is a large Earth satellite about a quarter of a million miles away?

The social scientist's reply was that truth is a social construct and therefore the tribe's view of the moon is just as true as ours. This made Dawkins wonder why sociologists or literary critics traveling to conferences did not choose to entrust their travel plans to magic carpets instead of Boeings. Dawkins verdict was: 'Show me a cultural relativist at 30 000 feet and I will show you a hypocrite' (Dawkins, 1994).

It is, as I said, rather unusual to hear such extreme relativist statements among sociologists of science. Still, there is enough to grapple with in the constructivist or relativist position of science as it is. One of the central claims is that facts are not as important as scientists think; for instance, facts can never settle a scientific controversy. How is this (fact?) demonstrated? It turns out that the proponents of the new social studies of science are wielding a surprisingly *unsociological* argument as their weapon: an abstract philosophical claim. First they point out that science cannot be justified philosophically (for instance the famous Duhem–Quine thesis states that scientific theories are always underdetermined by facts, which is generally accepted). However, the problem comes in the next step, which concludes that *therefore* in practice, too, scientists 'can' never have good enough factual evidence to convince themselves and each other. It 'must' be something else that influences scientific judgment. You guessed it: social factors!

One of the most potentially irritating doctrines for scientists in general, not only pro-science activists, was probably Collins' 'empirical program of relativism'. This programmatically refused to grant science any epistemological privileges. The burden of proof was rather on *science* to demonstrate its superiority over common sense (Collins, 1982, 1985). Indeed, it seemed to be exactly in response to Collins that Lewis Wolpert in his book *The Unnatural Nature of Science* insisted that science was indeed different from common sense. According to him, science's very wish to understand the world was 'unnatural' in the sense that science is not oriented toward practical utility but toward abstract understanding. But when it came to all those purported philosophical obstacles to science, Wolpert simply ignored them. He responded by invoking scientific practice. Scientists do not need philosophy, he declared. They have their own criteria for judging scientific theories: parsimony, comprehensiveness, fruitfulness, elegance, and so on. These rules of thumb may not be philosophically justified, but they work. And that is what counts in science!

The politics of the Science Wars

An example of how traditional science may be seen as deeply political is the following reconstruction of 'postmodern' anthropological reasoning, provided by Napoleon Chagnon, a subject of recent vicious attacks for his studies of the Yanomamö Indians. Chagnon explains why the new brand of anthropologists consider scientific anthropologists like him the real enemy:

> The logic I have heard goes something like this: Most people now being studied by anthropologists are victims of oppression and live in bad conditions. Fieldwork now means that you are present at a crime scene and should become a witness whose first duty is to report crimes. You should use 'interpretation' to identify crimes, not empirical data. This oppression is, in turn, caused by states. States wield power. Power rests on authority. Science is a kind of authority that the powerful will appropriate for oppressive goals. Therefore, scientific anthropologists are oppressors and are to be condemned for ethical, moral and even criminal wrongdoing (Chagnon, 1995).

When postmodernist humanists and standpoint theorists said that science is socially or culturally constructed, they were primarily interested in *values and ideology*. Science, despite its pretense, was seen as inherently value-laden (political, sexist, pro-Western, and so forth) and its pretense to objectivity suspect. In contrast, the social constructivists within the sociology of scientific knowledge have been primarily interested in *epistemology*, particularly in showing that the traditional rationalist philosophical explanatory model could no longer be justified. They saw themselves as epistemologically radical.

Whatever the reason, fundamentally epistemological or fundamentally political, it is upsetting for any scientist to hear that science is not the objective and rational enterprise it purports to be (or worse, that it cannot be objective). On the objectivity issue, the social constructivists appeared to have joined forces with feminists and 'postmodernists' in an assault on science. Gross and Levitt did not inquire into the groups' different rationales for science criticism but classified both under the common term 'cultural constructivism'.[2] Because, whatever the intent, the social *consequences* might well be the same. If an impression was created that science had no particular privileged status as a knowledge system in relationship to other ways of knowing, or was 'socially constructed' (whatever that meant), then this could be seen as a *de facto* admission that anything goes. The burden would be on scientists to demonstrate that they were doing something worthwhile. Thus, the seemingly esoteric battle in the Science Wars was at the same time a battle for credibility in the eyes of the public, with potential practical consequences for both sides (Bauer, 2000). (For a discussion of the relationship between purported anti-science sentiments and the cut in the science budget in the US and UK, see the discussion in Segerstråle, 2000, Chapter 5.)

What, then, of political oppositions in the current Science Wars? Many have regarded the Science Wars as a simple opposition between Right and Left, an interpretation almost invited by the subtitle 'the academic left' in Gross and Levitt's book. The political distinctions now seem to be much more subtle. It has become increasingly clear that the political conflict is *within* the contemporary academic left. Strong indications of this appeared particularly in conjunction with Alan Sokal's famous hoax (1996a,b). Sokal, a youngish leftist physicist, fooled the cultural journal *Social Text* into accepting a purported 'postmodern' piece on quantum gravity, where he drew far-reaching political conclusions from obscure-sounding (but impeccably referenced) statements in modern physics. A hoax is, of course, no fun if nobody knows about it. Accordingly, Sokal immediately revealed his underhanded deed to another journal, *Lingua Franca*, who published his explanation simultaneously with the original article. Sokal's hoax even made the first page of *The New York Times*, which brought the idea of the Science Wars to many who had not known about this phenomenon before. For Sokal himself, his fame meant lecture tours and follow-up books written with Jean Bricmont (1997, 1998a,b) this time attacking French postmodernists.

Sokal's hoax emphasized the silly features of postmodern interpretations of science, in a victory that was almost too easy. Sokal himself admitted he got the idea by checking Gross and Levitt's references; he had wondered whether they had perhaps taken the postmodernist quotes out of context. But, as Sokal told an audience in Lawrence, Kansas on 2 February 1997, the quotes were even worse *in* context! However, it is important not to lose track of the political dimension of the Science Wars.

Many have taken it for granted, guided by the subtitle of their book, that Gross and Levitt were conservatives criticizing the left. In fact, they were self-described *leftists* (Heller, 1994). But their leftist convictions were of a different, earlier brand—in fact of a type which made them have to directly oppose the 'cultural' left. There are clear signs in their book that they feel that the cultural left have betrayed the cause of the left-wing movement. They note that 'the left itself—not only the peculiar ideological tribe we have dubbed the "academic left," but the far broader tradition of egalitarian social criticism that properly deserves such a designation—is, potentially, one of the ironic victims of the doctrinaire science-criticism that has emerged . . .' (p. 252). Levitt indicated during a panel debate in 1995 that the current academic left focused on useless issues. The left ought to study things that directly affected society—large-scale electric networks, urban development, and so on—and the connections of these things to money and power. But it was not only that the current academic left was not serious. Gross and Levitt, true to *their* left-wing convictions, saw *objective science as a moral weapon in the struggle for better living conditions and social justice.*

This was also why science had to be as good as it could possibly be, engaging only the best minds. In other words, science could not be 'democratized' , because that would make it less useful to democracy (Levitt and Gross, 1994). But here was another bone of contention between the pro-science warriors and the cultural left. Statements like these easily made Gross and Levitt and other fighters against anti-science seem politically conservative. In the evolving liberal-left credo, an earlier emphasis on a *common* left-wing cause had given way to a focus on the political interests of various social *subgroups* instead. And in the new analysis' complete turnabout when it came to the view of the political role of science, science was now regarded as equivalent to social power rather than as a means in the fight for social justice. Science *criticism* had now become the new political weapon instead.

Another thing that seemed to unite the defenders of science against anti-science was a strongly emotional belief in the political importance of objectivity. They were at least partly fighting for *the cultural authority of science.* Science for them was a bulwark of universalism against the splintering efforts of the new postmodern left.[3]

I have been opposing the Gross-and-Levitt type of 'old' leftists to the current 'cultural left'. In between these fall the ''60s leftists', to whom the members of the Sociobiology Study Group of Science for the People belong. Not surprisingly, the positions taken by them—and Lewontin and Gould—often represent a transition between the old left and the cultural left, something that we will explore later in this chapter.

Anti-sociobiology and anti-science

Gross and Levitt did not simply declare their opponents mistaken. They went all the way, accusing them of 'anti-science'. This certainly got attention—and at the same time stopped serious discussion. In fact, they behaved in a very similar way to the critics of Wilson in the sociobiology controversy. Being declared 'anti-science' carries an immediate stigma, similar to that of being labelled 'racist', *if* the decent thing is to be pro-science and anti-racist. Thus, in both controversies, the attackers played on existing taboos and biases.

Can scientists be declared anti-science? That would seem to be a contradiction in terms. Indeed, Gross and Levitt did not include scientists among the 'academic left' that they were battling. But others believed that scientists *could* be anti-science. The philosopher Michael Ruse took issue with Gross and Levitt about exactly this in his review of their book (Ruse, 1994). Ruse was specifically asking why the authors, if they were critical of 'the academic left', did not single out such highly visible left-wing scientists as Stephen J. Gould and Richard Lewontin. After all, these two were well-known antagonists to science—more specifically, to research on the biological foundation of human behavior (sociobiology, behavioral genetics, and the like). Also, they were much appreciated and quoted by humanists and social scientists.

This very same sentiment was echoed by Wilson in his recent autobiography, *Naturalist* (1994). I was asked to read the manuscript and did indeed wonder why Wilson insisted on calling the critics of sociobiology 'postmodern', of all things. (In my view, the use of 'postmodern' for the Sociobiology Study Group was quite anachronistic.) But then I happened to pick up *Higher Superstition* and saw a glowing endorsement by Wilson on its back cover. I imagined what had happened. In reading about the threats to science and reason by the ideology of what Gross and Levitt termed 'the academic left', Wilson made an immediate association with his own painful experiences with left-wing academics in the 1970s and 1980s.

But there were also strategic considerations involved. By identifying his former enemies with postmodernism, while himself continuing to speak up for objective science and against ideology, Wilson was now able to find allies among the pro-science side in the Science Wars, including the National Association of Scholars. (Indeed, at an invited lecture at the History of Science Society meeting in New Orleans in 1994, Wilson mentioned that the sociobiology controversy taught him the importance of having allies.) And this time, unlike the sociobiology controversy, it was 'his side', the pro-science activists, who were on the warpath!

Consequently, Wilson produced two types of arguments designed to demolish his former enemies while boosting his own position. On the one hand, he reminded everybody of the Marxist ties of his opponents in the sociobiology controversy. On the other, he pledged allegiance to the credo and agenda of the National Association of Scholars. Both approaches were evident in a talk that he gave at the very first conference on science and anti-science arranged by the National Association of Scholars in Boston, 1994 and later published in the organization's journal, *Academic Questions* (Wilson, 1995). There he unearthed Levins and Lewontin's statement from way back in 1976: 'There is nothing in Marx, Lenin, or Mao that is or can be in contradiction with a particular set of phenomena in the objective world', at the same time as he included a brief ode to the Western origins of science.

Let us now go back to Michael Ruse's charge that the authors of *Higher Superstition* do not criticize Gould and Lewontin, even though these are notorious political critics of science. How might this be explained? A first suggestion would be that Gross and Levitt left Gould and Lewontin alone because they were aware of their overall position on science, and therefore simply knew that they were not anti-science. It is hard to tell what they thought about Lewontin, because he does not appear in their book at all. (Gross certainly knew Lewontin; they were at one time colleagues at the University of Rochester.) But a closer look shows that Gould was, indeed, mentioned by Gross and

Levitt—and they had nothing but *praise* for him! Gould was presented as the paragon of 'good' (that is, not constructivist) historical and cultural criticism of science. He was even quoted as an apt critic of feminist science, and of Jeremy Rifkin, that most persistent 'outsider' critic of science. Gould comes up smelling like a rose, standing *for* sound science and against all kinds of nonsense, a model critic of science.

Why were Gross and Levitt so enthusiastic about Gould, who was, after all, an outspoken political critic of science? The answer is: it was not left-wing criticism as such they were against, it was only any criticism that smacked of '*constructivism*'. For them, an acceptable humanistic or social critique of science was one in which the analyst somehow indicated a willingness to acknowledge science as *analytically* separate from politics. What they profoundly disliked was the mix-up of epistemology and politics characteristic of cultural critics of science. Scientific truth had to be kept clean. They saw Gould as fitting their bill.

So here we find an important political difference between the pro-sociobiologists, such as Wilson and Davis, and the pro-science activists, such as Gross and Levitt. The former did not recognize that *criticism* of science —or rather, of fields such as socio-biology, behavioral genetics, psychometrics and the like—was not necessarily the same as an *anti-science* stance.[4] Unlike Wilson and Davis, however, Gross and Levitt accepted that having political interests did not necessarily mean that one was not interested in 'good science'. Still, a political critic had to somehow signal correct belief in the re-lationship between science and politics. In contrast, Wilson and Davis used political belief as a convenient indicator of an anti-science stance.

As discussed in Chapter 11, Davis further reasoned that an anti-science scientist was also likely to be doing bad science himself. A blatant case here was Davis' article on neo-Lysenkoism (Davis, 1983). We saw how Davis first provided evidence for Gould's Marxism and then tried to demonstrate that Gould's science (punctuated equilibria) had suffered because of this. Wilson, in turn, was eager to point out Lewontin's Marxist affiliation (for example, Wilson, 1995). Note that Wilson did not make these kinds of assertions about Gould, although he occasionally did criticize Gould on scientific grounds, for instance, concerning the punctuated equilibria theory (Wilson, 1992). (Wilson was probably more ambiguous about Gould, anyway; after all, Gould was a fellow naturalist and extremely effective at popularizing the field of evolutionary biology. Also, it certainly became more difficult to attack Gould after his lionization by Gross and Levitt, Wilson's new comrades-in-arms.)

But here we have an interesting irony. *The Mismeasure of Man*, the book so highly regarded and recommended for its 'sanity' by Gross and Levitt, was the very same book that had provoked the fierce neo-Lysenkoism article by Bernard Davis, Wilson's earlier ally! Davis was especially shocked to see how readily the popular press had received the book (see Chapter 11). So, Wilson ended up seemingly caught between two positions on 'anti-science', each connected to the views of different allies. In practice, however, he did not have to choose allegiances. His friend Bernard Davis died just before Gross and Levitt started their campaign.

Here I have concentrated on continuities among the defenders of science in the sociobiology controversy and the Science Wars. Davis and Wilson saw the attack on fields dear to their hearts as an attack on science itself. For them, being against sociobiology, behavioral genetics, and psychometrics was automatically being against *science*. Although I have so far consistently argued that being against 'bad' science does not necessarily mean being anti-science, I will now turn to explore some possible points of connection between the earlier criticism of sociobiology and the later critique of science as a whole. We will see that some elements in the Sociobiology Study Group's overall position *do* indeed overlap with the current cultural left's criticism of science.

This means that, at least in some respects, we can see the sociobiology controversy as representing a *transition point* between the '60s 'New Left' and the new cultural left critique of science. What about the continuity between the critics themselves? There is, indeed, some connection. For instance, *The Science Wars* (1996), edited by Andrew Ross, contained a review of *Higher Superstition* by none other than Lewontin, and also an article by Richard Levins. For a discussion of this and other continuities between the sociobiology controversy and the Science Wars, we will turn to the next section.

Critical continuities and discontinuities

Yet Wilson may not have been totally wrong in labeling his opponents 'postmodernists'. There is no doubt that they have been an inspirational force for a younger generation of leftists. Gross and Levitt were right when they wrote that there is a sense of solidarity within the academic left, a solidarity of a political rather than an intellectual nature. Over the years, however, Gould's and Lewontin's inclination to support various left-wing causes may have occasionally landed them in epistemologically dubious company.

Indeed, if we look at the attitudes of the members of the Sociobiology Study Group in general, several parallels can be drawn between that group and the cultural or postmodern left. There was the preoccupation with science as power, rather than with social and political power directly. There was the distrust of experts, and distrust of objectivity. There was even the rather moving effort of Lewontin and others to 'democratize' science, although this was soon abandoned (see Chapter 11). Above all, there was the emphasis placed on ideological analysis of scientific texts. Indeed, this obsession with *textual analysis* is one of the most important bridges between the anti-sociobiologists and the current 'postmodern' left. Just as the sociobiology critics' opposition to 'bad' science in the Science Wars expanded into an indiscriminate criticism of all science, so the ideology–critical textual analysis from the sociobiology controversy later turned into 'total' textual deconstruction.

Still, there are important differences. The aim of the ideology criticism of the avid critics of sociobiology was, after all, to ferret out the Truth (see Chapter 10). In contrast, the postmodern attitude leaves nothing intact. The result of a deconstruction is not seen to be truer than the original text; it simply represents a different perspective and a different social power interest. And people with different standpoint epistemologies simply read texts differently.

Once again, we can see that the Sociobiology Study Group is occupying an inter-mediate position between an older left and the postmodern or cultural left in regard to science. The political aims were the same. Both the activists of the 1960s' left and the Marxists from an older left wanted to support the oppressed classes. But while old-style leftists like Gross and Levitt considered objective science exactly the weapon by which Truth could be wielded and held up against false claims by social power-holders, the members of Science for the People located the power to be opposed not in the Estab-lishment *per se*, but rather in science and scientific expertise, which they saw as its servants and legitimizers. For Gross and Levitt, objective facts were important as *moral* arguments. Any threat to the authority of science would undermine its strength as a political weapon. (And, indeed, the struggle of the left can be seen as a history of appeal to reason and moral sentiments based on indisputable facts about social conditions.)

Where, then, do Gould and Lewontin fall among the Marxists? This is a good ques-tion. Gould appears to be the more traditional of the two, seemingly moving com-fortably in old left circles in New York (where Levitt appears to have become acquainted with him). He is more deeply grounded as a Marxist (he said himself that he learnt it 'at his father's knee'; Gould, 1981b) than Lewontin, who is a more recent convert (see Chapters 11 and 14). Lewontin's Marxism is an interesting mix of 'total' dialectical Marxism, anti-racialism from the 1950s, and activist notions from the 1960s, somewhat uncomfortably combined with a hardnosed experimentalist approach to science. It is Gould who has more clearly spoken up for science, even biotechnology (against Rifkin), while Lewontin persists in a somewhat sneering attitude to science overall, pointing out failures rather than successes. Both, however, continue resisting 'bad' science. (I believe it is fairly safe to speculate that Wilson, if he were a Marxist, would be 'old left' of the Gross and Levitt style; see Chapter 14.)

In the mid-1980s, sociologist of science Edward Shils had claimed that there existed an anti-science movement with a connection between leading anti-science scientists and the new social constructivists in the sociology of science (Chapter 11). By 'anti-scientist' he meant largely opponents to sociobiology and biological research in human behavior. If this was supposed to be a descriptive statement, he was empirically wrong, I believe. At least Lewontin and his colleagues, in *Not in Our Genes* (1984), explicitly voiced their *disapproval* of constructivism, particularly the Strong Programme. I will turn to discussing this in a moment.

First, however, let us see why one might assume that Lewontin would agree with the constructivist program. The claim that science is socially constructed would indeed seem to fit his and Levins' idea that it is the capitalist system that is responsible for the type of atomistic, reductionistic science we have—one of the more pervasive themes in *The Dialectical Biologist* (Levins and Lewontin, 1985). Presumably, then, a different society would give rise to a different type of science. Is this not constructivism at its most rampant?

In the light of this it is interesting to note that Lewontin, together with Rose and Kamin, explicitly *dismissed* the position of the Edinburgh school, the originator of the Strong Programme, the core of the social constructivist paradigm. Particularly in its early days, the Strong Programme typically employed a 'social interest' approach, later superseded by a more general social-constructivist approach to the production of scientific knowledge, including facts. In the early approach, social interests were seen as connected to the objective, class-based interests of individual scientists and used to explain the success and failure of particular scientific theories at particular historic times. It was not scientific judgment about the tenability of a theory, but rather social factors that caused one theory to 'win' and the other to 'lose' a scientific controversy.[5] Isn't this just the kind of Marxist-like analysis, involving social factors, that would appeal to people like Lewontin?

It is true that the Strong Programme approach is quasi-Marxist, but that may be exactly the problem. The reason why Lewontin and the other authors of *Not in Our Genes* disapproved of the Edinburgh school was probably another aspect of the constructivist approach that they truly disliked. That had to do with the Strong Programme's insistence on the principle of 'symmetry' of explanation of true and false scientific claims. And here, the particular problem may have been the treatment of the IQ controversy.

The symmetry principle entails, for instance, that when investigating a controversy, it should not be assumed that the victorious theory won because of its greater rationality. Failed scientific claims should be given the same consideration as successful ones. The primary aim is to find the *social*, not scientific, reasons for one scientific theory's victory over another. This is probably where Lewontin gets off the train. After all, Lewontin *knows* that there is good and bad science. Take the demise of phrenology. From Lewontin's point of view, the credibility and fate of this science cannot be made dependent on social power interests and changing class relations in Britain, (see for instance Shapin, 1979), because we *know* (now) that phrenology is a pseudoscience. Any suggestion that the truth of phrenology was historically contingent implies that a different truth could in principle have prevailed.[6]

But what about the *The Dialectical Biologist*? Do not Levins and Lewontin there themselves do such things as trace the origin of atomism and reductionism to the market exchange in bourgeois society? Does not that make truth historically contingent, too? Yes, they do. But note the difference between their approach and that of the reasoning of Barnes and Shapin. Levins and Lewontin's Marxist approach at least implies the *possibility* of a true, non-ideological science. (A non-capitalist society would presumably give rise to a different science of a true and correct 'dialectical' kind.) Therefore, for Levins and Lewontin scientific truth is not a reflection of power relations at a particular time, so that in principle one theory or the other may equally well have prevailed. Truth is *not* contingent, but can be achieved if only the social conditions are right!

In other words, just like Wilson and Gross and Levitt, the authors of *Not in Our Genes*, too, believe that there exists a 'true science'. This is exactly why they worry that science may get contaminated by ideology. The only difference is that everybody means different things by 'ideology'. For Gross and Levitt, 'ideology' is various types of 'cultural left' ideologies; for Wilson it is typically political Marxist ideology. For the critics of 'biological determinism', again, 'ideology' is *bourgeois* ideology, an enemy of 'true science' and aimed toward supporting the social status quo. So, the authors of *Not in Our Genes* are clearly *not* anti-science. Indeed, it is just *because* they believe in true science that they liken themselves to a fire brigade, on constant alert to put out now this, now that, new and dangerous piece of scientific nonsense (Lewontin, Rose, and Kamin 1984, p. 266).

A further reason, perhaps the more acute one, is that nagging treatment of Arthur Jensen in one of the early landmark books of the Edinburgh school, Barry Barnes' *Scientific Knowledge and Sociological Theory* (1974). The time is one of a raging IQ controversy, with Jensen being declared scientifically and morally wrong by a large number of academics. Lewontin himself has demonstrated just how the paper's ideological bias leads Jensen to wrong conclusions (Lewontin, 1970). Kamin has written a whole book showing how Jensen is methodologically wrong (Kamin, 1974). But in the middle of all this, Barnes calmly pronounces: 'Jensen's (1969) does not represent a departure from normal practice. . .' (p. 134); 'the indefensibility of the paper is beyond dispute' (p. 133); and 'Jensen's findings lend themselves to being defended in terms of a pure science . . . ideology' (p. 136). Obviously, Barnes' 'symmetrical' treatment of Jensen seemed just too symmetrical for the critics of psychometrics, who simply '*knew*' it was 'bad' science.

So Lewontin cannot be tarnished with the constructivist brush. Still, it is true that Lewontin, although a serious critic of science, often comes out as something of a skeptic and negativist, and may therefore appear to show some of that 'hostility' to science that Gross and Levitt attributed to the cultural left. In a recent review of Carl Sagan's *The Demon-Haunted World*, for instance, Lewontin took the opportunity to remark on various overstatements and shortcomings of science (an example was the War on Cancer; Lewontin, 1997a). But some of his fellow scientists did not like his tone and felt he was being unfair; some progress had been made (Bernstein, 1997; Dorn, 1997; Krauss, 1997). Indeed, with such skepticism about science (although it is clearly 'internal' criticism, not criticism by 'outsiders'), Lewontin may seem to come close to the position taken by relativist sociologists Collins and Pinch (1993), who have argued that science is over-celebrated—it is really a rather mundane affair. Unlike Lewontin, however, these authors went on to argue that science is *inherently* contestable; it is just like DNA fingerprinting (for a review, see Segerstråle, 1994). Lewontin would regard *some* fields as contestable—perhaps exactly DNA fingerprinting—but he would not have extended this to all of science.[7]

Unlike these authors, Lewontin would not argue that it is because of the 'social negotiation' of truth and facts that scientific claims are less solid than meets the eye. This is something that Lewontin would not go along with. On the contrary: his strict criteria for good science requires facts and truth to be found—at the molecular level. We are dealing with a knowable reality (albeit extremely complex). Lewontin may be negativist, but he is not constructivist. If anything, he systematically goes too far in the *other* direction, requiring stronger scientific support than is usually available. For instance, criticizing Sagan for just assuming but not telling us how the scientific method might prove its claim to superiority, he wrote:

Sagan's intent is not analytic but hortatory. Nevertheless, if the exhortation is to succeed, then the argument for the superiority of science and its method must be convincing, and not merely convincing, but must accord with its own demands. *The case for the scientific method should itself be 'scientific' and not merely rhetorical* (Lewontin, 1997a, italics added).

Consequently, Lewontin responds with a list of scientific dilemmas and practices that make science look less unproblematic than Sagan would have it: theory-laden observations, scientists' tendencies to abandon facts and experiments that 'don't fit'; assertions without adequate evidence (here he brings in Wilson, Dawkins, and Lewis Thomas). Moreover, he argues that '[m]any of the most fundamental scientific claims of science are against common sense and seem absurd on their face'. And finally, there is the problem with arguments from authority. According to Lewontin, 'given the . . . inherent complexity and counterintuitive nature of scientific knowledge, it is impossible for anyone, including non-specialist scientists, to retrace the intellectual paths that lead to scientific conclusions about nature. In the end, we must trust the experts . . .'. These kinds of things, of course, are no news for scientists and writers on the nature of science (for example, Mahoney, 1976; Grinnell, 1992), but they may be surprising for innocent laymen who have only read 'hortatory' books. Again, the fact that Lewontin does not go on to tell us how science works *despite* all these problems makes him sound unnecessarily negativist.

Recently, however, it became clear that Lewontin does not see eye-to-eye with Gross and Levitt (and vice versa). He opened a book review with a gratuitous kick at Gross and Levitt, accusing them of 'obtuse ignorance of the actual state of science' (Lewontin, 1998a). The authors of *Higher Superstition* had claimed that '[s]cience is, above all else, a reality-driven enterprise . . . Reality is the overseer at one's shoulder, ready to rap one's knuckles or to spring the trap into which one has been led . . . by a too complacent reliance on mere surmise . . .'. Lewontin said he saw little connection between this and evolutionary biology, to which Gross and Levitt (1998) responded by declaring that Lewontin was by now 'quite gone' in his teeth (!). If science was *not* a reality-driven enterprise, they asked, why had Lewontin himself spent so much time testing population-genetic hypotheses? They also referred back to Lewontin's original (negative) review of their book, finding errors there (Lewontin, 1995).

It is interesting that Gross and Levitt should be so negative about Lewontin when they were so positive about Gould; after all, just like Gould, Lewontin had pointed out such things as ideological commitments in science. The problem was that he had also said that Gross and Levitt had an unproblematic high school view of science. Moreover, his original review of their book had been published in *Configurations*, a journal of cultural studies, and later republished in the collection *The Science Wars* (Ross, 1996). By his sheer actions and general critical attitude, then, Lewontin had signaled that he wanted to be with the new 'in crowd' in the academic left—a fact which did not escape Gross' and Levitt's attention.

In the next chapter we will examine Wilson's solution to the Science Wars.

CHAPTER 18

Interpreting the Enlightenment quest

Consilience—the new central dogma?

Consilience is a dramatic-looking book with a cover all in black and white. Published in the spring of 1998, it immediately made *The New York Times* bestseller list. Wilson had done it again! He had found a catchy title, written an eloquent book, and stirred up discussion. What is more, he had once again at least potentially irked the Brits. The idea which he launched had been originally developed on the other side of the Atlantic, but Wilson adapted it to suit his own special purpose. Just as Wilson in *Sociobiology* connected the new theories of Hamilton and others to his own brand of 'sociobiology', so in *Consilience* he borrowed the nineteenth-century scientist William Whewell's original notion, giving it a new connotation.

Whewell, in his *History of the Inductive Sciences* and *Philosophy of the Inductive Sciences*, employed the term 'consilience' to describe a particular phenomenon in science: the increased sense of truth perceived by scientists when an explanation seemingly belonging to one field turns out to be supported by a totally unrelated explanation of phenomena in another. Wilson's friend Paul Gross clarified this in great detail in an invited commentary on Wilson's book (Gross, 1998). That commentary, together with one by the philosopher Richard Rorty, were both accompanying Wilson's article 'Resuming the Enlightenment Quest' in the winter 1998 issue of *The Wilson Quarterly*. At roughly the same time, *The Atlantic*, one of the traditional opinion-leading magazines in the United States, sported on its cover: 'The Evolution of Morality', the title of another article by Wilson, adopted from his new book. All this signaled the urgency and importance of Wilson's message. What was it, then, he wished to convey?

If for Whewell consilience meant the conjunction of explanations from different scientific fields, for Wilson consilience meant more than that: it meant the unity of knowledge, and a particular type of unity, at that. Wilson traced the quest for universal 'consilience' or unity of knowledge all the way back to the Enlightenment. The Enlightenment's ideal was to unify all branches of learning under a common idea; the world could be rendered understandable with the help of universal science, and this understanding could be extended to man and society, too. However, ever since the decline of the Enlightenment, Wilson noted, the social sciences and humanities had been treated as intellectually independent: 'They are separated, conventional wisdom has it, by . . . possession of different categories of truth, autonomous ways of knowing, and languages largely untranslatable into those of the natural sciences' (Wilson, 1998b). But things were about to change, he envisioned:

> What most of the academy still takes to be a discontinuity is starting to look like something entirely different, a broad and largely unexplored terrain of phenomena bound up with the material origins and functions of the human brain. The study of this terrain, rooted in biology, appears increasingly available as a new foundational discipline of the social sciences and humanities (Wilson, 1998b).

Wilson argued that there were not different types of explanations, each one appropriate for a different discipline; there was 'intrinsically only one class', uniting 'the disparate facts of the disciplines by *consilience, the perception of a seamless web of causes and effects*' (Wilson, 1998a, italics added).

Elsewhere, again, Wilson was careful to present consilience not as a science but as *a metaphysical world-view*, a belief 'shared by only a few scientists and philosophers' (p. 9). Wilson regarded the world, too, as a 'seamless web of cause and effect'. The problem was how to capture this seamless web in an explanation which could span the existing gap between the natural sciences and the liberal arts, between nature and culture. But Wilson believed that he had found the answer. It was the idea of *Genes, Mind and Culture*, developed with Lumsden in 1981. At the core of *Consilience* was gene–culture co-evolution, and particularly the epigenetic rules.

But does not this kind of ambition, in spirit at least, sound vaguely similar to another attempt, that by Lewontin and Levins in *The Dialectical Biologist* in 1985? Did they not also want to capture the whole world in a causal manner? What is the difference? There is no difference in the ambition to capture the causal truth about the world, but there are different views about what the world is *like* and the best way to go about explaining it. Levins and Lewontin wanted to be able to correctly describe the world in all its complexity and everything's interaction with everything, including the capitalist system. For them, the world was full of processes of *interaction* at different levels, all with their own integrity. It was a vision full of feedback loops, a very complex type of causality, which they hoped to be able to express adequately by developing a new type of dialectical biology. For Wilson, however, interaction phenomena did not seem to get in the way. His appeared to be a traditional type of linear causality. He did, however, allow one big feedback loop—that between genes, mind, and culture.

Wilson compared his new approach with logical positivism, the well-known recent attempt to unify science. Consilience was superior. The logical positivists' 'fatal flaw' was that they could only use *subjective* terms; they could not 'track material phenomena of the outer world through the labyrinth of causal processes in the inner mental world, and thus precisely map outer phenomena onto the inner material phenomena of conscious activity' (Wilson, 1998b, p. 27). The logical positivists saw the criterion for objective truth as a *philosophical* problem. But that was a mistake, said Wilson. The problem is *empirical*, 'solvable only by a continuing investigation of the physical basis of the mind itself. In time, like so many searches of the past, it will be transformed into the description of a material process' (p. 27). The logical positivists simply did not know how the brain worked. 'That, in my opinion, is the whole story,' said Wilson (ibid.).[1]

We see here that Wilson never gave up his earlier idea of truth as direct corres-pondence or model building. From Chapters 3 and 8, we remember his belief that sub-jective meaning could be derived from an objective description of a physical process (his view of a synthetic god). Indeed, it seems that in the early 1980s he had already subscribed to a kind of hardline artificial intelligence vision of the mind. He put more trust into the development of cognitive science than many others at the time, including, for instance, Noam Chomsky.

Why exactly do we need consilience? Wilson lists a series of intellectual-cum-emotional-cum-practical reasons. Trust in consilience is the foundation of the natural sciences and one can only point to their consistent success. This is why Wilson believes it plausible that his unification project may work, too, although he admits there is no way of proving it (p. 10). Moreover, this kind of project satisfies our intellectual and emotional needs: 'the assumptions . . . about a lawful material world, the intrinsic unity of knowledge, and the potential of indefinite human progress are the ones we take most readily into our hearts, suffer without, and find maximally rewarding through intel-lectual advance' (p. 8). Wilson further argues that

> There is only one way to unite the great branches of learning and end the culture wars. It is to view the boundary between the scientific and literary cultures not as a territorial line but as a broad and mostly unexplored terrain awaiting cooperative entry from both sides. The misunderstandings arise from ignorance of the terrain, not from a fundamental difference in mentality. . . . *What, in final analysis, joins the deep, mostly genetic history of the species as a whole to the more recent cultural histories of its far-flung societies? That, in my opinion, is the nub of the relationship between the two cultures.* It can be stated as a problem to be solved, the central problem of the social sciences and the humanities, and simultaneously one of the great remaining problems of the natural sciences (1998a, p. 126, italics added).

Finally, consilience is the way to solve grave global problems. Because of the 'seamless web of cause and effect' when it comes to events in the world, the problems facing us are not part of either social science or natural science, they are part of both. And here the most urgent ones are unchecked population explosion, irreversible environmental degradation, and our own potential manipulation of the evolutionary process.

'We are drowning in information but starving for wisdom', Wilson notes (1998a, p. 269). It is important that there exist people capable of synthesis—in fact, the world 'henceforth will be run by *synthesizers,* people who are able to put together the right information at the right time, think critically about it and make important choices wisely' (p. 269). To this end, Wilson wants a reform of the undergraduate curriculum. He wants to rearrange the liberal arts in domains of inquiry which will unite the best of science and the humanities. At the same time, however, this new curriculum needs to be designed to provide answers also to important questions having to do with meaning and purpose: *What are we, Where do we come from, How shall we decide where to go?* (p. 269, italics in original). This, after all, is one of the important potential missions of the liberal arts. However, currently, theology is 'encumbered by precepts based on Iron Age folk knowledge' and Western philosophy is too timid when it comes to formulating 'humankind's noblest and most enduring goals' (p. 269). The future for the liberal arts, Wilson believes, lies in

> addressing the fundamental questions of human existence head on, without embarrassment or fear, taking them from the top down in easily understood language, and progressively rearranging them into domains of inquiry that unite the best of science and the humanities at each level of organization in turn . . . I find it hard to conceive of an adequate core curriculum in colleges and universities that avoids the cause-and-effect connections among the great branches of learning —not metaphor, not the usual second-order lucubrations on why scholars of different disciplines think this or that, but material cause and effect. There lies the high adventure for later generations, often mourned as no longer available. There lies great opportunity (1998a, pp. 269–70).

Of course, consilience could be wrong, says Wilson. But the current pace is such that we might find out 'in a few decades' if his consilience view is correct (p. 268).

Which, then, are the gaps or blank spaces on the map of the material world that have the greatest potential for this kind of consilient exploration? On Wilson's list are the following: 'the final unification of physics, the reconstruction of living cells, the assembly of ecosystems, the coevolution of genes and culture, the physical basis of mind, and the deep origins of ethics and religion' (p. 268). But what happened to wisdom, and meaning and purpose? They somehow got swept up in Wilson's great synthesis. Meaning, for instance, does not appear as an independently ascertainable aspect of reality. In fact, in Wilson's model there seems to exist no realm in which meaning can be formed and social goals and human values discussed *independently* of their causal connections to brain functions, and ultimately to genes and culture. But is not this exactly the traditional strength and function of the liberal arts: to give students some kind of *competence* and criteria when it comes to orienting themselves in a world of values? Without such training, how will students learn to think critically and make important choices wisely?

Wilson has an answer. The arts, too, are to be integrated in the big unification project! Imagination and its products are part of the project. The arts are also pursuing truth, because they 'embrace not only all physically possible worlds but also all conceivable worlds innately interesting and congenial to the nervous system and thus, in the uniquely human sense, true' (p. 268). Meaning appears, but in a redefined form: 'What we call *meaning* is the linkage among the neural networks created by the spreading excitation that enlarges imagery and engages emotion' (Wilson, 1998a).[2]

Still, the question remains of how Wilson's consilience might be implemented in practice in the undergraduate curriculum. Interestingly, there may already exist an example of a successful application! From reading about his teaching method, it seems that Wilson himself had already experimented with consilience for some time in his undergraduate courses at Harvard. By his own example he had shown how it was in fact possible to teach students both science and humanities and demonstrate the link between them. Not surprisingly, the clue was in his own subject: evolution. While teaching the principles of evolution, he had also been offering evolution as an answer to the metaphysical and moral needs of starved young minds! This is what he said in 1995 when interviewed by *The Harvard Gazette* for an article about professors' teaching styles:

> I teach a Core Curriculum course to nonscientists and I do this deliberately. I realize as I look at this group of some 200 faces each September that I am looking into the faces of future senators, CEOs of multinational corporations, *Wall Street Journal* editors, and a whole array of other citizens that make an enormous difference to our society. Together we explore one science, evolutionary biology. I try to make it interesting to them from the outset by teaching from the top down. I ask, What is life? What is the meaning of life? Let's not be afraid to ask these questions. What is the meaning of sex? Why must we die? What's the significance of people growing old and dying?
>
> And once I've asked these almost mythic questions and suggested that maybe science can provide answers, then I begin to go deeper and deeper. Soon I'm in solid biology. And since these students are expecting an answer at the end, which I try to give them, they'll follow me—I won't say to the gates of hell—but they'll follow me to the chemistry of DNA. They'll follow me to the mathematics of probability, and they don't complain, because by that time they understand that they have to know these things if they are going to really understand the significance of life, the meaning of sex, and so on.
>
> It's a pleasure, then, when I finally release them at the end of the term, to think that maybe they really have picked up some science and the scientific way of thinking, and certainly some new literacy that will have an impact when they become senators and editors and CEOs (Wilson, 1995).

Now we know Wilson's pedagogical strategy—and, indeed, it seems to be the same approach that Wilson follows in *Consilience*. First he captures the reader's imagination with a broad vision and its supreme importance. Then he entertains—this time with with snake myths and snake dreams—to argue for the plausibility of gene–culture co-evolution as 'complete consilience' (p. 127). By now, the reader will already be curious enough to respond to light lecturing about evolutionary principles. And so on. Wilson leads the reader step by step toward acceptance of his overall argument.

Indeed, this very same strategy—complete with snakes and snake myths—may even be behind his remarkable attempt to communicate with one particular group of re-calcitrant potential readers: religious fundamentalists and others who do not even believe in evolution! Quoting a 1994 poll of the National Opinion Research Center (NORC), according to which 23 per cent of Americans don't believe in evolution and one third more are undecided, Wilson acknowledges that many people, including very well-educated ones, do prefer creationism to evolution. The typical reaction of many of his fellow evolutionists is to prove the creationists wrong. But Wilson chooses a differ-ent approach: he brings up his own background education as a Southern Baptist, and declares himself empathetic to the feelings of the creationists—'and conciliatory' (p. 129).

Here we have, then, yet another connotation for 'consilience'—a *reconciliation* be-tween science and religion. Since consilience is a metaphysical project, it can serve as *both science and belief* at the same time. It is a complete world view—Wilson's total answer to the current needs of mankind. I will return to this in the next chapter.

With *Consilience*, Wilson has sketched for us a new, all-encompassing scientific program with evolutionary biology as the core discipline. In the middle of the twentieth century, the epoch-making scientific breakthrough came in molecular biology with Watson and Crick, DNA, and the Central Dogma. On the eve of the new millennium, Wilson gave us his response to that challenge, derived from the deepest reaches of evolutionary biology instead of molecular biology, and adapted to the new needs of science. Wilson is offering the world of science nothing less than a new Central Dogma, and with it, a new direction for the growth of knowledge. With consilience, we can leave gloomy prophecies about 'the end of science' (Horgan, 1996) behind us and look forward to a new era of synthesis instead.

Concealed by consilience? The social sciences and the arts

What exactly, then, is the envisioned relationship between the natural sciences and the other great branches of learning? Is it that Wilson is aggressively extending his original bid from the first chapter of *Sociobiology*: to biologicize the humanities and social sciences to make them more scientific? Often it does seem so.

But in the new book, we also find suggestions that all the branches should 'co-operate' —which would seem to indicate that social scientists, say, would have something to contribute to the new enterprise. It is not quite clear, though, what that would be, because Wilson declares so much of current social science wrongheaded. Early on in the book, Wilson predicts that the social sciences will split into two parts: one will become part of the sciences and one part of the humanities (p. 12). This, of course, has already happened in anthropology. But also in the multifaceted field of sociology, for instance, many sociologists see themselves as social *scientists* while others feel closer affinity with the humanities. And among some of the scientific sociologists there are even people interested in the evolutionary bases of social behavior, in a very general sense. They have an interest in interdisciplinary research and in exploring the links between social theory and research results in such areas as, say, nonverbal communication, ethology, psychophysiology, and neurophysiology (see, for example, Segerstråle and Molnar, 1997, Introduction). With regard to time and space, however, what makes sense for social scientists are typically proximate rather than ultimate explanations, events taking place in historic rather than evolutionary time, and interactional and situational aspects of behavior.

So far, it is probably some aspects of social psychology that best fulfill Wilson's criterion of evolutionary grounding and the role of the mind—even so, this discipline can only tell us about typical responses in typical situations. Although many of the every-day biases documented by social psychologists may indeed be part of the architecture of the human mind, they may or may not be operative in a *specific* situation. Take helping behavior. In a specific helping situation, the challenge is exactly to find out which among the many possible factors may have induced a particular person to help another. A blind helping 'instinct' (people typically cannot explain why they dive into freezing water to save someone), reciprocal altruism, empathy, rational calculation in the style of social exchange theory, personality factors, moral education, a culture that encourages helping, various situational factors (for instance, few other bystanders), evaluational factors ('the person deserved help'), transient feelings (feeling guilty, or in a good mood), or what? Or some or all of them? (Incidentally, it is exactly because of this complexity of causes and reasons that many of us enjoy teaching social psychology and social science in general.)

Although Wilson would probably *like* to be sympathetic to the social sciences, his writing style sometimes carries him away, and it is then that the reader may wonder if he has a special grudge against sociobiology in particular. For instance, checking back to *Promethean Fire*, in many respects an earlier version of his present program, we see that Wilson and Lumsden there, when listing the social sciences, include the following: political science, economics, and sociobiology (*sic*) (Lumsden and Wilson, 1983, pp. 174–5). Is this a typographical error (uncaught by two authors), or is it that scientific sociology is, indeed, destined to be subsumed under sociobiology (genes-mind-and-culture type)?

Interestingly, it is economics that is most severely criticized. Economics is said to be totally on the wrong track, not having a realistic view of human nature and not factoring in the environment in its overall calculations. Here Wilson is in agreement with many other critics of economics, including sociologists and political scientists! But look at the irony here. Neo-classical economists typically use models of self-interest, optimization strategies, and the like—and these are exactly the models that underlie much of sociobiological reasoning, too. Irony number two: Pierre van den Berghe, whom Wilson approvingly upholds as one of the few 'scientifically correct' sociologists, has listed exactly various economics-based postulates among the few solid findings in the field of social sciences (Wilson, 1998a, p. 186).

But back to consilience. With *Consilience* Wilson had, in fact, come full circle from his initial position in *Sociobiology*. Wilson had done it again—in yet another respect! Just as he never gave up sociobiology, but rather reintroduced the idea of a biologically grounded human nature with the help of environmentalism and the biophilia idea, here he is in *Consilience* reintroducing his original desire in *Sociobiology* to unify the social and natural sciences (see Chapter 3). Wilson has not changed, but the cultural climate has. Over a quarter century, different parts of his complex message have been digested by different constituencies at different times.

Does Wilson himself agree with the view that he is now realizing his initial vision—that he has come full circle? I had the opportunity of asking him this question at the annual meeting of the Association for Politics and the Life Sciences in Boston, September 1998. Wilson had been invited to give the keynote address, entitled 'The Relationship between the Social and Natural Sciences'. 'Yes,' he said, '*but!*' 'But what?', I asked. 'With more evidence', he said. 'Really?', I ventured. 'Much more!', he assured me. Thus, in Wilson's opinion, science had now progressed so that he was getting closer to his original goal in *Sociobiology*.

What, then, of the relationship between the social and natural sciences? Wilson's talk was something of a disappointment. It certainly did contain more evidence, but it was more of the type of evidence offered in *Genes, Mind and Culture*, that is, more about such things as the universality of color terms, the genetic control of medical conditions affecting behavior, and esthetic preferences seemingly supporting the *Biophilia* hypothesis. The lecture was, as usual, informative and entertaining, with beautiful slides, including a misty one from the rainforest ('I am looking for the sublime', said Wilson).

In its own right, the evidence was suggestive. But to go from this evidence of particular epigenetic rules all the way to consilience would certainly take a large leap of faith. Also, and somewhat alarmingly—at least for me as a social scientist—it seemed again quite clear that the social sciences did not really exist for Wilson, at least not in the same sense as they existed for the audience (an interdisciplinary crowd, largely political scientists). We had all apparently been subsumed under the complete consilience of gene–culture co-evolution. (These were my private reflections—the audience seemed generally thrilled to hear Wilson speak and warmly applauded him.)

The real problem, however, when it came to the relationship between the social and natural sciences, had to do with the nature of scientific explanation. Was there really only one type of explanation? Were explanations in terms of motivations and other subjective states only what Wilson in his book disparagingly calls 'folk psychology'? For Wilson, a scientific explanation was a causal explanation of behavior from the 'outside', as it were. But would such an explanation really work in a satisfactory manner? We have a good example close to home. What of the explanation of the behavior of *scientists*? Scientists have typically been both baffled and irritated when they have found scientific judgment and behavior 'explained' by the new brand of sociologists of scientific knowledge in just this causal manner (see Chapter 17).

The matter is not only one of adequate explanation of behavior. Scientists also want to be *understood* in their professional quest for truth—and this certainly applies to Wilson himself! Why else bother to write one's autobiography? And so we all wish to be understood, for what we are and what we do in our everyday activities and aspirations. What, then, should we do with this real, palpable realm where understanding takes place, of human empathy and sympathy, of shared meanings, feelings, and convictions? If anything, during the course of the sociobiology controversy and the Science Wars, the importance of such a realm for scientists was becoming even clearer. It was there that trust and support and a sense of common cause were established across disciplines, between scientists who had not earlier known of each others' existence.

This realm—I will call it the moral realm—operates rather differently from the scientific realm of explanation and demonstrable proof. It involves, instead, people's subjective perceptions of shared motivations, intentions, and the like, just those things which Wilson is banning as 'folk psychology'. What is more, it is based on exactly these kinds of shared convictions (regarding, say, sociobiology or the university curriculum), that scientists will take concrete action (say, form a Sociobiology Study Group or join the National Association of Scholars). When they do this, they may of course be acting on incorrect information or unsubstantiated belief, but that is not the point. The point is that their subjective beliefs about, say, sociobiology, have *consequences* for their actions, *independently* of whether they are right or wrong 'objectively'.

What is operative here is what sociologists call 'the definition of the situation', W. I. Thomas' well-known dictum. It is a plea for taking seriously what people believe, however odd-seeming or false, because this is an important factor in explaining their actions. As Thomas reminds us: 'If men define situations as real, they are real in their consequences'. This is why an important aspect of the sociologist's work, when it comes to human behavior, involves a *combination* of understanding and explanation. This methodological problem was, of course, expounded in detail by Max Weber, one of the greatest social scientists of all times and one of the three big classics in sociology (together with Durkheim and Marx). Weber contributed to the fields of sociology, political science, economy, history, and the study of religion. Interestingly, however, Wilson's list of social science gurus names Durkheim and Marx, and additionally Boas and Freud—but not Weber (Wilson 1998a, p. 184).

Weber is relevant particularly when it comes to a sociological criterion for truth. In the Weberian tradition, a good criterion for truth for a sociologist would be the correspondence between her account and a person's self-understanding. People studied should in some way be able to recognize themselves in the sociological story offered:

> Sociological concepts cannot be models of thought imposed from without (as positivists of all descriptions are wont to do), but rather must relate to the typifications that are already operative in the situation being studied . . . Or, using Weberian language, sociological concepts must be meaning-adequate (*sinnadequat*)—that is, they must retain an intelligible connection with the meaningful intentions of the actors in the situation (Berger and Kellner, 1981, p. 40).

Conversely:

> [I]f the human beings to whom a concept is applied can not 'recognize themselves' in it—in the case of living persons, by protesting verbally through their own definitions of their situation; in the case of people in the past, by what could be called 'protesting texts'—then the sociologist will be constrained to construct new concepts that will be more adequate to the situation in question (ibid., p. 42).

I believe these are important considerations when it comes to the adequacy of a sociological explanation of individual human behavior (see also Segerstråle, 1993; Schmaus, *et al.*, 1992).

But Wilson had a surprise in store. We had been taken on flights into high spheres, invited to consider the deepest quests of mankind and the reorganization of all knowledge. Social scientists and humanists were now courted, now chided, but basically urged to join in the consilience project, for their own sake and for the sake of mankind's future. It then comes as something of a shock to learn one additional reason why Wilson wished for a coherent system of explanation for human existence: *he wanted science to become more popular among non-scientists* (p. 268)!

So the problem was not, after all, with the humanities and social sciences! The problem was with *science*. People don't understand science, Wilson complains, they prefer science fiction:

> The productions of science, other than medical breakthroughs and the sporadic thrills of space exploration, are thought marginal. What really matters to humanity, a primate species well adapted to Darwinian fundamentals in body and soul, are sex, family, work, security, personal expression, entertainment, and spiritual fulfilment—in no particular order. Most people believe, I am sure erroneously, that science has little to do with any of these preoccupations. *They assume that the social sciences and humanities are independent of the natural sciences and more relevant endeavors.* Who outside the technically possessed really needs to define a chromosome? Or understand chaos theory? (Wilson, 1998a, p. 268, italics added.)

This is interesting. Is this a true assessment? Do people really prefer the social sciences and the humanities? At least according to John Brockman (1995), and echoed by Gould (1995), the opposite is true: science is today perceived as *more* interesting than the traditional humanities. There is an emerging Third Culture of popularized scientific concepts, exactly such things as chaos theory, complexity—and evolution, for that matter. This is what people want to read about, Brockman asserts in *The Third Culture*.[3]

Wilson is primarily concerned, however, with serious science education. He describes the apparently dismal situation in the US. In 1997 only a third of universities and colleges required students to take at least one course in the natural sciences (p. 13). Public intellectuals and media professionals have been trained almost exclusively in the social sciences and humanities. 'They consider human nature to be their province and have difficulty conceiving the relevance of the natural sciences to social behavior and policy' (p. 126). Worse, the vast majority of political leaders are trained exclusively in the social sciences and humanities. At the same time, they desperately need to know the facts of science, because 'only fluency across the boundaries will provide a clear view of the world as it really is, not as seen through the lens of ideologies or religious dogmas or commanded by the myopic response to immediate need' (p. 13). Consilience, then, becomes part of a larger program for the education of future leaders, a restoration of the ideal of the unity of learning from the Renaissance and the Enlightenment—still upheld some thirty years ago, according to Wilson (p. 13).

Enlightenment and hyper-Enlightenment quests

The philosopher Richard Rorty, however, questioned Wilson's very equating of the unification of knowledge with the Enlightenment quest. According to Rorty:

> [O]ne can be utterly devoted to the Enlightenment's project of a decent life for all the inhabitants of the planet, a life as free citizens of a cooperative commonwealth, while remaining in brutish ignorance of how computers, brains, or anything else works. I know quite a few people of this sort. I also know some who entirely share his devotion to Enlightenment ideals, but, having no taste for philosophy, poetry, or cultural politics, remain largely ignorant of all three (Rorty, 1998).

More importantly, Rorty pointed out that it was unclear how knowledge of science would be helpful for solving moral or political problems. Unlike Wilson, Rorty believes in a division of labor between the natural sciences and the humanities:

> [W]hen we know what we want but don't know how to get it, we look to the natural sciences for help. We look to the humanities and arts when we are not sure what we should want. This traditional division of labor has worked pretty well. So it is not clear why we need the further consilience which is Wilson's goal (Rorty, 1998).

Rorty is puzzled in general as to why Wilson thinks the unity of science is so important. The logical positivists hoped to unify culture by finding a method for replacing unscientific claims with scientific ones. In their zeal, they 'managed to make a lot of people feel guilty: mostly social scientists, but also a few philosophers and literary critics. This guilt caused these people to waste a lot of time trying to make their disciplines scientific', Rorty pointed out. Now philosophers look back on logical positivism 'with some embarrassment'. Wilson, on the other hand, described logical positivism as 'the most valiant effort ever mounted by modern philosophers'. Its only failure was that it didn't know how the brain works (Rorty, 1998, p. 32).

But why did Wilson believe that a seamless *causal* web would have to necessarily go together with a seamless *explanatory* web, asked Rorty? Might one not use different vocabularies to refer to the same seamless causal web? Academic disciplines are not supposed to be reflections of the real world; rather, they provide different ways of doing things, they are useful for different *purposes*. And so it should be, because humans have many different purposes, noted the pragmatist philosopher (Rorty, pp. 30–1).

And as to Wilson's basic tool for unifying knowledge, the epigenetic rules, Rorty said he did not doubt their existence. In his opinion, however, the examples Wilson cited were simply not *persuasive* enough. '[T]he hallucinatory power of dreams, the mesmerizing fear of snakes, phoneme construction, elementary preferences in the sense of taste, details of mother–infant bonding' will not be enough to drive humanists, social scientists, and artists toward evolutionary biology (p. 32). Even Wilson's supposed *prototype* for research of this new consilient kind, 'the breaking of light into the colors of the rainbow', failed to convince. How would the knowledge of 'a causal sequence running all the way from genes to the invention of vocabulary', help humanists and social scientists provide better insights, new vocabularies, and tools for thinking— which was, after all, what academics in these fields could offer best? In contrast to Wilson, Rorty argued for keeping the great branches of learning *apart*, as a way to *better* fulfill the Enlightenment project.

Rorty's concerns were seconded and expanded by another philosopher, Jerry Fodor, a specialist in cognitive science. He objected to Wilson's idea of the unity of the sciences on the grounds that it did not seem to be true to the facts. Yes, the natural sciences had been successful, but they had been successful in explaining science in their own many different 'dialects', *not* in the language of basic physics, Fodor noted. Moreover, rather than a unification process, what was typically going on in the natural sciences was a *proliferation* of new disciplines. The web of causal explanation was extended *horizontally* as well as vertically (as Wilson would have it): the result was new hybrid disciplines such as physical anthropology, developmental psycholinguistics, evolutionary psychology, and the like. In fact, Fodor argued, if we were looking for a good example of science's *failure* to unify vertically, it was exactly the discipline Wilson is betting his project on: cognitive neuroscience, the attempt to model how the brain implements the mind. And this despite heroic efforts and great expenditure (Fodor, 1998).

Admitting that his own negative evaluation of the progress of cognitive neuroscience might be an extreme position, Fodor still found Wilson's arguments in favor of this field 'pretty thin'. What Wilson saw as compelling evidence (such as: 'disturbance of particular circuits of the human brain often produces bizarre results') according to Fodor paled in comparison with the really big contributions to this field: Turing's computational theory of thought and Chomsky's discovery of the mathematical structure of language. And neither of those had anything to do with neurological research! Fodor observed that Wilson seemed to have 'swallowed whole' the recent brain science literature, which Fodor saw as mere 'Associationism with engineering jargon'. (Here he pointed to Wilson's own description of memory as involving nodes, linkages, and resonance of circuits, and creating meaning in the form of linked concepts simultaneously experienced.)

Just like Rorty, Fodor was puzzled as to why Wilson would assume that a view of the unity of *explanation* should entail the view of a unity of *reality*, too. There was a difference between epistemology and metaphysics. Consilience of the Wilsonian type was not the only way to go if we didn't want to fall into the swamp of postmodernism, deconstruction, and the like. We do not have to assume that everything has to be reducible to physics, Fodor protested; a view of scientific realism is quite compatible with a view of reality as made up of different levels of organization of the world. The heterogeneity of scientific discourse may even reflect this, he suggested. Thus, Fodor was convinced neither of the necessity nor of the feasibility of the consilience program.[4]

Another fruitful contrast can be made between Wilson's view of the Enlightenment project and someone with impeccable credentials as a promoter of the Enlightenment ideal, the German social theorist Jürgen Habermas. Habermas has been examining precisely the relationship between the great branches of learning for a considerable time. But he has from the outset taken exactly the *opposite* approach to the one now suggested by Wilson. If anything, Habermas' fear has been that scientific rationality will *take over* the type of reasoning that is characteristic of the humanities and social sciences, that is, discussion about desirable values and goals. In academia, as in everyday life, his worry is that the 'lifeworld' of norms and values will get 'colonized' by the logic of science and technology (see, for example, Habermas, 1970, 1984, 1987). If anything, Habermas wants to keep the world of values *away* from the world of science. This is because *the types of rationality involved in these two areas are fundamentally different, and complementary: practical reason vs means–end rationality.* (Habermas regards science itself as unproblematically progressive and truth-generating; his concern is with protecting the more vulnerable world of norms and values.)

Habermas' concern, in turn, derives exactly from *his* vision of the Enlightenment quest, which is one of a rational society. A rational society is not the same as a scientifically managed society; it is a society whose goals and values are settled on by a process of rational discourse. In fact, it is this type of social 'communication ethic' that constitutes Habermas' central Enlightenment ideal (see, for example, Habermas, 1979). This is also why he has been preoccupied with the structure and conditions for rational discourse in today's societies. (Interestingly, one of his models for rational discourse is science.)

Wilson, of course, does recognize the democratic process; in fact he relies on it (see Chapter 11). But he has not so far incorporated this process into his models about humans. The reason may be that he believes in democracy as an ultimate aggregate result of individual decision-making, a kind of 'mass response'. (Indeed, it was Bernard Davis who initially criticized Wilson precisely for his disregard of the political negotiation or bargaining process. According to Davis (1982), social level phenomena were not predictable, even based on the most complete information about individual minds, something that Wilson seemed to assume. There was no indication that Wilson had later changed his mind.)

The conclusion, then, is that Wilson in *Consilience* has a rather unusual interpretation of the nature of the Enlightenment quest. For him, this quest is primarily about the unity of knowledge, not about such things as universal standards of truth, justice, and morals, or about Reason in science and human affairs. Those who disagree with him, again, do not doubt the truth of science, but they see scientific truth as a *limited* one, which has to be supplemented with *other* Enlightenment truths.

Wilson's interest in the unity of all disciplinary realms—over and above each of them devoting themselves to their own Enlightenment quests—might be called a *hyper-Enlightenment* quest. In this respect, Wilson is different from 'regular' sociobiologists and pro-science activists, who might be described as pursuing merely 'regular' Enlightenment quests, eager to keep the realms of science and values apart. I will return to these differences in Chapter 19.

What is confusing is that Wilson can be found to oscillate wildly between a regular and a hyper-Enlightenment quest. Speaking as a scientist, he vehemently defends the objectivity of science and is outraged by his 'postmodern' opponents, whom he considers ideologically biased (see Chapter 11, Chapter 17). Speaking as a visionary, with concern for the future of Man and the world, he operates in his other, 'evangelist' or advocacy mode, where he freely embraces values (and some would argue, ideology). Readers get confused, and reviewers feel there is a double message (Todorov, 1998). Not even his close colleagues always know what he is up to.

It is perhaps typical of Wilson that in the first chapter of *Consilience* he cites both 'The Ionian Impulse'—the quest for knowledge and truth over belief—and the story of Icarus, who perished when he flew towards the sun. In his Ionian mode, Wilson upholds the importance of true knowledge over false—although perhaps comforting—belief. Here, of course, he is in good company with many other defenders of science in the sociobiology controversy and the science wars. For instance, in his comment on Gould's Spandrels talk at the Royal Society in 1978, Arthur Cain interpreted the Enlightenment quest as involving following reason and knowledge rather than, like Gould and Lewontin, invoking emotional arguments (Cain, 1979). Lewis Wolpert, too, emphasized the 'unnatural' nature of science: the wish to understand how the world really works (Wolpert, 1993). And Gross and Levitt (much to Lewontin's dismay) wrote about 'the unrelenting angel of reality', with which scientists have to wrestle (Gross and Levitt, 1994, p. 234; see Chapters 17 and 19).

In his Icarian mode, however, Wilson does not listen to anybody. He knows. And it is here that he parts ways with most of his scientific colleagues. It is indicative that Gross' article, accompanying Wilson's 'Resuming the Enlightenment Quest', was entitled 'The Icarian Impulse' (Gross, 1998). In his otherwise sympathetic review, Gross reminded the readers that Icarus' wings, made of feathers and wax, worked well until he flew too close to the sun. More specifically, Gross suggested that, like Icarus, Wilson's wings might fall off—if it turned out that he was not supported by other scientists.

Gross, here acting in a relentlessly Ionian mode, was simply emphasizing the fact that scientific success depends on what other scientists do. Truth is not revealed, but in the hands of the scientific community. For Wilson's new research program to succeed, others would have to find consilience fruitful. Wilson, of course, has recognized this himself. In his own allusion to the Icarus story, he presented consilience as an admittedly vaulting ambition. Still, he insisted that his approach was at least worth trying.

What are the predictions? Can we draw any conclusions based on experience, say, with Wilson's (and Lumsden's) earlier synthetic effort of a similar kind, *Genes, Mind and Culture*? At the time, Wilson reported considerable interest, particularly from psychoanalysts and mathematicians. Anthropologist Napoleon Chagnon found the Lumsden–Wilson approach useful for his Yanomamö data. Biologically oriented anthropologists found his ideas compatible, while social anthropologists were often offended. Some ethologists found the idea plausible. Maynard Smith condemned the models as unrealistic and the mathematics as flawed (see Chapter 8). But this time we are not dealing with models as such, we are invited to consider a new *approach* to science, 'consilient explanation'. Although Wilson admits that only a small number of researchers so far are doing the kind of research he is recommending, his footnotes contain the names of many potential allies. Close scrutiny, however, shows that among putative allies appear also people who have quite different views of the relationship between genes and culture from the Wilson and Lumsden model; notably, they typically do *not* believe that the genes hold culture on a leash in the same way Wilson does.

A real source of tension between Wilson and many of his potential allies has to do with Wilson's reluctance to leave the world of values alone. There are quite a number of researchers today who are genuinely interested in exploring the connections between evolutionary theory and human nature. The difference between these researchers and Wilson is that the former see their own inquiry as purely *knowledge-oriented*. In addition, many are acutely aware of the earlier history of biologization of human behavior, making them feel distinct unease at any suggestion of a connection between their science and politics.[5] In fact, one illustration of the difficulties for Wilson in trying to convince his most immediate scientific colleagues was an occasion when he first tried to introduce his consilience project.

The occasion was his keynote address in 1996 at the annual meeting of the Human

Behavior and Evolution Society in Evanston (June 1996). The organizers of this meeting had gone out of their way to make up for the past tension between the society and Wilson. ('We gave him a rough deal earlier,' explained the local host John Beckstrom, 'and we wanted to make up for it.') It is true that the society had distanced itself from Wilson and the name 'sociobiology' precisely because of the political associations of that name. Wilson, in turn, had distanced himself from the society—at least he had let his membership lapse. In an attempt to bring him back, the organizers had now decided to honor Wilson properly, asking him to deliver the keynote address.

The title of Wilson's address was 'The Unity of Science', but nobody really knew what that meant. Wilson was cheerfully introduced by his friend, former HBES president Nap Chagnon. The surprise came in the middle of the address when Wilson lashed out against Jacques Derrida and deconstruction, of all things. (My first reaction was that Wilson had brought the wrong manuscript, or mistaken the HBES audience for another one—say, a gathering of the National Association of Scholars.) It was all rather embarrassing: Wilson went on to treat the audience as a kind of big 'in-group', using a conspiratorial tone and acting as if we all knew what he was talking about and automatically agreed (an activity describable as 'drafting'; see Chapter 13). And it was not only the Derrida-tangent that seemed odd in the context. Although Wilson's keynote address was entitled 'The Unity of Science', the audience was not prepared for what he actually had to say. What baffled and annoyed many—including the conference organizers— was Wilson's insistence that there was only one science, and that the humanities should learn from science, because science prescribes the correct values for us! It seemed that after a twenty-year pause, Wilson had again shamelessly reiterated in public that controversial point from his first chapter in *Sociobiology*—the extrapolation from *is* to *ought*—and with a new vehemence.

For the organizers of this HBES conference, Wilson's talk was disquieting. They had invited him in a spirit of reconciliation, but it seemed he had only made matters worse. Had he really said what he seemed to have said? After serious discussion, Beckstrom felt compelled to write a letter to Wilson, a copy of which was also sent to each member of the society. Beckstrom asked Wilson to explain exactly what he meant:

> I hope I misunderstood you. Among other things, you seemed to be (1) promoting the use of evolutionary history of human behavior in establishing values for 'the humanities' and society in general and (2) denigrating philosophers who point out the follies of the Naturalistic Fallacy. In other words, you seemed to be advocating normative uses of sociobiology. If you were, I would have to oppose vigorously your position and I expect many in attendance with whom I later discussed your speech, would do likewise.
>
> That sort of usage was behind Social Darwinism and that unfortunate chapter set the Darwinian Paradigm back by decades. We just cannot suggest to political and social activists that they should use sociobiology/evolutionary biology/behavioral history in a normative manner again. I hope you will agree with me (letter from Beckstrom to Wilson, 2 July 1996; with copies to HBES 1996 registrants).

With hindsight, everything falls into place. Although at the time the audience didn't have a clue, Wilson's keynote address was obviously adapted from his newest book, then in progress. *Consilience* in different ways, indeed, urges the natural sciences and humanities to unite around the tenets of evolutionary biology. It is also clear why Derrida and postmodernism were introduced: they were perfect as anathema to Wilson's proposed unification scheme, because they epitomized 'the skeptical and relativistic accounts of "socially constructed" realities supplied by intellectuals who have lost faith in the original Enlightenment quest for unified knowledge', as Wilson later formulated it (Wilson, 1998b).

Silverman (1997) described the audience response as 'a vocal standing ovation', which he attributed to Wilson's 'call for sociobiologists to use their science for the betterment of society'. Many may have perceived this as the gist of Wilson's message. Others, again, including the organizers, were troubled by Wilson's normative-seeming approach. How, then, did Wilson respond to Beckstrom? I quote from his brief, hand-written note (not distributed to HBES members):

> Not to worry about my resuming normative reasoning; I will never open that Pandora's box. I realize now that I should not have dismissed the philosophers so cavalierly—it was bound to be misunderstood. But I will make the point that over the years they have done very little to further the biological sciences, and some have impeded them (letter from Wilson to Beckstrom, 9 July 1996).[6]

But had not Wilson said explicitly that the humanities should take their lead from science? How can Wilson be interpreted as saying something else than what a significant portion of the audience thought he said? The explanation is probably that Wilson did not see himself as making normative statements, because he was speaking about his new idea of consilience of knowledge. At this point he saw himself as promoting *science*, not naturalistic ethics. He was just showing the social sciences and humanities the way to become more scientific and thus help solve global problems. In any case, Wilson did not see himself in his speech as *directly* advocating the normative use of sociobiology or evolutionary biology for either ethical or political aims. [7]

Thus, while many of Wilson's colleagues would agree that there should exist some kind of *coherence*, consistency, or compatibility of explanations at different levels in science, that explanations at one level should not be contradictory to explanations at another level (see, for instance, the formulations by Cosmides and Tooby, 1992), this did not mean that they would necessarily be willing to take the next step. For a 'regular' scientist, Wilsonian consilience does require an unusual set of commitments: a belief that the unity of the world entails the unity of explanation; a belief that explanation can only mean explanation in the language of physics; a belief in the identity of brain and mind, explanation and understanding; finally, a sense of a deep connection between knowledge of evolutionary biology and human values. Wilson himself charmingly declared himself 'guilty, guilty, guilty' to all kinds of possible epistemological crimes: '*conflation, simplism, ontological reductionism, scientism*, and other sins' (italics in original), although he classified these as the objections of 'a few professional philosophers' to his unification project (p. 11). Wilson argued that his project was at least worth a try. In Chapter 20 we will encounter Wilson's arguments for the metaphysical importance of his new agenda.

Know thyself: a long-range Enlightenment goal

The 'real' message of *Sociobiology* was never adequately addressed on its own terms. *Sociobiology* can actually be seen as Wilson's particular solution to a problem that others had already grappled with: the problem of mankind's future in a radically changing environment. Like Lorenz and other ethological and anthropological writers of the 1960s and early 1970s, and Jacques Ellul and other technological pessimists before that, Wilson believed that mankind was in danger: technological development is outrunning our capacity to cope. Culture is proceeding faster than evolution. We are stuck with behavioral patterns that were once adaptive but are not any longer. This is why it is important for us to know who we really are and do something about this discrepancy between culture and nature.

Sociobiology, then, was Wilson's contribution to a larger Enlightenment project already in progress. However, as soon as the controversy started, Wilson's long-term concern for mankind as a whole got overshadowed by his critics' more short-term political concerns. For a long time the prevailing climate of opinion was so strongly pro-environmentalist (or rather, pro-culturalist), that it was simply not possible for Wilson to convince people that his book was *not* meant as a political contribution but as a long-range scheme for saving mankind. Consequently, the controversy became one of political accusations and defenses, rather than a serious discussion about the situation for mankind. Wilson was simply outdefined by the critics.

Wilson seems to have especially taken up the problem as it was formulated by Konrad Lorenz in the last two chapters of *On Aggression*, 'Ecce Homo' and 'Avowal of Optimism'. There, Lorenz emphasized the extreme importance for mankind to know about its own evolutionary heritage. While the serious themes raised by Lorenz had been an inspiration for the participants at the Smithsonian Man and Beast conference in 1969 (see Chapter 5), there had also been much protest by the liberal left. In *Sociobiology* Wilson tried cautiously to disassociate himself from the writings of the popular ethologists. Still, the fact that Lorenz in 1973 shared the Nobel Prize in physiology with Niko Tinbergen and Karl von Frisch must have felt like an encouragement to those who believed that finding out about mankind's adjustment to human nature was crucial for the future of humanity.

In his 1972 Croonian lecture Tinbergen had discussed the possible contribution of ethology to man's influence on his environment. He worried about global issues such as the depletion of non-renewable resources and population growth, and also about the increased pressure on human adjustment that every new cultural change was producing, including the strain this was putting on families and individuals. Tinbergen finished his lecture by urging 'all sciences concerned with the biology of Man to work for an integration of their many and diverse approaches and to step up the pace of building a coherent comprehensive science of Man' (Tinbergen, 1972, quoted in Hinde, 1991a). However, in a *Science* article Tinbergen had already criticized Lorenz' view of aggression as innate and argued for a more complex approach (Tinbergen, 1968).

Wilson differed from his ethologist and anthropologist colleagues in one important respect. They were basically raising questions about human adaptability, or pointing out the discrepancies between our basic 'human biogram' and the pressures of our current environment. Their approach was descriptive. But Wilson wanted to find a clear *prescription* for how we ought to live. Finding out about human nature would help us understand the realistic range for social and cultural experimentation, and thus aid social planning.

And this was, of course, why he committed the so-called naturalistic fallacy—which for him was not really a fallacy at all, but rather part and parcel of his overall program. What his liberal East Coast critics did not realize was that Wilson in his biological world view represented an older, venerable tradition in evolutionary biology, whose recent exponents included C. H. Waddington and Teilhard de Chardin.[8] For that tradition, the aim was precisely to look for moral messages in nature. For Wilson, the idea would be to probe deeply into human nature instead. 'Know thyself' was what Lorenz had argued for in his last chapter of *On Aggression* as the means for mankind to avoid self-destruction. But Lorenz had gone even further. Knowing biology, we would also know our true goal: 'Sufficient knowledge of man and of his position in the living world, as I have said, automatically determine the ideals for which we have to strive' (Lorenz, 1968, p. 288).

Wilson took this yet one step further. It was not only a question of understanding biology: we might come to understand *morality* itself! As he later formulated it (together with Michael Ruse):

> Human beings face incredible social problems, primarily because their biology cannot cope with the effects of their technology. A deeper understanding of this biology is surely a first step toward solving some of these pressing worries. Seeing morality for what it is, a legacy of evolution, rather than a reflection of eternal, divinely inspired verities, is part of this understanding (Ruse and Wilson, 1985).

Wilson and Ruse described morality as but one of the many products generated by the 'epigenetic rules'. Morality does not exist as an objective given; rather, we are evolutionarily induced to believe in morality, altruism, and so on because they are adaptive. And this also meant that our moral rules were species specific:

> If like the termites we needed to dwell in darkness, eat each others faeces and cannibalize the dead, our epigenetic rules would be very different from what they are now. Our minds would be strongly prone to extol such acts as beautiful and moral (Ruse and Wilson, 1985).

This termite comparison was a favorite of Wilson's—he had originally used it in his 1980 Tanner lectures—but it did not sit well with all audiences. The academics who were most uncomfortable with Wilson's move toward naturalistic ethics were probably professional moral philosophers. For these, morality typically resided in a transcendental realm, where the fundamental questions could be traced to Plato and Aristotle (see, for example, Williams, 1985). Among scientists, too, the question of the possible relationship between sociobiology and morality had been causing some turbulence ever since the beginning of the controversy (for example, Stent, 1977). Many felt that the matter needed serious discussion. In 1978, a Dahlem conference was devoted to the examination of the possible relationships between sociobiology and morality (Stent, 1980). There were even those philosophers who felt inspired by sociobiological insights (for example, Peter Singer in his *The Expanding Circle*, 1980).

To the potential annoyance of some, and the delight of others, the termites made their reappearance in *Consilience*—this time complete with the Termite Code of Ethics, republished from Wilson's original (1980d) lectures. Here is a snippet from the state-of-the-colony speech of a termite leader, ghost-written by Wilson:

> It is now possible to express the imperatives of moral behavior with precision. These imperatives are self-evident and universal. They are the very essence of termity. They include the love of darkness, . . . the sanctity of the physiological caste system; the evil of personal rights (the colony is ALL!); . . . and the ecstacy of cannibalism and surrender of our own bodies when we are sick or injured (it is more blessed to be eaten than to eat) (Wilson, 1998a, p. 148).

One avenue for Wilsonian expansion, then, was to do the 'deep history' of human morality. But there was room for further development, too, with regard to the concerns for mankind's future. The 1969 Man and Beast conference, as one of its many aspects, had been asking for a 'new morality', with the biosphere as a focus and 'Nature is my friend' as the rallying cry (Sebeok, 1991). After *Sociobiology*, Wilson extended his salvation project beyond mankind to life on Earth as such.

One thing that Lorenz had worried about was the difficulty with which mankind would be able to unite in one larger humanity, considering the tendencies for people to divide the world into in-groups and out-groups. Worrying about the threat of nuclear war, he could offer no solution except hope that reason would prevail, working together with natural selection, so that we would eventually come to love our neighbors. The threat of nuclear war, however, was soon to be supplanted by the threat of extinction of life on Earth as a whole. Here Wilson—supported by a general neo-catastrophist trend with tales of dinosaur deaths, asteroids, and the like—was able to make a convincing case for the importance of the preservation of biodiversity. In 1996, a reviewer in *The New York Times Book Review* noted that '[i]n the past decade or so Mr. Wilson has become best known as an eloquent doomsayer on the subject of declining natural resources . . . and the need to preserve "the diversity of life", which we are so recklessly diminishing through species extinction' (Bouton, 1996).

In *Consilience* Wilson reiterated this point. It was no longer only mankind but the whole world that was at risk. What had taken mankind into the current dangerous situation was the seemingly unavoidable 'Ratchet of Progress': 'The more knowledge people acquire, the more they are able to increase their numbers and to alter the environment, whereupon they need new knowledge just to stay alive' (Wilson 1998a, p. 270). In other words, Wilson declared, while the natural environment shrinks and resources diminish, '*advanced technology has become the ultimate prosthesis*' (italics added). We are back to Wilson's Ur-theme—repressed in the initial discussion about *Sociobiology*.

Wilson does not support the idea of human exemptionalism: the whole planet is involved. The Biosphere 2 experiment, the dream of freeing man from the natural environment, had failed miserably. Life is fragile, and exemptionalism neglects the fragility of life. We cannot just move on as if mankind could solve each crisis as it came along, including the decline of the global biosphere. We are caught in a spiral of technological progress and environmental destruction, and the reason is human nature:

> Each advance is also a prosthesis, an artificial device dependent on advanced expertise and intense continuing management . . . Human history can be viewed through the lens of ecology as the accumulation of environmental prostheses. As these manmade procedures thicken and interlock, they enlarge the carrying capacity of the planet. Human beings, being typical organisms in reproductive response, expand to fill the added capacity. The spiral continues. The environment, increasingly rigged and strutted to meet the new demands, turns even more delicate. It requires constant attention from increasingly sophisticated technology (Wilson, 1998a p. 289).

In this situation, the solution is one of sustainable development. 'The common aim must be to expand resources and improve the quality of life for as many people as heedless population growth forces upon Earth and do it with minimal prosthetic dependence' (p. 289). Full-cost accounting is needed, and new indicators of the state of the natural world and human well-being developed. We need a powerful conservation ethic: we have a responsibility not only to our own species but also to 'The Creation'—life on Earth (p. 292). In turn, this means preserving natural ecosystems (p. 297; here Wilson shows his Teilhardian colors).

We might say that throughout his career Wilson has been tracking the problem of the Ratchet of Progress, experimenting with different solutions. In 1969, he tried to find a way to speed up human evolution, using a simple population-genetic formula according to which change could take place in ten generations, or 200–300 years (Wilson, 1971c; see also Wilson, 1975a, pp. 146–7, 'Tracking the Environment with Evolutionary Change'). In *Sociobiology*, again, he relied on the multiplier effect, connecting genes to culture and thus keeping culture on a leash, preventing it from running amok, as it were. This he later modeled mathematically with Lumsden's help in *Genes, Mind and Culture*. In *On Human Nature*, he discussed both his alternatives: the leash principle and the possibility of man-made evolution through gene selection, either through traditional means or by new molecular techniques. Obviously, Wilson had more techniques at his disposal than Lorenz. Yet there is the same caution with regard to changing the gene pool. And just like Lorenz, who pointed out the link between aggression and other important traits, Wilson discussed the social costs—and benefits—of changing behaviors and circumventing certain innate predispositions (Wilson 1975, p. 575; 1978a, p. 134, pp. 147–8).

But it was in *Promethean Fire* that he, with Lumsden, developed in detail his most unusual scheme for matching culture and human nature: an explicit program of social engineering. Through social engineering, unwanted human behaviors might be finally curbed and others enhanced:

> Social engineering has the potential of profoundly altering every part of human behavior . . . Some very human propensities, which may have been of great adaptive value in the stone

age, are now largely self-destructive. *The most virulent of these, aggression and xenophobia, can be blunted. Other equally human propensities for altruism and cooperation may be enhanced.* The value of institutions and forms of government can be more accurately judged, alternative procedures laid out and steps carefully suggested (Lumsden and Wilson, 1983, pp. 183–4, italics added).

How did Lumsden and Wilson think this could be achieved? The answer is: societies could employ knowledge of the epigenetic rules 'to guide individual behavior and cultural evolution to the ends on which their members may someday agree' (p. 184).

So what would be an example of this kind of hypothetical social engineering, based on knowledge of epigenetic rules? Lumsden and Wilson produced one of their model examples: incest. How would a society go about *promoting* incest, if it wanted to, they asked? The engineering answer would involve using the knowledge we have about epigenetic rules to manipulate the environment and thus to achieve the desired outcome. We know that children raised together during the first six years or so are not physically attracted to each other (the Westermarck principle). Therefore, society might simply arrange for sisters and brothers to be raised apart, while at the same time in various cultural ways encouraging siblings to marry.

Lumsden and Wilson compared this type of social engineering to the way in which genetic defects of the phenylketonuria type were being corrected by the right diet. Through close knowledge of gene–environment interaction it is possible to select the precise environment that *reverses* the usual response—phenylketonuria or sister–brother incest, they noted (p. 177). But we can go much further: 'A sufficient knowledge of genes and mental development can lead to the development of a form of social engineering that changes not only the likelihood of the outcome but the deepest feelings about right and wrong, in other words, the ethical precepts themselves' (p. 179).

Tinbergen, too, in his 1972 Croonian lecture had considered the need for social engineering: 'The prevention of possible disadaptation and the creation of a new adaptedness will be a matter of behavioural planning'. In his view, 'while functional ethology helps us in identifying these pressures, *it will be knowledge of our behavioral mechanisms, and of mechanisms of behavioral development, that will have to form the basis for whatever engineering will have to be undertaken*' (Tinbergen, 1972, quoted in Hinde, 1991a, italics added). It is interesting to see that Wilson and Lumsden apparently agreed with Tinbergen about the importance of development and environment for the modification of behavior. In their model, then, culture could in principle drive the genes–mind–culture system *backwards*, as it were. Still, Wilson and Lumsden did not, like Tinbergen, take behavioral mechanisms seriously; they did not let proximate factors interfere with the ultimate predictability of their genes–mind–culture model. (Wilson later seems to have abandoned this particular social planning idea.)

In the last chapter of *In Search of Nature*, a book of essays published in 1996, Wilson asked 'Is Mankind Suicidal?' More specifically, he wondered '[i]s the drive to environmental conquest and self-propagation so deeply embedded in our genes as to be unstoppable?' This he answered in the negative. We were smart enough and would have time enough to avoid global environmental catastrophe. In *Consilience*, Wilson formulated what he saw as the two existing alternatives for mankind. Either it could maintain its 'greed' with the help of technology, or consider altering the genetic nature of the human species. He regarded both as Faustian bargains, although for him the second choice was 'strangely echoing the Enlightenment' (p. 270). (Indeed, considering his distaste for 'prostheses', Wilson might well be expected to be more enthusiastic about the latter option.) But Wilson saw this option, too, as problematic. 'Volitional evolution', changing our nature, would present mankind with the most profound intellectual dilemma it had ever faced, Wilson observed:

> It is entirely possible that within fifty years we will understand in detail not only our own heredity, but also a great deal about the way our genes interact with the environment to produce a human being. We can then tinker with the products at any level: change them temporarily without altering heredity, or change them permanently by mutating the genes and chromosomes.
>
> If these advances in knowledge are even just partly attained, which seems inevitable unless a great deal of genetic and medical research is halted in its tracks, and if they are made generally available, which is problematic, humanity will be positioned godlike to take control of its ultimate fate. It can, if it chooses, alter not just the anatomy and intelligence of the species but also the emotions and creative drive that compose the very core of human nature (1998a, p. 274).

But was this not exactly what Wilson had been warning about and promising ever since *Sociobiology*, most clearly in *On Human Nature* and *Promethean Fire*? *On Human Nature* contains many of the same problematics as *Consilience*. There we have the same suggestion that we need to know our true nature and choose our genes based on better knowledge and techniques (1978a, p. 208). And there we are also faced with the same dilemma of choice: if and when we have explained religion as a material force, we will have no external moral guidelines to follow, and will have to rely completely on ourselves. Where will we then take our values from? The answer Wilson gave in 1978 was that these values may *also* be part of our heritage. Perhaps something deep within us will be telling us not to change our genes, even if we could (1978a, p. 208).

Indeed, one of Wilson's overriding concerns has been the conservation of the human gene pool, a concern that he shares with Lorenz. Lorenz briefly considered conventional eugenics but discarded it in favor of cultural measures for discharging and sublimating aggression. One reason was the link he perceived between aggression and other important traits. Wilson, too, has from the beginning emphasized the possible link between desirable and undesirable behaviors (1975a, p. 575), and in general seems exceedingly unwilling to recommend tampering with our genetic heritage. But Wilson wants to conserve *all kinds* of species on Earth, not only humans. He is a conservationist at heart (1998a, p. 277).

This makes it perhaps less surprising to learn that Wilson believes that future generations will in fact be conservative and resist hereditary change. 'They will do so in order to save the emotions and epigenetic rules of mental development, because these elements compose the physical soul of the species', Wilson asserts (1998a, p. 277). '*If one alters the emotions and the rules, people might be more rational, but would no longer be human*. Why should a species give up the defining core of its existence, built by millions of years of trial and error?' (p. 277, italics added). Wilson does not believe we will 'surrender our genetic nature to machine-aided ratiocination' either (p. 298). Artificial intelligence will not, after all, be possible. The reason is that people want both rationality and emotion. People will not want to be soulless robots or lose their humanity! This is a rather remarkable turnaround from Wilson's earlier apparent infatuation with artificial intelligence. Indeed, as we shall see in the last chapter, it is this new emphasis on the importance of *emotion*—also as an ingredient in science—that creates a potential wedge between Wilson and his scientific colleagues.

Still, Wilson's discussion, straightforward as it is, appears rather mild in comparison with some other suggestions. When at the 1989 Man and Beast Revisited conference the question was raised once again, 'Can man endure?', one of the participants, Thomas Sebeok, decided to make this question more specific by asking: 'How, in what form, and for how long?' As an answer he came up with 'the same short-term answer as Lynn Margulis in 1986: "through the commingling of human and manufactured parts in new life-forms", a cybersymbiotic process that will enable us to rebuild our species' (Sebeok, 1991). Beat that!

CHAPTER 19

The tension between scientific and moral truth

Evolutionary biology: between science and values

There is no doubt that the sociobiology controversy has a strong metaphysical dimension. Underlying the crisp scientific and political interchanges are deep concerns about such things as the nature of human nature, free will vs determinism, essentialism vs existentialism, the body–mind relationship, and so on. And connected to these issues are, in turn, particular visions of the nature of science. In Chapter 14 I tackled some ontological issues having to do with the physical world, particularly holism vs reductionism. In Chapter 16 I discussed different scientific conceptions of the nature of genes and the nature of evolution. In this chapter and the next I will address some metaphysical and quasi-metaphysical themes that underlie and inform the positions taken by different parties in the sociobiology controversy: the nature of evolutionary biology as a science; the connection between scientific facts and social values; the opposition between free will and determinism; finally, the relationship between science and religion. We will see that scientists' positions on these matters are usually connected to deep moral and political concerns. Meanwhile, it is exactly the involvement of these kinds of themes that makes the sociobiology controversy important also as a *cultural discourse*.

I will begin with an examination of the nature of evolutionary biology itself—a root cause of the problems dealt with in this book. Evolutionary biology is a rather special type of discipline. On the one hand, like all sciences, it is trying to extend objective knowledge about the world. On the other, it is dealing with issues that impinge on the very origin of mankind. Evolutionary biological claims compete with other existing creation myths and human self-perceptions (cf. Durant, 1980). This characteristic makes it hard to consider it as just a science like any other. It seems unavoidable to attribute to evolutionary biology an *implicit moral function* as well. Another question is whether evolutionary biologists themselves recognize this as a problem, and if so, how they cope with it.

Indeed, in their different ways, sociobiologists and their critics have only been reminding us about the unintended consequences of theorizing in evolutionary biology. The talk about such things as the naturalistic fallacy is for academics, not for people who are desperately looking for guidelines for their lives. There is no doubt that evolutionary biology has an implicit moral/political message, at least for those who are not trained to guard themselves against these kinds of inferences, or do not have an alternative moral framework firmly in place.

One specter haunting the biological study of human behavior has been Social Darwinism. Others have worried about biological information being used for political control. For instance, at an early point in the sociobiology debate, Wilson's Harvard colleague, physicist Gerald Holton, wrote:

> The sheer instinct of self-preservation may be sufficient to account for the fact that people are suspicious as never before about any new scientific theory or technological development that might enlarge the potential for the control of human behavior. We ask, 'Control by whom? According to whose values? For whose benefit and whose risk? With what institutional constraint?' (Holton, 1978, p. 83.)

He noted that crimes had been committed in the name of science, some with the full collaboration of scientists. Still, recognizing these risks, Holton—with many others— took the position that knowledge is of supreme importance for us, and that science is our way of finding out about the world. (Later, he was to refer to this attitude as 'The Ionian Enchantment'; Holton, 1995.)

Others, however, do not even discuss these kinds of problems, but emphasize that in principle it is possible to combine a progressive social outlook with a defense of the objective nature of science. Among evolutionary biologists, it is particularly Dawkins who has become the spokesman for this kind of vision. Dawkins keeps pointing out that Darwinism is not 'advocating' anything! Values cannot be derived from nature; DNA does not care one way or the other—it just is (for example, Dawkins, 1995a). In fact, Dawkins can sound quite emotional defending the objective nature of his subject against the critics of sociobiology. After all the public spectacle, the general public's 'default' assumption may now well be that sociobiology is somehow associated with political conservatism. It is this sort of thinking that Dawkins has been regularly confronted with on public occasions and in interviews. Here is an example from a few years back, when he was asked why sociobiology is often associated with right-wing sentiments. You can almost hear the exasperation in Dawkins' voice as he told the interviewer:

> Because the opponents of sociobiology are too stupid to understand the distinction between what one says about the way the world is, scientifically, and the way it ought to be politically. They look at what we say about natural selection, as a scientific theory for what is, and they assume that anybody who says that so and so is the case, must therefore be advocating that it ought to be the case in human politics. They cannot see that it is possible to separate one's scientific beliefs about what is the case in nature from one's political beliefs about what ought to be in human society (Roes, 1997).

Dawkins makes the point about the fact–value distinction, and how it *ought to* be treated from a strictly logical point of view. But logic may be quite beside the point when it comes to people's actual reasoning in these matters. So let us ask a different question. Why is it that a statement of fact is somehow seen as a moral justification of a state of affairs? This is what the critics of sociobiology have constantly pointed out, and their targets equally steadfastly denied. By what mechanism does a 'mere statement of fact' in the world of science become a seeming prescription for action, although there is no *logical* connection? The answer is: a society where people perceive an intimate connection between a fact and its *utility*. Under such conditions a mere statement of fact is never really a 'mere' statement of fact.

This is why the critics attacked Wilson even when he presented views that were considered quite unexceptional in evolutionary biology. But what is even more interesting is that the perceived close connection between facts and utility applied also to the critics' *own* reasoning with regard to the political views they felt that they themselves could legitimately hold. The best example here is the response I got from a member of the Sociobiology Study Group when I asked him what he would do if there were ever incontrovertible facts about racial differences. He declared that in that case he would have to become a racist (see Chapter 11).

Obviously, statements of (presumed) facts in evolutionary biology or any other field are read as political prescriptions only if you believe that scientific facts will (or must!) be *acted* upon! Since for someone like Dawkins this is not the *obvious* fate of what he considers purely descriptive or illustrative biological statements, his reaction to the critics' accusations has, understandably, been one of strong protest. (In Chapter 9 we saw that he went as far as calling the alleged political intentions of sociobiologists a 'simple lie'.) Dawkins' persistent refusal to draw political conclusions from biological facts has obviously frustrated interviewers, who may or may not believe that Dawkins really believes what the critics believe he believes. Here we have Dawkins continuing his exchange with the interviewer we met before.

> *Q*: On the other hand, some people favored Darwinism because it appeared to support a political idea.
> *A*: Yes, Darwinism has been misused politically in this century, by Hitler and by others. Social Darwinism flourished at the end of the last century and the beginning of this century with people like Herbert Spencer and John D. Rockefeller. Rockefeller, an immensely rich and powerful man, had imported a form of Social Darwinism into his political beliefs. He really felt that the weakest should go to war, and the strongest should survive, it was right in business, it was right in capitalism that the economically strongest and most ruthless should prevail.
> *Q*: Is evolutionary theory telling us this?
> *A*: No! It is telling us this only if you say that what is going on there in nature ought to be true in political and social life. What I am saying, along with many other people, among them T. H. Huxley, is that in our political and social life we are entitled to throw out Darwinism, to say we don't want to live in a Darwinian world. We may want to live in, say, a socialist world which is very un-Darwinian. We might say: Yes, Darwinism is true, natural selection is the true force that has given rise to life, but we, when we set up our political institutions, we might say we are going to base our society on explicitly anti-Darwinian principles.
> *Q*: This is what you favor?
> *A*: Yes. (Roes, 1997)

Dawkins emerges as a boy scout, giving all the 'correct' answers. The interviewer could simply not 'get' him (not that there would have been anything to 'get', since Dawkins' own political sympathies are on the liberal-left).

Another interviewer, for *The Skeptic* a couple of years earlier, did not fare much better when it came to getting Dawkins to comment on presumed political inferences from sociobiological statements. Dawkins started off by refusing to see any connection between *The Selfish Gene*, *Sociobiology*, and *The Bell Curve*. Here he again vented his irritation with the critics, who 'instead of just calmly and peacefully sitting down and thinking about what is actually the truth: "Are there genes that influence behavior?", respond by "flaming up fires about old political issues". That kind of thing bores me rigid! *I care about what's actually true!*', Dawkins declared (Miele, 1995, italics added). Here we see a clear example of the difference between a *knowledge-oriented* and a *utility-oriented* approach to evolutionary biology in the opposition between Dawkins and the critics, over and above the deep-seated intellectual differences that we have discussed.

What are, then, the basic strategies among evolutionary biologists when it comes to handling this particular field and its potential value implications? There seem to be three. The first strategy is to keep science separate from values. The second strategy actively connects science with values: you criticize science you don't like or you do scientific research that corresponds to your values. The third also connects science with values, but in a more intricate and proactive way: it involves choosing or developing theoretical approaches with seemingly desirable social implications.

Who belongs where among the sociobiologists and their critics? It turns out that the dividing line does not run neatly between the sociobiological and critical camps. What we have instead is a division between scientists representing what I call Enlightenment and hyper-Enlightenment approaches. The former wish to pursue a 'pure' knowledge agenda, clearly separated from a moral/political one. This strategy aims at keeping scientific and moral truth apart, and this state of affairs is seen as both possible and desirable. The second group of scientists regard it as desirable and/or necessary to pursue truth in the scientific and moral/political realm at the *same* time. This distinction between Enlightenment and hyper-Enlightenment scientists may sound rather clear cut. There is at least one complication, however, when it comes to the sociobiology debate: Wilson has *two* modes of operation, an objectivist and a normative one. In other words, he is a member of *both* the Enlightenment and hyper Enlightenment camps, shuttling between them as his writing requires.

Among the personalities in the sociobiology controversy, the first strategy, the fact–value distinction, is probably upheld most strongly by Maynard Smith and Dawkins, by Davis, and by Wilson in his objectivist mode. This is the 'objectivist' school, which regards evolutionary biology as a regular descriptive and explanatory science, just like other sciences. Members of this group point out the need to keep science separate from ideology, usually warning about the Lysenko case. Wilson, Davis (see Chapter 11), and Maynard Smith (1989b) have all done this. Here Dawkins has recently taken a step further than his colleagues with his active crusade against 'viruses of the mind' (Dawkins, 1993). Viruses are all kinds of irrational belief systems, including the Catholic religion.

Dawkins is at pains to point out the lack of divine purpose and plan in evolution, using computer simulation to demonstrate that even the most complicated features—such as the eye—could have come about by the processes of evolution alone at least forty times (see Dawkins, 1996, Chapter 5).

The second strategy is to let values inform what you *count* as established fact or acceptable theory. You may, for instance, find very severe scientific flaws in science you consider morally/politically undesirable, while refraining from doing the same with science of whose (apparent) social implications you approve. Here we have the typical moral-cum-scientific criticisms of sociobiology as seen throughout this book, including that of the adaptationist program and its purported Panglossianism (see Chapter 6). You may also try to do science which satisfies both scientific and political criteria (for example, the liberatory and Marxist approaches in Chapter 9). In other words, one version of the second strategy is a type of 'critical' science.

The most intricate strategy is the third one. This strategy also combines science with values, but now in an explicitly or implicitly normative way. Here our prime candidates are on the one hand Wilson—Wilson this time in his normative, not objectivist mode —on the other, Gould and Lewontin.

From the beginning, Wilson emphasized the need to directly derive values for mankind from evolutionary biology, sometimes embarrassing his objectivist colleagues by being so unashamedly normative. And Wilson has been persistent in his wish to go from *is* to *ought*, sometimes seemingly retracting it, but soon snapping back. Over the years, Wilson has conceived multiple avenues for bridging the fact–value gap in terms of social intervention when it comes to our genetic heritage: 'sublimation' and diversion of negative traits (1975a); education and positive eugenics (1978a); social engineering by changing the environment for the epigenetic rules (with Lumsden, 1983); and in *Consilience* (1998a), providing a whole spectrum of suggestions: education, 'science, ethics and political choice', and, of course, consilience.

Throughout his writings, Wilson has practiced what he has preached and derived various conclusions from a scientific state of affairs. In contrast to the opponents of sociobiology, however, the social implications Wilson saw were *liberal*. In *Sociobiology* he played down the significance of IQ and declared race not a useful biological concept. In *On Human Nature* he discussed 'the cardinal value' of the survival of the human gene pool (p. 196) and the need for genetic diversity (p. 198). He argued for universal human rights, 'not because of some abstract principle, but because we are mammals' (p. 198), pointed to 'the failure of slavery' (p. 80), and noted that 'the longterm consequence of inequity will always be visibly dangerous' (p. 199). Further, he advocated a more liberal sexual morality (p. 141) and defended homosexuality as a socially useful trait (pp. 142–7).

These were relatively straightforward normative applications of biological knowledge to human affairs. I will now move to a more complicated type of normative maneuver.

Knowing people's seemingly unfailing tendency to draw practical conclusions from evolutionary biological theory, could one try to capitalize on this somehow? Could one not try to *induce desired moral/political consequences* by formulating a theory so that it would seem to have these kinds of implications? Indeed, this has been tried. This was in fact what Popper tried to do in developing his falsificationist epistemology. According to his autobiography (Popper, 1976), he wanted an epistemology that, if implemented also in social affairs, would be guaranteed to have politically desirable qualities. Just as bad scientific theories would be falsified and superseded by better ones, so bad governments would be 'falsified' and replaced by better ones. In other words, Popper was pursuing a hyper-Enlightenment quest for a combined scientific and moral/political truth. The third strategy, therefore, may be seen as a variant of the Popper principle.

Gould is probably our best example. His continuous search for theoretical alternatives to the adaptationist program, starting with punctuated equilibria and continuing with the idea of historical contingency (particularly in *Wonderful Life*) can be seen as one long argument for social reform and social justice. If everything is optimally adapted in the best of all possible worlds, there is no point in trying to effect social change. But if instead of adaptation you emphasize discontinuity, contingency, and chance, you indicate that in a radically new environment new types of individuals will flourish. Everybody gets his chance: it is not a question of the selection of the fittest. Or in Lewontin's apt quote from Ecclesiastes: 'the race is not to the swift, nor the battle to the strong, nor yet bread to the wise . . . but time and chance happeneth to them all' (Lewontin, 1981d). Unlike Gould, however, Lewontin has not really formulated an alternative scientific theory for generating 'positive consequences' in the Popper sense; his taste seems to confine him largely to the critical mode of the second strategy. Still, what he has done and keeps doing is to promote a *metaphysical* research program, where organisms are seen as subject and object, wholes as implying parts and parts as implying wholes, and so on (for example, Lewontin, 1981f; Levins and Lewontin, 1995).

But Gould is not the only one who may be affecting people's social perceptions with his theoretical work. There are recent movements also in the adaptationist camp, notably the attempts to restore group selection. As discussed in Chapter 6, it is not by accident that proponents of group selection tend to have strong moral convictions, and the moral appeal of group selection may be one reason for its popularity, particularly in the United States.

Telling the truth about biology

Obviously my classification of strategies or approaches is purely analytical. In practice, it is often hard to know which strategy is being followed, even when it comes to a seemingly obvious dichotomy such as that between an objectivist Enlightenment approach and a value-informed hyper-Enlightenment one. We can already see this in the disagreement between scientists as to what motivates a particular colleague to take a particular stance (quite an amount of conversational energy is sometimes spent trying to establish the truth in this matter).

Take, for instance, ethologists such as Pat Bateson and Robert Hinde. Bateson has kept emphasizing the role of developmental factors in the course of evolution. Initially, at least, someone like Dawkins thought that the whole thing was a misunderstanding between concerns of embryology and evolution. But it wasn't. Bateson had in mind such things as the evolution of the ability to 'track the environment'. Developmental processes proceed in a direction that is appropriate for particular conditions; they 'involve multiply influenced systems with properties that are not easily anticipated, even when all the influences are known' (Bateson, 1986, pp. 90–1). At a simple level, this may take the form of a conditioned response; for instance, the African grass-hopper's suppression of the genes for either green or black color depending on the environment (fresh or scorched savanna). For animals with more elaborate nervous systems, more and more powerful rules of tracking the environment have been pro-vided through learning. And just because of the dependence of an animal's behavior on external conditions, Bateson pointed out, 'it will be no more possible to predict pre-cisely what an animal will do from the knowledge of its genes than it will be possible to predict the detailed course of a game of chess from the knowledge of the game's rules and what the pieces look like' (p. 91). And when we get to humans, '[t]he view that a simple relationship exists between genes and behaviour, especially human behaviour, is nonsense' (Bateson, 1984, p. 344).

Other biologists have pointed out other reasons why prediction is difficult. The following comes from a review of Dawkins' *Climbing Mount Improbable*, by ecologist Valerius Geist:

> Mr. Dawkins pays no attention to adaptive phenotypic plasticity—an organism's ability to alter its physiology to accommodate changes in its environment—which normally thwarts natural selection on genes. Thus a false impression is conveyed that genes (mutations) generally produce the same results. They rarely do . . . Mutations whose effect can be overridden by the normal abilities of individuals spread randomly and, at best, become part of the genetic load of the species. We expect evolution (genetic change) to be rare, and when it does occur, it is proof of incompetence, of extinction barely avoided. Successful forms do not evolve noticeably as they deal competently with environmental vagaries. To be a 'living fossil' is the hallmark of biological success (Geist, 1996).

On the other hand, objections to the model of gene selectionism may easily go 'too far' for the horizon of a particular biologist, and at this point suspicion easily sets in. Here is an interesting example. Maynard Smith went as far as admitting that Darwin's theory of evolution by natural selection, although correct, was not 'enough', because it did not explain development: 'Since the kinds of varieties that can arise in a given species depend on development, and since the course of evolution is constrained by the variations that can arise, it is obvious that Darwinism is not all that we need to know', he emphasized. But having said that, he immediately added:

> My fear is that when people argue that Darwinism is not enough, it is not the absence of a theory of development, or of ecology, that they are worried about. Often I suspect that they are hankering after some kind of Lamarckian inheritance of acquired characters, or some Teilhardian inner urge towards the omega point. If so, they would be better to stick with Darwin (Maynard Smith, 1986b, pp. 45–6).

In other words, Maynard Smith drew a very clear line as to what was and was not 'acceptable belief'. He backed up his standpoint with the empirical observation that, although mutations of large effect exist, so-called macromutations or hopeful monsters —that is, mutants with new complex structures not present in any ancestor and able to perform a complex function—are *not* observed in genetics laboratories (pp. 44–5) (see Chapter 6).

Something similar was observed by Hamilton with regard to macromutation. In his autobiographical notes, Hamilton said he regarded himself as a gradualist, believing in small changes in existing structures, and assuming that genes which cause large changes would usually be selected out. According to him, those who believe in a mutation 'causing' a whole complex behavior pattern all at once are in fact setting up a strawman, because big-gene world concerns are not valid when it comes to standard gradual neo-Darwinist change:

> I think that a lot of the objection to so-called 'reductionism' and 'bean-bag reasoning' directed at Neodarwinist theory comes from people, who, whether through inscrutable private agendas or ignorance, are not gradualists, being instead inhabitants of some imagined world of super-fast progress. Big changes, strong interlocus interactions, hopeful monsters, mutations so abundant and so hopeful that several, may be under selection at one time—these have to be the stuff of their dreams if their criticisms are to make sense . . . However, in general it is certainly unfair to project the unrealistic difficulties of such a fast moving and major-gene world into that of normal Neodarwinism as if the difficulties of the former were the usual truth (Hamilton, 1996, p. 28).

When humans are explicitly involved, suspicions increase that colleagues are straying from the truth. Take, for instance, the so-called Seville Declaration on Violence. This was drafted by an international committee of twenty scholars at the Sixth International Colloquium on Brain and Aggression in 1986. UNESCO adopted the Seville statement in 1989, and it was later formally endorsed by a number of scientific organizations. This statement also met with criticism, however. In 1994, E. O. Wilson said the following to the Boston conference 'Objectivity in the Sciences and the Humanities':

> On 16 May 1986, a group of academic luminaries, including Robert Hinde, John Paul Scott, and several other prominent behavioral scientists, issued the Seville Declaration (following a conference in Spain), declaring invalid any theories or claims that aggression and war have a genetic basis. Such thinking is according to them 'scientifically incorrect'. 'Wars', the Declaration said, 'begin in the minds of men'. Warfare is a capacity to invent wars. Case closed. The authors of the Declaration suggested, in effect, that if you have any thoughts otherwise about these matters, keep your mouth shut. The Seville Declaration was adopted the same year as the official policy of the American Anthropological Association. Eighty per cent of the members who returned ballots on the motion to adopt voted in favor. *Virtually all the main premises and conclusions of the Seville group are contradicted by the evidence*, but no matter—the Declaration seemed to its signers and ratifiers the politically and morally correct thing to do (Wilson, 1995, p. 81, italics added).

Wilson went on saying that the participants 'must have felt good about supporting it'. But, he warned, '*feeling good is not what science is all about. Getting it right*, and then basing social decisions on tested and carefully weighed objective knowledge, *is what science is all about*' (p. 81, italics added).

One way of commenting on this statement would be to say that it was in fact a social, rather than a scientific, statement, and that its basic purpose was to counteract misconceptions about the inevitability of war. Even so, it has been criticized by scientists, who have typically emphasized the beginning of the statement which says that warfare is a peculiarly human phenomenon and that its radical change over time indicates that it is a product of culture (see, for example, Silverman, 1998, p. 278; Tiger, 1996). In other words, Wilson was not alone. But what if Hinde truly *believed* in what he signed? It seems that Wilson excluded this possibility, because he took for granted that he 'knew' the real truth. Still, the matter of aggression and violence had been of great concern for Hinde, who had clearly and carefully developed views with regard to these issues (for example, Hinde 1989, 1991a, 1991b).

Let us take a look at the Declaration itself. It says, among other things:

> *It is scientifically incorrect* to say that war or any other violent behavior is genetically programmed into our human nature. While genes are involved at all levels of nervous system function, they provide a developmental potential that can be actualized only in conjunction with the ecological and social environment . . . While genes are co-involved in establishing our behavioral capacities, they do not by themselves specify the outcome.

It also notes that '[w]ar is biologically possible, but it is not inevitable', pointing to cultural differences in this respect. Moreover, it declares it to be scientifically incorrect to say that humans have a 'violent brain', which would be automatically activated by internal or external stimuli, or 'that war is caused by "instinct" or any single motivation'. When it comes to modern warfare, the Declaration continues, it involves the institutional use of such things as obedience, suggestibility and idealism, rational planning, and modern war technology and training. The Declaration concludes 'that biology does not condemn humanity to war, and that humanity can be freed from the bondage of biological pessimism . . . Just as "war begins in the minds of men", peace also begins in our minds' (Seville Statement on Violence, 1986; reprinted in *American Psychologist*, October 1990, pp. 1167–8).

It seems to me that Wilson may have over-interpreted the Declaration; perhaps he did not study it first hand. The Declaration clearly does not dismiss the role of genes in aggression and war. It does admit that we have a *capability* to act aggressively. However, what it says is that aggression is not innate in the 'instinctive' sense, that is, that it will *always* be expressed. In contrast, people like Hinde are interested in the *conditions* under which we typically act aggressively, and these conditions may include particular *cues* from the environment and the situational context. The concern with situational and interactional factors,[1] means that here biology overlaps with social psychology (see, for example, Myers, 2000, Chapter 21). There is no denying, for instance, that in-group and out-group allegiances are easily formed, as social psychologists have shown (Tajfel, 1978), but as Hinde's colleague Bateson had pointed out earlier, '[w]e should do well to look carefully at the *conditions* in which this sense of allegiance is formed and the circumstances in which the cooperation collapses' (Bateson, 1986, p. 98, italics added).

Wilson's disagreement with Hinde may have to do with Wilson's retaining more of a sense of an opposition between innate and learned behavior, or perhaps, a stronger sense of genetic programming with regard to learning. Hinde, on the other hand, in the 1960s had been the leader in the attempt to bridge the gap between the dichotomization of innate and learned in Lorenzian ethology, and to reconcile ethology with the critique from Lehrman and other comparative psychologists. In 1966, he had achieved a successful synthesis of ethology and comparative psychology. According to Barlow (1991), Hinde's book 'effectively demonstrated the intricacies of behavioral explanations, particularly the delicate interplay of genome and environment that results in the behavioral phenotype'.[2] Wilson, of course, in turn has been criticized precisely for having a too narrow, 'determinist' view of development: 'Wilson believed that he could treat development of the individual merely as a complex process by which genes were decoded. It was this belief that enabled him to blend evolutionary and developmental arguments, and it is this that made him a genetic determinist' (Bateson, 1985). (And clearly Wilson would be incensed if anyone suggested that, because of his blueprint view, he was not telling the truth about, say, aggression.)[3]

So, is an emphasis on the complexity of behavior an expression of an 'Enlightenment' or a 'hyper-Enlightenment' quest? It is hard to say, since a scientist's 'true scientific belief' may often *coincide* with a sense of its having acceptable social implications. An emphasis on the complexity of behavior, for instance, if socially implemented, would seem to suggest a larger number of ways for potential social intervention than a more narrow focus on the genetic basis of behavior. But, as I argued in Chapter 15, scientists may be naturally oriented towards theories and issues that simultaneously satisfy their scientific and moral/political concerns.

In the sociobiology controversy, of course, we had two sides who distrusted the other, and who may or may not have sincerely believed that the opponents distorted the truth for political reasons. With regard to the allegations against sociobiologists, it was not always clear whether they were accused of deliberate distortion of the truth, of being lackeys of bourgeois ideology, or of reckless negligence in presenting 'dangerous' pieces of science to the innocent layman. It may not have mattered in practice, since the perceived result was the same: sociobiological claims were seen as defending the (unequal) social status quo as the natural state of affairs. The sociobiologists, again, typically believed that the critics were deliberately suppressing what the latter *knew* to be the truth, in the service of a political cause. John Krebs helpfully gave me some sense of prevailing belief at Oxford in the early 1980s. Lewontin seems to have been under greater suspicion than, say, Steven Rose, since Lewontin was said to 'know the issues'. (In this book, I have tried to rebut this type of straight political explanation of Lewontin's motives.) Some suspected Gould was 'really' an adaptationist, although he spoke against adaptationism. The sense that truth was being suppressed is also reflected in a comment by Dawkins at the time: he told me that he could see how one might wish to discourage research in some area, but he himself would never say that something was not *true*.

An interesting case of an apparent conjunction between scientific and moral truth can be found in the theory of group selection. Group selection has natural associations with such good things as co-operation and altruism, community spirit, small-scale socialism, and what have you, and despite the new paradigm of kin selection, many academics in their hearts may still have wanted group selection to be true. For instance, Brandon and Burian's excellent 1984 overview book took group selection more seriously than people like Maynard Smith and Williams would have 'allowed'. Sober and Lewontin (1982), too, seemed to want to give group selection a chance (although in 1981 Lewontin, in interview with me, appeared to have temporarily accepted Maynard Smith's verdict that group selection was a very rare phenomenon). For those in ontological denial of the gene-selectionist view of the world, D. S. Wilson's continuous effort to demonstrate the truth of group selection may have provided great comfort, just as it did for Wynne-Edwards in the early 1980s. And with regard to humans, some may have never converted to kin selection in the first place (see Chapter 7).

Starting in 1994, David Sloan Wilson and Elliott Sober have made a strong move for the reconsideration of group selection. In *Unto Others* (Sober and Wilson, 1998a), they cite various cases in which altruistic groups have in fact outcompeted selfish groups. The crucial problem is how to prevent selfish members from becoming free riders or taking over an altruistic group. But, they argue, humans have a battery of psychological and social tricks for making life difficult for non-co-operators—ostracism, shame, shunning, etc. Meanwhile, there are the many positive benefits of belonging to a group. And as soon as you have groups collaborating with one another, they have an advantage. I believe it is not only because of shared scientific convictions that two recent reviews have been surprisingly sympathetic: Kitcher (1998) and Lewontin (1998a). Interestingly, both reviewers seem to indicate that they would *like* the book's results to be true.

Maynard Smith (1998), on the other hand, is rather critical, but appears to oppose group selection on strictly scientific grounds. Maynard Smith informs us that he was taught by his mentor Haldane to be suspicious of group selection. He has consistently disapproved of Wilson's use of the term 'group selection' for what is actually trait group selection (for example, Maynard Smith, 1984b). Added to this is the irritating fact that Sober and Wilson have appropriated and *relabeled* his and Price's game-theoretical model of animal conflict, interpreting it, too, as an example of 'group selection'! Dawkins, too, has indicated that he dislikes group selection on purely scientific grounds (for example, Dawkins, 1981a, 1995b). This does not mean that the exchange between him and D. S. Wilson has not been intense. Dawkins has called Wilson a 'zealot' (Dawkins, 1994) and Wilson has returned the favor. Two scientists accusing each other of zealotry in the name of scientific truth?

Indeed, D. S. Wilson has been trying to establish group selection for about three decades, just as intensely as Dawkins has been fighting *against* the group-selectionist paradigm. In 1989, for instance, Dawkins declared group selection 'out of favor' (that is, group selection 'in the sense in which we have all long understood it'). He went on to say, however, that this was *not* the case in the United States:

> You could be forgiven for thinking the opposite: a generation has grown up, especially in America, that scatters the name 'group selection' around like confetti. It is littered over all

kinds of cases that used to be (and by the rest of us still are) clearly and straightforwardly understood as something else, say kin selection ... the whole issue of group selection was very satisfactorily settled a decade ago by John Maynard Smith and others, and it is irritating to find that we are two generations, as well as two nations, divided only by a common language (Dawkins, 1989a, p. 297).

Dawkins went on to recommend his student Alan Grafen's 1984 essay as a clear-thinking sorting out of 'the neo-group selection problem'. But, as we see, this was to no avail. Matters only got worse with Wilson and Sober's (1994) *Behavioral and Brain Sciences* article, later culminating in their 1998 book.

What, then, about this 'neo-group selection problem'? Trivers (1998a, 1998b) got himself involved in an interesting dispute with Sober and Wilson. Like Maynard Smith, he protested against their reformulation of gene-selectionist ideas in group-selectionist terms; in addition, he thought that they had got the group-selectionist idea wrong. But Sober and Wilson retorted that it was, in fact, *Trivers* who had misunderstood group selection (Sober and Wilson, 1998b). Because what they had done was build further on Price's (1970, 1972) covariance formulas, in the same way as Hamilton had done in 1975. They were right about Hamilton: in his revised derivation of his inclusive fitness formula, Hamilton had demonstrated, among other things, the continuity between kin selection and group selection, and pointed out the all-important criterion that altruists should be able to interact with one another; inclusive fitness should be applicable also to 'viscous populations'. This Sober and Wilson took to include their trait groups (see Chapter 7).

Sober and Wilson's allegiance to group selection may be a good example of a hyper-Enlightenment quest of combined scientific and moral/political truth. Sober and Wilson (with many others) *know* that group selection exists; the scientific truth in this case is of an *ontological* type. Dawkins, or Maynard Smith, on the other hand, do not dispute that group selection exists, but they believe that group selection *explanations* muddle clear thinking and that neologisms only make the situation worse. They want to explicate mechanisms clearly in terms of a gene-selectionist model; they dislike group selection for sheer *logical* reasons, whatever they may think about its political appeal. This is why I classify their objective as an Enlightenment quest.

What about Trivers? Trivers, too, may not like group selection models for logical reasons. From the beginning he has been thinking in terms of individual actors, using game-theoretical models, and has made significant contributions within this framework of thinking. But unlike Dawkins and Maynard Smith, Trivers' models are explicitly applied to *human* behavior, and this raises the question: does he or does he not believe that a game-theoretical conflict model in fact better describes the 'truth' of human interaction than group-selectionist models emphasizing co-operation? (See Chapter 5.)

As we saw, Sober and Wilson invoked Hamilton's authority and his new explication of inclusive fitness for the validity of their group-selectionist argument. Hamilton had actually constructed this derivation as a tribute to Price, and Price, in a sense, had helped him overcome what he called his 'allergy' to group selection at a technical level. But did the fact that he had worked in this way with group selection formulas now make him more positively predisposed to group selection in general? The answer is no—and a surprisingly vehement no. Unlike Dawkins and Maynard Smith, Hamilton's resistance to group selection was not strictly scientifically motivated. This became clear from his direct reference to Wilson and Sober (1994) in his autobiographical notes.

> 'Liberal' thinkers should realize from the outset that fervent 'belief' in evolution at the group level, and especially any idea that group selection obviates supposedly unnecessary or non-existent harsh aspects of natural selection, actually starts them at once on a course that heads straight towards Fascist ideology. This is not difficult to see from Fascist propaganda and, reading a little more between the lines, a route that is similar and was perhaps initially even identical, has always been signposted from Marxist propaganda (Hamilton, 1996, p. 192).

This was no small charge. Where might this type of reaction come from, seemingly directed against various types of political 'groupism'? Hamilton's 'allergy' could well be connected to his own experiences as a boy, growing up with a father active in the British mobilization against a potential German invasion in the Second World War. As a boy, he lost the terminal digits of one hand while trying to help his father make a bomb (Wilson, 1994, p. 320).

And there is more to telling the truth for someone like Hamilton. In general, his vision of the implications of his own theories for humans is a bleak one (see Chapter 7). We remember (Chapter 5) the *pain* that Hamilton experienced when he believed it necessary to tell the truth at two conferences, just as biologists have probably always felt when their findings about the truth of human nature go against moral or liberal beliefs. In contrast, it is easy to imagine the satisfaction of all those who in Sober and Wilson's book see new support for group selection. For these scientists, it has opened up a new joyous possibility of 'telling the truth'.

As we have seen in this book, there are clearly many motives for individual scientists' preferences for particular approaches and theories. And there are clearly taste preferences, too: there will be those who prefer to formulate themselves in more cautious terms, and those who like more dramatic language. Imageries of conflict or co-operation may be chosen for scientific and/or moral/political reasons, or even for dramatic effect. Bateson (1984) argued for the imagery of co-operation on the grounds that co-operation is a more widespread phenomenon than conflict, and that a notion of co-operation may work as a self-fulfilling prophecy, but Dawkins (1982) commended the new 'dog-eat-dog' language that 'now dominates the textbooks' (Dawkins, 1982, p. 56). He saw it as a good antidote to lingering group-selectionist thinking. Overall, it seems to me that the best working hypothesis is really that scientists are 'telling the truth' as they see it—although their colleagues may not always believe this.

For science, the situation depends perhaps less on individual scientists telling the truth than one would believe. Scientific truth is, after all, not dependent on particular individuals: the criterion for truth is a *communal* one. It is up to the scientific collective to accept or reject particular ideas, independently of their motivational source. Theories and models have to be 'true' in the sense that they 'work' and generate testable research (at least within a particular thought style; see Grinnell, 1992). That is good enough for most scientists—except for those with deep ontological cravings.

But what about the social consequences of scientific statements? This is the topic we will turn to in the next section.

Truth and consequences

The exaggerations in the sociobiology debate and the Science Wars may have left the impression of science as *certain* knowledge. In the sociobiology controversy, you either had 'bad' or 'good' science, and in the Science Wars, you either had science or anti-science—even in the case of largely tentative results in some fields. Who is there to emphasize that facts are often tentative? Scientists themselves understandably wish to put their best foot forward, in order to convince their colleagues, the public, and granting agencies. The media often make matters worse, with sensationalist attention to scientific 'news'. Take, for instance, the recent hype around 'the gene'. The publicity around achievements in the medical realm easily give people the impression that more is known than is, in fact, the case. There is little discussion of what a gene is or how it works, or of the fundamental differences between the notion of 'gene' in different fields: molecular genetics, Mendelian 'Drosophila' genetics, the quantitative genetics of psychometrics and behavioral genetics, and the different conceptions of the gene used in sociobiology. What the general public and decision-makers get is simply 'the gene'.

Meanwhile, nobody seems to require scientists in different fields to make clear what they are talking about. Sociobiologists and psychometricians, for instance, are not required to state that their genes are hypothetical, and that they are actually dealing with traits, rather than genes. Yet scientists can be very lucid about these things, and explicate and defend their approach (see, for example, Grafen, 1984 on a defense of the 'pheno-typic gambit', and Chapter 14 in this book).

Scientists from different fields feel perfectly confident telling the public about their latest research findings, but what the public does not know about are the deep differences and disagreements when it comes to conceptions of 'good science'. Thus, we have, for instance, psychometricians presenting facts that they truly *believe* reflect an objective reality—say, about cognitive differences between races—based on research that has undergone due scientific peer review in their field. Meanwhile the whole statistical approach used by the psychometricians is typically questioned by laboratory geneticists. The former say they are doing good, objective science, in accordance with the highest standards in their particular field. The geneticists retort that the psychometricians have indeed produced measurements and correlations, but this does not mean they have said anything about *real* genetic differences. These two camps—geneticists on the one hand, and psychometricians and sociobiologists on the other—typically have not seen eye-to-eye when it comes to the question of what is acceptable scientific methodology. But whom should the public believe, and why?

Obviously, the social use of scientific results would merit more general scientific and public discussion. As we have seen, some scientists think it is only natural that the latest scientific findings be used for policy-making. They feel that their science is on the right track and want it to be useful for society. Others argue that only knowledge that is as *certain* as possible and has been obtained through 'good' (that is, molecular level) science should be considered, not tentative results produced by fields using 'bad' (that is, psychometric, correlational) methods (Chapter 14). Finally, there are those who argue for a radical *disjunction* between scientific findings and social policy. In other words, science as an enterprise directed at understanding and explaining the world should be explicitly uncoupled from any consideration of social consequences (Dawkins' position). And we should probably not dismiss a fourth possibility: the idea of using science in the service of 'useful false beliefs' (Stent, 1978). And there were moments in the sociobiology controversy when (some) scientists on one side thought that (some) scientists on the other were distorting the truth for political reasons. (Lewontin went one step further, asserting that scientists sometimes tell deliberate lies see Chapter 3.)

One thing that is clear is that people in general, and decision-makers as well, do not really require a high degree of certainty in order to form an impression: tentative results will do the job. If social psychology has taught us anything, it is that people will jump to conclusions based on however scanty information (see, for example, Myers, 1994; Tversky and Kahneman, 1974; Nisbett and Ross, 1980). If this is the case, what can be done? Can people be discouraged from drawing overstrong conclusions from the stream of claims about genes 'for' human behavioral traits and new statistics about racial and group differences?

Clearly, many academics actually do *not* trust the public's judgment, and have therefore put the burden of responsibility on the scholarly community instead, suggesting various forms of control or censorship of dangerous ideas. What are some of these? For some, it is enough to emphasize the principle that scholars should make absolutely clear the difference between fact and speculation, *is* and *ought*. 'This requires total respect for the line between informing and advocating', argued sociobiological psychologist Irving Silverman (1998), and added: 'The dictum that we not invoke our science to promote moral and social judgments should be etched as deeply in our professional ethos as the mandate not to allow moral and social judgments to influence our science.' However, political scientist Vincent Falger got into a long-standing dispute with Silverman exactly about this issue. In Falger's view, there will always be a 'grey zone', scientific statements which have undeniable political implications without being obvious advocacies (Falger, 1995). For this reason, Falger argued, statements in the grey zone need to be avoided just as rigorously as real advocacies. But it was precisely this that Silverman had refused to accept (Silverman 1995a,b), being concerned about the potential lack of limits with regard to grey zones:

> Grey zones have a way of spreading, and can easily introduce another element of politics into our enterprise; the censorship and self-censorship of authentic scientific inquiries that may be perceived as having 'politically incorrect' overtones (Silverman, 1998).

As an example of how widely grey zones can spread he presented an excerpt from a 1993 York University (Canada) faculty committee report on standards for research ethics. It called for the prohibition of projects which *'can be interpreted* as [emphasis in original report] prejudicial or as promoting prejudice to persons because of differences such as culture, nationality, ethnicity, race, religion, gender, marital status, sexual preference, physical or mental disabilities, age, socio-economic status, and/or any other preference or personal characteristic, condition, or status' (quoted in Silverman, 1998, p. 280). This is why he stood by his belief that '[t]he line between legitimate scientific reporting and advocacy can and should be precisely delineated'. Behind the line, he argued, endeavors should be strongly defended in the name of freedom of inquiry; beyond the line, efforts should be equally strongly disavowed as outside the province of science.

It is hard to say how common Silverman's position is among practicing scientists (let alone sociobiologists); that is, the idea that there is a line and that it is possible to tell objective science from political advocacy. One problem with his position, of course, is exactly what the sociobiology controversy was all about, and that is: *who shall draw the line?* Different scientists draw it differently. Moreover, they often believe that political factors affect their colleagues' line drawing. The systematically different interpretations in the sociobiology controversy suggest that the line tends to be in the eye of the beholder—a phenomenon which may come to prevail even with clear guidelines.

Kitcher (1985) came up with another suggestion for coping with the potential political misuse of biological information about human behavior. According to him, 'pop' sociobiologists had thrown away their caution when they wrote about human behavior. He suggested that the *standards needed to be raised* when it came to statements about humans. When there were implications for humans, some usual practices of science, such as bold generalization, should be curtailed and the standards of evidence needed to be higher than in other, less sensitive areas of science. Again, it is not clear *who* would set these standards, and how high they would need to be. As we have seen, whether for scientific or moral/political reasons, or both, the critics of sociobiology have kept insisting on molecular-level proof of such things as behavioral traits before they would 'allow' such traits even to be *discussed* —thus invalidating any scientific employment of hypothetical genes 'for' behavior. There is also, clearly, the question of fairness between different scientific fields, taking into account their particular objectives and methodological possibilities; it is not *obvious* that experimentally oriented scientists should be setting the standards for others.

Finally we may ask, what is the status of moral/political argumentation itself? At least in principle, invoking moral considerations may well be one of the tools in the overall battle against sociobiology (some sociobiologists have suggested that this was the case in practice, too, for instance, Trivers, when he complained that the critics 'are wasting our time'). We also know from the reasoning in Chapter 15 that anyone requesting a raising of the standards for sociobiology is bound to get brownie points from its long-standing opponents. And indeed Beckwith (1987) seemed pleased with Kitcher's 'worry that unfettered sociobiological speculation based on poor science is being used to support social injustice'.

This does not mean that some kind of standards could not be set for a field by practitioners *within* that same field. But how would one go about raising standards? On my analysis, it is not so clear that a line can be drawn between 'serious' sociobiology and 'pop' sociobiology when it comes to implications for humans, since people systematically tend to draw conclusions for themselves from information about animals, too. Does this mean that an *overall* raising of standards is in order, for moral/political reasons? And what about experimentalists? They are not scot-free either. There has recently been concern about rampant data selection practices in laboratories (see, for example, Segerstråle, 1995; Goodstein, 1992), and this raises legitimate questions about experimental research in general, including, say, blood-factor data studies and their interpretation.

One clear possibility is to keep the public better informed. The burden may be on geneticists in particular to better explain the complex workings of genes, the different meaning of 'gene' in different subfields, and such things as the difference between single-gene genetics and the genetics of complex traits. Probably we also need a better public understanding of gene–environment interaction, and of the *complexity of behavior*. It is particularly important to emphasize the legitimacy of different levels of explanation of human behavior. Currently, because of the hype about genes, there may be a widespread assumption that genetic explanation is somehow the most important one. (The problems were certainly compounded by the critics of sociobiology, who tended to reinforce incorrect biological belief.) Here it is the ethologists (Hinde, Bateson, Blurton-Jones, and others) who have for a long time made explicit efforts to integrate levels of explanation of behavior (and seem recently to have been joined by leading behavioral ecologists, for example, Krebs and Davies, 1997). A recent attempt to integrate research on social behavior across levels and disciplines in the social and biological sciences is Segerstråle and Molnar (1997).

But are there not scientific truths with 'positive' consequences? Many have quoted Ernst Mayr, who some time ago introduced the idea of 'population thinking' instead of 'typological thinking'. He believed that emphasizing the great variation between individuals within any human population contained an anti-racist message (Mayr, 1982). Lewontin's 1972 bloodgroup studies showing larger within-group than between-group variation of genes have been widely cited, and recently the population genetic studies by Luigi Cavalli-Sforza and his associates have been hailed as progressive in just the same spirit (for example, Cavalli-Sforza *et al.*, 1994).[4] In political culture, including the liberal-left's, there seems to exist a pervasive belief that moral/political arguments *should* be backed up by facts. (Among those who have gone furthest in this area is, surprisingly, Wilson; see the discussion of his liberal arguments in *On Human Nature* in Section 1 of this chapter.)

Here, then, we have seemingly positive conclusions to be drawn from scientific facts. The problem is that arguments from facts—even progressive ones—will only reinforce the idea that our moral judgments ought somehow to be tied to the latest scientific knowledge. In my view, it is exactly this connnection between scientific understanding and perceived social utility that needs to be broken, not least for the reason that scientific knowledge and the interpretation of facts changes over time. Perhaps what needs emphasizing is that there is legitimacy in just trying to understand how the world works—this is, after all, what motivates most scientists to go into science in the first place! Can science in today's world be defended as a 'mere' quest for understanding? It appears that this is a position which people like Wolpert and Dawkins are publicly defending in their active efforts to uncouple scientific and moral/political truth.

Still, it is clear that some scientific theories and imageries appear to have more negative immediate social consequences than others, if and when taken out of their scientific context. What to do? It seems to me that a moral/political debate around the potential implications of science may be the only possible way to go. Considering that most people do not keep facts separate from values, and the policy-makers look to science as a social arbiter (Goldberg, 1994), perhaps a general debate about sensitive scientific issues is a healthy social phenomenon (particularly in a country like the US which does not have a broad spectrum of political parties). And, as I shall argue in the next and last chapter, this morally/politically inspired criticism may also be a tool for keeping *science* in these fields on track.

CHAPTER 20

The battle for the soul—and for the soul of science

Free will, determinism, and the attribution of guilt

In this last chapter I will return to the heavy metaphysical underpinnings of the socio-biology controversy, one of the reasons why it attracted so much interest and such deep engagement on the part of many academics. Throughout this book we have seen scientists with great concerns about the true depiction of reality, and I have distinguished between 'realists' and 'modelers', or 'metaphysicians' and 'logicians'. But there is no doubt that the central issue in the sociobiology debate had to do with the true nature of human nature. And here the sociobiology controversy continued an important debate in the wake of the Second World War: the grand opposition between existentialism and essentialism, or between free will and determinism.

Indeed, one of the most persistent themes throughout the sociobiology controversy has been that of free will and determinism. We saw it coming up again and again, particularly in the writings of the members of the Sociobiology Study Group and their associates. Anything having to do with genes was identified with genetic determinism, a seemingly unchangeable fate. Of course, Wilson, Dawkins, and others took pains to point out that the involvement of genes did *not* mean unchangeability of behavior. Wilson explained how phenylketonuria could be circumvented with the right diet, or myopia eliminated with glasses. Dawkins discussed at length the fact that there was no clear relationship between a trait being under genetic control and its being subject to modification (Dawkins, 1982). Still, many took at face value the critics' suggestion that invoking genes 'implied' an unchanging human nature, and this was certainly reinforced by contributions by the opponents of sociobiology (for example, Gould, 1978a; Nabi, 1981; Lewontin, Rose, and Kamin, 1984).

What the critics of sociobiology seemed to believe in was a 'totally free' free will, not a will in any way influenced by genetic constraints. This, in turn, followed from their belief in a separate realm of culture. Because of culture, there were no constraints on what humans could do, nor on our social and cultural arrangements. This was one of the early arguments in the sociobiology controversy promoted by Gould in 'Biological Potentiality vs Biological Determinism' (1976). Lewontin (1981a) and Levins (Levins and Lewontin, 1985) added that humans, with the help of technology (culture), could overcome their biological limitations. Since the critics had no sense that culture was in any way connected to biology, it is not surprising that Wilson's revised sociobiological program, with mind and culture linked to genes, did not fare better among the critics. Not even evolutionary psychology, arguably the most revised approach to sociobiology, met with approval. Gould, for instance, recently classified evolutionary psychology together with sociobiology as an example of 'fundamentalist Darwinism' (Gould, 1997b).

Although the critics generally resisted the idea of human universals, they did accept one: the human predisposition for language. But language was regarded as originating in a fortuitous evolutionary step—it was certainly *not* seen as a product of adaptation. Indicative of the different positions here are the reactions to the work of MIT psycholinguist Steven Pinker, who has recently argued for the adaptiveness of language (for example, Pinker, 1994). Sociobiologists of various stripes and evolutionary psychologists do like Pinker's work. Gould does not (Gould, 1995).

What was all this about? Why was the topic of genes and free will continuously brought up in the sociobiology controversy? Here is the explanation of one Sociobiology Study Group member, Stephen Chorover, my guide to the minds of the critics (see Chapter 10). Chorover described the sociobiology debate as part of the great struggle between free will and determinism. According to him, the social mythology underlying sociobiological theorizing could be traced all the way back to Genesis and the doctrine of original sin, and precedents to the sociobiology debate could be found throughout Church history.

Chorover tells the story of Pelagius who, against St Augustine's support of the doctrine of original sin, emphasized the importance of free will and individual responsibility. The result was that Pelagius was officially declared a heretic. And this is what has been going on ever since, he continued: 'Sides have continued to be taken and skirmish after skirmish has been fought across the lines of free will and predestination which divided them . . . Augustinian concepts continue to prosper today in many forms of sociobiological determinism, and these continue to be opposed by more contemporary versions of Pelagian thought' (Chorover 1979, p. 19).

But who is who in this tale? In Chorover's scenario, sociobiological theories automatically become part of the 'doctrine of the Church', that is, social mythologies devised to uphold the status quo. The determinist Church doctrine, in turn, is bravely fought by 'heretics' who are on the side of individual free will. In this tale, the critics of sociobiology appear as martyrs on the side of Truth in the sociobiology controversy, which represents only the latest episode in the age-long struggle between free will and determinism.

But what about that purported high priest of the Church, E. O. Wilson himself? It turns out that he *also* saw—and sees—himself as a heretic! Wilson was also fighting the doctrine of the Church. For him, the 'Church' represented both prevailing religious doctrine and prevailing culturalist doctrine; he was waging a battle on two fronts at the same time. In *On Human Nature* Wilson was worrying not about supporting the status quo but about *changing* it. And how might social change be effected? His answer was: through 'visionaries and revolutionaries' (Wilson, 1978a, p. 186). There is no doubt that Wilson saw himself as one of those revolutionaries and visionaries, who were typically given a hard time, to the degree that the 'reigning code has been sanctified and mytho-logized' and regarded as beyond question.

So *both* Chorover and Wilson identified themselves with those heretics who were for truth and against established dogma. Wilson's critics regarded him as a pillar of the establishment and themselves as challenging the status quo. Wilson, again, saw his critics as supporters of the prevailing doctrine—the left-wing–liberal culturalist dogma —and himself as a revolutionary. Both sides wanted freedom of thought, both wanted to see themselves as heretics. They just interpreted differently the nature of the heretic cause.

And now we come to the gist of the matter. It was apparently important for the critics of sociobiology to identify freedom with *individual responsibility*. If behavior could be 'explained away', say as part of original sin, then it would not be easy to hold individuals morally responsible for their actions. The problem with determinist explanations was that they seemingly *exonerated* individuals; no guilt could be attributed. Throughout the controversy, there was a great preoccupation with guilt among the critics of socio-biology. In their original letter, they stated that it was in the interest of power-holders to sustain the idea of a biologically determined human nature, because that could exonerate them from guilt about insufficient social reform. But note that the members of the Sociobiology Study Group were quite consistent in their rejection of explanations that seemingly denied individuals free will. They disliked Skinner, too, exactly because of his emphasis on the possibility of conditioning of humans—another determinism taking away individual responsibility (for example, Miller, 1978).[1]

Why this focus on individual responsibility and guilt? We are touching a larger concern in the general culture after the Second World War, impacting also on recent nature–nurture controversies: the opposition between existentialism and essentialism. The existentialist vision of man as free to make choices and therefore responsible for his actions had become particularly important in the post-war discussion of Nazi war crimes and the trial of Eichmann and others who argued that they were 'only following orders'. Jean-Paul Sartre and the existentialists would retort that every man had free will and therefore could choose not to obey.[2]

It was exactly this kind of discussion that formed the background to the ethological books in the late 1960s. References to an aggressive instinct or other genetic traits became absolute anathema for the liberal left. Enormous effort was spent on declaring aggression non-existent—and here the absolute champion was Ashley Montagu (1968, 1972, 1976, 1978). In the sociobiology controversy, it was probably Lewontin who worked hardest to demonstrate that aggression did not exist (for example, Lewontin, 1976a). In his Introduction to *Man and Aggression* (1968), an anthology of critical reviews of Lorenz and Ardrey, Ashley Montagu suggested that

> perhaps the principal reason for the popularity of works of this kind . . . [is that] *it provides relief for that heavy burden of guilt* most individuals carry about with them for being as they are. If one is born innately aggressive, then one cannot be blamed for being so. . . . Hence when books like those of Ardrey and Lorenz appear they are welcomed with all the fervor of a sinner seeking absolution from his sins. Ardrey and Lorenz stand in a sort of apostolic

succession to those who with millennial ardor have sought to restore the wicked and the unregenerate to the true faith (Montagu, 1972, p. xviii, italics added).

But this view is incorrect, Montagu pointed out. Science does not provide support for any idea of 'innate depravity'. According to him, the real danger with this kind of thinking is that it 'diverts the focus of attention from the real causes of "sin," of aggression, and encourages a Jansenist view of the nature of the human condition' (p. xix). So far, however, all attempts to saddle humans with instincts have failed, Montagu said: 'The notable thing about human behavior is that it is learned. It is nonsense to talk about genetic determination of human behavior' (p. xvii). For Montagu, then, any potential evidence for a human biological 'essence' would be necessarily associated with the doctrine of innate depravity and used as a tool to exculpate people.

According to Vernon Reynolds, however, the existentialist objection did not have to do with the *evidence* as such. Evidence might or might not exist for essentialist ideas about 'human nature', but nothing followed from that. Reynolds helpfully formulated the existentialist objection in the following manner:

> In saying that 'l'existence precede l'essence' Sartre resolutely denies the appeal to any religious, psychic or evolution-based inner programme of inherited tendencies in the explanation of human actions. As I see it, he is not denying the *existence* or the possible existence of such forces or tendencies, but only the *appeal* to them as undeniable and inescapable sources of, or controls on, what we think, say, and do. To make such an appeal is to act in bad faith. To act in good faith is to acknowledge the primacy of freedom and choice.
>
>   Thus, for present purposes, scientific efforts at any form of objective analysis or theorizing about human action or behaviour, including an appeal to 'drives', to 'innate behavioural tendencies', to the 'wiring' or the human 'biogram', to past experiences, or to the prevailing social order (including both institutional and linguistic structures) can only shed light on 'essence'. Whatever can be learned from an objective standpoint can never provide more than a background for the explanation of action, the foreground being occupied by the subjective choices of free individuals (Reynolds, 1980, p. 25, italics added).

Note here that Reynolds included among unacceptable essentialist appeals *also* social and cultural determinist explanations of various kinds; in fact, *any* appeal to external 'forces' as responsible for our actions. According to him, the existentialist position dismisses even such notions as Tiger and Fox's 'biogrammar' of society, a position which states that man is a cultural animal and that culture is the human special form of adaptation. What is wrong with that? According to Reynolds, this view assumes we are all variations of *a common essence*, which can be traced to our common hunter-gatherer past (1980, p. 24).

Here we may now have a clue as to why, for people like Gould, evolutionary psychology did not seem a solution to the problems associated with sociobiology (Gould, 1997a). At first blush, evolutionary psychology would appear more palatable, because it is after all dealing with the human mind, rather than with genes. In fact, unlike Wilson and others who focus on various types of gene–culture co-evolution, evolutionary psychology investigates the culture-generating capabilities of the mind. But now we see the problem for the critics of sociobiology: evolutionary psychology, too, posits an *essence* (complete with modules for specific behaviors, at that), and we do not want an essence, because we want no easy way to escape from the burden of individual responsibility! Gould, indeed, may be a kind of existentialist Marxist. In his article about biological potentiality and biological determinism (1976a) he invoked exactly Simone de Bouvoir's dictum that the human being is 'l'être d'ont l'être est de n'être pas'. This he used to drive home the point that '[o]ur biological nature does not stand in the way of social reform'.

A good final example of the persistence of the free-will theme among the critics and their assumptions about sociobiological reasoning can be found in Dawkins (1989a, p. 331). Dawkins rebuts the critics, and in doing so provides a complex answer to the critics' continuing allegations. He singles out a particular passage in *Not in Our Genes* discussing a purported dilemma for sociobiologists like Dawkins and Wilson:

> Brains, for reductionists, are determinate biological objects whose properties produce the behaviors we observe and the states of thought or intention we infer from that behavior . . . Such a position is, or ought to be, completely in accord with the principles of sociobiology offered by Wilson and Dawkins. However, to adopt it would involve them in the dilemma of first arguing the innateness of much human behavior that, being liberal men, they clearly find unattractive (spite, indoctrination, etc.) and then to become entangled in liberal ethical concerns about responsibility for criminal acts, if these, like all other acts, are biologically determined. To avoid this problem, Wilson and Dawkins invoke a free will that enables us to go against the dictates of our genes if we so wish . . . This is essentially a return to unabashed Cartesianism, a dualistic *deus ex machina* (Lewontin *et al.* quoted in Dawkins, 1989a, p. 331).[3]

To this Dawkins responds that the critics seem to believe that Wilson and he must *either* be genetic determinists or believe in free will. But, he goes on to say,

> it is only in the eyes of Rose and his colleagues that we are 'genetic determinists'. . . . [I]t is perfectly possible to hold that genes exert a statistical influence on human behaviour while at the same time believing that this influence can be modified, overridden, or reversed by other influences. . . . We, that is our brains, are separate and independent enough from our genes to rebel against them. . . . [W]e do so in a small way every time we use contraception. There is no reason why we should not rebel in a large way, too (Dawkins, 1989a, pp. 331–2).

Dawkins said he believed he was speaking for Wilson, too. But Wilson's view was more complicated. He and Lumsden addressed the question of free will in 1983. Does not the very fact that the brain is programmed by genes destroy free will, the authors asked? They answered in the negative:

> The biases in mental development are only biases; *the influence of the genes, even when very strong does not destroy free will*. In fact, the opposite is the case: by acting on culture through the epigenetic rules, *the genes create and sustain the capacity for conscious choice and decision* (1983, p. 182, italics added).

In fact, they explained, there is a lot of room for choice. Since predispositions result from an interaction of genes and environment, predispositions can be altered. Ethical precepts, in turn, are based on these predispositions, and can also be altered (p. 182; see the previous chapter's discussion of reversing incest taboos).

In other words, both sides in the controversy paid homage to the idea of free will, one by dismissing genes and the other 'despite' genes. But in the meantime the general public's view of the matter of genes and free will was undergoing an interesting transformation. At the end of the millennium, the problem of genes and free will looked rather different than it did fifty years ago. In fact, one might argue that we have now come to a point in the overall development where the new essentialism meets the new existentialism.

The new essentialism meets the new existentialism

By the early 1990s, the tide appeared to have changed. Many noted a new acceptance of biological explanations for human behavior (for example, Degler, 1991; Barkan, 1992). What was more, a total turnaround seems to have happened in regard to the gene. From being viewed with suspicion the gene had now become accepted. What was more, it had acquired a new aura! In *The DNA Mystique* (1995), Dorothy Nelkin and Susan Lindee argued that DNA had turned into something of a cultural icon. It now appeared in cartoons, on lapel pins, and even in names of perfumes. This may seem like a harmless development, but the authors pointed out that this, in fact, signaled something else. According to Nelkin and Lindee, we had now entered a new era of '*genetic essentialism*'.

In practice, they suggested, this meant that a whole new excuse was now available in the moral sphere. The substitute for the more traditional 'the Devil made me do it' was now: 'It's not me, it's my genes.' Genetics had now become explicitly connected to questions of good and evil. What a turn of events! From the point of view of Montagu and others, their worst fears appeared to have been realized. It would now be possible to do exactly what he and the critics of sociobiology considered absolute anathema—to stop referring to free will and individual responsibility and instead blame behavior on factors related to the human 'essence', in this case genes. Moreover, this was now turning into an acceptable public excuse.[4]

And it was not only the gene that had become presentable. The 1990s also saw a new set of books about animals, no longer aggressive, as in the 1960s, but instead moral and intelligent; books such as Frans DeWaal's *Good-Natured* (1996) and Robert Wright's *The Moral Animal* (1994), which was on *The New York Times* bestseller list for two years. New research presented animals as quite sophisticated communicators, including popular books and films on chimp language—a field where research has resumed after the controversies in the 1970s and early 1980s (Savage-Rumbaugh *et al.*, 1993)—and studies in cognitive ethology and animal proto-language (for example, Griffin, 1992; Cheney and Seyfarth, 1990; Evans and Marler, 1997).

In other words, toward the end of the millennium, there seemed to be a 180-degree turn in regard to human morality. Morality was no longer seen as linked to the notion of free will in an existentialist vision, but instead as *connected* to the genes responsible for the human essence. Instead of being carefully separated from essentialism, morality was now intimately connected to it. Moreover, this type of genetic explanation of moral behavior sometimes seemed to have the additional quality of being practically unfalsifiable. Consider that bestseller, *The Moral Animal*. What impresses the reader is that this book appears to go much further than traditional sociobiology. In *The Moral Animal*, *every conceivable kind of behavior*, both moral and immoral, is attributed to our genes' shrewd strategizing efforts. In fact, we learn that even the most apparently moral behavior is in fact 'nothing but' a self-serving strategy for survival—and we are just deceiving ourselves if we think otherwise. (The book, incidentally, uses this scheme to explain Charles Darwin's motivations, too. Darwin may have believed that he was acting in a gentlemanly and unselfish way, but in fact his behavior was self-interested. He was just outsmarted by his selfish genes!)

The genes thus appear as active agents, running our lives, and we look like rather stupid puppets on strings. It seems to me that not even 'hardline' human sociobiologists usually attempt such a psychological analysis (see, for example, the collection in Betzig, 1997), and evolutionary psychologists also seem to me more restrained (for example, Barkow *et al.*, 1992). On the other hand, it does seem to correspond with Trivers' and Alexander's notions about self-deception. Judging by its bestseller status, there seems to be great appeal in this kind of 'total' explanation. D. S. Wilson, however, in his review (1995) of *The Moral Animal* suggested that the book's cynical flavor came from the author's focus on selfish genes and his identification of morality with altruism in the strict sociobiological sense. A better alternative would have been to operate with a concept of *authentic morality*, based on such things as group solidarity and the punishment of deviants, and to look for a possible biological basis for that (in other words, the Sober and Wilson approach, 1994, 1998).

The shift toward a seeming unproblematic acceptance of 'the gene', of course, did not mean that the general public knew much about genes and the complexity of genetics—not to mention the complexity of human behavior. People might well have continued thinking in terms of nature vs nurture, genes vs environment, instead of in terms of gene–environment *interaction*. Much of the new emphasis on 'the gene' appeared to be fueled by something quite external to the sociobiology controversy: the excitement around the Human Genome Project. In their eagerness to advocate the project, leading scientists did, indeed, make pronouncements as if human beings were nothing but the sum of their genes. This new celebration of essentialism further helped to fuse metaphysics and genetics. Proponents did not hesitate to compare the genome to the Holy Grail (Walter Gilbert) or claim it to be 'the very essence of what it means to be human' (Jim Watson) (both quoted, among others, in Kevles and Hood, 1992).

But the story does not stop here, in the dark abyss of genetic essentialism. No sooner have we been doomed to blaming our genes than a new ray of hope shines forth. To the rescue: *a new type of existentialism*—and its advocate, E. O. Wilson! (It is I who am making this connection; Wilson himself does not discuss the new genetic essentialism.) What is, then, the 'new existentialism'? It turns out that it is nothing other than the idea of 'volitional evolution' mentioned in the previous chapter: mankind taking its own future in its hands, based on deep knowledge about its evolutionary heritage. It seems to me that the new existentialism comes in handy in coping with the genetic essentialist scare, because it suggests subjecting genes to human *choice*. According to Wilson, the choice in this new existentialism is much more far-reaching than in the old type of existentialism: in principle we will be able to change even those features that fundamentally make us human. (In an existentialist-sounding gambit in *Consilience*, Wilson goes as far as warning humankind that we will be making a choice even if we decide not to tamper with human nature.) The new existentialism also does not involve individual choice in the same way as the earlier one:

> We are entering in a new era of existentialism, not the old absurdist existentialism of Kierkegaard and Sartre, giving complete autonomy to the individual, but the concept that only unified learning, universally shared, makes accurate foresight and wise choice possible (Wilson, 1998a, p. 297).

Wilson, of course, is no stranger to the existentialist dilemma. If anything, he addressed it in the very first line of *Sociobiology*, where he quoted Albert Camus' famous statement that the only serious philosophical question is suicide. But Wilson brought it up only to immediately declare it 'wrong, even in the strict sense intended'. We are not really making a free choice in the sense of its being a rational choice, because our consciousness is 'flooded with emotions'. This, in turn, is a result of the make-up of our brain, a product of evolution. (From this, Wilson famously concluded that ethicists should study evolution.)

In *Promethean Fire* (1983) the authors ended up dismissing existentialism as an illusion: people may believe that they have moral intuition, 'those satisfying visceral feelings of right and wrong', but they in fact remain enslaved by their genes and culture. What counts as free will is just a passing moment of decision: 'while they exercise free will in moment-by-moment choices, this faculty remains superficial and its value to the individual is largely illusory' (1983, p. 183). According to Lumsden and Wilson, a truly free free will would have little to do with moral intuition. Moreover, free will would not mean freedom from societal norms; even social rebels were just substituting one set of goals for another, without knowing that what was really driving them were 'deep impulses and feelings prescribed by their genes'. The point would be instead to try to create 'some measure of intellectual independence from the forces that created us': '*Real freedom consists of choosing our masters by a procedure that allows us to master them*' (p. 174, italics added).

Wilson, then, in his own way has answered the existentialist dilemma by giving an essentialist answer. As he had already said in 1971: man makes himself genetically as he goes along (1971, p. 208). At the same time, the new essentialism—the idea of genes as the ultimate legitimators of human action—appears to be at least partly undermined by the very possibility of *choosing* these genes. If we are looking to allocate blame in such a scenario, the blame might no longer go to the individual's genes, as in Nelkin and Lindee's genetic essentialism, but instead to the chooser of the genetic make-up of this individual. This defers the question further: who gets to choose the genes? And of whom? And so on, in complicated hypothetical moral/political scenarios, ready for prospecting for those concerned about genes and free will.

No other gods?

Two things have been emphasized by the pro-science activists of recent years: science as the search for truth and science as the embodiment of Reason. Some scientists have gone even further: the late Carl Sagan presented science as a candle in the dark in a demon-haunted world (Sagan, 1996). For Sagan, science in its capacity as Reason could naturally battle religion and ideologies. As Lewontin tells the story (Lewontin, 1997a), it was after an occasion in 1964 where he and Sagan were invited to debate with creationists in Little Rock, Arkansas, that Sagan decided that his response henceforth would be to try to spread the message of science to the masses. It was clear that Sagan believed that science would help inspire a critical and skeptical attitude (something he was accordingly hailed for in *The Skeptic*, a magazine emphasizing rational belief over superstition and pseudoscience). But this was the same man who had taught us to appreciate billions and billions of stars, instilling a feeling of wonder and awe in the audience of his famous *Cosmos* program on television! Indeed, scientists sometimes wondered whether Sagan's popularity had to do with the nature of his particular subject matter—the cosmos and its mythical connections—rather than with the power of science. Still, they obviously appreciated what he was doing for science.

This is the time to tackle one of the more metaphysical questions informing the socio-biology controversy—and beyond. That is the question of the relationship between science and religion. Here we can find three basic positions advocated by the participants in the sociobiology debate: separation, confrontation, and merger.

Gould is a representative of the first approach, an unconfrontational one. According to him, 'Science and religion are not in conflict, for their teachings occupy distinctly different domains. . . I believe, with all my heart, in a respectful, even *loving* concordat.' The emphasis is Dawkins'; he found the quote in Gould's *Natural History* column and used it to illustrate a particular point in his own article 'When Religion Steps on Science's Turf', published in *Free Inquiry*, a scientific humanist journal (Dawkins, 1998d). The context was the Pope's attitude to evolution. For Dawkins, Gould was a typical example of 'a dominant strain of conciliatory thought, among believers and nonbelievers alike', who tend to believe in a division of labor between science and religion. 'The net of science covers the empirical universe: what is it made of (fact) and why does it work this way (theory). The net of religion extends over questions of moral meaning and value' (Gould quoted in Dawkins, 1998d see also Gould, 1999).

In Dawkins' article the Gould quote becomes a foil for his own position. Dawkins expressly does *not* want to leave religion alone. Religion belongs to those myths, legends, and recent cultural relativist beliefs that he sees as his responsibility to attack as superstition. Do not believe that science and religion can exist together in harmony, warns Dawkins in another article in *The Humanist* (1997b). The ambition of religion is to explain the *same* things as science! For Dawkins, religion occupies exactly the same slot as science in people's minds—a world-view slot—which is why they are in direct competition. But, continues Dawkins, unlike religion, science is supported by evidence; it gets results. This is why science is not just another belief system.

Like other evolutionists, Dawkins is worried about the rise of fundamentalist religions, but unlike most others, he appears to have a particular grudge against the Catholic Church. Dawkins explains how this religion particularly steps on science's turf: Catholic morals have direct scientific implications, and these are fundamentally anti-evolutionary. Catholicism demands the presence of a gulf between *Homo sapiens* and the rest of the animal kingdom. 'Catholic morality . . . is speciesist to the core.' This is why Gould is wrong when he says that religions restrict themselves to morals and values, notes Dawkins. On the contrary, *religions make direct existence claims of a scientific* nature: major doctrines of the Catholic Church—such as the Virgin Birth and the survival of our souls after death—are in fact *scientific* claims, according to Dawkins (1998d).

But for Dawkins God is not needed. Nor do we need any other myths; only science is needed! Science can be our source of inspiration, beauty, and wonder (1995a). And it seems, indeed, that this is the case for Dawkins himself—at least with regard to the theory of evolution. Here is an example. *Climbing Mount Improbable* (1996) starts with Dawkins listening to a lecture about the fig. The lecturer dicusses the fig in all kinds of ways, but it is a literary lecture, not a botanical one. Dawkins now tells the reader that he wants to 'tell the *true* story of the fig' (Dawkins, 1996a, p. 3, italics added). 'The fig story is among the most satisfyingly intricate in evolution . . . There is genuine paradox and real poetry in the botanical explanation of the fig, with subtleties to exercise an inquiring mind and wonders to uplift an esthetic one' (Dawkins, 1996a, pp. 3–4). Also, it can 'illustrate a scientific way of tackling questions which may serve as a salutary example to that literary dilettante' (p. 308).

For Dawkins, then, just as for Sagan, the clarity and beauty of science was all that was needed. (Dawkins rather movingly said in his review of *The Demon-Haunted World* that he would have liked to have written that book himself; Dawkins, 1996b.) Both wanted to share their visions with people to liberate them from dogma and false beliefs. Indeed, for Sagan it was hard to understand why everybody would not accept science, but rather hold on to other beliefs. For him, it was the existence of these other beliefs that was the biggest obstacle to the public understanding of science.

As a promoter of the public understanding of science, however, Dawkins appears to be going one step further than Sagan. He is advocating Darwinism not only as a candle in the dark against pseudoscientific beliefs, but also as a direct *substitute* for personal religion. Dawkins goes about this in a number of different ways. He identifies and dismantles arguments for the existence of God, particularly the Argument from Design (in *The Blind Watchmaker*, 1987). He addresses the questions that are typically held up by creationists and religious people as 'impossible' chance events, and painstakingly explains these with the help of Darwinian theory instead. His favorite example is the evolution of the eye, which he triumphantly reports has come about independently at least 40 times in different species, and for which even computer models have now been developed (Dawkins, 1996, Chapter 5). He convinces the reader that through the accumulation of small changes over a very long period, evolution can indeed climb Mount Improbable (1996). He debunks claims by creationists. And, perhaps most provocatively, he systematically uses biblical imagery in his own writings. The River out of Eden is the river of DNA, flowing through time. God's utility function is DNA survival. Mitochondrial Eve is replacing the mythical Eve. Still, he notes that there is one form of resistance among anti-evolutionists that it is hard to combat: 'The argument from incredulity'. The more incredible a belief, the more you stick to it, and in this way prove your worthiness as a believer (Dawkins, 1993).

People keep challenging Dawkins' position. He tells us himself:

> I have lost count of the number of times a member of the audience has stood up after a public lecture I have given and said something like the following: 'You scientists are very good at answering 'How' questions. But you must admit you are powerless when it comes to 'Why' questions' . . . Behind the question there is always an unspoken but never justified implication that since science is unable to answer 'Why' questions there must be some other discipline that *is* qualified to answer them. This implication is, of course, quite illogical (Dawkins, 1995a, p. 97).

Illogical it may be, but many individuals may actually not be hankering after *logic*—which may be exactly why they feel a need to go beyond science to various types of religions, myths, and pseudoscientific beliefs. So clearly *if* people are fundamentally looking for something that science cannot provide (answers to 'why' questions), it probably would not help to provide them with even the most brilliant explanation of science. Interestingly, exactly this problem was brought up by Lewontin in his review of Sagan's *The Demon-Haunted World* (Lewontin, 1997a). He noticed that Sagan, like most other scientists, believed it was self-evident that science provided the best approach. Moreover, according to Lewontin, Sagan thought that 'a proclivity for science is embedded deeply within us in all times, places and cultures'. But if that was so, Lewontin asked, why did so many believe in 'demons' *instead* of science? Sagan seemed to have no explanation for this, he said, except his suggestion that 'through indifference, inattention, incompetence, or fear of skepticism, we discourage children from science'. Also, Lewontin fingerpointed, Sagan did not tell us how he used the scientific method to arrive at his view that we have a natural proclivity for science (Lewontin, 1997a).

Dawkins, however, is not interested in this aspect of the problem. His mission is not to explain why people want answers to '*Why*' questions. In his recent books, he steadfastly presents a universe without a God, evolution without purpose, and a nature that does not care about us or give us any source of guidance. Nature should not be seen as a struggle between good and evil. Nature lacks all purpose: it is only maximizing the survival of DNA. So far so good. But at the same time, Dawkins disqualifies all available sources of solace: myths, legends, and religions: they are all viruses of the mind (Dawkins, 1993). Not many, except people with very strong minds, can live in such a world. Dawkins wants readers to believe in Darwinism as a substitution for myth, but his Darwinism carries the encrypted message that the world is empty of meaning. It would seem that Dawkins, if taken seriously, is actively creating a sort of meaning vacuum. If so, how do his readers fill that vacuum?

It is on exactly this point that Wilson differs from Dawkins. Wilson's books, particularly *On Human Nature*, *Promethean Fire*, and *Consilience* have been permeated with a concern for the emotional side of human nature. Emotions are what make us human. Wilson understands there is a need for answers to those '*Why*' questions that Dawkins—with most other scientists—perceives as being outside the scope of science. Wilson is operating with a different model of the human mind from Dawkins. And in *Concilience* Wilson in fact tells us why we keep wanting answers to why questions. The reason for our metaphysical quest is an evolutionary one: *religious belief can be seen as adaptive*. The submission of humans to a perceived higher power, in the case of religion, derives from a more general tendency for submissive behavior which has showed itself to be adaptive. By submitting to a stronger force, animals attain a stable situation. In other words, Wilson here uses ethological insight to argue that *we cannot eliminate our metaphysical quest*—it is part of our nature.

And this goes straight to the heart of the matter. Dawkins and Wilson represent dramatically different views of evolutionary biology as a science. Unlike Dawkins, Wilson believes that science (evolutionary biology) will (and *should*) be able to satisfy *all* our needs: our need for knowledge, for esthetic stimulation, and for deep emotional and metaphysical satisfaction.[5] This was, in fact, what he said already in *On Human Nature* in conjunction with his statements about 'the evolutionary epic' (and what he continued saying in *Consilience*):

> [T]he mind fights to retain a certain level of order and emotional reward. . . . [T]he mind will always create morality, religion and mythology and empower them with emotional force. When blind ideologies and religious beliefs are stripped away, others are quickly manufactured as replacements. . . .
>
> This mythopoeic drive can be harnessed to learning and the rational search for human progress if we finally concede that scientific materialism is itself a mythology defined in the noblest sense. . . .
>
> The core of scientific materialism is the evolutionary epic. . . . What I am suggesting, in the end, is *that the evolutionary epic is probably the best myth we will ever have*. It can be adjusted until it comes as close to truth as the human mind is constructed to judge the truth. And if that is the case, the mythopoeic requirements of the mind must somehow be met by scientific materialism so as to reinvest our superb energies (Wilson, 1978a, pp. 200–1, italics added).

So, in 1978 Wilson had already pointed out that, although the evolutionary epic might well be a myth, it would be better than other myths, 'probably the best myth we will ever have'. ('No other isms allowed but Darwinism!', I once heard Wilson tell an undergraduate class at Harvard.) According to Wilson, our brains are myth-making machines. If we don't give them something that can satisfy that need, they will fill up anyway—with myths of *less* adaptive value! But Wilson also realizes that for evolution to function as a myth, *it would have to take the full responsibility of a creation myth*. And this is why it would not do to reduce the evolutionary epic to merely an objectivist explanation of the world.

We saw that Lewontin asked how Sagan had used science to arrive at his conclusion that humans had an 'embedded' proclivity for science.[6] Well, here we have a scientific-ally grounded answer, offered by Wilson rather than Sagan, and interestingly suggesting the absolute opposite: that our minds are spontaneous *myth-makers* rather than spon-taneous scientific reasoners! If this is so, we may legitimately ask: in what way does the general public actually read and understand popular books about science—say, books on evolutionary biology?

Let us take a final overview of the different positions on science, and religion or myth. In *Consilience*, Wilson ends up seeing convergence, not conflict, between the religious and scientific quests for understanding. (If anything, he is more conciliatory now than a quarter of a century ago.) Over the years, Wilson has participated in a number of gatherings devoted to discussion of the relationship between science and religion.[7] Although Wilson, a self-described scientific humanist and materialist, has declared traditional religious belief and scientific knowledge 'at bedrock' incompatible, he still sees a link between religion and science in 'the undeniable fact that faith is in our bones, that religious belief is part of human nature and seemingly vital to social existence' (Wilson, 1991b).[8] We have, then, a situation where *Dawkins* now appears as a new type of critical weeder (of viruses, that is) while *Gould* joins Wilson as something of a positive planter (or at least a gardener who allows different flowers to blossom)! Still, Wilson, quite unlike Gould, seems to be wishing for some kind of *merger* of science and religion. Where does Hamilton stand? Hamilton, like Gould, sees science and religion as separate realms. He thinks that people should be allowed to pursue religious ideas if this makes them happy, and actually cannot understand Dawkins' fierce stance (personal communication).[9] Finally, what about Maynard Smith? What does he think about these issues? Based on what he said in 1984, it would seem that his own position is similar to Gould's and Hamilton's:

> Three views are tenable. The first, sometimes expressed as a demand for 'normative science', is that the same mental constructs should serve both as myths and as scientific theories . . . Although well-intentioned, it seems to me pernicious in its effects. If we insist that scientific theories convey moral messages, the result will be bad morality or bad science, and most probably both. . . .
>
> The second view is that we should do without myths and confine ourselves to scientific theories. This is the view I held at age twenty, but it really won't do. If, as I believe, scientific theories say nothing about what is right, but only about what is possible, we need some other source of values, and that source has to be myth in the broadest sense of the term.
>
> The third view, and I think the only sensible one, is that we need both myth and scientific theories, but that we must be as clear as we can which is which. . . . Yet to do science, one must first be committed to some values—not least to the value of seeking the truth (Maynard Smith, 1984, p. 24).

Maynard Smith, then, recognized the need for both science and myth, but as separate realms. Although he here did not directly address either Dawkins or Wilson, Maynard Smith can actually be construed as telling them 'a plague on both your houses!' We cannot do without myth, but it would be 'pernicious' to combine science with myth. Maynard Smith's own example of someone who 'got it right' was Jacques Monod. In his view, Monod had correctly emphasized that, while values cannot be derived from science, science in fact depends on values—that is, prior moral commitments—to be possible at all.

Keeping science on a leash—the importance of emotions and moral concerns

We have come a long way from the discussion about *Sociobiology* a quarter of a century ago—or have we come full circle? More facts have been gathered and theories elaborated, while the climate has changed from anti-genetic to pro-genetic. Still, individual scientists' perspectives on sociobiology as a research program have to do with where they stand on a number of epistemological and methodological issues. No one involved in the controversy has really substantially changed his mind over these twenty-five years, although the original agendas continue evolving. The sociobiology debate has been largely a vehicle for the scientists involved to promote their more long-term goals, including their particular visions of evolutionary biology.

There are several gratifying developments. We have a relative vindication of the sociobiologists unfairly accused at the beginning of the controversy. Also, over the course of the debate, there has been an increasing engagement with serious scientific and meta-scientific issues, and the deep-seated epistemological, methodological, and ontological differences between the participants have become more visible. The partial merger between the sociobiology debate and the Science Wars further helped clarify matters and the actual positions of the protagonists. Still, the Science Wars may have left the impression of science as *certain* knowledge—you either have science or you have anti-science—even in the case of largely tentative results in many fields.

There is a tendency among scientists writing for the general public to present science as a ready-made product, a body of knowledge or set of truths, which only need good explication. Although the general public may gain fascinating new insights and greater clarity with regard to scientific explanations of the world, what is presented here is typically science as a kind of *revealed truth*. The same is the case when the aim is to give the public a sense of a scientific approach to reasoning about evidence. This is what Dawkins is doing, for instance, in a recent story about a scientific vs legal approach to data (Dawkins, 1998a, b). We learn how a scientist would approach the data, say in the O. J. Simpson case, and how it was actually handled by lawyers. The difference is, no doubt, illuminating and it may improve people's reasoning skills. But very seldom these days do we get glimpses of the actual *uncertainties* involved in scientific decision-making, data selection, and the like—together with an explanation of how things work out right, after all (or wrong, for that matter).

Dissatisfied with the official picture of science, a new brand of sociologists of scientific knowledge and ethnographers of science have tried to capture how science is actually done. During the last twenty-five years or so, they have gone to laboratories and other places, documenting what they regard as 'the social construction of scientific facts'. Based on this body of research, science comes out looking so fluid that it makes one wonder that science can say anything at all! Compared to pro-science writers, these researchers have gone to the other extreme, acting as if scientists have *no* good reasons for making particular scientific claims at any particular time. On this view, science does not appeared constrained by facts or experiments. This challenge, again, has led people like Wolpert (1992) and Holton (1995) to only try harder to expound the special nature of science as a unique type of approach to the world.

What is missing is the emphasis on process. Scientific truths do not spring out of Zeus' head like Pallas Athena; they are the end products of a long collective process, and it is when they are not challenged any longer that they become 'established truth'. The 'harder' the data involved, the less likely are scientific claims to step back from their truth status, although it happens. In this respect scientific truth works like a ratchet. It is this end product that many pro-science writers emphasize as 'science'. But what was the *process*—often tortuous—through which the knowledge was assessed and debated and finally achieved the status of uncontested knowledge?[10]

A recent clash between Lewontin, and Gross and Levitt illustrates what happens when two idea-oriented conceptions of science come in conflict. According to Lewontin (1998a), Gross' and Levitt's view of science in *Higher Superstition* appeared to have little to do with a field like evolutionary biology. Lewontin argued that the authors' claim that science was 'above all else, a reality-driven enterprise', and reality 'the unrelenting angel with whom scientists have to wrestle', indicated

> ignorance of the immense diversity of canons of evidence that characterize different sciences, of the powerful role that metaphors play in the conceptualizations of the sciences and in directing their experimental programs, and in the degree to which prior ideological commitment governs what scientists say about the real world . . . (Lewontin, 1998b).

He concluded that, for Gross and Levitt, science consisted of uncontroversial, law-like statements that described what was 'really' true about the physical world, like Newton's or Mendel's laws or the law of combining proportions in chemistry.

What was the problem here? Did Gross and Levitt 'really' believe that science consisted of such statements, and were they blind to the influence of social and cultural factors? Did Lewontin 'really' believe that science, because it was influenced by ideological factors, involved metaphors, and the like, was largely unconstrained by reality, while still somehow enabling us to manipulate the material world? The answer to both is no. The exchange between Lewontin and Gross and Lewitt nicely illustrates the need for the distinction between process and product also when it comes to the question of *ideological influences* on a scientific claim and the scientific *truth* of this claim.

One problem in the sociobiology debate was that the critics located truth at the beginning of the production line, as it were. They regularly acted as if the truth of scientific claims somehow depended on the political ideologies of individual scientists, such as Wilson, rather than on the subsequent validation by an elaborate communal procedure in science. (Gould, however, on occasion pointed out the distinction between the so-called context of discovery and the context of justification; for example, 1982.) Incidentally, with regard to political influences on science, some scientists I met at the International Ethological Congress in Oxford in 1981 believed that not only science, but also the political positions of scientists, gets criticized in the process of mutual criticism. In other words, unlike Lewontin, these scientists trusted the system of mutual checking in science to eliminate not only scientific but also *political* 'error'!

Still, the sociobiology and IQ controversies clearly demonstrated the fact that there were several different criteria for 'good science' simultaneously in use among scientists, even in the same field. As we have seen, much of the sociobiology controversy was in fact about the epistemology, methodology, and even ontology of science, although these abstract issues were seldom addressed as such. The discussion took place in a very in-direct way, in the form of individual scientists attacking fellow scientists for producing politically and scientifically 'bad' science.

The sociobiology controversy has been permeated with moral/political concerns. Has this been good or bad for the field of sociobiology, and the broader field of evolutionary biology? Has it hindered or speeded up progress in these fields?[11] Of course, much muddle was created by the tendency of opponents of sociobiology to classify as 'erroneous' what proponents (and many mainstream scientists) regarded as perfectly legitimate scientific positions and plausibility arguments. One reason for this was that influential critics of sociobiology came from fields far away from evolutionary biology, or from a non-naturalist tradition within this field. In many respects, the sociobiology debate might be seen as an acting out of unarticulated and unresolved differences between scientists from different traditions (see Chapters 13 and 14). And this went far beyond the opposition within evolutionary biology. Because of the interdisciplinary nature of its subject matter—and its moral and metaphysical appeal—the sociobiology controversy attracted scientists from a wide variety of fields, all with different conceptions of 'good science'.

But precisely the fact that *moral concerns* were involved may have had a beneficial effect on sociobiology. It may have kept the evolving field, if not on the straight and narrow path, at least on some kind of leash—methodologically and epistemologically. As we have seen, morally concerned scientists spent enormous amounts of time criticizing sociobiology as a science.[12] Later, as Wilson's sociobiological program evolved, some of his critics even learnt population genetics in order to be able to present a competent scientific criticism (this was true of, for instance, astronomer David Layzer's, chemist Joe Alper's, and physicist Bob Lange's critiques of *Genes, Mind and Culture*). And while sociobiologists often dismissed their opponents' scientific criticism as politically motivated, there is no doubt they felt challenged by the criticism to clarify what they meant and clear up any obvious scientific misunderstandings.[13]

Wilson responded to his critics by changing his sociobiological program completely with regard to humans, going from Sociobiology I where genes were seen as directly affecting behavior, and thus in turn society and culture, to the genes-mind-and-culture type, Sociobiology II, with the mind factored in and epigenetic rules channeling its choice of 'culturgens'. The mathematical treatment meant that the new models could be more specifically appreciated (for example, Krebs, 1981; see Chapter 8) or criticized (for example, Maynard Smith and Warren, 1982). Dawkins' reaction was to express himself ever more lucidly. He explained what he meant by a 'gene'; he sorted out the difference between development and evolution; he made a distinction between replicators and vehicles, and so on. (His ultimate triumph may well have been to be given the green light in 1988 by hard-nosed philosopher Philip Kitcher, whose 1985 demolition job on Wilsonian sociobiology made even Jon Beckwith wince; see Chapter 16.)

In the IQ controversy, in a parallel fashion, the moral/political criticism drove the science of psychometrics into ever better formulations of its exact scientific position. The uproar around Jensen's 1969 *Harvard Educational Review* paper triggered great interest in the details of the methodology of this field (much of this reviewed by Block and Dworkin, 1976). Leon Kamin (1974), in particular, challenged Jensen's seemingly too-high estimates for the heritability of IQ in Caucasians. The Cyril Burt scandal further contributed to the suspicion about the existing heritability estimate of IQ. And *voilà*, in 1998 we have Wilson quoting it as a fact in his *Consilience* that the heritability of IQ for Caucasians is around 0.5 (Wilson, 1998a, p. 142). The lowering of the heritability estimate from roughly 0.8 to 0.5 in some thirty years surely has something to do with the relentless questioning of the psychometricians by their critics. At the same time, it had spurred Jensen in 1979 to write the book *Bias in Mental Testing*, defending his methods, which again triggered a critique by Gould (1980, 1981a). Later, in a new round, we had *The Bell Curve* (Herrnstein and Murray, 1994) with its critique (for example, Frazer, 1995; Gould, 1996a; Fischer *et al.*, 1997). The upheaval around the book, again, prompted a statement by educational psychologists in the *Wall Street Journal* specifying exactly what was the consensus in the field of psychometrics at the time and new discussions about the status of *g* and mental testing (for example, Sternberg and Grigorenko, 1997).

In fact, it is hard to believe that the relentless critique of sociobiology, IQ research, and the like would *not* have had consequences. When challenged, scientists typically respond. (Recall, for instance, Lewontin in Chapter 8 telling us that if someone finds a hole in a theory, the response is to find a way to patch it.) This notion of challenge in scientific disputes—just as in duels—has been usually explored by Biagioli (1993).

And there is another feature of scientific behavior. In general, scientists tend to look harder for errors when they do not like the outcome of a piece of research, and are less critical with themselves and others when the results come out as expected (Goodstein, 1992). Add to this a moral/political reason for scrutiny of error, and you have released a fearsome intellectual force![14] Of course, sometimes the error-finding business may get slightly out of hand, particularly if there is a perceived premium on error-finding (see Chapter 15). Still, for a scientist, accusations of error will typically be hard to ignore, and regarded as requiring a response.

Finally, the moral outrage felt—either with regard to sociobiology or with regard to the critics of sociobiology—linked scientists from a wide variety of fields, creating personal connections of trust between them, a process which may have also speeded up exchange of scientific information and thus helped the synthesis of knowledge from different fields. No doubt the 'truths' thus accumulated in the divided academy were different (see Chapter 13). At regular intervals, however, the arguments gathered on both sides got pitted against each other, thus furthering the 'arms race' of scientific truth-seeking, continuously upping the ante for each side.

Maynard Smith recently told me that he thought the sociobiology controversy had been healthy for the field, on the whole. What he meant was that, over time, the unnecessary political content had been gradually eliminated from the discourse, so that the 'real' scientific debate could finally begin (interview in 1998). In this book I am making a rather different point. I am arguing that moral/political concerns, far from being an obstacle to be eliminated, were in fact a *driving force* both in generating and criticizing scientific claims in this field, and that the field was better off because of this.

We see, then, the importance of moral and metaphysical commitments in science. They motivate scientific work, they sustain it in the face of adversity, and they drive scientists to closely scrutinize the claims of opponents. It seems to me that moral/political criticism is an important and healthy phenomenon in science, particularly in fields which depend largely on plausibility arguments. (This critique does not *have* to take the form of an attack on individuals, as happened in the sociobiology debate.)

As we saw, one of Wilson's leading concerns in *On Human Nature,* expressed again in *Consilience,* was his wish to somehow tap the emotional potential inherent in the 'mythopoeic requirement of the mind' and bring it into science as an energizing force. Wilson was clearly right about the importance of the emotional realm for humans, and the motivating force of commitment and belief. It is somewhat ironical that Wilson, smack in the middle of the cross-fire of controversy, should have worried about *introducing* these elements into science. What he wished to bring to science—emotion and belief—was already there.

Notes

Chapter 1

1 I have borrowed this passage from Sherwood Washburn's article 'The Behavior of Humans and Other Animals', *American Psychologist*, Vol. 33, No. 5, May 1978.

2 I discuss this further in Chapter 6. The tip in this case comes from 'the horse's mouth'.

3 The artist was someone unusually familiar with the sociobiological scene.

Chapter 2

1 For an overview of the IQ controversy see Block and Dworkin (1976); for Jensen's own account of actions taken against him, see Chapter 1 in Jensen (1972a).

2 Although the article was widely believed to have focused exclusively on racial differences in IQ, this topic covered only part of the 123 page article. According to Jensen, it was in fact the *editors* who had asked him to add this discussion to his original text. For the background to the article and the role of *Harvard Educational Review* in producing the Jensen scandal, see Jensen (1972a), Chapter 1.

3 For Herrnstein's account of events, see Herrnstein (1973), Chapter 1.

4 The piece was perhaps less sensationalistic than simply pro-sociobiology.

5 The first of the above quotes appeared in an article in the weekly newspaper *The Harvard Crimson*, written by Sociobiology Study Group member Miriam Rosenthal (Rosenthal, 1977); that article was reproduced as a CAR flyer. The second quote is from a flyer distributed just before a public lecture by Wilson in the Harvard Science Center (CAR, 10 February 1982).

6 There may have been more profound sentiments among leading ethologists against Wilsonian sociobiology. Unfortunately, neither Eibl-Eibesfeldt nor Tinbergen wanted to be interviewed. I will return to the reactions of other ethologists in later chapters.

7 Of course, there is no *obvious* connection between scientific results and social consequences. However, in a utility-oriented culture such as the United States, this type of reasoning is quite common, and it was clearly taken for granted in the sociobiology controversy. Very few, if any, academics took the position that no social conclusions could be drawn from scientific findings. I will return to this theme in Chapter 19.

Chapter 3

1 Wilson returned to this theme in *On Human Nature* (1978a), which can in fact be read as an analysis and critique of the manipulative powers of the Church. This point, however, was totally missed by the members of the Sociobiology Study Group. For a closer analysis of this, see Chapter 20.

2 For instance when Gould, in *The Mismeasure of Man* (1981a), says that a racist society inevitably produces racist science.

3 Wilson is probably at his best when having to face a challenge and his amphetamine or internal opiates kick in. I remember briefly visiting him in his office in April 1990. He was in an excited state because of a major crisis that had just happened. One of the employees at the Museum of Comparative Zoology had become violent and threatened people, but Wilson had successfully handled the incident. This was Wilson in full gear, as full of positive energy and fighting spirit as during our interviews at the height of the sociobiology controversy. A visitor whom I had brought with me got only this one-shot impression of Wilson's personality. He came to believe that Wilson was always like this: someone with a glint in his eye and even something of a provocateur type. So later, at the AAAS meeting in Atlanta in 1995, he was surprised and disappointed to hear Wilson's very low-key, standard biology evening lecture on biodiversity. But soon he again had a chance to see what he believed to be the 'true' Wilson. That was at the 1996 Human Behavior and Evolution Society meeting, where Wilson actually ended up shocking part of his audience (see Chapter 18).

Chapter 4

1 Among these, Wright was able to participate in the sociobiology controversy; one of his last contributions was published in *Evolution* in 1980 when Wright was in his nineties. (Haldane had died in 1964 and Fisher in 1962.)

2 Wright had worked out the coefficient of relationship used by Hamilton in his 1964 paper.

3 Maynard Smith here presented his 'haystack model' of mice populations (see also Maynard Smith, 1976a, reprinted in Brandon and Burian, 1984).

4 As to Hamilton's explanation of haplodiploidy in Hymenoptera, this is what Maynard Smith wrote in 1995: 'When I first came across this point in Hamilton's 1964 paper, I felt furious with myself for not having seen it, but slightly comforted that Haldane had missed it too' (Maynard Smith, 1995a, p. 183).

5 Incidentally, Hamilton did get his PhD (in 1969)—with Maynard Smith as an external reviewer. This fact we learn from Maynard Smith (1976b/1989, p. 205).

6 He had been a physicist and a chemist but later turned to science journalism (Hamilton, 1996, p. 172).

7 It turns out that others around the same time as Price had independently derived part of his formula. Still, none of these employed Price's nested analysis of levels of selection, which Hamilton thought was the beauty of Price's approach (Hamilton, 1996, p. 176). (Later on, Sober and Wilson, 1998a, would be making use of Price; see Chapters 16 and 19 in this book.)

8 It was also this formula that Hamilton later used and extended in his 1975 paper to actually reformulate his initial idea of inclusive fitness. Hamilton saw that paper as a tribute to Price (see Chapter 7).

9 As he explained (and later reiterated in interview), Price had submitted a paper to *Nature*, which was sent to Maynard Smith to referee. Maynard Smith goes on: 'Unfortunately the paper was some fifty pages in length and hence quite unsuitable for *Nature*. I wrote a report saying that the paper contained an interesting idea, and that the author should be urged to submit a short account of it to *Nature* and/or to submit the existing manuscript to a more suitable journal' (Maynard Smith, 1976b/1989, p. 205).

10 Price was later offered office space at the Galton Laboratory.

11 Dawkins' book was written quite independently of *Sociobiology*. He started it during a power breakdown in his lab in 1972, and continued again in 1975 (Dawkins, 1989, p. x). He did not read Wilson's book until later (Dawkins, 1981a, p. 577).

12 Dawkins' own example of complex behavior is reading. 'All we would need in order to establish the existence of a gene for reading is to discover a gene for not reading, say a gene which induced a brain lesion causing specific dyslexia' (Dawkins, 1982, p. 23).

13 Dawkins gives credit to Michael Wade (1978) for having come up with the idea first (Dawkins, 1981a, p. 570).

Chapter 5

1 Trivers is now cured. In an interview in 1985, he told *Omni* that he believed the chief concern of the Harvard faculty was the fact that he was mentally unstable (interview, Robert Trivers, *Omni*, July 1985, pp. 77–8, 80, 82, 108, 110). (The interviewer had mentioned that it had been said that Trivers was denied tenure because Harvard was bowing to pressure from leftist groups concerned about the political implications of sociobiology.) Trivers describes his horrible experience with schizophrenia in this interview.

2 According to interviews both in *Omni* and *Time*, Trivers had also been active in civil rights demonstrations. According to *Omni*: 'Growing up in suburban Washington, D.C., Trivers had developed a strong identification with blacks and black causes, an identification that eventually led him to join the Black Panther party. One colleague called Trivers "the blackest white man I know"' (*Omni*, 1985, p. 78).

3 The error was later corrected in conjunction with the republication of Hamilton's

paper in Williams' 1971 book *Group Selection*. For an explanation of the nature of the error, see Wilson (1994, p. 326).

4 Crook's (1976) review of *Sociobiology* in *Animal Behaviour* is somewhat critical, but not more than some other of the collected peer commentaries. Basically, although Crook calls the book 'magnificent' and declares the overall quality of the work 'very high', he wonders at Wilson's 'advocacy' and 'political game' of renaming a field which may as well be called evolutionary ethology. Crook classifies Wilson's work as 'closer to that of his great Harvard forebear W. M. Wheeler and the ecological school of G. E. Hutchinson and R. MacArthur than to the traditions of European ethology as transplanted to the U.S.A.'. He concludes that Wilson's book 'fails to break new ground in the end'. According to Crook, 'our present need is for major advances in developmental ethology'; he asks for 'a developmental understanding of the social dynamics underlying societal change'.

5 Wilson defined sociobiology as 'the systematic study of the biological basis of all social behavior'.

6 This, of course, goes against another conspiracy scenario arguing that the brouhaha was needed to sell an expensive and massive book.

7 And later, Trivers was struggling with the mathematics involving Hymenoptera sex ratios and consulting Wilson about it, perhaps in this way again emphasizing this specific example.

8 In his autobiography, Wilson notes parenthetically, 'few learned about the theory until I highlighted it in the 1970s' (1994, p. 317). It is not clear whether he refers here to his 1971 or 1975 book, or both. Also, he may have independent information, for instance from colleagues, that would indicate that this was the case, or he may be referring to the Seger and Harvey study.

9 Hamilton himself mentions that his 1967 paper contained at least the following ideas:

    1 the levels-of-selection debate;

    2 the idea of conflict within the genome;

    3 the 'evolutionarily stable strategy';

    4 the initiation of game-theoretic ideas in evolutionary biology;

    5 more indirectly, by emphasizing the costliness of male production for females and for population growth, as well as the ever ready 'option' (among small insects, for example) of parthenogenesis, the paper helped to initiate debate over the adaptive function of sex (Hamilton, 1996, p. 133).

10 The paper that inspired Hamilton was by G. C. and D. C. Willimas (1957).

11 Williams, personal communication to George Barlow (Barlow, 1991).

12 In the 1990s, however, ethology and behavioral ecology started moving back toward a more integrated approach; see, for example, Krebs and Davies (1997a). We will return to this in Chapter 16.

13 Wilson went on to discuss the various studies that human geneticists would have to undertake in order to provide the answer (pp. 207–8).

14 Thus, in discussing rapid behavioral evolution, Wilson appears to have had in mind some kind of social engineering—it was less a descriptive statement of the relationship between genetic and cultural evolution than a *prescriptive* one of potential measures that could be taken by planners.

15 Later, Hamilton imagined what he might have told her (Hamilton, 1996, pp. 193–5).

16 Indeed, also when discussing human evolution, Wilson included ecological and population parameters in addition to Fisher's formula of genetic evolution. Culture, of course, was recognized and factored in, but Wilson saw its role as largely to speed up evolution.

17 In early 1975 Bateson, together with Nick Humphrey, as Fellows of King's, had suggested the establishment of a research project in behavioral ecology. The project appointed research fellows for short or longer terms, and invited people for talks and discussions.

Chapter 6

1 Hamilton said he had also been fascinated with the idea of applying the Prisoner's Dilemma to evolutionary theory; he presented this briefly in his paper at the Man and Beast conference in 1969 (Hamilton, 1971d).

2 In 1972 Maynard Smith had already discussed Lewontin's game-theoretical approach and distinguished it from his own Price-inspired approach.

3 Indeed, it was in this spirit that he argued for the preservation of the human gene pool as a 'cardinal value', and also why he did not believe in the possibility of the accumulation of genes for certain social groups or classes (see closer discussion in Chapter 10).

4 Maynard Smith referred to Lewontin's views as expressed in two papers (Lewontin 1977b, 1978a) that Lewontin had sent to him.

5 Maynard Smith explicitly noted in his 1978 paper that it was the two Lewontin papers that had inspired his review of optimization theory.

6 John Maynard Smith commented that it was in fact Haldane who first invoked Pangloss and Panglossianism in evolutionary biology, although he used it in a somewhat different sense.

7 Before the Gould and Lewontin paper, the following papers had been presented at the Royal Society Discussion Meeting:
L. E. Orgel on 'Selection *in vitro*';
B. S. Hartley on 'The Evolution of Enzyme Structure';
B. C. Clarke, on 'The Evolution of Genetic Diversity';
J. Maynard Smith on 'Game Theory and the Evolution of Behaviour';

R. Dawkins and J. Krebs on 'Arms Races Between and Within Species';

D. and C. Charlesworth on 'The Evolutionary Genetics of Sexual Systems in Flowering Plants;

T. B. D. Kirkwood and R. Holliday on 'The Evolution of Ageing and Longevity';

T. Clutton-Brook and P. Harvey on 'Comparison and Adaptation';

G. C. Williams on 'The Question of Adaptive Sex Ration in Outcrossed Vertebrates'.

8 Here Gould gave an example from his own profession, geology. Most geologists believe that Charles Lyell's *Principles of Geology* was a textbook, whose persuasive power came from his abundant documentation of evidence for uniformitarianism. But, Gould continued, almost all modern studies recognize that Lyell in fact proceeded almost entirely by rhetoric. *Principles* was basically 'a brief for a partisan argument' (and, indeed, Lyell was a barrister by profession) (Gould, 1993b, p. 323).

9 Indeed, Williams (1992) adopted the term 'spandrels' to describe one type of new structure arising in evolution.

10 A sign of this was a conference on developmental constraints later published as a review article by Maynard Smith *et al.* (1987) (I will return to this in Chapter 16).

11 The scientist seems to have referred to Gould, rather than to Gould and Lewontin.

12 Spandrels, technically, are the triangles formed between vaults in a straight line, for example, between the arches on a Roman aqueduct.

13 The professor of civil engineering and architecture also discusses the ceiling of King's College. The author suggests that rather than providing an appropriate ceiling to carry the Tudor symbols (as Dennett would have it), 'it is far more likely that fan vaulting was selected for the college hall in order to adopt an up-to-date, high architectural style'.

14 John Krebs, in an interview in 1981, believed that Gould was still an adaptationist: 'he has to be'.

15 It did not escape the attention of the students of rhetoric that in his anti-adaptationist Spandrels article Gould happily quoted his own earlier adaptationist work in support of his argument *without* telling the reader about his later change of mind. 'He in fact rewrites those articles after the fact by quietly assimilating them into an opposite position', noted Bazerman (1993).

16 Gould may well have exaggerated the extent to which his audience would be 'resisting' his message; many were quite sophisticated adaptationists. One analyst of the symposium papers noted that 'in fact, only two of the ten primary papers fall into Gould and Lewontin's characterization of adaptationism. The remainder move across the spectrum, some ultimately adopting positions rather close to Gould and Lewontin's' (Bazerman, 1993). But, I was told, Gould disappointed his audience by completely ignoring Clutton-Brock and Harvey's paper, which had anticipated his attack.

17 When the authors introduced Dr Pangloss as the patron saint of optimization theorists, they did not feel it sufficient to let the statement about the Lisbon

earthquake as 'being for the best' stand alone; they had to rub in the point that 50 000 people lost their lives.

18 It is not obvious that the initiative had come from Futuyama (at SUNY, Stony Brook). According to a note, the letter signers were alphabetically organized. In addition to Futuyama, they included the following scientists from Harvard: R. C. Lewontin, G. C. Mayer, J. Seger, and J. W. Stubblefield III.

19 Here 'saltationist' is used instead of 'punctuationist' (or 'punctuativist').

Chapter 7

1 At this point Dawkins decided it would be important to signal that he, too, held the 'correct' belief in regard to hierarchies: 'At every level the units interact with each other following laws appropriate to that level, laws which are not conveniently reducible to laws at lower levels. This has all been said many times before, and is so obvious as to be almost platitudinous. But sometimes one has to repeat platitudes in order to prove that one's heart is in the right place! Especially if one wishes to emphasize a slightly unconventional sort of hierarchy, for this may be mistaken for a "reductionist" attack on the idea of hierarchy itself' (Dawkins, 1982, p. 113). Indeed, Dawkins told me in 1981 that one of the reasons he wrote his chapter on hierarchical organization in Bateson and Hinde's 1976 *Growing Points in Ethology* book was to demonstrate that he was not 'against' hierarchies (Dawkins, 1976b).

2 For this idea of reproduction, and against Dawkins' conception, Eldredge found support in Alexander and Borgia, who had argued, *contra* Dawkins, that species *were* replicators: 'Species give rise to species; species multiply' (Alexander and Borgia, 1978, p. 456, quoted in Eldredge, 1985, p. 6).

3 According to Eldredge, Williams in his 1966 book had seen organismic adaptation as the central problem in evolution, which had led him to discuss ecological inter- actions in terms of 'effective strategies' of individuals and such statements as 'the goal of the fox is to contribute as heavily as possible to the next generation of a fox population'. From there it was not a great leap to Dawkins' view of evolution as 'the process by which some genes become more numerous in the gene pool' (Dawkins, 1976a, p. 48). Eldredge noted that Dawkins' statement in fact represented the standard definition of evolution according to the Modern Synthesis (Eldredge, 1985, p. 106).

4 Eldredge pointed out, however, that Williams (1966) did not dismiss all forms of group selection out of hand; he 'merely argued that there would be no need for an onerous, higher-level process such as group selection if it were possible to show that simple natural selection alone would suffice to produce a given phenomenon. In- deed, Williams thought that higher-level selection was a virtual truism in evolution.' However, Williams in 1966 wondered about the relative *importance* of higher-level processes in relation to natural selection (Eldredge, 1985, p. 105).

5 'Culture is not inherited through genes, it is acquired by learning from other human beings. . . . In a sense, human genes have surrendered their primacy in human evolution to an entirely new, nonbiological or superorganic agent, culture' (Dobzhansky, 1963).

6 Wilson, of course, had from the very beginning protested against such rampant culturism, also pointing to its political dangers (Wilson, 1975c). This view of human nature as being constantly recreated in a historical process later got the Sociobiology Study Group in trouble with Chomsky (see Chapter 10).

7 This would later put Gould in opposition to Stephen Pinker, the young MIT linguist, who declared language to be exactly that—a specialized system among many others existing in the adapted human mind (Pinker, 1994; Barkow *et al.*, 1992).

8 Later, there have been studies showing that animals—including humans—may be able to tell kin from non-kin based on smell (for example, Wells, 1987). For a thorough early critique of Sahlins, see, among others, Etter (1978).

9 Harris' own theory of cultural materialism accepts that genes have shaped human nature until the agricultural revolution some 10 000 years ago. After that, there were major cultural changes. According to Harris, 'the major transformations of human culture, as well as regional cultural practices, can be explained as adaptations to ecological and economic conditions. Societies', he says, 'repeat cycles of exploiting new technology, overpopulating their land, and intensifying the use of resources to the point of ecological catastrophe, whereupon a new technology or resource is devised to start the new cycle' (Rensberger, 1983, p. 45).

10 Still, in 1969 Mead in her presentation at the Man and Beast conference had indicated strong dislike for Wilson's statement 'that it is possible, even in ten generations, to make a considerable change in a population. This also tends to lead people into a kind of passive despair. In many cases it emphasizes our dependence upon specific genetic traits of one sort or another and tends to deprecate the possible results of improved nutrition, education, and environment' (Mead, 1971, p. 373). Perhaps Mead accepted the general idea of biological foundations of behavior, but disliked the idea of 'genes'.

11 I believe that Lévi-Strauss' attitude to sociobiology was more supportive than that, having in the early 1980s seen a review in which he actually defended sociobiology.

12 The distinction between 'open' and 'closed' programs is Ernst Mayr's. In a closed program, the young in a species are born with 'a genetic program containing an almost complete set of ready-made, predictable responses to the stimuli of the environment'. In an open program, organisms 'have a great capacity to benefit from experience, to learn how to react to the environment, to continue adding "information" to their behavioral program' (Mayr, 1976, p. 23, quoted in Freeman, 1980, p. 201).

13 Among proponents of this view, Freeman lists Waddington (1961), Medawar (1976), and Popper (1976).

14 In 1983 Freeman wrote *Margaret Mead and Samoa*, a book basically arguing that Mead's famous book *Coming of Age in Samoa* (1928) did not agree with the facts.

15 They added:

What is meant, we suspect, is that we can test evolutionarily inspired optimality models of human behavior without reference to culture. But human culture does get in the way of fitness maximization. For instance, cultural traits can spread even at the expense of direct genetic benefits to their carrier. Cultural evolution has its own dynamics, constrained, but not fully determined by human evolutionary adaptability. A satisfactory understanding of human behavior requires examining the articulation of formerly adaptive traits with present cultural circumstances (Kacelnik and Krebs, 1997, p. 28).

16 Durham saw similarities between his own approach and Ruyle (1973), Campbell (1975), Boyd and Richerson (in press), Cloak (1975) and Dawkins (1976, Chapter 11).

17 Hamilton had referred to a quote from a 1965 article in *Science* on Old World monkeys and apes by S. L. Washburn, P. C. Jay, and B. Lancaster. The offending quote was as follows:

It has become clear that, although learning has great importance in the normal development of nearly all phases of primate behaviour, it is not a generalized ability; animals are able to learn some things with great ease and other things only with the greatest difficulty. Learning is part of the adaptive pattern of a species and can be understood only when it is seen as a process of acquiring skills and attitudes that are of evolutionary significance to a species when living in the environment to which it is adapted.

18 In fact, DeVore represented the type of anthropologist whom Dawkins would later admonish for 'misunderstanding' of kin selection theory—see the next and last section in this chapter.

19 Wrangham went on to say that because the choices, in turn, depended on biologically determined individual characteristics, natural selection was, after all, the ultimate arbiter of cultural change.

20 He added that, of course, the logic involved was 'genetic' in the sense that it reflected evolved characteristics of the species.

Chapter 8

1 See Chapter 18 for a closer discussion of sociobiology and the social sciences.

2 Leach probably referred to the King's College Sociobiology Group; see Chapter 7.

3 Of course, Wilson had argued from the very beginning that, even so, small existing differences could be blown up with the help of a multiplier effect.

Chapter 9

1 While the critics saw this as major proof of the correctness of their analysis, the critics themselves, of course, had virtually *told* the world's right-wing forces just how

sociobiology might be used politically. And how desperately did these right-wing forces really need sociobiology to boost their cause? I remember Mary Midgley's husband, a former member of the Communist Party, laughing at the idea that the National Front would need sociobiology.

2 And Nabi has a prehistory. 'Nabi' is the well-known pseudonym for a group of French artists in the 1890s. The word means 'seer' in Hebrew. In other words, 'Nabi' represents an older collective effort than Nicholas Bourbaki, the name under which a group of French mathematicians published their highly original work in the 1930s.

3 And following Mazur's (1981) conspiracy theory, the piece about Wilson was made into 'news' exactly *in order to* provoke strong critical reactions (see Chapter 6).

4 In turn, it was this letter that inspired Wilson's later attempt to unveil Nabi's identity.

Chapter 10

1 See Segerstråle (1990c) for a critique of tendencies in academic criticism.

2 As mentioned in Chapter 2, in 1984 I had my class at Smith College compare Chorover's interpretation to Wilson's original text, and despite their dislike of sociobiology, many students were dismayed at their own findings.

3 According to Wilson, in reality 'there is little evidence of any hereditary solidification of status' (p. 555), even though there exists in the literature some argument for the theoretical possibility for social stratification on the basis of genetic ability. Here Wilson cites the model of a single gene for success: Dahlberg in 1947. (Later Lewontin, 1981a, was to point out that this 'Dahlberg gene' was not even a model, it was a textbook example! Even so, it shows Wilson's eagerness to find an example in the literature that he can dismiss.)

4 Even if selecting only the 'best' data may be rather common practice in science, this is not consistent with ethical standards, and has been much discussed in recent cases of error and fraud. On the other hand, data selection *is* justified if a scientist has 'good reason' to believe that certain data are erroneous (for a discussion see, for example, Segerstråle, 1995).

Chapter 11

1 As we saw in Chapter 6, scientists easily perceive views that they disagree with as 'erroneous'. The critics seem to have taken the error-labeling tendency to an extreme.

2 In this, interestingly, he was supported by Beckwith, who together with others signed Davis' position statement in 1992.

3 In Wilson's 1994 description, the molecular biologists invading Harvard's biology department after Watson's Nobel prize appear to have acted in a very superior manner toward their colleagues in traditional fields of biology.

4 'The Lysenko affair' refers to the fact that from about 1935 to 1965 the development of genetics in the Soviet Union was halted. Mendelian genetics was replaced with a doctrine about the inheritance of acquired characteristics championed by Trofim Lysenko, a political figure put in charge of attempts to improve agriculture. For discussions of this affair see Joravsky (1970), Levins and Lewontin (1976), and Soyfer (1995).

5 This was in the context of his paper presented to the Philosophy of Science Association (1976a), an article that neither Davis nor Wilson saw. However, the argument resurfaced later in Lewontin (1979a).

6 There was also the question of the timing of Davis' article; it was in fact published after some delay. While Davis had prepared and circulated his draft and was ready to publish, Gould had come down with a nasty type of cancer. I strongly urged Davis to delay publishing his article (I assume others told him the same). And Davis did indeed wait. Later, Gould had a remission and miraculously recovered, and the article was published.

Chapter 12

1 Compare this with his experience with Hamilton's long paper (see Chapter 4), where he also struggled with the mathematics, but was persuaded!

2 In this respect, Luria was close to the position of Bernard Davis, who had struggled long and hard against what he considered exaggerated fears in regard to recombinant DNA. In general, Luria could understand Davis' position quite well, as he indicated in his discussion. After all, both he and Davis were molecular biologists. The biggest difference had to do with their views on IQ research and (consequently?) their views on Gould.

3 In fact, although Luria did not believe in IQ, he did believe in genes 'for' cognitive traits (see further discussion in Chapter 14). This position is also reflected in his biology textbook *A View of Life*, written in 1980 with Gould and Singer as co-authors.

4 At the time, the Whitehead Institute was widely rumored to be involved with secret defense research.

5 Luria's position may have represented a particular political line of the academic left at the time. The same attitude was shown by Miller and Beckwith, quoted earlier in this chapter: 'Scientists must take the lead in encouraging . . . criticism and informed discussion, rather than using the banner "freedom of inquiry" to stifle discussion' (Miller and Beckwith, 1977).

6 Davis, himself, of course, considered IQ tests useful. He wished to support the person whom Luria responded to, the headmaster of a school for gifted children, who thought IQ tests were useful for picking out exceptional talent.

7 Arguably, for Luria (1974b), the freedom to criticize other people's research may have extended as far as attempting to *discourage* their research. But it is hard to see how labeling their research 'racist' would not serve to prejudge the case.

Chapter 13

1 Testimony to this is the fact that in a 1989 poll, the officers and fellows of the International Animal Behavior Society rated *Sociobiology* the best scientific book of all time (Wilson, 1994, p. 330).

2 Midgley reported opposition to Dawkins among geneticists at the University of Newcastle upon Tyne. Also, in 1981 at least two people told me that Peter O'Donald in Cambridge disagreed with Dawkins' approach (John Krebs and Vernon Reynolds, interviews). O'Donald's chapter in the King's College Sociobiology Group's edited work (1982) indicates that at the time he was particularly concerned with the concept of fitness and the different ways in which this was used by sociobiologists and population geneticists.

3 The historian of science Alistair Crombie discusses this in his monumental *Styles of Scientific Thinking in the European Tradition* (1994).

4 Sarah Blaffer Hrdy, an anthropologist, was Irven DeVore's first female graduate student at Harvard. She represents an unusual brand of sociobiological feminism and is the author of *The Woman that Never Evolved* (1981, 1999).

5 The first one to suggest to me this opposition between a naturalist and experimentalist tradition within the sociobiology controversy was sociologist Nathan Glazer at Harvard. He also thought this correlated with cultural background.

6 As discussed in Chapter 6, the critics charged that sociobiologists assumed that every trait was adaptive, and then invented an 'adaptive story' to explain how this trait may have come about through evolution.

Chapter 14

1 Harvard psychologist Sheldon White took just such a view of a basic American interest in measuring performance, which existed much before any IQ testing (White, interview in 1982).

2 Lewontin rebutted the suggestion that this was the case quite specifically in a note to his republished 1970 article (Lewontin, 1976d).

3 In their 1980 article, Levins and Lewontin had used Daniel Simberloff's article on changing paradigms in ecology (Simberloff, 1980a) as a foil for a long Marxist critique of this field.

Chapter 15

1 The quest for moral recognition-capital sometimes appeared to be a direct motivating force for scientists involved in controversies of the sociobiology and IQ type, and responsible for getting them involved in the first place.

2 Those who say that there is no merit in mere criticism may actually underestimate the wish of some academics to see something 'well criticized'. In other words,

scientists may get credit for 'good criticism'—at least credit of a 'philosophical' kind. The philosopher Stuart Hampshire, for instance, greatly appreciated Lewontin's (1978b) critique of adaptationism (Hampshire, interview). Lewontin, in turn, enjoyed Hampshire's critique of *On Human Nature* in *The New York Review of Books* the same year (Lewontin, interview). This kind of philosophically oriented moral recognition may be the easiest type of recognition to obtain from members of other fields in academia. Gould, with his debunking attitude, for instance, is popular among social scientists, who often quote him as a representative of current thought in evolutionary biology. However, it is not clear to what extent this kind of general moral recognition counts toward *scientific* recognition in a particular scientist's own field.

3 Dawkins (1985), noted that the authors desperately sought to distance their own 'dialectical' interactionist models from existing interactionist models.

4 So was the fact that Davis was behind the first hiring of a black doctor to Harvard Medical School (see Chapter 11).

5 Wilson's close colleague at Harvard during this time, German entomologist Bert Hölldobler, characterized the opponents to sociobiology as 'sandbox Marxists'.

6 For the traditionalists, there was no obvious need to change the reward system; they got automatic credit just by doing what they did anyway (produce new knowledge, which was seen as an unproblematically good and useful activity), and defending the planter view of science in public.

7 A third one could be that, psychologically, getting to know the targets for criticism may interfere with carefully constructed 'working models' of these targets.

8 I here except those few who stepped in for the purpose of sorting out the confusion (see Chapter 12).

9 See, for instance, Lewontin's (1982) and Hamilton's (1996) comments about the popularity of ESS, and Grafen (1982), and Seger and Harvey (1980) on the popularity of kin selection.

10 Clearly, Lewontin's politically satisfying bloodgroup research also gave him moral recognition from anyone wishing to fight racism with science.

11 It was this review that Luria had sponsored and Lewontin briefly checked (see Chapter 12). Wilson had found this review 'strange', as he said in interview. On the other hand, he was rather pleased with it—he took its mere existence to mean that his critics were now taking him seriously and were moving in on his turf.

12 Bateson (1985), too, raised the question of the critics' narrow focus on genetic determinism. Would eliminating genetic determinism result in the rich distributing their possessions to the poor, he asked? 'Fat chance', was his answer.

Chapter 16

1 At the same time, what might be considered 'counterpoints' abound: Bill Irons is said to have had a 'scales-falling-from-my-eyes experience' when he read Alexander's

1974 paper (p. xiii). Napoleon Chagnon is described as 'in the early '70s trying to analyze Yanomamö marriage and kinship using Sewall Wright's inbreeding co-efficients' (p. xiii).

2 For instance, one of its early conferences, in Israel in 1987, included an anthro-pologist-led trip to the Neanderthal findings at Mount Carmel, as well as a bird watching tour to the Negev desert led by Amosz Zahavi, where we found Zahavi's birds behaving in exact accordance with his theories.

3 Incidentally, there was a third knight (whose comments reached the more limited audience of the *Human Behavior and Evolution Society Newsletter*). In 1993 Martin Daly, then president of HBES, did some empirical research to find out whether it was really true, as Gould claimed *contra* Cronin, that gene selectionism had nothing to do with the fact that the notion of female choice had recently come back to prominence in evolutionary biology:

> This claim seemed incomprehensible to me. Every page I turn lately seems to have some new attempt to test the Hamilton-Zuk hypothesis or to ascertain whether females care about male symmetry . . . or some such. But who knows? Maybe I don't read widely enough. Out there beyond that bad old sociobiological literature, there might be a whole 'nother world of more Gould-endorsable research that I've been missing! I figured I'd better go to the library and check.
>
> I pulled down the 1991 volumes of *Biological Abstracts* . . . and I looked up everything listed in the subject index under 'sexual selection'. That gave me 44 abstracts. . . .90% of the papers were framed and interpreted in sociobiological language. The substance of all five purely theoretical papers was explicit gene-selectionist modeling, and about half of the empirical studies would have had no point . . . but for their testing of implications derived from particular competing gene-selectionist models.
>
> *So Cronin was right and Gould was wrong.* No surprise here. The journals are full of research inspired by the theoretical tools provided by Hamilton and Williams and Trivers and Maynard Smith and a host of other gene-selectionists. There is no alternative research agenda regarding sexual selection (or altruism or parental effort or foraging, etc., etc.) because there is no alternative conceptual framework; the alternatives to be sorted out by further theorizing and research are *gene-selectionist* alternatives (Daly, 1993, italics added).

4 We may ask if this is really a correct description of Dawkins' position. Already in *The Extended Phenotype*, Dawkins, in fact, explained that his view did not preclude a recognition of macroevolutionary forces. It was just that he was focused on a *particular* one of these evolutionary forces: the process of adaptation through natural selection. And in that book he also pointed out that the unit of selection did not have to be the gene—it could, for instance, be a much larger chunk of the genome. However, it did have to have certain characteristics in order to be able to function as a replicator. Finally, he also did not resist the idea of hierarchical levels of selection (for example, 1982, p. 112).

5 The Cambridge psychologist pointed out that biological systems may be more or less adapted to evolve (the evolution of evolvability); for instance, certain types of DNA are better at evolving than others, and mentioned interesting mechanisms at

the biochemical level. 'A lot of the dispute between Gould and Dawkins could be resolved by these new ideas', Humphrey concluded (1995, p. 69). But Dawkins, at least, had already written exactly on the evolution of evolvability (1989b).

6 However, this may of course reflect a more general idea of packaging popular evolutionist books together, since Dawkins has also been sold together with Wilson in this way.

7 Wilson realized that he had already encountered one such 'philosopher'—Larry Slobodkin—at an early stage (see Chapter 14).

8 Sober and Lewontin went on to say that genic selection coefficients were 'reifications; they are artifacts, not causes, of evolution'. But immediately afterwards, in an interesting moment of self-reflection, they admitted that '[f]or this to count as criticism, one must abandon a narrowly instrumentalist view of scientific theories; this we gladly do, in that we assume that selection theory ought to pinpoint causes as well as facilitate predictions' (Sober and Lewontin, 1982).

9 According to Dawkins, people like Gould and Eldredge insist on talking about vehicles. Vehicles can be groups or higher level organized systems, organisms or genes; vehicles can be hierarchical. But when it comes to replicators, only genes or memes can be replicators. As a replicator, a 'gene' is a *logical* unit, not a 'real' entity in a hierarchy.

10 It seems to me that Williams' distinction is actually very similar to Dawkins' distinction between replicator and vehicle. Dawkins is not as 'physical' about the replicator as Williams appears to assume.

11 Maynard Smith told me he felt so insulted by Eldredge's treatment of himself that he refused to review the book for *Nature*. Later in 1995 he said the following about Gould:

> Gould occupies a rather curious position, particularly on his side of the Atlantic. Because of the excellence of his essays, he has come to be seen by non-biologists as the pre-eminent evolutionary theorist. In contrast, the evolutionary biologists with whom I have discussed his work tend to see him as a man whose ideas are so confused as to be hardly worth bothering with, but as one who should not be publicly criticized because he is at least on our side against the creationists. All this would not matter, were it not that he is giving non-biologists a largely false picture of the state of evolutionary theory (Maynard Smith, 1995b).

12 Steven Rose, too, has joined the new gambit in his recent book *Lifelines* (1998), attacking 'ultra-Darwinism', although he does not seem to have an umbrella title for the alternative. His new approach seems to be informed not only by Levins' and Lewontin's musings in the *Dialectical Biologist*, but also by such things as Maturana and Varela's ideas about self-organization, Brian Goodwin's notion of 'morphic fields' constraining the forms that organisms can take, and by the Gaia hypothesis—in other words, a bunch of non-reductionist, holistic approaches.

13 Goodwin, however, criticized that computer program for being too artificial, not describing real processes (Goodwin, 1995).

14 And look what she tells us about Lewontin, the radical champion. Lewontin gave a
    lecture to an economics class at the University of Massachusetts, using neo-
    Darwinian mathematical cost-benefit analysis to demonstrate some points. He
    ended his lecture saying that none of the consequences of his analysis had been
    shown empirically. But Margulis took this statement seriously. If he was aware of
    serious flaws in the assumptions of the formulas and the lack of empirical support,
    she asked, why, then, did he continue with this nonsense? Lewontin now admitted
    that his discipline, just as other disciplines, suffered from 'P.E.' (this turned out to
    be 'physics envy'). In fact, Lewontin conceded, 'if he didn't couch his studies in the
    neo-Darwinist thought style . . ., he wouldn't be able to obtain grant money that was
    set up to support this kind of work!' (Margulis, 1995, p. 132).

15 One new view of the genome interprets it as a kind of miniature society, exhibiting
    all kinds of social phenomena, including conflict, co-operation, and social contracts.
    The presence of 'selfish' genetic elements show how the interest of an individual
    may not coincide with the interest of a gene. A good example of this is 'genomic
    imprinting', in which the gene is expressed differently depending on whether it
    originates from the father's or the mother's side. Game theory can be used to model
    intragenomic conflicts of various kinds, suggesting that there may have evolved
    'evolutionarily stable strategies' of interacting genes. In other words, in practice, the
    genome may behave in a stable way, after all (Haig, 1997).

16 The authors also warn about the trap of anthropomorphic language. For instance,
    students of animal behavior may be labeling a behavior 'mate searching' instead of
    finding out what actually is going on. Researchers tend to conflate stimuli to which
    animals respond with the functional reasons for their response. But there is a differ-
    ence between, say, describing parents as responding to stimuli, including those of
    hungry offspring, and saying that 'parents allocate resources in response to the
    needs of individual nestlings'. It may well be true, but that would have to be deter-
    mined separately. 'Allocation' and 'need' have to do with functional explanations of
    optimal reproductive strategies, not with causal explanations of behavior, Krebs and
    Davies point out (p. 5).

17 In this context it was very interesting to learn from a friend of mine attending a
    dinner party with Mayr, that Mayr had been very critical of Wilson's *Consilience*.
    Mayr may have been particularly disturbed by this book's central suggestion that the
    same type of explanation should be employed in all sciences—that of physics.

Chapter 17

1 Kuhn himself very much disliked this appropriation of his ideas by sociologists of
   science, as I found out during an interview with him in the early 1980s.

2 Later, in what appeared to be an alarm call to scientists, Gross explicitly collapsed
   the humanistic and social scientific criticisms, charging that STS, Science and Technology Studies, as a whole had an anti-Western agenda (Gross, 1997).

3 For the cultural critics of science, it was not as obvious as for the pro-science activists that objectivity might be a formidable *political* weapon. One example is the educational policy after the Second World War, where science was deliberately given a central role in American higher education because it was seen as a *cultural* force that would promote universalism and rationality (for more discussion see Segerstråle, 2000, Chapter 5; Hollinger, 1994).

4 Much of the criticism of these fields was, of course, political in tone. Still, there had also been serious methodological objections, some of which seemed not easily dismissible as politically motivated (by, for example, Peter Medawar, John Thoday). As we saw in Chapter 12, Wilson was not convinced that there could be 'purely' methodological disagreement.

5 Just such an analysis was made by Donald McKenzie, for example, for statisticians in Britain (MacKenzie, 1981).

6 Of course, Lewontin tends to judge cases in the history of science from a quite 'presentist' vantage point. See, for instance, his treatment of Agassiz, Chapter 3.

7 Lewontin was, indeed, involved in a dispute exactly about DNA fingerprinting. As a result of his (and others') critique the accuracy of the test was increased.

Chapter 18

1 Wilson told philosophers that he and they had 'the common goal of turning as much philosophy as possible into science' (Wilson, 1998a, p. 12), and assured them that '[s]ymbols and concepts might in time finally be exactly defined and objective truth more precisely triangulated' (Wilson, 1998b).

2 In Rorty's opinion, this was an unhelpful definition of meaning. He considered it akin to saying: 'What we call a *program* is a disposition on the part of millions of electrical circuits to switch states in certain sentences. Both sentences are perfectly true, but neither tells you anything that might help you choose a meaning for your life, or a program for your computer' (Rorty, 1998, p. 33).

3 Perhaps not coincidentally, Brockman is also the literary agent of bestselling popularizers of science (including Dawkins, but not Gould) and his book is in fact a showcase for many of them.

4 Ernst Mayr in a similar way pointed out the difference between physics and biology in his recent book *This Is Biology* (1997).

5 Others had to learn it the hard way. For instance, many were taken aback by an unexpected interchange about racism showing up on the electronic bulletin board of the Human Behavior and Evolution Society in 1996 (this episode is documented by Tennov, 1998).

6 One might wish to disagree with this. In fact, many biologists have found the work of philosophers such as David Hull, Philip Kitcher, Elisabeth Lloyd, Elliott Sober, and Michael Ruse very useful. Perhaps Wilson had other philosophers than philosophers of biology in mind, when he wrote about 'the philosophers'?

7 Moreover, he had already stated in *On Human Nature* that Social Darwinism was a 'biologically untenable' doctrine.

8 Gerald Holton traces the phylogeny of sociobiology to the proponents of a mechanistic conception of life in the mid-19th century, such biologists as Ernst Haeckel and Jacques Loeb. He calls Wilson's *Sociobiology* 'an exercise in understatement and objectivity in comparison to these biologists, who also included ethics in their grand materialistic-mechanistic syntheses' (Holton, 1978, pp. 88–9).

Chapter 19

1 Over and above such things as ecological conditions, which Wilson would surely consider (see his 1971c).

2 There is, of course, the puzzling circumstance that Wilson himself, in 1969 at the Man and Beast conference, eloquently spoke up against the 'innateness' of aggression, invoking ecological and other factors in a proto-model of his sociobiological explanatory ambition. However, he did not particularly emphasize the role of development, which was not then, nor later, part of his sociobiological focus on 'ultimate' explanations.

3 Indeed, just this kind of 'blueprint' view of development was also one of the major reasons why, in the 1980s controversy about the risks of release of genetically engineeered organisms into the environment, ecologists opposed molecular biologists (one leader on the molecular side was, interestingly, Bernard Davis) (Segerstråle, 1990b).

4 Interestingly, in 1995 in an advertisement in the *The New York Review of Books*, Cavalli-Sforza's book was said to 'flatten *The Bell Curve*' also 'proving that racial differences are only skin deep' (March 23, 1995, pp. 45, 46). The conflict generated by Herrnstein and Murray's 1994 bestseller was widely perceived as a new round of the IQ controversy.

Chapter 20

1 This was why they approached Chomsky, the perceived demolition champion of determinist theories about behavior; see Chapter 10.

2 In the 1960s and 1970s, sociologists and social psychologists got in on this matter. Some tried to establish an attitude scale for identifying an 'authoritarian personality' to explain Nazi behavior. This idea lost popularity, especially when it was shown that authoritarian personalities existed among the left as well as among the right. Stanley Milgram (1974) tried to put an end to ideas about evil persons with his controversial 'obedience of authority' experiments and focus on the *conditions* under which people—anybody—would feel that they had to obey orders. Milgram thus emphasized the power of the situation as against personality theories. Still, the

existentialist view came to predominate, dovetailing nicely with the post-war environmentalist paradigm.

3 Here we see a welcome acknowledgement that Wilson and Dawkins are 'liberal' men—a novelty in the debate. This, of course, does not stop the opponents of sociobiology from attacking Wilson and Dawkins.

4 The worry about essentialism is nothing new. For instance, Jan Goldstein (1987) describes how in France in the 1800s there were serious discussions about how to distinguish criminal behavior from illness. In a cartoon of the time, a defendant pleads innocent on the basis that he had 'monomania for stealing', upon which the judge retorts that he, on the other hand, has 'monomania for convicting'.

5 Although Wilson elsewhere discusses the 'Ionian Enchantment', which emphasizes the wish to know over the wish to believe, he also recognizes the profound human need for belief. This is what Wilson has been arguing since *Sociobiology*, suggesting, for example, that 'human beings are absurdly easy to indoctrinate—they seek it', much to the irritation of his critics (1975a, p. 562).

6 Incidentally, it is interesting that Sagan, who with such eloquence expounded Paul McLean's theory about the 'triune brain' in his *The Dragons of Eden* (Sagan, 1977), would believe that science, a rational endeavor connected to the more recently developed neocortex, would be somehow primary, considering the plausible links of 'demons' and other irrational beliefs to older regions of the brain.

7 In 1986, for instance, he was invited by the Committee on Human Values of the Roman Catholic Bishops of the United States to be one of four scientists to join about fifteen bishops and cardinals for a two-day retreat (Wilson, 1991b). The other scientists were the theoretical physicist Freeman Dyson and the neurobiologist Roger Sperry, both scientific humanists, and Jerome Lejeune, a member of the Pontifical Academy of Science and the discoverer of Down's syndrome.

8 He has kept warning contemporary religions, however, that in order to be credible to modern man, they would have to move from an 'Iron Age' view of tribal wisdom and become more knowledgeable about science (Wilson, 1998a).

9 In October 1998, Hamilton, together with representatives of different fields in science, was called to a conference at the Pontifical Academy at the Vatican. From biology, Gould and Rose were also invited (Hamilton, personal communication).

10 The need for seeing science as a process is pointed out by, among others, Hull (1988) and Dunbar (1995).

11 I am not now addressing the fact that the particular expression of these concerns in the sociobiology controversy was highly unpleasant for targeted individual scientists.

12 In Chapter 6, I showed that for Gould and Lewontin, unlike the rest of the Sociobiology Study Group, the sociobiology controversy may have been a Trojan horse to promote their alternative, anti-adaptationist program.

13 I am here not referring to the various caveats that sociobiologists and other evolutionists started appending to their scientific statements, but to the scientific part of this business.

14 Of course, the atmosphere of criticism can become so strong that not even a reasoned discussion is possible. This was what happened early on in the sociobiology debate. Later, the same thing seems to have happened with another, even more heated question on the American scene: the debate about genetic factors in crime. In 1992, because of various pressures, a conference arranged to discuss scientific and ethical aspects of this matter—including several critical presentations—was cancelled by NIH (Coleman, 1992). Thus, some issues may simply be too hot to debate.

References

Adams, D. *et al.* (1986). The Seville Statement on Violence. *American Psychologist*, **45**, (10), 1167–8.

Adams, D. (ed.) (1991). *The Seville Statement on Violence: Preparing the Ground for the Construction of Peace*. Geneva: UNESCO.

Albury, W. R. (1980). Politics and rhetoric in the sociobiology debate. *Social Studies of Science*, **10**, 519–36.

Alcock, J. (1975). *Animal Behavior: An Evolutionary Approach*. Sunderland, MA: Sinauer Associates.

Alexander, R. D. (1974). The evolution of social behavior. *Annual Review of Ecology and Systematics*, **5**, 325–83.

Alexander, R. D. (1977). Review of the use and abuse of biology. *American Anthropologist*, **79**, 917–20.

Alexander, R. D. (1980). *Darwinism and Human Affairs*. London: Pitman.

Alexander, R. D. (1987). *The Biology of Moral Systems*. New York: de Gruyter.

Alexander, R. D. (1996). A view from the President's window. *Human Behavior and Evolution Society Newsletter*, **5** (1), 1–2.

Alexander, R. D. and G. Borgia (1978). Group selection, altruism, and the levels of organization of life. *Annual Review of Ecology and Systematics*, **9**, 449–74.

Allen, E. *et al.* (1975). Letter. *The New York Review of Books*, **13**, November, 182, 184–6.

Allman, W. (1994). *The Stone Age Present*. New York: Simon and Schuster.

Alper, J. (1978). Ethical and social implications of sociobiology. In M. S. Gregory, A. Silvers and D. Sutch (eds), *Sociobiology and Human Nature*, pp. 195–212. San Francisco: Jossey Bass Inc.

Alper, J. (1982). Book review of *The Legacy of Malthus*. *Science for the People*, March-April, 30–1.

Alper, J. *et al.* (1976). The implications of sociobiology. *Science*, **192**, 424–5.

Alper, J., J. Beckwith, and L. F. Miller (1978). Sociobiology is a political issue. In A. Caplan (ed.), *The Sociobiology Debate*, pp. 476–88. New York: Harper & Row.

Alper, J. S. and R. V. Lange (1981). Lumsden–Wilson theory of gene–culture coevolution. In *Proceedings of the National Academy of Sciences USA*, **78**, 3976–9.

Alvarez, L., W. Alvarez, F. Asaro, and H. Michel (1980). Extraterrestrial cause for the Cretaceous-Tertiary Extinction. *Science*, **208**, 1095–108.

Ann Arbor Collective for Science for the People (1977). *Biology as A Social Weapon.* Ann Arbor, MI: Michigan University Press.

Anonymous (1978). Editorial. Truth at any price. *Nature,* **271,** 391.

Anonymous (1981). Editorial. Isidore Nabi, RIP. *Nature,* **293,** 2.

Anonymous (1998). The gene is jumping. Book review, *Consilience. The Economist,* **11,** July 15–16.

Ardrey, R. (1966). *The Territorial Imperative.* London: Collins.

Ardrey, R. (1970). *The Social Contract.* New York: Atheneum.

Armstrong J. and **B. Drummond** (1981). Letter. *Science,* **211,** 773.

Axelrod, R. and **W. D. Hamilton** (1981). The evolution of cooperation. *Science,* **211,** 1390–6.

Barash, D. (1977). *Sociobiology and Behavior.* New York: Elsevier.

Barkan, E. (1992). *The Retreat of Scientific Racism.* Cambridge: Cambridge University Press.

Barkow, J. (1980). Sociobiology: Is this the new theory of human nature? In A. Montagu (ed.), *Sociobiology Examined.* Oxford and New York: Oxford University Press, pp. 171–97.

Barkow, J. H., L. Cosmides, and **J. Tooby** (1992). *The Adapted Mind.* Oxford: Oxford University Press.

Barlow, G. W. (1989), Has sociobiology killed ethology or revitalized it? In P. P. G. Bateson and P. H. Klopfer (eds), *Whither Ethology? Perspectives in Ethology* **8,** pp. 1–46.

Barlow, G. W. (1991). Nature–nurture and the debate surrounding ethology and sociobiology. *American Zoologist,* **31,** 286–96.

Barlow, G. W. and **J. Silverberg** (eds) (1980). Sociobiology: *Beyond Nature/Nurture?* AAAS Selected Symposium 35. Boulder, CO: Westview Press.

Barnes, B. (1974). *Scientific Knowledge and Sociological Theory.* London and Boston: Routledge and Kegan Paul.

Barnes. B. and **S. Shapin** (eds) (1979). *Natural Order: Historical Studies of Scientific Culture.* Beverly Hills, CA and London: Sage.

Barnett, S. A. (1980). Biological determinism and the Tasmanian native hen. In A. Montagu (ed.), *Sociobiology Examined.* Oxford and New York: Oxford University Press, pp. 135–57.

Bateson, P. P. G. (1978). Review, *The Selfish Gene. Animal Behaviour,* **26,** 316–18.

Bateson, P. P. G. (1981). Sociobiology and genetic determinism. *Theoria to Theory,* **14,** 291–300.

Bateson, P. P. G. (1982a). 1980 Preface. In King's College Sociobiology Group (ed.) *Current Problems in Sociobiology.* Cambridge: Cambridge University Press, pp. ix–xi.

Bateson, P. P. G. (1982b). Behavioural development and evolutionary processes. In King's College Sociobiology Group (ed.), *Current Problems in Sociobiology*. Cambridge: Cambridge University Press, pp. 133–51.

Bateson, P. P. G. (1982c). Synthesizing views about the origins of behaviour. In S. Rose (ed.), *Toward a Liberatory Biology*. London and New York: Allison and Busby.

Bateson, P. P. G. (1982d). Centenary plea. *Nature*, **298**, 414.

Bateson, P. P. G. (1984). The biology of cooperation. *New Society*, 31 May, 343–5.

Bateson, P. P. G. (1985). Sociobiology: the debate continues. Book review, *Not in Our Genes*. *New Scientist*, 24 January, 58–9.

Bateson, P. (1986). Sociobiology and human politics. In S. Rose and L. Appignanesi (eds), *Science and Beyond*. Oxford: Basil Blackwell, pp. 79–99.

Bateson, P. P. G. (1987). Familiarity out-breeds. Peer commentary on *Vaulting Ambition. Behavior and Brain Sciences*, **10** (1), 71–2.

Bateson, P. P. G. and R. Hinde (1976). *Growing Points in Ethology*. Cambridge: Cambridge University Press.

Bateson, P. P. G. and P. H. Klopfer (1989). Preface. In P. P. G. Bateson and P. H. Klopfer (eds), *Whither Ethology? Perspectives in Ethology* **8**, pp. v-viii.

Bauer, H. (1999). The anti-science phenomenon in science and technology studies. In U. Segerstråle (ed.), *Beyond the Science Wars*. Albany: SUNY Press.

Bazerman, C. (1981). What written knowledge does. *Philosophy of the Social Sciences*, **11**, 361–87.

Bazerman, C. (1988). *Shaping Written Knowledge: Essays in the Growth, Form, Function, and Implications of the Scientific Article*. Madison: University of Wisconsin Press.

Bazerman, C. (1993). Intertextual self-fashioning: Gould and Lewontin's representation of the literature. In J. Selzer (ed.), *Understanding Scientific Prose*. Madison, WI: University of Wisconsin Press, pp. 20–41.

Beckwith, J. (1976). The scientist in opposition in the United States. In W. Fuller (ed.), *The Social Impact of Modern Biology*. London: Routledge and Kegan Paul.

Beckwith, J. (1981–2). The political use of sociobiology in the United States and Europe. *The Philosophical Forum*, **13** (2–3), 311–21.

Beckwith, J. (1982). Evolution, sex and ideology. *Nature*, **295**, 631.

Beckwith, J. (1987). Criticism and realism. Peer commentary on *Vaulting Ambition. Behavior and Brain Sciences*, **10**, 72–3.

Beckwith, J. and R. Lange (1978). AAAS: Sociobiology on the run. *Science for the People*, March/April.

Beckwith, J. *et al.* (1975). Letter, *Science*, **187**, 298.

Bell, D. (1972). On meritocracy and equality. *The Public Interest*, 29–68.

Berger, P. and H. Kellner (1981). *Sociology Reinterpreted*. New York: Doubleday Anchor Books.

Berghe, van den P. (1978). Bridging the paradigms: biology and the social sciences. In

M. S. Gregory, A. Silvers, and D. Sutch (eds), *Sociobiology and Human Nature*. San Francisco: Jossey Bass, pp. 33–52.

Berghe, van den P. (1980). Sociobiology: several views. *BioScience*, **31**, 406.

Berman, M. (1981). *The Re-Enchantment of the World*. Ithaca, NY: Cornell University Press.

Bernstein, R. (1997). Science and 'The Demon-Haunted World': an exchange. *The New York Review of Books*, 6 March, 50–1.

Berreby, D. (1996). Scientist at work: David Sloan Wilson: enthralling or exasperating; select one. *The New York Times*, 24 September, Section C Science Desk, 1.

Betzig, L. (1997). Preface. In L. Betzig (ed.), *Human Nature*. Oxford: Oxford University Press, pp. xi–xiv.

Betzig, L. (ed.) (1997). *Human Nature*. Oxford: Oxford University Press.

Biagioli, M. (1993). *Galileo, Courtier*. Chicago: University of Chicago Press.

Bingham, R. (1980). Trivers in Jamaica. *Science 1980*, 56–67.

Blinkhorn, S. (1982). What skulduggery? *Nature*, **296**, 506.

Block, N. J. and G. Dworkin (eds) (1976). *The IQ Controversy*. New York: Pantheon Books.

Bloor, D. (1976). *Knowledge and Social Imagery*. London: Routledge, 2nd edn, 1991, Chicago: University of Chicago Press.

Blurton-Jones, N. G. (1976). Growing points in human ethology: Another link between ethology and the social sciences. In P. G. Bateson and R. A. Hinde (eds), *Growing Points in Ethology*, pp. 427–50. Cambridge: Cambridge University Press.

Blurton Jones, N. G. and V. Reynolds (eds) (1978). *Human Behaviour and Adaptation*. London: Taylor and Francis.

Bourdieu, P. (1973). The specificity of the scientific field and the social conditions of the progress of reason. *International Social Science Information*, **14** (5–6), 19–47.

Bodmer, W. F. and L. L. Cavalli-Sforza (1970). Intelligence and race. *Scientific American*, **223**, 19–29.

Boorman, S. A. and P. R. Levitt (1980). *The Genetics of Altruism*. New York: Academic Press.

Borgia, G. (1994). The scandals of San Marco. *Quarterly Review of Biology*, **69**, 373–7.

Bouchier, D. (1977). Radical ideologies and the sociology of knowledge. *Sociology*, **11**, 29–46.

Bouton, K. (1996). Review of '*In Search of Nature*'. *The New York Times Book Review*, September 22, p. 24.

Boyd, R. and P. J. Richerson (1985). *Culture and the Evolutionary Process*. Chicago: University of Chicago Press.

Brandon, R. (1982). The levels of selection. Philososphy of Science Association (1),

315–22. Reprinted in R. Brandon and R. Burian (eds), *Genes, Organisms, Populations*. Cambridge, MA: MIT Press, pp. 133–41.

Brandon, R. and R. Burian (eds) (1984). *Genes, Organisms, Populations*. Cambridge, MA: MIT Press.

Brinton, C. (1959). *The Society of Fellows*. Cambridge, MA: Harvard University Press.

Brockman, J. (1995). *The Third Culture*. New York: Simon and Schuster.

Brown, D. E. (1991). *Human Universals*. Philadelphia: Temple University Press.

Brown, J. (1975). *The Evolution of Behavior*. New York: Norton.

Bull, J. and H. Wickman (1998). A revolution in evolution. Editorial. *Science*, **281**, 1959.

Buss, D. (1994). *The Evolution of Desire*. New York: Basic Books.

Cain, A. (1964). The perfection of animals. In J. D. Carthy and C. L. Duddington (eds), *Viewpoints in Biology*, 3. London: Butterworths.

Cain, A. (1979). Introduction to general discussion. *Proceedings of the Royal Society of London*, **205 B**, 599–604.

Callahan, D. (1996). Calling scientific ideology to account. *Society*, **33** (4), 14–19.

Callon, M. (1999). Whose imposture? Physicists at war with the third Person. *Social Studies of Science*, **29**, 261–86.

Campbell, D. T. (1975). On the conflicts between biological and social evolution and between psychology and moral tradition. *American Psychologist* **30**, 1103–26.

Campbell, C. (1986). Anatomy of a fierce academic feud. *The New York Times*, 9 November, Section 12, pp. 58–60, 62, 64.

Caplan, A. L. (1978). *The Sociobiology Debate*. New York: Harper & Row.

Caplan, A. L. (1981). Popper's philosophy. Letter. *Nature*, **290**, 623–4.

Capra, F. (1982). *The Turning Point*. New York: Simon and Schuster.

Carson, H. L. (1977). Introduction to a pivotal subject. *Science* **197**, 1272–3.

Carson, H. (1981). Letter. *Science*, **211**, 773.

Cavalli-Sforza, L. (1992). Interview, *Le Nouvel Observateur*, 7 February.

Cavalli-Sforza, L. L. and M. W. Feldman (1981). *Cultural Transmission and Evolution*. Princeton, NJ: Princeton University Press.

Cavalli-Sforza, L. L. and M. W. Feldman (1982). IQ testing and the media. *The Atlantic Monthly*, December, **6**, 8.

Cavalli-Sforza, L. L. and M. W. Feldman (1983). Cultural versus genetic adaptation. *Proceedings of the National Academy of Sciences USA*, **80**, 4993–6.

Cavalli-Sforza, L., L. Menozzi and A. Piazza (1994). *History and Geography of Human Genes*. Princeton, NJL: Princeton University Press.

Chagnon, N. (1989). Yanomamö survival. Letter. *Science*, **243**, 1141.

Chagnon, N. (1995). The academic left and threats to scientific anthropology. *Human Behavior and Evolution Society Newsletter*, **4**, 1, 1–2.

Chagnon, N. A. and W. Irons, (eds) (1979). *Evolutionary Biology and Human Social Behavior: An Anthropological Perspective*. North Scituate, MA: Duxbury.

Charney, D. (1993). A study in rhetorical reading: how evolutionists read The Spandrels of San Marco. In J. Selzer (ed.), *Understanding Scientific Prose*. Madison, WI: University of Wisconsin Press, pp. 203–31.

Chase, A. (1977). *The Legacy of Malthus*. New York: Knopf.

Chasin, B. (1977). Sociobiology: a sexist synthesis. *Science for the People*, May–June, 27–31.

Cheney, D. and R. Seyfarth (1990). *How Monkeys See the World*. Chicago: University of Chicago Press.

Chomsky, N. (1959). Review of 'Verbal Behavior' by B. F. Skinner. *Language*, **35**, 26–28.

Chomsky, N. (1975). *Reflections on Language*. New York: Pantheon Books, Random House.

Chorover, S. (1979). *From Genesis to Genocide*. Cambridge and London: MIT Press.

Clarke, B. (1974). Causes of genetic variation. *Science*, **186**, 524–5.

Cloak, F. T. (1975). Is a cultural ethology possible? *Human Ecology*, **3**, 161–82.

Clutton-Brock, T. H. and P. H. Harvey (1979). Comparison and adaptation. *Proceedings of the Royal Society of London*, **205 B**, 547–65.

Collins, H. (1982). Knowledge, norms and rules in the sociology of knowledge. *Social Studies of Science*, **12**, 299–309.

Collins, H. (1983). The sociology of scientific knowledge. *Annual Review of Sociology*, **9**, 265–85.

Collins, H. (1985). *Changing Order: Replication and Induction in Scientific Practice*. Beverly Hills, CA: Sage.

Collins, H. and T. Pinch (1993). *The Golem: What Everybody Should Know about Science*. Cambridge: Cambridge University Press.

Collins, R. (1998). *The Sociology of Philosophies: A Global Theory of Intellectual Change*. Cambridge, MA and London: The Belknap Press of Harvard University Press.

Cordes, C. (1994). 2 scholars examine the 'bizarre war' against science they say is being waged by the academic left. *The Chronicle of Higher Education*, 27 April.

Cosmides, L. and J. Tooby (1992). The psychological foundations of culture. In J. Barkow, L. Cosmides, and J. Tooby (eds), *The Adapted Mind*. New York and Oxford: Oxford University Press, pp. 19–136.

Crombie, A. C. (1994). *Styles of Thinking in the European Tradition*. London: Duckworth.

Crook, J. (1964). The evolution of social organization and visual communication in the weaver birds (Ploceinae). *Behaviour*, **10** (Suppl.), 1–178.

Crook, J. (1965). The adaptive significance of avian social organization. *Symp. Zoological Society London*, **4**, 181–218.

Crook, J. (1971). Sources of cooperation in animals and man. In J. F. Eisenberg and W. S. Dillon (eds), *Man and Beast*. Washington, D.C.: Smithsonian Institution Press, pp. 235–60.

Crook, J. (1976). Multiple reviews of Wilson's *Sociobiology. Animal Behaviour*, **24**, 703–4.

Crook, J. and J. S. Gartlan (1966). Evolution of primate societies. *Nature*, **210**, 1200–3.

Cronin, H. (1991). *The Ant and the Peacock*. Cambridge: Cambridge University Press.

Curio, E. (1973). Towards a methodology of teleonomy. *Experientia*, **29**, 1045–58.

Daly, M. (1996). The view from the President's window. *Human Behavior and Evolution Newsletter*, 2 (1), 1–2.

Daly, M. and M. Wilson (1978). *Sex, Evolution and Behavior*. North Scituate, MA: Duxbury.

Daly, M. and M. Wilson (1980). Discriminative parental solicitude: A biological perspective. *Journal of Marriage and the Family*, **42**, 277–88.

Daly, M. and M. Wilson (1981). Abuse and neglect of children in evolutionary perspective. In R. Alexander and D. Tinkle (eds), *Natural Selection and Social Behavior*. New York: Chrion Press, pp. 405–16.

Darlington, P. J., Jr. (1971). Genes, individuals, and kin selection. In *Proceedings of the National Academy of Sciences USA*, **78**(7), 4440–3.

Dart, R. (1953). The predatory transition from ape to man. *International Anthropological and Linguistic Review*, **1**, 201–8.

Davies, N. (1991). Studying behavioural adaptations. In M. S. Dawkins, T. R. Halliday, and R. Dawkins (eds), *The Tinbergen Legacy*. London: Chapman and Hall.

Davis, B. D. (1974). Letter (rejected). *The New York Review of Books*, 7 May.

Davis, B. D. (1975). Social determinism and behavioral genetics. *Science*, **26**, 189.

Davis, B. D. (1976a). Novel pressures on the advance of science. *Annals of the New York Academy of Sciences*, **265**, 193–205.

Davis, B. D. (1976b). Speech at the Cambridge Forum, 10 April, 1976. The Davis Controversy. *The Present Illness*. Special Issue.

Davis, B. D. (1976c). Letter. *The Harvard Crimson*, 19 May.

Davis, B. D. (1976d). The dangers of regulating research by adverse public policy. *Harvard Magazine*, October, 26–30. Reprinted as Chapter 17 in B. D. Davis (1986), *Storm Over Biology*. Buffalo, NY: Prometheus Books.

Davis, B. D. (1976e). Academic standards in medical schools. Editorial. *New England Journal of Medicine*, **294**, 1118, and in B. D. Davis (1986), *Storm Over Biology*. Buffalo, NY: Prometheus Books, pp. 168–70.

Davis, B. D. (1978). The Moralistic Fallacy. *Nature*, **272**, 390.

Davis, B. D. (1979). Limits in the regulation of scientific research. In T. Segerstedt (ed.), *Ethics for Science Policy*. Oxford and New York: Pergamon Press.

Davis, B. D. (1980). The importance of human individuality for sociobiology. *Zygon*, **15**, 275–93. Reprinted in *Perspectives in Biology and Medicine*, 26 (Autumn 1982), 1–18.

Davis, B. D. (1982). Molecular genetics: a new foundation for evolution. Paper presented at the Darwin Centennial symposium 'Darwinism: The Expanding Synthesis with Molecular Genetics' at the American Academy of Arts and Sciences, Cambridge, MA, May 7–8, 1982.

Davis, B. D. (1983). Neo-Lysenkoism, IQ and the Press. *The Public Interest*, Fall, pp. 41–59.

Davis, B. D. (1984). A reply. *The Public Interest*, **75**, Spring, 152–5.

Davis, B. D. (1985a). Molecular genetics and the foundations of evolution, *Perspectives in Biology and Medicine*, **28**, (Winter), 251–68.

Davis, B. D. (1985b). Review of 'Not in Our Genes'. *Commentary*, January, 71.4.

Davis, B. D. (1986). *Storm Over Biology: Essays on Science, Sentiment, and Public Policy*. Buffalo, NY: Prometheus Books.

Davis, B. D. (ed) (1991). *The Genetic Revolution*. Baltimore and London: Johns Hopkins.

Davis, B. D. *et al.* (1992). The human genome and other initiatives. *Science*, **249**, 342–3.

Dawkins, M. S., T. R. Halliday and R. Dawkins (eds) (1991). *The Tinbergen Legacy*. London: Chapman and Hall.

Dawkins, R. (1976a). *The Selfish Gene*. Oxford: Oxford University Press.

Dawkins, R. (1976b). Hierarchical organization: a candidate for ethology. In P. P. G. Bateson and R. A. Hinde (eds), *Growing Points in Ethology*. Cambridge: Cambridge University Press.

Dawkins, R. (1978a). Replicator selection and the extended phenotype. *Zeitschrift für Tierpsychologie*, **47**, 61–76.

Dawkins, R. (1978b). Rejoicing in multifarious nature. *Nature*, **276**, 121–3.

Dawkins, R. D. (1979a). Defining sociobiology (review of M. Ruse, *Sociobiology: Sense or Nonsense?*). *Nature*, **280**, 427–8.

Dawkins, R. (1979b). Twelve misunderstandings of kin selection. *Zeitschrift für Tierpsychologie*, **51**, 184–200.

Dawkins, R. (1981a). In defence of selfish genes. *Philosophy*, October, 562–79.

Dawkins, R. (1981b). Selfish genes in race or politics. *Nature*, **289**, 528.

Dawkins, R. (1982). *The Extended Phenotype. The Gene as Unit of Selection*. Oxford and San Francisco: Freeman.

Dawkins, R. (1985). Sociobiology: the debate continues. Review, *Not in Our Genes*. New Scientist, 24 January, 59–60.

Dawkins, R. (1986). Sociobiology, the new storm in a teacup. In S. Rose and L. Appignanesi (eds), *Science and Beyond*. Oxford: Basil Blackwell, pp. 61–78.

Dawkins, R. (1987). *The Blind Watchmaker*. New York: W. W. Norton.

Dawkins, R. (1989a). *The Selfish Gene*. 2nd edn. Oxford: Oxford University Press.

Dawkins, R. (1989b). The evolution of evolvability. In C. Langton (ed.), *Artificial Life*. Santa Fe: Addison-Wesley.

Dawkins, R. (1990). Book review, *Wonderful Life. The Sunday Telegraph*, 25 February.

Dawkins, R. (1991a). Darwin triumphant. Darwinism as a universal truth. In M. H. Robinson and L. Tiger (eds), *Man and Beast Revisited*. Washington, D.C.: Smithsonian Institution Press, pp. 23–39.

Dawkins, R. (1991b). Introduction. In M. S. Dawkins, T. R. Halliday, and R. Dawkins (eds), *The Tinbergen Legacy*. London: Chapman and Hall, pp. ix–xii.

Dawkins, R. (1993). Viruses of the mind. In B. Dahlbom (ed.), *Dennett and His Critics*, pp. 13–27. Oxford: Basil Blackwell.

Dawkins, R. (1994). The moon is not a calabash. *Times Higher Literary Supplement*, 30 September, 17.

Dawkins, R. (1995a). *River out of Eden*, New York: Basic Books.

Dawkins, R. (1995b). A survival machine. In J. Brockman (ed.), *The Third Culture*. New York and London: Simon and Schuster, pp. 74–95.

Dawkins, R. (1996a). *Climbing Mount Improbable*. New York: W. W. Norton.

Dawkins, R. (1996b). Review of *The Demon-Haunted World. The Times*, February 15.

Dawkins, R. (1997a). Human chauvinism. Review, *Full House. Evolution*, **51** (3) 1015–20, June.

Dawkins, R. (1997b). Is science a religion? *The Humanist*, January/February, 26–9.

Dawkins, R. (1998a). *Unweaving the Rainbow: Science, Delusion, and the Appetite for Wonder*. Boston and New York: Houghton Mifflin.

Dawkins, R. (1998b). Arresting evidence. *The Sciences*, November/December, 20–5

Dawkins, R. (1998c). Postmodernism disrobed. Review of Sokal and Bricmont, *Intellectual Impostures. Nature*, **394**, 141–3.

Dawkins, R. (1998d). When religion steps on science's turf. *Free Inquiry*, **18** (2), Spring.

Dawkins, R. and J. R. Krebs (1978). Animal signals: information or manipulation. In J. R. Krebs and N. B. Davies (eds), *Behavioural Ecology*. Oxford: Blackwell Scientific Publications.

Degler, C. (1991). *In Search of Human Nature: The Decline and Revival of Darwinism in American Social Thought*. Oxford: Oxford University Press.

Dennett, D. (1993). Confusion over evolution: an exchange. *The New York Review of Books*, 14 January, 43–4.

Dennett, D. (1995a). *Darwin's Dangerous Idea*. New York: Simon and Schuster.

Dennett, D. (1995b). Intuition pumps. In J. Brockman (ed.), *The Third Culture*. New York: Simon and Schuster, pp. 181–8.

DeVore, I. (1971). The evolution of human society. In J. F. Eisenberg and W. S. Dillon (eds), *Man and Beast: Comparative Social Behavior*. Washington, D. C.: Smithsonian Institution Press, pp. 299–311.

DeWaal, F. (1996). *Good-Natured*. Cambridge, MA: Harvard University Press.

Dickemann, M. (1979). Female infanticide, reproductive strategies, and social stratification: A preliminary model. In N. A. Chagnon and W. Irons (eds), *Evolutionary*

Biology and Human Social Behavior: An Anthropological Perspective. North Scituate, MA: Duxbury Press, pp. 321–67.

Dickemann, M. (1981). Paternal confidence and dowry competition: A biocultural analysis of Purdah. In R. D. Alexander and D. W. Tinkle (eds), *Natural Selection and Social Behavior: Recent Research and New Theory*. Oxford: Blackwell, pp. 417–38.

Dickson, D. (1979). Sociobiology critics claim fears come true. *Nature*, **282**, 348.

Dobzhansky, T. (1937). *Genetics and the Origin of Species*. Reprint edn. New York: Columbia University Press.

Dobzhansky, T. (1963). Anthropology and the natural sciences – the problem of human evolution. *Current Anthropology*, **4.138**, 146–8.

Dobzhansky, T. (1968). On Genetics and Politics. *Social Education*, February, 142–6.

Dobzhansky, T. (1973a). *Genetic Diversity and Human Equality*. New York: Basic Books.

Dobzhansky, T. (1973b). Is genetic diversity compatible with human equality? *Social Biology*, **20** (3), 280–8.

Doolittle, W. F. and C. Sapienza (1980). Selfish genes, the phenotype paradigm and genome evolution. *Nature*, **284**, 601–3.

Dorn, H. (1997). Science and The Demon-Haunted World: an exchange. *The New York Review of Books*, 6 March, 50.

Dunbar, R. (1995). *Grooming, Gossip and the Evolution of Language*. Cambridge, MA: Harvard University Press.

Durant, J. (1980). How evolution became a scientific myth. *New Scientist*, September 11, 765.

Durham, W. H. (1978). Toward a coevolutionary theory of human biology and culture. In A. Caplan (ed.), *The Sociobiology Debate*. New York: Harper & Row.

Edge, D. (1996a). Stop knocking social sciences. Letter. *Nature*, **384**, 106.

Edge, D. (1996b). Editorial. *Social Studies of Science*, **26**, 723–32.

Ehrlich, P. and E. O. Wilson (1991). Biodiversity studies: science and policy. *Science*, **253**, 758–62.

Eibl-Eibesfeldt, I. (1979). Human ethology: concepts and implications for the sciences of man. *The Behavioral and Brain Sciences*, **2**, 1–57.

Eldredge, N. (1985). *The Unfinished Synthesis*. New York: Oxford University Press.

Eldredge, N. (1995a). *Reinventing Darwin. The Great Debate at the High Table of Evolutionary Theory*. New York: John Wiley and Sons.

Eldredge, N. (1995b). A battle of words. In J. Brockman (ed.), *The Third Culture*. New York: Simon and Schuster, pp. 119–25.

Eldredge, N. and S. J. Gould (1972). Punctuated equilibria: An alternative to phyletic gradualism. In T. J. M. Schopf (ed.), *Models in Paleobiology*. San Francisco: Freeman Cooper.

Elkana, Y. 1978. Two-tier-thinking: Philosophical realism and historical relativism. *Social Studies of Science*, **8**, 309–26.

Ellul, J. (1964). *The Technological Society*. New York: Alfred Knopf.

Evans, C. S. and P. Marler (1997). Communication signals of animals: Contributions of emotion and reference. In U. Segerstrale and P. Molnar, *Nonverbal Communication: Where Nature Meets Culture*. Mahwah, NJ: Lawrence Erlbaum, pp. 151–70.

Fahnestock, J. (1993). Tactics of evaluation in Gould and Lewontin's The Spandrels of San Marco. In J. Selzer (ed.), *Understanding Scientific Prose*. Madison, WI: University of Wisconsin Press, pp. 158–79.

Falger, V. (1995). Biology as a scientific argument in political debates: A European illustration. *Social Science Information* **34** (2), 321–33.

Falger, V., P. Meyer and J. van der Dennen (eds) (1998). Sociobiology and Politics. *Research in Biopolitics*, Vol. **6**. Stamford, CT and London: JAI Press.

Feder, M. (1997). Speedbumps for adaptationism. Review of *Adaptation*. *Science*, **277**, 189.

Feldman, M. W. and R. C. Lewontin (1975). The heritability hang-up. *Science*, **190**, 1163–8.

Fischer, C. S., M. Hout, M. S. Jankowski, S. R. Lucas, A. Swidler, and K. Voss (1996). *Inequality by Design: Cracking the Bell Curve Myth*. Princeton, NJ: Princeton University Press.

Fisher, R. A. (1930). *The Genetical Theory of Natural Selection*. Oxford: Clarendon Press.

Fletcher, R. (1991). *Science, Ideology, and the Media: The Cyril Burt Scandal*. New Brunswick, NJ: Transaction Press.

Fodor, J. (1998). Look! Review of *Consilience*. *London Review of Books*, 29 October, 3, 6.

Fox, R. (ed.). *Biosocial Anthropology*, New York: John Wiley and Sons.

Fraser, S. (ed.) (1995). *The Bell Curve Wars*. New York: Basic Books.

Freedman, D. (1979). *Human Sociobiology: A Holistic Approach*. New York: Free Press.

Freeman, D. (1980). Sociobiology: the antidiscipline of anthropology, In A. Montagu (ed.), *Sociobiology Examined*. Oxford and New York: Oxford University Press, pp. 198–219.

Freeman, D. (1983). *Margaret Mead and Samoa*. Cambridge, MA: Cambridge University Press.

Freedman, D. (1997). Is nonduality possible in the social and biological sciences? In N. L. Segal, G. E. Weisfeld, and C. C. Weisfeld (eds), *Uniting Psychology and Biology*. Washington, D.C.: American Psychological Association, pp. 47–80.

Freeman, D. (1999). *The Fateful Hoaxing of Margaret Mead—An Historical Analysis*. Boulder, CO: Westview Press.

Fukuyama, D. J., R. C. Lewontin, G. C. Mayer, J. Seger, and J. W. Stubblefield (1981). Macroevolution conference. *Science*, **211**, 770.

Fuller, S. (1995). Two Cultures II: Science studies goes public. *EASST Newsletter*, Spring.

Geist, V. (1996). The origin of eyes. Book review, *Climbing Mount Improbable. The New York Times*, 29 September, Section 7 Book Review, 34.

Ghiselin, M. T. (1974). *The Economy of Nature and the Evolution of Sex*. Berkeley, CA: University of California Press.

Gilbert, G. N. (1977). Referencing as persuasion. *Social Studies of Science*, 7, 113–22.

Giraldeu, L.-A. (1997). The ecology of information use. In J. R. Krebs and N. B. Davies (eds), *Behavioural Ecology*. 4th Edition. Oxford: Blackwell Scientific Publications, pp. 42–68.

Goldberg, S. (1994). *Culture Clash: Law and Science in America*. New York: New York University Press.

Goleman, D. (1992). New storm brews on whether crime has roots in genes. *The New York Times, Science Times*, September 15: B 5–6.

Goldstein, J. (1987). *Console and Classify: The French Psychiatric Profession in the Nineteenth Century*. Cambridge: Cambridge University Press.

Goodell, R. (1987). The role of mass media in scientific controversy. In H. T. Engelhardt and A. L. Caplan (eds), *Scientific Controversies*. New York: Cambridge University Press, pp. 585–97.

Goodstein, D. (1991). Scientific fraud. *The American Scholar*, 60 (4), 505–15.

Goodwin, B. (1986). Is biology an historical science? In S. Rose and L. Appignanesi (eds), *Science and Beyond*. Oxford: Basil Blackwell, pp. 47–60.

Goodwin, B. (1995). Biology is just a dance. In J. Brockman (ed.), *The Third Culture*. New York: Simon and Schuster, pp. 96–106.

Gottfried, K. and K. Wilson (1997). Science as a cultural construct. *Nature*, 386, 545–7.

Gould, S. J. (1966). Allometry and size in ontogeny and phylogeny. *Biological Review*, 41, 587–640.

Gould, S. J. (1976). Biological potential vs. biological determinism. *Natural History*, May. Reprinted in A. L. Caplan, *The Sociobiology Controversy*. New York: Harper and Row, (1978), pp. 343–51.

Gould, S. J. (1977a). *Ontogeny and Phylogeny*. Cambridge, MA: Harvard University Press.

Gould, S. J. (1977b). Caring groups and selfish genes. *Natural History*, 86 (12), 20–4.

Gould, S. J. (1977c). *Ever Since Darwin*. New York: W. W. Norton.

Gould, S. J. (1978b). Sociobiology and human nature: a post-Panglossian vision. *Human Nature*, 1 (10). Reprinted in A. Montagu (ed.), *Sociobiology Examined*. Oxford and New York: Oxford University Press, pp. 283–90.

Gould, S. J. (1978c). Sociobiology: the art of storytelling. *New Scientist*, 16 November, 530–3.

Gould, S. J. (1978d). *Ever Since Darwin*. New York: W. W. Norton.

Gould, S. J. (1979). The episodic nature of change versus the dogma of gradualism. *Science and Nature* (2), 5–10.

Gould, S. J. (1980a). Sociobiology and the theory of natural selection. In G. Barlow and J. Silverberg (eds), *Sociobiology: Beyond Nature-Nurture*. AAAS Selected Symposium 35, pp. 257–69.

Gould, S. J. (1980b). Is a new and general theory of evolution emerging? *Paleobiology*, **6**, 119–30.

Gould, S. J. (1980c). Jensen's last stand. *The New York Review of Books*, 1 May, 38–44.

Gould, S. J. (1980d). The *Panda's Thumb*. New York: W. W. Norton.

Gould, S. J. (1981a). *The Mismeasure of Man*. New York: W. W. Norton.

Gould, S. J. (1981b). Museum debate. *Nature*, **289**, 742.

Gould, S. J. (1981c). The ghost of Protagoras. *The New York Review of Books*, 22 January, 42–4.

Gould, S. J. (1982). Darwinism and the expansion of evolutionary theory. *Science*, **216**, 380–7.

Gould, S. J. (1983). Genes on the Brain. Book review, *Promethean Fire*. *The New York Review of Books*, June 30, 5–6, 8, 10.

Gould, S. J. (1984). Who has donned Lysenko's mantle? *The Public Interest*, **75**, Spring, 148–51.

Gould, S. J. (1987). *An Urchin in the Storm*. New York: W. W. Norton.

Gould, S. J. (1989). *Wonderful Life*. New York: W. W. Norton.

Gould, S. J. (1992). The confusion over evolution. *The New York Review of Books*, November 19, 47–54.

Gould, S. J. (1993a). Confusion over evolution: an exchange. *The New York Review of Books*, 14 January, 43.

Gould, S. J. (1993b). Fulfilling the spandrels of word and mind. In J. Selzer (ed.), *Understanding Scientific Prose*. Madison, WI: University of Wisconsin Press, pp. 310–36.

Gould, S. J. (1994). The evolution of Life on the Earth. *Scientific American*, October, 85–91.

Gould, S. J. (1995). The pattern of life's history. In J. Brockman (ed.), *The Third Culture*. New York: Simon and Schuster, pp. 51–64.

Gould, S. J. (1996a). *The Mismeasure of Man*. 2nd edition. New York: W. W. Norton.

Gould, S. J. (1996b). *Full House: The Spread of Excellence from Plato to Darwin*. New York: Harmony Books.

Gould, S. J. (1996c). Self-help for a hedgehog stuck on a molehill. Review of *Climbing Mount Improbable*. *Evolution*, **51** (3), 1920–3.

Gould, S. J. (1997a). Darwinian fundamentalism. *The New York Review of Books*, 12 June, 34–7.

Gould, S. J. (1997b). Evolution: the pleasures of pluralism. *The New York Review of Books*, 26 June, 47–52.

Gould, S. J. (1999). *Rocks of Ages: Science and Religion in the Fullness of Life*. New York: Ballantine Publishers.

Gould, S. J. and N. Eldredge (1977). Punctuated equilibria. *Paleobiology*, **3**, 115–51.

Gould, S. J. and R. D. Lewontin (1979). The spandrels of San Marco and the Panglossian paradigm: A critique of the adaptationist programme. *Proceedings of the Royal Society of London*, **205 B**, 581–98.

Gould, S. J. and E. Vrba (1982). Exaptation: a missing term in the science of form. *Paleobiology*, **8**, 4–15.

Grafen, A. (1982). How not to measure inclusive fitness. *Nature*, **298**, 425–6.

Grafen, A. (1984). Natural selection, kin selection and group selection. In J. Krebs and N. B. Davies (eds), *Behavioural Ecology*. 2nd edn. Oxford: Blackwell Scientific Publications, pp. 62–84.

Gragson, G. and J. Selzer (1993). The reader in the text of The Spandrels of San Marco. In J. Selzer (ed.), *Understanding Scientific Prose*. Madison, WI: University of Wisconsin Press, pp. 180–202.

Graham, L. R. (1977). Political ideology and genetic theory: Russia and Germany in the 1920s. *Hastings Center Report*, **7**, 30–9.

Graham, L. R. (1980). *Between Science and Values*. New York: Columbia University Press.

Gregory, M. S., A. Silvers, and D. Sutch (eds) (1978). *Sociobiology and Human Nature*. San Francisco: Jossey Bass.

Griffin, D. A. (1992). *Animals Minds*. Chicago: University of Chicago Press.

Grinnell, F. (1992). *The Scientific Attitude*. 2nd edn. New York: The Guilford Press.

Gross, P. (1997). Opinion: The so-called Science Wars and sociological gravitas. *The Scientist*, 28 April, 8.

Gross, P. (1998). The Icarian impulse. *The Wilson Quarterly*, Winter, 39–49.

Gross, P. and N. Levitt (1994). *Higher Superstition: The Academic Left and Its Quarrels with Science*. Baltimore, MD: Johns Hopkins University Press.

Gross, P. and N. Levitt (1995). Knocking science for fun and profit. *The Skeptical Inquirer*, **19**, 2, 38–42.

Gross P. and N. Levitt (1998). Higher Superstition: an exchange. *The New York Review of Books*, 3 December, 59.

Gross, P., N. Levitt, and M. Lewis (eds) (1996) *The Flight from Science and Reason*. Annals of the New York Academy of Sciences, Vol. 775. Republished by Johns Hopkins University Press, 1997.

Grove, J. W. (1989). *In Defence of Science*. Toronto: University of Toronto Press.

Guston, D. (1995). The flight from reasonableness. (Report from the Flight from Science and Reason conference). *Technoscience*, **8**, (3), 11–13.

Habermas, J. (1970). *Toward a Rational Society*. Boston, MA: Beacon Press.

Habermas, J. (1979). *Communication and the Evolution of Society*. Boston, MA: Beacon Press.

Habermas, J. (1984). *The Theory of Communicative Action. Volume I: Reason and the Rationalization of Society*. Boston, MA: Beacon Press.

Habermas, J. (1987). *The Theory of Communicative Action. Volume II: Lifeworld and System*. Boston, MA: Beacon Press.

Haig, D. (1997). The social gene. In J. R. Krebs and N. B. Davies (eds), *Behavioural Ecology*, 4th edn. Oxford: Blackwell Scientific Publications, pp. 284–304.

Haldane, J. B. S. (1932). *The Causes of Evolution*. London: Longman Green.

Haldane, J. B. S. (1938). *Heredity and Politics*. New York: Norton.

Haldane, J. B. S. (1955). Population genetics. *New Biology*, **18**, 34–51.

Hamilton, W. D. (1963). The evolution of altruistic behavior. *The American Naturalist*, **97**, 354–6.

Hamilton, W. D. (1964). The genetical theory of social behavior. I and II. *Journal of Theoretical Biology*, **7**, 1–16; 17–32.

Hamilton, W. D. (1967). Extraordinary sex ratios. *Science*, **156**, 477–88.

Hamilton, W. D. (1970). Selfish and spiteful behaviour in an evolutionary model. *Nature*, **228**, 1218–20.

Hamilton, W. D. (1971a). Geometry for the selfish herd. *Journal of Theoretical Biology*, **31**, 295–311.

Hamilton, W. D. (1971b). The genetical theory of social behavior. I and II. In G. Williams (ed.), *Group Selection*. Chicago and New York: Aldine/Atherton, pp. 23–87.

Hamilton, W. D. (1971c). Addendum. In G. Williams (ed.), *Group Selection*. Chicago and New York: Aldine/Atherton, pp. 87–9.

Hamilton, W. D. (1971d). Selection of selfish and altruistic behaviour in some extreme models. In J. F. Eisenberg and W. S. Dillon (eds), *Man and Beast: Comparative Social Behavior*. Washington D. C.: Smithsonian Institution Press, pp. 57–91.

Hamilton, W. D. (1975). Innate social aptitudes of man: an approach from evolutionary genetics. In R. Fox (ed.), *Biosocial Anthropology*. New York: John Wiley and Sons, pp. 133–57.

Hamilton, W. D. (1977). The selfish gene. *Nature*, **267**, 102.

Hamilton, W. D. (1996). *Narrow Roads of Gene Land: The Collected Papers of W. D. Hamilton*. Oxford and New York: W. H. Freeman.

Hampshire, S. (1978). The illusion of sociobiology. *The New York Review of Books*, 12 October, 64–9.

Haraway, D. (1981–2). The high cost of information in post-World War II evolutionary biology: Ergonomics, semiotics, and the sociobiology of communication systems. *The Philosophical Forum*, **13** (2–3), 244–78.

Harpending, H. (1986). Peer commentary on P. Kitcher's Precis of *Vaulting Ambition*. *Behavior and Brain Sciences*, **10** (1), 78.

Harris, M. (1979). *Cultural Materialism*. New York: Random House.

Harris, M. (1980). Sociobiology and biological reductionism. In A. Montagu (ed.), *Sociobiology Examined*. Oxford and New York: Oxford University Press, pp. 311–35.

Hartung, J. (1981). Paternity and inheritance of wealth. *Nature*, **291**, 25 June, 652–3.

Harvard Medical Alumni Bulletin (1976). Davis seen as impugning minority students. (Overview) July/August.

Hearnshaw, L. S. (1979). *Cyril Burt, Psychologist*. Ithaca, NY: Cornell University Press.

Hearnshaw, L. S. (1981). *Cyril Burt: Psychologist*. New York: Vintage Books.

Heber, R. (1968). *Rehabilitation of Families at Risk for Mental Retardation*. Madison, WI: University of Wisconsin Regional Rehabilitation Center.

Heinen, J. (1993). The uncertain outlook for life on Earth. Review of *The Diversity of Life. American Scientist*, March/April, 179–80.

Heller, S. (1994). At conference, conservative scholars lash out at attempts to 'de-legitimize science'. *The Chronicle of Higher Education*, 23 November, A18, A20.

Herrnstein, R. (1971). IQ. *The Atlantic*, September, 43–64.

Herrnstein, R. J. (1973). *IQ in the Meritocracy*. Boston, MA: Little, Brown & Co.

Herrnstein, R. J. (1982). Encounters with the press. *The Atlantic Monthly*, August, 68–74.

Herrnstein, R. and C. Murray (1994). *The Bell Curve: Intelligence and Class Structure in American Life*. New York: Free Press.

Hicks, L. H. (1973). Behavior and heredity: A reply. *American Psychologist*, **28** (January), 83.

Hinde, R. (1974). *Biological Bases of Human Behaviour*. New York: McGraw-Hill.

Hinde, R. (1982). *Ethology*. Oxford: Oxford University Press.

Hinde R. (1987). *Individuals, Relationships and Culture*. Cambridge: Cambridge University Press.

Hinde, R. (1989). Towards integrating the behavioral sciences to meet the threats of violence and war. *Medicine and War*, **5**, 5–15.

Hinde, R. (1991a). From animals to humans. In M. S. Dawkins, T. R. Halliday, and R. Dawkins (eds), *The Tinbergen Legacy*. London: Chapman and Hall, pp. 31–9.

Hinde, R. (1991b). *The Institution of War*. London: Macmillan.

Hirsch, J. (1969). Behavior-genetic analysis and its social consequences. Address presented at the Nineteenth Congress of Psychology, London, July 30, 1969, and dedicated to Professor T. Dobzhansky on his seventieth birthday. Reprinted in N. J. Block and G. Dworkin (eds), *The IQ Debate*. New York: Random House, 1976, pp. 156–78.

Hirsch, J. (1975). Jensenism: The bankruptcy of science without scholarship. *Educational Theory*, **25** (1), 3–27.

Hirsch, J. (1976). Multiple review of Wilson's *Sociobiology*. *Animal Behavior*, **24**, 707–9.

Hirsch, J. (1979). Sociobiology and environmental determinism. *Nature*, **279**, 188.

Hirsch J. (1981). To unfrock the charlatans. *Sage Race Relations Abstracts*, **6**, (2), 1–65.

Hirsch, J., T. R. McGuire, and A. Vetta (1980). Concepts of behavior genetics and misapplications to humans. In J. Lockard (ed.), *The Evolution of Human Social Behavior*. New York: Elsevier.

Holden, C. (1993). NIH kills genes and crime grant. Random samples. *Science*, **260**, 619.

Hölldobler, B. and E. O. Wilson (1990). *The Ants*. Cambridge, MA: Belknap Press of Harvard University Press.

Hölldobler, B. and E. O. Wilson (1994). *Journey to the Ants*. Cambridge, MA: Belknap Press of Harvard University Press.

Hollinger, D. (1995). Science as a weapon in Kulturkampfe in the United States during and after World War II. *Isis*, **86**, 440–54.

Holton, G. (1978). The new synthesis? In M. S. Gregory, A. Silvers and D. Sutch (eds), *Sociobiology and Human Nature*. San Francisco: Jossey Bass, pp. 75–97.

Holton, G. (1993). *Science and Anti-Science*. Cambridge, MA: Harvard University Press.

Holton, G. (1995). *Einstein, History, and Other Passions*. Woodbury, NY: American Institute of Physics Press.

Horgan, J. (1993). Eugenics revisited. *Scientific American*, June, 122–31.

Horgan, J. (1994). Revisiting old battlefields. Profile: Edward O. Wilson. *Scientific American*, April, 36, 38, 41.

Horgan, J. (1996). *The End of Science: Facing the Limits of Knowledge in the Twilight of the Scientific Age*. New York: Addison-Wesley.

Howe, H. and J. Lyne (1992). Gene talk in sociobiology. *Social Epistemology*, **6** (2), 109–63.

Hrdy, S. (1991). *The Woman that Never Evolved*. Cambridge, MA: Harvard University Press.

Hrdy, S. *et al.* (1996). *Sociobiology's successes*. Letter. Science, **274**, 162–3.

Hull, D. L. (1974). *Philosophy of Biology*. Englewood Cliffs: Prentice Hall.

Hull, D. (1978). Scientific bandwagon or traveling medicine show? In M. S. Gregory, A. Silvers, and D. Sutch (eds), *Sociobiology and Human Nature*. San Francisco: Jossey Bass, pp. 136–63.

Hull, D. (1980). Sociobiology: another new synthesis. In G. Barlow and J. Silverberg (eds), *Sociobiology: Beyond Nature-Nurture*. AAAS Selected Symposium 35, pp. 77–96.

Hull, D. (1981a). Units of evolution: A metaphysical essay. In U. L. Jensen and R. Harre (eds), *The Philosophy of Evolution*, Brighton: Harvester Press, pp. 23–44. Reprinted in R. Brandon and R. Burian (eds), *Genes, Organisms, Populations*. Cambridge, MA: MIT Press, 1984, pp. 142–60.

Hull, D. L. (1981b). Reduction and genetics. *Journal of Medicine and Philosophy*, **6**, 125–43.

Hull, D. (1988). *Science as a Process*. Chicago: University of Chicago Press.

Humphrey, N. (1995). The thick moment. In J. Brockman (ed.), *The Third Culture*. New York: Simon and Schuster, pp. 198–205.

Hurst, L. D., A. Atlan, and B. O. Bengtsson (1996). Genetic conflicts. *Quarterly Review of Biology*, **71** (3), 317–64.

Huxley, J. (1942). *Evolution: The Modern Synthesis*. London: G. Allen and Unwin.

Ingelfinger, F. J. (1978). Biological buffet. *The Sciences*, **18**, 28–9.

Israel, J. (1972). Stipulations and construction in the social sciences. J. Israel and H. Tajfel (eds), *The Context of Social Psychology: A Critical Assessment*. London and New York: Academic Press.

Jackson, N. (1981). Mystery genre. *Nature*, **292**, 792.

Jacoby, R. (1973). The politics of subjectivity: Slogans of the American New Left. *New Left Review*, **79**, 37–49.

Jaisson, P. (1993). *La fourmi et le sociobiologiste*. Paris: Editions Odile Jacob.

Jencks, C., M. Smith, H. Acland, M. J. Bane, D. Cohen, H. Gintis, B. Heynes, and S. Michelson (1972). *Inequality: A reassessment of the Effect of Family and Schooling in America*. New York: Basic Books.

Jensen, A. R. (1969). How much can we boost IQ and scholastic achievement? *Harvard Educational Review*, **39**, 1–123.

Jensen, A. R. (1970). Race and the genetics of intelligence: A reply to Lewontin. *Bulletin of the Atomic Scientists*, May, 17–23.

Jensen, A. R. (1972a). *Genetics and Education*. London: Methuen.

Jensen, A. R. (1972b). Interpretation of heritability. *American Psychologist*, **27** (10), 973–4.

Jensen, A. R. (1979). *Bias in Mental Testing*. New York: Free Press.

Jensen, A. R. (1982). The debunking of scientific fossils and straw persons. *Contemporary Education Review*, Spring, 121–35.

Jensen, A. R. (1985). The nature of the black-white difference on various psychometric tests: Spearman's hypothesis. With peer commentary. *Behavioral and Brain Sciences* **8**, 193–263.

Jensen, A. R. (1991). IQ and science: the mysterious Burt affair. *The Public Interest*, **105**, 93–106.

Jones, J. S. (1982). But is man a worm? *Nature*, **298**, 873–4.

Jones. S. (1995). Why there is so much genetic diversity. In J. Brockman (ed.), *The Third Culture*. New York: Simon and Schuster, pp. 11–18.

Jones, S. (1996). Up against the wall. Review of *Dinosaur in a Haystack* and *Full House:*

The Spread of Excellence from Plato to Darwin. The New York Review of Books, 17 October, 33–4.

Journet, D. (1993). Deconstructing the Spandrels of San Marco. In J. Selzer (ed.) *Understanding Scientific Prose*. Madison, WI: University of Wisconsin Press, pp. 232–55.

Joynson, R. B. (1989). *The Burt Affair*. London and New York: Routledge.

Kacelnik, A. and J. Krebs (1997). Yanomamo dreams and starling payloads: the logic of optimality. In L. Betzig (ed.), *Human Nature*. Oxford: Oxford University Press, pp. 21–35.

Kagan, J., N. Sniderman, D. Arcus, and J. S. Reznick (1994). *Galen's Prophecy: Temperament in Human Nature*. New York: Basic Books.

Kamin, L. J. (1973). The misuse of IQ testing. An interview with Kamin, by John Edgerton. *Change*, **5**, 40–3.

Kamin, L. J. (1974): *The Science and Politics of IQ*. New York: Halsted Press.

Kauffman, S. (1995). Order for free. In J. Brockman (ed.), *The Third Culture*. New York: Simon and Schuster, pp. 333–40.

Keeton, W. T. (1980). *Biological Science*, 3rd edition. New York: W. W. Norton.

Kevles, D. and L. Hood (eds) (1992). *The Code of Codes*. Cambridge, MA: Harvard University Press.

King, J. (1980). The genetics of sociobiology. In A. Montagu (ed.), *Sociobiology Examined*. Oxford and New York: Oxford University Press, pp. 82–107.

King's College (University of Cambridge) Sociobiology Group (1982). *Current Problems in Sociobiology*. Cambridge and New York: Cambridge University Press.

Kitcher, P. (1985). *Vaulting Ambition*. Cambridge, MA: MIT Press.

Kitcher, P. (1987). Author's Precis of *Vaulting Ambition: Sociobiology and the Quest for Human Nature*. With Peer Commentary. *Behavior and Brain Sciences*, **10**, 61–100.

Kitcher, P. (1998). You win, I win. Review of *Unto Others*. *The London Review of Books*, 15 October, 28–9.

Koertge, N. (ed.) (1998). *A House Built on Sand*. Oxford: Oxford University Press.

Kogan, J. (1976). Professor assails blacks' performance. *The Harvard Crimson*, 14 May.

Konner, M. (1999). One man's rainbow. Book review, *Unweaving the Rainbow*. *Scientific American*, March, 107–9.

Krauss, R. (1997). Science and 'The Demon-Haunted World': an exchange. *The New York Review of Books*, 6 March 51.

Krebs, J. (1985). Sociobiology ten years on. *New Scientist*, 3 October, 40–3.

Krebs, J. R. and N. B. Davies (1978). *Behavioural Ecology*. Oxford: Blackwell Scientific Publications.

Krebs, J. R. and N. B. Davies (1984). *Behavioural Ecology*, 2nd edn. Oxford: Blackwell Scientific Publications.

Krebs, J. R. and N. B. Davies (1997a). *Behavioural Ecology,* 4th edn. Oxford: Blackwell Scientific Publications.

Krebs, J. R. and N. B. Davies (1997b). The evolution of behavioural ecology. In J. R. Krebs and N. B. Davies, *Behavioural Ecology,* 4th edn. Oxford: Blackwell Scientific Publications, pp. 3–12.

Krebs, J. and A. Kacelnik (1997). Yanomamo dreams and starling payloads: the logic of optimality. In L. Betzig (ed.), *Human Nature, a Critical Reader.* New York and Oxford: Oxford University Press, pp. 21–35.

Ladd, E. and S. M. Lipset (1975). *The Divided Academy: Professors and Politics.* New York: McGraw-Hill.

Latour, B. and S. Woolgar (1979). *Laboratory Life.* Berkeley, CA: Sage. 2nd edn, 1989.

Lawler, A. (1996). Support for science stays strong. *Science,* **272,** May, 1256.

Layzer, D. (1972). Science or superstition? A physical scientist looks at the IQ controversy. *Cognition,* **1,** 265–300.

Layzer, D. (1975). Review of Leon Kamin. *Scientific American,* **233,** 126–8.

Layzer, D. (1981). A misguided mathematical model. *Technology Review,* **84,** 31.

Leach, E. (1968). Ignoble savages. *The New York Review of Books,* October 10, 24–9.

Leach, E. (1978). The proper study of mankind. *New Society,* 12 October, 91–3.

Leach, E. (1981a). Biology and social science: Wedding or rape? *Nature,* **291,** 267–8.

Leach, E. (1981b). Men, bishops and apes. *Nature,* **293,** 19–21.

Leeds, A. (1981–2). The language of sociobiology. *The Philosophical Forum,* **13** (2–3), 161–206.

Lerner, R. M. (1992). *Final Solutions: Biology, Prejudice, and Genocide.* University Park, PA: The Pennsylvania State University Press.

Lester, R. (1981). Naming names. Letter. *Nature,* **291,** 696.

Levins, R. (1968). *Evolution in Changing Environments.* Princeton, NJ: Princeton University Press.

Levins, R. (1981). Class science and scientific truth. *Working Papers in Marxism and Science,* Winter, 9–22.

Levins, R. and R. C. Lewontin (1976). The Problem of Lysenkoism. In H. Rose and S. Rose (eds), *The Radicalization of Science.* London and Basingstoke: Macmillan.

Levins, R. and R. C. Lewontin (1980). Dialectics and reductionism in ecology. *Synthese,* **43,** 47–78.

Levins, R. and R. C. Lewontin (1985). *The Dialectical Biologist.* Cambridge, MA: Harvard University Press.

Levinton, J. S. (1982). Charles Darwin and Darwinism. *BioScience,* **32,** 495–500.

Levitt, N. and P. Gross (1994). The perils of democratizing science. *The Chronicle of Higher Education,* 5 October, B1–B2.

Lewin, R. (1976). The course of a controversy. *New Scientist*, 13 May, 344–5.

Lewin, R. (1978). The biology of capitalism. *New Scientist*, 13 April, 100.

Lewin, R. (1980). Evolutionary theory under fire. *Science*, **210**, 883–7.

Lewin, R. (1981a). Do jumping genes make evolutionary leaps? *Science*, **213**, 634–6.

Lewin, R. (1981b). Cultural diversity tied to genetic differences. *Science*, **212**, 908–9.

Lewin, R. (1992). *Complexity: Life at the Edge of Chaos*. New York: Macmillan.

Lewontin, R. C. (1961). Evolution and the theory of games. *Journal of Theoretical Biology*, **1**, 382–403.

Lewontin, R. C. (1964). Selection in and out of populations. In J. A. Moore (ed.), *Ideas in Modern Biology*, pp. 299–311. New York: Natural History Press.

Lewontin, R. C. (1967). Spoken remark. In P. S. Moorhead and M. Kaplan (eds), *Mathematical Challenges to the Neo-Darwinian Interpretation of Evolution. Wistar Institute Symposium Monograph*, **5**, 79.

Lewontin, R. C. (1970a). Race and intelligence. *Bulletin of the Atomic Scientists*, March, 2–8.

Lewontin, R. C. (1970b). The units of selection. *Annual Review of Ecology and Systematics*, **1**, 1–18.

Lewontin, R. C. (1972a). Testing the theory of natural selection. *Nature*, **236**, 181–2.

Lewontin, R. C. (1972b). The apportionment of human diversity. *Evolutionary Biology*, **6**, 381–98.

Lewontin, R. C. (1974a). *The Genetic Basis of Evolutionary Change*. New York: Columbia University Press.

Lewontin, R. C. (1974b). The analysis of variance and the analysis of causes. *American Journal of Human Genetics*, **26**, 400–11.

Lewontin, R. C. (1975a). Genetic aspects of intelligence. *Annual Review of Genetics*, **9**, 387–405.

Lewontin, R. C. (1975b). Transcript of Nova program, WGBH Boston, #211. Transmission by PBS, 2 February.

Lewontin, R. C. (1975c). Interview. *The Harvard Crimson*, 3 December.

Lewontin, R. C. (1976a). Sociobiology—a caricature of Darwinism. In F. Suppe and P. Asquith (eds), *PSA 1976, 2*. East Lansing, MI: Philosophy of Science Association.

Lewontin, R. C. (1976b). Interview. *The Harvard Gazette*, 16 January.

Lewontin, R. C. (1976c). Review of Leon J. Kamin. *Contemporary Psychology*, **21**, 97–8.

Lewontin, R. C. (1977a). Caricature of Darwinism. Review, *The Selfish Gene. Nature*, **266**, 283–4.

Lewontin, R. C. (1977b). Adaptation. In *The Encyclopaedia Einaudi*. Torino: Giuglio Einaudi Editions.

Lewontin, R. C. (1978a). Fitness, survival and optimality. In D. H. Horn, R. Mitchell, and G. R. Stairs (eds), *Analysis of Ecological Systems*. Columbus, OH: Ohio State University Press.

Lewontin, R. C. (1978b). Adaptation. *Scientific American, 239*, 156–69.

Lewontin, R. C. (1979a). Sociobiology as an adaptationist program. *Behavioral Science*, **24**, 5–14.

Lewontin, R. C. (1979b). Work collectives, utopian and otherwise. *Radical Science Journal*, **9**, 133–5.

Lewontin, R. C. (1981a). Sleight of hand. Review, *Genes, Mind and Culture. The Sciences*, July–August, 23–6.

Lewontin, R. C. (1981b). The inferiority complex. Review, *The Mismeasure of Man. The New York Review of Books*, 22 October.

Lewontin, R. C. (1981c). Evolution/creation debate: A time for truth. *BioScience*, **31**, 559.

Lewontin, R. C. (1981d). Credit due to Nabi. *Nature*, **291**, 608.

Lewontin, R. C. (1981e). On constraints and adaptation. *Behavioral and Brain Sciences*, **4**, 244–5.

Lewontin, R. C. (1982a). Keeping it clean. Review, *Evolution and the Theory of Games. Nature*, **300**, 113–14.

Lewontin, R. C. (1982b). Are the races different? *Science for the people*, March/April, 10–14.

Lewontin, R. C. (1982c). Is intelligence for real? An exchange. *The New York Review of Books*, 4 February, 40–41.

Lewontin, R. C. (1983). The corpse in the elevator. *The New York Review of Books*, 20 January, 29, 34–7.

Lewontin, R. C. (1986). Personal introduction. In M. Schiff and R. Lewontin, *Education and Class: The Irrelevance of IQ Genetic Studies*. Oxford: Clarendon Press, pp. xii–xiii.

Lewontin, R. C. (1991). *Biology as Ideology*. New York: HarperPerennial (HarperCollins).

Lewontin, R. C. (1992). Foreword 1991. In R. M. Lerner, *Final Solutions: Biology, Prejudice, and Genocide*. University Park, PA: The Pennsylvania State University Press, pp. vii–ix.

Lewontin, R. D. (1995). A la recherche du temps perdu. Review, *Higher Superstition* and *On Looking Into the Abyss. Configurations*, **3** (2), 257–65. Reprinted in A. Ross, *The Science Wars*, 1996, pp. 293–301.

Lewontin, R. (1997a). Billions and billions of demons. Review, *The Demon-Haunted World. The New York Review of Books*, 9 January, 28–32.

Lewontin, R. (1997b). Science and 'The Demon-Haunted World': an exchange. *The New York Review of Books*, 6 March, 51–2.

Lewontin, R. C. (1998a). Survival of the nicest? Review, *Unto Others. The New York Review of Books*, 22 October, 59–63.

Lewontin, R. C. (1998b). Higher Superstition: an exchange. *The New York Review of Books*, 3 December, 59–60.

Lewontin, R. C. and L. C. Dunn (1960). The evolutionary dynamics of a polymorphism in the house mouse. *Genetics*, **45**, 705–22.

Lewontin, R. C. and J. L. Hubby (1966). A molecular approach to the study of genic heterozygosity in natural populations. *Genetics*, **54**, 595–609.

Lewontin, R. C., S. Rose, and L. Kamin (1984). *Not in Our Genes*. New York: Pantheon Books.

Lloyd, E. (1988). *The Structure and Confirmation of Evolutionary Theory*. New York: Greenwood Press.

Longino, H. (1990). *Science as Social Knowledge*. Princeton, NJ: Princeton University Press.

Lorenz, K. (1966). *On Aggression*. London: Methuen.

Lumsden, C. L. and E. O. Wilson (1981a). *Genes, Mind and Culture: The Coevolutionary Process*. Cambridge, MA and London: Harvard University Press.

Lumsden, C. L. and E. O. Wilson (1981b). Genes, mind and ideology. *The Sciences*, November, 6–8.

Lumsden, C. L. and E. O. Wilson (1981c). Genes and culture. *The New York Review of Books*, 24 September, 73–74, Reply to P. B. Medawar.

Lumsden, C. L. and E. O. Wilson (1981d). Letter (rejected). *Nature*, 9 June.

Lumsden, C. L. and E. O. Wilson (1982a). Precis of *Genes, Mind and Culture*. *Behavioral and Brain Sciences*, **5**, 1–37.

Lumsden, C. L. and E. O. Wilson (1982b). Authors' response. *Behavioral and Brain Sciences*, **5**, 31–7.

Lumsden C. L. and E. O. Wilson (1983). *Promethean Fire*. Cambridge, MA: Harvard University Press.

Luria, S. E. (1974a). What can biologists solve? *The New York Review of Books*, 7 February, 22–8.

Luria, S. E. (1974b). Reply. *The New York Review of Books*, 2 May, 45.

Lynch, W. (1994). Ideology and the sociology of scientific knowledge. *Social Studies of Science*, **24**, 197–227.

MacArthur, R. H. and E. O. Wilson (1967). *The Theory of Island Biogeography*. Princeton, NJ: Princeton University Press.

MacKenzie, D. A. (1981). *Statistics in Britain 1865–1930*. Edinburgh: Edinburgh University Press.

Mackie, J. L. (1978). The law of the jungle. *Philosophy*, October, **53**, 455–64.

Mackintosh, N. J. (1979). A proffering of underpinnings. *Science*, **204**, 735–7.

Mahoney, M. J. (1976). *The Scientist as Subject*. Cambridge, MA: Ballinger.

Mann, C. (1991). Extinction: Are ecologists crying wolf? *Science*, **253**, 736–53.

Mannheim, K. (1946). *Ideology and Utopia*. London: Routledge and Kegan Paul.

Marcuse, H. (1955). *Eros and Civilization*. Boston: Beacon Press.

Margulis, L. (1981). *Symbiosis in Cell Evolution*. San Francisco: W. H. Freeman.

Margulis, L. (1995). Gaia is a tough bitch. In J. Brockman (ed.), *The Third Culture*. New York: Simon and Schuster, pp. 129–40.

Mark, R. (1996). Architecture and evolution. *The American Scientist*, **84**, 383–9.

Markl, H. (ed.) (1980). *Evolution of Social Behavior: Hypotheses and Empirical Tests.* Report of the Dahlem Workshop, Berlin, 1980. Weinheim and Deerfield Beach, FL and Basel: Verlag Chemie.

Marler, P. and C. Evans (1997). Communication signals of animals: Contributions of emotion and reference. In U. Segerstråle and P. Molnar (eds), *Nonverbal Communication: Where Nature Meets Culture*. Mahwah, NJ: Lawrence Erlbaum Associates, pp. 151–70.

Masters, R. D. (1982). Is sociobiology reactionary? The political implications of inclusive-fitness theory. *Quarterly Review of Biology*, **57**, 275–92.

May, R. M. (1976). Sociobiology: A new synthesis and an old quarrel. *Nature*, **260**, 390–2.

May, R. M. and M. Robertson (1980). Just so stories and cautionary tales. *Nature*, **286**, 327–9.

Maynard Smith, J. (1964). Group selection and kin selection. *Nature*, **201**, 1145–7.

Maynard Smith, J. (1972). Game theory and the evolution of fighting. In J. Maynard Smith, *On Evolution*. Edinburgh: Edinburgh University Press.

Maynard Smith, J. (1973). Can we change human nature? The evidence of genetics. In J. Benthall (ed.) *The Limits of Human Nature*. London.

Maynard Smith, J. (1974). The theory of games and the evolution of animal conflicts. *Journal of Theoretical Biology*, **47**, 209–21.

Maynard Smith, J. (1975). Survival through suicide. *New Scientist*, **28**, 496–7.

Maynard Smith, J. (1976a). Group selection. *Quarterly Review of Biology*, **51**, 277–83. Reprinted in R. Brandon and R. Burian (eds), *Genes, Organisms, Populations*. Cambridge, MA: MIT Press, 1984, pp. 239–48.

Maynard Smith, J. (1976b). Evolution and the theory of games. *American Scientist*, January/February, 41–5. Reprinted in J. Maynard Smith, *Did Darwin Get It Right?*, New York: Chapman and Hall, 1989, pp. 201–15.

Maynard Smith, J. (1978a). Constraints on human behavior. Review, *On Human Nature*. *Nature*, **276**, 120–1.

Maynard Smith, J. (1978b). Optimization theory in evolution. *Annual Review of Ecology and Systematics*, **9**, 31–56.

Maynard Smith, J. (1978c). The evolution of behavior. *Scientific American*, **239**, 176–92.

Maynard Smith, J. (1981a). Did Darwin get it right? *London Review of Books*, June/July.

Reprinted in J. Maynard Smith, *Did Darwin Get It Right?* New York: Chapman and Hall, 1989, pp. 148–56.

Maynard Smith, J. (1981b). Genes and race. *Nature*, **289**, 742.

Maynard Smith, J. (1982a). Genes and memes. *London Review of Books*, February, 4–17.

Maynard Smith, J. (1982b). Descending sloth. *London Review of Books*, April, 1–14.

Maynard Smith, J. (1982c). Mind and the linkage between genes and culture. *Behavior and Brain Sciences*, **5**, 20–1.

Maynard Smith, J. (1982d). *Evolution and the Theory of Games*. Cambridge: Cambridge University Press.

Maynard Smith, J. (1982e). Introduction. In King's College Sociobiology Group (ed.), *Current Problems in Sociobiology*. Cambridge: Cambridge University Press, pp. 1–3.

Maynard Smith, J. (1982f). The evolution of social behaviour—a classification of models. In King's College Sociobiology Group (ed.), *Current Problems in Sociobiology*. Cambridge: Cambridge University Press, pp. 29–44.

Maynard Smith, J. (1982g). Storming the fortress. *The New York Review of Books*, May. Reprinted in J. Maynard Smith, *Did Darwin Get It Right?* New York: Chapman and Hall, 1989, pp. 8–14.

Maynard Smith, J. (1983). Current controversies in evolutionary biology. In M. Grene (ed.), *Dimensions of Darwinism*, Cambridge: Cambridge University Press. Reprinted in J. Maynard Smith, *Did Darwin Get It Right?* New York: Chapman and Hall, pp. 131–47.

Maynard Smith, J. (1984). Science and myth. Natural History **11**, 11–24. Reprinted in J. Maynard Smith (1989), *Did Darwin Get It Right?* New York: Chapman & Hall, pp. 39–52.

Maynard Smith, J. (1984a). Paleontology at the high table. *Nature*, May. Reprinted in J. Maynard Smith, *Did Darwin Get It Right?* New York: Chapman and Hall, 1989, pp. 125–30.

Maynard Smith, J. (1984b). 1983 Preface to Group selection. In R. Brandon and R. Burian (eds), *Genes, Organisms, Populations*. Cambridge, MA: MIT Press, 1984, pp. 238–9.

Maynard Smith, J. (1985a). Do we need a new evolutionary paradigm? Review of M. W. Ho and P. T. Saunders' (eds), *Beyond Neo-Darwinism*. *New Scientist*, 14 March. Reprinted in J. Maynard Smith, *Did Darwin Get It Right?* New York: Chapman and Hall, 1989, pp. 157–61.

Maynard Smith, J. (1985b). Biology and the behaviour of man. Review of Philip Kitcher, *Vaulting Ambition*. *Nature*, **318**, 121–2.

Maynard Smith, J. (1985c). The birth of sociobiology. *New Scientist* 26 September, 48–50. Reprinted in J. Maynard Smith (1989), *Did Darwin Get It Right?* New York: Chapman & Hall, pp. 53–60.

Maynard Smith, J. (1985d). *On Being the Right Size and Other Essays* by J. B. S. Haldane. Oxford: Oxford University Press.

Maynard Smith, J. (1986a). Natural selection of culture? Review of *Culture and the Evolutionary Process. The New York Review of Books*, November. Reprinted in J. Maynard Smith, *Did Darwin Get It Right?* New York: Chapman and Hall, 1989, pp. 114–21.

Maynard Smith, J. (1986b). Molecules are not enough. *The London Review of Books*, 6 February, 8–9.

Maynard Smith, J. (1986c). Structuralism vs selection—is Darwinism enough? In S. Rose and L. Appignanesi (eds), *Science and Beyond*. Oxford: Basil Blackwell, pp. 39–46.

Maynard Smith, J. (1988). *Games, Sex and Evolution*. New York: Harvester Wheatsheaf.

Maynard Smith, J. (1989a). *Did Darwin Get It Right?* New York: Chapman and Hall.

Maynard Smith, J. (1989b). Science, ideology and myth. In *Did Darwin Get It Right?* New York: Chapman and Hall, pp. 39–50.

Maynard Smith, J. (1991). Dinosaur dilemmas. *The New York Review of Books*, 25 April, 5–7.

Maynard Smith, J. (1992). Taking a chance on evolution. *The New York Review of Books*, 14 May, 43–46.

Maynard Smith, J. (1993). Confusion over evolution: an exchange. *The New York Review of Books*, 14 January, 43.

Maynard Smith, J. (1995). *Genes, Memes and Minds*. Review of D. Dennett, *Darwin's Dangerous Idea: Evolution and the Meanings of Life. The New York Review of Books*, 30 November, 46–8.

Maynard Smith, J. (1998). The origin of altruism. Review of E. Sober and D. S. Wilson, *Unto Others. Nature*, **393**, 639–40.

Maynard Smith, J. and G. Price (1973). The logic of animal conflict. *Nature*, **246**, 15–18.

Maynard Smith, J. and M. G. Ridpath (1972). Wife-sharing in the Tasmanian native hen, Tribonyx mortierii: a case of kin selection? *American Naturalist*, **106**, 447–52.

Maynard Smith, J. and E. Szathmary (1995). *The Major Transitions in Evolution*. Oxford: W. H. Freeman.

Maynard Smith, J. and N. Warren (1982). Models of cultural and genetic change. *Evolution*, **36**, 620–7.

Mayr, E. (1963). *Animal species and evolution*. Cambridge, MA: Harvard University Press.

Mayr, E. (1975). The unity of the genotype. *Biologisches Zentralblatt*, **94**, 377–588.

Mayr, E. (1976). The evolution of living systems. In E. Mayr, *Evolution and the Diversity of Life: Selected Essays*. Cambridge, MA: Belknap Press. Original publication 1964.

Mayr, E. (1980). Prologue: some thoughts on the history of the evolutionary synthesis.

In E. Mayr and W. B. Provine (eds), *The Evolutionary Synthesis*. Cambridge, MA: Harvard University Press, pp. 1–48.

Mayr, E. (1982). *The Growth of Biological Thought*. Cambridge, MA: The Belknap Press of Harvard University Press.

Mayr, E. (1983). How to carry out the adaptationist program. *American Naturalist*, **121** (3), 324–34.

Mayr, E. (1984). 1983 Preface to The Unity of the genotype. In R. Brandon and R. Burian (eds), *Genes, Organisms, Populations*. Cambridge, MA: MIT Press, 1984, pp. 69–70.

Mayr, E. (1991). *One Long Argument: Charles Darwin and the Genesis of Modern Evolutionary Thought*. Harmondsworth, England: Penguin Books.

Mayr, E. (1997). *This Is Biology*. Cambridge, MA: Harvard University Press.

Mazur, A. (1981). Media coverage and public opinion on scientific controversies. *Journal of Communication*, Spring, 106–15.

Maxwell, M. (1990). *The Sociobiological Imagination*. Albany: SUNY Press.

McGuire, T. R. and J. Hirsch (1977). General intelligence (g) and heritability (H, h). In F. Weizman and I. C. Uzgiris (eds), *The structuring of experience*. New York: Plenum Press.

Mead, M. (1928). *Coming of Age in Samoa*. New York: Morrow.

Mead, M. (1971). Innate behavior and building new cultures. In J. F. Eisenberg and W. S. Dillon (eds), *Man and Beast*. Washington, D.C.: Smithsonian Institution Press, pp. 369–81.

Medawar, P. (1963). Is the scientific paper a fraud? *The Listener*, 12 September, 377–8.

Medawar, P. (1969). *Induction and Intuition in Scientific Thought*. Philadelphia: American Philosophical Society; London: Methuen.

Medawar, P. B. (1974). On inequality. *New Statesman*, 8 February, 184–5.

Medawar, P. B. (1976). Does ethology throw any light on human behaviour? In P. P. G. Bateson and R. A. Hinde (eds), *Growing Points in Ethology*. Cambridge: Cambridge University Press, pp. 497–506.

Medawar, P. B. (1977a). Unnatural science. *The New York Review of Books*, 3 February, 13–18.

Medawar, P. B. (1977b). Reply. *The New York Review of Books*, 31 March, 36.

Medawar, P. B. (1977c). Reply to Miller and Beckwith. Letter. *The New York Review of Books*, March 31, 37.

Medawar, P. B. (1981a). Back to evolution. *The New York Review of Books*, 19 February, 34–6.

Medawar, P. B. (1981b). Stretch genes. *The New York Review of Books*, 16 July, 45–8.

Medawar, P. B. (1982). *Pluto's Republic*. Oxford: Oxford University Press.

Medawar, P. B. and J. S. Medawar (1977). *The Life Sciences*. New York: Harper & Row.

Mermin, D. (1996). What's wrong with this sustaining myth? Review of Collins and Pinch, *The Golem. Physics Today*, March, 11, 13.

Merton, R. K. (1942/1973). The Normative Structure of Science. In R. K. Merton, *The Sociology of Science*. Chicago: The University of Chicago Press, 1973, pp. 267–78.

Meselson, M. (1981). Bicentennial address. *Bulletin of the American Academy of Arts and Sciences*, **35**, 24–9.

Midgley, M. (1978). *Beast and Man*. Ithaca, NY: Cornell University Press.

Midgley, M. (1979). Gene-juggling. *Philosophy*, **54**, 439–58. Reprinted in A. Montagu (ed.), *Sociobiology Examined*, 108–34. Oxford and New York: Oxford University Press, 1980.

Midgley, M. (1980). Rival fatalisms: The hollowness of the sociobiology debate. In A. Montagu (ed.), *Sociobiology Examined*, 15–38. Oxford and New York: Oxford University Press.

Miele, F. (1995). Darwin's dangerous disciple. An interview with Richard Dawkins. *The Skeptic*, **3** (4), 80–5.

Miele, F. (1998). The Ionian instauration. An interview with E. O. Wilson. *The Skeptic*, **6** (1), 76–85.

Milgram, S. (1974). *Obedience to Authority*. New York: Harper & Row.

Milkman, R. (1977). Molecular evolution. *Evolution*, **31**, 456–7.

Miller, L. G. (1978). Philosophy, dichotomies, and sociobiology. In A. Caplan (ed.), *The Sociobiology Debate*. New York: Harper & Row, pp. 319–24.

Miller, L. and J. Beckwith (1977). Letter. *The New York Review of Books*, 31 March, 36–37.

Monod, J. (1969). From biology to ethics. In J. Monod, *Occasional Papers of the Salk Institute of Biology*, Vol. I, October, 1–22.

Montagu, A. (1965). *The Human Revolution*. Cleveland: The World Publishing Company.

Montagu, A. (ed.) (1968). *Man and Aggression*. Oxford and New York: Oxford University Press.

Montagu, A. (1976). *The Nature of Human Aggression*. Oxford and New York: Oxford University Press.

Montagu, A. (ed.) (1978). *Learning Non-Aggression*. Oxford and New York: Oxford University Press.

Montagu, A. (ed.) (1980). *Sociobiology Examined*. Oxford and New York: Oxford University Press.

Morris, D. (1967). *The Naked Ape*. London: Jonathan Cape.

Mulkay, M. and G. N. Gilbert (1982). Accounting for error. *Sociology*, **16**, 165–83.

Murray, C. (1984). *Losing Ground: American Social Policy 1950–1980*. New York: Basic Books.

Myers, G. (1990). *Writing Biology*. Madison, WI: University of Wisconsin Press.

Myers, G. (1993). Making enemies. How Gould and Lewontin criticize. In J. Selzer (ed.), *Understanding Scientific Prose*. Madison, WI: University of Wisconsin Press, pp. 256–73.

Myers, D. (2000). *Exploring Social Psychology*, 2nd edition. New York: McGraw-Hill.

Nabi, I. (1980). On evolution and the English sonnet: A satyrical comment on the reductionist theory of Edward O. Wilson and Co. *Science and Nature*, no. 3, 70–4.

Nabi, I. (1981a). On the tendencies of motion. *Science and Nature*, no. 4, 62–6.

Nabi, I. (1981b). Ethics of genes. *Nature*, **290**, 183.

Nabi, I. (1981c). It wasn't me. Letter. *Nature*, **291**, 374.

Nelkin, D. and M. S. Lindee (1995). *The DNA Mystique*. New York: Freeman.

Nisbett, R. and L. Ross (1980). *Human Inference: Strategies and Shortcomings of Social Judgment*. Englewood Cliffs, NJ: Prentice-Hall.

O'Donald, P. (1982). The concept of fitness in population genetics and sociobiology. In King's College Sociobiology Group (ed.), *Current Problems in Sociobiology*. Cambridge: Cambridge University Press, pp. 65–85.

Orgel, L. E. (1979). Selection in vitro. *Proceedings of the Royal Society of London*, B **205**, 435–442.

Orgel, L. E. and F. H. C. Crick (1980). Selfish DNA; The ultimate parasite. *Nature*, **284**, 604–7.

Oster, G. F. and E. O. Wilson (1978). *Caste and Ecology in the Social Insects*. Princeton, NJ: Princeton University Press.

Page, E. B. (1972). Behavior and heredity. Resolution. *American Psychologist*, 27 (July), 660–1.

Papineau, D. (1995). Natural selections. Review, *Reinventing Darwin, River out of Eden, Darwin's Dangerous Idea*. *The New York Times*, 14 May, Section 7 Book Review, 13.

Parker, G. A. (1978). Selfish genes, evolutionary games, and the adaptiveness of behavior. Review article. *Nature*, **274**, 849–55.

Parker, G. A. (1984). Evolutionarily stable strategies. In J. Krebs and N. B. Davies (eds), *Behavioural Ecology*, 2nd edition. Oxford: Blackwell Scientific Publications, pp. 30–61.

Parker, G. and J. Maynard Smith (1990). Optimality theory in evolutionary biology. *Nature*, **348**, 27–33.

Pennisi, E. (1998). A genomic battle of the sexes. *Science*, **281**, 1984–5.

Pinker, S. (1994). *The Language Instinct*. New York: HarperCollins.

Pinker, S. (1995). Language is a human instinct. In J. Brockman (ed.), *The Third Culture*. New York: Simon and Schuster, pp. 223–36.

Pinker, S. (1997). *How the Mind Works*. New York: W. W. Norton.

Planck, M. (1949). *Scientific Autobiography* (F. Gaynor, trans). New York: Philosophical Library.

Popper, K. R. (1945). *The Open Society and Its Enemies. Vol. II*. London: Routledge and Kegan Paul.

Popper, K. (1974). Darwinism as a metaphysical research program. In P. Schilpp (ed.), *The Philosophy of Karl Popper*. LaSalle, IL: Open Court.

Popper, K. (1976). *An Intellectual Autobiography: Unended Quest*. Glasgow: William Collins.

Popper, K. (1978). Natural selection and the emergence of mind. *Dialectica* **32**, 339–55.

Popper, K. (1980). Evolution. Letter. *New Scientist*, Aug. 21, 611.

Price, G. R. (1970). Selection and covariance. *Nature*, **227**, 520–1.

Price, G. R. (1972). Extension of covariance selection mathematics. *Annals of Human Genetics*, **35**, 485–90.

Proshansky, H. M. (1973). Behavior and heredity. Statement by the Society for the Psychological Study of Social Issues. *American Psychologist*, **28** (July), 620–1.

Provine, W. P. (1973). Geneticists and the biology of race crossing. *Science*, **182**, 790–6.

Queller, D. (1995). The spaniels of St. Marx and the Panglossian paradox: a critique of a rhetorical programme. *Quarterly Review of Biology*, **70** (4), 485–9.

Raup, D., S. J. Gould, T. J. M. Schopf, and D. S. Simberloff (1973). Stochastic models of phylogeny and the evolution of diversity. *Journal of Geology*, **81**, 525–42.

Ravitch, D. (1982). IQ. *Commentary*, February, 66–70.

Rensberger, B. (1975a). Updating Darwin on behavior. *The New York Times*, May 28, 1, 52.

Rensberger, B. (1975b). The politics in a debate about sociobiology. *The New York Times*, Sunday, 9 November, 16 E.

Rensberger, B. (1983). Becoming human. The nature–nurture debate II. *Science*, **83**, 38–46.

Reynolds, V. (1976, 1980). *The Biology of Human Action*. Oxford and San Francisco: W. H. Freeman.

Reynolds, V. (1980). Sociobiology and the idea of primordial discrimination. *Ethnic and Racial Studies*, **3** (3), 303–15.

Richardson, G. Editorial. *Harvard Medical Bulletin* November/December.

Richerson, P. and R. Boyd (1978). A dual inheritance model of the human evolutionary process. I. Basic postulates and a simple model. *Journal of Social and Biological Structures*, **1**, 127–54.

M. H. Robinson and L. Tiger (eds) (1991). *Man and Beast Revisited*. Washington, D.C.: Smithsonian Institution Press.

Roes, F. (1997). An interview with Richard Dawkins. *Human Ethology Bulletin*, **12** (1), 1–3.

Rorty, R. (1998). Against unity. *The Wilson Quarterly*, Winter, 28–38.

Rose, H. (1996) 'My enemy's enemy is—only perhaps—my friend.' *Social Text*, 1/2 (Spring/Summer), 61–80.

Rose, H. and S. Rose (eds) (1976). *The Radicalization of Science*. London and Basingstoke: Macmillan.

Rose, H. and S. Rose (1982). On opposition to reductionism. In Rose, S. (ed.), *Against Biological Determinism*. London and New York: Allison and Busby.

Rose, M. R. and G. V. Lauder (1996). *Adaptation*. San Diego: Academic Press.

Rose, S. (1978). Pre-Copernican sociobiology? *New Scientist*, **80**, 45–6.

Rose, S. (1979). 'It's only human nature': the sociobiologist's fairyland. *Race and Class*, **20** (3). Reprinted in A. Montagu (ed.), *Sociobiology Examined*. Oxford and New York: Oxford University Press, pp. 158–70.

Rose, S. (1981a). Genes and race. Letter. *Nature*, **289**, 335.

Rose, S. (1981b). Genes and free will. Letter. *Nature*, **290**, 356.

Rose, S. (ed.) (1982a). *Against Biological Determinism*. London and New York: Allison and Busby.

Rose, S. (ed.) (1982b). *Toward a Liberatory Biology*. London and New York: Allison and Busby.

Rose, S. (1986). The limits to science. In S. Rose and L. Appignanesi (eds), *Science and Beyond*. Oxford: Basil Blackwell, pp. 26–36.

Rose, S. (1995). The rise of neurogenetic determinism. *Nature*, **373**, 381–2.

Rose, S. (1998). *Lifelines*. Oxford: Oxford University Press.

Rose, S. and L. Appignanesi (eds) (1986). *Science and Beyond*. Oxford: Basil Blackwell.

Rosenberg, A. (1986). Peer commentary on P. Kitcher's Precis of *Vaulting Ambition*. *Behavior and Brain Sciences*, **10** (1), 80–2.

Ross, A. (1996). *The Science Wars*. Durham, NC: Duke University Press.

Ruse, M. (1979, 1985). *Sociobiology: Sense or Nonsense?* (First and second editions). Dordrecht, Holland: Reidel.

Ruse, M. (1994). Review of Gross and Levitt's *Higher Superstition*. *The Sciences*, **34** (November/December), 39–44.

Ruse, M. and E. O. Wilson (1985). The evolution of ethics. *New Scientist*, 17 October, 50–3.

Ruse, M. and E. O. Wilson (1986). Moral philosophy as applied science. *Philosophy*, **61**, 173–192.

Russett, C. (1966). *The Concept of Equilibrium in American Social Thought*. New Haven: Yale University Press.

Ruyle, E. E. (1973). Genetic and cultural pools: Some suggestions for a unified theory of biocultural evolution. *Human Ecology*, **1**, 201–15.

Sagan, C. (1977). *The Dragons of Eden*. New York: Random House.

Sagan, C. (1996). *The Demon-Haunted World: Science as a Candle in the Dark*. New York: Random House.

Sahlins, M. (1976). *The Use and Abuse of Biology*. Ann Arbor: University of Michigan Press.

Salzman, F. (1979). The sociobiology controversy continues. *Science for the People*, March/April.

Samelson, F. (1978). From 'race psychology' to 'studies in prejudice'. *Journal of the History of the Behavioral Sciences*, **14**, 265–78.

Samelson, F. (1979). Putting psychology on the map: ideology and intelligence testing. In Allan Buss (ed.), *Psychology in Social Context*. New York: Irvington Publishers, pp. 103–68.

Samelson, F. (1982). Intelligence of man. *Science*, **215**, 656–7.

Samelson, F. (1992). Rescuing the reputation of Sir Cyril Burt. *Journal of the Behavioral Sciences*, **28**, July, 221–33.

Savage-Rumbaugh, S. and R. Lewin (1994). *Kanzi: The Ape on the Brink of the Human Mind*. New York: John Wiley.

Savage-Rumbaugh, S., J. Murphy, R. Seveik, D. Brakke, S. Williams, and D. Rumbaugh (1993). Language Comprehension in the Ape and Child. *Monographs of the Society for Research in Child Development*, **58**. Chicago: University of Chicago Press.

Scarr-Salapatek, S. (1971). Unknowns in the IQ equation. *Science*, **174**, 1223–8.

Schiff, M. and R. Lewontin (1986). *Education and Class: The Irrelevance of IQ Genetic Studies*. Oxford: Clarendon Press.

Schmaus, W., U. Segerstråle, and D. Jesseph (1992). 'The hard program in the sociology of science. A manifesto.' *Social Epistemology*, **6** (3), 243–65.

Science as Ideology Group of the British Society for Social Responsibility in Science (1976a). The new synthesis is an old story. *New Scientist*, 13 May, 346–8.

Science as Ideology Group of the British Society for Social Responsibility in Science (1976b). Sociobiology: a reply. Letter. *Nature*, **261**, 13 May, 96.

Seabright, P. (1981). Review of *Genes, Mind and Culture. The New Republic*, 2 December, 26–31.

Searle, J. (1990) The storm over the university. *The New York Review of Books*, 6 December, 34–42.

Sebeok, T. (1991). A personal note. In M. H. Robinson and L. Tiger (eds), *Man and Beast Revisited*. Washington, D.C.: Smithsonian Institution Press, pp. ix–xiii.

Segal, N. L., G. E. Weisfeld, and C. C. Weisfeld (1997). *Uniting Psychology and Biology*. Washington, D.C.: American Psychological Association.

Seger, J. (1981). Social scientists and sociobiologists get their lines crossed. *Nature*, **291**, 690.

Seger, J. and P. Harvey (1980). The evolution of the genetical theory of social behaviour. *New Scientist*, **87** (1208), 50–1.

Segerstråle, U. (1983). Whose truth shall prevail? Moral and scientific interests in the sociobiology controversy. Ph.D. thesis in sociology. Harvard University (unpublished).

Segerstråle, U. (1986). Colleagues in conflict: An 'in vivo' analysis of the sociobiology controversy. *Biology and Philosophy*, **1** (1), 53–87.

Segerstråle, U. (1987). Scientific controversy as moral/political discourse. *Contemporary Sociology*, **16** (3), 544–7.

Segerstråle, U. (1989). Bringing the scientist back in. *EASST Newsletter*, **9** (3/4), 5–7.

Segerstråle, U. (1989). The (re)colonization of science by the life-world: problems and prospects. In H. Haferkamp (ed.), *Social Structure and Culture*. Berlin and New York: De Gruyter.

Segerstråle, U. (1990a). The sociobiology of conflict and the conflict about sociobiology. In Vincent Falger *et al.* (eds), *Sociobiology and Conflict: Evolutionary Perspectives on Group Behaviour*. London: Chapman and Hall.

Segerstråle, U. (1990b). Negotiating 'sound science': Expert disagreement about release of genetically engineered organisms. *Politics and the Life Sciences*, **8**, 221–31.

Segerstråle, U. (1990c). Taboos and the distortion of academic discourse: a meta-critique of academic reasoning. In A. Elzinga *et al.* (eds), *In Science We Trust?: Moral and Political Issues of Science in Society*. Lund: Lund University Press.

Segerstråle, U. (1990d). Scouting for fraud and error: A new form of scientific work? Paper presented at the XIIth International Congress of Sociology, Madrid, 7–14 July 1990. (Abstract in *Sociological Abstracts*, December 1990.)

Segerstråle, U. (1992). Reductionism, 'bad science' and politics: A critique of anti-reductionist reasoning, *Politics and the Life Sciences*, **11** (2), 199–214.

Segerstråle, U. (1993). Bringing the scientist back in. In T. Brante, S. Fuller, and W. Lynch (eds), *Controversial Science*, 57–84. Albany: SUNY Press.

Segerstråle, U. (1994). Science by worst cases. Review of Collins and Pinch, *The Golem: What Everyone Should Know About Science*. *Science*, **263**, 837–8.

Segerstråle, U. (1995). Good to the last drop: Millikan stories as 'canned' pedagogy.' *Science and Engineering Ethics*, **1** (3), 197–214.

Segerstråle, U. (1997). Understanding the Science Wars. Paper presented at the Annual Meeting of the American Sociological Association, Toronto, 9–13 August.

Segerstråle, U. (1999). Anti-antiscience: a phenomenon in search of an explanation. Part I and II. In U. Segerstrale (ed.), *Beyond the Science Wars: The Missing Discourse about Science and Society*. Albany: SUNY Press.

Segerstråle, U. and P. Molnar (eds) (1997). *Nonverbal Communication: Where Nature Meets Culture*. Mahwah, NJ: Lawrence Erlbaum Associates.

Selzer, J. (ed.) (1993). *Understanding Scientific Prose*. Madison, WI: University of Wisconsin Press.

Shapere, D. (1986). External and internal factors in the development of science. *Science and Technology Studies*, **4** (1).

Shapin, S. (1979). Homo phrenologicus: Anthropological perspectives on an historical problem. In B. Barnes and S. Shapin (eds), *Natural Order: Historical Studies of Scientific Culture*, 41–67.

Shapin, S. and S. Schaffer (1985). *Leviathan and the Air-Pump: Hobbes, Boyle and the Experimental Life*. Princeton, NJ: Princeton University Press.

Sheehan, T. (1980). Paris: Moses and Polytheism. In A. Montagu (ed.), *Sociobiology Examined*. Oxford and New York: Oxford University Press, pp. 342–55.

Sherman, P. W., H. K. Reeve and D. W. Pfennig (1997). Recognition systems. In J. R. Krebs and N. B. Davies, *Behavioural Ecology*. 4th edn. Oxford: Blackwell Scientific Publications, pp. 69–96.

Shermer, M. (1996a). An interview with Stephen Jay Gould. *The Skeptic*, **4** (1), 86–90.

Shermer, M. (1996b). Gould's dangerous idea. *The Skeptic*, **4** (1), 90–5.

Shils, E. (1985). Preface to B. Davis, *Storm over Biology: Essays on Science, Sentiment, and Public Policy*. Buffalo, NY: Prometheus Books.

Shweder, R. A. (1999). Humans really are different. Review, *Three Seductive Ideas. Science*, **283**, 798–9.

Silverman, I. (1995a). Sociobiology and sociopolitics. *Social Science Information* **34** (1), 79–86.

Silverman, I. (1995b). Rejoinders to Falger and Salter. *Social Science Information* **34** (2), 347–8.

Silverman, I. (1997). Changing the world: Comments on E. O. Wilson's and Vincent Sarich's addresses at the 1996 HBES conference. *Letter to the editor. Human Behavior and Evolution Society Newsletter*, **6** (1), Spring, 9–10.

Silverman, I. (1998). Can behavioral science change society? In V. S. E. Falger, P. Meyer, and J. M. G. van der Dennen, *Sociobiology and Politics. Research in Biopolitics*, **6**. Stamford, CT and London: JAI Press, pp. 275–81.

Simberloff, D. (1980a). A succession of paradigms in ecology: Essentialism to materialism and probabilism. *Synthese*, **43**, 3–39.

Simberloff, D. (1980b). Reply. *Synthese*, **43**, 79–93.

Simpson, G. G. (1981). Exhibit dismay. *Nature*, **290**, 286.

Singer, P. (1981). *The Expanding Circle: Ethics and Sociobiology*. New York: Farrar, Straus & Giroux.

Skinner, B. R. (1981). Selection by consequences. *Science*, **213**, 501–4.

Smith, E. A. (1994). Semantics, theory, and methodological individualism in the group-selection controversy. *Behavioral and Brain Sciences*, **17** (4), 636–7.

Snyderman, M. and R. Herrnstein (1983). Intelligence tests and the Immigration Act of 1924. *American Psychologist*, **38**, September, 985–6.

Sober, E. (1980). Holism, individualism and the units of selection. In P. Asquith and R. Giere (eds), *PSA 1980*, vol. 2., Proceedings of the 1980 Biennial Meeting of the Philosophy of Science Association, East Lansing, MI.

Sober, E. (1984). *The Nature of Selection*. Cambridge, MA: MIT Press.

Sober, E. and R. Lewontin (1982). Artifact, cause, and genic selection. *Philosophy of Science*, **49**, 157–80.

Sober, E. and D. S. Wilson (1998a). *Unto Others*. Cambridge, MA: Harvard University Press.

Sober, E. and D. S. Wilson (1998b). The golden rule of group selection. Reply to Trivers review. *The Skeptic*, **6** (4), 83–6.

Sociobiology Study Group of Science for the People (1976a). Sociobiology—another biology determinism. *BioScience*, **26** (3), **182**, 184–6.

Sociobiology Study Group of Science for the People (1976b). Response to E. O. Wilson. *Science for the People*, May.

Sociobiology Study Group of Science for the People (1976c). Minutes. 10 May.

Sokal, A. (1996a). Transgressing the boundaries: Toward a transformative hermeneutics of quantum gravity. *Social Text*, **46–47**, 217–52.

Sokal, A. (1996b). Sokal's response. *Lingua Franca*, **6** (4), 62–4.

Sokal, A. and J. Bricmont (1997). *Impostures Intellectuelles*. Paris: Odile Jacob.

Sokal, A. and J. Bricmont (1998a). *Intellectual Impostures*.

Sokal, A. and J. Bricmont (1998b). *Fashionable Nonsense*. New York: Picador.

Soyfer, V. N. (1995). *Lysenko and the Tragedy of Soviet Science*. New Brunswick, NJ: Rutgers University Press.

Stagner, R. (1973). Behavior and heredity comment slightly off target. *American Psychologist*, **28** (1), 84–5.

Stebbins, L. and Ayala, F. (1981). Is a new evolutionary synthesis necessary? *Science*, **213**, 967–71.

Steen, W. van der and B. Voorzanger (1984). Sociobiology in perspective. *Journal of Evolution*, **13**, 25–32.

Stent, G. S. (1977). You can take ethics out of altruism but you can't take the altruism out of ethics. *Hastings Center Report*, **7**, 33–6.

Stent, G. S. (1978). *Paradoxes of Progress*. San Francisco: W. H. Freeman.

Stent G. S. (1980). Introduction. In G. S. Stent (ed.), *Morality as a Biological Phenomenon* (Dahlem Workshop, Berlin 1977). Berkeley and Los Angeles: University of California Press.

Sterelny, K. and P. Kitcher (1988). The return of the gene. *Journal of Philosophy*, **85** (7), 339–61.

Sternberg, R. J. and E. L. Grigoenko (1997). *Intelligence, Heredity and Environment*. Cambridge: Cambridge University Press.

Sutherland, S. (1981). IQ gladiators in separate combat. *Nature*, **290**, 636–7.

Symons, D. (1989). A critique of Darwinian anthropology. *Ethology and Sociobiology*, **10**, 131–44.

Symons, D. (1992). On the use and misuse of Darwinism. In J. Barkow *et al.* (eds), *The Adapted Mind*. New York: Oxford University Press, pp. 137–59.

Tagliabue, J. (1996). The Pope pronounces evolution fit. *The New York Times*, 27 October, Section 4, 2.

Tajfel, H. (ed.) (1978). *Differentiation Between Social Groups*. London: Academic Press.

Tennov, D. (1998). The public image of sociobiology and evolution. In V. Falger *et al.* (eds), *Sociobiology and Politics*, Research in Biopolitics, Vol. 6, pp. 231–7. Stamford, CT: JAI Press.

Thoday, J. R. (1972). Genetics and educability. *Journal of Biological Education*, **6**, 323–9.

Thoday, J. M. (1981). Probity in science: The case of Cyril Burt. *Nature*, **291** 517.

Thomas, L. (1981). Debating the unknowable. *The Atlantic Monthly*, July, 49–52.

Thompson, P. (1983). Tempo and mode in evolution: punctuated equilibrium and the modern synthetic theory. *Philosophy of Science*, **50**, 432–52.

Tiger, L. (1969). *Men in Groups*. New York: Random House.

Tiger, L. (1996). My life in the human nature wars. *Wilson Quarterly*, Winter, 14–25.

Tiger, L. and R. Fox (1971). *The Imperial Animal*. New York: Holt, Rinehart, Winston.

Tiger, L. and R. Fox (1973). Animal, venerable, imperial: an adventure story. *The Columbia Forum*, Fall, 26–31.

Tiger, L. and M. H. Robinson (1991). Introduction. In Robinson, M. H. and L. Tiger (eds), *Man and Beast Revisited*. Washington and London: Smithsonian Institution Press, xvii-xxiii.

Timpanaro, S. (1974). Considerations on materialism. *New Left Review*, **85**, 3–22.

Tinbergen, N. (1963). On aims and methods of ethology. *Zeitschrift für Tierpsychologie*, **20**, 410, 433.

Tinbergen, N. (1968). On war and peace in animals and man. *Science*, **160**, 1411–18.

Tinbergen, N. (1972). Functional ethology and the human sciences (Croonian lecture). *Proceedings of the Royal Society of London*, **182 B**, 385–410.

Tinbergen, N. (1978). Use and misuse in evolutionary perspective. In W. Barlow (ed.), *More Talk of Alexander*. London: Gollancz, pp. 218–36.

Todorov, T. (1998). The surrender to nature. Review of Consilience. *New Republic*. 27 April, 29–33.

Tomkow, T. and R. Martin (1982). Is intelligence for real? An exchange. *The New York Review of Books*. 4 February, 40.

Trivers, R. L. (1971). The evolution of reciprocal altruism. *Quarterly Review of Biology*, **46**, 35–57.

Trivers, R. L. (1974). Parent-offspring conflict. *American Zoologist*, **14**, 249–64.

Trivers, R. L. (1976). Foreword to *The Selfish Gene*. Oxford: Oxford University Press, pp. v–vii.

Trivers, R. L. (1985). *Social Evolution*. Menlo Park, CA: Benjamin Cummings.

Trivers, R. L. (1997). Genetic basis of intrapsychic conflict. In N. L. Segal, G. E. Weisfeld, and C. C. Weisfeld (eds), *Uniting Psychology and Biology*. Washington, D.C.: American Psychological Association, pp. 385–95.

Trivers, R. L. (1998). As they would do to you. Review of E. Sober and D. S. Wilson, *Unto Others*. *The Skeptic*, **6** (4), 81–3.

Trivers, R. L. (1998). Think for yourself. Trivers replies to Sober and Wilson. *The Skeptic*, **6** (4), 86–7.

Trivers, R. L. and H. Hare (1976). Haplodiploidy and the evolution of the social insects. *Science*, **191**, 249–63.

Turner, J. R. G. (1981). Apes or angels? Letter. *Nature*, **291**, 374.

Tversky, A. and D. Kahneman (1974). Judgment under uncertainty: heuristics and biases. *Science*, **183**, 1124–31.

Van den Berghe, P. L. (1980). Sociobiology: Several views. *BioScience*, **31**, 406.

Van Valen, L. M. (1981). Nabi—a life. *Nature*, **293**, 422.

Varela, F. (1995). The emergent self. In J. Brockman (ed.), *The Third Culture*. New York: Simon and Schuster, pp. 209–16.

Vetta, A. (1973). Amendment to the 'Resolution on Scientific Freedom Regarding Human Behavior and Heredity'. *American Psychologist*, **28** (May), 444.

Vrba, E. and N. Eldredge (1984). Individuals, hierarchies and processes: towards a more complete evolutionary theory. *Paleobiology*, **10**, 146–71.

Wade, M. J. (1977). Review of *The Selfish Gene*. *Evolution*, **220**, 221.

Wade, N. (1976). Sociobiology: Troubled birth for new discipline. *Science*, **191**, 1151–5.

Wade, M. (1978). A critical review of the models of group selection. *Quarterly Review of Biology*, **53**, 101–14.

Waddington, C. H. (1960). *The Ethical Animal*. New York: George Allen and Unwin.

Waddington, C. H. (1961). The human evolutionary system. In M. Banton (ed.), *Darwinism and the Study of Society*. London: Tavistock, pp. 63–81.

Waddington, C. H. (1975). Mindless societies. *The New York Review of Books*, 7 August, 30–2.

Wald, G. (1978). The human condition. In M. S. Gregory, A. Silvers, and D. Sutch (eds), *Sociobiology and Human Nature*. San Francisco: Jossey Bass, pp. 53–74.

Walgate, R. (1978). Race and IQ: Jensen retains fellowship. *Science*, **191**, 1033–5.

Walsh, J. (1996). Science for the people: Comes the evolution. *Science*, **191**, 1033–5.

Washburn, S. L. (1976). Sociobiology. *Anthropology Newsletter*, **18** (3), 3.

Washburn, S. L. (1978a). Animal behavior and social anthropology. In M. S. Gregory, A. Silvers, and D. Sutch (eds), *Sociobiology and Human Nature*. San Francisco: Jossey Bass, pp. 53–74.

Washburn, S. L. (1978b). Human behavior and the behavior of others. *American*

Psychologist. **33** (5), May. Reprinted in A. Montagu (ed.), *Sociobiology Examined.* Oxford and New York: Oxford University Press, pp. 254–82.

Washburn, S. L., P. C. Jay, and B. Lancaster (1965). Field studies of Old World monkeys and apes. *Science*, **150**, 1541–7.

Wells, P. A. (1987). Kin recognition in humans. In D. J. C. Fletcher and C. D. Michener (eds), *Kin Recognition in Animals.* New York: John Wiley, pp. 395–415.

Werskey, P. G. (1978). *The Visible College: A Study of Left-Wing Scientists in Britain, 1918–1939.* New York: Holt, Rinehart, Winston.

West-Eberhard, M. J. (1975). The evolution of social behavior by kin selection. *Quarterly Review of Biology*, **50**, 1–33.

West-Eberhard, M. J. (1976). Born: Sociobiology. *Quarterly Review of Biology*, **51**, 89–92.

Wheeler, D. (1996). An eclectic biologist argues that humans are not evolution's most important result; bacteria are. *The Chronicle of Higher Education*, 6 September. A23–4.

White, E. (ed.) (1981). *Sociobiology and Human Politics.* Philadelphia, PA: Temple University Press.

Wiegele, T. (ed.) (1979). *Biopolitics: Search for a More Humane Political Science.* Boulder, CO: Westview Press.

Wilkie, T. (1993). *Perilous Knowledge: The Human Genome Project and Its Implications.* Berkeley, CA: University of California Press.

Williams, B. (1976). Review, *The Selfish Gene. New Scientist*, 4 November, 291.

Williams, B. (1985). *Ethics and the Limits of Philosophy.* London: Fontana Press/Collins.

Williams G. C. (1966). *Adaptation and Natural Selection.* Princeton, NJ: Princeton University Press.

Williams G. C. (ed.) (1971). *Group Selection.* Chicago: Aldine Atherton.

Williams G. C. (1992). *Natural Selection: Domains, Levels and Challenges.* Oxford: Oxford University Press.

Williams, G. C. (1995). A package of information. In J. Brockman (ed.), *The Third Culture.* New York: Simon and Schuster, pp. 38–47.

Williams, G. C. and D. C. Williams (1957). Natural selection of individually harmful social adaptations among sibs with special reference to social insects. *Evolution*, **11**, 32–9.

Wilson, D. S. (1980). *The Natural Selection of Populations and Communities.* Menlo Park, CA: Benjamin Cummings.

Wilson, D. S. (1995). Holding a mirror to human evolutionary psychology. Review of *The Moral Animal. Quarterly Review of Biology*, **70** (1), 53–6.

Wilson, D. S. and E. Sober (1994). Reintroducing group selection to the human behavioral sciences. *Behavioral and Brain Sciences*, **17** (4), 585–654.

Wilson, E. O. (1971a). *The Insect Societies.* Cambridge, MA: Harvard University Press.

Wilson, E. O. (1971b). The prospects for a unified sociobiology. *American Scientist*, **59**, 400–3.

Wilson, E. O. (1971c). Competitive and aggresssive behavior. In J. F. Eisenberg and W. S. Dillon (eds), *Man and Beast: Comparative Social Behavior*. Washington, D.C.: Smithsonian Institution Press, pp. 181–217.

Wilson, E. O. (1975a). *Sociobiology: The New Synthesis*. Cambridge, MA: Harvard University Press.

Wilson, E. O. (1975b). Human decency is animal. *The New York Times Magazine*, 12 October, 38–50.

Wilson, E. O. (1975c). For sociobiology. *New York Times Review of Books*, 11 December, 60–61.

Wilson, E. O. (1976a). Academic vigilantism and the political significance of socio-biology. *BioScience*, **26**, 183–90.

Wilson, E. O. (1976b). Sociobiology: a new approach to understanding the basis of human nature. *New Scientist*, **70**, 342–4.

Wilson, E. O. (1976c). Author reply to multiple reviews of *Sociobiology*. *Animal Behaviour*, **24** (3), 716–18.

Wilson, E. O. (1977a). The social instinct. *Bulletin of the American Academy for Arts and Sciences*, **30** (1), 11–25.

Wilson, E. O. (1977b). Letter. *The New York Review of Books*, 31 March, 36.

Wilson, E. O. (1977c). Biology and the social sciences. *Daedalus*, **106** (4), 127–40.

Wilson, E. O. (1978a). *On Human Nature*. Cambridge, MA: Harvard University Press.

Wilson, E. O. (1978b). The attempt to suppress human behavioral genetics. *Journal of General Education*, **29**, 277–87.

Wilson, E. O. (1978c). Foreword. In A. Caplan (ed.), *The Sociobiology Debate*. New York: Harper & Row.

Wilson, E. O. (1978d). Introduction: What is sociobiology? In M. S. Gregory, A. Silvers, and D. Sutch (eds), *Sociobiology and Human Nature*. San Francisco: Jossey-Bass.

Wilson, E. O. (1979). *On Human Nature*. New York: Bantam Books.

Wilson, E. O. (1980a). The relation of science to theology. *Zygon*, **15**, 425–34.

Wilson, E. O. (1980b). A consideration of the genetic foundation of human behavior. In G. W. Barlow and J. Silverberg (eds), *Sociobiology: Beyond Nature/Nurture?* AAAS Selected Symposium 35, 295–306. Boulder, CO: Westview Press.

Wilson, E. O. (1980c). Caste and division of labor in leaf-cutter ants (Hymenoptera: Formicidae: Atta) I and II. *Behavioral Ecology and Sociobiology*, **7**, 143–56, 157–65.

Wilson, E. O. (1980d). Comparative social theory. The Tanner lecture on human values, University of Michigan 1979. In S. M. McMurrin (ed.), *The Tanner Lectures on Human Values*. Salt Lake City: University of Utah Press/ Cambridge: Cambridge University Press, pp. 48–73.

Wilson, E. O. (1981a). Genes and racism. *Nature*, **289**, 627.

Wilson, E. O. (1981b). Who is Nabi? *Nature*, **290**, 623.

Wilson, E. O. (1982). Sociobiology, individuality, and ethics: A response. *Perspectives in Biology and Medicine*, **26** (Autumn).

Wilson, E. O. (1984). *Biophilia*. Cambridge, MA: Harvard University Press.

Wilson, E. O. (1991a). Sociobiology and the test of time. In M. H. Robinson and L. Tiger (eds), *Man and Beast Revisited*. Washington, D.C.: Smithsonian Institution Press, pp. 77–80.

Wilson, E. O. (1991b). Scientific humanism and religion. *Free Inquiry*, **11** (2), 20–3.

Wilson, E. O. (1992). *The Diversity of Life*. Cambridge, MA: Belknap Press of Harvard University Press.

Wilson, E. O. (1994). *Naturalist*. Washington, D.C.: Island Press.

Wilson, E. O. (1995). Science and ideology. *Academic Questions*, **8** (3), 73–81.

Wilson, E. O. (1998a). *Consilience: The Unity of Knowledge*. New York: Alfred Knopf.

Wilson, E. O. (1998b). Resuming the Enlightenment quest. *The Wilson Quarterly*, Winter, 16–27.

Wilson, E. O. (1998c). The biological basis of morality. *The Atlantic Monthly*, April, 53–70.

Wilson, E. O. and M. Harris (1978). The envelope and the twig. *The Sciences*, **18**, 10–15, 27.

Winsor, D. (1993). Constricting scientific knowledge in Gould and Lewontin's 'The Spandrels of San Marco'. In J. Selzer (ed.), *Understanding Scientific Prose*. Madison, WI: University of Wisconsin Press, pp. 127–43.

Wolpert, L. (1993). *The Unnatural Nature of Science*. Cambridge, MA: Harvard University Press.

Wrangham, R. (1980). Sociobiology: Modification without dissent. *Biological Journal of the Linnean Society*, **13**, 171–77.

Wright, S. (1980). Genic and organismic selection. *Evolution*, **34** (5), 825–43.

Wright, R. (1994). *The Moral Animal*. New York: Random House.

Wynne-Edwards, V. C. (1962). *Animal Dispersion in Relation to Social Behaviour*. Edinburgh: Oliver & Boyd.

Wynne-Edwards, V. C. (1963). Intergroup selection in the evolution of social systems. *Nature*, **200**, 623–6.

Wynne-Edwards, V. C. (1972). Ecology and the evolution of social ethics. In J. W. S. Pringle (ed.), *Biology and the Human Sciences*. Oxford: Clarendon Press, pp. 49–69.

Wynne-Edwards, V. (1984). Preface to intergroup selection in the evolution of social systems. In R. Brandon and R. Burian (eds), *Genes, Organisms, Populations*. Cambridge, MA: MIT Press, (1984), p. 42.

Wynne-Edwards, V. (1986). *Animal Sociality and Group Selection*. Oxford: Blackwell.

Glossary

This glossary is intended as a quick guide to some terms used in the text.

adaptation A product of evolution, for instance a particular anatomical structure, behavior, or trait that is well-adjusted for fulfilling a certain function in a certain environment. Also: the process of adjustment or modification involved in the production of this structure or behavior.

adaptationism The attempt to study all traits of an organism as if they were adaptations. According to critics (notably Gould and Lewontin), sociobiologists tell 'adaptive stories', in the style of Rudyard Kipling's 'Just-so stories', explaining how a particular trait may have come about through evolution. The critics, in contrast, point to reasons why individual traits may *not* be adaptations (for instance, they may be linked to other traits, they may be the product of allometry, and so on), in this way engaging in what could be termed 'critical' 'Just-so stories'.

allele Alternative form of a gene, for instance a gene resulting in a green or yellow pea phenotype.

allometry Relative growth of a part in relation to an entire organism (if the organism is big, so is typically the part). Allometry is one of the reasons why a part of a body may not require an independent adaptive explanation.

altruism Any behavior that promotes another organism's 'fitness' (number of offspring) at the expense of its own fitness. (Note that 'altruism' is here used in a strictly technical, behavioristic sense, which does not involve motives). A puzzle for Darwinian theory until Hamilton developed the idea of 'inclusive fitness' in 1964.

anti-science Used in the so-called Science Wars by some vocal scientists to label what they perceived as irrational and dangerous claims by postmodernists and constructivists in the humanities and social sciences.

'bad science' A term with both scientific and moral/political connotations, used by critics of sociobiology, behavioral genetics, and IQ research to describe science in these fields. Conversely, sometimes used by the proponents of these same fields to suggest that the *critics'* science, because of their political interests, 'must' be scientifically bad.

Bauplan The Continental theory that pre-existing structural patterns or body plans pose constraints on evolution.

Central Dogma The view associated with Watson and Crick and early molecular biology that the process of protein synthesis goes from DNA to RNA to protein, but never the reverse. (Later it was discovered that in some cases genetic information can flow from RNA to DNA).

cognitive commitments Scientists are typically driven by scientific convictions about such things as the nature of 'good science', acceptable evidence, treatment of error, and the like. These commitments are typically linked to the particular tradition the scientists come from, for instance an experimentalist or a naturalist one.

competition for recognition In science the most coveted reward for a contribution is peer recognition. This is typically given for new information or an approach that opens up a new field of inquiry. But it has to be new. This can explain why scientists are so concerned with matters of priority. I argue that in the sociobiology controversy, the competitive spirit spread beyond science to the moral realm as well, and that many of the scientists involved in the controversy were soon pursuing 'moral recognition' as well.

culturalism In this book sometimes used instead of 'environmentalism' to denote an approach that emphasizes the cultural shaping of human nature.

deme A local population of closely related interbreeding organisms, hence the largest population unit that can be analyzed by the simpler models of population genetics.

environmentalism The doctrine, prevailing in academia at the time of the start of the sociobiology controversy, that human behavior is exclusively shaped by the environment or culture. To avoid confusion with the environmental protection movement, better called 'culturalism'.

epigenetic rule A rule describing the process of epigenesis, that is, the chain of developmental processes involved in the interaction between a genotype and its environment resulting in the phenotype. In *Genes, Mind, and Culture* (1981a) and *Promethean Fire* (1983) Lumsden and Wilson suggest that epigenetic rules channel the development of the mind. An example of an epigenetic rule is incest avoidance; the rule in this case would say: don't mate with someone you grew up with. According to Lumsden and Wilson, knowledge about such rules would make it possible to circumvent them by cultural means, if we wished to.

epistemology Dealing with how we acquire 'true' knowledge about the world. Profound epistmological differences exist between the opponents in the sociobiology controversy.

essentialism The attempt to explain human behavior by referring to a human 'essence' or nature, and its biological, psychological, social, or historical shaping. (From an existentialist point of view, such explanations are typically used to exculpate persons from their ultimate responsibility for their actions).

ethology The study of whole patterns of animal behavior in natural environments.

evolutionarily stable strategy (ESS) A pattern of behavior ('strategy') which is 'evolutionarily stable', that is, it will prevail against any alternative behavior pattern when it is the dominant one in the population. Natural selection tends to produce populations of organisms that use an ESS. ESS involves game-theoretical reasoning from economics, applicable to situations where the best outcome for an individual depends on what other individuals do. ESS is associated with Maynard Smith and Price (1973); an early version was Hamilton's 'unbeatable strategy' (1967).

existentialism A philosophical position arguing that humans fundamentally have free choice and therefore responsibility for their actions. An existentalist would not accept an explanation or excuse for a person's action that invokes such things as human nature, psychological idiosyncracies, or social or situational factors—anything that would seem to limit the exercise of free will.

fitness In biology, 'fitness' refers to the number of offspring produced by an organism. (Involves no evaluation of any other type of 'fitness'.) In sociobiology, 'inclusive fitness' is used to adjust for the effects of relatives on one another's reproduction.

gene A particular DNA sequence that is the functional unit of inheritance. A gene works by specifying the structure of a protein or by controlling other genes. In the sociobiology controversy, some of the conflict is created by different conceptions of the nature of the gene. Sociobiologists operate with hypothetical genes 'for' behavior, such as altruism, using population genetics formulas. Molecular geneticists study concrete DNA sequences coding enzymes and other proteins important for physiological processes. So far, the link between genes, physiology, and behavior remains quite obscure (except in a few rare cases of single-gene diseases).

gene pool All the genes in a population. Large gene pools are important for prevention of extinction.

genetic determinism In biology the idea that the gene represents a blueprint that will in practice always be followed, disregarding the potential influence of factors affecting development in a particular environment. Used as a political term to denote that 'genes are destiny'.

genome All the genes of an organism of a species, for instance the human genome.

genotype All or part of the genetic constitution of an individual. Population-genetic theory typically regards the genotype as resulting from a random process of recombination of alleles. Ernst Mayr, however, in 1975, emphasized 'the unity of the genotype'.

'good science' In the sociobiology and IQ controversies, used by both sides to denote the type of science they were doing themselves.

gradualism The evolution of new species by gradual accumulation of small genetic changes over long periods of time. Also a theory of evolution that emphasizes this.

group selection A process of natural selection among groups rather than individuals. An early assumption was that individuals sacrificed themselves 'for the good of the group', for which Wynne-Edwards first formulated a possible mechanism in 1962. Biologists soon, however, declared group selection an unlikely phenomenon and preferred the new paradigm of kin selection (one exception was E. O. Wilson). Recently D. S. Wilson and Sober reintroduced group selection, this time as 'trait group' selection, which they traced to Price's (1972) and Hamilton's (1975) later broadly conceived view of inclusive fitness. While many, following Maynard Smith's early formulation, see kin selection as opposed to group selection, Hamilton himself (following Price) includes both of these (and also trait group selection) among the alternative ways in which altruism can evolve by natural selection.

inclusive fitness This concept, developed by Hamilton in 1964 and further in 1975, explains how natural selection can favor altruism. This can happen if the benefits of altruism can be made to fall on individuals who are likely to be altruist rather than random members of the population. A typical case is a group of relatives (kin selection), but Hamilton intended 'inclusive fitness' to be a broader concept than 'kin' selection, 'group selection', or 'reciprocal altruism'. Inclusive fitness has been typically used to formalize reasoning about natural selection in kin groups. Natural selection can favor altruism between genetic relatives if the reduction in fitness (number of offspring) of the donor is more than made up for by the increased fitness (number of offspring) of the recipient. The point here is that an individual's genes are represented also in relatives, in proportions corresponding to their genetic relatedness. This is why the degree of relatedness between donor and recipient is an important consideration in the formula for calculation of inclusive fitness.

kin selection A process of selection in which individuals are postulated to behave altruistically towards relatives with whom they have genes in common. Kin selection provided a solution to the mystery of animal altruism by focusing on 'inclusive fitness' (Hamilton, 1964) rather than the fitness of an individual organism; in this case inclusive fitness takes into account the effect that living in groups of relatives has on fitness (something that can be expressed in population-genetic terms). One way of understanding this is to see it from a 'gene's eye's perspective' (Dawkins): what ultimately counts is not the survival of the individual organism but rather the survival of copies of the gene itself—and since relatives share genes, copies of the gene can be found in them as well. Kin selection has been contrasted with group selection, following Maynard Smith's (1964) formulation, but Hamilton's (1975) reformulation of inclusive fitness includes both kin selection and group selection among the alternative ways in which altruism can evolve by natural selection.

linkage disequilibrium When there is linkage and interaction between genes on a chromosome, they may produce certain stable combinations, 'linkage disequilibria'. Under these conditions the usual assumptions and calculations of population genetics, which is based on single genes and free competition between their alleles, do not hold. In 1974 Lewontin suggested that such linkage disequilibria were common enough to make the whole chromosome respond to selection as one unit ('the genome as the unit of selection').

macroevolution Large-scale processes over long time spans having to do, for example, with morphological changes in the fossil record, or species formation.

The Modern Synthesis A fusion of Mendelian genetics and Darwinism in the early decades of the 20th century, whereby many branches of evolutionary biology were reformulated in the language of population genetics, thus making it amenable to mathematical treatment. This approach expresses evolution (or rather micro-evolution) mathematically as a change in gene frequencies in a population. The architects of the Modern Synthesis saw the new approach (also called neo-Darwinism) as compatible with macroevolutionary change.

moral capital Using a quasi-economic model, scientists' quest for peer recognition can be described as a competition for 'symbolic capital' (Bourdieu, 1975). According to this model, scientists are trying to accumulate new capital and protect their existing investments, while taking calculated risks. I argue that in morally/politically involved controversies such as the sociobiology debate, the competition for recognition spread to the moral realm as well, resulting in a pursuit of moral capital in parallel with (or sometimes in lieu of) the scientific quest for credit.

moral reading A special type of exegesis of sociobiological texts to extract the worst possible social implications from sociobiological statements.

norm of reaction The full range of phenotypes associated with a particular genotype. For instance, a plant that has a short stalk in one environment may have a longer stalk in other environments.

ontology Another word for metaphysics. Dealing with the way the world or human nature 'really' is. In the sociobiology and IQ controversies, many critics of socio-biology were deeply concerned to present a true picture of the evolutionary process, or the nature of human intelligence, and criticized their targets for their models and assumptions.

phenotype The visible properties of an organism that are produced by the interaction between its genes, and between the genotype and the environment.

planter A scientist with a traditional belief in the growth of scientific knowledge through new contributions and the unproblematic benefit for society of this activity. A planter scientist encourages new explorations, because the growth of knowledge is the way to truth.

pleiotropy The term for one gene influencing many traits at the same time. Critics of sociobiology see this as a problem for the study of adaptation.

population genetics In the Modern Synthesis many branches of evolutionary biology were reformulated in the language of population genetics and (micro)evolution was expressed mathematically as a change in gene frequencies in a population. Selection, for instance, was expressed as the increase of one genotype at a greater rate than another in the population. Other processes for altering gene frequencies, such as mutation pressure, meiotic drive, genetic drift, and gene flow, were also math-ematically formulated. Population genetics is based on single genes and assumes there are no constraints on the process of free competition and recombination of alleles (such as strong linkage or interaction). The opponents of sociobiology have typically criticized the lack of realism of these assumptions.

postmodernism Originally a trend in French philosophy, coming to the United States with some 20 years delay, and picked up enthusiastically by a younger generation of politically oriented humanists, who saw this as a tool to empower minorities and fight various types of oppression (Western, male, white, etc.). In practice, the political activity takes place through the analysis of 'oppressive texts', including scientific ones.

presentism An evaluation or explanation of the views of historical actors from the standpoint of present-day knowledge and belief. It ignores what the actors actually knew or believed at the time. When such an evaluation involves a moral judgment (for instance, of the fact that these actors operated with what we now know to be incomplete or erroneous knowledge), it may be called *moral presentism*.

punctuated equilibria Evolution that is characterized by long periods of stability in the characteristics of an organism and short periods of rapid change during which new forms appear. Also a theory of evolution that emphasizes this. Eldredge and Gould coined the term in 1972 and developed it later. Many well-known evolutionists, however, do not see punctuated equilibria as a novel problem for the Modern Synthesis.

reciprocal altruism The repaying of altruistic acts among unrelated individuals, or at least the promise of repayment in the future. The term is associated with the work of Trivers (1971).

reductionism The idea of explaining a theory or concept in terms of another more elementary theory or concept. In science, this approach has been successful in many fields, for instance in the reduction of Mendelian genetics to molecular genetics. Sociobiologists have been accused for trying to reduce the complexities of behavior to the action of genes and thereby ignoring important interaction processes.

   The criticism is not only theoretical and methodological, however. In the sociobiology and IQ controversies critics have often assumed that reductionists (i.e., most practicing scientists) automatically hold various types of *ontological* convictions as well, such as an atomistic view of society, or a belief in the reality of averages. This may or may not be the case for individual 'reductionists', but would need independent demonstration.

relativism The idea that science has no privileged epistemological status when it comes to other 'ways of knowing'.

The Science Wars A mid-1990s conflict between on the one hand a vocal minority of activist scientists, on the other postmodern humanists, and constructivist and relativist social scientists, engaged in various types of critical analyses of science.

social constructivism A popular approach in recent social studies of science. Roughly, the idea that truth is in various ways socially influenced, or 'negotiated', and that what is presented as scientific truth has no special epistemological status—the outcome could in principle have been different had the prevailing power relations been different. In this approach, scientists' own scientific and moral commitments are ignored in favor of an explanation based on social factors attributed to the scientists.

sociobiology E. O. Wilson defined sociobiology in 1975 as 'the scientific study of the biological basis of social behavior' in all kinds of organisms including man'. British biologists typically preferred the name 'behavioral ecology' or 'functional ethology' instead, to sharply distinguish the new kin selectionist approach from older group selectionism (something Wilson did not do in his book). The uproar around Wilson's *Sociobiology* (1975) obscured the fact that most 'sociobiologists'/behavioral ecologists/functional ethologists are quite *uninterested* in humans. 'Sociobiology' today has a broad range of uses. Professional 'human sociobiologists' often call themselves Darwinian anthropologists or evolutionary psychologists.

standpoint epistemology A perspective in radical humanism that says that there are different coexisting truths (for instance for different social minorities), and that one truth is as good as another. Again, science has no special epistemological status.

W. I. Thomas' theorem Also referred to as 'the definition of the situation': 'If men believe situations are real, they are real in their consequences'. People act on the basis of meaning, and to understand their behavior, we have to find out how they reason.

Tinbergen's Four Questions The idea that four types of questions regarding animal behavior are equally important and legitimate: questions about (adaptive) function, (proximate) causation, development, and evolutionary history. Sociobiologists and functional ethologists have typically concentrated on only the first of these questions.

weeder A type of scientist, visible in the sociobiology and IQ controversies, who is concerned that 'bad science' will have bad social consequences and therefore needs to be weeded out before it can do social harm.

Index

The page numbers in bold represent major sections of the text which deal with that particular topic
Book and Journal titles are represented in *italics*